PETERBOROUGH AT
1939-1945

By
David Patrick Gray

Published by David Patrick Gray

PETERBOROUGH AT WAR
1939-1945

ISBN 978-0-9554517-3-7

First Published 2011
David Patrick Gray

Printed in Great Britain for
David Patrick Gray

PETERBOROUGH AT WAR
1939-1945

Mother's Pride

My boy's a sailor, my boy is…,
His ship's as long as our street.
I call it a boat and it teases him so
but its really the best in the fleet.

He wrote me a letter from Malta,
the number of places he's been…!
I can't really say I know where they all are
but he tells me the things that he's seen.

He always remembers his mother,
his picture stands proud on the shelf.
I can't help the tears when he says how he cares
and I tell him, "look after yourself."

There's times when we never hear nothin'
and I picture the sea in my sleep.
His ship crashing down on the fists of the waves
and the hands reaching up from the deep.

And then bold as brass he'll turn up at the door
and I'll faint in his arms with the shock!
"I'm here for three weeks," he'll declare, just like that!
"We're in for repairs at the dock."

He's out with them fighting the U-boats,
a gunner who knows every trick.
He says when the buggers come up to the top
he sends them back down just as quick!

Contents

Dedicated to Jan and Douglas

Foreword

At the heart of the city centre, tucked at the end of Priestgate, is a grand Georgian townhouse which is home to Peterborough Museum. Behind the Museum is the Trinity Street car park, patrons of which may have noticed a couple of curious signs painted onto the back of the building. One proclaims 'contamination, male entrance', the other invites passers-by to discard their clothing and place it in the bins. Fortunately, I'm not aware of anyone taking up this particular invitation in recent times and stripping off in the middle of the car park!

Many people come into the museum and ask about the signs, often assuming that they are in some way connected to the building's previous use as the Peterborough Infirmary (between 1857 and 1928). In fact they date to the Second World War and are connected with a bath house which stood on the site of the modern car park. The bath house was originally built for use by the Infirmary, but was reopened in 1935 as a municipal slipper baths after the main building had been turned into the museum. During the war the baths were set aside for decontamination purposes in the event that poison gas was used by the enemy. Gas had proved to be a deadly weapon during the First World War and it was feared that it might be used in the new conflict, hence the issue of gas masks to the entire British population. Mustard gas was not only dangerous to inhale but blistered the skin; hence the instruction on the sign to remove any contaminated clothes. Once stripped, the afflicted person could be taken into the bath house to be scrubbed down and decontaminated. Fortunately this never needed to be used…

Whilst the signs (and a literal reading) may raise a smile today, they are a reminder of a potentially grim chapter in our history. The signs provide a visible reminder of Peterborough's wartime past.

Peterborough got off incredibly lightly compared to many other places in terms of damage inflicted by enemy bombing, something we can be very grateful for, but also slightly mystified by, given the city's importance as an engineering and railway centre. The local engineering companies were significant for their production of wartime resources, and indeed benefited from the munitions contracts. Perkins Engines, for example, were able to build the Eastfield works in 1947 as a result of their expansion from wartime production.

The city was home to a flight training school (RAF Peterborough), a training centre for special forces (the Jedburghs at Milton Hall), many thousands of evacuees, and hundreds of visiting American servicemen. These included no less a person than the film star Clark Gable, stationed at RAF Polebrook in 1943 (and from many ladies of a certain age that I have spoken to, he certainly had hearts a-fluttering during his frequent social visits into the city!)

This volume provides for the first time a comprehensive account of this period in our history, written by one of the foremost researchers in this area. David Gray (aided by his partner-in-crime Roger Negus) has, over the last decade and more, done much to research and promote Peterborough's story during the two World Wars. His publications have highlighted the stories of those who joined up and went away to fight, particularly those who made the ultimate sacrifice in the service of their country. David's work has been instrumental in compiling a definitive Roll of Honour for the city. This volume includes the stories of some of these service personnel.

Principally, this book provides a detailed social history of the city in this period. It gives an insight into the effect that the war had on local people and recounts fascinating stories of those Peterborians who experienced life on the Home Front.

It is a great honour to have been asked to write this foreword and duly commend David for his work, another volume which adds to the growing library of local studies that gives the lie to the idea that Peterborough has no history. As someone who takes occasional groups on guided walks around 'Wartime Peterborough', I'm also very grateful that this book has been completed as it gives me even more material to work with!

Stuart Orme
Historian and Tour Guide
Interpretation Manager, Peterborough Museum Service

Introduction

When I originally set out to write the complete history of Peterborough in World War Two I saw it as being contained in a number of volumes. After writing and publishing the first one I soon realised that the story needed to take the form of one single book, in which the whole story could be recorded and read without people waiting for further volumes to be published and perhaps missing them. The people who bought the first volume will recognise the early part of this book, although it has been revised and corrected. The majority of it however, from 1942 to 1945, is new, and completes the story of Peterborough At War 1939-1945.

I was born in Peterborough and I love this city and I hope it will show in the way this book has been written. As I have stated, this is the *complete* story, covering the Home-Front and the Battle-Front. Peterborough's contribution to the war effort in terms of manpower and money was massive. Other towns and cities, of course, were also making their contributions but that is their story, I am only interested in ours. The numbers of men and women that left our city to serve in the armed forces was phenomenal. The toll of those that died while carrying out their duties was exceedingly heavy, and those that were taken into captivity numbered many hundreds, some of those prisoners of war returned, others succumbed to their cruel deprivations in squalid camps, behind barbed wire.

At home, the city rose to the challenge of total war. The Civil Defence Services including the Wardens Service, National Fire Service, Women's Voluntary Service, Supplementary Fire Parties, Ambulance Service, Rescue Parties, Salvage Parties, First Aid Service, Home Guard and Fire Watchers, to mention but a few, were fully manned. Other essential work was also carried out by volunteers such as manning services canteens, and collecting salvage of all kinds in the never ending struggle to raise funds for the war effort. The incredible contribution made by children was staggering and is rightly covered here in detail. Peterborough continued to raise money for many different funds throughout the war, but their contribution to the three national fundraising efforts during those years, Wings Week, Salute the Soldier Week and Warship Week, was nothing short of astounding. So much so, that the Chancellor of the Exchequer visited the city on more than one occasion to thank the people personally for their hard work. This is, perhaps, a lesser known part of the city's contribution but this book tells the full story.

One of my main priorities before writing this story was to "tell it like it was," and not to gloss over any part of the history of those years which might be seen as unsavoury or unflattering. Although I believe that we should feel nothing but pride with regard to Peterborough's wartime role, nevertheless, this history was not written while gazing through rose-tinted spectacles. Within its pages will be found murder, vandalism, drunkenness, fraud, assault, burglary and a multitude of different thefts. Other law breaking, specific to wartime restrictions, such as infringing the blackout, are also here. All of these things are a feature of human society and will always be present. I am a firm believer that although times change, people don't, and in spite of these indiscretions, which were dealt with firmly by the law at the time, the city continued to endure and succeed, and still does.

Of course, hundreds of men, and some women, from the city died while serving their country, and their stories are covered here. Many are tragic in their detail and yet other people vanished in the lonely jungle or desert, at sea and in the air, and nothing is known of the details of their passing. People died at home also, as in the few air raids on the city, when the members of a small family died after being dragged from their bombed home. Two Fire Watchers also perished in the city streets, but sometimes it is the unexpected and totally unnecessary death which makes us stop for a moment when we come across it, and perhaps allows us to take a measure of the stupidity and waste of war. I am talking particularly about the little boys, on separate occasions that fell into deep water basins installed on street corners for use in putting out fires, and drowned before they could be reached. Fathers were serving in the Forces, mothers were compulsorily obliged to carry out war work, what were the children to do? Where were they to go? When they were not at school, the street was their only home. The war forced these circumstances upon people and the war killed those little boys.

You will find humour here as well as sadness, bravery as well as cruelty, kindness as well as crime. Humour, bravery and kindness; these are the words I think best describe the people of our city and it is here in this history in abundance. One picture that sticks in my mind's eye comes from the description of the Thanksgiving Parade in the city on Sunday 13th May, 1945, after the German surrender. Women and children had climbed onto the roofs of the communal air raid shelters in Bridge Street to watch the parade go by and couldn't get back down again afterwards. Soldiers who had been marching by, British, American and other nationalities, stood at the bottom and caught each one as they jumped off. I find this such an affecting image and feel that it encapsulates everything people in the city had been fighting and dying for.

The basis for the stories in this history comes from the local newspaper published at the time, the Peterborough Standard. Each story has been checked using a number of sources including the Commonwealth War Graves Commission and other specialist web sites. Much detail has been added and, corrections made where necessary.

The Rolls of Honour at the end of each chapter have been deliberately set out chronologically, not alphabetically. This is so that the reader can see the order in which people were being killed, and who they were, as they read through the book. Individuals can be looked up in the Roll of Honour Index if that makes things easier, however there are also many stories relating to these men throughout the text of the following chapters.

The Roll of Honour has been compiled using a number of sources that include contemporary newspapers, the Commonwealth War Graves Commission, web sites and war memorials. The criterion for inclusion has been primarily that they were people who were natives of the city or that they had resided here as a result of circumstances such as marriage or employment. If there was a slight doubt then invariably they have been given the benefit and have been included. It is acknowledged that there may be the odd omission but it is as complete a record as has been possible to compile and it is hoped that the reader will appreciate this.

I must end by thanking my best friend Roger Negus, whose encouragement kept me going through many months of research and typing, and stopped the writing of this book taking as long as the war. Roger also helped with the final compilation of the Rolls of Honour and his help and advice with the Index and cover was also invaluable. Finally, special thanks to Stuart Orme, Curator of Peterborough Museum, for writing the Foreword to this book.

1939

On Friday 25th August 1939, the citizens of Peterborough woke up to what they may have thought would be a day much like any other. There was a political crisis in the air, but this was a country town, and the troubles of Europe must have seemed very remote to the people of the city as they carried on with their normal daily lives.

Lovell's Garage in Westgate was selling new Morris Eights from £128, Wallace Beery was starring in "Sergeant Madden" at the Broadway Kinema, and Jeanette MacDonald and Nelson Eddy were appearing in "Sweethearts" at the Princess. The main worry of the day, if you didn't count the threatened strike by 500 local railwaymen, fighting for a minimum wage of 50 shillings a week, were the injuries suffered by two members of Peterborough United Football Club during the pre-season friendlies, with the prospect of playing Notts. County Reserves in the first game of the season the following day.

The day before, on the 24th, the City Mayor, Lily Violet Bryant, wrote an open letter to the people of Peterborough, which was printed in the local newspaper of the time, the "Standard." This news was what the people of the city would be waking up to, and this perhaps, was the final proof that from that moment on they would be working to provide for their own safety, and for some, fighting for their very existence.

Mayor Bryant stated that it was her duty now to bring certain points to the notice of the citizens of Peterborough. She requested that they make preparations, in case the order came to, "screen completely, after dusk, all windows, skylights, glass doors etc. in private houses, shops, factories and other premises so that no light would be visible from the outside."

The instruction was to prepare only, and not carry out the work until the order was given.

The new street lighting restrictions were already in place from the night of the 23rd, and the Mayor advised everyone to take care on the roads in the dark. Ominously, she also requested that all those skilled in first aid should attend the various practice meetings that were being arranged throughout the area.

Residents were also reminded at this time that homes would be required for evacuees from London. Householders were asked to be prepared to give shelter to unaccompanied children and advise on how many they could take. The rates were 10 shillings per child per week, 8 shillings and sixpence each where more than one child was taken in, beds and blankets would be supplied. This 'request' however, had a sting in the tail, in that a refusal to take an evacuee meant a £50 fine or three months in prison or both!

The Chief Constable, Mr. T. Danby, also had a letter published alongside that of the Mayor's, in it he mentioned the leaflets that were available giving information on blacking out homes, shops etc. and screening car and industrial lights. Posters were to be distributed regarding air raid warnings:

"These will consist of a fluctuating, or warbling, signal of varying pitch, or a succession of intermittent blasts sounded by hooters and sirens. The signals may be supplemented by sharp blasts on police whistles. The 'raiders passed' signal will be a continuous signal at a steady pitch.

If poison gas has been used, warning will be given by hand rattles, and the ringing of hand bells will announce that the danger from gas has passed." These last few lines surely must have been the most shocking.

Another leaflet: 'Aids to Movement In Darkened Streets,' outlined procedures for local authorities in the screening of traffic signals, and also in applying white paint to sidewalks, trees, lamp standards etc. to aid the motorist at night, who would be driving with lamps "not exceeding 7 watts, shining through an aperture of not more than 2 inches in diameter and obscured with white tissue paper!"

Black out tests for business people were carried out on the nights of Wednesday 23rd and Thursday 24th at the request of the police, in which it was said "most people co-operated."

It must be remembered that up to this point war had not been declared, however, construction had started on the sixty-five air raid shelters that were to accommodate 3,250 people who might find themselves in the streets during a raid. Each shelter, able to hold fifty people, would be 43 feet long, 7 feet wide and have 6 feet 4 inches of headroom. Each would be provided with three rows of benches. The locations would be as follows:

Bishop's Road Car Park	19 Shelters	950 People
New England Recreation Ground	7 Shelters	350 People
Fletton Recreation Ground	7 Shelters	350 People
Stanley Recreation Ground	22 Shelters	1,100 People
Burghley Square (two sites)	7 Shelters	350 People
Trinity Street Slipper Baths	3 Shelters	150 People

Each shelter had one entrance and one emergency exit, the latter being about 2ft. 6ins. across, and could be easily pushed aside by someone inside. In addition each shelter had three lavatories. Although splinter-proof and gas-proof, the shelters would not withstand a direct hit. The reason for this weakness was somewhat strangely justified by the explanation that underground shelters which would be proof against direct hits would cost the public £12 to £15 a head! It was stated that "the shelters, in an emergency," (when else would they be used?) "would be able to hold about twice the official accommodation figure."

Peterborough was deemed by the authorities as not being in a very vulnerable area, and that being so, shelters were not issued to householders, although they could be purchased.

The public shelters would be open all day and an attendant would be present, employers however, were bound to provide shelters for their own employees during the hours of work.

The employees of Joseph Farrow and Co.'s works and offices at Old Fletton certainly had enough shelter.

Three great reinforced concrete underground shelters, able to accommodate 400 to 500 workers, an underground hospital, warning sirens and a fire fighting system, all designed by the firm's architect, had been under construction since May. Each shelter had ventilation, electric lighting, telephones and lavatories and the occupants were protected against direct blast. Two were constructed near the railway bridge and one on the works premises. The firm also had its own decontamination squad and fire brigade.

City Services Blackout

By the end of August, the Town Hall had been completely blacked out. All windows were covered with thick brown paper fitted into wooden frames. Skylights and

14

fanlights were screened, and felted on the outside. The A.R.P. Committee made a close inspection and were satisfied that the scheme was 100 per cent efficient.

The Dean of Peterborough had made provision for buckets of sand to be placed in the cathedral to deal with any small fires, but admitted that they would have to rely on the town fire service for anything more serious. It was decided that if the "lights out" order was given, any service which was taking place at the time, would be abandoned. A good sized trench had been dug in the gardens of the Bishop's Palace, which would be available for the residents of the Palace, the domestic staff, and the officials of the Diocesan Office.

In case war was declared the hospital management had made arrangements for all removable patients to be evacuated to make room for air-raid casualties. Patients were to be 'graded' daily as to whether they could be sent elsewhere or home in case of emergency. Most of the hospital windows were darkened by the application of blue paint to the glass, and others with paper screens which could be removed during the day. To get a proper lighting effect with the blue paint, yellow electric light-bulbs were fitted. Both operating theatres and the whole of the roof were protected with sandbags.

A large number of sandbags were filled for the protection of the North Station of the L.N.E.R., beginning with the telegraph office on the up platform, and provision was made to darken all office windows. Railway travel was heavy at this time, but not much more than usual. It was difficult to say how many people had cut short their holidays and were returning home, the number was not enough to upset the seasonal average travelling by rail. The increase in road traffic however, was more marked. Traffic to the coast, particularly Hunstanton, had been well below normal for the last week-end of the month. On the other hand, the inland flow appeared heavier, and many cars were drawing caravans.

It was thought an impossible task to protect everything in the huge collection at the city museum, but probably some of the more valuable articles would have to be moved to places of safety in the event of war. The huge windows at the museum could not easily be darkened, so it was decided not to use those particular rooms after dark.

A wireless appeal now went out for blood donors, and the Women's Voluntary Service were taking names at the Town Hall. Mrs. Arthur Mellows, in charge of the W.V.S. was asking for "200 for blood transfusion, 200 Auxiliary Nurses, and many more car drivers."

The Auxiliary Fire Service was practicing dealing with incendiary bombs, and over 300 men had been enrolled. A force of up to 500 was planned, and uniforms were on the way.

Mr. Lister Robinson and Major De Gray, the chiefs of the wardens department were satisfied that everything was in hand, although there were still some vacancies in the ranks. The warden's posts and telephones were all ready for immediate use. Alderman Snowden, Chairman of the City A.R.P. Committee made a final appeal for 120 more firemen, 150 rescue and demolition men, and more women drivers. "Untrained men," he said, "were a damned nuisance."

Mrs. S.G. Cook was the local representative for the Women's Land Army for Peterborough and Rural, and began enrolling women at the Garden House, Cathedral Precincts.

Children

It was estimated at this time that there were 3,521 children in the city under five years old, who would require respirators. That was the number of births since June 30th 1934. The registration of children was continuing.

It was expected that the number of children evacuated to the city from London would total 6,000 from elementary schools, and 850 from secondary. There was no indication of the probable age range. The children would be met by Mr. Hankins, the reception officer, and taken to Bishop's Road School, from there they would be sent by bus to ten selected schools throughout the city, and finally on to their foster parents. One problem that this created was that there would be more visitors than city children in the schools, and two school sessions were planned, city children in the morning and evacuees in the afternoon.

Deacons School had its windows darkened so it could be used as a reception area after dark for the distribution of evacuees. Likewise, ten other elementary schools for the same purpose. Consideration was being given to the possibility of digging trenches at the King's School before its reopening on September 21st. The High School at Westwood Park was fortunate in having, what an expert called, "the best cellars in Peterborough," for A.R.P. purposes. A portion of these had been gas-proofed and could comfortably accommodate the whole school and its staff.

Business (almost) As Usual

September had now arrived, and the city had taken on a new life. A large percentage of people, some travelling to work, others out shopping, were now carrying their gas masks. Police, A.R.P. personnel and others had their steel helmets as well. There were also many new faces in the city, away from their hometowns for the duration. In the streets there were fewer cars from other towns and foreign registration numbers were rarely to be seen.

The painting of white lines down the centre of all Class 1 roads and at junctions with main roads was now complete and hydrants were painted orange-red. Zinc-screened hurricane lamps marked corners for those out at night. All key points in the city - fire and police stations, warden's posts, petrol pumps and banks - were securely sandbagged. The fire station doors were open day and night with a crew ready.

At night the streets were comparatively deserted, and those who were out walked quickly. The city black-out had been very successful with few cases of failure to comply with the regulations. Offenders were warned but repeated offences would bring more stringent action.

Old fashioned blinds and curtains that had lain in the back rooms of shops were now suddenly in great demand, as shopkeepers were pressed for black-out materials.

There was no abatement of trade on market days and the cattle market continued as usual, although the extra urgency of the harvest kept some farmers away. Practically everywhere people were trying to carry on with their normal daily lives, the news was however, that if the worst came, Peterborough was ready.

The work of the respirator department at the Town Hall was going on apace. The registration of children had been complicated by the influx of refugee mothers with babies, and the children's respirators had not yet arrived in the city, the Home Office having sent supplies to the more vulnerable areas of the country first. Peterborough would get theirs in due course.

Another group who were causing unexpected trouble was the large number of

Peterborough residents who had laughed at the whole idea of gas masks when they were originally being issued, and had not bothered about them. These people were now clogging up the system by clamouring for their masks, and the supply of respirators was rapidly becoming exhausted, particularly the larger sizes. These laggards would not be supplied until more masks arrived. Also, one or two members of pacifist organisations, who refused respirators before the war started, later decided that they needed them after all.

The new lighting restrictions and the desire to save petrol was now having an effect on the local buses. The Eastern Counties Bus Company now announced that there would be no buses from Peterborough to the country after 7:30 p.m. and a limited city service after that hour.

On September 3rd 1939 Britain was at last at war with Germany, only time would tell if the city would pass through unscathed. The people of Peterborough were ready for the test.

The Entertainment World
By the end of the first week of September, all local amusement places had been closed by order of the government. Everyone hoped that they would all be reopened soon, but in the meantime, all of their many employees were out of work. The government would only say that a reopening would be considered in the light of experience. Cinema and theatre performances, even sporting events were brought to an end at this time.

The following plays and films were all cancelled:
EMBASSY - "Giving The Bride Away."
THEATRE ROYAL - "Whiteoaks."
ODEON - "Stagecoach."
BROADWAY KINEMA - "The Little Princess."
CITY - "Sword Of Honour."
PRINCESS - "Stand Up And Fight."
NEW ENGLAND - "Charlie Chan in Honolulu."

The football season, which had just begun, was put off until further notice, and the town's remaining cricket fixtures were cancelled. Mr. Sam Haden, the manager of Peterborough United Football Club, closed down proceedings on Saturday 9th September, and applied for a full time post in a first aid squad. A number of players took jobs in local factories, two went back to their homes outside the city and the rest were looking for employers to take them on. Mr. Haden kept in touch with all the men ready to recall them at short notice should the season begin again.

A week later the government allowed all theatres and cinemas in neutral or reception areas to open again, they had to close at 10 p.m. and no children were admitted without an adult. All places of entertainment were immediately packed to capacity.

Evacuees and Shelters
5,479 evacuees had been sent to the Peterborough area by the middle of September, and already the first tribunal was set up for the hearing of complaints by, or regarding evacuees. Twelve members sat on the tribunal, which split into threes in order to get through the business. It was found that there were a number of very real grievances on both sides. A number of evacuees had simply gone home without the council being given any notification, and others had switched from one billet to

another, again without any warning. Extra washing facilities situated, somewhat offensively, at the cattle market, which had been provided for Evacuees, were at first little used, however, they soon became more appreciated.

It was now decided that all schools in the city would remain closed until they had been equipped with air raid shelters. Eighty-three shelters were originally ordered, and their construction was divided up between 36 builders who had promised to have them ready inside a fortnight. Some delay was caused by the hold up of reinforcement for the concrete roofs. The number of shelters required was soon raised to 116 however, and schools opened in succession, as and when the shelters were ready. The pupils from some schools helped to dig trenches in the playing fields until proper shelters had been erected, and most school buildings had their interiors fortified with sandbags.

Of the general shelters for public places, it was estimated that 70 percent had been completed by September 15th. This construction work was also held up due to the fact that the corporation was only allowed to receive pre-cast concrete slabs for four shelters a week. Some complaints had been made that the slopes at the entrances to the shelters were too steep, but the City Engineer pointed out that the Home Office provided for a slope of one in four, and in Peterborough the gradient was one in ten!

The completed shelters were now under constant supervision by the police, and the public were again reminded that the shelters were for people caught in the street during a raid, and not for people to rush to from their homes. A shelter was now being placed in Hill's Yard and there would be two instead of three in Trinity Street. Orders were also issued for the erection of three cleansing stations and decontamination centres at the St. John's Street depot, Tennyson Road, and Mountsteven Avenue. The three warden's posts at the Territorial Hall, London Road, Itter Park, and the Paul Pry were now completed. During this week many more streets were painted with white dotted lines. This was only in the main streets - about 50 miles of them - and the paint had to be continually renewed.

In darkly shaded places like Park Road, trees and lamp posts were painted with broad white bands. Traffic islands, kerbs, entrances to garages or private houses, and other points were being treated as rapidly as possible.

One animal, which obviously needed more than a few white dotted lines to show him the way, was involved in a collision of an unusual kind on Wednesday 26th September. A sheep, part of a flock being taken to the cattle market, saw its reflection in 'Fairway's' shop window and promptly decided to join itself! With one bound the sheep crashed through the plate glass window causing £10 worth of damage, and smashing a large crockery display. The store manager quipped that his bargains were obviously too good to resist.

Rationing and Identity Cards
Fuel control started on Monday 18th September at the Old Vicarage in Priestgate, opposite the museum. Food control had not yet commenced as instructions were still awaited. There had been a steady stream of applications all week for petrol ration books. The applicant, after producing his registration document, would receive two books of coupons, each valid for one month. The coupons varied according to the size of the car's engine, and each coupon provided for about 200 miles of travelling. Coupons could not be hoarded as they were only valid for the stated month.

The National Registration Bill now provided for the compilation of a National

Register, and the issue of identity cards for all. This was to help with National Service requirements, provide up to date statistics concerning man power, the preservation of contact between family members dispersed by evacuation and to facilitate the proof of identity for the purpose of claims for special payments. After the returns had been collected, the cards would be issued to each person, or to whoever may be in charge of them. Registration would take place on Friday September 29th by 101 local enumerators covering the 80,000 people, (85,000 including evacuees), living in the city and rural district. Each enumerator would have on average about 850 identity cards to make out. There were an estimated 21,259 houses to cover.

The new food rationing cards would be issued on the completion of the identity card schedules; each identity card holder would get their own food ration book. Some guidance was given on how to describe various occupations when completing the identity card application schedules. The word "unemployed" could not be accepted, and a person's "real" occupation in life should be stated, as for example, 'waiter, (unemployed)' or 'waiter (retired).' A housewife could not be described as 'married woman,' but as 'domestic duties, unpaid.'

After the enumerators had finished their work, only two people had absolutely refused to give any information. As soon as they received notes to say they would get no ration books, their schedules found their way swiftly into official hands! The final total of identity cards issued for the Peterborough area reached almost 90,000.

Across the top of each identity card was a row of letters and figures. The letters indicated the Peterborough area, and all combinations started with 'R'; the following letters indicated the enumeration district in which the person lived, such as 'RQBM' (which, incidentally, was the code belonging to the Deputy Registration Officer). Next was a figure, for example '184', which denoted the number of that person's schedule in that area, and thirdly, a small figure, for example '1', that denoted the position on that schedule. From this code, a search could be made at the local record office, and all the details relating to that person could be instantly found.

These identity cards were to be carried at all times by each citizen, parents had to carry their children's cards. A week after they were issued, a 'Standard' reporter surveyed 20 people in the street, asking them if they had their cards on them - 19 said "No!"

Vandalism

As a number of schools were still closed due to building work at the beginning of October, a lot of children were on the streets, and considerable damage was being done to the public shelters, both those completed, and others under construction. Sandbags at the entrances had been thrown down, boxes of lighting sets overturned, bulbs removed from lamps, seats overturned, emergency exits filled with rubbish and other such mischief.

"Still worse," said the 'Standard', "is the improper use made of the places by older boys and girls."

An appeal was made to parents to keep their children away from the dangerous excavations. The parents in turn suggested that their children would be far safer back at school than roaming the streets. The work at two schools was almost complete, and Walton reopened on Monday 9th October, and Woodston C of E, on Wednesday 11th.

The First Military Tragedy

"Boy Herbert Michael Bradley, aged 17, youngest son of Mr. and Mrs. J.T. Bradley, of Tower Street, New Fletton, Peterborough, was one of sixteen naval men killed in the German air raid on warships in the Firth of Forth on Monday." This was the stark headline in the 'Standard' on Friday October 20th, 1939. The counting had begun.

Herbert Bradley was the first city man to die; he had been a member of a gun crew on the Royal Navy cruiser, HMS SOUTHAMPTON, when they were attacked by 14 German dive bombers at 2:30 p.m. on Monday, 16th October 1939. A bomb glanced off the bow of the ship destroying the Admiral's barge and a pinnace, (small boat), which were tied up alongside. Splinters from the bomb caused the deaths of three men on the ship. It was thought that the sailors were running to man the guns when they were killed which was why they were caught in the open. Four of the German aircraft, mostly Dornier Do17s, were shot down by fighters and anti-aircraft guns.

Boy Bradley had celebrated his 17th birthday only two months before, and had been in the navy for a year and eight months, serving on the Southampton for ten months. He was educated at All Souls' Catholic School, in Peterborough, leaving there at the age of 14. He went to work in the brickyards, but had always wanted to join the navy, and he soon joined up at Cambridge.

In his short career he sailed to Canada, America, Portugal, Spain and Malta. It was at Malta that he reached the final of the boxing championships between the Home and Mediterranean Fleets. He did not compete in the final however, as he had a damaged hand, but later met the other finalist and beat him.

Herbert had two brothers, John Francis Bradley, who was serving with the 402 Anti-Aircraft Unit, and Chris Bradley, who was employed at the power station. His father had served 12 years with the King's Own Yorkshire light Infantry, and had seen action in the Battle of Mons during the First World War.

On being asked by the Admiralty whether they wanted Herbert's body to be buried at Rosyth or at Peterborough, his parents requested that he be brought back home.

Every seat in All Soul's Roman Catholic Church was taken on Friday 20th October 1939, the day of Herbert Bradley's funeral, and 500 people crowded into Woodston Cemetery to see him buried. The Royal Air Force provided an escort and a firing party at the cemetery, and Major J.C.S. Musk was present with a detachment of the National Defence Company. The coffin was draped with the Union Jack. Many friends and townspeople who filled the church, lined the route of the procession along Park Road from Fitzwilliam Street to Westgate.

On the same day that Herbert Bradley was killed, the Ministry of Labour figures for the unemployed in Peterborough were announced, 786, a drop of 66 from the previous month. The figure broke down as 332 men, 19 boys, 374 women and 61 girls. It seemed that the authorities would have no problem in replacing the likes of Herbert Bradley.

48 Wardens Posts in the City and Soke

The soundness of city A.R.P. shelters and the sandbag protection of many public and private buildings were severely tested by very heavy rainfall on Sunday 15th and Tuesday 17th of October. However, great strides had been taken in the provision of A.R.P. services and the public were informed of this fact.

On October 20th 1939, a list was published of all the A.R.P. Service Posts in the area, although revisions were being made all the time. The following was the current list for that date:

CITY A.R.P. STATIONS.
First Aid Posts.
1 Bridge Street (Bridge Foot).
2 St. John's Church Hall, Mayor's Walk.
3 Millfield Congregational Hall, St. Martin's Street.
4 Keeton Road Hut.
5 Mountsteven Avenue clinic.
   South Ward: City combines with Old Fletton Urban Council, at ex-Service Men's Club, High Street.

Auxiliary Fire Stations.
1 Central Fire Station, Deacon's Street.
2 Hall and Co.'s works, Queen's Walk.
3 Read's Garage, Lincoln Road.
4 Sage's Lane.

DISTRICT DEPOTS.
Engineer Services.
1 Corporation Depot, St. John's Street, (also cleansing station).
2 Bread Street, Woodston.
3 Tennyson Road, new building in course of construction; until completion at Lawn House, Dogsthorpe Road, (also cleansing station).
4 Mountsteven Avenue, new building in course of erection; until ready at Barn in Sage's Lane.
5 Barnack (combined with the Soke County Council).

Ambulance Stations.
1 Swimming Pool, Bishop's Road.
2 Princes Street.
3 Paston Hall.

WARDENS POSTS.
City.
1 Meadow's Fruiterers, Westgate.
2 Old Town Hall.
3 Nutt's harness room, Eastgate.
4 George Street, Sunday School.
5 London Road, Shortacres, (new building).
6 Warehouse basement at Mr. Dobson's, 28, London Road.
7 Mayor's Walk Church Hall, (also First Aid Post).
8 The Gaol, Thorpe Road.
9 Outbuilding, Manor House, Longthorpe.
10 Cobden Street, Methodist Sunday School.
11 Store No.6, Cutlack's Brewery, Monument Street.
12 Gladstone Street, Boy's School.
13 Corporation Depot, St. John's Street.
14 The Blue Peter, Star Road.
15 St. Martin's Street, Church Hall, (also First Aid Post).
16 Summer House at Mr. Hill's, Princes Gate.
17 Agricultural Society's offices, Eastfield Road Showground.

18 Newark School.

19 Harris Street Baptist schoolroom.

20 Garage at Hazell's, 96, Northfield Road.

21 Mr. Cracknell's Manor House, Dogsthorpe Road.

22 Committee Room, St. Paul's Church Hall.

23 Keeton Road School.

24 Garage at Paul Pry Inn, Walton.

25 Schoolroom, Chapel Lane, Werrington.

26 Itter Park, Paston.

48 Garton End.

WARDENS POSTS.

Soke.

27 Mr. G. Mathews, High Street, Eye.

28 Mr. A.E. Harris, Belmont House, Newborough.

29 Timber Yard Office, (Mr. C.W. Neaverson), Peakirk.

30 School House, (Mr. V.W.W. Rawbon), Glinton.

31 Arbomfield Mills, (Mr. V. Jackson), Helpston.

32 The Vicarage, (Rev. C. Curtis), Etton.

33 Vine Farm, (Mr. D.G. Morton), Bainton.

34 Tower House, (Mr. C.B. Allerton), Barnack.

35 Middle Farm, (Mr. J. Bettinson), Southorpe.

36 Mr. Burbidge, Pilsgate.

37 Burghley Houise, Stamford.

38 The Rectory, (Rev. J.W. Rodgers), Wittering.

39 Bleak House, (Mr. T. Gibbs), Wansford-Thornhaugh.

40 Fitzwilliam Arms, (Mr. A.J. Cole), Castor.

41 Glover's Garage, (Mr. A.R. Glover), Ailsworth.

42 Sutton Manor, (Mr. J. Button), Sutton.

43 Mr. J.W. Whitsed, Northborough.

44 The Vicarage, (Rev. A.H. Smith), Maxey.

45 Fairfax House, Deeping Gate.

46 Milton Hall, (Mr. H. Elliot), Castor.

47 Manor Farm, (Mr. F.S. Glover), Marholm.

What to do in an Air Raid

At the same time that the above tables were produced, a letter from a Spaniard who had lived through the Spanish Civil War a few years earlier, and who "went through more than 400 raids," was published in the 'Standard', for the guidance of the townspeople. It read as follows:

"At the sound of the alarm, keep a cool head, follow instructions, but above all do not rush. Always know the shortest way to the nearest air raid shelter. Have warm clothing with you in winter. If there is no shelter available, get down into a basement. Keep close to corners. Avoid being near doors and windows. If no warning has been given against gas, keep your windows and doors open. Do not stand in the middle of a room, but get close to the main inside walls. If actual bombing finds you in the street, rush into the nearest doorway and lie down flat close to the wall with the head pointing inwards, while if caught in the open, far from any shelter or house, lie flat in the lowest ground, and if there is grass or soft ground lie there. Bombs falling on soft ground sink in and the explosion is upwards.

Carry with you a lead pencil, a piece of soft rubber or cork to put between your teeth in order to keep the mouth open. This avoids internal injury or the bursting of the ear drum by concussion. If lying in the open, cover your head with a folded coat or open book to avoid injury from splinters from anti-aircraft gun shells.

For information, a bomb falling in the immediate vicinity makes a loud whistling sound, (would this small piece of information be of much use under the circumstances?). Bombs falling from 100 to 500 yards distance make a loud hissing sound. Strips of paper pasted over the window panes do not prevent them from breaking; they do keep splinters in place."

Black Week for the Black-out

The grave increase in the number of deaths on the roads of the country during the blackout hours was brought home to the city people during the week ending 28th October, when four fatalities occurred on the district's roads. The first blackout accident in the city occurred at 10:35 p.m. on the night of Wednesday 5th September, when two cars came together while approaching the traffic lights in Long Causeway. In that incident the only things that were damaged were two car wings, but it was obvious that more serious accidents would inevitably take place.

One of the four people killed during this "black" week was a local man, Mr. Fryer Hooper, aged 87, of 8, Green Lane, Werrington. He was cycling home after working in a beet field, and was killed when he swerved and caught the side of a coal lorry passing Werrington Green.

During the first month of the black-out, in September, 1,130 people had died in accidents on the roads in Great Britain, compared with 554 in the same month the year before. The increase in deaths however, occurred chiefly among pedestrians, 633 in September as opposed to 238 in the previous month.

As an example, the black-out times published in the 'Standard', on October 20th 1939, are presented below:

DATE	BEGINS P.M.	ENDS A.M.
Friday 20th	5:59	7:38
Saturday 21st	5:56	7:40
Sunday 22nd	5:54	7:42
Monday 23rd	5:52	7:44
Tuesday 24th	5:49	7:47
Wednesday 25th	5:46	7:50
Thursday 26th	5:44	7:52

Ration Books Ready

By the end of October there were nearly 90,000 ration books at the Town Hall, ready to be sent out. On the word "go," they were to be sent to everybody living in the district under the direction of the Local Food Controller. Also ready were 2,500 forms on which applications could be made for extra rations for "heavy workers." These forms had to be endorsed by the man's employer and returned to the Controller for adjudication. There were also special forms for commercial travellers, enabling them to get rations at any place. The ration books would all be sent out by post.

The first items to be rationed would be: Meat, bacon and ham, butter and margarine, cooking fats and sugar. There were blank pages in the books where additions could be made as other items went on ration.

The ration books would be prepared by about 120 volunteer workers, mainly elementary school teachers, W.V.S. and other ladies and these would be supervised by the City Treasurer's Staff.

Evacuees and Militia
The first baby to be born to an evacuee mother in Peterborough arrived in the middle of October. Mrs. Lax, who was billeted with Mrs. Deboo at 303, Cromwell Road, gave birth to Eric in the maternity ward at St. John's Hospital. The Mayor gave little Eric a souvenir spoon bearing the city arms. Mother and baby both returned to Mrs. Deboo's later.

Another 23 evacuee school children were expected to arrive in the city from London at any time. They were to join their friends at Walton. They came from the Bentall Road Mixed School, and were in the government's No.2 scheme, which gave a second chance to those who refused the first opportunity. More children were also expected to arrive in the Norman Cross district.

On Saturday 21st October, another group of men aged 20-22 were called upon under the militia scheme to register at the Peterborough Employment Exchange. A total of 397 actually signed, and more names were coming in by post. The total from the city and Soke was just about the same as when the last group were called in June. Men could not choose their units, but those with a preference for the Air Force or Navy as opposed to the Army were invited to say so. 61 men opted for the Navy and 150 for the Air Force. This compared with 20 and 56 respectively on the last occasion. Half a dozen conscientious objectors also registered that day.

The largest number of men registering was brickmakers, with men engaged in engineering running a close second. Men employed in exempted trades would be combed out at Cambridge where they all went for their medical examinations.

Guy Fawkes Blacked-out
At the end of October the city police made it clear that the lighting of fireworks which gave light, (did they know of any other type?), between the hours of sunset and sunrise would be an offence under the Lighting Restrictions Order, 1939. Bonfires were also prohibited. Further to this, letting off a firework "causing a report within the hearing of the general public," would constitute an offence under the Noise (Defence) Order, 1939. Obviously the only person letting off fireworks in 1939 would be Hitler!

The A.R.P. services had been carrying out experiments in the use of luminous paint to direct people to the public shelters at night. "Shelters," it was stressed, was the correct description, even though temporary signs still read "To Trenches." The paint experiment was not very successful, and a scheme of positive lighting was submitted to the Ministry, who would have to pay the cost.

If the failed experiments and continuing vandalism to shelters was not enough to cope with, the local A.R.P. services were now asked to undertake a review of their personnel, with a view to possible re-organisation. The city whole-time personnel had already been reduced from 78 to 28.

Still more bad news was that helmets and masks for very young children had still not yet been received in Peterborough, nor was it known when they would arrive. For the youngest children - infants from birth up to two - the box helmet was specified. For those over two, there was the small respirator, similar to, but simpler than the adult mask. It was hoped that in an emergency some of the children between three and four might be able to use the adult respirator. Depots were waiting to issue the equipment as soon as it turned up.

Bad News, Good News

It may be thought unusual that during a time of war, a manufacturer producing items such as aeroplanes should find itself in receivership. But that was just what happened to the 'Peterborough Aircraft Company Limited,' on Friday 3rd November 1939, in the Chancery Division of the High Court. The claim was for the District Bank Ltd. to be entitled to the sum of the assets of the company. A similar motion was received on behalf of the bank in connection with the 'Aircraft Exchange and Mart Ltd.'. Both companies were associated with each other and both shared the same offices.

An investigation of the books showed that there had been elaborate inter-dealings between the two companies. The bank's claims were upheld.

It was on this same day that the ration books were finally sent out by post to the citizens of Peterborough, although the exact day for the beginning of rationing had not yet been fixed by the government.

On a happier note, the Odeon Theatre was crowded on the night of Sunday 5th November, for the concert of Jack Jackson's Band, some compensation surely for the absence of fireworks.

It was the first purely business concert - as opposed to a charity event - ever held in a Peterborough theatre on a Sunday. Mr. Peter Broomhall, the Odeon Manager, was very pleased with the turnout, particularly in view of the bad weather. "The enthusiasm and the support were nothing less than terrific," he said.

There was a liberal helping of comedy laced with war songs. Favourites such as "Run Rabbit Run," and "Three Little Fishes," were put over well by Jackie Hunter, the drummer. Gene Crowley sang "Bon Voyage, Cherie," "There'll always be an England" and "Lords of the Air."

Jack Jackson sang "Berlin or Bust" and "We're Gonna Hang Out the Washing on the Siegfried Line." Another great hit was the parody of "Boomps a Daisy" by "Hitler, Goering and Goebbels."

Christopher Gill, described as a "young coloured baritone," sang two groups of songs, including "Moses go down," "Solitude," and "Old Man River."

How wonderful that concert must have been then back in 1939. Thinking about the excited atmosphere, we can imagine the laughter and applause as our own townspeople made the most of their happiness. What would some of us give to be there now and experience that night?

It was the War Office, of course, who during that period could always bring the people back down to earth. They now issued a reminder in the city that places of military and national importance such as camps, bridges, factories, gasometers, electrical plants, railway junction lines, etc. were all guarded by armed sentries day and night. The public were warned against trespassing and were advised that when visiting such places on business they would be challenged. This also referred to searchlight and anti-aircraft gun sites. On being ordered to halt they should do so immediately, announcing their presence with the word "Friend." They must then be prepared to give their names and state the nature of their business.

In view of the fact that all sentries were armed with ball cartridge, it was "most essential that the precautions be strictly observed."

Arcade Black-out Problems

The Westgate Arcade in Peterborough, was, and still is, an interesting piece of 'Old World' Edwardian architecture. Lined both sides with small shops, it was probably the only undercover shopping arcade in the city at that time. Almost the entire length of the Arcade roof was glazed, and in order to comply with the black-out regulations the glass was painted on the inside, and, as an extra precaution, a black paper screen was hung underneath.

These measures, it would seem, should have been adequate enough to prevent any light escaping. However, on the night of October 31st 1939, at 7:15 p.m. Inspector Frost of the City Police, while on patrol in Westgate, came across a shaft of light beaming brightly out of the Arcade, and picking out the front of the Bull Hotel opposite like a spotlight.

On investigation, Inspector Frost found five lamps blazing in the Arcade which were operated from a switchbox, unfortunately this was locked and he could not extinguish the lights. Also inside the Arcade was Mr. George Dewberry of 197 Gladstone Street, Peterborough, who was responsible for switching the lights on in the first place. Inspector Frost warned Mr. Dewberry that he would face prosecution for permitting an unobscured light to be displayed in the Arcade, and it was at the beginning of November when Mr. Dewberry found himself in front of Peterborough Magistrates in order to answer the charge, and being represented by Mr. Mellows. He pleaded 'not guilty.'

It was deduced that lights from the shops in the Arcade could not be seen from outside and that it must have been the lights that Mr. Dewberry, the caretaker, had turned on which had been showing. There were lights in the Arcade that were meant to be left on at night, but these had been specially treated, the offending lamps had not. Mr. Dewberry said that the lights in question were always left on until the shops closed, but as there was not much light in the Arcade after that he had decided to "leave them on for the first time, to see what it was like." "I didn't know it was so bad."

Mr. A.W. Ruddle, part owner of the Arcade was called for the defence, and he stated that as Mr. Dewberry had previously been a member of the City Police Force for 24 years, he did not think he was a person who would deliberately infringe the regulations!

Mr. Dewberry also stated that he did not think that the lights showing would have attracted enemy aircraft, and that other police officers had passed through the Arcade and said nothing.

Mr. Ruddle explained that the caretaker's duties were to keep the lights on until the shops closed and then switch over to three red lights which were left on all night. Mr. Dewberry had to clean the Arcade every morning for which he turned the lights on, and no comment had ever been made. Dewberry also stated that there were hundreds of other places where the reflections were worse than that from the Arcade. This notwithstanding, a fine of ten shillings was imposed.

Walter Turpin of 56, Elmfield Road, Peterborough, was also summoned on the same day, for permitting an unobscured light to be displayed in the Arcade at 6:45 p.m. on November 1st 1939. He also pleaded not guilty.

It was Inspector Frost again who had investigated in response to a telephone call. Again, he found a shaft of light coming from the Arcade. The first display window in Rose's Fashion Centre was illuminated by five unscreened lights. In the second window there were about ten unscreened lights, and there were nine or ten further lights in a third display window. Turpin was the shop manager, and on being shown the lights, was reluctant to turn them out. When the lights were eventually switched off everything was as it should have been, even with a light still shining over the shop doorway. Turpin said he had seen lights on in other shops and couldn't see why he should not have his on. However, it was pointed out that the other shops were not near the entrance to the Arcade as his was.

On telling the court that he did not think that the lights had been all that bad, Turpin was fined £1.

More Preparations
By the first week of November, the Peterborough Red Cross Depot had got into full swing at its Cowgate premises. Quantities of flannel had been received from official sources, cut up and sent to working parties to be made up for hospital purposes. Wool, which had been obtained locally, was sent out for knitting into gloves, helmets (Balaclava), and other comforts. There were a large number of helpers who were in the charge of Miss Shipley Ellis, the Secretary, and Mrs. Sheckleton. The Depot was open from 10 a.m. to 4 p.m. daily.

The Engineer's Department was now making excellent progress with shelter construction, and the 65 called for in the first scheme were practically complete. The second scheme for a further 32 shelters was sanctioned and would go ahead as fast as the concrete sections were received. The ten shelters specified in the third scheme were waiting official sanction.

The shelter provision was now:

No. 1 Scheme - 65 shelters, with room for 3,250 occupants.

No. 2 Scheme - 32 shelters, 1,600 occupants.

No. 3 Scheme - 10 shelters, 500 occupants.

Total accommodation - 5,350 occupants.

Another team from the Engineers department was carrying out a systematic survey of sandbag protection at this time. The breastworks, (sandbags stacked up against outside walls for blast protection), were being removed, and bad bags replaced, and then the whole breastwork was treated with a cement preparation, which was applied under pressure.

More air raid wardens (unpaid), were now required to supervise public air raid shelters in the event of enemy attack. Residence close to the shelters was deemed a great advantage. Men aged over 30 years were eligible.

The locations of shelters in Peterborough at that time were as follows: Bishop's Road car park, Stanley Recreation Ground, New England Recreation Ground, Fletton Recreation Ground, and Trinity Street.

Only two elementary schools, All Souls and Dogsthorpe, were now still closed due to their shelters not yet being finished.

Recruiting
Voluntary recruiting for the army was now going on steadily at the Recruiting Office, at Rothesay Villas, Lincoln Road. Men chose their units, and as far as possible, they were sent to them. All the infantry regiments were open, the Artillery, Royal Army Service Corps, Veterinary Corps, Auxiliary Military Pioneer Corps (35 to 50), and Anti-Aircraft (22 to 50).

Drivers of motor vehicles, private, light and heavy were required for mechanised units (22 to 35). The normal age range for the infantry was 20 to 30.

The National Defence Corps was also open to older men (35 to 50), and the Military Police were looking to recruit ex-service men of the Regulars or Territorials with at least four years service, and a discharge character of not lower than "very good."

In the short period up to the 10th November, numbers of men from the following towns signed up for the army at Peterborough:

Peterborough	84	Farcet	2	Warmington	1	Glinton	1
Whittlesey	6	Oundle	2	Polebrooke	1	Bourne	1
Stanground	6	Ailesworth	2	Great Gidding	1	Warboys	1
March	4	Fletton	2	Washingley	1	Marholm	1
Elton	1	Market Deeping	3	Nassington	1	Holbeach	1
Crowland	3	Orton Waterville	1	Tansor	1	King's Lynn	1
Yaxley	2	Water Newton	1	Thorney	1		

The Northamptonshire Regiment was by far the most popular amongst the volunteers, but there was also a strong liking for the Leicestershire Regiment. The Sherwood Foresters and Lincolns also had their supporters. The Artillery was popular but not as much as the Royal Armoured Corps, and the rush to join the tanks led to recruiting being "rationed out" to various recruiting depots. Army Recruiter Fenton was in charge of the Recruiting Office, and he had recently gone into residence there.

A new soldiers club was about to open at this time in Long Causeway. Donations and gifts were asked for in order to equip the canteen for the benefit of servicemen passing through the city. The premises were situated next to Lloyds Bank and there was a canteen on the ground floor, and a games room upstairs.

At the same time, the local Divisional Unionist Association decided to start a collection in order to provide a parcel of "Christmas cheer," for every man from the area who was serving abroad, or on the high seas.

There was no way of obtaining a complete list, so relatives and friends were asked to provide names and addresses, in order that no man missed out on his "comforts."

It may, or may not, have been a comfort for the city people to know that November 5th was also the beginning of "Rat Week." Apparently, there was no official action, but there was a man engaged on rat destruction regularly, and he was paid a per capita fee by the City Council.

Conscientious Objectors

Seven conscientious objectors attended a tribunal in Cambridge on Thursday 16th November, 1939, in order to support their claims to exemption from military service. Six of the seven came from Peterborough.

His Honour Judge Lawson Campbell presided over the tribunal, and over the weeks it would have to deal with over 300 applications for exemption.

The first case was a Water Newton man named Dennis Standing Gray, and then came the Peterborough men.

Gordon Jones, of 66, Alexandra Road, Peterborough, said he was applying for registration in the register of conscientious objectors because, as a member of the Christian church and his belief in Christ's teaching, he could not undertake to prepare himself in any way whatever for war, which to him meant mass murder.

Believing as he did that all work turned out by war preparation conflicted with his convictions, he submitted that it would be impossible to undertake work of this nature. He could only accept unconditional exemption, leaving him free to carry on with his present occupation, and the social service he was able to render to the needy.

He was employed at Baker Perkins, and was, by trade, a draughtsman, although owing to the firm reducing trainees, he had gone back into the works as a machine hand.

The Chairman of the tribunal asked him if he would go into the Royal Army Medical Corps.

"I am afraid not," replied Jones, "if I did so I would have to take the military oath." Jones stated that in joining the R.A.M.C. he would be avoiding the main issue by preparing people who were injured to go back and fight again. "A thing that is wrong for me," he said, "is wrong for everyone else in my opinion."

The Rev. L. Lloyd Lister, of Westgate Congregational Church, Peterborough, said he had known Jones for about three and a half years, and had found him sincere in all his pacifist convictions.

Jones was unconditionally registered as a conscientious objector.

The next man was John Daniel, of 187, Oundle Road, Peterborough. He said in his statement that he was a Christadelphian, and as such he held religious conscientious objection to participating in war, which he believed to be contrary to the commandments of Christ. This belief had been characteristic of the Christadelphian body since its inception. Daniel gave his occupation as a G.P.O. draughtsman.

Asked if he did not think he could help his country in some way, Daniel said he was quite willing to help in any way possible if it was not contrary to the laws of God.

Albert J. Lander, of Peterborough, said he had been a Christadelphian for 47 years and had taken a leading part in the movement. He added that Daniel was a sincere member. He was unconditionally registered as a conscientious objector.

At the afternoon session Wilfred Ronald Jeffrey, an L.N.E.R. employee residing at 12, West Parade, Peterborough, said he regarded military training as an offence against man. He did not consider for a man to defend his country by force of arms was in the best interests of the people, no matter how worthy the cause. Asking for complete exemption he said the only service he could conscientiously accept was the work he was at present doing.

The Rev. F.H. Cumbers, of London Road Methodist Group, handed in a letter from Jeffrey's own minister and said he also had known Jeffrey for over three years. He could testify as to the sincerity of his beliefs.

Jeffrey was unconditionally registered as a conscientious objector.

Victor Newton, of 30, Alderman's Drive, Peterborough, was a diesel engine inspector; he sought complete exemption and said the people in this country were as down-trodden as in any other country. Conscription was placed upon us without a vote being taken. He could not offer any form of service except his job. He had refused to join the A.R.P. squad at his works. Answering questions he said the diesel engines which he inspected were used for commercial work. Some were made for the Air Ministry, but he was still on commercial work. The Chairman told him, "You have to be very careful; some of these commercial engines you are inspecting may be taken over by the War Office.

Evidence was again given by the Rev. F.H. Cumbers, and Newton was unconditionally registered as a conscientious objector.

Ronald Frederick Stocks, an employee of the Old Fletton Urban District Council, and residing at 83, High Street, Old Fletton, was also unconditionally registered. He objected on religious and ethical grounds to be trained for the killing of others, or assisting in the training of others for that object. He was not against civilian work.

Finally, for the Peterborough men, Harold Livingstone Cave, of 23, Cecil Road, said he was a Nonconformist lay preacher. He applied for exemption on religious grounds, but said he would accept civilian work if he was satisfied that it was not helping in the war. When Cave said he was actively training for the ministry, the Chairman told him he could secure exemption if that fact was certified by a minister of his denomination. The tribunal was then adjourned.

A.R.P. at the Brickyards

By November 17th, another local "institution" had completed its A.R.P. arrangements. The London Brick Company at Fletton stated that all of its A.R.P. arrangements were completed, and in all the works at Fletton, some form of protection was available. A number of old tunnels, with 15ft. to 20ft. of earth covering, had been utilised as shelters. Where necessary, baffle walls had been built at the tunnel ends to make them safe from blast and splinters, seating and emergency lighting had been installed.

In other cases tunnels under the press sheds had been used, one had three large entrances and five emergency exits. It had its own water supply, emergency lights and toilets. Where there were no convenient tunnels, brick lined trenches were dug, all to a depth whereby a seated person would be below ground level. These trenches were covered with sheets of corrugated iron which in turn was covered with several feet of earth, providing maximum protection.

For A.R.P. organisation purposes the whole area was taken as one unit. The area control centre was in the engineer's shop, and it was there that reports from all units were collated and sent to headquarter services, such as decontamination, rescue and demolition squads. The fire brigade and ambulance service were also close at hand, awaiting instructions from the centre.

A.R.P. at Westwood Works

Mr. D.Y.B. Tanqueray was the Director in charge of all A.R.P. services at Baker Perkins, on Westfield Road, Mr. F.B. Willows was secretary and Mr. T.W. Blake, the chief instructor. A five figure sum had been expended on A.R.P. protection of all kinds at the works. There were 26 underground and above ground shelters, with steel-plated tops, to accommodate about 2,500 persons; A.R.P. stores, a cleansing and decontamination room complete with every facility, and a fully furnished ambulance room. The shelters had toilets, fresh water, and even a gramophone, and were camouflaged. They also had luminous paint applied so that they would be distinguishable at night.

A special feature of the ambulance room was a gas filtration pump, which automatically divided pure air from foul inside a sealed tank, and circulated the fresh air through the room. The pump could be switched on when colour detectors fitted on the outside indicated gas.

30

A new works fire station had been built with its own brand new trailer pump; the men who operated it were accommodated at the station. An efficient wardens organisation was supported by watchers in every part of the works, whose duty it was to report the first sign of an outbreak of fire. Seventy to eighty members of the personnel had gone through a course of training on how to deal with incendiary bombs. There were 45 rescue and 20 decontamination workers; 48 firemen (including auxiliaries), and 80 ambulance men who had formed their own division of the St. John Ambulance Brigade. Added to these were women first aid workers under the supervision of Nurse Savage and Mrs. Gabbertas. Twenty had already been awarded their first aid certificates.

Lectures, demonstrations and exercises were all devised and no employee needed to go further than the works for the best training in A.R.P. precautions.

By the end of November over 400 employees had received instruction and had duties assigned to them. The nerve centre of the scheme was the control room, situated at the top of the office block. Messages and warnings were received, and orders issued from this point.

The firm had built gas chambers for training and already over 1,000 people had passed through them. There was also an incendiary bomb training building. Baker Perkins was probably the best equipped factory, with the most highly trained staff, in the whole city area.

Another service proud to show the citizens that it was ready for action was the Auxiliary Fire Service. At 2:30 p.m. on Saturday 18th November, 150 men of the A.F.S. paraded in full uniform with their equipment through the streets of the city centre. This was about half the city force, with them they had 4 large trailer pumps, each with 8 men, 14 small pumps, each with 6 men, one 1,000 gallon dam and two 500 gallon dams. All of this equipment was spread between four separate stations.

The parade started at its headquarters in Bishop's Road car park and entered Bridge Street under the direction of the City Engineer, as Fire Brigade Superintendent and Chief Officer E.G. Haylett. They then passed down Long Causeway, Broadway, Lincoln Road East, Park Road, Westgate, St. Leonard's Street, Cowgate, and back into Bridge Street.

By the 24th November the long awaited baby's gas helmets had finally arrived in the city. The helmets, intended for the use of babies up to 2 years old, were issued from the following centres between 10 a.m. and 12:30 p.m. and 2 p.m. and 4 p.m. on Tuesday 28th November:

Congregational Church Hall, Westgate.
George Street Schoolroom.
St. John's Mission Hall, Mayor's Walk.
Cobden Street Schoolroom.
St. Mary's Church Hall, St. John's Street.
St. Martin's Street First Aid Post.
Harris Street Schoolroom.
St. Paul's Schoolroom.
Mountsteven Avenue School.
Chapel Lane Warden's Post, Werrington.
They were also available at the Infant Welfare Clinic, Town Hall, at 2:30 p.m. on Thursday 30th November, and Friday 1st December.

Parents had to attend the nearest centre to their homes and take with them their identity cards; people living in Longthorpe and Newark had theirs delivered to their homes. The helmets had to be handed back when the child reached two years of age and it was exchanged for a small child's respirator for two to four year olds.

Over a thousand helmets were handed out at the ten centres on the Tuesday, leaving about 300 left. These were available the following Tuesday from 2 p.m. to 4:15 p.m. at five different centres.

Still with children, the last two schools to open, All Souls and Dogsthorpe, began accepting pupils back again on Monday 27th November, after their shelters were finally completed.

Twenty-three more evacuee children arrived in the last week of November, 17 went to Fletton, 3 to Woodston and 3 to houses in the City.

About the same time, the Regional Officer of A.R.P. wrote to the city services indicating that he was prepared to allow light gates or doors at the entrances to public air raid shelters, the keys to be kept at the nearest A.R.P. post. The first duty of the wardens in a raid would be to see that the gates were immediately opened. Presumably this measure was to be brought in to deter vandals from whom the shelters were suffering significant damage. The City A.R.P. Committee decided to make no alteration to the city's arrangements, an alternative, having the keys in a wooden frame, was also rejected, the feeling was, as we might have guessed, that the keys would be stolen by vandals.

City Sirens Tested

The public were also warned at this time, that for testing purposes, the air raid warnings would be sounded at 10 o'clock on Wednesday 6th December. Factories were asked not to "join in" with their hooters.

From this time onwards the sirens would be tested at 10 a.m. on the first Wednesday of each month.

The official air raid sirens were situated at the Town Hall, Gas Works, Electricity Works, Police Station, East Station, Brotherhood's Works and Baker Perkins, and on the day of the test, were considered satisfactory.

In order to show that it was only a test, the all clear long drawn out note was given first, followed by the intermittent blasts of the raid warning. The all-clear was repeated at the end. The Mayor listened in her parlour in the Town Hall and other officials in various places. Reports indicated that the down-wind sirens were heard distinctly indoors and out, but up-wind (to the north) people indoors did not hear a thing. It was pointed out that in the event of a real raid, the sirens would be supplemented, probably to the extent of 100 per cent, by works hooters, and the whistles of air raid wardens and others in the streets. Sirens sounded during the night would probably be much more effective. The main object was to make sure that the sirens were in working order, and this was fully achieved.

A number of people were interviewed after the siren test, and their observations are printed below:

Mrs. A. Bains, Lincoln Road, Werrington: "We listened, but never heard a sound. Four other people in the village to my knowledge never heard it either."

Mr. Edward G. Hadman, Churchfield Road, Walton: "I barely heard it. I was at Walton School at the time, and Mr. Avery the headmaster, complained that he did not hear it."

Mrs. N. Pailing, Keeton Road, New England: "I heard it, but it was not very loud. I should never take any notice of it if it was for an air raid. I should keep on working. My husband at Werrington Pump House did not hear it."

32

Miss W. Madderson, Headmistress of St. Mary's Infants School: "We were listening, but we didn't hear anything at all."

Mr. W. Rolph, Mayor's Walk: "We heard the sirens quite clearly, especially the one at Westwood." (Baker Perkins).

Mrs. J. Peach, Midland Road: "I was very busy in my shop, and although the doors were shut I could hear the warning very well."

Mr. E.W. Barrett, Oundle Road Post Office: "The sirens were heard very clearly."

Mrs. C. Mathews, Palmerston Arms: "We had the doors shut, and although the warning was only faint we could tell what it was."

A Dogsthorpe woman: "As I was listening for the sirens I heard them, otherwise I am sure I should not have done so."

A Longthorpe man: "I could not distinguish the difference between the sirens and railway whistles."

Christmas 1939

Men up to the age of 23 were now due to register for military service, should they be required, and an estimated 400 men from the city were thought to come into this band. Not particularly good news to the families of those men, especially coming at a time of celebration and reconciliation. Bad news too was the first fatal blackout accident to occur at Fletton. 67 year old Richard Ireland of 219, Fletton Avenue, was knocked down and killed by a bus at White Hat Corner.

If the war escalated, and that was out of everyone's control, there would be few enough of the good times, and so as far as the city people were concerned, this first wartime Christmas was going to be as good, if not better than any before it. The Mayor (Mrs. Bryant) and the Mayoress (Lady Craig) were visitors to the Memorial Hospital and the Isolation Hospital on Christmas morning, where they tasted turkey and Christmas cake, served by Alderman Whitsed.

The Services Canteen and Restroom in Long Causeway had "ever open doors", and there was a ceaseless flow of 'city lads' who were home on leave from the services.

The Rotary Club distributed 403 Christmas puddings to deserving cases, over 50 more than the previous year.

There were 40 weddings at churches and chapels in the city and district, of these, ten bridegrooms were in service uniform. One of these was Lance Corporal R.W. Caswell, of the staff of Barclays Bank, Church Street, who married Miss Mary Keene at All Saints on Boxing Day.

Places of entertainment reaped a harvest. The Embassy Theatre was "packed to capacity at both performances", and the Empire had a "full house three times", all cinemas were well attended.

As with the places of public entertainment, the football season was now, also allowed to continue. The attendance at the Peterborough United v Boston Midland League match on Boxing Day - 1,765 - was not as big as had been anticipated, this being put down to the poor weather.

Rail and bus traffic was heavy, but the roads were relatively free of problems, only two minor accidents in the city reported.

Between December 18th and Christmas Day 615,000 postal packages passed through the Peterborough Head Post Office, an increase of 15,000 on 1938. Letters numbered 50,000 more.

Eight dances were arranged in the city for New Year week. The Grand Hotel had three, and the Angel two. Others were at the Dujon Restaurant, Elwes Hall, and the Mansfield Hall.

Peterborough United won their two home matches during the holiday, and lost away. The results were:

Saturday 23rd: United 15, Royal Navy Depot 2 (Friendly).

Christmas Day: Boston 2, United 1 (Midland League).

Boxing Day: United 3, Boston 1 (Midland League).

Peterborough set up a new club record by beating the Royal Navy Depot side 15-2. The previous best scoring feat by the first team had been 12-0 against Boston the previous season.

The forces did however have one success on the football field, An RAF team played Fairways on Westwood Works ground on Christmas morning, for the Canteen Fund, and won 6-3.

BRADLEY, Herbert Michael – 12 Tower Street, Peterborough. C/JX 157789 Boy 1st Class, Royal Navy. Died, aged 17, on the 16th October 1939 when the cruiser HMS Southampton was bombed by aircraft in the Firth of Forth when most casualties were incurred as the men were running along open deck to man the anti-aircraft guns. The son of Mrs M. Bradley, of Fletton, Peterborough. Buried in Woodston Cemetery, Peterborough, Section 6, Grave 64.

COWAN, Stanley – Leading Seaman P/JX 152626, HMS Cossack, Royal Navy. Died, aged 36, on the 8th November 1939 when the Tribal Class Destroyer, HMS Cossack, collided with another Allied ship, the SS Borthwick, resulting in the death of five of her crew. The ship returning to Scotland for repairs. The husband of H. Cowan of Peterborough. Buried in Edinburgh (Seafield) Cemetery. Sec. P. Grave 703.

COCKS, Percival Rowland Henry – 42 Fulbridge Road, Peterborough. Chief Officer Merchant Navy. Died, aged 42, on the 5th December 1939 when the SS Navasota, in convoy OB-46, was hit by one torpedo from U-47 in the Atlantic. The son of Rowland and Emily Alice Cocks and the husband of Muriel Ernestine Cocks of Ladybrand, Orange Free State, South Africa. He has no known grave and is commemorated on the Tower Hill Memorial, London, Panel 72.

DRAWWATER, Matthew Infield – Pilot Officer (Pilot) 40374, 37 Squadron, Royal Air Force. Died, aged 28, on the 18th December 1939. He was the pilot in a Wellington, Serial No 2935, that took off from Feltwell on a reconnaissance mission. The aircraft was shot down by fighters and fell into the sea west of Schillig Point, Germany when all five crew died. The son of John and Florence Drawwater of Peterborough. Buried in Sage War Cemetery, Germany. Grave 7.A.4.

1940

At the beginning of the New Year there was yet another proclamation from the government under the National Service Acts. The liability to register their names under the acts was now extended to men of 19, but these men would not be called up until they were 20. Also included were men who had reached the age of 20 since December 1st, and men whose ages on January 1st were 23, 24, 25, 26 and 27. Around 2,500 men from the city were estimated to fall into these groups and around 2,000,000 men nationally.

Unfortunately 80 percent of the unemployed men in the city were above the age limits specified in the new call up, so this burden would be little affected, slackness in the brickyards accounting for a large number of men being out of work. Businesses however, would suffer, and the Co-operative Society, for instance, confirmed that they would eventually lose up to 50 percent of their staff, with the added drawback of a fall-off in trade in the city for men's clothing.

Lost at Sea

News of the death of another city man reached his home in Fulbridge Road in the first few days of 1940. Chief Officer Percival Rowland Cocks, was serving on the Royal Mail Steamer NAVASOTA, when it was torpedoed by a German submarine on the night of 5th December during a violent storm in the Atlantic.

Mr. Cocks, 42 years of age, had been home on leave on November 22nd, and then had sailed from a West Coast port on the 26th. His wife, Mrs. Muriel E. Cocks, a dispenser at the Friendly Societies' Medical Institute, heard from a survivor that her husband was last seen trying to launch one of the ship's lifeboats. The bad weather conditions would have made survival extremely difficult and the launching of lifeboats almost impossible. 43 of the ship's crew were posted as missing, most of them being sucked down by the NAVASOTA, sinking to the bottom in just eight minutes.

From Monday 1st January 1940 the maximum hours that a young person (under 16), could be employed was reduced to 44 hours per week. Mr. J.D. Medcalf, the Secretary of the Peterborough Chamber of Trade, said that grocers and provision traders would be mainly affected, with the new ruling mostly applying to errand boys. An appeal had been made to people to take their own goods home with them, the plea, however, was having little effect. The main reason for the cut in hours was due to the blackout, and the fear of boys being kept on the job after "lights out."

On Monday 8th January food rationing was finally introduced, and it was about this time also that the local council decided to allow the keeping of pigs on allotments. There had been a bye-law against this as the styes were thought to take up much needed land for cultivation, however, as long as the styes were properly constructed, pigs were food too weren't they?

The taking out of a council loan of £2,800 was approved in chambers for the purchase of the Palmerston and Glebe Road allotment estate, Woodston, and purchase of Tebbs and Sons land at Fulbridge Road was adjourned pending applications for allotments there. Corporation land at Lincoln Road, Walton was ploughed, and offers to hire allotments were invited. 29 allotments were also taken on the Tennyson Road estate. The Ram Fair Meadow was also ploughed to meet requirements, as was the Padholme Road estate.

On a more sombre note, instructions were now received for the provision of 200 war graves, for members of the armed forces, on land that had been set aside for the purpose at a cost of £290. Mr. Stafford, some would say rather shortsightedly, proposed that the decision be reversed as the anticipated emergency might never happen, and the shallow drainage on the proposed land could be done any time.

The original proposal had been to use 1.8 acres of land to accommodate 1,600 graves, the revised alternative for 200 was later accepted. At the time the chosen site was a field full of cattle, and the £290 was the price for fencing and draining the land. The City Engineer added that if they waited until there was a raid, and they suddenly had 50 bodies arrive, they would not be able to deal with them without work being carried out straight away. The committee eventually decided to go ahead with the preparation of the 200 graves.

The demolition of the caretaker's house at the Broadway cemetery also provided the space for another 113 graves for the impending emergency.

Civil Defence Matters

At the beginning of January the A.R.P. Senior Regional Officer decided that the public should be allowed to use school air raid shelters after school hours, although the consent of the Local Education Authority was required. An A.R.P. grant would not be forthcoming unless it was shown that the public shelters were substantially relieved. It was stressed that the shelters must not be invaded by the public during school time. To prevent this from happening, the gates to the Lincoln Road Senior School were locked during daytime, and there were shelters in the recreation ground opposite anyway.

Other matters brought up at the council meeting at that time included the Agricultural Society agreeing to a request to allow the use of the dressing room under their grandstand as a temporary cleansing station. The London Brick Company, on the other hand, said that their sports pavilion was the only facility their men had, and it was in daily use. They could not, therefore, agree to a request.

It was decided at this time that wages would not be paid to A.R.P. wardens who were off duty due to medical illness. A decision on applications for rate relief for people called for military service was put off for discussion at a sub-committee, and schoolchildren, it was decided, should continue to carry their gas masks with them at all times.

Among other items: the City Engineer was accepting local tenders for underclothing for the male personnel of civil defence who wore heavy protective clothing. The cost was about £60. A military unit was to be allowed to use the slipper baths at 2d. per head. No.61 Padholme Road was now made ambulance station No.1, in lieu of the swimming pool. Rental was £60 per annum plus rates. A new warden's post was to be made at Keeton Road, on corporation land. A hut in Crown Street would be used for recreational purposes by the wardens. Approval was received for the appointment of two whole-time members of the Women's Auxiliary Police Force. A committee was set up to estimate the cost of providing toilets for the emergency clearing stations. School air raid shelters, it was decided, would now be lighted by oil lamps at a cost of £1 per shelter, and head teachers were asked to arrange for older children to knit mittens and scarves for county regiments. No one could accuse the members of Peterborough Council of not doing their bit!

There was another, city wide, siren test on Wednesday 3rd January, with much better results than the first one the previous December. The brickyards', works', and factories' sirens were all brought into use to augment the eight at the Town Hall (electric and compressed air), the East Station, the Police Station, Baker Perkins, Brotherhoods, the Electricity Works and the Gas Works. Beyond the city boundary there were also sirens at the beet factory, Stanground police station and Fletton fire station.

A still morning helped the sound to travel, and from all quarters came reports of much better reception. At Walton and Werrington, where few people heard them in December, the sirens were heard very clearly. However, a new Gents 4 h.p. electric siren was ordered, to be erected at Werrington, similar to those at the Town Hall. The cost would be £59 15s. and would rank for a grant.

More Objectors

Five people from the city attended the Eastern Counties Conscientious Objectors Tribunal at Cambridge on Tuesday 16th January 1940. Harold John Wheatley, a schoolteacher of 141 Dogsthorpe Road said in his statement: "I am convinced I can do more useful service both to Europe and to Germany by peaceful example than by armed opposition with its attendant distress". He said he was, however, willing to assist in civil defence, "as in this he was, to some extent, counteracting the unhappiness caused by war."

He was unconditionally registered as a conscientious objector.

Arthur William Wheeler, of 69, Exeter Road, wrote that from childhood he was taught by his parents that war could not be condoned in any circumstances. At the age of 16 he had joined the Peace Pledge Union. He objected to taking part in this war or any other war and was striving to put the principles of Christianity into practice. Wheeler was a clerk in the Engineers department of the L.N.E.R. which had been evacuated to Peterborough from London. He was placed on the conscientious objectors register on condition that he continued in that occupation.

Reginald Stanley Town, of 8, Bamber Street, based his objections on Christian pacifism; he was convinced that all war was murder. His father had suffered for his conscience in Wormwood Scrubs during the First World War. Town was employed as a tyre distributor and driver with the Marsham Tyre Co. and said he wouldn't mind the sack if it was brought about by his refusal to help fit tyres to military vehicles. He said he considered A.R.P. work wrong as it indirectly helped the war to continue, and that he was a member of the Harris Street Baptist Church. He was registered as an objector.

Leonard Bush of 13, St. Marks Street, wrote, "I believe that there is a way of life that can bring the world to peace. That is the way of reconciliation. I believe it is right to love in all circumstances. Every act of love brings the world closer to the ideal of peace; every act of hate makes it more remote." This interpretation, he said, was based on the teachings of Christ, and he felt it wrong to take part in war or to engage in any of its auxiliary services. He was an invoice clerk, and Secretary of the local branch of the Peace Pledge Union. He was unconditionally exempted.

Frederick Stanley Kemmenoe, a 20 year old railway clerk, of 68, Exeter Road, wrote in his statement: "I recognise the great debt that I owe to my country for the benefits that I derive from it. But when I am asked to perform a duty which conflicts with the greater claim of universal mankind and with the infinitely better way of life revealed by the Lord Jesus Christ, I must come to a decision as to whom I owe greater allegiance. I have no quarrel with the people of other countries and cannot recognise the right of the government to compel me to take part in any form whatever in any organisation designed for the express purpose of killing my fellow beings."

Kemmenoe said he was an evacuated railway clerk, and attended the Pentecostal Church. He was registered on the condition that he did not change his employment.

Submarine Disaster

Chief Petty Officer John Frederick Shaw, second son of Mr. and Mrs. H. Shaw, of 28, Huntley Grove, Peterborough, was a member of the crew of H.M. Submarine UNDINE, one of three submarines reported by the Admiralty on Tuesday 16th January, to have been lost while, "engaged on a hazardous enterprise." Aged only 25, C.P.O. Shaw was thought to have been the youngest officer of that rank in the whole submarine service.

Three submarines were sunk in close succession in that January, SEAHORSE, on the 10th, UNDINE, on the 15th, and STARFISH, on the 20th. They were all lost in the Heligoland Bight; UNDINE was hunted down by German minesweepers and sunk with depth charges.

C.P.O. Shaw's father, an insurance broker and travel agent at 11, Broadway, had a feeling that his son was still alive. A message had been broadcast over German radio that some members of UNDINE's crew had been picked up, although it was not known at the time if the information was correct.

"We are confident," Mr. Shaw had said, "knowing his capabilities and knowing how he can adapt himself, that if he escaped from the submarine he has reached safety all right." A friend had broken the news to Mr. Shaw of the loss of the submarine after having heard it on the wireless. C.P.O. Shaw had been married for less than a year, he had been a fine swimmer and two brothers, T.A. Shaw and G.R. Shaw, were prominent members of Peterborough Swimming Club. Mr. G.R. Shaw and a third brother were both serving with the forces.

After being educated at Huddersfield College, where he won the swimming and diving championships, C.P.O. Shaw went on to Huddersfield Technical College spending five years in the Engineering department. He went on to become a Petty Officer on board an aircraft carrier before volunteering for submarine service. After special training he was appointed to the UNDINE as C.P.O.

In the official Admiralty list, published on Thursday 18th January, C.P.O. Shaw, described as an engine room artificer, 4th class, was posted as missing.

The A.R.P. Bill Rise

On Wednesday 17th January, approval was given by the Board of Education for the construction of a number of shelters at schools in the area. At Fletton Secondary, six shelters at £708. Fletton Council School, five shelters and the strengthening of some rooms, £994. Stanground C. of E. mixed, four shelters, £472; infants, three shelters, £354. Woodston Council junior, four shelters, £472. Total estimated cost, £3,000, to be met by loan.

The Fletton Urban District Council also asked for five additional public shelters to be built. Reasons put forward for these were the large number of people working in the district and passing to and fro at all times of the day and night, and the large number of people carried by buses from and to the city centre, especially on market days. A decision was made to provide the extra shelters at a cost of about £900. The building of a central air raid warden's post in Fletton was also asked for at the estimated cost of £100 excluding fittings, but expenditure above £50 for this purpose could not be approved.

It was at this time that the A.R.P. Committee received a report from H.M. Inspector of Schools, who had recently visited the county, recommending the hiring of further halls in the Fletton district for school accommodation to enable normal sessions to be worked, instead of the alternate day system that was being implemented at the time. If this was to be done, further air raid shelters would have to be constructed for the halls, which would be solely used for evacuees and therefore the cost would be entirely met by the government as an evacuation charge. There were 196 infants and 86 mixed senior elementary children for whom accommodation had to be found.

New Year Arctic weather
January 1940 went down in the record books as being the coldest spell of winter weather since 1895. One of the worst stretches of road, according to the police, was the Ailesworth-Helpston road, along which one Peterborough driver had his van completely buried by drifts, forcing him to abandon it. This was the first time the Eastern Counties Omnibus Company had to withdraw buses from local services due to the bad state of the roads. One night the whole of the town services were withdrawn from 7 o'clock onwards, the roads being "like a sheet of glass," and about 30 buses were stranded in the gutter on different parts of the road. Workmen from Brotherhood's could not drive their vehicles home because of the ice, and had to walk, as did people leaving the theatres and cinemas. The buses were eventually taken back one by one after the roads had been gritted.

The worst day for the buses was January 20th. Mr. Baker, the district superintendent, said that the frost was so severe that the bus radiators and hot water pipes froze up as they ran on the roads. No fewer than 20 buses were put out of commission with burst radiators, and certain routes had to be cancelled. Conditions improved after that, but the buses ran late. The worst road in the city, as far as the bus drivers were concerned, was Lincoln Road with its pronounced camber.

Approximately 8,000 tons of snow was shifted from the city streets, by some 200 men from the Highways Department, 60 of whom had been secured from the Employment Exchange. All this had been accomplished with one mechanical snow-plough, eight motor vehicles, and four horse-drawn carts. The snow was piled up at the pleasure fair and horse fair meadows. The mail and train services were less affected, but were behind schedule.

There was, at this time, what was described as a "plumbers' harvest," with an estimated 1,260 burst pipes in the city. One out of every four of the 1,100 houses owned by the Corporation was affected in this way. Whole rows of houses were frozen up, some being without water for over a week.

On the farms hundreds of acres remained to be ploughed, and horses and tractors stood idle. There was a shortage of labour on the farms, and a shortage of coal generally, due to transport problems. The Nene was completely frozen over, but was unsuitable for skating. Many birds, particularly waterfowl, were frozen to death.

The Chief Constable issued a statement to the public stating: "Everybody, under the bye-laws, is liable for the cleaning of snow from the footpath in front of his or her premises. The co-operation of householders in doing that would be greatly appreciated, it makes it easier for pedestrians.....The Corporation cannot do everything."

UNDINE Survivor

Listening to a broadcast in English from the German Bremen transmitter on the night of Thursday 25th January, Mr. and Mrs. Shaw, heard the name of their son, Chief Petty Officer John Frederick Shaw, mentioned in the third list of survivors from the British submarine UNDINE. The following day C.P.O. Shaw's wife received a telegram from the admiralty confirming the German broadcast. Shortly afterwards Mrs. Shaw received a card from her husband dated January 20th, the card was printed in German with deletions in ink and pencil and stated only that he was well, and a prisoner of war. Also pencilled on the card was: "My address is: Prisoner of war, J.F. Shaw, E.R.A. D/MX 54419, OFLAG IX A, Germany."

Next Group to Register

On Saturday 17th February, another group of men was called to register. This applied to men who on December 31st had reached the age of 20, but not 24, that is men who were born between January 1st 1916 and December 31st 1919 inclusive, this would now exhaust the number of men who were born during the First World War. About 500 men from the city were expected to register. There was now a new reserved category, "Quarries," but this was thought unlikely to affect the area, although there were many trades under the general heading of engineering.

Plans were also in preparation at this time for the overhaul of the nation's gas masks. Many of these had been issued in September 1938, and had not been checked since then. Apart from cases of perished rubber or cracked eyepieces, there was concern that other faults may have developed without the owners being aware.

It was proposed to establish a servicing organisation throughout the country, largely furnished by A.R.P. wardens. They were already trained in the inspection and care of gas masks and would be capable of effecting minor repairs and re-adjustments.

Help in the Blackout

After five black months, street lighting finally re-appeared in the city again, although in a restricted form, on Friday 9th February 1940. The new official lamps made their first appearance in Bridge Street and Long Causeway, and although illumination was described as "very, very faint," it was enough to prevent many footpath collisions and false steps at kerbs.

Mr. Rowland, the Deputy City Electrical Engineer, stated that the number of lamps authorised for Peterborough was 291. About 40 had been put into operation during the first week. "There is a tremendous rush for them," said Mr. Rowland, "and we have got to get them when we can. They are coming in driblets, and as they arrive we are getting them out."

The lamps would continue to be fitted, one on each pillar, from Oundle Road, over the Town Bridge, to Fitzwilliam Street, Broadway. Other streets which would eventually have them were Westgate, Church Street, Cowgate, St. Leonard's Street, and Midgate as far as City Road.

Selected posts would also be fitted in Thorpe Road, London Road, Fletton Avenue, Thorpe Park Road, Mayor's Walk, Russell Street, Westwood Street, Gladstone Street, Cromwell Road, Lincoln Road, Park Road, the remainder of Broadway and Eastfield Road.

Lamps would also be fitted at other points in streets on the routes to air raid warden's posts. The cost of fitting and erecting the whole job was 15 shillings per lamp, the work was carried out by the Corporation Electricity Department. The special lamps were designed to be attached to existing street lighting fittings. They were made of metal, with reflecting surfaces, cut down to a minimum, and were manufactured to a standard specification agreed by a joint committee of the Illuminating Engineering Society and the Home Office A.R.P. Department.

The maximum illumination allowed at that time was .0004 foot candle, the average being .0002 foot candle, (a foot candle was a measurement indicating the light on a surface given by a candle a foot away). The maximum intensity of the beam of light projected could not exceed one candle power in any direction, and the stringent conditions imposed for the use of this limited lighting made it compulsory for lamps to be at least 100 feet apart, and not less than 10 feet above street level. However, as far as Mr. Rowlands knew, they would not be required to be extinguished during an air raid.

Tests had been carried out by the Home Office, and no direct light was found to be visible from the air, (at .0004 foot candle 10 feet above street level, it's hard to imagine any direct light being visible from the ground!) and there was not sufficient reflected light to be seen from above. As far as was known, the new lamps would be used for the duration of the war, subject to further government alterations. The lamps would be lit every night from blackout time, and, like ordinary street lamps, be operated by a time switch.

News from the Front
News of recognition for two Peterborough men was now reaching the city. Flight Lieutenant Reginald William Gautrey, aged 26, younger son of Mr. and Mrs. J.F. Gautrey, 127, Cromwell Road, was mentioned in dispatches, and 25 year old Stoker Burnell Willis, fourth son of the late Private William Willis who was killed in the Great War, and of Mrs. S. Pendred of 1a, Eastfield Road, who was serving on the destroyer HMS ANTELOPE when she sank two U-boats in one day.

Flight Lieutenant Gautrey had been educated at Deacon's School and later had worked in the City Treasurer's department at the Town Hall for five years. He had received his commission as a pilot officer in February 1936 and had been on the RAF Reserve for the past twelve months. In the previous September he had been promoted to Flight Lieutenant and was based at Calshot.

It was not known for what specific action he received his mention, but among the list of official announcements made at that time were awards for offensive and reconnaissance patrols over the North Sea and elsewhere, including attacks on submarines and as Flt. Lt. Gautrey was serving on flying boats, these would seem the most probable.

Stoker Willis was expected home on leave as his ship had gone into port, and although it was the second half of February, the Christmas decorations were still up at his home waiting for his return and the beginning of the celebrations.

Coal and Compulsion
Since the beginning of the war a shortage of coal had been affecting the whole of the country, worse in the south, but Peterborough had been struggling more than most, and all the schools had been kept closed due to the cold weather and lack of coal for heating. However, on Monday 19th February the situation was eased somewhat when a special 37 wagon train, carrying 350 tons of coal was received in the city. The coal was sent on to distributors and, with other small quantities arriving, the situation

improved. The schools re-opened the same day, and continued with periodical rations.

Churches, clubs and institutes were allowed 50 percent of their ordinary rations, and householders were able generally to get by on a moderated supply, however, it was stated that in one home it was found to be necessary to break up a chair in order to boil a kettle!

Public services were still being well maintained during this time of shortage with another special train-load of coal arriving at the electricity works that same week, there was however, still a great shortage of coke.

Another Government Evacuation Scheme was now set to tax the patience of local householders with a request for homes for another 400 children evacuated from London. The billeting allowance for children over 14 was increased from 8s. 6d. to 10s. 6d. The method for securing the homes for the children was to send an application form to every householder who had to complete it and return it stating how many children they could take.

The previous evacuation census in the district received 1,200 offers to which 500 children were allotted. Of those who came, only 271 were still left in the area. It was accepted that should the number of offers this time fall short of the required amount, compulsory powers would be resorted to by the government.

More Men Register
Out of over 500 men who registered in the 23 age group at the Peterborough Labour Exchange on Saturday 17th February 1940, only five - less than one percent - raised a conscientious objection.

The actual number attending to sign was 490, of these, 64 elected for service with the Navy and 130 with the Air Force. The rest did not specify. In addition five enrolled by post on account of illness and ten more due to living a long distance from the exchange. The total included about 40 who had reached the age of 20 between December 2nd and 31st last. A number of recruits, more than usual, were in reserved occupations, mainly engineering.

Notification was received that the 24 year olds would be called to enroll on March 9th. This speeding up was due to the services rapidly absorbing the lower age groups, and more and more reserved occupations applying in the older groups as they became affected. The March registration would involve all men who became 24 during 1939, and also those who became 20 between January 1st and March 9th 1940. These were expected to be called up in the April. No decision had been reached by the War Office to call up in August men over 28. According to the present arrangements the registration of the 24 year olds would take place in March, and age groups up to 28 would follow. The call for men over 28 years of age would mean another Royal Proclamation.

There were 120 deaths recorded in Peterborough and district in the first seven weeks of 1940, many due to the cold weather with a few put down to accidents in the blackout, this compared with 73 for the same time the previous year. Mortality, as might have been expected, was highest among people between 70 and 80, 38 deaths recorded. The 60 to 70 age group came next with 33. The following table compares 1939 and 1940:

AGE GROUP	1940	1939
Over 90	2	4
80 to 89	13	9
70 to 79	38	23
60 to 69	33	20
50 to 59	15	9
30 to 49	10	6
Under 30	9	2
Totals	120	73

In January 1940 there were 55 burials at the Eastfield cemetery and 15 at Broadway, a total of 70 as compared with 37 in the corresponding month of 1939.

A.R.P. Matters

Intensive training of wardens in how to deal with incendiary bombs was now going apace. On Monday 19th and Wednesday 20th February, Sgt. Gilder gave evening lectures on the use of the stirrup pump in incendiary fires. Pump tests were also carried out every Thursday and Saturday at the Ram Fair Meadow where practical exercises were carried out. Other training also took place at some of the larger business houses in the city.

As far as the city shelters were concerned though, the news was not necessarily all good. The heavy snows of January had imposed a severe test on the air raid shelters, although they had stood it well. In no case did the water penetrate the roof, but there were a few instances during the thaw where water had run down the sloping entrance approaches. Generally the sumps had managed to cope with this minor flooding, however, some shelters had accumulated water up to a depth of a few inches.

One of the lowest portions of Stanley recreation ground was the worst. But even there the trouble was not bad enough to make the shelter unusable had the need arisen. A fire pump was eventually used to pump out the excess water.

The main problem with the city shelters, was again, wanton vandalism. The police were constantly on the look-out for offenders but the blackout made their job almost impossible. In the Burghley Square shelters it was said that, "damage of a disgusting nature had been perpetrated," and again a number of lamps had been stolen or damaged.

Notwithstanding these problems, work on the second section of the city shelter scheme was proceeding; those at West Town recreation ground were well under construction, although the problem of sites for shelters in the centre of the town had still not been solved.

As a comparison to the damage that was being done to Peterborough shelters, it was stated that 62 of the 163 air raid shelters in Norwich had been damaged wantonly during February. In some cases glass panels protecting the keys had been smashed and the keys removed.

Another threat to the city A.R.P. Committee was received late in February in the form of an order from the Senior Regional Officer for two of Peterborough's five first aid posts to be closed. The S.R.O. said he could not justify the retention of five posts fully manned, neither did he feel that there was a special case for retaining ambulance paid personnel in excess of 14. The members of the city council were so upset by this request that the Town Clerk informed the S.R.O. that they were not prepared to take the responsibility of the reduction, and told him that he would have to name the posts which would have to go. The five posts were at Bridge Street, Mayor's Walk, St. Martin' Street, Keeton Road and Mountsteven Avenue.

Bridge Street was important because there was nothing over the bridge; Mayor's Walk served a thickly populated neighbourhood; St. Martin's Street was right in the centre of the city; Keeton Road served New England, and Mountsteven Avenue served Walton.

The two posts were to be closed temporarily and re-opened in the event of an air raid, but it was feared that if they did close the staff would go to other war work and the facilities would be lost at a crucial time.

The A.R.P. Committee thought that the citizens should know the position, and decided to take it to the Houses of Parliament; they also asked Lord Burghley to see if he could do anything about the situation.

More Black-out Offences

Black-out offenders were now regularly being brought before the Peterborough magistrates. One reason for this slackness was obviously that, up to this time, (March 1940), there had been no sign of enemy bombers over the city, and people had difficulty in appreciating the fact that they were under wartime emergency conditions. However, this did not mean that offences of this kind stopped as the war progressed; the simple reason was that people were just too careless.

On Wednesday 30th February the following people appeared before the magistrates in order to answer for various offences committed against the black-out regulations:

Donald Victor Christmas of 13, Huntley Grove, allowed a light to shine from a garage skylight in Queens Street at 6:05p.m. on 11th January. Christmas had given a youth permission to work on a lorry in the garage using an unscreened lamp, allowing light to escape through the roof of the building. He was fined £2 with 10s. costs.

Eva Smith of 73, Broadway, had allowed a light to shine from a side window of her house at 8p.m. on 3rd February. P.C. Hubble noticed that the whole of her garden and a wall 30 feet away were lit up. Mrs. Smith said: "quite right, I know when I have done wrong." She was fined £1.

Charles Lewis Winter, of 153, Cromwell Road, had allowed light to escape from his lavatory window at 7p.m. on the evening of 1st February. P.C. Briggs discovered that a screen had been provided for the window, but it had not been erected. Mr. Winter, who was renting a room at the house, said he was sorry, but his landlady usually blacked-out that particular window. He was fined 10s.

William Short of 19, Queen's Drive, allowed a light to shine from his upstairs bedroom window at 1a.m. on the night of 11th February. He told the police that he had just come in and lit the gas, which went low. He then went downstairs to put a shilling in the gas meter, and the light then suddenly became bright. He was fined 10s.

Edwin Leslie Ward of 104, Fulbridge Road, had lights burning in his hall and an upstairs room at 8:15p.m. on the evening of 11th February. P.C. Jenkins said that there were only light curtains covering the door and windows which did not prevent the light from being seen. Mr. Ward said that he had only been at the house for ten days and had trouble blacking all of it out. He said he regretted unwittingly committing the offence under difficult circumstances. He was fined 15s.

George Goodyear, of 71, Queen's Road, (10s.), and Annie Quin, of 79, Scotney

Street, (5s.), were both fined for using unauthorised front lamps on their pedal cycles.

Harold Wadsley Laxton, of 191, Lincoln Road, was summoned for riding a motorcycle displaying an unauthorised front lamp at 5:45p.m., on 30th January. P.C. Mayes stopped him in Long Causeway and found that he only had a thin strip of black paint or paper around the edge of the glass. Mayes said that the light was governed by the speed of the engine; he was in second gear owing to the snow. In top gear the light would not have been so bright! He was fined 10s.

George Robert Smith, of 28, Hankey Street, was also summoned for driving a lorry with unscreened lights and unblacked reflectors at 5:40p.m., on 20th January. Smith said that the lorry, as a rule, was not used at night. He was also fined 10s.

Costly Defence
The defence in this case was on the football field, but, although they let in six goals, Peterborough United still managed to win their game against Frickley Colliery 7-6, putting them at the top of the Midland League in a terrific match played at London Road on Saturday 26th February.

Using the terminology of the time, it was stated that the half-backs and backs on both sides were frequently beaten, but they were not entirely to blame. A soft surface gave them little foothold, and, once beaten, they found it impossible to recover.

There were three goals in the first six minutes, and then from being 3-2 down Peterborough pulled up to lead 4-3 at half-time. After the interval they took the score to 7-3 before the colliery rallied and scored three times in a quarter of an hour. The United team was:

Shelton, Tasker, Smith (J), Fletcher, Warnes, Hewitt, Fielding, Rowbotham, Macartney, Johnston and Rudkin.

The attendance was 1,205. The takings were: Tickets - £53 10s. 3d. Programmes - £1 13s. 2d. Car Park - 10s. 3d.

Defence of a more costly nature was brought home to the local people on the afternoon of Saturday 2nd March 1940, when a training aircraft from Peterborough (Westwood) airfield crashed just outside Wansford. Two young Sergeant Pilots, James Fife Wales, 20, of Mewslade, Mizenway, Cobham, Surrey, and Robert Shirra Spratt Black, 24, of Beechwood House, Kilnhurst, near Rotherham, died when their Hawker Hart, K4997, went down during a training flight.

Their bodies were brought back to Peterborough for a double funeral with full military honours, which took place on the afternoon of Wednesday 6th March at the Eastfield cemetery, after a service in the Broadway cemetery chapel. The two coffins were carried side by side on an RAF tender, each draped with the Union Jack, and surmounted by the two men's caps.

Witnesses who ran to the scene of the crash said that when they came across the plane it was upside down in a field, as they approached it to look for survivors it suddenly exploded and burst into flames, causing them to back off. The charred bodies were eventually recovered, and the RAF medical officer was satisfied that their deaths had been instantaneous.

There were about seventy airmen present at the funeral, wreaths were laid, three volleys were fired by the firing party, and the Last Post was played by an RAF bugler.

On a happier note, Stoker Burnell Willis now arrived at his home in Eastfield

Road on ten days leave. It will be remembered that he had been serving on HMS ANTELOPE when she sank two U-boats in one day. He was welcomed at the railway station by his family and friends, many city people and the Mayor. He had been below on watch in the engine room when the first depth charges went off, and then was told of the destruction of the first U-boat. About half an hour later they attacked the second submarine and witnessed heavy oil coming to the surface. They stayed over the sunken submarine for eight hours, but no survivors were seen.

Raid Warning
On March 15th, obviously concerned about the number of black-out offences being committed, the police made an official announcement through the local press. They said that they and the air raid wardens had instructions to enforce very strictly the lighting order, and, in view of the possibility of enemy air raids during the next few weeks, the police earnestly requested the co-operation of all householders in effectively screening all lights in shops and houses during the black-out.

In order to emphasise the scale of the problem, a report from an airman flying at three thousand feet over the city was published, in which it was stated that at 9p.m. on a previous evening, a very large number of lights were clearly visible in different parts of the city. Many people, it was stated, were in the habit of going upstairs, switching on the electric lights, and then screening the windows, which should have been done before the black-out.

Householders were also urged at this time to get their respirators examined by a warden at the Old Town Hall, the warden's post, St. Paul's Church Hall, George Street Church schoolroom, or at Cobden Street Church schoolroom. It was said that unless care was used, "The valve may become displaced, rendering the respirator ineffective."
Children's respirators would be examined at schools.

Demand for allotments was increasing by the middle of March; the "Dig for Victory" campaign bringing forth many applications, and more land was still required. Land was bought up in the Crown Street field, New England, with a further five acres still being used for games being recommended for ploughing. Land close to Fulbridge School was also earmarked for ploughing at this time. A number of plots had been let on the Westwood Estate, but about two acres were held back by the council for the planting of potatoes. The whole of the land on the Ram Fair meadow had been let apart from one or two plots. More land at Padholme Road was also being considered.

Conflicting Movements
There were two contrasting problems causing concern in the city during the middle of March. The amount of people volunteering to put up evacuees coming into the area had been, to say the least, disappointing, and at the same time there was concern that too much of the locally produced beef was being sent out of the district.

Billets were needed for 4,000 evacuees, but up to Wednesday 13th March, only about 250 had been offered with some people sending in forms stating that they could not receive children for a variety of reasons. Failure to return the official form, which had been sent out to all households, was construed as a refusal. Mr. Frank Smith the City Treasurer and Chief Billeting Officer still had faith in a good response saying: "I am sure that if people realised that a lot of children were in real danger of losing their lives they would do anything for them and that if a whole lot

47

arrived in an emergency, they would re-consider their decision."

The Mayor sent out a personal appeal to the people of the city encouraging them to come forward and volunteer.

Butchers were having a problem of a different kind during this week with the transfer to other parts of the country of large numbers of cattle being produced in the local area. On Wednesday 15th for example, over 150 beasts passed through the cattle-market, with only 75 being left for local requirements, the others going to other districts.

Butchers, at this time, were given buying permits for supplies equivalent to 1s. 10d. worth of meat per registered customer, plus an allowance of two and a half percent for manufacture and wastage. Under this arrangement each butcher carried enough stock to cover each customer he had registered with him, and each customer therefore, had his or her supply guaranteed. Butchers made fortnightly returns to the Food Office, sending in the coupons they had taken as evidence of sales, and it was on this basis that they received their subsequent buying permits. In this way each butcher would always be able to stock the exact amount of meat needed for supply to his registered customers.

A number of locally produced beasts may have been leaving the area, however, with this system in place, it would seem that the city would always have enough meat for its citizens.

A Clipsham stone headstone to the memory of Boy Herbert Bradley, of Tower Street, who lost his life the previous October while serving on the cruiser HMS SOUTHAMPTON, was now erected in Woodston cemetery. The memorial was presented by Messrs. Robert Cox and Sons, stonemasons, of Eastfield Road, in grateful appreciation and remembrance. The stone stood 4ft. high, and an inscription at the centre read:

"In grateful memory of Boy Herbert Michael Bradley, who was killed on war service on HMS Southampton, October, 16th, 1939, aged 17 years, R.I.P."

There were plenty more from where he came from.

On Saturday 9th March 605 local men registered in the 20-24 year group for service in the forces. 98 applied for service in the Navy or Marines, and 144 in the Air Force. Only three men put their names forward as conscientious objectors. The 25 year old class would soon follow but no decision had been reached about the 26 and 27 year classes at this time. It was usual to have a months interval but this all depended on the requirements of the services.

By Saturday 6th April over 3,000 local men had registered for service with the forces. The 582 men on that day took the total to 3,046. The figures were: 20-25, 582 (including 6 conscientious objectors); 20-24, 605 (3); 20-23, 505 (5); 20-22, 407 (14); 20-21, 397 (6); 20, 460 (7). The 41 conscientious objectors represented 1.34 percent of the full number of signatories, in some parts of the country it ran as high as 3 percent.

Of those registering on Saturday 6th, 85 asked for Navy service, 11 for the Marines, 180 for the Royal Air Force, and the remaining 306 either plumped for the Army or had no preference.

The first combined A.R.P. exercise in the city took place on the morning of Sunday 10th March. The personnel on duty numbered approximately 700, including 300 members of the casualty services, and about 150 men of the Auxiliary Fire Service. Others taking part were the police, wardens, rescue and decontamination squads and the report centre staff.

The full scale exercise took place at Werrington. The air raid sirens were assumed to have sounded at 9:50a.m., when the A.R.P. workers left their homes for action stations. Three "enemy aircraft" were supposed to have dropped eight 500lb. high explosive bombs, four clusters of incendiary bombs and five 50lb. gas bombs. Wardens from sectors in which there were no incidents assisted as casualties and as umpires. The programme was drawn up by Mr. K.H. Thorpe, the Deputy City Engineer, and an element of surprise was maintained throughout.

"Bombs" were dropped at 10 o'clock, and the "incidents" were cleared up by 11:30, the whole exercise was thought to have been a great success.

Deaths in the Air and at Sea

Reports now reached the city of the death of Acting Pilot Officer Ronald Arthur Sims, aged 19, younger son of Mr. and Mrs. Edward Sims, of Cambria, 73, Alexandra Road, Peterborough, who lost his life when the plane which he was piloting crashed at 3 o'clock on the morning of Sunday 31st March.

The accident occurred at an aerodrome in the West of England where he had been taking part in night flying training. It was understood that he was attempting to land after his second solo flight when the port wing of the aircraft hit a tree. His death was reported as being instantaneous, and his parents received the news at about 10 o'clock on the same morning of the crash when they were informed by the police of a telephone message that had been sent. A confirmation telegram from the Air Ministry was received by the parents later the same day.

A.P.O. Sims, whose father was employed in the Traffic department of the L.N.E.R. at New England, was educated at Lincoln Road and King's Schools, he also sang in the cathedral choir. On leaving school he became a draughtsman in the Engineer's Department of the G.P.O. in Park Road. He started his Air Force training in July 1939, gaining his wings by the end of that year. His brother, Harry, was also in the R.A.F.

A second local man, Telegraphist, George Dillon, Royal Navy, younger son of Mr. and Mrs. J. Dillon, of 34, Star Road, Peterborough, was at this same time reported as "missing, believed killed."

George was serving on HMS GLOWWORM, a 1,345 ton destroyer presumed lost in action off the Norwegian coast. On April 11th, about 5p.m. a telegram arrived which read: "Regret to report that your son, George Dillon, Telegraphist, P/SSX 23638, is missing, believed killed, on war service, R.A. R.N. Barracks, Portsmouth." The next day they received another letter, this time from Rear Admiral C. Tait, confirming the death of their son.

George Dillon was educated at New Road, Boys School, and on leaving joined the staff of the L.M.S. goods offices at Crescent Wharf. After turning 18 in 1938 he joined the Navy, eventually being posted to HMS RAMILIES and seeing service in South African and Australian waters. He was home on leave in January 1940 after which he was instructed to report to HMS GLOWWORM.

Mr. Dillon was an air raid warden in the city, and his elder son, Bernard, was called up with the 22 age group and was at this time serving with an infantry battalion at Colchester. A memorial service to George was held at St. Mary's Church on Sunday 21st April.

Due to strict censorship rules the exact circumstances of a man's death were rarely revealed in the press during World War Two, as this could divulge important information to the enemy such as troop and ship movements, and war losses in air squadrons etc. However, we now know that HMS GLOWWORM was part of a destroyer screen for a minelaying force, which was mining Norwegian waters in order to prevent iron ore being shipped to Germany. They had lost a man overboard on April 6th and on turning back to look for him they had lost contact with the rest of the squadron. At this same time a German force was invading Norway, being supported by the German heavy cruiser ADMIRAL HIPPER, and it was this ship that the little GLOWWORM met on April 8th. Although hopelessly outgunned the destroyer turned at full speed and under the pounding of 8-inch salvoes from the German ship, rammed the HIPPER abreast of 'B' turret, inflicting serious damage before capsizing. Moments later, GLOWWORM'S depth charges exploded beneath her, administering the coup de grace, only one officer and 37 men survived to be rescued by the HIPPER out of a complement of 145.

Even though one or two "Forces" deaths had now been reported, the "land war," had yet to take its first soldier victim from the city area. A high spirited letter was received in the city in August by a member of the local British Legion, from two Peterborough brothers, Private A. Dickens and Sergeant T.C. Dickens, from "somewhere in France." It displays a somewhat innocent attitude to the war, harking back to the traditions of the First World War and fighting the "Hun," and marching out to make the world a better place, a fine sentiment, but one feels that these two brothers have much to learn and much to see before they achieve their goal, and the boys in the men shine through from their words.

"We were very pleased indeed to hear from one of the 'Steelbacks' of 1914-18. They are worthy of the good name, as they helped to knock the Huns out. My brother and I have landed again 'somewhere in France.'

We think it is encouraging to see the land girls doing their bit for the country, but we are afraid they will have to work harder, as you know, a strong home front means a good battle front. The lads out here are as bright and happy as can be expected.

We trust the British Legion will carry on with the good work; the men of 1914-18 standards know the meaning of comradeship and nobody knows what you men went through. The lads out here have one determination - the spirit to win and to hit first and answer afterwards! We can assure you if we have that spirit there will be no cause to worry about the German nation. 'There'll always be an England,' and at times like these if we want to live and make a better world for our mothers, fathers, brothers and sweethearts then we must fight for our freedom, for our loved ones. Will you please call on our parents?

With kind respects to the men of the British Legion; also the women's section."

That last little plea, "Will you please call on our parents?" has an almost childlike quality, and does not sit well with the mature impression they have tried to create in the rest of the letter. For the Dickens brothers as well as the other volunteers, the real war could not yet be imagined.

A Death Not Worth Mentioning

An inquest on Private George William Longley, aged 26, of 91, Eastgate, Peterborough, was adjourned by the Paddington Coroner on Saturday 6th April, for further enquiries to be made. On Tuesday 9th, when the inquest was resumed, it was stated that Private Longley, a dispatch rider in the R.A.S.C., stationed at Kensington Barracks, was involved in a collision with a railway goods wagon in Bayswater Road, at the junction of Hyde Park Road, on the 4th April. He died in St. Mary's Hospital, Paddington, the same day.

Mr. Longley was formerly a landscape gardener in Peterborough and he joined the R.A.S.C. in November 1939, three months before he was due to register. He was the second son of Mr. and Mrs. C. Longley, of Forest Row, near Ashes Wood, Sussex, and just over three years before had married Miss J. Folksworth, adopted daughter of Mrs. Folksworth of Wisbech, and the late Mr. J.G. Folksworth. Private Longley had been home on 48 hours leave that Easter, and this was to be the last time his wife and two-year-old son, Raymond, would see him.

Private Longley's parents must have wanted him near them, as it seems on their request his military funeral took place at Forest Row on Tuesday 9th April.

After the war a list was compiled of the names of all the men and women from Peterborough who had been killed in the service of their country during the war, these included civilian victims of enemy bombing, and it was placed in Peterborough cathedral. The name of Private Longley does not feature in this list, neither for that matter does Percival Rowland Cocks, who, as mentioned earlier in this book, was killed when the Royal Mail Steamer NAVASOTA was torpedoed in the Atlantic in November 1939.

Private Longley was a soldier who was killed in an accident while on service, Percival Cocks was not in the Royal Navy, but was a merchant seaman instead. The subtle differences between these two deaths and those of the others who are mentioned in the cathedral list, those being servicemen killed due to direct enemy action, do not in my opinion warrant their omission; particularly when civilian victims of indiscriminate bombing are named. It is one of my main aims in writing this book to track down these omissions, and create a complete list of Peterborough war dead, so that they can be placed equally, side by side, in the sight of the citizens of today, and be recognised for their individual sacrifices.

A Word of Advice

The war, which it has to be said, hadn't started out to be quite as spectacular as the city people had first imagined, now suddenly took a turn for the worse with the German invasions of Norway and Denmark on April 9th. Alderman Snowden, Chairman of the City Council A.R.P. Committee, stated that Peterborough was prepared for any emergency, and added: "A Word Of Advice: If bombs drop don't get panicky; if you are caught in the streets, take refuge in the nearest shelter; if you are at home, stay there."

Mrs. A.A. Mellows stated that she now had 1,425 W.V.S. enrolled on her books who were ready for any emergency. Departments manned by the W.V.S. included evacuation duties, ambulance drivers and attendants, first-aiders in first aid posts supplementing the St. John workers, clerical workers in F.A.P.; Services canteen workers and transport drivers.

Another, little known task, came under the heading of "panic squads." In raids, when many people might become homeless, three large halls would be earmarked to house them for 48 hours. During this time they would be looked after by between 60 and 100 W.V.S. volunteers who would be standing by ready in these special squads.

Outside actual A.R.P. duties, some 25 members were engaged in digging. They had already done good work at Thorpe Road House, and at a number of vacant allotments. They also went on to get some house gardens into order for planting food. The city ladies were indeed doing excellent work.

It was also at about this time that the already famous fighter ace, E.J. "Cobber" Kain, visited the city. The 21 year old R.A.F. pilot, who had by this time shot down five enemy planes, thus gaining the title of "Ace," was in the city to meet Miss Joyce Phillips, who was with the Court Players Repertory Company and appearing in a show at the Empire Theatre. Kain was on ten days leave after having been injured while parachuting to safety from his crippled aircraft, and while still in Peterborough, he and Miss Phillips announced their engagement.

The Northamptonshires Carry the Torch

No history of Peterborough during the war would be complete without mention of the Northamptonshire Regiment. This was our local regiment, and more Peterborough men fought in it than in any other during the First World War. Naturally it had a certain attraction during the second war too, although with different recruiting methods, it was not, as before, made up of large groups of city men volunteering en masse. However, because of its history, and through the local connection that was still adhered to by many men who joined its ranks, the Northamptonshire Regiment still held a position of pride in the hearts of the city people. The soldiers of this regiment represented "Our Boys," and any news of them was always received with great interest.

It was for this reason that on April 5th, 1940, the "Standard" reported with great pride that the Northamptonshire Regiment had had the honour of putting the first Territorial battalion in the front line. The majority of the officers and men of this battalion, the 5th, had been recruited under the Territorial scheme and had come from Peterborough, Huntingdon, Oundle and St. Neots. A number of Reservists and Militiamen were with them to bring the battalion up to full strength. The men had moved into a French village somewhere just to the rear of the Maginot Line, and it was there that some reporters managed to speak to them.

"We suffered no casualties," said the commanding officer, "and did not see a lot of Germans. Occasionally we spotted working parties. We had our patrols out in No-Mans-Land and the fact that many men come from the country was probably useful. We heard the dogs out with the patrols, but all we got was one German spade, and we shot one dog."

A story was related of the experiences of another patrol that was led by a young subaltern.

"The patrol silently entered a certain village that stands, uninhabited and deserted, in No-Man's-Land. Cautiously they moved down the dark and empty main street. They surrounded a cottage which German soldiers were believed to have used. No sound came. They went inside. The rooms were all empty.

But signs of recent German occupation were discovered. In one room the Germans had obviously had the possibility of a musical evening. Evidently they had changed their minds in a hurry, and left so quickly that they left behind them a radio set and an old German gramophone, together with 22 German gramophone records. One was 'Romeo and Juliet.' The Northamptonshire men carried the gramophone and all the records back to their lines. There were no needles.

The next night the same subaltern took out a patrol and visited the same cottage. Again the place was unoccupied. When they went in they saw that the radio set had been taken by the Germans.

The gramophone will be placed in the unit's museum in its headquarters in England."

One soldier who was interviewed at this time was Private Walter Gray, a bricklayer from Peterborough.

More Register
On Saturday 27th April, 585 men of the 20-26 class registered for service with the forces, at Peterborough Employment Exchange. Of this number, 67 elected for service with the Navy, two for the Marines, and 183 for the Air Force. The remainder asked for the Army, or expressed no preference. There were eight conscientious objectors, bringing the total number at Peterborough in this category to 49. Of the number registering for service on that Saturday, about half were in reserve occupations, and would not be accepted into the forces, being retained instead on their civilian duties.

The subject of servicemen was at the centre of discussions at the Town Hall at this time. The city council had just decided to make up the wages of local men who had been called up; to the levels they were being paid in their previous civilian jobs. This decision however, did not turn out to be as popular as might have been expected.

The Chamber of Trade "expressed concern....in view of the heavy additional burden placed upon the ratepayers."

The Property Owners Association "learned with some anxiety" of the decision, and asked if it were irrevocable.

The Meat Traders Association asked the council "to reconsider their decision."

The Associated Road Operators wrote "protesting against the decision."

For the time being, the council decided to stick to their decision, and wrote to the various associations informing them of the fact. They did however state that they would reconsider the present arrangement when it expired in the following September.

First Full A.R.P. Test
The A.R.P. services for the whole of the North Midlands Defence Region took part in the first full scale test mobilisation on Sunday 5th May, 1940. For the purposes of the Peterborough test it was supposed that 124 bombs had been dropped, causing 68 deaths, and injuries to another 157 people. All the A.R.P. services were brought into action. The test was set by A.R.P. Headquarters at Nottingham, and the Regional Commissioner, Lord Trent, was in touch by telephone with the Control Centre at intervals from 10:30 to 12:00, the effective period of the raid.

At 9:35 the air raid message Yellow was received, followed at 9:51 by the air raid message Red. At 10:50 seven enemy aircraft were supposed to be seen approaching from the direction of Leicester, flying low over the city. They dropped 24 large high explosive bombs and 100 incendiary bombs.

Sixteen high explosive bombs made effective hits, causing 208 casualties, 68 of whom were killed. Only nine of the incendiary bombs were effective, and these caused large fires, which spread rapidly. Seventeen persons were seriously injured in the fires which occurred, bringing the casualty list to a total of 68 killed and 157 injured in the raid.

The more spectacular action took place directly in the city centre. The L.N.E.R. Sheet Stores building was struck by two high explosive bombs, and one incendiary bomb scored a hit on a crowded passenger train in a siding. There were 35 casualties, two being trapped under debris at one end of the building, and 20 in one of the coaches. A goods train was on fire, and the hydrants were covered in debris.

On the railway, the L.N.E.R. first aid personnel and fire party were called into action, rescuing and bandaging the injured, (the roles of the injured were acted out by Boy Scouts and young women of the W.V.S.). The firemen, working in relays, brought water from the river, and with stirrup pumps checked the spread of the fire.

Near at hand there was another major incident. In Trinity Street, one high explosive bomb fell between the road and the air raid shelter, and another outside the slipper baths. The entrance to the shelter was blocked by sandbags, and a fallen tree, and ten injured people were trapped. Two people had been blown on to the roof of the baths. The wardens called in police assistance, and the wounded in the shelter were rescued via the emergency hatch. The two people on the roof were dressed for fracture of the spine, and were lowered on stretchers to the ambulances.

The old Occupational Centre in Bridge Street was the target for two high explosive and two incendiary bombs. Ten injured people were trapped on the first floor, and the staircase was burnt out. There were 15 other cases outside, and the water mains were out of action. A crowd of over a thousand were controlled by the police, while firemen rescued the injured with the aid of ladders, and attacked the fire with water pumped from the river into a canvas reservoir. First Aid parties carried the injured into the Bridge Street first aid post. In Baker Street a house was on fire with six people inside, and 14 others in the vicinity were hurt.

The reports that reached the Control Centre were as follows:

Lodge in Oundle Road recreation ground wrecked and on fire, 6 casualties.

Wharf Road School hit by high explosive bomb, 6 casualties.

County School for Girls on fire, 30 casualties.

Gladstone Street Girls School struck by three bombs and on fire, 35 casualties, 9 being in the partially collapsed building; road made impassable by bomb crater.

Die Casting Co. premises in Princes Street damaged and on fire, 30 casualties, 10 trapped, and wall in danger of collapse, hindering rescue work.

Three bombs on Eastern Counties bus depot, 26 casualties and big fire involving petrol pumps.

High explosive bombs fell at new viaduct, junction of New Road and City Road, junction of Park Road and Westgate and Fulbridge Road - Paston Lane cross-roads, none exploding.

L.N.E.R. Clothing Store, Walpole Street on fire, 10 casualties, 2 trapped.

Paston All Saints former parish hall, Lincoln Road, Walton, on fire, and partly demolished, 15 casualties, 3 trapped.

Old building next to 99, Church Street, Werrington, on fire, and in danger of collapse, 10 casualties, 2 trapped.

As can easily be seen, these tests called for considerable initiative, ingenuity and large amounts of local knowledge. Official umpires from neutral towns made constant observations during the exercise, at all points, and reported to the Regional Office afterwards that they were "well satisfied," with the manner in which the jobs were tackled.

The W.V.S. provided 71 members for the exercise, and the Scouts sent along almost 100 boys. Owing to a last minute hitch the RAF from the local aerodrome had been unable to co-operate. It had been planned that the city services would cover the railway incident, but the railway company turned out their own service, another example of the initiative that would undoubtedly be needed, if and when, the real bombing began.

During a lunch held later that day at the Angel Hotel, which had followed a conference with the umpires at the Old Town Hall, Alderman Snowden declared that on the days showing, "Peterborough had nothing to fear."

The War Becomes Real

On May 10th 1940, the Battle of Flanders began. In less than a month the Germans took France and the Low Countries, which began with the invasion of Belgium, Holland and Northern France. The famous Maginot line was pierced with ease as the German Blitzkrieg spread quickly towards the Channel ports. Chamberlain resigned, and Churchill gave his first address to the House of Commons as prime minister on the 13th, saying: "I have nothing to offer but blood, toil, tears, and sweat."

The intensification of military operations now began to bring home the fearful toll of war.

Mr. and Mrs. A. Sharp, of 69, Park Road, received an Admiralty telegram on Saturday 11th May informing them that their eldest son, Paymaster Commander William Arthur Sharp, R.N. aged 40, had been killed while on active service. Commander Sharp had been in the navy since 1916 and had served for two years during the First World War. During his service he had two periods at the admiralty, first as assistant secretary to Admiral of the fleet Sir Charles Madden when he was First Sea Lord. His second spell was as Assistant Paymaster-Director-General. He was a gifted linguist and was appointed by the Admiralty as official interpreter of Russian, French and German. He was a fellow of the Royal Geographical society and had travelled extensively. He was unmarried.

On the same day as Mr. and Mrs. Sharp, Mr. S.G. Poole, of Cromwell Road, a mains engineer at the electricity power station, received an official message that stated his younger son, Sergeant C.J.S. Poole, RAF, was "missing, believed killed."

Sergeant Poole was known to be serving somewhere on the Western Front, and the date of his death was given as the 10th, just the day before. A letter followed on the following Monday evening (13th), confirming the news and intimating that there could hardly be any justification for hope that he had escaped by any means. This would seem to indicate that in official circles at least, the exact cause of his death was known, but that the authorities were not prepared to pass this information on to the parents.

Sgt. Christopher John Stafford Poole, (generally known as John), was 20 years of age, he had been in the Air Force for two years and in France since the outbreak of hostilities. Educated at Miss Mansfield's High School and then at King's School, he had left to join Barclay' Bank. He served as an observer in the RAF, and in peace time was known as a very good rugby player.

Petty Officer Harry Carter, aged 36, of H.M. Submarine SEAL, was posted as "missing on war service; believed to be a prisoner of war." His experience was just the beginning of a strange story if he did but know it. His wife, Mrs. Violet Carter, and two sons, Gordon (11) and Tony (9), of 69, Crown Street, received the Admiralty message on the 11th May and she was quite happy he was a prisoner as long as he was safe. P.O. Carter had been home on leave just three weeks before; he seemed to have been through a wearying time according to his wife, as his hair, apparently, had turned white. He had been in the submarine service for 13 years and was due for a pension after the next three. He saw action during the First World War in 1918 when he was aged 15, the ship in which he served was cut in two and he was picked up only after many hours in the water. Posted to the SEAL in 1939, they were assigned to the China Station, reaching Aden at the outbreak of the war, when they were recalled.

On June 9th 1931, P.O. Carter was in the submarine POSEIDON, which sank in the China Seas. He had the amazing luck to be brought to the surface by an air bubble as the vessel went down, being picked up by the RAWALPINDI. He also served on the submarines REGULUS, SEAHORSE and STERLET, the last two of which were reported missing earlier in the war.

The story of the SEAL is interesting because of the following reason. The submarine was a minelayer, and at the time P.O. Carter was serving on board her she was captured by German aircraft and motorboats on the May 5th 1940, trying to enter the Baltic. Later, refitted, and manned by a *German* crew, she served with the German navy as U.B., finally being scuttled at Kiel on May 3rd 1945.

A tragedy of a different kind befell 20 year old Private James Montague Francis, son of Mr. and Mrs. Charles Francis, of 5, Lime Tree Avenue. He had been on the staff of the City Council before being called up, and died in the Royal Herbert Hospital, Woolwich, on Saturday 11th May.

Since the beginning of March, Private Francis had been in military training in the Essex Regiment. His father, who worked at Baker Perkins Ltd., received the news that his son, who had never been of strong physique, had contracted a cold which had developed into bronchitis and he had been taken to hospital some three weeks prior to his death. X-rays subsequently showed that he had been suffering from pulmonary tuberculosis.

Private Francis had been born in 1919 at Werrington House, Werrington, and was educated at Miss Back's School, Lincoln Road, and then went on to the King's School. On leaving school he went to work for the Corporation in the City Treasurer's department.

The Race Is On
With the sudden escalation of the war, recruiting in the city for a wide range of civil defence organisations went into overdrive. There was an intensive campaign to recruit all men in reserved occupations, all men over the calling up age, and literally, ALL WOMEN.

The official recruiting depot for these services was the W.V.S. depot at the old Town Hall, which was run by Mrs. Arthur Mellows, and she emphasised that there was a job for everyone. The A.R.P. services were, at that time, well equipped with personnel, however, many of the men were under the age of 36, and would in their turn be called up to the fighting forces. Their places must eventually be filled, mainly by women.

Among the volunteers being asked for were men and women with first aid certificates, car owner-drivers, (men and women), motorcyclists, to be used as dispatch riders to link up with Nottingham and other towns which might be cut off by bombing. Stretcher bearers, clerical workers for first aid posts, and volunteers to offer temporary shelter to those who had been bombed out of their homes. In fact the only service that was not being recruited at the old Town Hall was that of the new Defence Volunteers, who were to combat parachute attacks. These were signing on at the police station.

With the real threat of invasion now hanging over the country due to the rapid German advance, the government sent out an appeal in the form of a wireless broadcast by Mr. Anthony Eden, the Secretary of State for War, on Tuesday 14th May, for men to join a new force, the Local Defence Volunteers, (L.D.V.). Originally set up to assist the local defence forces, and combat an invasion by parachutists, the L.D.V., who soon acquired the nickname of "Parashots," went on to become what we now know as the Home Guard.

By midday on Thursday 16ᵗʰ May, there had been 418 men from the city, enrolling for the new L.D.V., including 26 ex-officers and 52 ex-N.C.O.'s. There had also been 77 men enrolling from the outlying district. The first volunteer was at the police station before the wireless broadcast, announcing the formation of the new force was finished, he was Mr. J.H. Skinner, of 47, Bright Street. Among the first to enroll were the Town Clerk (Mr. A.J. Reeves), the Engineer (Mr. F.J. Smith), Col. A.H. Mellows and Sir Arthur Craig.

The force was voluntary and unpaid, and was open to British subjects between 17 and 65 years of age. The period of service would be for the duration of the war, and volunteers, once accepted, would be provided with uniforms and armed. Service was part-time and would not interfere with the volunteers' occupations or mean they would have to live away from home. All classes responded, including schoolmasters, farmers, other professions, and tradesmen.

Mrs. S.G. Cook, the local representative for the Women's Land Army, was not having as much success with her recruiting campaign. The numbers were, "dribbling in," as she put it, but they were not enough for requirements. The girls who did volunteer were completely untrained, although this was generally given at a college, it had now been reduced to one month on account of the urgency, and training was completed on the job.

The slackness of the blackout in the city was still causing some concern, and Mr. Lister Robinson, the Chief Air Raid Warden, went to the top of St. John's Church steeple one night in the middle of May, to see for himself how well it was being observed. He recorded an improvement from previous months, but saw two infringements coming from the direction of Trinity Street. When he came back down to earth however, he was unable to track them down. He stated that the skylight was the most dangerous form of infringement, and urged people to give special attention to this area. The Chief Constable issued a number of hints to aid compliance with the blackout regulations.

"Will people do their ENTIRE blackout BEFORE the dark period?"

Many people, he believed, left their bedrooms until they went to bed, and then turned the light on while they put up the screens, thereby committing a temporary breach of the regulations.

"A thin streak of light down the side of the window is also a frequent form of infringement."

Another A.R.P. matter giving cause for concern was that very few people so far, had come forward to have their gas masks tested. A large number however, who had not bothered until this late hour, were now turning up to collect respirators for their children.

A new scheme was also being introduced at this time, in which the fire fighting services were to be strengthened by members of the public, working in small teams in emergencies, as firemen in their own streets. Such groups of dedicated citizens, no doubt, were extremely impressed on hearing the announcement that each team would be supplied with a free stirrup pump, on a loan basis of course.

City householders at this time were still being very slow in coming forward to offer homes for the 4,000 child evacuees from London that had been allocated to the city. The Ministry of Health was beginning to put pressure on the city council and yet another appeal appeared in the local newspapers. It was stated that the children would only be sent to the city if their homes were in imminent danger of aerial bombardment, and it was hoped that on realising this, more people would come forward. The fact was however, the number of voluntary billets registered fell far short of the required amount.

Fourth Proclamation Signed, and L.D.V. takes Shape

The King had now signed the fourth Proclamation under the National Service (Armed Forces) Act, and men up to the age of 36 would now eventually register. The proclamation took in:

1. Men born between January 2nd 1921, and May 9th 1921, inclusive.
2. Men born between May 10th 1903, and January 1st 1912, inclusive.

The procedure of men registering in successive age groups in an ascending scale would continue, with no one being called upon until he had reached the age of 20.

The first age group included in the new proclamation would be the 28's in June, following the last of the third Proclamation, the 27's at the end of May. At this rate the 36 year olds would register in February 1941.

It was estimated that the additional age groups would contain 2,500,000 men, although, as in previous call ups, the number would be reduced by men in reserved occupations.

The Local Defence Volunteer force for the Soke and City took actual shape on the evening of Wednesday 22nd May 1940, when Col. Mellows explained details to a large gathering of officers and N.C.O.'s who had registered for service.

The County Commander of the L.D.V. for Northamptonshire was Major-General Sir Hereward Wake.

Divisional Commanders for the five divisions of the county were:

Kettering: Lieut. Col. H. Burditt.

Wellingborough: Brig. Gen. A.F.H. Ferguson.

Northampton Borough: Major T.E. Manning.

Soke and City of Peterborough: Col. A.H. Mellows.

Towcester: Lieut. Col. P. Lester Reid.

There were now 1,073 men enrolled in the Soke and City area, a military force, subject to military law. They were divided into companies, sections, and sub-sections and each were allocated defined areas of responsibility. Colonel Mellows listed the main personnel:

Group Commander: Mr. R.J.C. Crowden (who was second in command under Col. Mellows).

Assistant Group Commander and Adjutant: Mr. George Baker.

Assistant Adjutant: Mr. W.A. Heighton.

Transport Officer: Sir Arthur Craig.

Assistant Transport Officer: Mr. A.W. Wilson.

Liaison Officer: Mr. A.F. Percival.

Records Officer: Mr. W.B. Buckle.

Quartermaster: Mr. H.P.E. Dawson.

Regimental Quartermaster Sergeant: J.L. Jones.

Company Leaders and Seconds-in-Command:

City.

No.1, Mr. D.C. Banks; Mr. J.E.G. Hassall.

No.2, Major Staton, Mr. G.H. Farrow.

No.3, Mr. H.A. Goodacre, Mr. B. Bunfield.

Soke.

No.1, Mr. H.L. Samson, Mr. S.W. Goodale.

58

No.2, Mr. H. Elliot, Mr. J.G. Warwick.

No.3, Vice Admiral A.H. Alington, Major G.H.S. Fowke.

Colonel Mellows stated that anyone who had a uniform "saved from the moths," was at liberty to use it. Arm bands would be issued and a form of battle dress. Works and other vulnerable points would organise their own sections, which would become part of the L.D.V. This included the railway.

Rifles and ammunition, when available, would be issued to the Company Commanders, and would be kept at company headquarters. No ranks would be given, but there was no reason why men should not use the rank with which they left the army. Each company would have a dilution of very young men who would require training and experience. Until they were trained they would be useful as messengers and for other non-combatant duties.

Officers both in the Division and groups lost no time in getting their sections, sub-sections, and patrols going with the facilities that were already available. On Monday 27th May, the Peterborough unit moved its headquarters to Messrs. Fox and Vergette's horse repository in Lincoln Road, and every night there was great activity. On that Monday evening nearly seven hundred men formed a giant hollow square in the repository yard, men of all ages and all walks of life. Colonel Mellows stood on a bale of straw in the centre and addressed his men. He told them they were all volunteers and comrades, and were all equal in their desire to do their part in that difficult moment of their county's history.

That night, and on succeeding nights, Regimental Sergeant Major Atkinson drilled squads of those who had never seen service. They learned the technicalities of the Lee Enfield rifle, how to march and drill in time, and how to respond to the word of command.

Not a post of danger in the town or the rural area was unwatched, and liaison was kept up with bordering counties. The work also involved a number of men being present all night at the headquarters, and there were long hours of watching and waiting. The Post Office Club, which had its building on the repository premises, was put at the disposal of the L.D.V., and although the licensed part of the club was closed, the games rooms were left open all night, which was a great boon to the soldiers.

While more ordinary recruits were still wanted, there was a greater need to form a Transport Company, and men with their own cars, vans, and lorries, (they already had 49), were encouraged to get in touch with the Transport Officer, Captain Sir Arthur Craig, as a matter of urgency.

The question of arming the new force was also creating a problem, namely the acquisition of weapons. The Chief Constable made a request through the local press for people with rifles, revolvers, and ammunition, to loan them to the L.D.V., these would be returned after the war. Those people, who held weapons without permits, would not have to face proceedings if they took this opportunity to surrender them.

Gas, Food, Rabbits and Aliens

By the end of May, the Town Council had received 61,000 new respirator smoke filters which had been provided in order to afford greater protection against enemy gasses, in particular, arsenic smoke. Arrangements were made for the filters to be attached to all respirators which had to be taken to the depots at times advertised by posters, and on police loud speakers. Arrangements were made to attach the new filters to children's respirators at the different schools. The new filter was called the

59

"CONTEX," standing for Container Extension, and it was hoped they would be fitted during the evenings.

Adapting the respirators turned out to be a bigger job than had first been expected. The fitting of Contexes began in the first week of June, and every post soon found that they were suffering from a shortage of the adhesive tape with which the extensions were attached. The Home Office rules allowed for only two feet of wastage in every two hundred feet of tape supplied, in practice, much more was inevitably wasted. The worst affected station was Mountsteven Avenue School, where 1,200 masks were dealt with on Monday 3rd June; it had to close the next day as they had run out of tape. At nine o'clock the same day, St. Mary's church hall ran out too, but Mr. H.J. Bass, Head Warden of Group 5, came to the rescue with a fresh supply.

The Home Office had intended that the extensions should be fitted by hand, but most of the workers in Peterborough soon had a variety of jigs constructed which enabled the fitting to be much quicker. Mr. Percy Crowson invented the first machine, he was in charge of the station in the old Gaol in Thorpe Road and he claimed he could deal with four respirators in a minute. Further jigs were developed on the basis of Mr. Crowson's design, and Mr. A.E. Curd of the St. Martin's Street post claimed he could fit six respirators per minute. One of the originals had already been sent to the Home Office at Nottingham.

At Cracknell's, Dogsthorpe, 850 masks were dealt with on Tuesday 4th, while at Fulbridge School several wardens had large blisters on their hands as proof of the heavy workload. Queues formed outside the posts at the Town Hall and in Westgate, and two tiny tots each brought a pramload of respirators.

The Chief Warden feared that many people were leaving the matter too late, and expected the fittings to go on well into the night.

The city people were now reminded that it was time for them to send in the cards, (found at the back of their ration books), as applications for new books, and to be sure they filled in the code numbers and letters printed on their identity cards. The cards had to be at the Town Hall by Saturday 1st June.

From June 1st to the 15th the new ration books would be written up, and addressed; from the 15th to the 22nd they would be posted to the holders; and from the 24th to July 6th the holders had to fill in the counterfoils and register with their retailers.

The new books would come into operation on July 8th. School teachers and other voluntary workers would assist with the large amount of sorting and clerical work. Amazingly enough, two weeks after the deadline, 4,000 city people had still not applied for the renewal of their ration books. When their old books were fully used up, they would not be able to draw rationed articles. On top of this, 3,000 people had filled out the application forms incorrectly!

By the end of June the number of city people who had still not applied for new books had dropped to around 1,000, and the following week would find themselves unable to buy rationed food. The number of incomplete applications had also dropped to 2,000. These latecomers were putting an increasing strain on the hard pressed clerical workers, most of whom had offered their services on a voluntary basis.

In another food related item, it was decided at a meeting of the Soke War Agricultural Committee, on Wednesday 29th May, to take a strong line to get rid of the rabbit pest. Notice was given that if the people affected did not carry out this work, the committee would act and charge the expenses.

It was also decided to take firm action in certain cases where farming was not satisfactorily carried out. Two extra members were invited to strengthen the personnel of two district committees.

Approximately 50 aliens in the City and Soke were affected by the new curfew order issued on Wednesday 29th May. The order stated that aliens over 16 of all nationalities and stateless persons must be in their homes between 10:30p.m. and 6a.m. as from Monday 3rd June. Neither were they allowed to be in possession of any bicycle, motor vehicle, seagoing craft, or aircraft. If they wished to possess any of these items, they had to apply to the police for a permit.

News of the Wounded

Mr. and Mrs. Frank Gray, of Glendorn, Exeter Road, had three sons in the forces, Walter Francis, Horace Cooper, and John Charles. During the last weekend of May, they heard from Walter, who was a casualty in hospital. He stated that it was nice to be back after seeing what they had seen at the front - sights he should never forget. He added: "Several of our platoon are here, including Sergeant Bull, (son of Jack Bull, the Loco footballer, of New England). We have most certainly done a bit to steady Hitler, for we must have wiped thousands out with our little gun, which is what they deserve, and will get in due course."

Mrs. George Hitch, of 211, Fletton Avenue, received only a telegram on the morning of Tuesday 28th, stating that her husband, Gunner George Hitch, of the Royal Artillery, had been seriously wounded in action. It stated that he was lying in an emergency hospital in Wales and requested that she should visit him.

She left immediately with her sister and found him with his right arm shattered, his right thumb severed, his right hand deeply cut, his teeth blown out and chin badly cut. He was injured when the Germans attacked with hand grenades and his friend standing next to him was killed. George was taken prisoner, and the Germans took away all his rations, his money and his personal belongings. Later the Germans were pushed back and George was rescued by a stretcher party. Even on the hospital ship he was not safe, as it was bombed incessantly.

Gunner Hitch was a Reservist, having served eight years in India, and was called up when hostilities broke out. He was at Westwood Works for some time and had married Miss Joan Stimpson the previous November.

First Raid

The first air raid on the city took place at 12.45 a.m. on the morning of Saturday 8th June. Five high explosive bombs fell causing some damage but no casualties. One bomb fell in the centre of Bridge Street at the foot of a lamp standard and windows on both sides of the road were shattered for a distance of 150 yards, tiles were also stripped from roofs.

The swimming pool was damaged with one corner of the wall and kiosk demolished. The pool was drained, windows screened, the broken glass cleared and the pool refilled and "back in business" by 4p.m. Fifteen houses were damaged, and the Bishop's Palace and gardens in Bishop's Road. Shop premises in Bridge Street and the Saracen's Head Hotel also suffered.

Dunkirk

With the Allied forces now split by the German Army reaching the Atlantic coast,

61

and the surrender of the Belgian Army, the British had no alternative but to withdraw back to Dunkirk. Between May 28th and June 4th, British naval forces, plus a flotilla of other smaller boats and ships, evacuated 220,000 men of the British Expeditionary Force from the beaches, plus 130,000 French soldiers, and a small number of Belgians.

Local men played their part bravely during the evacuation, many escaped back to England to fight another day, some of them seriously wounded, all with terrible stories to tell of what they did and what they saw. Some men, as every family waiting for news knew, would never come back to Peterborough. They lie there still, men of our city, holding their piece of French soil, never giving ground to the enemy.

Private Victor Garfoot, Royal Army Medical Corps, of 2, Lister Road, died of wounds in a French military hospital on the 20th May, he was 20 years old. He was the second son of Mr. and Mrs. W. Garfoot and came to Peterborough from Bourne six years earlier. For a time he had been with the London Brick Company, later going to the Viaduct Motor Co., London Road. He joined the R.A.M.C. a year before the war broke out. His brother Douglas was serving in the Northamptonshire Regiment, and after seven weeks without any news, they finally heard from him on Wednesday 5th June, saying that he was safe in England. Their father was a local postman.

Corporal Thomas James Davis, Green Howards, of 30, West Parade, was killed in action on the 31st May, aged 21. News of his death reached the city on Monday 10th June, just two days after his wife had given birth to their son. Corporal Davis had been called up the previous July with the first batch of militiamen, previously he had been a fireman on the L.M.S., and played the accordion in the L.M.S. Harmonica Band. As a boy he had sung in the St. John's choir. Two years earlier, he had married Miss Edith Speechley, of West Parade. His younger brother, Joseph William, was in the Tank Corps in Egypt.

Corporal Horace William James Stanford, 5th Northamptonshire Regiment, of 16, Fengate Close, had not been heard of for over a month when the news finally reached his wife that he had been killed in action. On contacting the War Office however, in an attempt to confirm what she had been told, she was informed that no casualty of that name had been reported. It was some time after this that her worst fears were confirmed with the official news that Corporal Stanford had been killed in action on the 22nd May. Before the war, he had been a games attendant at the New England recreation ground.

Mr. and Mrs. A. Sewell, of 109, Lincoln Road, Walton, received news on Saturday 22nd June, that their only son, Private Frederick John Sewell, Northamptonshire Regiment, had died in France on 22nd May, from wounds received while fighting in the thick of the action at Dunkirk. Before the war he had been an assistant groundsman at a local aerodrome.

Many more city men were wounded, some so severely that they would never serve in the forces again.

Sergeant John Cyril Bayes, of 70, Cowgate, had been wounded in the knee, and lay in a northern hospital. 22 years of age, he had been a fireman on the L.M.S.

Sergeant E. Copestake, of Saxon Road, had been wounded in action and was sent to a hospital in Liverpool. He was the son of Mr. and Mrs. Copestake of Palmerston Road. He was married, and had a daughter of 8, and a son of 14 months. Before the war he had been a salesman with Avery's.

Sergeant Eric Arthur Smith, of St. Paul's Road, son of Mrs. and the late Mr. E. Smith, had sustained severe shrapnel wounds to his lower legs, and had been sent to a hospital in Birmingham. His wife had received the news on Monday 3rd June, and the following day travelled with her sister, Mrs. F. Habbins, to see him. They learned that he had lain on the battlefield for some time before he was rescued by Private A. Parkinson, another Peterborough man. Sgt. Smith had been at Brotherhood's before he was called up, and had been a Territorial for some years.

Corporal Donald Gow, of 52, Orchard Street, had sustained shrapnel wounds to his right arm. He was 34 years old and had been a Territorial from the age of 16. Before the war he had been an electrician with the London Brick Company, he was also an entertainer at concerts, and a footballer of some repute. His father, Mr. A. Gow, had served with the Canadians during the Great War, and was now in the L.D.V.

Corporal Roger Freeman, of 221, Cromwell Road, was in hospital with shrapnel wounds to his shoulder and legs. He was 31 years of age, and had been a lorry driver for the Corporation. Married, with a boy of 9, and a girl of 7, it was doubly unfortunate at that time that his wife was seriously ill.

Lance Corporal J.H. Dexter, of 31, Goodyer's Yard, had been sent to a Hertfordshire emergency hospital with three wounds in his right leg.

Private George Walter Pepper, of 37, Clarence Road, had been hit in the calf of his left leg by shrapnel. Before the war he had been a labourer with J.R. Horrell and Sons.

Driver Frank Crisp, of 17, St. Paul's Road, was lying wounded in hospital at Aldershot. He had written to his wife telling her he would soon be home. He had been an Eastern Counties bus driver.

Wounded men were being sent all over the country at this time to hurriedly prepared emergency hospitals. Another local man recuperating in the north was Private Frank Nundy, of Alderman's Drive, he, like many others, was suffering from shrapnel wounds, this time in his right hand.

Sapper William Thomas Newton, of 44, Chapel Street, Stanground, was older than most at 40 years of age. He was still lying in a military hospital in France at this time, one small part of the country that was yet to be overrun. He had seen action with an Engineers unit which had suffered a great deal of heavy bombardment and was seriously wounded. The son of Mr. and Mrs. Newton, of Palmerston Road, he was married, and had joined the army during the First World War at the age of 17. In civilian life he had been a fitter's assistant on the L.N.E.R.

Suffering from wounds of a different kind was Sergeant William Bull, of 15, Norton Road. He was in hospital recovering from a motorcycle accident in which he had injured his hand; the wound had later become septic. His mother, Mrs. W.I. Bull, of 141, New England, and his wife, visited him twice in hospital while he was undergoing electrical treatment and massage. Sgt, Bull's father, Mr. W.I. (Jack) Bull, had been a well known Peterborough and New England footballer.

Driver Thomas German, of West Parade, had certainly come into contact with the enemy, and had been sent to the County Hospital, Farnborough with serious injuries. He had been hit by a number of bullets, one going through his upper lip, and others narrowly missing his lungs and spine. For over 30 hours he had lain unconscious on German occupied soil, but was finally brought home from Dunkirk on 31st May and was made comfortable in hospital. Driver German had been an employee of Mr. George Read, removal contractor, of Stone Lane, and had been a member of the Peterborough Motor Cycle and Light Car Club and the Weight Lifting Club.

Bandsman Frederick Westwood, of 26, Cobden Street, was lying in Basingstoke Hospital recovering from gunshot and shrapnel wounds, and had been visited by his wife. Before the war he had been a foundry labourer at the Westwood Works, and, like his brother Bernard, who was a painter's labourer in the same firm, played football for the works team.

Fate could deal its cruelest blows to men who thought they had escaped the terror of the beaches. Men who having managed to find a boat at Dunkirk and board it, and be on their way to safety, often found themselves suddenly facing death again, coming under attack on the voyage home. Private Noel Woodward, of 70, Garton End Road, considered himself lucky to be in hospital in England. Aged 22, he was the only son of Mr. and Mrs. Charles W. Woodward, and had been in France since November 1939 as batman to Colonel Tuck.

After marching under fire to Dunkirk, his unit waded into the sea up to their necks to reach the boats which took them to the transport ships. While the men were drying their clothes in the engine room and when the ship had been under steam for 20 minutes, a German bomber scored three direct hits. Private Woodward was wounded when he was assisting the injured into the lifeboats. He was eventually able to get into a boat which then drifted for eight hours before the English coast was sighted.

Another man whose boat was attacked by aircraft was Driver Arthur Hollis, of 33, Oxford Road, although thankfully he was not injured. He was the eldest son of Mr. and Mrs. C. Hollis, and had returned from Dunkirk in a drifter, being sent on afterwards to Doncaster. While being visited by his parents on Sunday 16th June, he told them that his party was bombed all the way over. Before that, he and another soldier had been guarding a stores dump in France when it was attacked by German aircraft and blown up. Driver Hollis had been an engineer at the Westwood Works before the war, being a member also of Harris Street, Baptist and Westwood Works' tennis clubs; he was also for a time Scoutmaster of Harris Street Troop of Boy Scouts.

Private B. Bowd, of Clifton Avenue, had shrapnel wounds to his head and arms but was doing well in hospital.

Private C.R. Rollings, of 4, Harris Street, was in the city on a month's sick leave from a St. Albans hospital. He had been back from France to undergo a serious operation, and had worked in the Post Office Engineering department.

Private Harry Hurst, of 16, Peveril Road, was in Horton Hospital, Surrey, where he had been visited by his parents Mr. and Mrs. J. Hurst, and his fiancee, Miss Margaret Ringrose. He was suffering from shell shock but was doing well. Before the war he had worked at the Mayor's Walk branch of the Co-op and was one of the first in the city to be called up into the militia. He had his medical examination the day after his 21st birthday, and reported a month later on July 15th

Trooper Robert Drake, of 170, Dogsthorpe Road, was missing. His brother, Private George Drake, who was in a regiment of Hussars, however, was safe in England. It can be imagined how desperate his widowed father, Mr. George Drake, who worked in the brickyards, was for news of his eldest son; even a message to say that he was wounded and in hospital would have been a relief. Like thousands of other relatives, he could only wait. On Friday 5th July 1940, it was announced in the 'Standard' that Trooper Robert Drake, 15/19 Hussars was a prisoner of war. By July

19th, George would be posted as missing.

Private Bert Ludlow, 2nd Northamptonshire Regiment, of 7, G.N. Station Road, fourth son of Mr. and Mrs. A.J. Ludlow, had also been posted missing. The Ludlows had five sons and one daughter, and had lost their eldest boy in the first war. Bert had been a bus conductor before he joined up, and two of his brothers, Cecil and Stanley George, were both bus drivers. Bert was later found to be a prisoner of war in Germany.

Also among the missing was Private Cecil Horace Lightfoot, he had worked for the London Brick Company for two years before joining up in November 1938.

Private George Fincham, Royal Warwickshire Regiment, of 151, Belsize Avenue, had been in the army for eight years, and for some time had been based at the Ordnance Depot at Walton. He had married Miss H. Anthony the previous year, and it was she who received the news late in June that he too was missing in action. A month later she received the news that he was a prisoner of war in Germany.

Determined to get home was Private David Sayer, of 32, Churchfield Road. He was the third son of Mr. and Mrs. A. Sayer, and had marched so far that he was in hospital with septic feet. Called up eight months previously, he had been fighting in the Somme area of France. Before the war he had been a baker's roundsman with A. Fowler and Sons.

Great Escapes

Although some Peterborough men were killed in the retreat to Dunkirk, and during the evacuation, and others were seriously wounded, some less so, there were also great stories of bravery and survival to come out of, what was in effect, a great military defeat.

Mr. and Mrs. E.M. Fox, of Holbrook House, Eastfield, received the news in the middle of June that their only son, Driver George M. Fox, of the R.A.S.C., was safe in England. Driver Fox, in a letter to his parents, said that after fighting in the neighbourhood of Brussels for 14 days with practically no rest, his unit was forced towards the coast, and was machine gunned, shelled and bombed all the way.

At Dunkirk they were on the beach from early on Monday 3rd June, until the following Thursday, awaiting transport. No rations were served, and sleep was impossible, as the gun barrage and bombing was incessant. "I owe my life to the fact that I had a full water bottle," he wrote.

When he reached England he posted a card to his parents to say he was safe. Driver Fox used to help his father in the business of George Sangster Ltd., grocers of Long Causeway. News of the safe return of two other members of staff was soon received, men who had not been heard of for weeks. One was Corporal John Boniface, of the Grenadier Guards. He took part in the epic rearguard action at Calais, and his home was at 43, Cromwell Road. The other man was Private Stanley Broughton of the Northamptonshire Regiment, of 73, Grange Road.

Two brothers, Privates Arthur and Charlie Dickens, sons of Mr. and Mrs. S.A. Dickens, 18, Wellington Street, came home on the morning of Wednesday 12th June. They had been in a camp in England since their arrival from Dunkirk.

"It was hell," said Arthur. "We never thought we would get away....Charlie fetched in four wounded and one killed. He risked his life for the dead man because he could not bear to see him out there."

For five days they had neither food nor drink, that was until Charlie killed, cooked and dressed, as well as possible, six chickens from a farmhouse. He also attempted to milk a cow, and did in fact get half a bucketful until the animal decided to knock it over. Undaunted, he caught another cow, and milked another half-bucketful.

Arthur told of how he arrived at Dunkirk "wearing a dead man's boots" as his own were worn out, two days later than Charlie, whom he had believed to be dead. He found Charlie in a farmhouse fast asleep, and when he woke him, offered him a parcel of soap and cigarettes from home. Overjoyed at seeing each other they eventually returned to England in a destroyer under heavy gunfire.

A strange tale of courage performed by Trooper James Manley Cook, of 20, Exeter Road, gained him more than a little notoriety in the city. Under heavy machine gun fire, he climbed onto a blazing tank to rescue his mascot, a brassiere, which had been tied to the aerial. One wonders if it was for this reason only that he was promoted to Corporal soon afterwards.

Mr. and Mrs. R. Cook, his parents, had moved to the city from Grimsby six years earlier, about the same time that James, now aged 23, joined the Tank Corps. Mr. Cook had known nothing of his son's exploit until he had read it in the newspaper.

"He brought the brassiere with him when he last came home on leave," said Mr. Cook. "There must be a story behind it, but what it is he won't say. It was a foolish thing to risk his life like that, but who can help admiring his courage? He wrote and told us of the tank action at Calais. His tank caught fire and they had to run for it with machine guns all round them. But he did not tell us the bit about the brassiere.

We chaffed him about it when he was home, and we tried to get it from him. He would not give it up, and he would not tell us anything. 'Where I go, this goes,' was all he would say."

Corporal Cook was a radio operator in the tank which caught fire. Later, at a rest camp, he spoke to a reporter:

"When we set out to meet the enemy I tied the brassiere on the aerial. It seemed to be in keeping with the mood of the men. They did not give a damn for anything. They were singing and laughing, and anybody would have thought it was a motor coach trip setting out."

Another member of the tank crew told the reporter that Cook risked his life to save the "battle flag" after the tank had been set on fire by an incendiary shell.

"We had stopped a few enemy tanks when an incendiary shell whizzed through Cook's legs. He looked a bit surprised, but he was not hurt. The next second the tank was filled with brilliant blue flame. It was impossible to see anything, and it got damned hot. The commander told the driver to reverse, and then gave orders to abandon the tank. Cook suddenly leapt on the tank and snatched the brassiere from the aerial. How he escaped being hit was a miracle."

There were quite a number of local men arriving safely back from the beaches, as the following list shows. However, these may not necessarily be all of them:

C.Q.M.S. G.H. Buttifant, 9, Portland Road.
Company-Sergeant Major Rufus Adams, formerly steward of Lincoln Road Drill Hall.
Engineer Officer George A. Rodgers, 231, Eastfield Road.
Sergeant Gerald Beardsall, 111, Granville Street.
Sergeant L.A. Wade, 130, New England.
Sergeant J.W. Boyden, 324, Clarence Road, Eastern Counties bus driver.
Corporal William Murdoch, 166, New England.
Corporal Harry Curd, 42, Dogsthorpe Road.

Lance Corporal W. Ralph Steadman, Padholme Road.
Lance Corporal John William Sharp, M.M., 56, New Road.
Private Douglas George Jolly, School Place, Albert Place.
Private Samuel Sharp, 56, New Road.
Private Percy Ambrose Partridge, 32, Westwood Row, Westwood Street; Postman at the G.P.O.
Private Gordon Piggott, Walpole Street, formerly at the G.P.O.
Private Percy Saunders Swiffen, 28, Fulham Road.
Private R. Markley, City Road.
Private Jack Ball, Farcet Road, Stanground.
Private Robert Curtis, (20), 26, Padholme Road, a dispatch rider, formerly an L.M.S. fireman.
Private Roland H. Roberts, 83, Park Road.
Private R.W. Coulson, R.A.M.C., 69, Gladstone Street.
Private G.W. Goodman, 107, Bishop's Road.
Private A.V. Stocks, 93, Dickens Street.
Private Alex T. Gill, Broadway.
Private W.F. Bradley, 8, Crawthorne Road.
Private Ronald A. Read, 171, Eastfield Road.
Private George E. Shaw, 185, Padholme Road.
Driver Percy Chambers, 622, Gladstone Street; Eastern Counties bus driver.
Driver Chas Savage, 320, Clarence Road, was a labourer at Baker Perkins.
Driver E.G. Bellairs, 243, Gladstone Street.
Driver E. Birch, 28, Percival Street.
Driver Broughton, 12, High Street, Old Fletton.
Lorry Driver Leslie Theodore Wise, 4, High Street, Old Fletton.
Signaller Bert Allen, 5, Willesden Avenue, was at Baker Perkins.
Bandsman Kenneth George Parker, 23, Church Street, Stanground.
Drummer Frederick Baker, Russell Street.
Drummer Ronald Baker, Russell Street.
Leading Seaman James Henry Bean, (HMS Scimitar), 332, Clarence Road. Formerly G.P.O. postman.
Able Seaman Sidney James Fountain, (HMS Codrington), Craig Street. He had fifteen years in the navy and re-enlisted for the duration. Formerly at Baker Perkins for two years.

Seven trains carrying British Expeditionary Force men stopped at Peterborough station during the weekend of 31st May, 1st June. In most cases this had been their first stop after being landed in England and many of them still had wet clothes from swimming and wading to the ships. Some were exhausted and sound asleep, many had some day's growth of beard, and others had no boots.

The city women of the W.V.S. were asked to meet the trains and arrange refreshments. Tea, lemonade, cakes, buns and biscuits were placed on railway trolleys all along the platform, with helpers at each one. The men got out and had their food and the platform was a mass of khaki. Cigarettes and postcards were given out, with huge numbers written there and then being posted for them, telegrams were also sent. This was the first time any of them had had to inform their families that they were safe, and the W.V.S. did a wonderful job. As one train left, another one arrived within 20 minutes, and hundreds of teacups were constantly being washed, as always, the ladies of the Peterborough Women's Voluntary

Service were ready.

Emergency Measures
The city people were now warned that on Friday 21st June they would hear the church bells rung at two set times. These warnings, designed to alert the public in case of a German invasion, were part of tests which were being carried out by the L.D.V. The exercise would be conducted throughout the country.

The City Fire Brigade were also stepping up their vigilance by equipping new Supplementary Fire Parties of three men in various sectors of the city with a stirrup pump each, and training them in their use. Stirrup pumps had proved to be very efficient in dealing with incendiary bombs around the country, and Chief Officer Haylett asked for every householder to keep a bucket of water standing by, so that when the stirrup-pumpers came they would not have to wait.

The Ministry of Supply was now speeding up the collection of salvage, and local authorities in towns having a population of more than 10,000 were being called on to organise a campaign. Collecting in Peterborough was already going on apace, waste paper, cardboard, scrap metals, household bones and rags were constantly being collected, and the city service was helping the Rural District by picking up waste in bulk from their two or three central dumps. "Every piece of paper, old bone, or scrap of metal is a potential bullet against Hitler," was the official cry.

The W.V.S. was in need of rubbish also, in their case, old mattresses. These were for fixing on top of ambulances and cars as protection against shrapnel. The condition of the mattresses did not matter, and Mrs. Mellows would arrange to collect them if desired. "You may be helping one of your own folk by a gift of this sort," she said.

Although there was still a problem with obtaining places in the city for evacuees from London, about 150 local children had now been registered for evacuation to the Dominions. By the last week of June, approximately 100 children from city elementary schools, 44 from secondary schools and 5 at rural elementary schools had been registered, and more were expected. The children would be medically examined, and school teachers would escort them.

A week later there were over 200 more applications for the evacuation of city elementary school children, approximately one in thirty of the total in the city. Those applying would not necessarily be automatically accepted. Preference was being given to children from evacuation areas, and at this time, Peterborough was still officially a reception area, putting it in the third category for consideration. Parents were expected to pay a sum for their children to be evacuated, six shillings being the agreed amount. They were also allowed to express a preference for a particular Dominion or country - Canada, U.S.A., Australia, New Zealand or South Africa.

On Saturday 22nd June another 578 men registered for the services. They were nearly all 29's but there was a good sprinkling of 20's. The total included six conscientious objectors. Men were not asked individually for their preference, but they had the opportunity of expressing it. 31 went for the Navy or Marines, and 74 for the Air Force. Up to this time the city registrations had reached a total of 5,380, including 63 conscientious objectors.

Plane Obstructions
The order was given at the beginning of July that, "every field in the area which is

capable of being used as a landing ground for aircraft is to be rendered dangerous forthwith for any such operation."

The Commissioner for the North Midland Region, (Lord Trent), appealed for co-operation in this task so that within a few hours, and certainly not later than a couple of days, not a single available field would be without substantial obstructions. After a period had elapsed, a military survey would be carried out, and where necessary, work that had not been satisfactorily undertaken would be completed by the services.

The need for these precautions against a threatened invasion of this part of England were thought to be vitally urgent. Even the presence of standing crops was not to be regarded as an excuse for non-obstruction. Farmers were told that they would cause the least damage to their crops if they placed the obstructions themselves, rather than leaving it to the military.

Generally speaking any field, (grass or arable), which provided a runway of 300 yards or more was a potential landing ground and had to be obstructed. Anything could be used to create the obstructions as long as it was substantial and at least four feet high. Old farm carts or other farm implements, strong posts planted firmly in the ground; anything likely to damage a plane on landing. Although it was accepted that it may not be possible to destroy a plane completely, enough damage could be caused so as to make it impossible for it to take off again, enabling it to be dealt with on the ground. Troop-carrying planes were especially susceptible to damage in this way and it was imperative to ensure that they would not be in a condition to make a second journey.

The names of five more city men now appeared in the 'Standard' on July 5th, reported as missing in action:

Corporal J.W. Smith, 68, Saxon Road.

Private J.H. Stamper, 232, Clarence Road.

Private G.T.F. Hasdell, 261, Lincoln Road.

Private W.A. Garner, 62, St. John's Street.

Private J.L. Topham, (21), 18, Dryden Road, New England, he was also listed as being wounded.

More Black-out Cases
The number of people being brought before the magistrates for infringing the black-out restrictions was relentless. There were six more summonses on Wednesday 3rd July. A.E. Baxter and Co. had been showing a light from an unscreened second storey window at 10:40 p.m. on the night of June 13th. Mr. Baxter said he could not trace the person responsible for leaving it on and that from then on the mains would be switched off when the offices closed. They were fined £4.

Basil George Barnaby of 88, St. Paul's Road, had been showing a light through the thin curtains of a back bedroom window at 11 p.m. on the same night. He said he had seen the curtains closed and had assumed that the black-out was in place, "I had been working 14 hours," he added.

"I don't mind if you had been working 24 hours," the Chairman told him. "This desperate carelessness has got to stop. You will be fined £3."

John Harvey Spires, of 286, Dogsthorpe Road, had left a bathroom light on in an unoccupied house at 10:40 p.m. on the night of June 22nd, he was fined £3.

Albert Reginald Barton, of 157, Clarence Road, had a light showing through thin curtains on the same night. He told the court that a child had left the light on. Having already been previously cautioned, he was fined £2.

Mary Searle had left a light showing through thin curtains at the rear of 6, Cavendish Street at 11:45 also on the night of June 22nd, she was fined £1.

And finally for that session, William Cecil Harlowe, of 46, Craig Street, pleaded guilty to leaving a light showing in 33, Boroughbury at 11:45 on June 23rd, he had left at 2 p.m. and thought he had switched the light off. He was fined £4.

During a council meeting on Friday 5th July, in which great disappointment was expressed at the fact that in a city of 50,000 people, there were only four volunteers as stretcher bearers, the Electrical Manager asked for instructions from the A.R.P. Committee as to the use of the air raid shelters in the school premises in Albert Place. Mr. Swain said that a lot of people had no room in their backyards for a shelter, and wondered if they could use the school shelters as they were standing idle.

Alderman Snowden said that it was definitely laid down that public shelters were only for people caught out in a raid, and householders would have to stay indoors, away from their windows, this way they would be safe.

Mr. Howard asked if the public could be advised on the best means of constructing a shelter within their own homes, and was told that a special panel of local architects had been set up for that purpose and were authorised to charge 10s. 6d. for their advice.

Mr. J. Hall asked if the council could supply materials to householders who wished to build shelters. Alderman Snowden said they could only do that if the city was a vulnerable area.

Mr. Hall: Aren't we a vulnerable area?

Ald. Snowden: No, we are not.

Mr. Hall: I thought we had been turned into one when I heard that the children were not going to be evacuated here.

The Town Clerk: Aren't they? That's news to me.

Mr Hall: Why don't we have Anderson shelters?

The Mayor: Again, because we are not a vulnerable area.

Mrs. Wood asked if any complaints had been received about nurses having to go to their posts without tin helmets.

The Town Clerk: They are not entitled to tin hats. The Controller hasn't got one, and he has to walk down.

Ald. Snowden said Lord Trent had told him that until the fighting services were fully supplied there would be no more helmets for the civil population.

At the Education Committee on the same day, Mr Hall expressed the hope that an appeal would be made to the public, particularly mothers, not to fetch their children out of school during air raid warnings.

The children were well protected, and mothers who went to schools endangered their children's lives and their own. The schools had been provided with shelters, and mothers should not interfere.

At the same meeting it was decided that the erection of air raid shelters at Eastholm Council School should begin. A suggestion that children should bring salvaged bones to the schools for collection by the Engineer's department was not adopted.

An official notice was indeed published to the effect that it was suicidal for parents to gather up their children from school and rush to the shelters. At the same time, residents at a distance from shelters were asked to open their doors so as to afford temporary protection to passers-by. Old lace curtains stuck to windows, they

70

were told, provided the best protection against glass splinters according to experiences in Welsh air raids. Beneath the stairs was a good refuge, after a direct hit the stairs were often the only structure left intact, furniture provided next to no protection. Sulphur fumes from exploding bombs had also created gas scares, but, people were told, these soon passed off. So far no splinter had yet penetrated an Anderson shelter.

Rumour mongers were now abroad in the city, and strenuous efforts would be made to find and prosecute them. Two examples were quoted by the Town Clerk to the 'Standard' on July 5th. One was that the Germans had a poison sprayer which would destroy whole towns. The other had come from a man in a car who had said that the enemy had landed, and that all mothers should fetch their children from school.

One statement that definitely was not a rumour was a new Defence Regulation which required that private persons surrendered all fireworks capable of being used to give visible signals to the enemy. The main types were: rockets, maroons, shells, Roman candles, and coloured flares. These had to be handed in immediately with offenders being subject to heavy penalties.

On Saturday 6th July, 599 men of the 30's group registered for service with the forces, there were also a score or more late entries. Of these, 51 expressed a preference for the Navy or Marines, and 186 for the Air Force. There were no conscientious objectors. A week later, 603 of the 31's registered, 56 Navy, 169 Air Force. This time there were 4 conscientious objectors.

New Programme of Domestic Shelters
On July 12th it was announced that domestic communal shelters would be erected in various parts of the city on the instruction of the government. The programme would provide for nearly 200, and when complete, would accommodate about 9,000 people. The construction would be carried out by local builders and all the shelters would be made of brick, with arched brick tops, covered with cement, and be above ground. They would, as a rule, hold 48 people each and be sub-divided for parties of 12.

The shelters would be unfurnished, but the nearby inhabitants could provide what items they liked from their own homes. The entrances would be secured by locked gates, the keys of which could be kept at one of the nearby houses by arrangement with other residents. There would be no artificial lighting provided.

In addition, the City Engineer submitted a scheme to the Senior Regional Officer (S.R.O.), for the provision of surface shelters for Bridge Street, Long Causeway and the Minster Precincts, having regard to the concentration of people in the market-place on market days. Owners of cellars and basements in the vicinity were asked to allow them to be used by the public, and this received a good response with 17 offers made. The City Engineer made a survey of 13 of them, and he estimated the cost of strutting 7 of these would come to approximately £600, and they would accommodate 295 people.

Mr. W. Pentney offered the use of a large garden at the rear of his business premises in Church Street for the construction of a splinter-proof shelter; the A.R.P. committee accepted this with thanks.

The North Midlands Regional Commissioner now asked through the 'Standard' for efforts to be continued to increase the number of shelters everywhere, however, there was heavy military demand on supplies of cement, and bricklayers were almost wholly engaged on government contract work. The Commissioner therefore asked that where possible, air raid shelters in factories, offices and shops should be adapted and placed at the service of the general public.

The Board of Education also issued new instructions now. In the event of bombs dropping without warning near schools, the children should take up the safest positions in the building itself, away from the windows and lying on the floor. In no circumstances should they be allowed to leave the building, whether to go to the school shelters or for dispersal to domestic shelters.

On July 12th, the following letter, signed by the Peterborough and District Branch of the British Legion, and addressed to the Town Clerk, appeared in the 'Standard'.

"Dear Sir - We note from a recent announcement in the local press that the two guns in the park are advertised for disposal by the Parks and Recreation Grounds Committee of the City Council.

The guns in question were captured by the 6th battalion of the County Regiment, (Northamptonshire), with which many local citizens, also members of this branch of the Legion, served with valour and distinction during the last war. So the guns are of historical interest to them and their relatives who reside in the city.

At a recent meeting of the British Legion it was resolved:

1. That the two guns in the park, which were presented to the citizens of Peterborough, be GIVEN back to H.M. Government to help to defeat 'Hitlerism.'

2. That we view with dismay the action of the Parks Committee in advertising the guns for sale as scrap.

3. That we suggest application for permission to dispose of the trophies be made by the council to the appropriate Department of the War Office.

4. That, should such permission be forthcoming from the War Department, the British Legion members respectfully suggest that the proceeds realised be given to the Red Cross.

We are sending a copy of this letter to the press."

At the beginning of August it was announced that a tender for the two guns had been received from Mr. W. Evans, and this had been accepted. The total offer, £8 10s. was donated to the National Red Cross Association. This tender had beaten another from Mr. H. Parker of £6 12s. 6d.

Two more local men were mentioned in the 'Standard' on July 12th as missing in action, they were:

Lance Corporal A.J. Miners, 2nd Northamptonshire Regiment, 37, Taverner's Road.
Private A.N. Long, 90, Padholme Road.

Having already provided a canteen and rest room for the servicemen in the city, moves were now afoot during the middle of July to provide the same facilities for the women of the Auxiliary Services. Mrs. Hester Blagden, writing from the Palace, in the Minster Precincts, said that the women's needs were very great. "They may not be so many in numbers but they are away from home, they are in camp or billets, they have only moderate wages; and their officers are pressing us to give them some place to which they can go in their leisure hours, where they can sit, have refreshments, read, write, and talk with their friends."

The Ecclesiastical Commissioners put 7, Minster Precincts at their disposal at a nominal rent, and an appeal was started for monetary contributions as well as for items of equipment such as beds, tables, crockery and games.

Salvage

Since the first appeals for salvage and scrap metal went out, the stocks in Peterborough had been increasing steadily. There was an enormous range between the amounts that were brought in, from six year old Marion Davis who took in her doll's tea set which was made of metal, to Mr. H.J. Amies who took in a large stock of aluminium goods from his shop. A lot of the articles sent for scrap were brand new and were of an endless variety - kettles, tea-pots, hot water bottles, collanders, fish kettles and even shoe stretchers. Most articles were made of aluminium but others were copper kettles, brass candlesticks and lamps, pewter tea-pots, iron pots, hanging lamps etc. Appeals were made at local cinemas by the Mayor and Mrs. Mellows, and cars driven by the W.V.S. took the articles from there to the Town Hall.

By the middle of July Mrs. Mellows estimated she had four tons of scrap, three tons being aluminium. New articles were damaged with an axe in order to deter thefts, and the scrap would be sent away when they had reached five tons. The target was achieved by the 27th July when Mrs. Mellows officially ended her collection, not being anxious, as she said, to see any more aluminium for a very long time!

Ten tons of paper a week was also being baled and shipped to the pulpers as fast as it could be carried, and by July 19th, 170 tons of paper had been sent away.

Other collections included 20 tons of tin, 8 tons of scrap iron, three and a half tons of rags, 450 milk bottles, 80 gross of mixed bottles, and a small quantity of copper and brass.

On July 19th, more Peterborough men appeared in the 'Standard', posted as missing in action:

L/A.C. Eric Smith, Geneva Street, (believed prisoner).

Private A.G. Drake, Dogsthorpe Road, R.A.S.C. (ex Hussars).

Sapper Eric Victor Reynolds, 5, Haddon Road, Royal Engineers.

Sapper Reynolds was 24 years of age and had been employed at Baker Perkins since he was 15. His brother, Private F.A.W. Reynolds, Suffolk Regiment, was called up just three weeks before, and also worked at Westwood, in the foundry. Their father, Mr. V. Reynolds, worked with the L.N.E.R.

Of the 150 stirrup pumps promised for official use in Peterborough, only 50 had turned up by the end of July. A few people had acquired pumps early on before demand had become too great, but further deliveries were, at this time, not very likely. One person who inquired was told "ten weeks."

People were being recommended to buy garden hose instead; the price of this was starting to go up, but not too much as yet. A special fitting which provided the required spray was easily obtainable.

There were 607 registrations of men of the 32's group at Peterborough on Saturday 20th July. 51 asked for service in the Navy, and 189 in the Air Force. There were 4 conscientious objectors.

The L.D.V., who were still recruiting in the city, were now to get a name change. Mr. Anthony Eden, the Secretary of State for War, stated in parliament on Tuesday 23rd July that the Local Defence Volunteers were to be given the title "The Home Guard." Armlets would be issued bearing the initials "H.G."

On July 26th, the 'Standard' announced that Private Donald George Taylor, R.A.S.C., son of Mr. and Mrs. G. Taylor, 338, Lincoln Road, was missing in action. His wife, Mrs. E. Taylor, was at that time living with her parents in Bright Street, with their two children, the youngest of whom Private Taylor had not yet seen. He had last been on leave in February, and his wife had received only one field card from him since. That had been ten weeks earlier. A keen cricketer, Private Taylor had joined the army before the war, after being with the London Brick Company as a lorry driver. It wasn't until the beginning of August that it was discovered that he was a prisoner of war.

Spitfire for the City

On Tuesday 23rd July, the Peterborough Chamber of Trade passed the following resolution:

"This chamber desires to inaugurate a scheme for the city to raise £5,000 to present a Spitfire to the government."

The Mayor promised to preside over a public meeting to discuss the next step, and this took place in the Reception Room of the Town Hall on the night of Thursday 1st August. It was hoped that the whole city would pull together, from small children taking pennies into school, to large companies donating grander sums. Collection boxes in shops, flag days and dances were all suggested as ways of raising the required amount.

It was also stated that if the total sum raised exceeded that of £5,000, but was not enough to purchase a second Spitfire, the money could be used to buy components. A list of examples was provided:

Engine - £2,000.

Airscrews - £350.

Tail - £300.

Machine Guns - £100.

Compass - £5.

Clock - £2. 10s.

Spark Plugs - 8s.

Rivets, (per 20), - 6d.

The morning of Tuesday 30th July brought mystery and excitement to the sleeping residents of Westwood Park Road.

The Mayor's telephone wires were cut, isolating the civic head. Across the road, 30ft. of tennis netting had been ripped from its iron supports and taken over the boundary hedge into the next garden. There it was left on top of an apple tree, whose full crop was widely scattered across the ground. Apparently the tree had been violently shaken to throw the fruit so far.

What was the explanation? Had Hitler been trying out a secret weapon during the night? The solution was not so sinister. A barrage balloon had escaped its moorings, and after causing excitement further afield, had come to Peterborough at 4a.m., where its antics were finally brought to an end.

Local defence forces went in pursuit and the sound of gunfire over Woodston announced the end of the intruder's games. It was fortunate that no damage had been done to any houses along its route.

Among a list of prisoners of war published in the local press on Friday 2nd August, appeared the name of Trooper R.L. Jinks, Royal Armoured Corps, of 286, Walpole Street, until this time nothing had been heard of his whereabouts and it was confirmation that he was still alive. However, in the following week's Roll Of Honour, Trooper Jinks appears, once again, in the missing in action column. Three other city men who had been posted as missing in action were also confirmed as prisoners at this time.

Another 658 city men registered for national service in the forces on Saturday 27th July, with 30 more being received later by post. There were two conscientious objectors.

A.R.P. News

A special committee on A.R.P. in schools now decided not to attempt any treatment of school windows. If children could not go to school shelters, they would have to keep away from windows and lie on the floor. It was announced at the beginning of August that: "Use of school shelters is to be permitted to the public between 5:30p.m. and 8a.m." On an air raid warning during school hours all gates would be locked.

Gates giving access to the shelters would be left open during the hours stated, and police and wardens were asked to supervise them.

Electric bells were fitted wherever teachers required them, and fire appliances, stirrup pumps and first aid equipment were supplied and maintained close by. The provision of this equipment came to a total of £230.

The A.R.P. Committee also reported to the council at this time that they had been approached by the Trades and Labour Council and the National Federation of Building Trades Operatives to support an application for Anderson Shelters. Alderman Snowden again stated that no Anderson shelters were available, and in any case, the Peterborough area was designated as being non-vulnerable, and so was not entitled to them. The city was allowed communal shelters and was getting on with them. This was not accepted by the other parties as being a satisfactory answer.

There was, however, some good news on the A.R.P. front. The City Fire Brigade had now received their new Dennis 350-500 gallon per minute capacity trailer pump. This joined equipment that they already had, including an escape ladder, and a 700 g.p.m. pump, purchased in 1931, a Commer fire tender equipped with first aid pump and foam apparatus, and a Dennis 250gal. trailer pump. The first 20 stirrup pumps had now arrived and had been issued to the new Supplementary Fire Parties, numbering around 150, and situated all over the town.

A meeting of the City A.R.P. Committee on Monday 5th August, heard particulars from the City Engineer, Mr. F.J. Smith, of a further scheme for the provision of more communal brick shelters able to accommodate about 30,000 people.

The Engineer said that 626 shelters, each accommodating 48 persons, would be required, at a total cost of £62,000. Allowing for the government grant, the council would have to find £12,960. The Town Clerk put forward the scheme and made an application for the grant.

Additional shelters were already being provided on the surface in Long Causeway, Bridge Street, Pentney's Yard, and the Precincts. The Guildhall had also now been sandbagged. 34 shelters would be provided under this plan, at a cost of £1,954.

An order was now published by the Town Clerk, Mr. Arthur J. Reeves, requiring occupiers of dwelling houses to clear and keep clear all articles in any loft which was not furnished for human habitation. This was a government order to reduce the risk of fire in roof spaces caused by incendiary bombs.

Causing more concern to a number of wardens was the news that uniforms would not be issued. They gave notice that they intended to claim for any damage to their clothing due to their having no uniforms or overalls. The S.R.O. stated that claims for damaged clothing would receive sympathetic consideration.

The wardens of 3b sector were now asking for a siren for Longthorpe. It was stated that the city sirens were not loud enough to be heard there. The Chief Warden said that complaints had been received from wardens and the general public in all parts of the city, except the centre and the South Ward, that the sirens were inaudible. The Chief Constable stated that he had received complaints that warnings had not been heard at night in the Alexandra Road, Garton End and Northfields districts. It was recommended that a remote control siren be installed at the Park Laundry.

It was at this time that a letter was received by the Town Clerk from the American Trailer Ambulance Committee. The Committee proposed to make an appeal on behalf of English towns to the Mayors of towns and cities in America bearing the same names, and asking if ambulances would be acceptable.

The Town Clerk was requested to reply thanking the Committee and stating that the A.R.P. Committee would be only too pleased to accept, provided, (and it is open to conjecture what the A.R.P. Committee thought passed for ambulances in America), that the ambulances were fitted with four wheels!

In the Roll of Honour published in the 'Standard' on August 9th, there appeared the name of Bandsman G.A. Wilkinson, Northamptonshire Regiment, of Fletton, in the missing in action column. Lance Corporal A.J. Miners, of 37, Taverner's Road, was confirmed as being a prisoner of war.

Mr. and Mrs. W.A. Smith, of 163, Belsize Avenue, Woodston, received news of a more tragic nature in the middle of August when they were notified that their youngest son, Aircraftman (1st. Class), Alex James Smith, had been killed in an air raid on Gosport while on active service on the South Coast. In civil life he had been a brick setter at the London Brick Company. He joined the Air Force Volunteer Reserve in September 1938, and was called up for full time duty as a transport driver on the outbreak of the war. Later he was attached to a balloon barrage crew, and he was due on leave in less than two weeks had his death not intervened. He was home in the February and his parents had heard from him only a week before receiving the terrible news. Alex's fiancée, Miss Edna May Bussey, of 86, South Street, Stanground, received a letter the day he was killed. Being educated at Fletton Council School, he was a keen swimmer. His father was also employed at the L.B.C.

The funeral at Gosport, took place on Thursday 15th August and was attended by his father and brother. Later, after permission was obtained by his parents, Alex's body was re-interred in Woodston cemetery on the 12th June 1941.

The Home Guard
The largest muster of the City Battalion of the Home Guard was seen on the evening of Friday 16th August, when it paraded past a saluting base that had been set up outside the Town Hall. The Peterborough Group consisted of two battalions, the City and the Soke; however, it was the City battalion only, commanded by Captain R.J.C. Crowden, that marched past on that evening. Brigadier-General Sir Hereward Wake, Commandant of the Northamptonshire Group was to take the salute but he was called to see the King that day and his deputy, Colonel Hobson, stood in for him. Also present was Major James A.D.C. to Sir Hereward, Colonel A.H. Mellows, Commander of the Peterborough Group, the Town Clerk and other dignitaries.

The battalion assembled at their headquarters, and moved off at 7:30, led, strangely enough, by a gramophone, with amplifier, mounted on a lorry! This arrangement however, did not prove satisfactory, for as the men marched quite well for such a new unit, it was thought that they would have done far better with a band or drums. Everyone hoped that before long they would be able to make up this deficiency, and advertisements were later put in the newspapers asking for bugles and other instruments to be donated. The route of march was along Westgate, St. Leonard's Street, Cowgate, Bridge Street, to the car park, and back via Bridge Street, Long Causeway, Westgate and Lincoln Road. As the column passed the saluting base the command "Eyes left" was given by the C.O.; and carried on by company and section commanders, being smartly obeyed by the men.

On the way back, the men, who were almost all in uniform and carrying rifles, were inspected by the Mayor. Besides the general companies, there were also special works and other sections including the railwaymen, who formed an entire company, Westwood Works (a large section of No.2 Company), the firemen, regular and auxiliary, who provided a contrast in their blue uniforms, and the Post Office contingent, composed of electrical and other Corporation personnel. At the head marched officers and other ranks of Group and Battalion Headquarters Staff, while the rear was brought up by the transport and motor cycle dispatch riders.

Complaints of abuse to air raid shelters were still causing great concern towards the end of August, with another appeal to the public to "protect the shelters which are built to protect them." The damage by pilfering, breaking and by "filthy conduct," was still terrible. The authorities stated that they could not do everything, and it was up to the city people generally, to realise their necessity, and help if they could.

Accommodation was also a problem for the men of the No.1 Warden's Post in Fletton. They wanted to be transferred from their wooden hut to the brick built library next door. The council agreed as long as a place could be found for the displaced books, the Old Fletton Council School or the Fletton Avenue Methodist Schoolroom was suggested. The condition was also made that the books would have to be returned, and the library restored to its original state after the war. The A.R.P. Authority then suggested that the library be removed to the old A.R.P. hut now occupied by the wardens, and the wardens to move into the library. The change was agreed, and it seems that the wardens got the better part of the deal. It would have been interesting to record the comments of some of the residents who had to sit in the old wooden hut while they used their library!

Perhaps it is understandable that after a year of being at war, the locals were becoming increasingly impatient with what many of them thought were over officious air raid wardens. After all, no one in the city had seen a single German aircraft overhead, what was all the fuss about? The magistrate's courts were continually hearing cases of black-out infringements without any sign of a decrease in the numbers, and at the end of August yet more were being summoned to appear.

Perhaps the best example, up to this time, of the attitude of many city residents towards the enforcement of the black-out, was reflected in the case of Arthur Malcolm Pulton, of Padholme Road Post Office, who was reported for an infringement at 11:30p.m. on the night of August 1st.

Thomas Stimson, the Padholme Road air raid warden, stated that he and his colleagues had seen a downstairs light on, and when they shouted a light came on upstairs. The defendant came down and said, "You wardens are all a ***** nuisance. You have all got the wind up. It's all ***** red tape." Pulton was told he would be reported, and he replied, "You can do what you ***** well like." Other wardens also gave evidence. Pulton denied in court that he had used bad language and said that the wardens had upset him with their bullying manner. He stated that he had lost a leg in the last war, and because of his disability he could not get round to see to the black-out like an ordinary man.

The magistrate fined Pulton £3 with 2s. 6d. costs. The Chairman said he disliked hearing a man in the defendant's position making remarks about red tape and getting the wind up, when public servants - for that is what wardens were - were doing their duty. The defendant had six or seven windows; he (the Chairman) had 60.

Fletton Urban District Council was not happy. At their monthly meeting on Monday 19th August, they deplored their inability to obtain or purchase a supply of stirrup pumps in excess of the district's allocation - ten. The Civil Defence and Emergency Committees had decided that the council should buy 40 more pumps for use by the Supplementary Fire Parties at an estimated cost of £50. The District Auditor however, had informed them that there was no way he could allow the expenditure out of the rates. The council then decided to approach the Home Office (Fire Brigades Division) for a further issue of 40 pumps, but was told that according to the population and vulnerability of the district, they were only allowed 10.

As there was nothing the council could do, they decided they might ask individuals to buy pumps. "We shall have to wait until the place gets on fire," said Councillor Goodwin, "and then we shall see!"

As they couldn't buy pumps and give them away, the council decided to purchase 60 pumps on a sale or return basis, and encourage Supplementary Fire Parties to buy them from the council at £1 each, thus, satisfying the District Auditor. The question was then turned to buckets, which were also in short supply.

To be fair, and broadly speaking, by the end of August the Ministry of Supply had completed the task of providing sufficient steel helmets, respirators, oilskin clothing, fire fighting appliances, medical stores, stretchers, rescue party appliances and a large number of other articles, to meet the demands of establishment strength in each area. In some cases however, volunteers had come forward in such numbers that establishment strength had been exceeded, although this was encouraged, as it was thought they would definitely be needed later on. Steps were being taken to increase the provision of personal equipment such as steel helmets, subject, however, upon the claims of the fighting forces.

Work was also forging ahead at Fletton with the construction of air raid shelters, continuing with Wootton Avenue and the High Street, on the basis of one shelter for every four houses. According to the Home Office there should be one shelter for 12 to 14 persons, a local census had been carried out and the average per house in the two streets was 4 to 5 persons, as opposed to the Home Office figure of three and a half! The principle was adopted that where necessary, bigger shelters would be constructed.

The sandbags protecting the council offices at Fletton had now collapsed, and window protection was provided instead, front and back. The sandbags were taken away and a shelter under the stairs was strengthened. Sandbags in Huntley Road and Wootton Avenue were also showing signs of decay.

Horses were now coming under the provisions of the A.R.P. rules. Drivers of horse drawn vehicles in the city were advised, on the sounding of the sirens, to take their horses out of the carts and tether them either at the back of the cart, or to iron railings (if the salvage men had left any standing), or lamp posts. If possible, they should be drawn into side streets.

Although the trivia of war was taking place, not only in the city, but all over the country, it was still occasionally being punctuated by spasmodic reports of the deaths and woundings of local men.

The Roll of Honour for August 23rd recorded that two men, Gunner James O. Hughes, of High Street, Stanground, and Gunner John W. Phillips, of 757, Lincoln Road, both in the Royal Artillery, were now prisoners of war. Also at this time though came the news that Aircraftman (First Class) Kenneth Albert Lewis, eldest son of Mr. and Mrs. A. Lewis, of 17, Milton Road, Fletton, had been seriously wounded during a German air attack on a British aerodrome. His parents went to visit him, his mother remaining at the hospital to be by his side.

Aircraftman Lewis, who had been in the volunteer reserve, had been employed by the Eastern Counties Omnibus Company as a conductor before being called up at the outbreak of the war. His father was employed on the L.N.E.R.

Spitfire Fund Grows
By the end of August the Spitfire Fund had grown to £1,236 11s. 6d. and money was coming in from every conceivable direction. The employees of many local firms, for example, raised money with collections, but it was the individual donations that best showed the will of the people.

Graham Aubrey, aged 11, of 7, Lime Tree Avenue, raised 5s. by the sale of old newspapers he collected in his street.

Mr. J.L.R. Beeton made a house-to-house collection in Norfolk Street, and raised £18 4s. 3d. only one household did not subscribe it was said.

Beryl Dale, of Orton Hall, wrote to the Treasurer: "Dear Sir, I am sending you my birthday money of 5s. for our Spitfire Fund."

A card with the words: "this is from a widow - an old age pensioner," accompanied 2s. 6d.

Ten three-penny pieces from the money box of Malcolm Thorpe, aged 18 months, of 7, Mayor's Walk, was received.

On Wednesday 28th August, £2 2s. was received from Mrs. Heath and "Jimmy," a donkey that was born on the Somme during World War One, and was brought back to Peterborough to raise money for the R.S.P.C.A. after the war.

Wardens groups, whist drives, the Ladies Orchestra, the Rotary Club, public houses, the St. John Ambulance Brigade, everyone was sending donations, the cause had certainly captured the imagination of the people.

Someone else who had aircraft, but of a different kind, on his mind at this time was Robert Wagstaff, a Peterborough market stall trader, who appeared in court at the end of the month on a charge of, "Making a statement likely to cause alarm and despondency on July 20th."

Wagstaff was accused of telling a woman at the city market that: "Norwich Station has been bombed and thousands of people have been killed.....if you don't get bombed, he is going to starve you out."

For spreading this unfounded rumour Wagstaff was fined £2 with 6s. costs, he said he would appeal, as he "definitely did not say it."

The original number of official evacuees received in Peterborough and its surroundings, who had all come from London, had been 545 adults and 1,088 children - 1,633 people. The number of houses used for billeting them had been 685. Out of that number of original evacuees, there were only 8 adults and 184 children still in the area by September 1940.

The reason for the voluntary return of the evacuees was put down to the fact that

London had not yet been bombed. Also, husbands had become lonely, and the houses had got in the condition that they would do with "mother away." "They said we were no safer; we had no Anderson shelters. So they trickled back."

During the last two or three months however, there had been a steady influx of unofficial refugees from various coastal towns, numbering just over 2,400. These people had arranged their own billets with friends or with other people. The local authority had found billets for about 200 of them. It was known how many had come to the city through the changes in the ration cards.

Second Raid

At 10.50 p.m. on Saturday 31st August, approximately 100 incendiary bombs fell over an area from the city to Milton Park. At the same time three or four big oil bombs, the first to be used by the Germans were also dropped. Theatres, cinemas and public houses in the city were all full when the drone of aircraft was heard overhead. Most of the people in the streets hurried into the shelters and within a few minutes three or four loud explosions were heard accompanied by brilliant flashes of light. Small fires were started in the meadows by the river just behind the City Engineer's house, and in the gardens and orchards of private houses. All of the fires were quickly extinguished by police and air raid wardens.

Fires started by four large bombs were put out by Auxiliary Fire Service patrols. The damage turned out to be slight, as in each case the fire was confined to a small area, and was brought under control within a few minutes. All of the bombs dropped clear of buildings. The only casualties recorded were a frog burned to death and a wasp's nest partly destroyed.

Air Raid Shelter Crisis

By September, the constant damage to the local air raid shelters was being regarded with the gravest concern in official circles. It was thought that the public should help guard the shelters, which were after all, built at enormous cost for their safety. The perpetrators of this damage were believed to be boys and youths of 15 to 20 years of age.

Lamps and guards were torn down, emergency exit covers broken, canvas screens ripped away, forms used as see-saws, and their legs broken, in several cases fires had been started. By far the worst damage had been caused in the Padholme Road area, but there were also complaints regarding Occupation Road, New England.

"Cannot some of those who are doing no war service," said Alderman Snowden, "come to an arrangement with their neighbours to keep, in turn, constant supervision over the shelters nearest to them."

In answer to this he was told that most damage was caused by children from the other end of the streets, and residents did not like to interfere with neighbours' children.

After they had been open only two days (in early August), there had not been a single electric light bulb left in the shelters at Saxon Road and Park Lane end. Stones had been thrown down the entrances, and concrete steps broken, Latrine seats were smashed. In one, the iron cover to the emergency exit had been lifted, thrown down into the interior, and broken. Lamps had been left switched on, so that the batteries which fed them were exhausted.

On the subject of appealing to parents there seemed small hope. More often than not, officials were met by jeers and boos. Shelters in other parts of the town were generally fairly decent, and at New England the Ranger looked after them. The Stanley Recreation Ground Shelters it was said were abused more than any through indecent misuse by adults.

The Chief Constable now issued another of his famous requests, this time for the city's theatres, cinemas and dance halls to close at 10p.m. each night, as from Monday 9th September. He was concerned about the large number of people leaving these places of entertainment during the time when hostile air attacks might be expected, due to the nights getting darker earlier. Up until this time the theatres and cinemas had been closing at 10:30 and the dance halls at 11:00 since the beginning of June, before then, dances had sometimes gone on until 2a.m.

The Scrap Piles Up

The Ministry of Supply wrote to the council at the beginning of September asking for the removal of unwanted metal railings for scrap. The council replied that the Ministry should arrange for the removal of the scrap already collected and still within the city. The City Engineer stated that the only railings he could suggest were round New England recreation ground - 450 yards and about fifteen and a half tons. It was not thought that railings should be removed from gardens. The railings at the old burial ground in Cowgate and between the grass and asphalt in Fulbridge Road playground were also mentioned.

The problem that the council faced were the growing piles of scrap metal at their salvage depots, they were unable to take any more, or to send the metal they did have on to the scrap dealers, as the dealers yards were in their turn, full to bursting also. There was obviously a bottleneck somewhere, and the suggestion was made that the dealers were holding on to the scrap in order to force the price up higher. There was talk of a "metal ring," and fingers were pointed at two or three people working in Fengate, but it was agreed that the blame could not be placed wholly at the doors of the local dealers, as it was said that the firms outside the city which took the metal off the local yards, were themselves moving very slowly.

Since November 1939, the council had collected 250 tons of paper, 35 tons of tins, 6 tons of rags, 2 tons of bones, 10 tons of scrap metal, 200 gross bottles, 35 gross milk bottles, half a ton of brass and lead, a quarter of a ton of copper and 4 cwts. of string. Although the scrap metal seemed to stay in the dealer's yards for weeks, there had been no serious delay with any of the other items.

Three more Peterborough men appeared in the 'Standard' on September 6th, confirmed as being prisoners of war, they were: Flight Sergeant, C.G.S. Poole, RAF, of Cromwell Road, Gunner Signaller, H.L. Hall, Royal Artillery, of Star Road, and Private K. Trimmings, Royal Army Ordnance Corps, of 36, Windmill Street.

By the beginning of September nearly 700 "Housewives" had enrolled for service to provide temporary resting places for people injured in raids who might have had to await the arrival of an ambulance. Mrs. Mellows had made an appeal earlier in the year, and the response had been wonderful. Each volunteer was supplied with a card to put in her window, and these became familiar objects in many streets.

It was at this time that the Red Cross and St. John War Organisation were asked by the Minister of Health to establish 20,000 beds for convalescent servicemen in private houses and other suitable buildings. They hoped to eventually equip 40 separate establishments. These would be used as auxiliary hospitals according to requirements. The only house that the local joint committee had at its disposal at that time was the Lindens, in Lincoln Road, lent for the duration by Mr. A.J. Paten, at that time it was still unused but would eventually take on this role.

Additions were once again being made to the city air raid sirens in order to make them more audible in all parts of the city, regardless of the wind direction. The Baker Perkins siren was now electrified and another had been put up in one of the towers at the showground. Next to be placed would be one in Tennyson Road, and a fourth at Longthorpe, all would be centrally controlled.

A story was circulating in the city at about this time also of an incident which occurred locally during an air raid warning. After the sirens had sounded one night, and a man was feverishly tucking in his trousers, he suddenly called out, "I've been hit! Take the children to safety."

His wife rushed off to the shelter with the children and returned to find her husband helpless - with laughter. He had tucked the curtain in with his shirt, and had brought the pole down onto his head!

On a more serious note, the School Management Sub Committee stated that on Friday 30th August, during a daylight air raid warning, the public smashed their way through a locked gate to get to the shelters in Cromwell Road school playground. The Chief Constable had been notified of the matter.

Images of school children, unable to get into packed shelters due to them being full of adult gatecrashers, and being left to the mercy of the bombers, throws a somewhat darker light onto the behaviour of some city residents.

Pals Safe

Pals since they attended Lincoln Road Council school, Private George Thomas Frederick Hasdell, 2nd Northamptonshire Regiment, and Lance Corporal John Stamper, Clarence Road, both reported on July 5th as being missing in action, were now confirmed as being prisoners of war. Following notification from the War Office that Private Hasdell was a prisoner at a Stalag, a letter and postcard was received from him by his mother, Mrs. Kate Hasdell, of 261, Lincoln Road. He was her second son, and had spent six years on the North West Frontier and some time in Canada before the war. Lance Corporal Stamper was the third son of Mr. and Mrs. Joe Stamper of 232, Clarence Road.

White butterflies took up five minutes on Wednesday 11th September at the meeting of the Soke County Agricultural Committee. Mr. S.M. Egar said that harm was being done by the butterflies to cabbages now wanted for food. In Huntingdonshire people had been paid 4d. for every 100 butterflies they caught. The County Land Agent had paid for many hundreds out of his own pocket.

The Chairman, Lord Exeter, told the committee that he could not allow the agent to pay out his own pocket, the country was full of these butterflies and the Committee would carry on with the payments. "I do not think it will break the council," he said. The Land Agent was instructed to accept further catches on behalf of the Committee.

The Supplementary Fire Service - the stirrup pumpers - were, by the middle of September, the latest A.R.P. body to be allocated arm bands, door plates, and window bills. The arm bands gave the wearers permission to enter places in danger; the plates notified the leader of the stirrup pump party, and the location of the pump; the bills indicated that the occupant of the house was a member of the service and could put anyone in touch with the team.

The Chief Officer, Mr. Haylett, now stated that there were 65 official pumps in use with Supplementary Fire Parties, and that over 300 civilians had been trained by him at the A.F.S. headquarters. Another 53 pumps had been allocated to the district and would soon be issued. A total of 175 pumps would soon be on hand in the city, and residents were constantly reminded to keep a bucket of water handy at all times.

Many of the groups had improvised scoops for handling bombs, and a considerable number of the pumps were privately owned. These pumps, with garden hoses fitted, would help reduce the danger of fire spreading. More volunteers were still needed, and many citizens saw it as a way of serving their country.

Even after twelve months of war, there were still complaints that sirens were not being heard. It was stated as a fact that it was impossible to hear them at Woodston School above the noise made by the children.

The headmaster of Old Fletton School wrote to the council saying that in one alarm, the first they had had when the school was assembled, he could not find one child who had heard it inside. A boy coming in from the outside was the first to tell him it was sounding, and he heard it as they were going into the shelters. Although the District Council thought that it was a problem for the County, they did accept that they had a moral responsibility and would discuss what progress could be made.

One council member asked how they heard the fire alarm when it was sounded. He was told there wasn't one!

By the third week of September there were nearly 5,000 people in Peterborough who had come from other areas, particularly the coast, on their own initiative. More were still coming at the rate of about 300 a week. A return was sent to the government every week, as these people were taking many of the billets already set aside for a possible official influx. The last list showed that Peterborough had 385 government evacuees, and 4,346 private visitors. Other "strangers" taking the total to well over the 5,000 mark.

Local tradesmen at least, were feeling the benefit of a large number of additional customers, and the Food Control Office stated that there had been no shortage of supplies. No retailer or buyer had gone short.

By the first week of October a steady stream of voluntary evacuees began to come in to the area from London, and between 700 and 800 found billets or had them hired for them. This took the city total to 5,300 evacuees, with only a tiny amount having official billeting vouchers. A large contingent of official evacuees was expected the following week. Provisions were being made by the Food Control for further supplies in anticipation of more mouths to feed. Compulsory billeting had so far been avoided, but residents accepted that it had to be getting closer.

Third Raid

At 1 a.m. on the night of September 19th, one high explosive bomb fell near the Corporation Farm; four houses were damaged including Fengate House and the Tannery. It is difficult to judge whether these odd, almost random attacks were much more than returning bombers ditching the remainder of their loads over enemy territory before heading back over the Channel. There seemed to be little gain to the enemy in these visits, and again in this case, no casualties were inflicted.

Shelters and More Shelters

The City Engineer now sent the S.R.O. a revised scheme for shelters in the precincts and near the Market Place, and for the strengthening of two private cellars offered by tradesmen - Messrs Barlow and Sons and Mr. H.W. Pickering, in Church Street.

The proposals were for brick built shelters in the precincts to hold 325, the cellars, 127, and a shelter in Mr. W.H. Pentney's yard for 50 - a total of 502. The precincts shelters would be on the green, to the left on entering the Foregate, and would not obstruct the view of the cathedral. Once these were on the way it was hoped to proceed with shelters in the centre of Long Causeway and Bridge Street. Other tradesmen had offered the use of cellars, and although some could not be officially accepted, their owners were prepared to let the public use them in emergencies at their own risk.

Meanwhile, the erection of other street shelters was going on apace. Construction had reached the bus depot in Lincoln Road, and was also going on in Exeter Road, Gladstone Street and Walpole Street.

This scheme would eventually spread all over the city, including Fengate, from where complaints of neglect had been received. There had also been a large number of requests for domestic communal shelters, in response to the Corporation's suggestion to provide them free of cost to those streets whose residents were receiving less than £250 per annum income.

By the end of the month the City Council had provided 310 domestic communal shelters in streets, and many more were in the course of construction. Those completed provided shelter for 9,000 people.

Ultimately there would be accommodation for between 30,000 and 35,000 people, but there would not be street shelters for all. Where possible, passages were to be adapted as shelters, and fitted with gas-proof curtains.

Wardens were being reminded at this time that in no circumstances should they attempt to heat or supplement the heating of their posts by the use of braziers or stoves which were likely to emit fumes.

There was a grave risk of gassing by carbon monoxide. The same consideration applied to the use of braziers or stoves in private garden air raid shelters, and in domestic communal, and public air raid shelters.

In answer to a previous appeal by the A.R.P. Committee, eight first aid posts for animals injured by enemy action had now been established in different parts of the city. A meeting was held at the Old Town Hall on Thursday 10th October to explain the details of the scheme and give some information on the prevention and treatment of animal casualties. Volunteers and anyone else interested in the scheme were encouraged to step forward.

Just for a change, instead of complaints, the A.R.P. service paid tribute to a set of residents for setting a good example in tending their local air raid shelters. On October 4th, Mr. C. Bothamley, warden of No.7 post (No.3 Group), had a letter printed in the local press in which he said:

"I would like to pay a tribute to the ladies living near the air raid shelters in Nicholls Avenue, Fulham Road, Haddon Road, and Almoners Lane; also to the Ranger of West Town Recreation Ground. These people keep the shelters spotlessly clean.

When one reads about the public shelters in other parts of the city, it looks as if there is a little war work the ladies in other parts of the city could do by three or four adopting a shelter near their homes. I would also like to thank the young people and the children for the respect they pay to these shelters. They are a credit to the city."

Sailor's Death

Mr. and Mrs. A. Pridmore, of 40, Tower Street, received a telegram from the Admiralty on Tuesday 17th September stating that their eldest son, Alan Harry Pridmore, had died as a result of an electric shock.

Pridmore, who was 21, was called up the previous October, and entered the navy as an electrician. He had last been home on leave in March, and until Monday 9th September, when four letters arrived, his parents had not heard from him for 13 weeks.

Before he joined up he was with the London Brick Company as an electrician. He had been a keen musician, and had played solo cornet in the Farcet Salvation Army Band. He had also been a Songster Leader, and was a pupil of Miss K. Bellairs. His father was foreman at Hicks No.1 yard.

Although at this time the government had no intention of requiring people to camouflage their vehicles, it had not stopped some locals from painting their cars "in order to render them less conspicuous." There was no objection to private owners taking these steps on their own account, even if the practice was of doubtful use, but there was a regulation which stated that private vehicles should not be painted in a manner that resembled camouflaged Service transport. A note was printed in the 'Standard' informing citizens that, "owners should not paint their cars with what is generally known as a disruptive camouflage, or with a jazz pattern. Cars painted in this way may be mistaken for Service vehicles, especially in a poor light."

People were told that whenever one or more colours were used, it was best to keep to dark neutral shades other than the grey and khaki already adopted by the Services. Also, the paint should always have a matt surface. Considering that most cars were painted black during the 1940's, efforts to tone down the colour seem a little pointless looking back on it.

Working Through the Siren

At the beginning of October a leaflet entitled "Working through the siren" was being widely distributed through the employers associations, trades unions and government departments interested in war production. It explained that one of the principle aims of the enemy's indiscriminate air attacks was to reduce the British war output; this could only be countered by all workers, both in works and offices, being ready to run the risks, which varied greatly from district to district, involved in treating the siren, not as a signal to stop work, but only as a warning that danger may be imminent.

There had been considerable modifications to the former order for certain departments of the Civil Service to stop work and rush to shelters every time the siren was sounded. The practice now was as follows:

Post Office: Major Routh, the Head-Postmaster, stated that the staff would not now cease work, nor would the public be excluded from the counter department. If a warning came of imminent danger it would be different; the staff would take cover, and the public would be asked to leave. The matter had largely been left to their discretion.

Taxation Offices: At the new No.1 and No.2 taxation district offices in Cross Street, they were given a free hand, and the staff unanimously elected to carry on. With the present heavy workload, they did not want to add to the difficulty. At first they were told to go to the big shelter below the building, but now a watcher would stand at the rear top windows and keep in touch with the watcher at the telephone exchange, and danger would lead to a quick dive down.

The Banks: Notices had now been placed in all the banks stating that they would remain open for the transaction of urgent business. If for reasons of immediate safety it became necessary for the staff to take cover during immediate local danger, banking services would be provided, but the doors must be closed, and not locked or bolted.

Town Hall: While the staff were at liberty to do what they pleased, first aid and fire parties would stand by. A number of the personnel would have to stop work to take up various A.R.P. posts outside.

Works: Most of the local factories had decided to carry on working during the raid-time. Brotherhood's started the practice on Monday 30th September, and Baker Perkins the following day.

As far as the actions of pedestrians who were caught out during an alert were concerned, the Government advice was to go on their way after the warning as long as they wished, but be prepared to take cover if they heard guns or bombs, or enemy aircraft nearby. When there was a reason to think that the enemy was near, it was the duty of all citizens to avoid taking unreasonable risks, not only for their own sake, but also for the sake of the civil defence services that might be called upon to look after them if they were injured. It was left to the pedestrian to decide whether to take shelter, and not for the air raid wardens to intervene, unless there was evidence of enemy activity in the vicinity. Even in that case they were only to advise, and not stop, or insist on anyone taking cover in a shelter if they did not wish to do so.

At a meeting of the Peterborough A.R.P. Committee the question was raised whether it was necessary for the sirens to be sounded so frequently, the present system was in line with the instructions from the Ministry of Home Security, and as such, no decision was made to take any other action.

Approval was now received in October for a grant to construct communal domestic shelters under two new schemes. Number One, for 8,112 people in 169 shelters at a cost of £6,900 for materials and £10,000 labour. Number Two, for 30,000 people in 626 shelters at a cost of £25,040 for materials and £37,560 labour. It was now also government policy that drinking water should be available in all public shelters, and the City Engineer stated that the cost of fixing water tanks to the shelters would cost an extra £103 not including the cost of having two men visit each shelter to maintain the supply.

At about this time a meeting of various representatives from a number of local industries took place, and Peterborough was made a centre for the giving of a course for roof watchers, or "Jim Crows" as they were nicknamed. The men would undertake the vital task of watching for the approach of enemy planes while their fellow workers carried on with essential war production during the period of the "alert." Peterborough was one of five training centres in the Midland Region. The trainees received theoretical instruction, including the recognition of various types of hostile aircraft in silhouette, and also a practical course in which the local RAF joined in by flying in their own aircraft.

Soon afterwards the Home Security (Fire Watchers) Order came into force on September 19th. This required the appointment of a whole-time fire watcher in every premises where 30 or more people were employed. Where two firms shared a building and their collective employees numbered more than 30, they could make a joint arrangement.

The stipulation was that the watcher had to be on the premises the whole time for which he undertook to watch, and at his post during the period of a raid or alert. He had to be ready to detect an outbreak of fire and to use the appliances to deal with it, or to take other action as required. Warehouses and sawmills also came under these regulations.

Compulsory Billeting
By the second week of October, organised parties of women and children from bombed areas in London were again arriving in the city. Although most had been distributed among the villages in the rural districts, the task of the Billeting Officers was not now proving to be easy, and at Fletton, for example, Mr. J.E. Clarke, Clerk to the Fletton Urban District Council, had to invoke compulsory powers in order to obtain the required number of billets. He also warned that further action would be taken in certain cases where there was a definite refusal. The number of arrivals on Saturday 5th was 430: 160 adults, 150 children between the ages of 3 and 14, and 120 under 3. 230 of these had been allocated to Fletton. All the evacuees were medically examined before being placed, and they were found generally to be in good health, although there were a number of cases where individuals were classified as suffering from bomb-shock. So far, school accommodation was not proving to be a difficulty.

Speaking of the rules of evacuation, Mr. Clarke said it seemed hardly fair that there should be compulsion at this end, and the necessity to use the "big stick" to get them in, when there is no compulsion on the visitors to accept what they were given.

We can only read from this statement that some evacuees were a little 'choosy' about where they were billeted. This could only have made the job of the billeting officer more difficult. The payment for accommodation was now 5 shillings per adult and 3 shillings per child, and they had to make their own arrangements when it came to food. All of them had to have registration cards, and had to make their own applications for free milk. For other assistance they had to get forms from the billeting officer and take them to the Employment Exchange.

The three W.V.S. officers for the district - Mrs. Allan, Mrs. Morley Wells and Mrs. Atkinson - did all they could for the mothers and children, including obtaining gifts of clothing and toys. Overcoats, pullovers and children's woollies were in most demand.

Some parents objected strongly about being put in different houses from some of their children, but with large families this was occasionally necessary. The mothers could not understand that they had to adapt to the conditions, and feared that a bomb might part them from their children forever. There were rumours that more mothers and children would soon be arriving, bad news indeed for the Fletton billeting officer.

First Blows Struck by the Home Guard
The Home Guard was ready for a fight, but the incident that took place on September 28th at Walton was not quite what their creators had had in mind. Magistrates sitting at the beginning of October heard the case of Harry Winters, of 44, Grove Street, who was summoned for assaulting Samuel Christopher, he pleaded guilty.

Christopher, a storekeeper at Walton, and a member of the Home Guard, said he was on guard duty, and went into the guard room. Winters, a skilled labourer, was also a member of the guard. Winters started an argument and made some "very uncalled-for remarks." He said that Christopher was "always trying to get the men into trouble," and that he was "an agitator." All of these were quite untrue. Christopher had lost his temper and called him something. Then Winters had struck him twice.

Sidney Smalley, also a member of the Home Guard, had been present on duty, and said there had been an argument started by Winters, and Winters had "put himself into a fighting attitude." Smalley had tried to make peace but Winters struck two blows at Christopher, drawing blood.

Mr. Sturton, who was acting for Winters stated that his client expressed deep regret. Unfortunately, the long hours he had worked were a trial to the nerves, and the other man (Christopher) using bad language had made matters worse. It was one of those unfortunate arguments that did arise. His client had suffered for it, he had lost his job, though he had since got another. He was very sorry, and had paid dearly for it.

The Chief Constable spoke of previous convictions for assaulting the police and two other assault cases. In imposing a fine of £1 and 6s. costs, the Chairman said it was a pity to see men wasting their energies like this.

The Spitfire Fund was finally wound up on Wednesday 16th October. The fund had grown as follows:

September 6th - £1,807.
September 13th - £2,925.
September 20th - £4,692.
September 27th - £5,000.

By the 16th October the total had reached £6,318 6s. 6d. and a cheque was drawn up in favour of the Ministry of Aircraft Production, and sent to Lord Beaverbrook. An acknowledgement was received from him the following month, thanking the city for its patriotism and self sacrifice, "...It is this spirit, so splendidly evinced by the contributors to your fund, against which the legions of Hitler will struggle in vain..."

Owing to the great success achieved by the Spitfire Fund, it was decided to have a War Weapons Week for the City and the Soke in order to try and raise £350,000 to pay for a destroyer. This new effort would commence on November 29th.

Yet More Evacuees
A headache for Fletton and every other part of the city arrived on Friday 11th October, when approximately a thousand official evacuees from London descended on the city. Their reception was not accomplished it was said, "Without difficulty and without demur."

By the following week billeting had still not been completed, but there were comparatively few "overs" then remaining.

The mothers and children arrived by train and were convoyed from the station to the Salvation Army Citadel in King's Street, where a meal was awaiting them, masses of trunks, bags and parcels being dumped on the pavement. From there they were taken in pre-arranged numbers to selected schools in all parts of the city, from where they would be escorted by the W.V.S. in cars to their billets. Reception was mixed. Some people took mothers and children in freely, others did so only under pressure, a number refused outright. At the end of the day, room had to be found for 60 or 70 more people at Thorpe Road House, and others were put up in the New England Wesleyan Schoolroom and in the Wesley Hall, Pipe Lane.

Some difficulties were due to mothers with large families refusing to be separated from any of their children. The problem of finding a billet for a family of 6 or 7 (there was one of 9), was obvious. Such cases were quartered in empty houses which had been requisitioned, with furniture provided by the Mayor. A number of Londoners were still not happy however, imagining that a full supply of empty houses were to be provided for all, with free furniture. A drift back to London by a few of them had started as early as the following day!

The Food Control Department still had ample supplies, and The Milk Office was keeping up under heavy pressure. The market stalls on the Saturday did an exceptional trade, the visitors apparently taking a particular liking to light pastries, compared with the more staple foodstuffs. This last intake had pushed the total number of evacuees who had come to the city to 8,562. All the empty houses in Peterborough not already booked for other purposes had been requisitioned for the large families, and thirteen houses had now been taken. The newcomers were spaced as evenly as possible in the 14 areas into which the city had been divided for billeting purposes. There were about 360 children of school age in this last batch that would have to be found space in the schools.

As previously stated, a drift back had already started, and by the end of the following week at least 17 had gone home. It was largely a matter of sheer boredom, they wanted to go out at night and enjoy themselves. They liked their hosts, but they didn't want to just sit around the fire in the evenings, reading or listening to the wireless. Strangely enough, they missed the "fun" of going to the shelters, "the good humour and the frolic of it," the sing-songs and little parties. Some thought had to be put into the lack of entertainment being provided, "when they came they were tired and weary, but two or three good nights' rest made them want town life again."

By the end of October there were over 9,000 evacuees in the city, official and unofficial. They were coming in at a rate of about 50 per day and were making their own billeting arrangements. A new depot for the reception and distribution of gift clothing for evacuees was now opened at 10, Cowgate. This was filled straight away with a large collection of clothes, including an enormous consignment of gifts from America.

Red Cross Work

Progress was now being made in getting ready the city's two Red Cross Convalescent Homes - The Lindens, Lincoln Road, and Paston Hall - £250 had been set aside for each towards the acquisition of equipment. Alterations for the Lindens would cost £150, at Paston there was very little to do other than blacking out, this however would be expensive as there was a large amount of glass. The Lindens had been offered by Mr. Paten, Paston Hall by Mr. Le Maistre. Beds would be the main items to requisition, it was obvious however, that due to the evacuee position, there were no spare beds in the city and these would have to be obtained from elsewhere.

Mrs. Ellis and her ladies had been busy at the City Red Cross depot, during the month of September she had sent away to hospitals 198 pairs of pyjamas, 23 dressing gowns, 36 tropical vests, 5 navy pullovers, 222 children's nightdresses and 36 bed jackets. They also sent two large parcels of clothing for children, mostly made from the scraps and cuttings from their work-tables. The R.N. Comforts Depot received 60 pairs of sea boot stockings, and 25 pairs of minesweepers' gloves were also dispatched. To Lowestoft were sent 40 helmets (balaclava), 30 pairs of gloves, 20 scarves, 50 pairs of mittens, 5 pairs of sea boot stockings and 970 pairs of socks.

Mrs. H.J. Farrow had started a knitting party for the Home Guard, and Mrs. W.T. Mellows had sent off a large quantity of assorted bandages to London, she was also appealing for prams, push-carts and folding chairs as well as warm clothing for the evacuees. Mr. J.W. Fowler, of the St. John's Ambulance Association was putting out a call of his own for 60 volunteer stretcher bearers for the Peterborough Memorial Hospital in the event of an emergency; a duty rota would be arranged. The work was never-ending, but there were always people in the city willing to carry it forward.

New vehicle lighting regulations affecting side, rear and stop lights came into force on Wednesday 23rd October, and one can only imagine the reaction of the local drivers when they read the new rules, these barely allowed any light to be seen at all. No wonder so many people were killed on the roads during the black-out.

The new regulations were intended to reduce lighting so that the lights were clearly visible at 30 yards, but invisible at 300 yards. Drivers were urged to comply with the following requirements:

"Apply black paint on the inside and outside of the front glass leaving a clear circle an inch in diameter - the size of a halfpenny. Dim the inch circle by applying white paint to the inside of the clear space; by fitting semi-opaque white paper inside the lamp glass; or by getting a garage or electrical firm to reduce the power of the bulbs by putting a resistance in the circuit....rear and stop lights should be treated similarly, with the obvious exception that the inch circle must be red."

The order to extinguish headlamps when the sirens sounded had been cancelled. Instead, masked headlamps could be used, but only while the vehicle was in motion! Fog-lamps were not permitted during either the purple or red warning. Public service vehicles could use one third of their normal interior lighting, and the police retained the right to order headlights to be extinguished during an attack. At this stage of the war, no one was now allowed to buy a new car unless they were engaged in work of vital importance.

The Chief Constable also warned at this time about the use of torches during air raid warnings, citing a case where people leaving a dance in a Midland town during an alert period, used torches to find their cycles and lit cigarettes, which, along with the light from the hall doorway, attracted an enemy aircraft, causing bombs to be dropped close by.

Shelter News and the Home Guard

By November 1st, rapid progress had been made with the construction of the domestic shelters. Manor House Street off Lincoln Road, Burghley Square and other parts close to the centre of the city had now been reached. The shelters in the Precincts were roof high, and the large underground shelters for public use, at the corner of Craig Street and Lincoln Road would soon be available. By the end of the month, the Engineer was asked to submit a scheme for domestic shelters for the whole of the city not covered by existing schemes. He was also requested to obtain a suitable site for shelters in Park Road and the Westgate district.

The public were now surprised to see a number of shelters being taken down, or at least being de-roofed. These were the shelters with round-arched tops. Owing to the shortage of cement at the time of construction, the old corbelled and cement roofing had been found to be impracticable, and a government design for arched roofs, made with lime mortar was ordered to be substituted.

These, in turn, were found to be faulty in design, and from many places, including Peterborough, came reports that the walls were being pushed outwards.

About 40 shelters of this design had been completed, or were nearing completion in the city, and rather than put public safety at risk, the round roofs were ordered to be removed. In due course the tops were replaced with four and a half inch corbling and reinforced cement.

Very considerable reforms of the Home Guard were announced in the House of Commons on Wednesday 6th November. The main points were the granting of commissions to all approved commanders, with a suitable complement of warrant and N.C.O. ranks bearing "traditional titles."

Compensation was to be paid for the loss of wages if called out for whole-time emergency service; arms were to be available for 1,000,000 men; conditions of service would not be changed and battle dress would now be issued, with denims being withdrawn.

Captain G. Baker, who had been administrative officer and adjutant of the Home Guard, first for the Group, and then for the City Battalion, found it necessary for professional reasons to give up the offices in November. Mr. J. Bradbury, who had been Coy.Q.M.S. for No.1, took over the administrative duties, and Mr. E.W. Bromige, then second-in-command of No.III, became adjutant, his place as second-in-command was taken by Lieutenant A.E. Stewart, R.A.

Fourth Raid
At 5.10 a.m. on Saturday 16th November, six high explosive bombs were dropped in the Fletton area. Thirty-one houses were damaged in Queen's Walk, Orchard Street, London Road and Park Street, two were demolished and two people were injured.

Mr. John Crowson, of 37, Queen's Walk, whose house was demolished, was cut about the head and face, and his wife and daughter, Miss Mary Crowson suffered from shock. Ambulance Officer, T.W. Blake found that when her bedroom floor had collapsed Miss Crowson had fallen, still in bed, into the room below; she was shaken but was rescued through the dining room window. Mr. and Mrs Crowson were in the front bedroom and were in danger of being trapped by falling masonry. An ARP rescue squad carried them out through the front bedroom window and down a ladder to safety.

In one of the wrecked rooms an unbroken electric light bulb still hung from what was left of the ceiling, and a bottle of milk stood among a pile of bricks. Two canaries in a cage were killed.

Mr. E. Goodson lived next door with his six children - Edward, aged 17, Edna 16, Sheila 14, Kenneth 13, Joyce 11, and George 10. Edna recalled: "Somehow we all found ourselves in the front room, and dad told us he'd been blown out of bed. The stairs had gone, and we could smell gas, so dad tied sheets and blankets together until they reached the front garden. He tied one end to the window frame, and Ted scrambled down the water pipe. He fell a little way but wasn't hurt. Dad then told the rest of us to go down the ladder, and ambulance men took us off at the bottom. We thought we had lost our cat, Snookes, but later on he came to the front bedroom window. We could not get him to leave the house."

A steel shelter in a garden on the very lip of one of the craters, stood undamaged. Mr. Goodman told of his providential escape. "A stone slab a yard square, off a cistern in the back garden, came hurtling through the roof and crashed beside my bed. Beams and most of the ceiling followed it, but I had my head under the clothes by then, and I didn't have a scratch to show for it."

A bomb fell on the pavement outside Mr. and Mrs. Walker's house in an

91

intersecting street, and a gas main was fractured.

The Coalheaver's Arms in Park Street was severely damaged by several bombs, the bar and front bedroom were wrecked. The landlord Mr. Haynes and his wife had been fortunate in sleeping in the back bedroom. Wine and spirit bottles and rows of glasses on shelves in the bar facing the street miraculously survived, and there was a roaring trade in the one undamaged room when opening time brought business as usual.

The biggest crater was made in a square formed by the gardens of four council houses. It was 30 feet across and 10 feet deep, and earth from it was flung over a wide area. At one of the houses Miss Beryl Stimson was in the back bedroom. She had a narrow escape, but "she has gone to work this morning," said her mother the next day.

Jack Allen, sleeping in the back room of another house, was struck on the head by falling plaster, but was not hurt. The garden shed took the main force of the shock and was lifted bodily four feet. Beetroot from the garden was strewn on the top of the shed.

Demolition squads were at work when daylight came, and by the end of the day many houses which had suffered badly were again inhabitable. Water and gas mains were repaired and debris cleared up.

Rations and Registrations

By the middle of November, the City Treasurer was in the throes of preparing the third issue of ration books, and he was not receiving as much help from the public as he would have liked.

It was estimated that 15,000 more books would be required, 105,000 as opposed to 90,000 the previous time. Applications (the tear-out cards in the old books) were coming in very slowly in spite of well publicised notices. Of the 20,000 applications that had been received up to that time, 20 percent had not been filled in correctly, the chief error being that people were not filling in their registration number. The last day for applying was 20th November, less than a week, and many people would have the issue of their new ration book delayed. The number was simple enough to find, it was printed on the front cover of their old book!

By the end of the month there were 15,000 residents who had still not applied for their new books, ten days after the deadline. Applications were drifting in at a rate of about 100 a day. By 5th December, the school teachers had completed their task of preparing the new ration books, although something like 10,000 could not be processed owing to errors in about 1,000 of them, and the fact that applications had not been received for the other 9,000. These defaulters, it would seem, would have a lean time over the Christmas period, as delays would be accentuated by the extra traffic going through the post office.

The W.V.S. at this time stated that their mobile canteens were not available for A.R.P. service, but that if the committee acquired a canteen, they would staff it. The committee decided to purchase a canteen for the city A.R.P. and at the same time the Town Clerk made an application for one of the American Red Cross canteens, located in Northamptonshire, to be allotted for use in the Soke.

486 men registered for service at the Ministry of Labour Exchange at Peterborough on Saturday 9th November. These included the half of the 1905 group who were born between July 1st and December 31st in that year, and those who reached the age of 20 between July 28th and November 9th 1940. Of the older

category a very large number were in reserved occupations. 196 chose the Air Force, and 60 the Navy. The older men could only elect ground duty.

Of the 20 year-olds, 25 applied for flying. Only two men pleaded conscientious objections - one from each age group. The remainder of the 1905 group registered for duty the following week on Saturday 16th the actual number on that day was 299, stragglers bringing the number up to over 300. Again, a considerable number were in reserved occupations. Of the total, 147 chose the RAF, and 26 the Navy, there were three conscientious objectors.

Raid Rest Centres

Due to experiences in raids elsewhere, the provision of Emergency Feeding and Rest Centres opened in the city to cope with the sudden distress arising from air raids was increased from three, to seventeen. Originally set up at the beginning of the war, the three centres, all in the city, were fully equipped and maintained and ready to be called into action, these had now been increased to eleven in the city and six in the rural area of the Soke.

The centres were set up to provide for people who had become homeless through air raid damage; and for people who had been required to move out of their homes by the police because of the presence of unexploded or delayed action bombs. They could be opened and made ready at any hour, day or night, on the orders of the Chief Constable, and they had washing, feeding and sleeping facilities which could be used until people could return to their homes.

The following is a list of centres set up and ready at the end of November:

IN THE CITY

Methodist Schoolroom, Wentworth Street.
Barrass Memorial Hall, Park Road.
King's School, Park Road.
St. Mary's Church Hall, St. John's Street.
Haig Memorial Hall, Brook Street.
Deacon's School, Deacon Street.
Methodist Schoolroom, New England.
Werrington C. of E. School, Werrington.
Werrington Parish Hall, Werrington.
Woodston Church Hall, Palmerston Road.
St. Margaret's Church Hall, Fairfield Road.

IN THE RURAL AREA

Helpston Council School.
Peakirk Parish Hall.
Eye C. of E. (Senior) School.
Castor and Ailsworth War Memorial Hall.
Thornhaugh Council School.
Barnack C. of E. School.

The provision was made on the basis of a percentage of the population, and with regard to the structural resources of the chosen buildings named for the feeding, washing, and sleeping of both sexes and all ages on an emergency footing.

A schedule of equipment for each centre was prepared, and the comprehensive list of items included: Beds, blankets, gas cookers and cooking utensils, field kitchens, supplementary sanitation, dish cloths, hand towels, kettles, jugs, baths, towels, bowls, buckets, scrubbing brushes, hot water bottles and so on. Not to mention gas, water and electricity. Large stocks of these articles were assembled at selected dumps, and from there they were parcelled out to the various centres by the W.V.S.

Stocks of non-perishable foods were also held at a number of points ready for immediate delivery. Transportation of this food to the centres that needed it would be attempted as long as the conditions at the time, such as the state of the roads, made it possible.

Special arrangements were in place for the removal and care of the disabled, and those with infectious diseases.

The halls and schools involved in the scheme did charge rent, but only a nominal amount, and, except for the food, the cost of the whole scheme was paid for by the government.

To help with both the rescue and resettlement of casualties, a request was now issued to householders to put up a notice outside their houses or front gate, stating how many people were sleeping on the premises. This would help first aid and rescue parties to know how many people they had to deal with should a house be bombed.

War Weapons Week

War Weapons Week in Peterborough began on Saturday 30th November, and by day five the "savings barometer" had risen to £300,000, towards a target of £350,000, the cost of buying the Navy a destroyer. This achievement was accomplished in spite of the fact that one military unit which was to play a conspicuous part in the programme of events was transferred at the last minute to another station.

The RAF and the Royal Artillery put on repeated static displays in the Market Place on the Thursday and Friday. Bomber and fighter aircraft flew in formation over the city all day on the Thursday, and the Auxiliary Fire Service gave a fire fighting demonstration at the Bishop's Road car park, following a parade, the following day.

Among the exhibits displayed on the Market Place were an armoured car, two 6-inch howitzers, two 40mm anti-aircraft guns, and two 25 pounders. Smaller arms consisted of Vickers and Lewis ground guns, an American Lewis with a 97-round magazine, and a Vickers with a 100-round magazine.

British aircraft engines included the Rolls-Royce 1,030 h.p. 12-cylinder Merlin II and 585 h.p. 12-cylinder Kestrel X and the supercharged Mercury VIII. The Merlin was the type of engine fitted to Spitfires, Hurricanes, Defiants and Whitleys at the time.

German engines included a Daimler Benz from a Messerschmitt fighter and a Jumo from a Junkers bomber.

Among other British exhibits were incendiary, smoke, and shrapnel bombs, high explosive bombs from 112 to 550 lbs., camera guns, light and heavy bomb carriers, flares, a Browning machine gun, as fitted to Spitfires and Hurricanes and capable of firing 1,150 rounds per minute, a Watts wooden airscrew, a de Havilland variable pitch airscrew from a Fairey Battle, and parachutes.

German exhibits included incendiary bomb baskets, parachute flares, bomb fragments, the whistle from a 'screaming' bomb, a 960 round per minute machine gun from a Dornier Do17 bomber, the cradle of a parachute mine, bomb release equipment, a bomb sight, a leaflet balloon, a wireless receiving set, portable oxygen apparatus, and a life jacket. All the exhibits were demonstrated by airmen and members of the W.A.A.F.

The exhibition that proved to be of the greatest interest however, was the one held at the King's School, where a downed German Junkers JU88 bomber was on display. The aircraft, used for dive bombing and reconnaissance, had been brought down by an RAF fighter over the Yorkshire Moors, and although relatively still in one piece, its fuselage was riddled with machine gun bullets.

Several different types of British and German bombs also turned up at the school during the week for display. Among the exhibits was a basin-shaped basket in which a German land mine had descended, a slightly charred silk parachute was still attached to it by cords. Another was the outer shell of a crude, 12 gallon oil bomb, and others included a German 100-kilo high explosive bomb, and British and German fire bombs.

Airscrews, supercharger casing, cylinders and parts of various types of German aircraft were on show, as well as an undamaged Junkers Jumo aero engine.

Hundreds of model aeroplanes were also on display at the school, British, American, German and Italian, some cut in half to show their internal details. There was also a full-size, single-seater sports plane still under construction that created great interest. A model port named Random, built by the pupils, was also on display, showing bomb damaged buildings and port facilities, representing a location on the East Coast that was suffering from enemy attacks.

On the last day of the week, there was a display on the Market Place of rifle drill and gas drill, carried out by new recruits in order to show what new men could learn in a relatively short time. Also during the day there was a parade of fire fighting personnel and their equipment, which assembled at the Bishop's Road car park and paraded past the Town Hall. They marched on through many of the city streets, concluding with a demonstration back at the car park of dealing with petrol fires and a blazing house.

The day to day totals of the money raised by the city went as follows:

Saturday	£75,000.
Monday	£150,000.
Tuesday	£200,000.
Wednesday	£225,000.
Thursday	£300,000.

By the end of the week the city people had raised a staggering £444,000, exceeding the target by £94,000, by buying Savings Certificates, bonds, and donating money.

The final sum was achieved in the following way:

National Savings Certificates	£55,903.
3 per cent. Defence Bonds	£73,066.
21 per cent. War Bonds	£245,408.
Trustee Savings Banks Deposits	£45,868.
Post Office Savings Bank Deposits	£23,581.
Interest Free Loan	£601.
Gifts	£11.

THE GIFTS

Dujon Staff	£1.
Fulbridge Road, Supplementary Fire Party (Women's Section).	10s.
8 Old Age Pensioners	£2 2s. 6d.

Miss Binns	2s. 6d.
Mr. W.E. Andrews (Half Sovereign).	19s.
Mrs. Butcher, collecting box	£4. 7s.
Mrs. Allen	10s.
Mrs. Banks	£1.

The city had responded very well to the appeal, and many large sums had been invested by firms, societies and private individuals, a large number of whom wished to remain anonymous. Many local savings groups had increased their normal savings twenty-fold, and in some cases groups had doubled their membership.

The King's School model aeroplane exhibition had been a huge success, thousands of people paid a total of £152 7s. for admission during the week.

Below are examples of some of the larger sums invested:

Prudential Insurance Co. Ltd.	£10,000.
Anonymous	£5,000.
Alexander Thomson (Furnishers), Ltd	£2,500.
Eagle Star Insurance Co. Ltd.	£2,500.
Mr. A.R. Baker and others	£2,000.
Hayward and Towell Ltd.	£1,000.
Mr. Arthur Gee	£1,000.
A. Fowler and Sons Ltd.	£1,000.
Luke Turner and Co. Ltd.	£500.

The last parade through the city at midday attracted enormous crowds. Three anti-aircraft guns manned by A.T.S. girls were followed by the City and Volunteer Fire Brigade engines, 14 pumps - including one from Westwood Works and one from Brotherhood's - and a mobile dam. One of the demonstrations that took place later at the car park showed how untrained people could deal with incendiary bombs using earth, sand, and a stirrup pump. Foam was used on burning oil, and a fireman wearing an asbestos suit walked through the flames. A wet drill - running out hose from a pump and striking a target - was won by Northfields Station.

On the following Monday evening, Peterborough was mentioned on the wireless as one of the places that had exceeded the Weapons week aim.

With all the problems that the city was facing during this time, billeting, damaged shelters, black-out defaulters etc., this week surely proved that the people of Peterborough were indeed, all pulling together.

Home Guard
The City Home Guard also played their part in War Weapons week. They assembled at the Repository in Lincoln Road on Sunday 1st December and route marched to the Market Square where they put on displays of various tactics and other demonstrations. An explanation of what was going on was relayed over a microphone.

Through the public spirit and generosity of lady philanthropist Mrs. F. Smith, of Eastfield, the City Battalion of the Home Guard finally got its own band. Mrs. Smith approached Captain Crowden and offered a substantial sum required to equip 23 musicians with instruments, brass and reed, to form a first rate military band.

Fortunately there were enough men already in the ranks of the battalion who were skilled in the use of the instruments, and Bandmaster B.V. Powe, who served with the Hunts. Battalion band, offered his services in training the players. The practices took place at the Unity Hall.

In a meeting held on Monday 23rd December, which was also attended by A.R.P. officials, various methods by which the Home Guard could help the A.R.P. services in certain eventualities were discussed. This would be at times when the Home Guard were not required as a fighting force. It especially applied to help with dealing with incendiary bombs during cases of heavy bombing, traffic direction, and other duties for which the A.R.P. services may not have enough personnel. In such duties, the Guard units would work under the direction of the trained men or police in any section of civil defence.

It was not often that a battalion could rely on the good will of people like Mrs. Smith, and, like other military units, the City Battalion always required regimental funds for everyday expenses. The C.O. had up to this time refrained from appealing to the public for donations as they were already continually being asked to give money to good causes. However, at the beginning of December, he finally made an appeal for help and the good citizens of Peterborough found that they could still come up with a few pounds for a worthy cause.

Teachers on Service
Since the war began two members of the City Education Committee's office staff, and 20 male teachers had joined the Forces. The following is a list in approximate order of their joining up:
Private R.S.W. Vergette, 5th Hunts. Battalion, office staff.
Lance Bombardier R.A. Smith, Royal Artillery, office staff.
Lance Aircraftman A. Quince, RAF, Walton Junior mixed.
Lance Bombardier, R.C. Robinson, Artillery (A.A.), Lincoln Road senior boys.
Gunner, G. Stimson, Artillery, New Road boys.
Private, T.A. Parker, R.A.O.C., New Road boys.
Private, J.C. Hynam, R.A.O.C., New Road boys.
Private, Stanley Bird, Pay Corps, Fulbridge junior mixed.
Sapper, Ralph Richards, R.E., Fulbridge junior mixed.
Aircraftman 2nd Class, J.A. Sainsbury, RAF, Walton senior mixed.
Airman, F.J.S. Davis, Fleet Air Arm, St. Mark's junior boys (temporary).
Corporal, R.F.M. Corder, RAF, Woodston boys.
Private, R.O. Wintle, Pioneer Corps, Lincoln Road senior boys.
Private, C.H.W. Furmidge, Pay Corps, New Road boys.
Aircraftman, C. Beresford, RAF, St. Mark's junior boys.
Gunner J.H. Roberts, Artillery, (search-lights), Orchard Street boys.
Gunner E.C. Blake, Artillery (A.A.), Lincoln Road senior boys.
Aircraftman 2nd Class, P.W. Branson, RAF, Walton senior mixed.
Private, N.L. Bradbury, R.A.M.C., Lincoln Road senior boys.
Signaller, F.I. Kershaw, R.C.S., Lincoln Road senior boys.
Aircraftman, G. Lowday, RAF, New Road boys.
Aircraftman 2nd Class, F.I. Judd, RAF, Walton junior mixed.

Appeals
There were always a large number of appeals being made, both official and unofficial, in the local press and through circulars, such as the one from the Home Guard. Some at the beginning of December consisted of one from the new Mayor, Councillor J.A. Bartram, in which he drew the attention of the public to the urgent necessity of dealing with incendiary bombs. Thousands were being dropped on

Coventry, Birmingham, Southampton and Bristol in order to light up the cities so that high explosive bombs could then be dropped with greater accuracy.

"It is no use sitting back and saying 'It is the fire brigade's job.' "He said, "Fire fighting is so urgent a matter that it cannot be left to the civil defence services alone. Any member of the public should do his utmost to extinguish a fire bomb, wherever it may fall."

The City Engineer now had bags filled with sand and placed against lamp-posts throughout the city. This sand was to be used by the public for fire-fighting, and the Mayor appealed for the citizens to see to it that it was used properly. He also asked householders to place a bucket of water, sand, or loose earth by their front doors for the same purpose, and lastly he appealed for more people to form Supplementary Fire Parties.

At the same time Mrs. A.H. Mellows, County Organiser of Women's Voluntary Services, was carrying out her own appeals. One for motor-cycle dispatch riders. "Recent experiences in other towns," she said, "have shown the importance of having an efficient dispatch rider service ready to operate immediately the telephonic communications are damaged. We did have a reasonable number of these volunteers at one time, but for one reason and another, the number is considerably reduced. Petrol will be supplied and the necessary equipment provided by the City Engineer." Volunteers could enroll through the W.V.S. office at the Old Town Hall.

Mrs. Mellows was also appealing for men's old gloves for use in rescue parties. "They are already provided with gloves for dealing with broken glass etc., but there are other unpleasant jobs they have to do for which they need gloves that can be destroyed afterwards. The gloves could be donated at the W.V.S. office.

The Post Office was also calling this time for volunteers to take on the duties of postmen or postwomen during rush periods, due to the heavy Christmas traffic. They received an immediate response, and in a short time enrolled 132 women, 47 men, 49 schoolboys and 14 girls over the age of 16. There were also 105 soldiers helping out with loading and unloading at the Corn Exchange and at the stations.

A Final Life for 1940

The last official news of 1940, as far as the city was concerned, was contained in a telegram from the Admiralty received by Mr. and Mrs. W. Laud, of 612, Gladstone Street, the day before Christmas Eve. It stated that their eldest son, Able Seaman William Laurence Henry (Laurie) Laud, had lost his life on active service on 17th December. Later, on the night of Thursday 2nd January 1941, the official news was announced on the radio that H.M. Destroyer ACHERON, (A.B. Laud's first and only ship since October 1939), had been lost. The ship had struck a mine while patrolling off the Isle of Wight.

A.B. Laud, who was 19, had joined the navy a fortnight before war broke out, and had been home on leave a month before his death. In civil life he had worked as a boy porter at the East Station and was well known for his connection with St. Paul's Church, having been a member of the choir for over ten years. He had also been a member of the L.N.E.R. Musical Society. Two of his brothers were also in the choir.

A special service was held for him at St. Paul's on Sunday 29th December when Handel's "Largo" was played in accordance with a wish he had expressed some time before in the event of him being killed. His parents, brothers and sister attended among others.

Christmas 1940

With many local men away in the forces and the rationing situation as it was, Christmas 1940 was never going to be celebrated in the city on a traditional scale. Men in the forces however, did receive parcels from home, and, although restricted in scope, the people still carried on the spirit of the season.

The Mayor and Mayoress carried out a Christmas morning tour, first visiting many of the city's first aid posts and ambulance stations. At eleven o'clock the Mayor kicked off at the Peterborough United versus the Army football match, and a quarter of an hour later he and the Mayoress visited the Isolation Hospital, the Memorial Hospital, Thorpe Road House and St. John's Hospital. The rest of the day they spent with their family.

At the market there were very few joints of beef or ham to be found, although poultry was plentiful, with game and rabbits also being scarce. There was a good supply of English turkeys at controlled prices, 2s. 10d. lb., geese, 1s. 10d. lb., ducks 2s. and roasting chickens 2s. As with the rabbits, pheasants and partridges were in short supply, but there were a few hares to be found be if you knew where to look.

Mincemeat and pudding ingredients were scarce and expensive, but ready made puddings could be found in the shops and ladies were advised to buy these due to the scarcity of ingredients. There were no figs or dates, and nuts were very highly priced, although in fair supply. Oranges were very scarce and eagerly sought after, 2d. or more each, and apples were very expensive, up to 1s. lb.

Holly and fern could be obtained from only one or two stalls but there was no mistletoe. Christmas trees could be bought from 6d. upwards, and flowers, which were easy to come by, and cheap, were used to supplement the lack of greenery.

Because of the war, Boxing Day was not declared a bank holiday, and this meant that the railways were offering no special rates during this period.

The usual round of festivities at the Memorial Hospital was curtailed, although turkey and plum pudding was served on Christmas Day. Patients were also allowed to invite two of their friends in for tea.

The 'Standard' held a party at the Salvation Army Citadel on Saturday 28th December for the children of city men serving in the Forces. 400 guests between the ages of 5 and 14 were catered for, and after what was described as "rollicking entertainment," they sat down to a "grand tea," and all received presents from Father Christmas. As crockery was in short supply, the children were asked to bring their own mugs or cups.

It is easy to lose sight of the fact that Hitler was trying to drop bombs on gatherings such as these.

No special Christmas arrangements were made for the services canteens - the men's in Long Causeway and the women's on Deans Court. At the Servicemen's Institute in Wentworth Street Church and the Recreation Centre at the Salvation Army Citadel informal sing-songs were arranged for Christmas night.

Due to the cancellation of the Boxing Day bank holiday, some of the local engineering firms were having just one day's holiday on Christmas Day, the brickyards however, closed from noon on Tuesday (Christmas Eve) to the Thursday morning.

Radio

Although it does not specifically relate to Peterborough, I think that it is worthwhile giving a mention to the Christmas radio programmes at that time. After all, most of the city people would have been listening in as television was still a long way off for ordinary people. The BBC broadcast a "Christmas Under Fire," special, consisting of sixteen separate items from all parts of the Empire.

The programme opened with the bells of one of Britain's bombed cathedrals striking two o'clock. The story then moved to a country rectory, where bombed out London mothers, their children and friends were heard thanking their hosts at the end of their first war-time Christmas dinner in the country. Other items featured the pilot and crew of a flying boat squadron of the RAF Coastal Command; the Army on guard in the Holy Land; an exchange of Christmas greetings with the Empire Forces in the Near East; a minesweeping trawler protecting shipping in home waters; the Home Guard at an isolated watching post; a North-Western port where British and Allied merchant seamen were spending Christmas ashore; a Polish Army camp; the ward of a Canadian Red Cross hospital; a Christmas pantomime in a Scottish town; an English village carol concert; South Wales, where steelworkers sang as they worked; an impression of Londoners on the alert at an Auxiliary Fire station and a London Fire Brigade station in the East End; a party in one of the deep shelters; and a brief glimpse of a family in a small suburban home.

Christmas wasn't the same, the city was full of strangers, and families had been split up. Local men had been called up and sent to places they were not allowed to mention. Food was short, the black-out was long, and civil defence seemed to take up everyone's spare time.

Sandbags, buckets of sand, air raid shelters and warning posters littered the streets, but everyone was still pulling together, still shaking their fists at Hitler. "If this is how it has to be," they said, "we can take it."

It was a good thing perhaps that for now, the people of Peterborough did not know what was ahead of them.

SIMS, Ronald Arthur – 73 Alexandra Road, Peterborough. Pilot Officer 42654, RAF Bomber Command. Died, aged 19, on the 31st March 1940. The son of Edward and May Sims, of Peterborough. Buried in Eastfield Cemetery, Peterborough, Grave 7059, Div. 1, Block 17.

LONGLEY, George William – 91 Eastgate, Peterborough. Driver T/116269, R.A.S.C. Died, aged 26, on the 4th April 1940 in a motorcycle accident. The son of Charles and Elizabeth Longley of Ashurst Wood and the husband of Elsie Longley of Ashurst Wood. Buried in Forest Row Cemetery, Sussex, Grave 1460.

DILLON, George – 34 Star Road, Peterborough. Telegraphist P/SSX23633, Royal Navy. Died, aged 20, on the 8th April 1940 when the Destroyer HMS Glowworm deliberately rammed the German Cruiser Admiral Hipper. The son of Jack and Rose Dillon, of Peterborough. He has no known grave and is commemorated on the Portsmouth Naval Memorial, Column 40, Panel 3.

SMITH, Cyril Reginald – Pilot Officer 77168, Royal Air Force Volunteer Reserve. Died, aged 40, on the 12th April 1940. The son of Claud Le Comte Thompson Smith and Ellen Smith and the husband of Joyce Langford Smith of Peterborough. Buried in Eastfield Cemetery, Peterborough. Div. 1. Block 17. Grave 7371.

SHARP, William Arthur – 69 Park Road, Peterborough. Paymaster Commander, Royal Navy. Died, age unknown, on the 10th May 1940 while serving on HMS Penelope. Next of kin is not known. He has no known grave and is commemorated on the Portsmouth Naval Memorial, Column 1, Panel 37.

POOLE, Christopher John Stafford – 28 Cromwell Road, Peterborough. Sergeant 580416, Royal Air Force. Died, aged 20, on the 10th May 1940 on bombing operations against German troops invading Luxembourg. He was an Observer in a Fairey Battle, serial number K9270, code letters PM. Aircraft took off at 1345 hours from Betheniville. The plane was shot down 9km NE of Marche-en-Famenne, Belgium. The pilot became a POW, two crew were killed. The son of Stafford George and Lillian Helen Poole, of Peterborough. Buried in Hotton War Cemetery, Belgium, Grave III.E.10.

THOMAS, Ivor Llewellyn – Sergeant (Pilot) 580177, 40 Squadron, Royal Air Force. Died, aged 24, on the 10th May 1940. He was the pilot of Blenheim, Serial No. L8831, which was one of five 40 Squadron Blenheim's lost on this day. It took off from Wyton. The cause of loss was not established. The aircraft crashed in the vicinity of Den Haag (Zuid Holland).The son of George and Annie Thomas of Llanrhidian, Glamorgan and the husband of Joyce Thomas of Peterborough. His brother Albert George also died on service. Buried in The Hague General Cemetery, Holland. Allied Plot. Row 1. Grave 7.

TOPHAM, John Leslie – 46 Northfield Road, Peterborough. Private 5886242, 5th Northamptonshire Regiment. Died, aged 21, on the 10th May 1940. The son of

Herbert and Clarice Topham of Peterborough. Buried in Dunkirk Town Cemetery. Joint Grave 29, Plot 1, Row 1.

FRANCIS, James Montague – 5 Lime Tree Avenue, Peterborough. Private 6020049, Essex Regiment. Died, aged 20, on the 11th May 1940 in the Royal Herbert Hospital, Woolwich of Pulmonary Tuberculosis. The son of Charles Edward and Fanny Francis of Peterborough. Buried in Eastfield Cemetery, Peterborough, Grave 4208, Div. 1, Block 11.

GARFOOT, Victor – 2 Lister Road, Peterborough. Private 5884630, 164 Field Ambulance, Royal Army Medical Corps. Died, aged 20, on the 20th May 1940. The son of William and Jessie Garfoot, of Peterborough. Buried in Avelin Communal Cemetery, France. Grave 2.

SEWELL, Frederick John – 307 Lincoln Road, Walton, Peterborough. Private 5886164, 5th Northamptonshire Regiment. Died, aged 20, on the 22nd May 1940. The son of Alfred and Ethel Sewell of Walton, Peterborough. Buried in Outtersteene Communal Cemetery Extension, Bailleul, France. Grave 42, Plot 3, Row B.

SMITH, J.W. – 68 Saxon Road, Peterborough. Corporal 5943242, 5th Northamptonshire Regiment. Died, aged 40, on the 22nd May 1940. The son of James and Susannah Smith of Peterborough and the husband of Mabel Jane Smith of Peterborough. Buried in Esquelmes War Cemetery, Belgium, Grave V1.B.28.

STANFORD, Horace William James – 16 Fengate Close, Peterborough. Corporal 5881626, 5th Northamptonshire Regiment. Died, aged 27, on the 22nd May 1940. The son of Sydney and Louise Stanford; husband of I. M. Stanford, of Great Yarmouth. Buried in Kaster Churchyard, Anzegem, West- Vlaanderen, Belgium, Grave 1.

SWALLOW, Robert Stanley – Trooper 7889738, 5th Royal Tank Regiment, R.A.C. Died, aged 19, on the 28th May 1940. The son of Stanley and Harriet Swallow of Peterborough. Buried in Beauvais Communal Cemetery, Oise, France. Mil. Plot. Grave 11.

GIBBS, Robert Alfred – 13 Swan's Place, Peterborough. Petty Officer C/JX 162567, Royal Navy. Died, aged 41, on the 29th May 1940 when the Destroyer HMS Wakeful was sunk by a torpedo fired from a German E-boat while participating in the evacuation of the BEF from the Dunkirk beaches. The son of Robert and Susan Gibbs and the husband of Clara Louisa Gibbs of Thorney, near Peterborough. He has no known grave and is commemorated on the Chatham Naval Memorial, Kent. Column 34,2.

DAVIS, Thomas James – 30 West Parade, Peterborough. Corporal 5830031, 5th Green Howards (Yorkshire Regiment). Died, aged 21, on the 31st May 1940. The son of Mr and Mrs Francis Edward Davis, of Peterborough and the husband of Edith Annie Davis of Dogsthorpe, Peterborough. He has no known grave and is commemorated on the Dunkirk Memorial, France. Column 49.

WRIGHT, Herbert Leslie – Lance Corporal 5882351, 2nd Northamptonshire Regiment. Died, aged 28, on or about the 1st June 1940. The son of Frederick and Amelia Wright of Peterborough. Buried in the Maroeuil Communal Cemetery, Pas de Calais, France. Grave 6.

JOHNSON, Harry Bernard – St Pauls Road, Peterborough. Gunner 1531762, 43 Battery, 101 Lt. A.A/Anti-Tank Regiment, Royal Artillery. Died, aged 19, on the 7th June 1940. The son of Harry and Florence Johnson, of Peterborough. Buried in St. Valery-En-Caux Franco-British Cemetery, Seine-Maritime, France. Grave A40.

WINDSOR, Thomas Samuel Frederick – 12 Padholme Road, Peterborough. Private 2185187, Aux.Mil.Pioneer Corps. Died, aged 22, on the 17th June 1940 when German aircraft bombed a troop train at Rennes that was carrying part of the B.E.F. evacuating France. The son of John and Dora Windsor of Peterborough. Buried in Rennes Communal Cemetery, France, Grave 104, Sec.18, Plot 1, Row A.

GRANT, Alphonso Kinmont – Orton Waterville, Peterborough. Private 2184064, 115 Coy. Aux. Mil. Pioneer Corps. Died, aged 25, on the 17th June 1940 when German aircraft bombed a troop train at Rennes that was carrying part of the B.E.F. evacuating France. No known next of kin. No known grave and is commemorated on the Dunkirk Memorial, France, Column 151.

JINKS, Robert Leslie – 286 Walpole Street, Peterborough. Trooper 7902192, Royal Armoured Corps. Died, aged 21, on the 17th June 1940 when German aircraft bombed a troop train at Rennes that was carrying part of the B.E.F. evacuating France. The son of Robert and Edna Jinks of Peterborough. Buried in Pornic War Cemetery, France, Grave 1.E.5.

BLOM, Walter Michael – 33 Vere Road, Peterborough. Flight Lieutenant, DFC, 150 Squadron, Royal Air Force. Died, aged 23, on the 27th July 1940 when, being the pilot of a Fairey Battle aircraft, Serial Number L5528, Code Letters JN, a bomb fell off the plane at its base at Newton, Nott's, and exploded killing Blom, his two crew and four ground crew. The husband of Catharine Winifred Blom of Peterborough. Believed to be the Brother in Law of Ronald Henry Orton who was also killed. Buried in East Bridgeford (St Peter) Churchyard, Nott's. Grave 3A.

SMITH, Alex James – 163 Belsize Avenue, Peterborough. Aircraftman 743465 1st Class, Royal Air Force Volunteer Reserve. Died, aged 26, on the 12th August 1940. The son of William Alderman Smith and Annie Smith of Woodston, Peterborough. Buried in Woodston Cemetery, Peterborough. Grave 73, Section 7.

PRIDMORE, Alan Harry – 40 Tower Street, Peterborough. Wireman C/MX 62075, Royal Navy. Died, aged 21, on the 3rd September 1940 serving on HMS Royal Sovereign. The son of Arthur and Floris Nellie Pridmore of Peterborough. No known grave and commemorated on the Chatham Naval Memorial, Kent. Column 39.1

WILDERS, Edward William – 72 Harris Street, Peterborough. Assistant Steward, Merchant Navy, S.S. Manchester Brigade (Manchester). Died, aged 20, on the 27th

103

September 1940. No known next of kin. No known grave. Commemorated on the Tower Hill Memorial, London. Panel 67.

KAY, Norman Douglas – Lance Bombardier 905441, 97 (The Kent Yeomanry) Field Regiment, Royal Artillery. Died, aged 19, on the 10th November 1940. The son of Gladys Stanton of Peterborough. Buried in Carmarthen Cemetery. Sec. K. Grave 1.

LAUD, William Lawrence Henry – 612 Gladstone Street, Peterborough. Able Seaman P/SSX31151, Royal Navy. Died, age not known, on the 17th December 1940 when the destroyer HMS Acheron was sunk by a mine off the Isle of Wight. The son of William and Ethel Laud of Peterborough. No known grave. Commemorated on the Portsmouth Naval Memorial, Column 1, Panel 39.

1941

Invaluable Sand

Two tons of sand - "Invaluable material for countering incendiary bombs directly they fall" - was given away on the morning of Sunday 5th January. The sand was donated by the Chief Air Raid Warden, Mr. Lister Robinson, who had it deposited on the square in front of Messrs. C.J. Robinson and Son's grocery store at 1, Harris Street, Millfield. Cynical readers may think, perhaps unfairly, that placing the free sand at this location would certainly have had the effect of bringing large numbers of people to the front of the aforementioned shop bearing a similar name, and with it the obvious passing trade. However, we should not doubt the sincerity with which the offer was made.

Anyone who turned up with a bucket or similar container was allowed to fill it up until the supply ran out. The idea was to supply the residents from the immediate district but anyone was able to take advantage of the offer - "free, gratis, and for nothing other than the fetching."

Mr. Robinson had been disappointed that more residents were not putting sand and water in their front gardens and he hoped to stimulate interest.

Almost as soon as it was dumped on the Saturday afternoon, people began to congregate with buckets and spades, and Mr. Robinson had to remind them that Sunday was the actual day of distribution.

The first people arrived at dawn the next day, and Mr. Robinson and his assistant, Mr. G.W. Collet, were ready with a spade and a long-handled shovel. People came with buckets, pails and sacks to be filled, and when the heap was cleared at midday, it was estimated that there had been 300 callers. They came from as far away as Russell Street and Newark Avenue. Sixty per cent of the callers were women, and most of the remainder were elderly men or little girls.

A woman who turned up with two buckets from over a mile away told Mr. Robinson that she had been evacuated from London and was billeted with a man and woman who had six children.

"They told me 'We are not going to bother'," she said, "and I said to them if you had seen what I have you would be only too glad to get up much earlier than nine o'clock to get free sand'."

Another woman arrived with a perambulator, and calmly requested that it be filled. She was politely reminded that there were others to be served.

Mr. Robinson then decided to arrange to have another two and a half tons of sand distributed freely on the following Sunday, with Mr. W.C. Hare, of Windmill Street, providing half of it. Mr. Hare canvassed Windmill Street between Gladstone Street and the blacksmith's shop, and enrolled a Supplementary Fire Party of 17, Mr. Hare being the Chairman and Mr. R. Burns, of 102 Windmill Street, the Secretary. They had three stirrup pumps and "plenty of ladders." A rota had been arranged, and two watchers were on duty every night until 1a.m. or for the full period of an Alert.

Most of the sand which had been provided on the Sunday was taken by members of the fire party. Large bins of it had been placed in front of Mr. Robinson's shop, and in Mr. Hare's garden, at 103, Windmill Street. In addition, plenty of tins were placed at convenient points along the road. Besides the fire party, there were many early callers for the sand, and the big heap was cleared before half past ten.

Mr. Robinson gave up a window of his shop to a display.

Under a banner "This is what you want", were buckets of water and sand, a stirrup pump, a rake, and a shovel. Beneath another notice - "This is what you must look for" - was a German incendiary bomb. Fortunately for Mr. Robinson, he could mix business with a desire to provide a public information service.

Mr. J.J. Crane, a builder, of Granville Street, also gave sand to householders in the district on that Sunday.

Appeals

Appeals featured constantly in the columns of the local and national press, and perhaps even at this early stage in the war the public were becoming a little immune to the persistent calls for increased action.

Featuring in the first "Standard" of the new year was a complaint concerning the "moderate" response to the City Engineer's request to be informed of the positions of old wells with a view to their adaptation as an emergency water supply in case of incendiary attack. A great many of the old Victorian terraces in the city had wells in their back gardens, and this was one source that Mr. Lister Robinson was surely hoping to exploit.

Further along the columns it was stated that sixty volunteers were still required at the hospital to act as stretcher bearers. There were just over 30 enrolled, but only 26 bothered to turn up for practice or to take their turn on duty, and this allowed only two on duty at any one time instead of four. The bearers had their own officers, Mr. Harris being Chairman and Mr. Royce, Secretary. The O.C. was Mr. J.W. Fowler, Hon. Secretary to the St. John Ambulance Association, who carried out the training. Members were trained to unload and load ambulances, carry patients, and put them to bed. The County Transport Officer, H.V. Sheppard, 21, Lincoln Road, East, was the Corps Transport Officer. Duties were carried out from 7p.m to 6a.m. each night, and might in themselves explain the lack of volunteers.

Mrs. M. Shipley Ellis was trying to contact a number of Red Cross working parties through the newspaper columns in order to let them know that she now had a large number of cut-out garments waiting to be sewn together.

The party working at Werrington Church Hall had completed the following articles by the end of 1940:

271 pairs of socks, 150 pairs of mittens, 23 pairs of bed socks, 6 heelless bed socks, 40 pullovers, 98 balaclava helmets, 20 scarves, 37 pairs of gloves, 13 pairs of minesweepers' gloves, 7 pairs of steering gloves, 68 night-shirts and pyjamas, 32 vests, 8 night-dresses and bed-jackets, 13 dressing gowns, and 15 shirts, approximately 800 articles. In addition, the party sent ten shillings to 51 local men in the forces as a Christmas present and cigarettes to three officers.

Still with the Red Cross, Paston Hall had now been taken over and was ready to receive convalescent patients, following hospital treatment. There was accommodation for 50 patients.

The Lindens was also being converted for the same use.

A further advertisement in the "Standard" gave particulars of a request for a better response to the Government's appeal for salvage. During the last two months of 1940 there had been a serious decline in the amount of waste paper returned to industry, partly due, it has to be said, to the reduced issue of paper, but much was going to waste as refuse.

Cereals for pig and poultry food were also in short supply, and farmers were only getting one third of pre-war requirements. The importance of maintaining the pig population and egg production was stressed, and householders were urged to collect every bit of kitchen waste.

People were asked to leave out "contraries," such as orange, grapefruit and banana skins, (most people must have thought 'If only'), rhubarb tops, tea leaves, egg shells, soap or soda. Fats and bones were also being asked for. The City Engineer had bins put out for this refuse and the council was collecting a ton a day, but they had to double this. There was no appreciable decline in local paper collection.

Fire Watching
At the beginning of the year the Government decided to introduce compulsory fire watching for all factories, shops, and business premises as a result of the fires being caused by incendiaries in the City of London.

Mr. Herbert Morrison, the Home Secretary and Minister of Home Security, stated in a radio broadcast on the night of Tuesday 31st December that details would shortly be announced, and there would be severe penalties for neglect. Householders were called upon to form parties to protect their homes.

A meeting was held at the Reception Room in the Town Hall on Wednesday 8th January, and owners and occupiers of factories and lock-up shops and offices, and representatives of trade associations were invited. The new regulations were to be explained by Mr. F. Skevington, Deputy Principal Officer, North Midlands Region.

Mr. Skevington urged that every occupier of a lock-up shop should have a fire watcher on his or her premises every night of the week until 8p.m. and that groups of neighbouring premises should join together to provide joint watchers to look after the place between 8p.m. and midnight.

The heavy raids on cities and towns at this time had been on such a scale that the Government had decided that voluntary measures could no longer be relied upon. Preventative measures were now made compulsory, and extended to everyone, employers, managers and employees.

"Every square yard of the city was a potential source of danger, and must be watched. It was a 100 per cent job, and they could not be satisfied without a 100 per cent defence."

Private houses were already provided for by the Supplementary Fire Parties, and churches and chapels, including the cathedral, now had to have their own watchers. Large business houses had to arrange to have employees stay behind to watch for the requisite time period. Alderman Snowden stated that the A.R.P. committee had agreed to put heaps of sand in the streets for people to take if the need arose.

Mr. Perkins, a tobacconist, asked who was going to vouch for the honesty of the fire watchers. Mr. Skevington said that they could not expect the town to vouch for the honesty of everyone. Mr. Perkins said that he did expect it. He sold cigarettes and had had two burglaries and the police had not caught them yet! His concern was met with laughter.

By the end of January, an organised fire watching strategy was developing rapidly. The Town Hall was under constant watch throughout 24 hours a day by a special staff detailed solely for the purpose. They were in positions to command every inch of the roofs, and fire-fighting equipment was ready to hand at many points.

Measures at the Cathedral had also taken shape, with Mr. S.O.G. Willson organising the watching. The central tower, which commanded a view of practically the whole of the roofs, and the bell tower, were excellent vantage points. Another post was in an upper chamber of Mr. Mellows' house, the Vineyard. From here there was an effective line of vision to the Eastern Chapel of the Cathedral.

To supplement the system of newel staircases in the Cathedral, a number of ladders were erected which gave quick access to any part of the roofs from the towers or from the ground. The watcher's post in the sacristy was connected by telephone with the "top." Sand, water, shovels and other equipment were positioned at many strategic points. There were also ready means to enter those "perilous places", (from the fire danger point of view), the great chambers between the ceilings and roof. The service was maintained from dawn to dusk.

The three precincts wardens were Mrs. Blagden, Miss Land and Mr. Robinson. A watch rota was arranged with women up to 10p.m. and Mr. Robinson organising the men from 10 to dawn. The watchers met in the sacristy, where they too, were in touch with the Cathedral sentries. Arrangements were made for the watchers to have access to any garden which could prove to be a dumping ground for German missiles.

Granville Street had had a Street Safety Committee for some months, and had purchased, or been given equipment in addition to the official issue. A regular system of patrols was in force. Warden Mrs. Lilley had loaned one of her garages in Granville Street for use as a fire station. This was the first of its kind in the city, and contained stirrup pumps, sand, water, ropes, ladders, spades, hatchets etc.

Every sector of wardens was divided up according to the number of active wardens in it. Each warden had charge of a section of streets to look after during an alert. In some parts builders, painters and other tradesmen left their ladders so that they could be used in case of emergency.

The Co-op., theatres and picture houses, Woolworths and Marks' and Spencer's all had their own systems in operation. The museum joined in a combined service with other occupiers of that end of Priestgate.

Wages were paid to watchers and varied from £3 to £5 a week for full hours. Others were engaged at 3 shillings a night (6 to 12).

Midgate shopkeepers met on Wednesday 15th January to formulate their plans for fire watching. It was decided to form five groups in the area, with the following appointed representatives:
1. Sharman to Tebbs. - Mr. A. Sharpe.
2. Perkins to Morley. - Mr. A. Smith.
3. Swan's Place. - Mr. Shrive.
4. Radford to Miller. - Mr. W. Colishaw.
5. White Swan Café to Dominion Café. - Mr. J. Heritage.

Nearly 100 watchers had been organised for Huntly Grove, following a meeting at King's School, where Mr. W.F. Shearcroft showed an official film. Mr. J.P. Bristow arranged another meeting at the school for people living in Park Road, between Burghley Square and Huntly Grove, and a system was soon in operation there.

Precautions were established in other churches. At St. John's a party had been formed to keep a close watch each evening from 6 to 10p.m. and from then on a modified basis. Ladders were erected to give access to the roof from the churchyard.

All Saints Church had formed a band as had Park Road Baptist church, every street had its dump of sand, and hundreds of people were taking advantage of lectures and demonstrations on how to tackle incendiary bombs.

St. Barnabas arranged a rota whereby two watchers would be on duty, and the whole of the church would be watched every night from 6 to 8p.m. and during alerts from 8 to 12 midnight.

It was estimated at this time that there were well over 600 stirrup pumps installed in the city; as many as 175 had been given out to fire parties. Some 200 had been sold by the local authority to anyone who wanted them. About 150 more were known to have been purchased privately. A further supply of 200 pumps was on order. Besides these, it was also known that a large number of people had installed garden hoses, with the requisite nozzle, which were quite as effective as long as the piped water continued.

Bridge Street, which was a typical example of what was being done, was divided into small groups of five or six premises each. Each person was responsible for their own premises until 8 o'clock, and from that time parties of two took over until midnight. All occupiers left their keys in sealed envelopes with the watchers. At the close of the watch these were handed to the Sector Leader.

Women were very keen to share in the duty, and a number of them took the earlier spell - 8 to 10. A comfortable rest room was provided by Mr. J.W. Fowler, the head warden of the sector.

Casualty of War
At 9:25a.m. on Wednesday 8th January, Lance Corporal Clarence Dubock, from Eastern Green, Coventry, of the Corps of Military Police, was riding his motorcycle combination along Lincoln Road towards the junction with Alma Road. The road surface was wet after some earlier rain, but Lance Corporal Dubock was not travelling at an excessive speed. Mr. Charles Duke, a wireless dealer, of 262, Lincoln Road was idly looking out of his window when he noticed the soldier go into a skid and swerve straight across the road hitting a car coming in the opposite direction. He saw the combination overturn and the rider trying to raise himself but then collapsing.

Mrs. Nellie Wood, of 439, Gladstone Street, had been walking to town along the east side of Lincoln Road at the same time when she heard the motor cyclist shout "Ooh!" The motorcycle then went out of her view behind an air raid shelter, and she heard a crash. She ran to the rider and heard him say. "Oh my leg, my leg."

Mr. George Bean Tucker, a salesman, of Rock Road, was driving the car that had been hit by the motorcycle. He was quite close to the air raid shelter when he saw the motorcyclist coming towards him. Suddenly the sidecar wheel lifted and the machine came across the road straight at him. He swerved to his left but there was a collision. Mr. Tucker pulled up on the footpath; the motorcyclist had been thrown over the bonnet of his car, hitting the end of the air raid shelter before falling to the ground between the shelter and a tree.

Lance Corporal Dubock, who was 28, was admitted to Peterborough Hospital at 9:40a.m., suffering from shock, and a compound fracture of the left tibia and fibula. His condition had been fair, but at 9:20p.m. he collapsed and died.

At the inquest, which was held on Thursday 9th, Mr. Tucker said that the air raid shelter, situated on the west side of the road, was in rather a dangerous position. This was echoed by the Coroner, who agreed that most of them were, being built on the roads due to the lack of space on the pavement. This led to vehicles having to pull out further than usual in order to see around bends and corners.

A verdict of accidental death was returned.

Fifth Raid

At 11 p.m. on the night of Wednesday 15th January, five high explosive bombs damaged 127 houses and 21 other premises in Walpole Street, St. Paul's Road, Lincoln Road and Clarence Road. One man was killed and five others were injured.

This had been a large raid aimed at industrial targets. Some factories were hit and a number of worker's houses damaged. The dead man was Mr. George W. Ruff, of 200 Palmerston Road, Woodston. He was a railwayman and had been killed whilst on duty.

Civil Defence

Experience gained from bombing raids in other parts of the country brought the news that the brick communal street shelters were standing up well to near misses by the heaviest bombs. Many lives had been saved. The explanation was that the squat and sturdy structures, whose walls were nearly twice the thickness of ordinary house walls, offered comparatively little surface for that blast of an explosion to strike.

The official advice was: "If there is a communal shelter near your home, seek its refuge when the siren warns. It will give you a full measure of protection in the direst emergency."

Someone who was relying on the safety of a shelter for a different reason, this time one built next to his office, was Mr. H.E. Plant, a coal merchant, of 110, Cobden Avenue. So confident was he of the soundness of his shelter that he had placed £95 inside for its certain protection. Imagine his surprise then, when on the night of Saturday 18th January, the shelter caught fire at approximately 11:40, and the City Fire Brigade had to be called out to deal with it. Wooden bunks and bedding were in flames but this was soon overcome with a first aid jet connected to a street hydrant. The furniture in the shelter was considerably damaged and the ceiling of the office was burnt away.

Fortunately for Mr. Plant the firemen managed to save the £95 from the fire, which appeared to have been caused by a stove.

Still with shelters, the S.R.O. wrote to the A.R.P. Committee at this time with reference to condensation in shelters caused through shelter doors, ventilators and emergency exits being closed. He suggested that shelters should be ventilated by a through draught of air at least once a day, and that the Wardens' service might undertake the duty. No doubt this would have been an unwelcome suggestion as far as the hard-pressed wardens were concerned, which is probably why the committee deferred a decision pending a report by the Chief Constable.

A meeting was held at the old Town Hall on Tuesday 21st January of leaders of the Rest Centres which the W.V.S. had been asked by the Public Assistance Committee to organise and run. There were 16 centres in all, and the W.V.S. volunteers were being arranged in shifts so that at whatever time an emergency might arise, a pre-determined number of helpers would be ready to go immediately. The same equipment and staff was allocated to each hall, and the purpose of the meeting was to co-ordinate the work.

Mrs. A.H. Mellows presided, and Lord Exeter, Chairman of the County Council impressed on those present the necessity for having the organisation ready to house and care for people who might be temporarily rendered homeless by bombs.
The centres and their leaders were as follows:

St. Mary's Hall, Mrs. Bosley.
Woodston Church Hall, Mrs. Atkinson, with Mrs. Laxton and Mrs. Smith.
King's School, Mrs. Shearcroft.
Wentworth Street School, Mrs. Stanley.
Barrass Hall, Mrs. Tucker.
Haig Hall, Mrs. G.B. Dickens.
Deacon's School, Mrs. Davies.
Werrington Church Hall, Mrs. Kirman.
Eye Church School, Mrs. Patston.
Castor Memorial Hall, the Hon. Mrs. Pelham.
Peakirk Hall, Mrs. L. Neaverson.
Helpston School, Mrs. Tanqueray.
Barnack School, Mrs. Fairweather.
Thornhaugh School, Mrs. F. Perkins.

There was also a call at this time from the W.V.S. for more women car drivers for service in the event of a severe raid. They were not necessarily required to go out into danger, but were wanted for work the next day.

The City Home Guard was also advertising for recruits at this time, from 17 to 19 years of age. It was thought to be a good grounding for when they came to join up in the regular army.

Following a conference at Leicester, the Town Clerk now wrote to the Headmasters of King's and Deacon's Schools concerning the engagement of senior boys, from 16 years of age, for service as messengers in the event of a serious raid. The boys would be under the control of the Headmasters. The City Engineer and City Treasurer were to draw up a scheme of rendezvous points. One wonders what the parents of these boys would have thought, had they known, about the idea of their sons running about with messages during heavy raids.

The City Treasurer, Mr. Frank Smith, who was Hon. Secretary of the National Savings scheme in Peterborough, now stated that amazing success had been achieved in the way of loans to the Government during 1940. Peterborough was asked to raise £850,000 in the twelve months, and this was nearly reached, leaving out of account the whole of the £450,000 got together in War Weapons Week. With this huge effort included, the amount raised in Peterborough for the year was £1,261,793.

The following details show how the loan was made up:
National Savings Certificates - £286,674.
Defence Bonds - £227, 997.
Two and a half per cent National War Bonds, (June 29th to Dec. 28th) - £194,429.
Deposits in Trustee Savings Bank and Post Office Bank - £553,093.

At a meeting of the Soke Savings Committee the secretary, Mr. Frank Smith, was asked to invite the Admiralty to name the destroyer for which Peterborough raised £444,000 in War Weapons Week, H.M.S. PETERBOROUGH. On doing so he received a reply stating that while no assurance could be given that the name would be adopted, it would be added to the list of city and town names from which future selections of names of H.M. ships would be made as and when the occasion arose. Unfortunately for Peterborough, the occasion never did arise!

Missing
During the middle of January, Mrs. Violet Burkey, of 18, Willesden Avenue,

111

Walton, suddenly received official notification that her husband, 1st. Class Air Gunner, Jim Burkey, was missing from one of H.M. Aircraft Carriers in the Mediterranean. Mr. and Mrs. Burkey had been married on the previous October, and had made their home at Willesden Avenue with Mrs. Burkey's mother, Mrs. Violet Stockman, who had a son and another son-in-law also serving as air gunners on aircraft carriers. "Jim" Burkey, who was 26, joined the navy at the age of 15. Mrs. Burkey was a cashier at the Theatre Royal and Empire. Her father, Mr. Tom Stockman, had been killed in a crane accident at Westwood Works about five years earlier, two years after the family had moved to the city from Willesden.

Football

A special meeting of the Board of Directors of Peterborough United Football Club was held on Tuseday 21st January, to consider the future of the club. After a good deal of discussion it was decided, in spite of the dwindling playing staff and supporters who were being taken away for war work, that an effort would be made to keep the club going for the time being. The next match had already been arranged and would take place on February 8th, against the Royal Engineers.

At a following meeting of the directors on Tuesday 4th February however, the club secretary, Mr. H.J. Poulter, tendered his resignation. Mr. Poulter, who had been secretary ever since the formation of the club seven years earlier, took the decision in view of the directors deciding to try to carry on.

"I felt it would be a good thing to try to provide a little relaxation for war workers," he said, "but support has been so poor that I now feel that my spare time can be better spent in civil defence duties."

The Police

Apart from punishing the odd blackout infringement, the city police were carrying on with their work with unsung determination, keeping track of all the normal offences which, despite the war, were constantly being committed.

The records for 1940 show that in spite of our rose-tinted view of that period in history, crime held tightly on to its place in society, and wherever there happened to be a law, someone would be prepared to break it.

The number of street accidents had gone down, from 736 in 1939, to 539 in 1940. But there were still frequent complaints from pedestrians about the speed and general dangerous driving of local motorists. War legislation had thrown a heavy burden on the police, increasing their working hours considerably, but so far they had met all the demands made on them.

There had been 661 indictable offences (such as house and shop-breaking, theft and fraud) reported to the police during 1940. Of those it was found that 161 cycles and other articles reported as stolen had either been misplaced, lost or taken in error. This left a total of 500, an increase of 15 compared to 1939.

The offenders in connection with 348 of the above offences were caught, and 137 were proceeded against, 59 more than 1939. They were dealt with as follows:

Summarily 130, of whom 53 were convicted, charges proved, orders made 68, and acquitted 9.

There were seven persons committed for trial at Quarter Sessions and Assizes. 62 persons were cautioned, and 16 dealt with elsewhere for indictable offences.

For non-indictable offences 593 persons were proceeded against and dealt with by the justices, 85 of this number were apprehended, and 508 were summoned. This was an increase of 227 compared with 1939.

510 persons were convicted, 2 dealt with under the Probation of Offenders Act, 13 discharged, 2 bound over, 6 dismissed under the P.O. Act, and 60 otherwise dealt with. 140 of these were for motoring offences, 131 being convicted, 5 discharged, and 2 dismissed, charges proved, and 2 bound over.

24 persons were dealt with for drunkenness (18 drunk and incapable, and 6 drunk and disorderly). This compared with 41 (32 and 9) for 1939. 15 were residents, 2 non-residents, and 7 vagrants.

During the year 460 robberies were reported to the police, as against 450 the previous year. The value of property stolen was estimated at £1,338 15s. 7d., that recovered at £327 9s. 11d. and that unrecovered at £1,011 5s. 8d. One lunch-hour robbery accounted for £450 of this total. The number of offences detected was 317, and undetected 143.

In 1939 the figures were, value of property stolen £922 3s. 3d. value of property recovered £288 8s. 3d. robberies detected 222, undetected 228.

The value of property and monies obtained by fraud was £20 2s. 10d. compared with £132 3s.0d. the previous year. There were 14 offences committed, and the offender was traced in 9 cases.

In 1940, four juveniles were proceeded against for house and shop-breaking, 49 for larceny of cycles and from shops, unattended vehicles, etc. and 23 for non-indictable offences, (i.e. offences against traffic laws).

During the year 1,034 persons were reported for offences against sundry statutes and bye-laws and warned and advised to exercise more care, as on repetition of the alleged offences proceedings would be taken; 219 of these were cautioned for motoring offences. 998 persons, (including 347 for motoring offences) were dealt with in a similar manner in 1939.

During the year 15 persons were arrested by the city police for other forces, as compared with 18 in 1939. In addition, 55 persons were arrested and handed over to the military authorities.

Enquiries had been made by the police and reports submitted to the Coroner in 73 cases of death. In 57 cases inquests were held. Five of the deaths were due to motor accidents in the city, and 17 to motor accidents in other police districts.

The following shows the verdicts at the inquests, at one of which the Coroner sat with a jury:
Suicide 5, accidental death or misadventure 50, natural causes 1, murder 1.

During the year a large number of circulars relating to wanted and missing persons, stolen and lost property, warnings to local tradesmen, etc. were widely circulated. From other forces 2,385 pieces of information relating to persons and property wanted and stolen were received for enquiry, and the necessary attention given. The work and enquiries for other forces created a great burden on the already hard-pressed city force.

During the year 539 accidents, in which traffic was involved were reported to the police, 163 resulting in 5 deaths and 183 persons being injured, and 376 without personal injury as follows:

Responsible	Total	Injury or Death	Damage Only	Killed	Injured
Drivers of Public Service Vehicles	18	3	15	-	3
Motor Cycles	18	8	10	-	10
Private Cars	185	39	146	-	50
Motor Cabs	7	1	6	-	1
Goods Vehicles	149	28	121	-	32
Horse Drawn	10	1	9	-	1
Pedal Cycles	83	46	35	1	51
Pedestrians	42	35	7	4	35
Dogs etc. running in front	27	-	27	-	-
Totals	539	163	376	5	183

The police on night duty found the doors or windows on 218 dwelling houses, 776 lock-up premises and 387 shops insecure, the total being 1,381.

There were 243 dogs found and placed in the kennels at the police station during the year. 29 horses, cattle etc. were found straying by the police and restored to their owners.

1,792 articles were reported to the police as lost during the year, and a large proportion was traced and restored to the owners.

During the year 2,545 articles, comprising money, jewellery, etc. were found and taken charge of by the police. Also, 29 prisoners were conveyed to H.M. Prison, Leicester, 3 to H.M. Prison Holloway, and one to Liverpool. Apart from these duties there were scrap dealers to be visited and their books to be checked, and lodging houses to be checked also.

The authorised strength of the city force was 55, plus 3 "additional", 1 policewoman and 4 civilian clerks. Actual strength: 50, plus 3 "additional", 1 policewoman and 2 civilian clerks. Four Army Reservist members of the force were recalled to military duties.

624 days were lost through sickness by members of the force during the year, as against 218 days during 1939. All members of the force held the St. John Ambulance certificate.

According to the census of 1937 the population of the city was 46,550. The length of the streets patrolled was 69 miles.

School Shelters
It was decided in February that all the elementary school air raid shelters in the city would be heated and lighted electrically. The cost, £3,137, would be paid for by the Board of Education. The council proposed to install electric radiators and doors to exclude draughts. The shelters were built on tarmac playgrounds or gravel, and it was proposed to eliminate dust as far as possible by laying concrete or tar-spray on the gravel.

There were 130 shelters for approximately 5,500 elementary school children and it was practice at Peterborough for the school teachers to marshal children to the shelters when an alert was sounded during school hours. These daytime alerts were seldom of long duration, but the children were in the shelters for sufficient time to be conscious of the cold after the warmth of the classrooms.

Also at this time, after an inspection by the A.R.P. Emergency Committee, Westwood House High School was named as an Emergency Civic Centre in the event of the Town Hall being damaged by enemy action.

Miss G.H. Mattock, who was head of the school in Thorpe Road, received a letter from the Committee stating that she would have to consider the possibility of arranging alternative accommodation for her school in the event of the existing premises being required. Miss Mattock's immediate reaction to the letter is not known. Later, the City Engineer asked the Committee for permission to use the High School basement as an alternative report and control centre, this was agreed to, and fitting up arrangements were soon underway.

At about the same time approval was given for the city council to construct nine public surface shelters in Long Causeway and Bridge Street, to accommodate 275 people, at an expenditure not exceeding £1,329, including lighting, sanitation etc.

Air Training Corps
Nation-wide recruiting for the Air Training Corps for boys from 16 to 18 years of age began on February 1st, 1941, and by the end of the first week over 100 youths had applied for enrolment in No. 115 (Peterborough) Squadron. A call also went out to any men between the ages of 32 and 55 who had previous experience in the Air Force to enroll as commissioned officers in the force. Applications were being made to Sir Arthur Craig, 9a, Westgate, Peterborough, although permission was soon given for the St. Mark's Hall, Cromwell Road, to be used as their headquarters.

A.R.P. Apathy
One hazy morning when the sirens sounded, the Chief Warden, Mr. Lister Robinson, came across 15 shops in one city street with their lights full on. Fourteen tradesmen, he said, complied with his request to turn the lights off, the other was "nasty," and would be reported.

It must have been a constant worry for people trying to ensure they had a complete black-out at night, considering the penalties they might incur, without being told by whom they might see as overzealous wardens, to turn their lights out during the daytime as well. Nit-picking or not, the Chief Warden was only doing his job.

"It was dangerous," he said, "for lights to be on in hazy daylight as at night, because it had been established that wherever a Nazi airman saw a light he would drop bombs. Remember this, and tell everybody - where there is light there is danger."

Mr. Robinson also said the R.A.F. had made a test flight over the city on January 17th, and the report was that the black-out was still not satisfactory. (The ex-A.R.P. Chief for Huntingdon, Alderman W.H. Clayton, had just been fined £2 for a black-out offence in his shop in Huntingdon High Street).

During this same week the A.R.P. staff at the Old Town Hall was having a busy time testing respirators, Sergeant Gilder described the demand as "overwhelming." People were asked to show their gas masks to their local warden first who would advise them if they needed to submit them for further tests.

It was amazing the number of gas masks that did not fit properly when their

115

owners took them in to be inspected.

"I don't blame the wardens who went round in the first place," said Sgt. Gilder, "I think the trouble is that wartime worries and broken rest have caused people to lose weight. This is especially true of women; they are thinner in the face and the respirators no longer fit. Others have slackened the head bands to make the masks fit super-comfortably, and again the result is a misfit. Another cause is the change in the style of women's hairdressing since the respirators were issued."

In the last few days Sgt. Gilder had taken two parties through the 'gas chamber'. In one party of 34 only four respirators were serviceable and a perfect fit; in the other party there was one good fit in 20.

Paston area wardens took 20 members of the public, including some school children, to the 'gas chamber' at the weekend, and it was said that they stood up well to the test.

School children's masks were also being tested at the schools by policemen, and many were found to be in an appalling condition. At Walton alone 73 replacements were necessary. Respirators had been found without filters, and with the eyepieces broken.

"I am certain that some of the parents have not looked at them since they were issued," Sgt. Gilder said, "or at their own, for that matter. Judging by the state of some of the respirators the boys have played football with them, and the parents have not had the foggiest idea of what was going on."

As a contrast to the general state of apathy that was enveloping the city as far as A.R.P. matters went, a letter sent to a local senior warden Mr. R.W. Chaplin, by an 83 year old lady residing in Lincoln Road, shows the other side of the coin:

"Dear Sir - I know you will understand that, being 83 and too deaf to hear Alerts or All Clears, I can't take an active part in fire-fighting. I had thought of calling on you as to duty, but most days lately I have been kept in by a cold.

If it is advisable to have a stirrup pump for this group of houses I should be pleased to bear a good part of the cost. My 'help' is over 64. Happily for me she is careful about black-out!"

Major R. de Gray, the Deputy Chief Warden, said the "grand spirit of this aged lady.... sets a fine example to the general public."

The Kitchen Front

City people were now being asked to double their collections of kitchen refuse. A month earlier in January, 24 tons had been carted away by the council, about 5 tons a week. Feeders, it was said, were "falling over each other," to get it. There were plenty of customers whatever the supply as it was found to be excellent feeding stuff.

People were advised to keep unsuitable refuse out of the bins, in one case some tin-tacks had been found, these, it was stated, "were not suitable for pigs." There were about 200 public bins out, and they were emptied every day.

The refuse was handed over to the pig keeper just as it was, which saved money on processing. The price paid was 24 shillings a ton, this did not quite cover the cost of collection, but with ten tons a week the scheme would be self supporting.

There was still an unsatisfied demand for allotments around the city, all council plots had been spoken for with many new applications coming in. Owners of earmarked land were generally ready to give up possession and the council were willing to take over any large gardens that were not being cultivated.

In all 289 war-time allotments had now been laid out, and 120 acres had been taken for cultivation, with seedling plants even being grown for sale in the city park.

P.O.W. Letter
Mr. and Mrs. A.C. Wilkinson, 143, High Street, Fletton, received a letter at the beginning of February, from their son, Private George Wilkinson, Northamptonshire Regiment, who was a prisoner of war in Germany. The letter had been written on November 10th and stated that the camp had lately received some Red Cross parcels, which eked out to one between four men. They contained cocoa, tea, milk powder, and tins of meat and fruit. - "just making a decent meal each."

The prisoners were short of clothes and Private Wilkinson still wore the uniform he had been captured in, "but we have got decent barracks to live in, with a bit of fire, so it is not too bad." He added that he was in the medical section of the camp and did no work, finding it rather monotonous looking at barbed wire all day. He told his parents to keep their chins up, as the war won't last forever.

For Steward, Edward William Wilders, the war was already over. His parents, Mr. and Mrs. G.E. Wilders, 72, Harris Street, received the news of his death in the middle of the month. William, whose 21st birthday had been just two weeks earlier on January 30th, had been their only son and he lost his life on 27th September 1940, when his ship, the S.S. MANCHESTER BRIGADE, was sunk. He had been in the Mercantile Marine for four and a half years, and before that had been a member of St. Barnabas' choir and of the Junior Imperial League.

New Ponds and Bad Luck
Emergency water supplies were now being planned for the city, in the form of ponds dug in certain areas. The sites provisionally approved were:
Stanley Recreation Ground, capacity 150,000 gallons; cost estimated at £600.
S.E. corner of the park, 100,000 gallons; £419.
Westwood Sports Ground, 100,000 gallons; £419.
L.N.E.R. ground, Walpole Street, 100,000 gallons; £419.
Paddock next to the Public Assistance Institution, 100,000 gallons; £419.

Someone who would have welcomed a little water was Annie Ginns, of Caverstede Road, Walton. She had the raw deal of being summoned for 'Allowing a chimney to be on fire' on February 4th. She pleaded guilty.

Special Constable Woods said that during the black-out flames rose one or two feet high from the chimney.

The defendant told the court that she had gone to London for a few days to see her brother, who was in the A.F.S. and who had been burned, and her father, who was in hospital with injuries due to bombing. When she came back she lit a small fire in a room that was not often used. She had been in the house a year and the chimney had not been swept in that time. Annie was fined 10 shillings.

"You were very unfortunate," the Chairman said, "but you would have been more unfortunate if there had been somebody overhead. That is just what they love to look for."

Home Guard Field Day
On Sunday 22nd February the Home Guard had the most comprehensive field day they had yet undertaken. They brought all their forces and arms into service, and manned all the most likely defensive posts in and around the city. The City Battalion

acted as defenders with the exception of one company which 'deserted' to the enemy. The Soke and the Hunts. Battalions were the chief attackers. Every approach to the city came into the sphere of operations some time during the day.

Considerable ingenuity, both in attack and defence was shown, with many tricks learned in lectures, brought into use. In one case attackers creeping up the concealed side of a road were detected by their reflection in a shop window on the other side.

A number of H.Q. and specialist officers who were delegated as umpires made notes throughout the day and submitted their reports that evening. The main features being looked at were the manning and preparation of certain barriers, and the various methods of attack.

On the following Saturday, 559 men born in 1921 registered for service at the Peterborough Labour Exchange. Of these, 319 expressed a preference for the Air Force, and 108 for the Navy. Three claimed to be conscientious objectors.

The Director of Scrap Supplies was now asking councils to remove all iron railings not clearly needed for public safety. It was reported that 20 tons could be had from the New England recreation ground, Bishop's Road gardens and gravel walk, instructions were issued however, that these should not be taken down.

Permission was given however, for the pavilion at Westwood Grange to be used as offices should the playing field be required as an emergency camp site in a serious raid.

Fool-Proof System
Local man Private Gordon Roll is credited with having evolved - in a prison camp in Germany - what he believed to be a fool-proof betting system.
In a letter to a friend in London he wrote:

"I have been making plans to make £120,000 a year at horse racing and roulette. I have worked out a system, and shall bring off some big coups with six horses I intend to buy and name 'Stalag,' 'Propaganda,' 'Buckshee,' 'Browned Off,' 'Junkers,' and 'Muck In',"

Private Roll, who was taken prisoner in Belgium, added that he was determined to win the Derby after the war with his entry to be called "Good Old Blighty."
These revelations seem to indicate the possibility of a head wound!

United as Casualties of War
The City Council showed a compassionate spirit to Peterborough United F.C. towards the end of the month, in dealing with the club's difficulties over rent arrears.

The Park and Recreation Grounds Committee reported to the council on Friday 28th February that they had met three representatives of the club - Mr. J.E. Swain (chairman), Mr. G. Creed and Mr. H.J. Poulter - who asked whether, in view of war-time conditions, the Committee would terminate the lease or grant a reduction of rent for the period of the war. The Treasurer reported that the present year's rent was still in arrears.

The Committee decided that, if the club were unable to pay the full rent of £50 a year, half may be paid and the arrears carried forward until after the war.

A certain Mr. Wright, and history does not record his status within the proceedings, asked if it was any use spoon-feeding the club in that way.

Alderman Snowden said the club would pay up after the war. They had had a bad time. It should be recorded that the city has Alderman Snowden, and not Mr. Wright, to thank for the continuance of the city team.

118

The report was adopted.

Not only were United short of money, they were short of players too, (and spectators, which created the cash flow problem). Owing to short notice, United and Phorpres fielded depleted sides at London Road on Saturday 1st March, and two reporters present joined in on opposite sides. United still won 4-1.

A.R.P. News

Plans were passed by the council at the beginning of March for the building of brickwork shelters for office records for the Co-operative Society at St. Paul's Road. Shelter provision costing £500 was also put in hand at St' John's Street depot.

From now on the lodge at Fletton recreation ground was to be used as a muster point for police and Special Constables, and the War Agricultural Committee were asked to allow Westwood Grange and Fulbridge Road playing fields to be used for grazing. Permission had already been given for the use of the pavilion at Westwood Grange to be used as offices should the field be required as an emergency camp site in a serious raid.

A decision was also made now to increase the charge to outside authorities, including the military, for patients admitted to the Isolation Hospital from 9 shillings to 10s. This may have been in order to offset the rise the Matron of the Isolation Hospital was given after she was asked to supervise the smallpox hospital as well.

Someone else with an interest in money at this time was the cleaner of an unnamed First Aid Post, who was dismissed for "an irregularity in making out a time sheet."

It was obvious now that the city needed more gas cleansing stations, and Mr. Mollison who was now appointed as A.R.P. Officer, was given the task of making people more "gas-minded."

The city's fire services were pretty good, but to make things even safer the Government had now advised that the water supply should be supplemented by the provision of static water supply basins placed at five selected points around the city.

The number of people able to carry out fire watching duties on business premises was showing a deficiency, and the A.R.P. Committee had approached the Regional Commissioner requesting that compulsory orders be made to all eligible males to register.

As far as residential areas were concerned, the wardens had done their job, but even now some streets were just not interested. The suggestion was made that the names of the streets that had not helped themselves should be published in an effort to shame them into action.

The first street, Saxon Road, was 'named and shamed' in the Standard on April 11th. At the time there were 481 fire watching parties that had voluntarily enrolled - 5,589 men and 2,799 women. In addition 64 city people were known to be acting as street watchers, but had declined to sign the official forms.

Salvage

The January figures for city salvage were published at the beginning of March and read as follows:

Paper 34tons, kitchen waste 25tons, milk bottles 1,056, tins 12tons, bones 3tons, and ashes 5,672tons.

Household refuse was now to be collected fortnightly instead of weekly due to shortage of labour and vehicles and the ongoing daily collection from the street bins

119

of kitchen waste.

One problem at this time was that some streets had no refuse bins, and the householders would not go into the next street with their kitchen waste. Extra bins were being put out onto the streets by the council as fast as they could get them.

Mr. Horrell, of Horrell's Dairies, was complaining to the council now that a lot of people would rather put their bottles in the dustbin than put them out for his milkmen. It seemed a scandalous waste that the council were selling his milk-bottles for salvage, and he joked that he ought to pay the council ten per cent to collect them for him.

Home Guard
As from February 1st 1941, the rank of Lieutenant-Colonel was conferred on Colonel A.H. Mellows, T.D., and Captain R.J.C. Crowden, M.C. Captain Crowden was Commanding Officer of the City Battalion of the Home Guard, and Colonel Mellows was Commander of the Group comprising the City and Soke Battalions. Commissions for other Home Guard officers were also expected and a week later they were published:
CITY BATTALION
Officers approved for the 1st. Northamptonshire (City of Peterborough) Battalion, Home Guard.
Headquarters:
Commanding Officer, Lieutenant-Colonel R.J.C. Crowden, M.C.
Second in Command, Major H.J. Farrow.
In Command, Headquarters Company, Major E.W. Bromige.
Second in Command, Headquarters Company, Captain W.A. Heighton.
Other Officers, Captain J.J. Campbell, Captain D.C. Banks, Acting Major H.H. Staton, M.B.E. Lieutenant A.W. Wilson, Lieutenant H.J. Wilson, Lieutenant H.P.E. Dawson, Lieutenant H. Ashling, Lieutenant A.W. Ruddle, Lieutenant F.A. Errington, and Chaplain O. Whiting.
'A' Company:
Officer Commanding, Major J.E.G. Hassell.
Second in Command, Captain E.A.W. Withers.
Lieutenants, H. Kettle, C.J. Thompson, F. Adamson, T.G. Spreckley, and T. Need.
Second Lieutenants, A. Chappell, J.H. Young, A.P. Allen, H.W. Knight, C. Bremer, and F. Dent.
'B' Company:
Officer Commanding, Major E.G. Hann.
Second in Command, Captain F.H. Plaistowe.
Lieutenants, F.R.H. Fuller, W.F. Pailing, A.L. Berridge, A.W. Clements, and W.P. Blackman.
Second Lieutenants, F.S. Rauld, T. Rowland, J.S. Barnes, R.G. Barber, and A.F.E. German.
'C' Company:
Officer Commanding, Major H.A. Goodacre.
Second in Command, Captain A.E. Stewart.
Lieutenants, A.C. Munton, W.D. Larratt, T. Reed, S.G. Rudge, W.F. Willis, and A.C.A. Thompson.
Second Lieutenants, G.S. Twiddy, W. Login, and A.L. Bickener.
'D' Company:

Officer Commanding, Major E.A.J. Bilham. M.C.

Second in Command, Captain C. Taylor.

Lieutenants, L.T. Howlett, T.A. Burnett, J.H. Booker, R.T. Hook and H. Collcott.

Other staff appointments were:

R.S.M. Atkinson, 1st class Warrant Officer; Armourer Sergeant, W. Beaver; Bandmaster, W. Powell; Permanent Staff Instructor, Staff Sergeant Joyce; Orderly Col. Sergeant, J.G. Lawson; Gas Sergeant, J.S. Alleson; Q.M.-Sgt. J.L. Jones; Admin. Officer, H. Cracknell.

SOKE BATTALION

Officers approved for the 2nd Northamptonshire (Soke of Peterborough) Battalion, Home Guard.

Headquarters:

Officer Commanding, Lieutenant-Colonel A.H. Mellows, T.D., D.L.

Second in Command, Major H.L. Samson.

Chief Guide, Captain C.M. Everard.

Liaison Officer, Lieutenant W.B. Buckle.

Musketry Officer, Lieutenant W.G.M. Roberts.

'A' Company:

Officer Commanding, Captain A.F. Percival.

Second in Command, Captain J.W. Goddard, M.C. and Bar.

Lieutenants, W.G. Ferrier Kerr, and R.W. Shorrock.

Second Lieutenants, H. Hicks, H.B. Paten, and J. Button.

'B' Company:

Officer Commanding, Captain J.G. Warwick.

Second in Command, Captain E.W. Canham.

Lieutenants, A.R. Allen, M.M., W.R. Wood, and T. Oldfield.

Second Lieutenants, G. Franks, A.G. Shelton, and H.S. Walker.

'C' Company:

Officer Commanding, Major H.W.A. Elliott.

Second in Command, Captain H. Dewhurst.

Lieutenants, W.H.E. Northcott, M.M., T.C. Bolton, S.G. Garford, R. Perkins, and G.M.A. Hall.

Second Lieutenants, C.W. Benstead, H.H. Pearson, R.G. Stiggers, J. Perkins, and F. Meeks.

'D' Company:

Officer Commanding, Captain J.C. Goodale, M.C.

Second in Command, Captain J.G. Avery.

Lieutenants, E.W. Macro, G.P. Little, N.T. Glenn, and F.W. Gilby.

Second Lieutenants, R. Briers, and E. Severn.

'E' Company:

Officer Commanding, Major A. Peasgood, D.C.M. M.S.M.

Second in Command, Captain L.G. Turnill.

Lieutenants, H.P. Parker, C.E. Wiseman, E. Iliffe, and J.E. Conington.

Second Lieutenants, H.G. Burgess, N.A. Pledger, and A.G. Teesdale.

There was great interest being taken in the Home Guard for other reasons at this time, due to rumours of impending changes, in particular with that concerning the scrapping of the arm band and the substitution of a sleeve label. A small step on the road to a full uniform!

A large amount of equipment had been received by the Home Guard at this time, and the band was kitted-out with first class instruments. There were also implements and materials for entrenchments, steel helmets for all, and water-bottles in good supply.

On Sunday March 23rd, the Home Guard escorted the Mayor and Corporation to the morning service at the Cathedral for the National Day of Prayer service.

Two announcements at this time showed the double effect of enemy action, first with the news that Sergeant C.W. Minn, R.A.F., V.R. of Star Road, was missing whilst on military service in the East. The second being the news that six cots destined for the Children's Ward at the Memorial Hospital, and provided by funds raised at a 'Standard Chums' children's concert in the city, had suddenly become a military target and had been lost to enemy action before they could be delivered. Alternatives were being sought after.

Shelter Scandal

At the beginning of April it had become apparent that the city air raid shelters were in a terrible state. This time however, their condition was not due to vandals, but to faulty construction. There had been a national shortage of cement at the time that the shelters were originally built, to a design and specification stipulated by the Ministry of Home Security. For example, forty arch-type shelters had been started and after the third one had been built the first one had collapsed. The others under construction were immediately demolished on the orders of the City Engineer, Mr. F.J. Smith.

Another problem was that the Government had decided to issue bunks for the 12-seat shelters, this reduced the accommodation to only seven people and the question was asked, "Where are the other five supposed to go?"

The Government's answer was: "When Peterborough people use the shelters regularly to sleep in at nights, then you will,(the Council), be authorised to provide additional shelters for the other five."

This astute piece of logic had already been superseded though, as a new design for a reinforced brickwork shelter that would take twelve bunks had already been sent out.

A Regional instruction had now been received, and not before time, that all shelters constructed in ungauged lime mortar, (lime and sand only, with no cement), were to be closed immediately pending demolition. Those built with lime mortar were to be examined, and any considered unsatisfactory were also to be closed prior to being pulled down.

This action, brought about by the bad shelter design, which in itself was due to the cement shortage, led to the closure of 1,300 12-unit shelters - i.e., accommodation for 15,000 city people.

Gas Matters

Always a matter of serious concern, the subject of enemy poison gas attacks was again brought to the fore on Monday 7th April, when the City A.R.P. Committee received a Ministry of Home Security circular on carrying gas masks.

It suggested that all Corporation employees should be asked to carry masks, as an example. A further suggestion was that at a given hour on days to be arranged, all should don their masks for a period of five minutes. Practice gas "attacks" were to be arranged in various parts of the city. One wonders what the council employees (dustmen, builders, clerks etc.) thought of the idea of standing about for five minutes a day wearing their gas masks. No doubt it would have done little for their morale, being held up to ridicule, as it is difficult to imagine that this would have encouraged others to do anything other than snigger.

Mrs. A.H. Mellows arranged to have Sgt. Gilder give four lectures on gas measures at the Town Hall on April 22nd and 29th, and May 6th and 13th. These were for the 'Housewives' of Service personnel, and those that attended would qualify for the W.V.S. badge. The subjects were: Latest information about gas; First Aid for gas casualties; How to protect yourself; and Incendiary bombs and fires.

At the first of these lectures about 450 ladies turned up. Sergeant Gilder, the city gas lecturer, told them that "people seemed terribly afraid of war gas. There was no need for it," he said, they "used gas for cooking and were not afraid, and there was no more danger with war gas than with domestic gas," (except they could turn off their cookers if they wanted to!), -"if they understood it."

He dealt with gases that might be used, explained their effects, methods of defence, and treatment of patients.

The local Education Officer was in discussion with the Chief Constable also at this time with regard to warnings to schools in the event of gas attack; mask drill was already receiving attention. Consent was given to use the Eastholm Infant's School, Walton senior mixed, and Walton junior mixed as gas decontamination centres. This did not interfere with their educational roles under ordinary conditions.

Tragedy

On a more sombre note, another family received news at this time about a lost relative. Mr. and Mrs. J.W. Steadman, of 211, New England, were informed that their eldest son, Seaman Harold Francis Steadman, A.B., was missing. Harold was 24 and had joined the navy in July 1940. Before the war he had been with Messrs. Petts, and was engaged to Miss Joan Moore, of Northfields Road.

Seaman Steadman was later confirmed as having been killed in action almost seven weeks earlier on 24th February 1941.

The same week, Sapper Bernard Stanley Hodson, of Oxford Road, was reported as having died in a northern hospital. Members of the Railway Company of the Home Guard formed a Guard of Honour at his funeral service at Park Road Baptist Church, on Saturday 12th April. The only son of Mr. and Mrs. F.S. Hodson, of 28 Oxford Road, Private Hodson died in a military hospital of meningitis on Sunday 6th April. Aged 20, in civil life he had worked in the L.N.E.R. Accountant's Office. There were nearly fifty wreaths.

On the 3rd April there was another accident involving an air raid shelter and a motor vehicle. Two airmen were detained in hospital after their car had crashed head-on into a street shelter near Paston Lane. The car was wrecked and a hole knocked in the brickwork of the shelter. Neither of the men was local.

Another item concerning shelters appeared in the newspapers at this time involving a list of towns where permission had been given to the authorities to supply refreshments in shelters.

The 'Standard' received a number of enquiries from townspeople asking if this meant that "charming waitresses will bring trays of tea - with sugar - and biscuits to the surface and other shelters at the time of an Alert."

"It does not," replied the 'Standard'. The permission applied only to the very large shelters which were provided in most towns for the temporary housing of people whose homes had been bombed. However, on the evening of Monday 5th

May, the A.R.P. Committee decided to make an application for sanction to provide canteen facilities for three groups of shelters: Bishop's Road, 19 shelters holding 950 persons; Stanley recreation ground, 22, holding 1,100; and Cathedral Precincts, 7, holding 325.

At the end of the month it was reported at a meeting of the A.R.P. Committee that the city district had indeed been nominated for inclusion in the area for the provision of canteens for serving the public in shelters.

Fire Watcher Crimes

At Peterborough Police Court on Wednesday 16th April, William Thomas Bigley, of 290, Gladstone Street, was sent to prison for six months for stealing articles of women's clothing from Trollope's store, while employed there as a fire watcher.

This sort of crime had been a worry from the beginning, with proprietors being concerned that their property was at risk from theft while people were present throughout the night. The Chairman of the court, General Strong, in perhaps overstating it slightly, told the accused that he was guilty of an offence almost amounting to looting, for which in war-time the death penalty could be enforced.

One charge specified 1 pair of women's shoes, 2 princess slips, 2 pairs of knickers, 3 pairs of stockings, and other articles, valued at £6. 11s. 4d. stolen from Trollope's on or about March 19th.

A second charge related to 1 pair of women's shoes, a boy's cap, 1 pair of gloves, 4 pairs of knickers, 2 nightdresses, 3 pairs of stockings, and other articles valued at £5. 3s. 8d. property of the same firm, and stolen on or about March 12th.

While Bigley had been fire watching one night, a member of Trollope's staff took a jumper from him before he had left the shop and this was reported to the police. Later, after searching his house, they recovered the rest of the items, Bigley admitted taking them, saying, "There you are, I took them from Trollope's when I was fire watching." After he had been charged he said, "I am very sorry. I would not have had it happen for ever so much, but it can't be avoided now."

Bigley had worked at Trollope's since 1935, latterly as a fire watcher, at 62 shillings a week and the management had asked the court that the charges should not be unduly pressed. However, the court considered it a serious abuse of trust, and no doubt hoped that the sentence would act as a deterrent for others. A woman was also charged with receiving some of the stolen goods, but she was later acquitted.

Another fire watcher, Jack King, of 121, Gladstone Street, also found himself in court, this time for being drunk in Russell Street and Gladstone Street on April 5th, while he should have been fire watching.

Albert Ernest Barratt, a fellow fire watcher, said King should have been on duty with him in Boroughbury, but at 8 o'clock he came and said he was ill. At 10:20 he returned drunk, and was very abusive. Barratt then went to look for a constable to have him ejected.

P.C. Bratley said that he went with Barratt to the repository, and found that King had gone into the Post Office Social Club without permission and was lying on the floor with a bottle of beer in his hands; a steward was trying to get him out.

P.C. Bratley put King into the street and watched him stagger along Russell Street, bumping into people and doors as he went. He then bumped into a man and became argumentative and this time P.C. Bratley took him home, he would have arrested him, he said, but all the cells at the police station were full!

King was fined 10 shillings, with 5 shillings costs. The Chairman said he was sorry he could not put on a higher penalty.

Warden Shortage
The calling-up of Air Raid Wardens for army service was now developing into a serious deficiency in several parts of the city, and was putting undue strain on the remainder of the force.

Warden enrolments at this time totalled 830, but for various reasons not all of the wardens were active. Even if they had been, there would only have been one warden for every 66 of the city population, taking into account the influx of some 10,000 evacuees.

Some sectors were fortunate in having a number of reserves over and above the "first line" strength of six wardens, but others were not so lucky. This was particularly the case in the North Ward and part of the Paston Ward, where railwaymen on awkward "turns" and munitions workers on long shifts predominated.

It was felt that there were a number of residents who should have been able to find a few hours a week to help out. The shortage existed particularly in Sectors 8D, E, F and G, which were based at Keeton Road School and covered the following district:

Fulbridge Road, Dryden Road, Keeton Road, Tennyson Road, Wilberforce Road, Shakespeare Avenue, St. James's Avenue, Portland Avenue, Lister Road, Cowper Road, Burns Close, Coleridge Place, Scotney Street, Crown Street, Burmer Road, Belham Road, and Thistlemoor Road.

Girls Register
Women were now being called-up. The first 814 city girls aged 20 years old registered on Saturday 19th April, a few of them failed to take along their registration cards, but the general attitude was one of cheerful acquiescence, and no one was kept for more than five minutes. Leaflets were provided explaining the different services that were available - A.T.S., W.A.A.F., W.R.N.S., and nursing.

Strangely, there was no opportunity for conscientious objection as there was with the men, but there was little argument. The main question was whether there was any likelihood of a speedy call-up for work. The next step would be interviews of the girls who were not doing work of national importance.

It was noted that "The general run of numbers was such as one is used to seeing passing in and out of the head Post Office in Cumbergate during an ordinary day."

Many of the girls were with their mothers or aunties, some had their boyfriends, and a number arrived with an army "escort" on either side. One girl was seen to arrive in work-grimed overalls; some came in cars, others on cycles. Not a few had perambulators to leave outside.

Some women in other parts of the country, working as full-time ambulance drivers and full-time first aiders were upset that they were not eligible for call-up, remaining in their necessary jobs until the end of the war, although permission was given to those who did not wish to stay in these occupations to resign before April 19th. There was no dissatisfaction at all in Peterborough, and not one resignation!

The First Gas 'Attack'
On April 25th 1941, a short article, which may have alarmed some city people, appeared in the 'Standard' warning of a forthcoming 'gas attack'. This 'attack' was

to be a test designed to make people aware of the dangers, carry their gas masks every day, and be prepared to wear them. The actual day, hour and place were not revealed, the only indication being that it would be made on a day during the week beginning May 5th. The gas to be used would be in the form of crystals which when heated gave off a type of tear gas. Gas masks, it was said, would be quite effective in dealing with it, and in a very short time it would disperse into the atmosphere.

On May 2nd, a little more information became available. The time and place of the test would be announced to the public only ten minutes beforehand by a loud-speaker van and posters. One assumes that the posters would have been of little value considering the time scale involved. Gas rattles would also be heard. The duration of the test would be half an hour, although this would depend on the prevailing wind conditions. People were warned that if the gas got into their houses or shops they should open their doors and windows to "give it a good getaway." Although one assumes they could have been letting more in!

Peterborough's first gas test finally took place on the afternoon of Friday 9th May, 1941, and was considered to be very successful. Many scores of people wore their respirators for close on half an hour - longer than many had ever done before - to discover that the masks were very good protection and not too uncomfortable.

The gas was released from four braziers at the Market Place end of Bridge Street, and Dr. Davies, chief of the gas identification service was superintendent of the operation. Rattles were sounded and masks were quickly donned. The only effect of the gas being a slight tingling in the skin of the neck and other exposed places.

Without the masks there was a slight irritation to the eyes affecting people in varying degrees. Only about a pound and a half of the gas-producing material was used, whereas a bomb would probably have held twenty pounds. During the test several buses passed the spot as well as cars and other vehicles. In some cases the drivers and passengers put on their masks, but not all of them. Apparently a quick dash through the area caused no bad effect.

Two platoons of military marched through with respirators adjusted, and the Bishop was also recognised in spite of his mask. The wind was a factor in dispersing the gas very quickly at the end of the test. Several ambulances with personnel and appliances were in attendance and others of the A.R.P. services for instructional purposes. There were no casualties, but one or two people caught unawares had to be helped into shops to recover their sight.

The public were warned afterwards that next time there would be no announcement beforehand.

'Casualties'

It is indeed a shame that, as I have mentioned before, information regarding servicemen who were killed or missing was quite often, very sparse in detail. As if to emphasise this point, on April 25th a small item was published in the 'Standard' reporting the news that Acting Leading Seaman Anthony John Davies, eldest son of Mr. and Mrs. T. Davies, of 125, Fletton Avenue, was officially reported by the Admiralty as missing whilst on active service. Leading Seaman Davies had been in the navy for six years. He had been educated at Fletton Secondary School, and had been an active member of the Cathedral Voluntary Choir. Mr. and Mrs. Davies had another son, A.V.M. Davies, who was also serving in the navy at this time, as a Writer.

Acting Leading Seaman Davies would later be confirmed as having been killed in action on April 6th 1941, serving as a gunner.

This report of a real casualty, no more than one column inch in length, sat alongside another, twice as long, describing how some "very practical tests were being carried out on two or three afternoons a week at ambulance stations, the personnel of which become 'casualties'."

Members of first aid parties were called to find 'casualties' labelled with details of wounds or injuries, including "mysterious unconsciousness, gas cases, wounds, fractures or lacerations." These they would have to treat, and also arrange for them to be transported to places appointed.

It seems strange that 'fake' casualties should get more attention than real ones, but censorship, and the need to keep up morale, were real considerations.

Immediately below this was an even longer column carrying an appeal from the Mayor for fellow-citizens to donate portable wireless sets to two service men's, convalescent homes in the city, - The Lindens and Paston Hall. Garden chairs and outdoor games were also required.

Railings
The government need for scrap iron from home supplies continued, and in order to maintain these supplies and to build up reserves it was essential to tap all sources. The Iron and Steel Control of the Ministry of Supply had already approached all Urban Authorities, and over 1,000 tons of scrap iron a week had been contributed during the five months since December 1940, from railings on the various properties which were administered by Local Authorities.

In many districts private owners had contributed railings, and through a voluntary scheme which was already in place, it was hoped that all property owners would be given full opportunity to make personal contributions to the national needs, by offering unessential boundary fences, front railings, or those which divided adjacent gardens.

To assist even more in this 'push', the Local Authorities were asked by the Ministry of Supply to assist in the collection of privately owned railings. An authorisation form could be obtained from the City Engineer at the Town Hall, which enabled the council to make the necessary arrangements for the removal of the railings. All the owner had to do was to sign the form and the council would go round and remove the railings, any types were required, wrought or cast iron.

The prices of iron and steel scrap were controlled, but it was generally thought that the price would cover the making good of the damage, with a little something left over. This 'little something', it was suggested, should be placed at the disposal of the Local Authorities to relieve rates, or be donated to the Red Cross, Spitfire, or other similar local voluntary funds.

Types of railings that were not required fell into three classes:
1. Fencings of light gauge wire type.
2. Railings or fencings serving essential purposes such as protecting the public from personal danger, protecting growing crops, or necessary for enclosing or keeping out of stock.
3. Railings of historical and artistic value.

The public were warned that their railings would not necessarily be taken straight away, as the need to build up reserves was just as important as obtaining immediate supplies.

127

More Sad News

On Monday 28th April, Mr. and Mrs. Topham, of 18, Dryden Road, New England, received the news from the War Office that their second son, Private John Leslie Topham, was officially reported as killed in action.

Private Topham, who in civil life had been with Mr. H.W. Hoyles, joined the 5th Northamptonshire Regiment as a Territorial before the war, and was with them when they were the first Territorial unit to go into the front line in France. The communication sent to Mrs. Topham stated that her son was killed on the Western Front between May 10th and July 3rd, 1940. Soon after the evacuation from Dunkirk Private Topham was reported missing, and a month before this final notification his family received the news that no further trace of him had been found.

During the same week that the Tophams received their tragic message, Mrs. Garner, of 62, St. John's Street, received from the International Red Cross a letter written eleven months earlier by her husband, Lance Corporal W. Garner, in France on May 31st, 1940.

The letter had no stamp, and it was assumed that L/Cpl. Garner wrote it hurriedly after he had been captured, and dropped it in the hope that someone would find it and post it. L/Cpl. Garner was posted missing after the fall of France.

There were only a few pencil-written lines in the letter, in which he told his wife not to worry about him, and hoped that his two children were well.

Lance Corporal Garner was a Territorial before the war, going to France with the 5th Northamptonshires. He married Miss Richardson, of St. Martin's Street, in 1938.

On Saturday 3rd, May, 575 women born in the year 1919 registered under the Registration of Employment Order.

Evacuees

Some comical, if not sad, examples of the difference in cultures between local people and the many evacuees coming into the area were reported at the beginning of May. Sixty-five more children from London arrived at Peterborough station at the end of April, bound for Stilton and the Ortons.

The "domestic incompetence" as it was described, astounded the families with which these newcomers were billeted.

"One of our London guests," it was stated, "was asked to cut some bread and butter for her host and family. This she professed herself as unable to do as she had always purchased her supplies already cut and buttered from her provision merchant.

A boiled egg was presented to an evacuee. She looked at it with interest, expressed surprise that it was given her for breakfast, asked what was its nature, and when told, asked how she should break the shell and eat it.

Another mother found her host washing her child's head. She expressed surprise and indignation. 'Face and hands might be washed,' she said, 'but heads never.'"

The 'Standard' published the words of the Earl of Beaconsfield who wrote in 1845: "Little do we know of the state of our own country that the general reader might suspect that the writer had been tempted to exaggerate. After nearly a hundred years two nations seem to exist still in this small island."

Women's Services Canteen

Volunteers were now needed at the Women's Services Canteen on Monday, Tuesday and Wednesday evenings. Mrs. Francis, the Warden, at 7, Minster Precincts, reported that the canteen was being much used, particularly in the evenings, and sometimes all night, weekends were also busy. In March they had over 370 visitors and April over 450. People used the canteen during the day, but 56 people slept there during March and 75 during April.

Hospitality had been extended to the wives and families of soldiers, sailors and airmen travelling by train and arriving in the small hours. All have been given a bed and breakfasted before carrying on with their journeys.

It is sad to have to record that, even in those days of mutual help and suffering, there were still people who found themselves in positions of trust and were unable to resist the temptation put before them. On Wednesday 14th May, four ladies who worked as voluntary helpers at the two Servicemen's Canteens at the Market Place and the North Station appeared before Peterborough Magistrates charged with the theft of cash and stock at times when they were working there.

In some cases marked coins had been placed in tills where suspicion had been aroused, small amounts of money ranging up to only a few pounds were involved, and in one case only two packets of tea. None of the ladies who were caught had ever been in trouble before, and in those days when everything was in such short supply, perhaps it is not too difficult to understand. All were volunteers and regularly gave up their time to help others, which is why I see no need to divulge names and addresses. Their fines, one of £5 and three of £3, and the shame of having the stories reported in the local newspaper were punishment enough.

Sunday Attack
An exercise in attack and defence was carried out on the afternoon of Sunday 27th April. The defenders were the City Battalion of the Home Guard, and the attackers an infantry battalion. The Zone Commander of the Guard (Col. Lister Reid) paid a visit with his Staff Officer (Captain Shillito), and inspected all the defences, with Colonel Crowden, and other H.Q. officers of the Guard. Colonel Herring-Cooper, C.O. of the attackers, visited his operations.

Considerable ingenuity was shown by both sides, and it was believed that in no instance did any notable number break through the defences. On Tuesday 29th, Col. Crowden received a letter from the Zone Commander, congratulating officers and other ranks on the keenness shown. He was surprised to see such a good turn-out.

Extra duties for men who had not chosen to enlist in the Home Guard could be found fire watching, for school teachers at least. At a meeting of teachers at the Town Hall on Tuesday 29th, it was decided that a census of all eligible males, under the Fire Prevention (Business Premises) Order, would be taken.

A list of teachers available for duty would be forwarded to the City Engineer, and a date would be fixed for registration at schools and public halls. All males between the ages of 18 and 60 were required to register, and in due course those considered eligible would be notified of their duties.

Steel Shelters
At another meeting, this time of the A.R.P. Committee on Monday 28th, the City Engineer reported that 1,000 Morrison steel indoor shelters which had been allocated to the city were on their way.

Each shelter accommodated two adults and one child, and after a survey had been made they were allocated to selected families. They could not be put where a) shelter accommodation had already been provided. b) On a floor where there was a basement below. c) in a house which was three storeys high. The room in which the

129

shelter was placed had to be carefully selected, so that the walls gave lateral protection.

Besides this free issue, the council were pressed to sell a number to people outside the income limit, at the price of £7 12s. 6d. The Committee decided to advertise for applications, both for free shelters and for purchase. The shelters were in the form of an iron table, 6ft. 5ins. x 4ft., and 2ft. 5ins. high. The top was a strong sheet of iron, and the legs were of thick angle-iron. Underneath there was a bed on iron slats. The shelters had to be erected by the householder.

By the following week 250 shelters had arrived in the city. The Committee decided to offer 25 per cent for sale, and the rest were issued free under the stated conditions.

More Home Guard News

Dr. Holmes and Mr. W.F.F. Shearcroft had now been enrolled into the City Home Guard. Dr. Holmes became the Medical Officer, and carried out instruction in ambulance duties, and Mr. Shearcroft began training N.C.O.'s as gas instructors.

There had been a generous response from the city for contributions to the Battalion welfare fund for which an administering committee had been set up under the C.O. and second-in-command. The Mayor had also donated a Platoon Efficiency Cup, which was competed for at the King's School ground. The first officer's mess night took place at the Dujon on Thursday 8th May, with about 60 members attending.

Promotions for the following Warrant Officers and Sergeants in the 1st. (City of Peterborough) Northamptonshire Battalion Home Guard were also now confirmed:
'B' Company:
W.O. Class II: C.S.M. A. Gow.
Sergeants: H.B. Miller, C.C. Worthy, G.D. Wilson, J.R. Gooding, W.S. Myers, F. Watkins, R.C. Eames, S.M. Carpenter, S.R. Taylor, G.W. Burrows, W.K. Wragby, E. White, T.W. Boyd, N.H. Harry, C.J. Cooke, G. Florence, T. Andrew.
'C' Company:
W.O. Class II: C.S.M. W.D. Cousins.
Col. Sgt.: C.Q.M.S. E. Eyles.
Sergeants: A. Gale, L.W. Titman, E. Barnes, A. Hart, L.G. Amabilino, H. Child, E. Stimson, A.M. Baxter, J.R. Condie, R.D. Frusher, W.V. Davies, G. Clark, J.W. Houseman, A. Sims, J.A. Turnbull, W. Smith, J.H. Goodliffe, G. Oliver, T. Pluck, E.C. Monck.
'D' Company:
W.O. Class II: C.S.M. B.W. Fisher.
Sergeants: F. Allwright, G.H. Graham, J.W. Mee, W.H. Oliver, W.E. Savage, E.E. Thompson, N. Coates, T. Henson, R. Methven, F. Roberts, C. Saunders, W. Wilson.
H.Q. Company:
Col. Sgt.: J.G. Lawson.
Sergeants: W. Beaver, J.S. Olleson.
Corporals: W. Simpson (administrative section), J.H. Brown.

Fire Duties Become Compulsory

In the middle of May, Lord Trent, the North Midland Regional Commissioner, directed that the Civil Defence Duties (Compulsory Enrolment) Order, 1941, be applied to Peterborough.

This meant that all male British subjects not less than 18 years of age but under 60, residing in Peterborough, were now required to apply to be registered for fire prevention duties unless they were in a class which was exempt from registration. The City Council was responsible for making all arrangements regarding registration and enrolment.

Persons exempt from registration, apart from "blind persons and mental deficients", were members of the Armed Forces (including the Home Guard), Constables (including Special Constables), members of the Royal Observer Corps, registered medical practitioners, and masters and crew of ships engaged in sea-going service.

The Fire Prevention (Business Premises) Order had been applied to Peterborough at the end of the previous January. Under that, occupiers of business premises were obliged to make satisfactory arrangements to combat the incendiary bomb menace. At the same time as this the Commissioner had directed that Regulation 27b of the Defence (General) Regulations should also apply to the city. It then became the obligation of the City Council to first make fire prevention arrangements in residential areas and for all other non-business premises; and secondly, to provide the personnel for fire prevention duties at business premises where proper arrangements or joint arrangements could not be made with staff available.

The City Council later reported to the Regional Commissioner that it would not be able to carry out the second obligation with the volunteers available and accordingly asked that the Civil Defence Duties (Compulsory Enrolment) Order, 1941, be applied to the city. The registrations took place on Saturday 24th May, at a number of schools across the city.

And so it was, that even with the enormous number of city people who volunteered for fire watching duties, it was simply not enough. Those who had decided not to lift a finger, had forced the council's hand, and in doing so had placed themselves at their disposal, to be directed to whatever fire watching duties the council wished them to undertake.

Sixth Raid

One understandable reason for the hesitation of many people to volunteer for fire watching duties became only too apparent at 3.35a.m. on Saturday 10th May, when four high explosive bombs fell on the Priestgate/Cowgate area of the city, killing two fire watchers, and injuring five other people.

The main area of damage was to the offices of Mr. R.Y. Norris, Messrs. Fox and Vergette, Messrs. Swallow, Crick and Co., Messrs. Wyman and Abbott, Milton Estates Ltd., and Messrs. Percival and Son; also to shop premises, and Mr. W.J. Deacon's house all in Priestgate; to premises of Messrs. Lamplugh, General Electric Co., and Williamson's Ltd, Cowgate; there were also some houses damaged in Thorpe Road. In all there were 21 houses and seven other properties damaged.

The two fire watchers, Mr. Benjamin Thompson, aged 69 years, of 155, Gladstone Street, and Mr. Sydney Everitt Wyatt, aged 48 years, of 128, St. John's Street, were both killed when a bomb demolished the back rooms of a block of offices occupied by a firm of Merchants. The men were buried beneath wreckage, and rescue workers were hampered by fire attributed to live coals in a grate in a rear room, and by escaping gas.

Three of the injured were from one family, and became trapped when their

131

quarters received a direct hit, but they were eventually rescued. A great deal of the surrounding property showed the effects of blast.

In the Thorpe Road area, flames rose from wooden premises near to where bombs fell. Firemen soon brought the flames under control. A nearby warehouse lost part of its roof and the top of a side wall, although the stock was not greatly affected.

Shortly after the bombs fell a searchlight crew in the area were machine-gunned, but there were no casualties.

Flying Officer Wounded

On May 16th, Flying Officer Donald A. Garner, formerly of Queen's Gardens, Peterborough, was reported wounded in the chest during operational duties against insurgents in Iraq. He was in hospital but his condition was not regarded as serious. An old Deaconian, Flying Officer Garner was granted a commission in the RAF after two years in the City Police Force. A few years earlier his father, Mr. A. Garner, was promoted from Chief Superintendent at Peterborough G.P.O. to Head Postmaster at Burton-on-Trent.

F.O. Garner was a Flying Instructor at an airfield in Iraq when it was attacked by Iraqi rebels. The Instructors and students constructed makeshift bomb racks on their bi-plane training aircraft and fought off the attackers over a number of days.

Two weeks later a telegram was received from Flying Officer Garner stating that he was in a military hospital in Bombay, and was "going on fine."

Post Office Home Guard

A Home Guard unit was formed in May among Post Office employees at Peterborough. The personnel consisted of members of the Head Postmaster's and Telephone Manager's staffs, and the officers were: Captain W.C. Whitehead (Telecommunications Branch), Lieutenant R.W. Clewer (Telecommunications), Second Lieutenant W.A. Watson (Telecommunications), and Company Sergeant Major J. Arnett (Postal).

At the inception of the L.D.V. the Post Office staff formed two sections of 'B' Company of the City Battalion, although the Post Office men were now a separate organisation.

All sections of the civil defence services, with the exception of fire-fighting, were brought into full operation by an A.R.P. exercise on Tuesday 20th May. A supper at the Dujon followed, and it was said that lessons were learned.

Airgraphs

Many airgraph letters were reaching the city by the weekend of 23rd May. The recipients of three of them being, Mrs. A.V. Hickling, of 31, All Saint's Road, from her brother, Warrant Officer C.T. Thomas; Mrs. G.C. Piggott, of 26, Huntly Road, Woodston, from her husband; and Miss Josephine Reading, from Mr. W. Whittlesey, a friend in the RAF.

The original letters from servicemen were photographed, and a copy, about the size of a man's thumb-nail was sent by air to this country. Here, an enlargement was made, and sent on to the addressee. The Airgraph service was designed to save shipping and aircraft space. The first packet of airgraphs sent from the Middle East weighed 15lbs.; the original letters would have weighed 3cwt.

1902's Register

On Saturday 17th May, 708 city men born in 1902 registered at the Employment Exchange. Preference was expressed by 248 for ground duty with the RAF, an unusual choice considering previous registrations, but a move calculated, no doubt, to keep most of them from being shot down. 51 asked for the Navy, and 63 elected for civil defence. There were six conscientious objectors.

Men born in 1901 registered on the 31st May being the final registration group arranged up to this time.

City Men in Bismarck Chase

On board HMS HOOD when she was sunk on Saturday 24th May, by a shell from the German battleship Bismarck which struck her magazine, was Marine Leslie Bertram Toogood, of 62, Orton Avenue, Woodston.

Marine Toogood was the second son of Mr. and Mrs. B. Toogood, and had been on HMS HOOD for only a fortnight. His parents received a letter from him on the day he was killed. Before joining the Marines 15 months earlier, he had been a clerk at the London Brick Company offices. He was 21 years old and was engaged to Miss V. Barnes, 12 New Road, Peterborough.

Also serving on board HMS HOOD, and killed when she was sunk was Marine Sydney George Layton, eldest son of Mr. and Mrs. G.M. Layton, of 22, Hampden Road, Eastgate. He had been in the Navy almost three years, and had served on the Hood all of that time.

Petty Officer Edward Crumpler, only son of Mr. and Mrs. A.E. Crumpler, of 841, Lincoln Road, was on the cruiser HMS SUFFOLK, which played an important part in shadowing the Bismarck until it was sunk. He was an Ordnance Artificer in the forward gun turret, and before he joined the Navy he had been at the brickyards, and later at Brotherhood's. He celebrated his 21st birthday on 30th May.

Two other Peterborough men, Stoker Savage, and Engine Room Artificer Mitchelson were also serving on board the SUFFOLK at this time.

Seventh Raid

At 3.37 a.m. on the morning of Saturday 24th May, a single low flying aircraft dropped a number of incendiaries and eight high explosive bombs, some with delayed action fuses. The areas hit were Lincoln Road, Towler Street, St. Mark's Street, Park Road, Church Walk, Henry Street, Crawthorne Road, Granville Street and Broadway. In all, 100 houses were damaged and three demolished, six people were injured. Of those injured, only three - Miss Mary Booth, with shock and bruises, Mr. Arthur Venables, with lacerations, and Mr. Chandler, with a suspected fracture - were detained in hospital.

The incendiary bombs were effectively dealt with. One particularly good piece of work was done by a police constable by the name of Richardson, who removed a burning bomb from the top of a house and threw it onto the roadway.

The civil defence services and restoration squads got busy directly the incident was over. Two doctors gave attention to the casualties on the spot, administering an injection to a girl who was trapped for between two and three hours. A mobile canteen, provided and serviced by the WVS was found to be of great value.

After this raid there had been much comment in the city because the siren had not been sounded until after the raid was over.

Second Whitsun of the War

There were marked variations in the working hours of many city firms and establishments on this second Whitsun of the war. Out of six large industrial firms in the city, one carried on as normal over the holiday weekend, four closed on the Monday, and the other broke up from midday on the Saturday to the following Tuesday. The banks remained open on the Monday, but solicitor's offices were closed, so too were all the shops of members of the Chamber of Trade.

There were no special facilities for bus or rail travel for pleasure, and indeed, the public were asked to keep the railway lines clear for war traffic, and gardening was suggested by the Government as a pleasant alternative to a break by the sea or in the country.

The Town Cricket Club arranged home matches with an Air Force XI on the Saturday and with Ramsey on the Sunday. The Corporation tennis courts and bowling greens in the Park Road and Itter Parks, and the New England, New Fletton and West Town recreation grounds were all open from 2p.m. to an hour after sunset on the Sunday and all day on the Monday. From that Sunday until September the Corporation Swimming Pool was open from 7a.m. to 10:30p.m. It seems difficult to believe that there was even a war on.

Bird on a Switch

This book is dedicated to recording the events connected with Peterborough during World War Two. So it may come as a surprise when I now record the goings-on at St. Ives on Monday 26th May. I do this partly because it is just too good to leave out, and because it highlights the differences between the various counties in their approaches to the multitude of temporary wartime restrictions in force at the time.

When Mrs. Hilda Newton, principal of Slepe Hall School, was summoned for a black-out offence at St. Ives on the Monday in question, the theory was advanced that a starling flew into the room, settled on the light switch, and turned on the light. Miss Suzanne Purnell, giving evidence for the defence, said that one afternoon she (Mrs. Newton) found a downstairs light on and saw a bird in the room. When she heard about the upstairs light showing in the black-out she went to the room concerned and found on the floor an enormous amount of soot and a dead starling.

Inspector Hall asked: "Do you seriously suggest that a starling could switch on an electric light?"

Miss Purnell: "It could have done the one downstairs, and I think it could have done the one upstairs..."

Amazingly, the bench dismissed the case under the regulation whereby a person is not responsible if he or she is judged to have made adequate provision. Maybe Mrs. Newton got off because she was the Headmistress of Slepe Hall School, and the Chairman thought she would have too much to lose if she were found guilty, we will never know. However, it is certain that if she had appeared before the Peterborough magistrates, she would have been given short shrift for relying on the story that a bird had turned two lights on, on two different floors, and surely no one would have been in the least surprised.

Those Rations

It was a strange fact during the war that the city people just did not seem interested in applying for their ration books. Perhaps they thought that if they ignored it, it would go away, a dangerous attitude to take considering the difficulties in getting

134

food that would result in not having a new ration book. The last day for applications to be in for the new books was Saturday 24th May 1941, however, as with the first issue; the Food Officer had received hardly any applications. In 1941 each person was going to be issued with two ration books, which meant that 200,000 had to be prepared, an enormous task. The method of applying was simple, a page from the old book had to be filled in, torn out, and posted. This was obviously still too much trouble for most city people.

A bigger talking point in the city came a week later, when clothing, cloth and footwear rationing came into force on Sunday 1st June. The whole thing had been cloaked in secrecy by the Government in order to prevent bulk buying by people, 'stocking up' before its enforcement and it was generally well accepted as being a fair way to spread out the declining stocks. The main question was whether shop window displays should show the number of coupons required for each article shown? Some thought that it would help customers know before they went in to purchase, and save them and the assistant a lot of time. Others however, shopkeepers included, thought that it might act as a deterrent to sales.

The other 'hot' topic of debate concerning clothes, related to ladies stockings, a serious problem to the "poorer woman's budget." Cheap stockings, it was said, "do not pay for repairs", once they were badly laddered there was nothing that could be done about them, and many young women could not afford to buy good stockings.

"If the weather is warm," said the 'Standard', "this is likely to be a stockingless summer."

Comments throughout the city trade were generally as follows:

Mr. Harry Nobbs, President of the Board of Trade:

"It is essentially a good scheme…everyone will get his or her fixed ration. I hope this will do away with the quota system, because we have been getting nothing extra under the quota for the city's 10,000 evacuees."

Mr. T.S. James, Co-operative Society:

"The scheme appears to me to be simply to restrict spending. There is plenty of money about, and in our tailoring, boots and drapery departments we have been putting big figures on in the last few weeks. Now we shall revert from maximum sales to minimum."

Mr. H.J. Farrow, Draper, Broadway:

"There will be a more even distribution than has been the case for some time, and that is what we have been after…A point that appears to have been overlooked is that furnishers who deal in curtain materials must collect coupons, for such materials…are easily made up into summer dresses." (Black-out material was not couponed, so long as it was black, however, this did not stop people trying. One plea was, "I want black-out curtains, but I don't want them black, we have enough gloomy things about us as it is." But shopkeepers were not allowed to sell coloured black-out due to the fact that it could be made up into clothing. So could black, come to that!).

Mr. P.G. Thompson, of Messrs. E. Abington and Sons Ltd., tailors, Broadway:

"The scheme will stop people with plenty of money, who, noticing that stocks are getting a bit low, decide to lay in a couple of suits, an overcoat, a few shirts and some underclothes. They can still do that, but when they have spent their year's allowance of 66 coupons they will be no better off than the man who has to think carefully before he spends on clothes."

The other main opinion amongst men and women, was that women should have been given extra coupons, because they needed more clothes than men.

Hero Missing
On Friday 30th May, Mr. and Mrs. J.F. Gautrey, of 127, Cromwell Road, received the news that their younger son, Flight Lieutenant Reginald William Gautrey, aged 28, was missing as a result of air operations.

Flt. Lt. Gautrey was serving with the Ministry of Aircraft Production and had been ferrying Catalina flying boats from the Consolidated Aircraft Corporation at San Diego to Britain. Later he had been engaged on, what were called, "other important duties."

Born at St. Neots, his parents brought him to Peterborough when he was five years old, and he was educated at Deacon's School. He had spent five years in the City Treasurer's Department, and for the last year of that, had been in the RAF Volunteer Reserve. In February 1940 he was Mentioned in Dispatches for gallantry and devotion to duty in the execution of air operations.

In April 1941 Flt. Lt. Gautrey was instrumental in saving the lives of survivors of a torpedoed merchant ship. While still several hundred miles out in the Atlantic, when he was flying a Catalina to Britain, he sighted lifeboats and sent out a wireless call for assistance. A destroyer raced to the rescue and the occupants of nine lifeboats and a raft were picked up.

Later, Mr. and Mrs. Gautrey would be notified that their son had been killed in action on May 23rd 1941.

Stage and Screen
There was always something going on in the city, even when the gloom was at its darkest that could raise the spirits, at least for a few hours. There were always shows and films to be seen, and in the first week of June, 1941, the great Billy Cotton and his band were entertaining crowds at the Embassy. At the Empire, the Court Players were presenting "Anne, One Hundred Per Cent.", a comedy apparently, but one perhaps not destined to be remembered by many, (unless you had seen it, of course).

Movies on show throughout the city starred a host of famous names:
City Cinema: "Hullabaloo" Frank Morgan. "Queen of the Yukon" Irene Rich and Charles Bickford.
"Dr. Kildare Goes Home" Lew Ayres and Lionel Barrymore. "Drums of the Desert" Ralph Byrd and Lorna Grey.
Odeon: "Escape" Norma Shearer, Robert Taylor and Conrad Veidt.
Broadway Kinema: "Old Bill and Son" Morland Graham, John Mills. "Meet the Wildcat" Ralph Bellamy and Margaret Lindsay.
New England: "Three Faces West" John Wayne. "The Carson City Kid" Roy Rogers. "Girl From God's Country" Chester Morris, Jayne Wyatt and Charles Bickford.
Princess: "Third Finger Left Hand" Myna Loy and Melvyn Douglas. "Primrose Path" Ginger Rogers and Joel McCrea, and on Tuesday only, the Phorpres Dance Orchestra.

Emergency Plans for 6,000
Emergency feeding arrangements which were to come into operation in the event of a heavy air attack had been completed by the second week of June. Food had been put into storage ready, and charges for the meals had been set: Adults 6d. school

136

children under 10, 4d.

The City Treasurer had arranged for seven schools to be opened as emergency feeding centres immediately the need arose. Cooking apparatus had been installed and arrangements had been made for the storage of food by the Co-operative Society.

The scheme was based on the provision of meals for not less than 10 per cent of the population, i.e. 6,000 for the city and district. Meals would be served in two sittings at each centre, and it was thought that many meals would be sold for consumption off the premises. Experience in other parts of the country had shown that for the first few days following a severe aerial attack, the feeding centres were crowded, but by the end of the week, the numbers declined rapidly. There was however, a small number who required feeding for a lengthy period. It was therefore decided to equip three of the centres with cooking ranges, as distinct from boilers, so that they could be used as communal kitchens to deal with the residue.

The 10 per cent basis was thought to be sufficient to cover emergency feeding requirements, but to provide a reserve; a list was compiled of commercial catering establishments, works canteens and the Public Assistance Institution for cooked food in bulk for delivery to the feeding centres.

In addition there were the W.V.S. and other mobile canteens to supplement the service, the Army had also agreed to send field kitchens.

These feeding centres were for those who were in a position to pay for their meals, and the prices were sufficient to cover all expenses, whereas the Rest Centres were for the destitute and homeless. Arrangements had also been made for the supply of hard fuel for each centre, sheds and equipment had been erected for storage, so that no centre was entirely dependent on gas or electricity, which might be put out of action. There was also an additional water supply over that from the mains.

The following schools were designated as Emergency Feeding Centres:

Walton senior, capacity in one sitting, 500.

Fulbridge junior, 500.

Lincoln Road girls, 450.

Cromwell Road mixed and infants, 500.

Eastholm infants, 300.

West Town junior mixed, 500.

New Fletton, 250.

Of these, Fulbridge, Eastholm and New Fletton were more fully equipped to act as communal kitchens after emergency feeding had finished. For all the seven schools, the nearest Co-operative Society branch was utilised for the storage of the food supplies for that centre, alternatives were also noted.

The food stocks were laid down according to the Ministry's own scale, the totals being as follows, the amount being divided up between the centres, in accordance with the sitting capacity detailed earlier:

Biscuits, 80.4 cwt.; tea, 6 cwt.; margarine, 26.761 cwt.; soup, 4,800 tins; sugar, 6 cwt.; beef, hash or meat roll, 32.16 cwt.; tinned milk, 1,680 tins; baked beans, 53.39 cwt.; salt, 47.8lbs.; thickening for stews, 375lbs.; oatmeal, 13.37cwt.; dried vegetables, 10.022 cwt.; baked pease pudding, 33.48 cwt.

40 Year Olds Register

On Saturday 31st May, 737 city men born in 1901 registered for service at the

Employment Exchange, a few more names were later received by post. 55 asked for service with the Navy, 251 the Air Force, and 66 for civil defence. The others expressed no preference. There were 3 conscientious objectors.

Points of Order
A number of minor, but interesting points were raised at the local council meeting at the beginning of June, the following examples being a taste of the subjects regularly talked about at these sessions. The Town Clerk was instructed to investigate and report cases of extortionate rents which had been brought to his notice.

A medical practitioner was asked for an explanation as to why a child suffering from scarlet fever was exposed to other people without a clearance certificate having been issued. (No answer was recorded).

The books at the central and branch libraries, valued at £10,000, were to be insured against war damage risks.

Hints on water purification were to be sent to all households.

A pleasure launch was to be hired and adapted as a fire float.

Some allotment holders had refused to pay extra rent for water and were to be given notice to quit.

Mr. Godfrey, of Newborough, had sent the Mayor two bags of seed potatoes!

A mechanical excavator was to be obtained, if possible, to dig a trench grave, failing which, manual labour would be employed.

Salvage for April: Paper 44t. 19c. 1qr. Tin, 5t. Bottles, 29doz. Bones, 2t. 14c. 3qrs. Milk bottles, 600. Kitchen waste, 26t. 19c. 1qr. Ashes, (ex-tip), approx. 3,500 tons.

Residents in Ashcroft Gardens were informed that abolition of their cesspools could not be considered on financial grounds.

Surplus plants at the park were to be offered for sale.

Static water supply basins which were being excavated in various parts of the city would be protected; fences that were already in stock would be erected as the basins were completed.

Queues and Schools
Examination of the school attendance returns at this time showed that the average was at only 89 per cent. There had been little sickness over this period, and the main reason for the absences was that many children had had half days off for shopping, or to be more accurate, queueing.

Due to the many shortages that were now being experienced, long queues were tailing back from most stores where rationed items could be found, and parents were sending their children out to save their places in the queues instead of sending them to school.

Teachers, on the other hand, were finding themselves with much extra work, filling in the new ration books for the city before they could be distributed. The City Education Committee decided to grant the teachers a 'long weekend' before half term; particularly because they would be called on again the next time the new ration books came around.

Apart from being asked to submit estimates for additional school shelters, the City Engineer was now tasked to provide outside ladders at Fulbridge School and improvements, including lighting, heating, sanitary fittings etc. at all school shelters, at a cost of £3,167 which would be paid for by a government grant. The school shelters had all been built using cement mortar, and as such, the brickwork was in excellent condition.

Parts of Queen's Drive and Orchard Street schools were now to be adapted for use as gas decontamination centres for the public, although this did not affect their use for school purposes.

When the schools reopened for the new term at the beginning of June, all the children's gas masks were examined. Intervals for subsequent examinations were arranged according to the findings of the first one.

The vandals had been at work again, and the head teacher of Eastholm (infants) School and the Chief Constable reported the breaking of 38 rain water gully covers around the school buildings on Sunday, May 4th. "Certain action taken was approved", it was said, concerning the three boys attending the school who were found guilty.

Missing

The families of more local men now received the news that they were missing in action.

Corporal James Manley Cook, aged 24, Royal Tank Regiment, only son of Mr. and Mrs. R. Cook, of 20, Exeter Road, was reported missing while serving in the Middle East. Corporal Cook joined the Royal Tank Regiment seven years earlier, and back in 1940 had been in one of the tanks which had made a last gallant stand at Calais to enable the British troops to make a safe withdrawal. It will be remembered that Corporal Cook leapt onto his burning tank to recover a brassiere mascot he had tied to the aerial. His father was proprietor of the Happy Circle Library in Westgate. Later, on July 4th, the 'Standard' confirmed that Corporal Cook had become a prisoner of war.

Mr. and Mrs. E. Bunting also received news that their only son, Gunner James Verden Bunting was posted missing on April 28th. He had been in Greece for about seven months. Educated at Deacon's School, he was employed by the Co-operative Society's tailoring departments at New England and at Park Road. He was engaged to Miss M. Long, of Walton.

Three months later, Mrs. Bunting would receive the news that her son was confirmed as being a prisoner of war in Germany.

Corporal Frederick William Parkinson, steward at the City and Counties Club in the city, was now missing. He was serving in the R.A.S.C. and had been called to the Colours as a reservist shortly before war broke out. He had served in France and had lately been in the Near East.

A week after his wife had received this information she received another letter informing her that Corporal Parkinson had been taken prisoner.

Sapper Stanley Arthur Wray, R.E. only son of Mr. and Mrs. Wray, of 61, Alderman's Drive, was now reported as missing in Greece since April 28th. Educated at Deacon's School, he joined the forces in November 1939, and as an indication of how desperate things were, was drafted to France the following month. He was evacuated from Dunkirk, and on January 9th 1941, he sailed for the Middle East. Before the war he had been a clerk in the commercial department of the L.N.E.R.

On a happier note, Master-at-Arms Sydney Brooksbank, R.N., third son of Mrs. Brooksbank, of 34 Hereward Road, was awarded the D.S.M. in connection with the evacuation from Greece. He was a member of the crew of H.M.S. AJAX, famous for the part it played in the Graf Spee episode. Mr. Brooksbank's wife and daughter resided at 198, Lincoln Road.

Another successful escape was made by the seaman son of Mr. and Mrs. W. Rawlinson, of 44, Montagu Road, Walton, who heard on Friday 6th June, that Supply Assistant Kenneth Rawlinson had been safely evacuated from Crete. Kenneth, who was 20, had been educated at Deacon's School and had joined the Navy in April of 1940. He had sailed for Crete in the September to take up a position at a shore base.

Driver Ernest Plumb, of 118 Star Road, was not actually missing, although the printing on a letter to his wife from a prisoner of war camp gave little away, apart from the faintest of clues that he was somewhere in Italy. Driver Plumb had been with Watkins and Stafford before he had joined the Army.

Killed

Private Thomas William Binns, aged 28, a dispatch rider, of 9, Towler Street, died in a military hospital on Friday 13th June, from injuries received in a collision with a lorry. He was in the 5th (Hunts.) Battalion, of the Northamptonshire Regiment, and took part in the evacuation of Dunkirk. The second son of Mr. and Mrs. Horace Binns, he was in civil life an L.N.E.R. employee. He left a wife and two children. He had a military funeral which took place at St. Mark's on Friday 20th June.

Registrations

On Saturday 14th June, women born in 1918 registered for national duty. The city total (minus a few late entries) was 514. This compares with 575 in the 1919 list and 814 in that for 1920.

The reason for the great fall was uncertain at the time, it was thought that more from the 1918 category may have migrated away from the city, and more were probably in necessary employment. It was also thought that births had been fewer in the last years of the First World War compared to the two following it. As usual, there were no female conscientious objectors.

On Saturday 21st, men born in 1900 registered for military and industrial duty. Men born between January and June were for industry, and those born between July and December for military service. There was only one conscientious objector in the 338 of the latter group. Twenty expressed preference for the Navy, 100 for the R.A.F., and 113 for civil defence.

On Saturday 28th June, 532 women born in 1917 registered at Peterborough Employment Exchange for work of national importance.

A high percentage of those who signed in previous age groups were already on war work, and at this time, not a great number of the remainder had been called into industry. Numbers in the three groups already registered were: April 19th, 21's 816; May 3rd, 22's, 575; June 14th, 23's 514.

An announcement in the 'Standard' on Friday 13th, stating that the Town Clerk had been authorised to take proceedings against people who had failed to register for civil defence duties had a salutory effect. The following weekend there had been a sudden spurt of men who, for various reasons, had omitted to "sign on" for fire watching duties at business premises. There seemed no way of avoiding some kind of war service.

More Ration Books

A last minute rush during the middle of June, brought applications for ration book renewals practically to 100 per cent., and very few people in the city were now endangering their food supply by omitting to send in their cards.

On the evening of Monday 16th June, school teachers began the task of preparing 180,000 books for distribution. This was double the previous number, due to the separate issue of supplementary coupons.

The work went on steadily into the evening on every day that week, and was finished by the Saturday. The books were then distributed by the Post Office.

American Ambulance

The gift of an ambulance to the city of Peterborough, from the people of the town of Peterborough, New Hampshire, U.S.A. was accepted in a ceremony that was held in the Market Place on Thursday 26th June, 1941.

Mrs. Somerville-Smith, of the British-American Ambulance Corps, presented the ambulance to the Duchess of Gloucester, who received it on behalf of the city people. Behind the platform, which was flanked with palms and pot plants from the Park greenhouses, were the Union Jack and the Stars and Stripes, crossed. The national flags also flew on either side of the facade of the Old Town Hall.

The east and south sides of the square were formed of members of A.R.P. units and Women's Voluntary Services. On the north were some 400 members of the 1st (Peterborough City) Battalion, Home Guard, under Lieutenant-Colonel R.J.C. Crowden, M.C. the Commanding Officer. The ambulance was located in front of the Gates Memorial Fountain.

After the Home Guard was inspected, the presentation was made, and Mrs. Somerville-Smith spoke:

"Your Royal Highness, your Worship, my Lords, ladies and gentlemen, and children of Peterborough. I include the children because the future of this world will depend on the children of Great Britain and America. If they do not grow up understanding and liking each other, then there is no hope for them nor for anyone else on this earth..."

Mrs. Somerville-Smith must have been a remarkable woman, and it is worth repeating some more of her words that show great humour, compassion and dedication:

"I come from the south where we are all of British blood, with the exception of the French families of South Carolina and Louisiana. I became what they call in America 'British-minded' at the age of 12. At that time one of my older sisters returned from school in the North filled with the idea that the one way of forwarding a social career was to become a member of a society called "The Daughters of the American Revolution." Now, most of my life had been spent on a cotton plantation 18 miles from the nearest railway, surrounded on three sides by swamps. There was nothing in the swamps but mud, snakes and mosquitoes, so there did not seem to be very much scope for a social career.

However, we began investigations into family records at once. There was an aunt staying with us at the time, and we plied her with questions until she asked what we were trying to do. We announced that we were joining the 'Daughters of the American Revolution'.

'Have you told them?'

'No but...'

'Then I shouldn't bother. They won't have anything to do with you'.

'But why? We have been here since colonial times, and five of our men fought in the revolutionary war.'

'You are quite right, so far, but, if you will look into the matter a little further, you will discover that your men did not fight *against* the British but *for* them'.

"That blighted my social career, but gave me another vocation. I promptly became the champion of Great Britain in America. Great events have a way of passing unnoticed, and neither the British Empire nor the United States seemed aware of my decision, but I maintain that this ambulance is the direct result of that decision.

I have lived in this country twenty-four years, ten months and twenty-four days. I do not claim that I always understand British mentality, but I have absorbed something of your atmosphere. By the time the war started I felt certain of two things. One, that Americans would give anything you needed if concise lists were sent to them quickly. Two, that you would never send concise lists quickly. I talked this over with various Americans in England, and they all agreed with me."

By June 1940, after seeing the lack of ambulances and hospital supplies, Mrs. Somerville-Smith went to America to tell them to send all they could quickly. She travelled approximately three thousand miles across America, trying to raise ambulances and supplies, finally meeting Mr. William V.C. Ruxton, in New York, head of the British American Ambulance Corps. Together they made it possible for towns in America to send money to purchase ambulances for towns in Britain. No one can doubt Mrs. Somerville-Smith's commitment to this country, and I am proud to commemorate her name within these humble pages.

More Casualties

The news of casualties was now becoming more frequent, with injuries and deaths being reported as well as the fate of men who had been taken prisoners of war. There were still the missing of course, but sometimes there was a happy ending. The lottery of war was constantly taking its toll, and would continue to do so.

Pilot Officer Ronald Orton, of The Gables, Vere Road, was now lying in a Royal Air Force hospital, severely injured while on active service. Aged 19, he was the son of Mr. and Mrs. L.H. Orton, who were called to his bedside along with his sister, Mrs. Gittins. P.O. Orton was educated at Deacon's School and joined the staff of A.E. Craig and Co. Ltd. He played cricket for Old Deaconians and occasionally for the Town, and football for the Auctioneers. He was accepted for a commission course in 1940. His sister's first husband, Flying Officer Blom, had already been killed on active service.

Only a few days would pass before she would lose her brother, as P.O. Orton finally succumbed to his injuries on Thursday 26th June.

Another man killed in action, this time on June 15th, was Private Albert Berrisford, aged 27, of the Sherwood Foresters. Killed by enemy action in the Middle East, Private Berrisford was the son of Mr. and Mrs. E. Berrisford, of 13, Windmill Street. He was previously in the London Brick Company's yards at Whittlesey and Fletton.

Sergeant Charles William Hancock, R.A.F. V.R., aged 25, of St. Margaret's Road, Fletton, was one of two more men who were missing at the beginning of July. He was reported missing after an operational flight over Germany on the night of June 25th-26th.

Sergeant Hancock was the eldest son of Mr. and Mrs. J.W. Hancock of Whittlesey. His wife, (formerly Miss Ivy Blessitt) received official notification that her husband was missing, and another letter shortly afterwards from his Wing Commander, extending the deepest sympathy of officers, N.C.O.'s and men of the station. Sgt. Hancock joined the R.A.F. just before Christmas 1939, and was a wireless operator and air gunner.

The other missing man was Driver Frank E. Doughty, R.A.S.C., son of Mr. and Mrs. Doughty, of Queen's Walk. He had been posted as missing in the Middle East since April 28th. Driver Doughty was called up in February 1940, and had previously been with the Co-operative Society. He was also a member of the Athletic Club.

Beer Shortage
A shortage of beer in the city had become acute by the middle of July. So much so that nearly all the licensed houses had drastically cut their opening hours, and several had been forced to close for as long as four consecutive days. After consultation with the Chief Constable on Tuesday 8th July, the Licensed Victuallers' Association fixed new opening hours as follows:

Weekdays: 11:30 a.m. to 1:30 p.m.; 8:30 p.m. to 10:30 p.m.

Sundays: 12 noon to 1:30 p.m.; 8 to 10 p.m.

These hours were applied to all houses for two weeks, after which they were reviewed. Apart from trying to conserve supplies for the residents of the city, it was also hoped that the new hours would stop people from going from pub to pub and creating large crowds.

All beer to licensed houses had been rationed by the brewers at the beginning of the month. Production at most breweries however, was well up in comparison with pre-war days, but consumption had greatly increased. One suggestion from brewers to their landlords was to supply strangers with a half pint and regular customers with a full pint, but it was thought that this would be too difficult to work.

Mineral waters were also extremely scarce owing to the sugar rationing, and people who preferred to drink Shandy were drinking beer instead, thus adding to the shortage of beer. The sale of other items in pubs such as tea, cheese, etc. was also impossible owing to rationing.

Shelter Review
On Wednesday 16th July, the City Engineer reported to the A.R.P. Committee on a Ministry of Home Security circular setting out a revised shelter programme.

The circular called for a review of the shelter accommodation at that time, with a view to the strengthening of existing shelters to cope with the mines being dropped by parachute, and the provision of dormitory shelters at points away from probable targets.

In assessing the requirements so far as dormitory shelters were concerned, consideration was only to be given to regular shelterers, which the Ministry said was between twelve and a half to twenty five per cent of the population. The suggested method of finding the number and identity of the regular shelterers was to advertise in the local press. The usual procedure for dormitory shelters was to issue passes to people entitled to use them and to provide shelter marshals. This would probably mean that some people wishing to take shelter would be turned away if they could not produce a pass.

Railway Accident
A non military casualty was sustained on Thursday 17th July, when railway fireman, George William Potkins, aged 43, of Evaine, Rock Road, Peterborough, suffered fatal injuries.

143

Potkins went on duty at 8 a.m. to work a train of empties to Doncaster. Past Marholm crossing the black-out curtain round the cab came adrift, and Potkins climbed on to the tender to retrieve it. As he was doing so his head was struck on the footbridge at Woodcroft crossing, and he was killed. The driver stopped the train at Helpston, and the body was removed.

Potkins was the son of Mrs. Potkins of 137, Belsize Avenue, and was married, with two sons - James, an apprentice at Westwood Works, and Anthony, a Deacon's schoolboy.

Registrations

On Saturday 12th July, 263 young men born between January 1st and June 30[th,] 1922 registered at Peterborough for military service. Sixty-four expressed preference for the Navy and 106 for the RAF. There were no conscientious objectors.

On Thursday 17th July there was military action taking place in the city itself. The City Battalion Home Guard carried out a tactical exercise in full view of the public. The idea was that an attack on the city had driven in the defenders of the perimeter, who had fallen back to protect certain points of special importance and vulnerability.

The attackers were Headquarters and 'D' Companies and one platoon of 'B' company, with 'A' 'C' and the rest of 'B' defending. Umpires followed the 'battle' and prepared reports. The attack lasted from 8 to 10 p.m. and the attackers and defenders were distinguished by the wearing of steel helmets and field service caps respectively.

Savings Targets Set

By the middle of July Savings Groups in the City and Soke area had chosen their targets for the summer campaign of ten weeks' duration. The targets ranged from heavy ambulances to machine gun bullets.

At a meeting at the Town Hall, the chairman said that people in Peterborough were earning good money, but they had to save a great deal more. The City Treasurer said the object of the meeting was to get savers to double their contributions. They had been set a target for the year of two million pounds, and at the end of June they had only got half a million. They now required £50,000 a week.

The 500 groups in the area averaged 50 members, a total membership of 25,000 out of a population of 70,000. Taking into consideration children and others, it was thought that they should have had a membership of 50,000.

There were four separate classes of groups:
1. Street groups.
2. School groups.
3. Factory, office and shop groups.
4. Social groups.

The Mayor appealed to the groups to make their tasks higher by saving more. At this time only 102 local groups out of a total of 498 had notified the Local Association Secretary of the target chosen for their summer savings drive, but by the following week most had forwarded the information as follows, bringing a total value to £17,650:

	£
1 25-pounder Field Gun	3,000
1 Bofors Gun	3,000

1 Heavy Ambulance	600
1 Nest of Sub-Machine Guns	400
1 Heavy Machine Gun	350
3 Light Ambulances	900
30 Machine guns	3,000
20 Bren Guns	1,000
4 Large Armour Piercing Bombs	400
5 Anti-Tank Rifles	225
1 Large General Purpose Bomb	45
15 Parachutes	600
5 Rubber Dinghies	175
21 Tommy Guns	630
7 Mortars	175
5 Rifles	35
10,000 Rounds S.A. Ammunition	55
34 Pistols	136
10 Field Gun Shells	30
62 Stretchers	93
16 Trench Mortar Bombs	20
10 Small Bombs	10
750 Hand Grenades	150
8 Soldiers' Equipment	56
18 Heavy Anti-Aircraft Shells	72
1 Anti-Aircraft Gun	2,500

By the beginning of August, enough information had been gathered to show the targets chosen in greater detail:

Baker Perkins Ltd: 1 25-pdr gun (£3,000), and 1 Bofors gun.

Kings School, Eastfield Road No.3, and Werrington: Heavy Ambulance (£600 each).

Fairways, Regent Buildings: Nest of machine guns (£400).

Newborough Village: A.A. Gun (£3,000).

Maxey Village: Heavy machine gun (£350).

"Valentine" 72, Westgate: 3 large armour piercing bombs (£100 each).

L.N.E.R. Loco running department, staff group: One large armour piercing bomb and a Bren gun (£100-£50).

Cleeve, Westwood Park Road: Large general purpose bomb (£45).

Patent Safety Ladder Co: Anti-tank rifle and rubber dinghy (£45-£35).

Fulbridge Junior School, Walton Junior Mixed School, and R. and W.H. Symington: Light ambulance each (£300 each ambulance).

L.N.E.R. loco running department, employees' group: 12 machine guns.

Minster Precincts: 2 machine guns.

Town Hall: 2 machine guns.

Grimshaw Road, Soke County Council, Peterborough 1st District Inspector of Taxes, F.W. Woolworth and Co., Vere Road Nos. 1 and 2, Princes Gate, Eastholm Senior Girls School, Norfolk Street: One machine gun each (£100 each gun).

Mountsteven Avenue No.1: 2 Bren guns.

Elmfield Road: 2 Bren guns.

Granville Street and Henry Street, Broadway No.1, Co-operative Society check office, Gilpin Street, Peterborough Food Office, Mayor's Walk, Charles Street, New

Road, Woodston: one Bren gun each. (£50 each gun).

Barnack School: 2 parachutes.

Montagu Road, Walton First Aid Post, Deacon's School, Springfield Road, St. Marks Junior Girls, Queen's Drive School, Fulbridge Infants, London Road No.1, Woodcroft: One parachute each (£40 each parachute).

Longthorpe Village: 10 Tommy guns.

Fletton Avenue: 2 Tommy guns.

W.V.S. Office, Rotary Inner Wheel, Thorpe Road No.2, Woodfield Road, Glebe Road, Holdich Street, Alexandra Road, English Brothers, T.L. Barrett Ltd., Alderman's Drive No.1, Queen's Walk, Star Road No.1: One Tommy gun each (£30 each gun).

L.N.E.R. Accountant's Office: 2 Anti-tank rifles.

Bamber Street, Vergette Street: One Anti-tank rifle each (£45 each rifle).

Sturton and Sons Ltd: One Bren gun and four pistols (£50-£4 each pistol).

W.M.S.A. Huntley Grove: Rubber dinghy and mortar (£35-£25).

Harris Street Women's Meeting: Parachute and rubber dinghy (£40-£35).

Newark School: Rubber dinghy: (£40).

National Deposit Friendly Society: one Bren gun and one Tommy gun (£50-£30).

Helpston Village: One machine gun and one parachute (£100-£40).

Warbon Avenue, The Mayor's Working Party: One mortar each.

Fengate No.1: Two mortars (£25 each mortar).

Casualties and Survivors

Mrs. Rose, of 57, St. Martin's Street, received the news in mid July, that her husband, Petty Officer Alfred John Rose, was one of the survivors when the Royal Navy Sloop, HMS AUCKLAND was sunk by aircraft bombs off Tobruk, Libya, on 24th June.

Petty Officer Rose had been in the Navy since he was sixteen, and he had been on HMS AUCKLAND since her pre-commissioned days when he supervised the erection of the detection gear when the ship was on the stocks. He was aboard when the AUCKLAND assisted in the evacuation of British troops from Norway.

Before her marriage, Mrs. Rose, formerly Miss Henson, was an assistant at Mr. F.J. Howe's stationery shop in Dogsthorpe Road.

Less happily, Mr. and Mrs. T. Davies, of 125, Fletton Avenue, received confirmation that their son, Acting Leading Seaman Anthony J. Davies, who had been reported missing in April, had in fact been killed in action.

Gunner Davies, who had been in the Navy for six years, had been educated at Fletton Secondary School, and had been a member of the Cathedral voluntary choir. He was killed on the 6th April.

Mr. Norman Clithero of Newark received the information from the War Office on Monday 21st July that Cpl. George Clithero, Lincolnshire Regiment, had been wounded in the Middle East on April 9th. Corporal Clithero had been educated at St. Mark's School, and had been in the withdrawal from Dunkirk.

Another city man who had now been taken prisoner was Driver Frank Doughty, Royal Army Service Corps, of 23, Queen's Walk, Fletton. Driver Doughty, eldest son of Mr. and Mrs. F.C. Doughty, and formerly in the Co-operative Society's Park Road butchery branch, was a prisoner of war in Germany.

Mr. and Mrs. R. Jinks, of 286, Walpole Street, finally ended a long vigil at the end of July when they received the news from the War Office that their youngest son, Trooper Robert Leslie Jinks, had been killed on the LANCASTRIA, when it was sunk by aircraft bombs off, St. Nazaire, France, almost exactly a year earlier on 17th July 1940. At the time they were told only that he was missing. This information turned out to be wrong, as Trooper Jinks had been killed when a troop train he was travelling on was bombed by German aircraft. The train was on its way to the coast to embark the troops on the Lancastria and this is where the mistake was made.

Trooper Jinks had been on the clerical staff of Westwood Works before he was called up. A member of the Works Sports Club, he had been a keen tennis player.

Driver George Drake, R.A.S.C. was reported missing in the Middle East on July 2nd. He was the elder son of Mr. George Drake, 170, Dogsthorpe Road, and the late Mrs. Drake. His brother Robert, of the Queen's Hussars, was already a prisoner of war in Germany.

In August, Private Joseph William Davis, Royal Tank Corps, of New Road, Peterborough, was reported as missing. He was later reported as being killed in action on 10th June 1941.

Kind Offer

An interesting snippet of well meaning information which was printed in the 'Advertiser' on Friday 25th July must have raised a few eyebrows, albeit for the wrong reasons, it went as follows:

"TO SERVICE MEN - Members of the Forces home on leave are invited to call at Mrs. E. Godfrey's house, "The Walnuts." A pleasant surprise awaits them there."

Queues

Efforts to abolish the long queues that were building up in the city were officially being regarded as meeting with more success by the 1st of August. One pork butcher had eased his problems by spreading his supplies evenly over his several branches, in this way he prevented the rush to his shop in town. There was still some congestion though, caused by some tradesmen selling at a fixed time on Wednesdays, Fridays and Saturdays.

At the end of July police officers could be found photographing queues and going down the lines taking names.

More rationing was regarded in some quarters as the only logical solution to the queue problem, but this presupposed a constant flow of supplies, and this could not be guaranteed with seasonal goods like tomatoes.

It was suggested that greater co-operation between retailer and customer would ease the problem. If the customers were convinced that the shopkeeper was going to share out his wares fairly, there would be fewer tendencies to rush into a queue the moment supplies arrived. One imagines that the sense of this argument would not convince most people as many were convinced that all shopkeepers had their favourites.

Thorpe Hall

Thorpe Hall, formerly the home of the Strong family, and later the residence of Mr. E.J. Meaker, was opened as an annexe of Peterborough Memorial Hospital on Friday 25th August.

Twenty-two patients - male and female medical and surgical cases - were transferred there from the Midland Road hospital by Corporation ambulances and that recently presented by the citizens of Peterborough, New Hampshire, USA. Voluntary stretcher bearers were on duty at the hospital and at the Hall, and the transfer was completed in just under two hours.

The adaptation of the Hall for use as a hospital had been in hand since the previous January. The big room to the left of the main entrance - the dining room in the days of the Strong family and the ballroom during the occupation of Mr. Meaker - was the female ward, and the smaller room in the same wing was the male ward. To the right were the domestic offices, a rest room and a dining room.

Only the ground floor was used at first, but eventually there would be accommodation for 100 patients.

Cinema Incident

As well as the usual black-out offences and petty thefts, the magistrate's courts dealt with a great assortment of crimes at the time, of which the following is one of the more interesting.

Arthur Isaac Israel Woolf, of 12, Council Houses, Fengate, was summoned for assaulting Mrs. Inez Kedgley, of Fengate, on July 18th. He pleaded not guilty.

Mrs. Kedgley said that on that date she had gone to the cinema, and Woolf sat next to her, on her right. She noticed his hand getting near her dress and she moved a little. He edged further down in his seat, and touched her leg above the knee. She said nothing to him, but slapped his face and knocked his glasses off. He said, "I'm sorry" and went away. She had no doubt that Woolf had been the man, or that his action had been deliberate.

Lilian Kate Harper, of 5, Council Houses, Fengate, said Mrs. Kedgley sat in front of her and Woolf came from the front to sit beside her. She saw nothing happen until Mrs. Kedgley slapped the man's face. P.C. Stone said Woolf had told him Mrs. Kedgley had made a mistake.

Woolf said that he had come to England in 1939, after two months in a German concentration camp. He fought in France and came back from Dunkirk. Then he was discharged from the Army because he had diabetes, and he came to Peterborough, where his mother-in-law lived. On July 18th, at the pictures, he rubbed his legs because they were causing pain. Someone smacked his face, and he left after apologising. He did not want to cause trouble, because he was a married man with a family. He was convinced that the lady had mistaken his intention. If he did touch her he did not realise it, because his privations in the concentration camp had caused him to lose the sense of feeling. He had been a professional musician, and because of that loss of feeling he could no longer play. The magistrate was unmoved and Woolf was fined £2, with 5s. costs.

Shelter Death

On July 31st, Walter Richmond, aged 67, a retired engineering turner, living at 43, Granville Street, with his nephew, George Robert Knighton, was sitting in a partly demolished air raid shelter in Lincoln Road, New England, cleaning bricks, when the roof collapsed on top of him breaking his neck and killing him.

The shelters had been built with defective mortar and were being taken down before rebuilding. Mr. Richmond had been cleaning the mortar off the bricks so that they could be reused. After the debris had been cleared, his body was found in a doubled-up position, with his knees bent towards his chin, and his head on his chest. He had been killed instantly.

More Group Targets

The National Savings Committee had asked the local W.V.S. in March to undertake the organisation of street groups in the city. By August, 254 streets out of a possible 276 had been visited by the ladies of the W.V.S. Some of the longer streets had more than one group, and some of the smaller ones made up one group. Altogether there were now 175 street groups in operation with a total membership of 3,645.

Savings Group targets were increasing rapidly by the middle of August. Mayor's Walk First Aid Post had purchased nine heavy anti-aircraft shells in July, and were now fixing a more difficult target for September. Midland Road was going for 12 trench mortar bombs instead of one, and Alexandra Road for two Tommy guns instead of one.

The following were additional targets:

Fulbridge Road, No.2: Machine gun and 2,000 rounds of ammunition.

Farrow's, Long Causeway: 2 Tommy guns.

Charles Street, who aimed at £50, now had over £100 and was trying or £150.

Longthorpe aimed for £200 but now hoped to raise £850.

L.N.E.R. Running Department Staff aimed at £150 during the twelve weeks ending October 10th had exceeded their target in four weeks.

On Tuesday 26th the Local National Savings Committee decided that they would hold a Warship Week from Thursday 27th November to Saturday 6th December. The Committee was aiming to raise £2,000,000 by the end of 1941, and to date they had raised £704,783. They hoped that the Warship Week would put the grand total well on its way to the two million mark.

It was proposed that the achievement of the area objective would be commemorated by a replica of the ship's badge, to be presented to the Admiralty for permanent exhibition in the Town Hall. In addition it was hoped that a plaque would be placed on the quarterdeck of the ship to commemorate the occasion. The Admiralty had already made it clear that for many reasons it was impossible to consider the actual naming of ships in connection with Warship Weeks.

Home Guard Operations

Some of the inhabitants of Stanground had been amazed to learn that their streets had been invaded by German parachute troops during the morning of Sunday 10th August.

The invaders were engaged by 'C' Company of the 1st Hunts. Battalion, Home Guard, under the command of Major G.R. Rumsey. This company was also busy at the same time repelling further invaders attacking Fletton from the south and severe fighting was taking place in the neighbourhood of the Phorpres Sports Club.

In these circumstances the commander of 'C' Company called for assistance from 'A' Company of the same battalion, which also operated in the Fletton district. Dispatch riders on motorcycles dashed through the Fletton streets, and within a very few minutes three heavily armed reserve sections were moving up in support. Soon the flags of 'A' Company's signal section reported the arrival of a reserve section at Stanground Church, and the reinforced 'C' Company then put the invaders to flight. It was understood that there were heavy casualties, but only of a notional character.

All posts in the district had been manned, and motorists who had left their identity cards at home found themselves in difficulties. Buses travelling along the Oundle Road were brought to a standstill by Home Guards with fixed bayonets, who, covered by the rifles of their concealed comrades, satisfied themselves that no fifth columnists were among the passengers before the vehicles were allowed to proceed.

Further exercises involving the manning of road blocks were planned, and the public were asked to co-operate with the Home Guard by always having their identity cards available for inspection. At the end of this exercise, a "reliable source" let it be known that a well known local works would be attacked by a hostile unit on the following Sunday morning, (17th), and travellers along the Oundle Road should not be surprised at what they saw or heard.

Sure enough, on the day in question 'A' Company of the 1st Battalion Home Guard were involved in a large exercise during the morning when 'a well known industrial establishment' was attacked by No.4 platoon under Lieutenant S.E. Rogers, No.2 platoon under Second Lieutenant Cooper and No.1 platoon under Sergeant A. Dodds.

The works in question was defended by No.3 platoon, assisted by the battalion assault section; the whole of the defence operations being under the command of P.S.M. Smith. The company signal section was on duty and busily engaged in sending messages to the umpires.

The perimeter of the works bristled with concealed machine gun and rifle posts, whilst snipers hidden in outlying trees took a heavy toll of the advancing "enemy" and bombers lay in wait for the unwary.

At different points the umpires had considerable difficulty in deciding who was dead and who was alive, so keen and close were some of the encounters.

Pedestrians passing along nearby roads were startled from time to time when the rattle of rifle fire broke unexpectedly on their ears. From time to time men could be seen rushing forward, tin helmets festooned with grass and branches.

The exercise lasted from 8:30 a.m. to 1 p.m. and was hailed as a great success. The prospect of week-end camps near Fletton with other companies was raised and preparations started.

Milk is Rationed
Saturday 23rd August was the last day for people to register for milk rationing. The main features of the new government scheme were:
Each child: One pint per day.
Expectant mothers: One pint per day.
Persons under 18: Half a pint per day.

Permanent residents in hotels and children in boarding schools before October 1st were not to register. Everyone else who held a ration book had to register. The rationed milk supply was expected to come into operation on October 1st.

The Co-operative Society's dairy on Midland Road was the largest local distributor, with sales of 779,000 gallons over the previous six months. Mr. J. Turner, the dairy manager was pleased that rationing was finally being brought in, as his milkmen had often had to bear the brunt of public disapproval.

Complaints such as "Why have Mrs. Brown and Mrs. Smith been given two pints and me only one?" were the kind of questions continually being asked. And, as he put it, while some roundsmen could "keep the peace", others were not so psychologically gifted for appeasement.

Water Danger
The actions of Mr. F. Jeffrey, of 50, Alderman's Drive, saved the life of a five-year-

old boy, who fell into the street's static reservoir on the evening of Monday 25th August.

The boy, Brian Musson, only son of Mr. and Mrs. H. Musson, of 51, Percival Street, was playing with friends at the side of the reservoir, (which was used to store water for fire fighting), at about 8 o'clock when he tried to retrieve a whip which had fallen into the water. The sides were steep and smooth and the boy slid down the bank. Mr. Jeffrey was just coming out of his house, which was opposite, and saw two or three boys near the edge of the water, he told them to get away.

One of the boys told him a boy was in the water. Mr. Jeffrey slipped off his jacket and dived in about eight feet of water to get to the boy. Then he had to shout for assistance to get out. A number of residents formed a chain which enabled Mr. Jeffrey and the boy to be pulled out. The boy was taken home, violently sick.

Mr. Jeffrey, who lost his spectacles during the rescue, received a glass of brandy and a glass of whiskey from neighbours for his efforts.

The Second Anniversary
The second anniversary of the outbreak of the war had now been reached, and it is interesting to recall how the city first faced up to the crisis.

The Town Hall and the hospital were the first public buildings to be completely blacked out. Seventy-five per cent of householders had laid in a stock of black-out materials, and this had caused such a shortage that these materials, along with drawing pins and candles, became the first "short" commodities of the war.

The hospital had been warned to be ready at a moments notice to evacuate patients who could be moved to their homes, in readiness for an influx of air raid casualties.

Civil defence measures, which had been in hand for some time were given their finishing touches, or were speeded up. Protective measures included the filling of 250,000 sandbags, of which 10,000 were sent to the hospital.

Plans were in hand to construct sixty-five air raid shelters, each to hold fifty people, in Burghley Square gardens, Bishop's Road car park, Fletton, New England and Stanley recreation grounds, Trinity Street and Hill's Yard. At this stage only 27 had been completed, and the digging of deep trenches was ordered.

The Report and Control Centre was manned day and night by a skeleton staff, warden's posts were fitted up with all requirements, with a staff on immediate call. Lawn House, Dogsthorpe, Walton House, and the Savoy Cinema were equipped as centres for decontamination, rescue and repair squads.

Premises at Hall's Works, London Road, Read's Garage, Lincoln Road, and Walton, were earmarked as A.F.S. substations, and all was made ready at the first-aid stations at Trinity Street schoolroom, Mayor's Walk Mission Hall, St. Martin's Street schoolroom, Keeton Road, and Mountsteven Avenue.

A big drive was launched to fill the gaps in the defence services. The W.V.S. appealed for 200 auxiliary nurses and as many women car drivers as could be found; the A.F.S. membership had to be increased from 300 to 500; and 150 men were wanted for rescue and demolition gangs.

Veterans from the First World War - men aged between 45 and 55 - responded well to the call for National Defence Companies, and Mrs. S.G. Cook had a fair influx for the Women's Land Army.

The 5th (Hunts) Battalion, the Northamptonshire Regiment, returning from camp, went into barracks at St. Peter's College, and the 306 Howitzer Battery Territorials were also called up.

Exactly two years before, the first evacuees arrived in the city. They came by special train from Tottenham, Islington and Crouch End for distribution to Fletton urban area and the Barnack district of the Soke. The following day's contingent, children in the morning and mothers and children in the afternoon, came principally from Stoke Newington, and went to the Norman Cross villages, parts of the Soke, and the Walton end of the city.

The last trainload of the first batch of official evacuees arrived at 11 a.m. on Sunday, September 3rd, the very hour that a state of war between Great Britain and Germany was declared.

City Air Crash

At 9 o'clock on the morning of Wednesday 17th September, an RAF aircraft crashed into the roof of 83, Willesden Avenue, in the city and penetrated through to the kitchen.

There had been three people in the house at the time - the tenant, Mr. Edward Goodson, and two daughters - Edna, aged 17, and Sheila, aged 15. Mr. Goodson had just got out of his downstairs bath when the crash occurred. The plane, a training aircraft, had been seen high up when it suddenly dropped out of the sky, the two airmen managed to bail out and make safe landings.

Mr. Goodson was employed at Baker Perkins; his wife had died six years earlier leaving him with six children to look after. The previous November he had been bombed out of another house in the city, on that occasion the whole family had been trapped upstairs and had to escape by climbing down a number of knotted bed sheets.

On this second occasion Mr. Goodson stated: "The blast knocked me back against the bath, causing a slight bruise across my back. The room was filled with thick dust and escaping fumes, and I could hardly breathe. I made my way to the scullery window and made my escape that way. My daughter Edna, who keeps house for me, was upstairs making the bed, and Sheila was in the front room collecting her books ready to go to a commercial school. Edna managed to climb out of the front bedroom window."

Mr. G.D. Ireland, of 76, Willesden Avenue, who was working in a surface shelter, saw the plane hit the house, and ran to give assistance, helping Edna out of the bedroom window. A member of the fire brigade for 17 years, he promptly went to the gas main and turned it off.

Mr. F. Biggin, a school attendance officer, had a narrow escape. He was riding his bicycle in a lane when an aeroplane wheel fell in the road just in front of him, he managed to steer clear.

A cycling errand boy who was passing Mr. Goodson's house swerved to the other side of the road.

Although no other property was damaged, No.83, being at the end of a row of eight, half of Mr. Goodson's roof had been ripped off, and the fuselage of the plane was lodged in the back bedroom and kitchen, which were completely wrecked.

Many people saw the two pilots gliding to earth in their parachutes. One landed on the roof of a wagon works and cut his eye; the other had a more comfortable landing in an allotment.

Mr. Goodson, who had fought in the previous war and was a member of the A.R.P. at Baker Perkins, was looked after, along with his children, by his friendly neighbours.

Another Home Guard Battle

The main feature of the third week-end camp held by the Hunts Home Guard near Peterborough was an exercise in which 500 men were engaged for the whole of the morning of Sunday 14th September.

Units of the Regular Army on foot and in lorries supported by detachments from the Soke of Peterborough Battalion Home Guard, formed a main attacking force designed to represent parties of German parachutists while the defenders (commanded by Major W.T. Cook), were drawn from the battalion in camp. The object was to test the speed with which the defending Home Guard could discover and destroy the "enemy" forces.

Attacks were made on a front nearly eight miles in length. About 5 per cent of the invaders succeeded in reaching their main objective, (Orton Hall), but were eliminated by a promptly organised counter-attack.

One lorry load of the "enemy" approaching from the east down the Oundle Road were caught at a road check; they were destroyed by rifle and machine gun fire and the lorry captured and driven in triumph to battalion headquarters. Another detachment attacking from the west in a lorry succeeded in surprising the sentries who stopped it by concealing one man under the back axle, and another man (the smallest in the unit), under the bonnet itself!

The men threw themselves into the whole operation; many of the attacking force had blackened their faces and wore camouflaged headgear.

The signal sections were in operation flashing messages to H.Q. which dispatch riders then rushed to the H.Q. of the defending battalion. The rattle of blank rifle fire and the use of dummy bombs all added to the realism of the exercise. One attacker had to be prevented from using a real cylinder of tear gas in order to reach his objective.

New Target for Warship Week

The city's aim in Warship Week, which was due to commence at the end of the year, was changed to a submarine, costing £425,000.

There were now 574 savings groups, 183 of which were street groups; 24 new groups had been started up during that September; a year before, there had only been 330 groups in the city. The amount saved up to this point was £782,362, an increase of £154,736 on the figure of the same time the previous year (1940).

At the last meeting of the City Local Savings Committee it had been proposed to buy a destroyer in Warship Week, at a cost of £450,000, but the cost had now risen to £700,000. A submarine could be bought for £425,000. If the city raised the money a ship could be given the name "Peterborough" and the Admiralty would present to the city a commemorative plaque.

Mr. W.D. Larrett said that King's School would be prepared to give a show on similar lines to that during War Weapons Week.

Mr. Grimwade suggested that the price of various components of a submarine be ascertained and that groups should have competitions in raising the required amounts.

Mr. Bailey suggested that the price of the Davis escape apparatus should be discovered. This would make a useful target for all the schools.

The meeting decided that the Warship Week aim should be £425,000, to purchase a submarine, a decision which would later come back to haunt the city people.

Shopgirls Withdrawn
It was now announced that all women between the ages of 20 and 25 working in the retail trade, other than food, were to be called-up for recruitment to women's auxiliary services or other vital war work.

This instruction was to cause serious inconvenience to local traders as they would lose their trained staff and would have to rely on younger, inexperienced girls. Trade was already slowing down because people were using up their coupons. Many a husband found that when he wanted a garment, his wife had used his coupons as well as her own. A lot of shop girls had already gone into munitions works in order to avoid being sent out of town, with the new 20-25 category disappearing, shops would be extremely short staffed.

The argument was made that girls should be taken from the railway offices, the Post Office, the Town Hall and government offices; it was not fair that the retail trade had to bear the whole brunt while others went clear. The government, however, had spoken.

Large stores, such as Marks and Spencer and Woolworths, lost 50-55 per cent of their staff, some departments, even establishments, had to close down. However, Mr. Compton, Drapery Manager at the Co-operative Society, put the whole thing into context when he said: "If it is essential, the girls must go, for winning the war is the most important job before us. If we don't win the war it will be no use opening at all!"

Labour Shortage
The shortage of labour on farms was again the predominant topic of conversation at the meeting of the Executive Committee of the Peterborough County Branch of the NFU on Saturday 4th.

Too much delay was being experienced securing soldiers, and women were not available to the extent of previous years as many were in munitions works. Irish labourers, it was added, wanted prohibitive prices as Government contractors were paying wages above those possible to the agricultural industry.

Town boys aged 14 to 19 years were soon to become available for placing on farms, although the period of training would be eight weeks. Pocket money would be provided by the War Agricultural Executives, and the boys would get free board and lodging. It was expected that the farmers would employ the boys afterwards and at the appropriate wages from 16-19 years.

Women Workers
There were 547 registrations for industrial employment at the Employment Exchange on Saturday 28th. October, of women born in 1914.

The interviewing of the women in the registered age groups was proceeding steadily, and generally speaking their attitude was helpful. A number of applications were being made for the ATS and other services. There was a great willingness on the part of the women to take work in the munitions factories, however, the same could not be said of some of the employers.

Generally speaking there had been a desire to co-operate, but in a few cases there had been a tendency to demur about taking women on. When it was pointed out that the welfare of the country depended on sacrifices, it was usually found that a little opposition disappeared.

The main objection was the doubt as to whether women could carry out "men's work". The fact was that women had been found capable of doing work which, under normal circumstances, they would never have attempted. For instance, two women were already engaged in road-work, this entailed weeding roads and footpaths, and generally cleaning the road sides. The two women concerned were Mrs. Tatman, of 15, Gladstone Street, and Mrs. Colthorpe, of 57, Clarence Road. They were obtained through the Exchange and their pay was 10d. an hour. Two other women who offered their services, Mrs. Pearson, and Mrs. Read, both of Saxon Road, were employed as labourers in the park and other gardens. Their work included hoeing weeds, cutting grass edges, sweeping drives and footpaths, cleaning flower beds, burying old materials, thinning vegetables, and (on wet days) washing flower pots and other indoor work. Their pay was also 10d. per hour.

Fire Guard Progress
By the middle of October there were over 300 fire parties registered and equipped, Mr. B. Coney being the staff officer. For this service the city was divided into nine groups, corresponding with the warden's divisions, and the following were the head fire guards, and (where appointed) the deputy heads:
Group Number:
1. Mr.J.C.Bessell; Mr. D.H. Ruff.
2. Mr. J.W. Scotney; Mr. F.J. Moore.
3. Mr. J.W. Calvert.
4. Mr. R.S. Mathews; Mr. H.W. Corbit
5. Mr. R.P. Palmer; Mr. W.H. Walker.
6. Mr. R. Hill; Mr. C.J. Robson.
7. Mr. R.E. Salman; Mr. S. Roper.
8. Mr. G.W. Forbear.
9. Mr. B.J. Plant; Mr. F.W. Brown.

To assist the head fire guard in the training of his personnel, each group had a group training officer. These officers were appointed so that all members could be trained, as far as possible, within the boundaries of their own area. They were:
1. Mr. H. Torode
2. Mr. D. Marshall.
3. Sergeant R.A. Beal.
4. Mr. N.H. Brewin.
5. Mr. H.V. Shepherd.
6. Mr. W.E. Hubble.
7. Mr. A.J. Gosling.
8. Mr. T.F. Sewell.
9. Mr. T.J.G.W. Pearce.

Arrangements had already been made in some groups for training to commence. Senior and deputy senior fire guards were in the course of appointment, and would be placed in control of each warden's sector, of which there were 90 in the city.

Everyone was expected to fire-watch in his own street and those who were prepared to do this were recognised by the government as members of the civil defence organization. The bulk of the fire guards already enrolled were drawn from the ranks of those who could, on various grounds, claim exemption from fire watching on business premises, including those over 60.

Those who had not enrolled, and could not claim exemption, were allocated for duty in the centre of the city. Equipment issued prior to the formation of the fire guard, was being supplemented by the issue of helmets, armlets, and stirrup pumps where required. A requisition for 4,000 steel helmets had already been sent.

At the same time an application was made for authority to purchase a further 100 mackintoshes for wardens. It was also agreed at this time that lights on street obstructions and blocks would remain for the time being, and not be complicated with new colours or combinations of colours or symbols.

Remarkable Shop
During these times of shortages, one shop still managed to provide city people with a decent supply of clothing. The shop, run by the WVS in Cowgate, was known as the Clothing Depot. In charge was Mrs. T. Dickens, and Mrs. A. Jordan, and the shop was open on Wednesdays and Fridays. There was never a lack of customers or stock.

The store was lined in two large rooms with shelves which were loaded with utilitarian clothing, almost entirely supplied from the consignments sent by the American Red Cross. The gifts were received at the Regional depot at Nottingham, where they were divided and allocated to areas in the Region on the basis of numbers of evacuees. "Customers," at least in the first instance, attended after investigation by the Public Assistance organization, and every article taken was booked to the recipient. In the case of each new article - and they formed the majority - the requisite coupons had to be provided, as without these the depot could not get the stock replaced. In no case was payment for goods permitted.

The clothing was in endless variety and of uniform good quality. It ranged from greatcoats to stockings; from rubber and other boots to wool cardigans. It served all ages and both sexes. The families of serving men in need were dealt with by the equally well equipped depot of the Soldiers', Sailors' and Airmen's Families Association, under the guidance of Lady Craig.

Another department of the WVS depot was that relating to sudden demands in cases of houses being bombed. In immediate readiness there were, at each of the 16 Rest Centres, 10 outfits each for men, women and children, who may have been driven from their home with the minimum of clothing. Some of this clothing had already been used, and the borrowed articles, after having been worn, were washed and returned to the depot after being finished with.

Another provision sent from America were a number of bags containing small necessities - torch, towel, tooth brush, etc. - these were also urgently required by those driven from their beds and homes.

Civil Defence
Units from three Home Guard battalions took part in another exercise on Sunday 4th, involving an attack on a Peterborough railway station.

By 10.30 operations were in full swing and civilians using London Road saw opposing parties of Home Guards armed with rifles, Tommy-guns and other equipment, busy firing blank ammunition at each other from behind bushes and gardens walls.

Two minor casualties from a visiting unit were taken to hospital for treatment but rejoined their company before cease fire.

The City Council was having its own problems in connection with Civil Defence matters. The Clerk had heard from the Hunts. County Council that the Ministry of Home Security had not approved the issue of Morrison indoor shelters either free or on payment. A decision was made to take the matter up direct with the Ministry.

The two reasons given by the Ministry for its decision were: 1. The area was not within the stipulated distance from certain likely targets; 2. The public had been given the chance of having baffle walls. A strong letter of protest was subsequently sent.

At the same time the Ministry had refused to grant a certificate for the erection of a strong room in which to house the Council's records and documents. The Council was not prepared to take this lying down either, and a motion was passed to immediately renew their application. Probably in the spirit of "nothing ventured, nothing gained," they decided also to apply to the Ministry of Health for the allocation of a Nissen hut to be earmarked as an emergency rest and feeding centre.

Iron Railings

Five members of the City Engineer's staff had been occupied for several weeks on a city-wide survey of iron railings. Workmen were now calling on citizens in order to take away all railings that were considered unnecessary for public safety or for the protection of stock. A standard rate of 25s. a ton was laid down, but there was a compensation provision for those whose claims were higher. Owners were of course encouraged to give up their railings free of charge.

Mr. Iliffe, of the City Engineer's department stated that the iron salvage from Peterborough would make a useful contribution towards the estimated national figure of 350,000 tons required for the manufacturer of weapons and to save shipping space.

One ton of scrap metal was equal to 150 18lb. Shell cases. Five tons of scrap was equal to 48 250lb. bombs, or 25 500lb. bombs, or 500 Bren guns, or 5,000 rifle barrels.

Ten tons was equal to one 3.7 anti-aircraft gun; 14 tons, a 4.5 A.A. gun; and 15 tons a medium tank.

Targets Topped

Thirty-one savings groups in the city and district had, by the middle of October, exceeded the targets they had set themselves in the twelve weeks drive in the summer. The Precincts and part of Park Road had initially aimed at £80 but had increased this by 1,500 per cent, reaching £1,200. Eastfield Road No.3 and Longthorpe each raised ten times their objective.

A full list is given below:

	Target £	Target Raised £
Eastfield Road No.3	100	1,000
Longthorpe	200	2,000
Mr. H.J. Farrow	60	160
County School	80	83
Newborough and Borough Fen	2,500	3,000
Alexandra Road	60	217
Bamber Street	45	80
Queen's Drive Infant's	40	90

Walton First Aid Post	45	54
Grimshaw Road	100	300
Norfolk Street	100	303
Fulbridge Junior School	300	450
Fulbridge Infant's School	40	69
Helpston	140	165
Paten & Co.	100	142
Cromwell Road Senior School	40	49
Wansford	50	674
Mayor's Working Party	33	211
LNER Loco Running Department		
(Employees)	1,200	1,420
(Staff)	150	256
Garton End	35	111
Baker Perkins	6,000	6,340
Town Hall	200	581
Newark School	35	45
Co-op Check Office	50	331
Magee Road	20	38
New Road, Woodston	50	85
Precincts & part of Park Road	80	1,200
Willesden Avenue, Mildmay Road	85	229
Charles Street	50	450
Summerfield Road	19	21

Bomb Talk

On Tuesday 14th, Sergeant R.A. Beal of the ARP gave a talk at the Town Hall explaining how to deal with incendiary bombs. The following are some of the points he made:

"You must pool your materials and equipment as well as your personal service, stirrup pumps, hose pipes, ladders, etc. must be readily accessible to all. They are no good kept in an outhouse. Fire brigades cannot possibly deal with all the fire bombs which may fall in a raid. The incendiary bomb, it has been found by experience, will generally pierce the roof to the upper storey, and it must be dealt with there. Courage and perseverance are wanted. Deal with it promptly. Throw it out of the window, or through it. Cover it with sand to make it easy to handle.

A bomb will probably burn for about seven minutes. A stirrup pump has proved its worth time after time. Do not throw a bucket of water on a bomb. It will make it explode.

The fire party is three. The strongest uses the nozzle of the pump, the next strongest pumps, and the third person keeps the bucket full. One can't work standing in a smoke filled room. Lie down with the face close to the floor where there is always a clear layer of air. Besides, one can see the bomb, and any fire it has caused.

Arrange to help in adjoining sectors, but don't leave your own without making sure that no bombs have fallen there. Incendiary bombs are announced by short sharp blasts on a whistle, which mean nothing else.

Coming down stairs which may be burning below, walk on the side nearest the wall. Keep the face towards the stairs; that is, come down backwards.

If you tie sheets together and tie them to a bed, before you attempt to come out

158

by the window, move the bed close to the window. In dropping from a window, face the wall, and lower yourself until you hang by the window sill. As you drop, push your knees against the wall. In lowering other people with a rope, get a ' brake' on the rope with your foot and over the window sill.

Don't clutch a person on fire. Throw him or her down and roll in a coat or Macintosh. Remove all old stuff from lofts. This is a legal demand."

At this present time compulsion applied only to business premises as far as fire watching was concerned. However, it was thought that enough street watches would come forward without the need to compel anyone. There were, it was said, people who preferred to remain in bed while others watched for them. The authorities knew how to deal with them, and would do so in such cases as were reported to them.

Missing

More local casualties were being reported in October at this time.

Pilot Officer (Observer), Walter (Titch), Barrett, of 697, Lincoln Road, was now reported missing from an operational flight over Germany on the night of October 13th. P/O Barrett had been an Old Petriburgian. A keen rugby player, he turned out for the Wasps and Blackheath XVs. He was the third son of Mr. and Mrs. W. Barrett, and was married in the previous August to Miss Dorothy Owen, a well-known pianist and daughter of Mr. and Mrs. D. Owen, 14, Clifton Avenue, Peterborough.

P/O Barrett had been on the staff of Baker Perkins before the war and had joined the RAF in September 1940. On Tuesday 28th October, news was conveyed to the family via a telephone call from the Red Cross in London, that P/O Barrett was a prisoner of war in Germany.

At about the same time, Sergeant H.C. Watson, RAF, was reported as being a prisoner of war. Sgt. Watson, a wireless operator and air gunner, was the adopted son of Mr. and Mrs. G. Gray, 181, Westwood Street. He was reported missing on September 15th.

Crime

In the same week that the news of the two airmen above was reported, the names of six other local men became known for more infamous reasons.

The LNER had been suffering from petty crime from its employees for some time, and the following employees appeared before the Peterborough Police Court on Wednesday 15th October, charged with stealing goods in transit, and other railway property.

Joseph Edward Burrows, railway shunter, 4, Gordon Avenue, Woodston, was sentenced to six weeks imprisonment with hard labour for stealing 254 Oxo cubes, value £1 12s. 4d.

Edward Driscoll, railway porter, of 31, Atkinson Street, had a case of stealing 12 sponge cloths, value 2 shillings dismissed on payment of 15 shillings costs, and sentenced to one month in prison for stealing two pillowcases, value 7shillings.

Richard Neal, railway porter, 12, Providential Place, was given six weeks for stealing cigarettes valued at £9.

James Alfred Fitzjohn, railway shunter, Whittlesey, had a charge of stealing 64 sponge cloths dismissed on payment of 15 shillings costs.

Wilfred John Capewell, railway checker, Stamford, was sentenced to one month for stealing five pairs of socks valued at 12s. 6d.

Lastly, George Alfred Luty, railway station foreman, Stamford, was given one month for stealing six pairs of socks valued at 15 shillings.

It is easy to criticise these men, but we should understand that most things were now being rationed, and the temptation when confronted with any kind of goods must have been tremendous.

'Volunteers' Required

During October, a number of city canteens found themselves struggling to provide a service due to staff shortages. The WVS canteen in Long Causeway was looking for an early shift worker, (7am-11am), and Captain W.S. Tyler, of the Church Army canteen at the North Station, was after another worker for each night, to work through the night. The canteen had two sections, one which served refreshments, and a dormitory containing twenty beds.

At the outbreak of the war in 1939, the Toc H Room in Priestgate had been opened as a temporary canteen while the premises in Long Causeway were being prepared. Members of Toc H met trains on the first night and were on duty in the canteen; they undertook to continue this work when the transfer to the new building took place, and did so from 7pm to 7am each night. The demands of the Services soon began to deplete the strength of a movement, most of whose members were of military age, and other volunteers joined them in this important work.

The number of troops using the canteen steadily increased, and two years later, the need for extra male helpers had become urgent. A public appeal was now made for the first time, men were needed for night or day shifts, the twelve hour periods were divided into two six hour shifts, (7-11pm and 11pm-7am), the latter being the more desperate in terms of shortages. Rev. F.M. Hodgess Roper, of 55, Park Road, was the canteen organiser.

Volunteers of a different kind, in the shape of voluntary refugees, were still arriving in the city at this time. During the second week of October the city's population grew by between two and three hundred.

More a case of being 'called-up' than volunteering, were the 380 local people who registered for industrial service at Peterborough Employment Exchange on Saturday 11th October. These were men born in 1895, and in each case the point for consideration was whether the man should be transferred to work which was of more national importance than that which he was already doing. The next local registration would be on October 25th for women born in 1912.

Preparations for 'Submarine Week'

By the middle of October there were 591 savings groups in the city, since January 1st the city had saved £886,551 and the new selling centre in Church Street had been doing very well. Warship Week was to commence on November 27th, and a target of £425,000 had been set with which to buy a Submarine.

The new shop was doing £100 worth of business each week, and a special five minute 'trailer' entitled; "Give Us More Ships" had been prepared and would be shown at local cinemas. A special plaque had also been designed which was to be presented to the city in commemoration if it succeeded in attaining its £425,000 target. The cost, £10, would be borne by the city.

A change was made, in that it was also announced now that the submarine would be named after the district, (not the city as previously stated), and the name would be revealed before Warship Week commenced.

The Warship Week Secretary, (the City Treasurer), now proposed that the Licensed Victuallers Association should be asked to display posters inside and out of their premises. It was also suggested that they might supply speakers for the Week and that the houses should set themselves targets. Mr. S.G. Farrow stated that all imports of wines had been stopped since the previous January, and for anything which went out of the front door, nothing was coming in the back door. He did not know how the licensed Victuallers were going to help as they were in such a poor way. If anyone had got a good job on offer would they let him know!

The Secretary said that the Region would allow a grant for expenses at the rate of 10 shillings per 1,000 population, which would total about £40. During the last War Weapons Week the expenses had come to around £190, and the bills were forwarded to the Region. The Secretary thought they could usefully use about £250.

A suggestion for a concert to be given by the RAF band at the Embassy was made, and an entertainments sub committee was formed to arrange this and other entertainments. The secretary also suggested that a sub committee be formed to seek subscriptions. Bank managers and stockbrokers would all be ex-officio members as they would "touch" people automatically "as was their wont".

King's School were to give an exhibition of model ships with Dunkirk in the background, cut out ships would be supplied to schools and it was hoped that shop owners would exhibit these models in their windows.

The Secretary also said that the cinema vans would be in the city during the Week. Messrs Baker Perkins had offered guns for static displays, and the Admiralty had sent 250 fine photographs for exhibition. The military were willing to give full co-operation for parades and it was hoped that the RAF would give another 'leaflet raid' (dropping leaflets over the city). Mr. Hoyles had promised a five guinea coat to the lady group secretary who had the best increase in her group's savings during the last three months of the year.

Mr. S.G. Farrow, who had been appointed honorary official agent organiser, reported on the progress of the scheme by which shop-keepers were asking customers to take their change in sixpenny stamps. He said that it had surprised him that the big company shops, which were run by Jews and who would be on the top of the list if Hitler came, would not allow their assistants to ask customers to take stamps for change.

On Tuesday 28th October news was received that arrangements had been made with the Admiralty for the city to adopt the submarine OLYMPUS following Warship Week, subject to the achievement of the financial objective - £425,000.

The committee decided to hold a naval exhibition at the Corn Exchange during the first week of December, and the RAF had promised to give a display on the Market Place. Information was received however, that because of the necessity to economise in the use of petrol, the RAF would be unable to carry out a 'leaflet drop', or do any special flying.

Fire Watching Exemptions and the Cathedral
The following information taken from the October report on the watching of premises under the Registration for Civil Defence Duties (Compulsory Enrolment) Order, 1941, shows the difficulty sometimes experienced when recruiting fire watchers in the city.

The local authority was given the power to register men between 18 and 60 years of age and to allocate them for fire protection duties, provided they could not claim exemption. The total number registered (on May 24th) was 10,485. Of these, the number successfully claiming exemption was 9,107. Of the balance of 1,378, 788 did not claim exemption and 590 claims for exemption were disallowed. Thousands of those exempted were already performing duties in their own business premises. One of the places where fire watchers were urgently needed was the Cathedral and £400 had been spent on equipment already.

Placed out of the view of the public eye were hundreds of gallons of water, countless sandbags, over a score of stirrup pumps, and hundreds of feet of hose scattered about the building. Four dry risers, (long pipes fixed to the side of the Cathedral to take water straight to the top of the roof) had been fixed. Special thick steel mesh had been erected over the organ with the hope that incendiary bombs would slide to the ground. Ladders were positioned in all necessary places and securely fixed to prevent slipping. A special wooden bridge had been constructed to make it easy crossing from the triforium to the West Front.

Axes, ceiling hooks, shovels and other equipment designed to pick up incendiaries were liberally placed throughout the building. A telephone had been installed to enable fire-watchers to phone from the Lantern Tower and Bell Tower to the Sacristy, in order to keep the 'nerve centre' fully informed.

Precautions had also been made to ensure the safety of the fire-watchers. Ropes and steel bars had been provided to prevent people from falling, and torches were available. There were many ways of escape to those who knew the building should one stair become blocked by masonry.

With the winter drawing on and the threat of longer nights, the call had gone out for more fire-watchers. These people would take some time to learn their way around the huge building and extra instruction was being provided. In comparison, St. Paul's Cathedral in London had a rota of hundreds of men, twenty-five of them taking their turn every night. Our Cathedral, it was said, meant every bit as much to us, as St. Paul's did to Londoners.

King's School
At the end of October, Mr. H.R. Hornsby, Headmaster of the King's School, who volunteered for service as a gunner in the Royal Artillery soon after the outbreak of war, received a commission.

The school staff was now represented among the officers of all three Services. Captain W.V. Garrard was in the Army, Sub-Lieut. Raymond Gillibrand was in the Royal Naval Volunteer Reserve, and Mr. R. Capper had been transferred to the Royal Air Force with commissioned rank.

Smiles
Among the many letters and forms which constantly flowed into the Food Offices were some that occasionally brought a smile to the faces of the officials.
"Please send me a form for cheap milk as I am expecting mother."
"I have a child nearly 2 years old, and I am expecting an increase in November, hoping that this meets with your kind consideration and approval."
"I have had a baby 2 months old fed entirely on cows, and another child 4 years old."
"Please will you allow me to change my fat retailer?"
"Please may I change my 2 children for meat?"

Fletton at War

A number of points were discussed at the meeting of the Fletton Urban District Council on Monday 20th October. The Surveyor reported that scheduled iron railings for salvage amounted to 22 tons 11cwt. An appeal by the owner of 244, Oundle Road, against the scheduling of his railings on the grounds that they possessed artistic merit and prevented cattle straying, had been disallowed. The total weight of railings was now 32 tons.

Thirty-two applications for allotments had been made in Fletton, Woodston and Stanground, however, there were none vacant and it was proposed that those found uncultivated should be let. An inspection was arranged.

Fletton had its own problems with fire watchers; registrations had numbered 1,472, but 1,097 forms for claims for exemption had been issued. However, rooms at the Secondary, Stanground and Woodston Junior Schools were made available for use by fire-watching parties, and an application for 1,000 fire guard helmets was made.

In reporting on progress in the erection and capacity of outside shelters, the Clerk said that many householders had not accepted baffle walls, and a shortage of labour had hindered work. The shelters and baffle walls built were expected to provide protection for 4,562 people. Designs had been proceeded with for shelters for caravan dwellers.

The Ministry of Home Security had written that Morrison indoor shelters could only be purchased or issued free in areas already selected on the basis of priority need. Fletton was not one of these areas.

At the end of October, Mr. Frank J.A. Shaw, Hon. Secretary of Old Fletton Urban District Local Savings Committee produced the following figures for savings in the area.

Joseph Farrow and Co. Ltd. aimed at a summer target of £675, the price of a heavy load of bombs, and actually raised £1,000. Old Fletton WVS set out to reach £445 - £300 for a light ambulance, £100 for a machine gun and £45 for 30 stretchers - and their result £540 12s 6d. Fletton Council School decided on £40 for a parachute, and their total was £17 15s. Complete group subscriptions had been:

	£	s.	d.
Stanground branch Co-op Soc.	6	1	0
A.W. Smith, Oundle Road.	324	0	0
Old Fletton WVS.	540	12	6
Stanground C. of E. Infants Sch.	67	13	0
Old Fletton Council School (PB)	198	8	0
Old Fletton Council School (SS)	70	18	0
Woodston Junior Council School	145	11	4
Woodston WVS.	25	12	6
Newall Engineering Co.	2,070	7	0
Stanground WVS.	615	9	0
Fletton LNER.	30	11	0
Hunts. County Sec. School (PB)	118	3	0
Messrs. Hawkins Ltd.	68	14	0
London Road, Woodston	211	13	0
London Brick Co.	4,620	15	0
Orton Ave. Branch Co-op Soc.	4	8	6
Joseph Farrow & Co. Ltd.	1,330	7	6

163

Stanground C. of E. mixed.	23	16	8
Old Fletton Fire Brigade	70	2	6
Old Fletton Urban District Public Health Department.	18	10	0
Fellowes Road branch Co-op Soc.	5	6	6

The amount subscribed through the three post offices at Old Fletton, Woodston and Stanground from October 1st 1940, to September 30th 1941, was £8,309 15s. and the total amount raised through the groups was £10,277 5s.

Registrations

On Saturday 25th October 627 women born in 1913 registered at Peterborough Employment Exchange with a view to being selected for war work.

This brought the number of personal registrations to 4,832, and as the postal applications for registration in each group had averaged nearly 100, the grand total was about 5,500.

Numbers in previous age groups had been: 27's - 547, 26's - 600, 25's - 621, 24's - 532, 23's - 514, 22's - 575, 21's - 816. In the later age groups the majority of women were married, with children. These would be passed over until every other category had been exhausted. In the earlier groups practically every person considered to be available for some form of war work had been placed.

Gestapo Methods

During a meeting of the Peterborough Chamber of Commerce on Tuesday 28th October, Mr. W.H. Hoyles complained that Board of Trade officials had been going into business houses and trying to get assistants to accept loose coupons - trying, in fact, to get them to break the law. Fortunately the attempt which he saw reported was not successful. The assistant went and consulted the management.

This, Mr. Hoyles said, was not British. We did not want Gestapo methods in this country. The Chamber should protest, and at the same time ask the public not to present loose coupons. It was reported that these agents had also been active in shops in Lincoln.

Mr. S.G. Farrow said that when money was spent in such work it was not much encouragement to them to collect savings. It was agreed that a letter of protest would be sent to the Board of Trade.

Head Lights

Major Mollison, the Chief Air Raid Officer, stated in the press at the end of October that he was "very worried over the brilliant car head lights which are to be seen in the streets". He stated that just after an alert, there had been a long stream of glaring lamps pouring down Broadway and Long Causeway. He was in no doubt that a plane above could have seen them from a great distance. And the streets were full of people at the time.

He commended the example of one picture house, where it exhibited a request to car owners to drive out of the car park as far apart as possible, with head lights switched off.

Missiles from the Cathedral

Although it was at risk from Luftwaffe bombers, and also short of fire watchers, the

Cathedral turned out to have its own inherent dangers one day at the end of October.

During the morning service on Sunday 26th, two youths, who had established themselves on the roof outside the East End, were happily discharging catapults at passers by.

At about 11:20 Leslie Gilbert, aged 18, of 183 Cromwell Road, and two younger brothers were on their way round the Cathedral when Leslie noticed the youths. They took cover behind the parapet, and brought their catapults into action. Gilbert walked to the other side, and without effect, told the youths to come down. One youth was said to have had his foot through a skylight, but fortunately no glass fell on to the Cathedral floor. As the two boys passed the east window, their shadows were seen from inside the building by Mr. D. Foreman and Mr. H. Hemmings, both men left the service to investigate.

They reached the roof by means of the fire watcher's scaffolding at the east end - the way the two boys had gained access, and eventually the intruders were caught, brought down, and detained in the Sacristy until the police arrived.

Death at Sea

Sub-Lieutenant George Andrew Rodgers, aged 27, of 231 Eastfield Road, Peterborough, son of Mrs. Rodgers and the late Mr. Robert Rodgers, was now reported killed at sea by enemy action.

On leaving King's School, George was apprenticed as an engineer at Brotherhood's. Joining the Royal Fleet Auxiliary Reserve, he became fourth engineer and was posted to the ship on which he met his death.

His wife, formerly Miss Mary Smillie, of Greenock, lost her father less than three weeks earlier and was spending a holiday with her mother at Mull when she received the news of her husband's death. Sub-Lieut. and Mrs. Rodgers were married in June 1940.

Sub-Lieut. Rodgers was killed in action on 22nd October 1941, while serving on the 8,145 ton tanker, DARKDALE. The DARKDALE had been a relatively new ship, completed 15th November 1940, and was torpedoed and sunk by a U-boat off the coast of St. Helena.

New Ration Books

By the beginning of November, Peterborough was ahead of much of the country in the circulation of the new ration books. The books were ready for distribution in the city on Saturday 8th, Fletton and district on the Monday, and by Saturday 15th November, the whole district had been supplied. The books were obtainable from the local food offices and at the large number of sub-offices that were opened specially for the purpose.

One person from each household was asked to collect the new books to cut down on queues, there were no forms to fill in but the old books had to be shown. It was also possible to collect books for friends as long as their present books were produced.

When the day arrived, the issue of the points ration books went very well, 67,830 having been distributed up to the Saturday night. During the day 15 schools had been in use as sub-offices, at Williamson Avenue it was found that many people were helping by collecting neighbour's books as well as their own. One caller even had a parcel of 40 books.

Bishop's Road school was not very busy as many people living in that neighbourhood had already collected their books direct from the Food Office. There, some applicants had presented the first ration books issued, and when it was explained that they should have brought the most recent, they said that they thought any old book would do.

At New Fletton, one caller had a perambulator stocked with books collected from both sides of a long street.

Lincoln Road School, New England, had had an endless flow of callers, mostly their own families only.

Dogsthorpe had a surprisingly large demand. The school opened at one o'clock and by 2:30 the allowance of 300 points books had gone.

Salvage

The Highways Committee's monthly salvage return, given on Friday 31st October, stated that the following had been sold: 32 tons 11cwt 2qrs. of paper; 5t. 14c. 1qr. of tins; 8 gross bottles, and 18t. 16c. of kitchen waste.

Alderman Howard said that the Committee's attention had been drawn to a man who regularly emptied the contents of the Croyland Road bin into a sack and took it away, and to a man and woman who did the same thing in Paston Lane. He asked members of the public to safeguard their own interests by immediately reporting anything of that nature. Speaking of the iron railings survey, he said the Committee had received a considerable number of letters objecting to railings being taken. He asked those people to think of those who had paid the supreme sacrifice, of the small towns in Greece; and of the scorched-earth policy in Russia. The Engineer was to proceed with requisitioning.

Navy News

Naval Wireless Telegraphist Ron Laxton, youngest son of Mr. and Mrs. T. Laxton, of Glebe Road, was serving on HMS PENELOPE, when, as part of a larger force of cruisers, she played a part in the sinking of eleven enemy ships off Taranto on the morning of Sunday 9th November. An Old Boy of King's School, and a cricketer and footballer, his father was manager of the Co-operative Society's Park Road butchery branch.

Another local sailor, Leading Supply Assistant, Oliver Blake, son of Mrs. E.R. Blake, Cherry Tree Farm, Garton End, was on the aircraft carrier ARK ROYAL when she was torpedoed and sunk on 14th November.

His mother received a cable saying that he was safe and well. LSA Blake, who spent much of his early life with his aunt, Mrs. C.W. Johnson, at Cherry Tree Farm, had been in the navy for two years.

Registrations - On Saturday 8th November, 600 women of the 1912 age group registered for national service at the Employment Exchange. As had been the case in other registrations, a large proportion of the women were married with families.

A.R.P. Matters

At the ARP Committee on Tuesday 11th November, P.c. P.W. Vincett reported on his examination of school children's respirators. Of 6,421 examined, 1,111 needed repair, and 268 were exchanged for larger sizes. These percentages were an improvement on the results of the previous examination when 25 per cent were defective. For repairs charges, £28 14s. 7d. had been collected.

An advertisement was now being displayed announcing the screening of an important A.R.P. film.

It related to noises to be expected in a big air raid, and demonstrated to the public that a lot of noise did not necessarily imply the greatest danger. It would be shown free of charge at the City Picture House, twice on Sunday 14th December, supervised by Dr. A.E. Carver, an eminent nerve specialist. The noise film was recorded during an actual air raid on London. Tickets could be obtained from Major Mollison, the Air Raid Officer.

At a meeting at the Town Hall on Wednesday 12th November, a Roof Spotters Club for Peterborough and district was formed; the object was to increase the efficiency of roof spotters in recognising aircraft. The London Brick Company had had a club since the March, and had 30 members.

Raid Victims Die

Twelve days after the death of his daughter, Miss Edna Kingston, Mr. Frank Kingston died at the Memorial Hospital on Wednesday 26th November, aged 66.

Mr. Kingston and his wife and younger daughter had been injured when a bomb demolished their cottage in Cross Street, at the rear of Mr. A.F. Percival's offices on the night of the 10th May.

Father and daughter never recovered from the shock. Miss Kingston was in a hospital for facial air raid casualties for several months after the raid, and soon after being discharged, her father was taken to the Memorial Hospital. Mr. Kingston had been employed at Godfrey's Wagon Works for 46 years, and had been retired for five years. Mrs. Kingston and her elder daughter, Mrs. Smith, were the only family members left. Mr. Kingston's funeral took place at Gedney Hill on Saturday 29th November.

Warship Week

Warship Week actually covered a period of ten days, officially beginning on Thursday 27th November and ending on Saturday 6th December. Each day had a set programme of events, described below, all listed in the official Souvenir Programme.

Friday 28th - Parade of the 70th Leicesters through the northern part of the city, followed by a weapon display by the same regiment on the Market Place; also on the Market Place, an exhibition by a searchlight unit and a display by the Fire and Civil Defence services.

Saturday 29th - Leicesters' route march in the centre of the city. At noon, the opening of the King's School exhibition by the Mayor.

Sunday 30th - Route march by the City Battalion Home Guard, the Mayor to take the salute at 12.30pm at the Town Hall.

Monday 1st - A display in the Market Place of field and anti-aircraft guns and other equipment manufactured by Baker Perkins Ltd. At noon the opening by the Mayor of the Admiralty exhibition at the Rechabite Hall, Lincoln Road.

Tuesday 2nd - Baker Perkins exhibition open all day.

Wednesday 3rd - Leicesters' route march for one hour in the city centre.

Thursday 4th - A display by the RAF on the Market Place, including captured enemy equipment; also a searchlight equipment display.

Friday 5th - RAF and other equipment display continued; also a Rescue Party demonstration on the Market Place.

Saturday 6th - Route march by the Leicester Regiment, the Mayor taking the salute at noon.

In addition there was to be a naval cinema show put on from a mobile van in the Market Place on each day of the week except Wednesday, when it would move to the King's School playing field. The King's School and Rechabite centre displays would be open every day, as would the selling centres in Church Street, King's School and the Trustee Savings Bank, where it was said: "loans to any amount, from 6d. to a million pounds" would be accepted. An indicator set up at the Market Place would show the day to day progress of the week.

Many other exhibitions and displays were organised for the week, far too many to list here, but the contributions of the city children towards the war effort may serve as an example of the kind of devotion the whole city was putting into the proceedings.

The main effort in the King's School push to raise funds rested on their model entitled, "The Evacuation of Dunkirk". This occupied the whole stage in the great hall and showed to scale the French seaport, with houses, docks, quays, beach and sand dunes. In the foreground was a wide stretch of the English Channel, covered with warships and other craft of every size and description, such as took part in the evacuation. Crowds of tiny soldiers and sailors were placed to give realism. Accuracy in the details was assured due to the loan of helpful data given by the War Office.

Every boy in the school had taken a hand in the making of the display. Three quarters of a ton of clay had been given from the brickfields with which to construct the several hundred separate parts that made up the complete model. The exhibition was open each day and at a charge of 6d. a time at the door. At an exhibition the previous year a total of 3,000 people had visited the school, it was hoped they would exceed this number.

The boys and girls at Fulbridge Council Junior Mixed had also been busy making models of warships, this time from plasticine. These ranged from battleships to motor torpedo boats. The models were placed in the window of the electricity showroom in Bridge Street, where they formed an impressive display. The plans sent to the school from the National Savings Movement were for models in wood. Wood, however, not being an easy commodity to get hold of at that time, was substituted with plasticine, thanks to Miss K. Bays, a member of the school staff.

Of the thirty-four models displayed, the pride of the school was the King George V battleship which was made by Colin Donette, Colin Frost, John Pudney, John Eames, Peter Elmer, John Russell, Cynthia Porter and Joan Rawlings. The model was 2ft. 4ins. in length and weighed over 5lbs. Complete in every detail, it had thick wire to represent the 14in. guns, pins for pom-poms, and thread for ropes. At the stern was a miniature Blue Ensign which took one boy nearly a whole afternoon to make. The signal flags it carried showed the message "SAVE", and it and all of the other ships were finished off with a smooth coat of mid-grey distemper. Fulbridge School had a fine record in saving, in the previous school year the savings group raised £1,400. During War Weapons Week the group had achieved the sum of £305, and in the three months of the present school year they had already raised £510.

By the night of Wednesday 3rd, the official target of Warship Week, £425,000, was reached. The adoption of HM Submarine OLYMPUS was assured and the organisers were now pressing forward to the three quarters of a million mark.

The indicator on the Market Place had shown the following day to day figures:

168

Friday	£150,000
Saturday	£200,000
Monday	£280,000
Tuesday	£310,000
Wednesday	£360,000
Thursday	£425,000

The largest subscriptions included:

Trustee Savings Bank	£25,000
Co-operative Society	£25,000
Barclays Bank	£15,000
Lloyds Bank	£15,000
National Provincial Bank	£15,000
Midland Bank	£15,000
Westminster Bank	£15,000
Wesleyan and General Assurance Society	£10,000
Peterborough Provincial Benefit Building Society	£10,000
Pearl Assurance Co.	£10,000
Royal Insurance Co.	£7,500
London, Liverpool and Globe Insurance Co.	£7,500
W.H. Symington and Co.	£5,000
Paten and Co. and associated Companies.	£5,000
Yorkshire Insurance Co.	£2,500
Norwich Union Fire and Life Insurance Societies.	£2,500
Royal London Mutual Insurance Society.	£2,500
County Fire Office and Alliance Assurance Co.	£2,500

Donations large and small came from all over the city, shops, schools, societies and individual citizens, the money flooded in. Finally, at the end of Warship Week, the grand total of £523,000 had been reached, £98,000 above the original target. On Friday 5th December, the Mayor received a telegram from Sir Kingsley Wood, Chancellor of the Exchequer carrying: "heartiest congratulations on success of Peterborough Warship Week."

No one could dispute the commitment of the city people; they deserved their submarine and were proud of it. In the future, the crew of HMS OLYMPUS would be able to rely on the city people to look after their welfare, that future however, would be anything but certain.

Pressure on Canteens

By December 5th there were six Canteens in the city for the Armed Forces and they were working at full stretch every day, so much so that the WVS were in consultation with the railway authorities in order to establish another canteen at the East Station.

The WVS Services Canteen on the Market Place had Honourable seniority. It had been established on November 9th, 1939, and had been manned day and night throughout the two years by WVS volunteers, with Toc H to help them at night. Toc H and the WVS had before this run a small canteen at Toc H. HQ. In the past two years countless thousands of hungry and tired servicemen had found a meal, warmth and facilities for a rest within the doors of the canteen. By this time it had 18 beds and had opened up a sleeping-house over T.L. Barrett's shop, 21, Midgate, where there were 42 more beds. The charge to the men was 6d. per night, and every night all the 60 beds were occupied.

The work at the canteen had increased enormously, and provision had to be made for the unexpected arrival of large parties of men at any time. Every Tuesday morning a party of some 100 naval ratings stopped there for a meal. Nearly 500 members of the WVS worked shifts at this, and the other WVS canteen at the North Station.

The North Station Canteen was open from 10am to 10:30pm and each session served from 1,200 to 1,400 men and women.

There were also three WVS mobile canteens - the Anne Norris, the Baker Perkins, and the Louis D - and these turned out regularly whatever the weather. They ploughed through snow, rain and mud to lonely camps and isolated spots during eight hour shifts in order to reach all the men who needed their services, they then had to clear out the vans, prepare them and garage them for the next day.

The Women's Services Canteen, which was solely for women in the Forces, had been established in August 1940. It was situated in the Precincts and was also being well used. The number of "sleepers" had trebled, and varied from three to seventeen per night. Over 350 meals were served there every week. This place provided numerous comforts including easy chairs, beds, books, radio and games. A tea room and hot baths proved to be very popular. Women were even allowed to take their boyfriends or husbands into the canteen to take meals with them.

Mrs. Francis, the Canteen Warden, told of a WAAF mother, who spent her seven days leave at the canteen. She had lost everybody and everything. Her husband had been killed while serving in the Navy; her daughter, aged 19, had been killed in a raid whilst at her fiancé's home; her brother had been killed in the RAF, and most of her near friends had been killed in London "blitzes." The woman's own home - a flat in London - had received a direct hit, and her clothes and belongings were lost. Mrs. Francis did all in her power to cheer the woman up, and arranged for her to go out for lunch and tea every day.

The Salvation Army Canteen in King Street, which had been established for over 14 months, had attained a reputation second to none with the troops in the neighbourhood. The canteen was open from 2 to 10:30pm and was in the charge of Major and Mrs. Albon, and a band of willing Salvation Army helpers. It was estimated that they served between four and five thousand servicemen and women every week. The canteen made a speciality of its home-made cakes and doughnuts. A sixpenny speciality was a plateful of chips, a cup of tea, and roll and butter. Troops for miles around knew when the doughnut nights were, and they sold like wildfire. A reading and writing room was also provided, and there was music in the evenings.

The Wentworth Street Service Men's Institute, which was run by the Free Churches, was the largest canteen, and each week they had well over 1,000 men and women go there. There was a strong recreational side which included table tennis, billiards, darts, table games and a piano.

The newest canteen was that of the Church Army, situated in the grounds of the Great Northern Hotel. It was in charge of Captain W.S. Tyler and had been open for four months; its speciality was a spruce-looking dormitory, with ten new bunk beds - 20 beds in all. They were provided with two pillows, two sheets and three blankets each and were always spotlessly clean. Arrangements were made to call the men in time to catch their trains, beds being 1shilling a night, or bed and breakfast 1s. 6d.

Some four to five thousand men used this canteen every week.

Registrations
On Saturday 6th December, 608 women born in 1910, registered at the Employment Exchange for National Service. As before, a large proportion of these were married women with domestic responsibilities.

On Saturday 13th, 258 men in the eighteen and a half group, the youngest so far, registered for military service. Preferences expressed were: RAF ground staff, 79, RAF flying duties, 31, ground or flying, 1, Royal Navy, 62, Royal Marines, 2, no preference, 82. There was one conscientious objector.

It was also decided at this time, that ten thousand young men who were presently working on the land, would be called to the Forces early in the new year. This may have been due to complaints from older men that it was unfair to call up men of 41 who had served in the previous war "while so many younger men were still in reserved occupations." This was certainly the view of Mr. W. Pratt, the Hon. Secretary of the Werrington branch of the British Legion who voiced his concerns; he was assured that each man in this older age group would be given the opportunity of attending a tribunal. It is probably fair to say that this was a countrywide concern and the government was sensitive to the issue.

Spy's Bad Luck
A Peterborough business man and his lorry driver who stopped to ask directions were responsible for the arrest and execution of a German spy at Wandsworth prison on Wednesday 10th December.

Mr. W.A. Spink, of 124, Park Road, managing director of Fairways Supply Co. Broadway, and his driver Mr. James Bonsor, of Fengate Close, were on their way home from London on May 13th 1941, with one of the firms removal vans when they lost their way. They spotted a man at the side of the road and stopped to ask him for directions to the north.

The man they spoke to was Karel Richard Richter, who had been dropped by parachute from a German aircraft in the early hours of that Tuesday morning in a field near the village of London Colney.

Richter, who was wearing a tweed overcoat, evening dress trousers and boots, spoke in broken English and immediately aroused suspicions. Bonsor went to a house and called the police while Spink stayed with the man. The police finally came and took Richter away.

At the local police station Richter was found to be carrying several hundreds of pounds in British and United States currency. He also had a map of the eastern counties and a pocket compass. He was wearing an overcoat and civilian suit, three pairs of woolen pants and two pairs of socks.

Richter had been dropped under cover of an air raid, precisely the same air raid that had caused the Peterborough men to detour and become lost in the first place.

"Scorch"
Exercise Scorch which took place on December 6th and 7^{th,} was, up to that time, the biggest mock invasion exercise of the war.

Units of the 1st Hunts. Battalion H.G., under the command of Lt. Col. C.W.D. Rowe, some of whom were on duty from 2pm on the Saturday to 6pm on the Sunday, played an important part in the army manoeuvres which affected the local district along with many others. News of 'enemy' infiltration soon reached the headquarters of the various companies concerned, and some platoons were in action within a very few hours. During the night men from 'A' Co. captured a battery commander with several of his staff and a number of vehicles including the officers mess stores!

The only complaint which the Army had to make concerning the fighting qualities of the Home Guard was that they were too kind to their prisoners. These prisoners were searched in accordance with normal routine, but one of them afterwards showed with great pride, a map which he had taken from the pocket of his searcher!

At one stage in the battle the headquarters of a company close to the Great North Road was stormed by 'enemy' troops who captured the H.Q. staff. News of this disaster quickly reached the other companies and a counter-attack was organised. Reserves were rushed up by lorry and the H.Q. was recaptured.

The factory unit's anti-sabotage posts were manned throughout the period of the exercise whilst reserve sections were held in readiness to be dispatched at a moment's notice in their own transport to any spot where the 'enemy' was located.

At one period of the night an 'enemy' detachment, comprising a number of vehicles left the road for an isolated farm in the hope of getting some rest. They had, however been spotted, and after a series of messages had made sure that all road exits had been blocked, fighting patrols went forward and succeeded in capturing all the vehicles concerned.

Several instances were reported of "rough and tumbles" between the opposing forces, and in some cases both prisoners and captors came in covered from head to foot with mud. It can only be assumed that at least unofficially, some of this mud would have been tinged with red.

Casualties

On Monday 8th December a telegram was received which told of a 'real' casualty of war. The recipient was Mrs. A.J. Pyle of 184, Star Road, and the telegram from the Air Ministry informed her that her husband, Pilot Officer Arthur John Pyle, 103034, an observer in RAF Volunteer Reserve, 40 Squadron, had been posted as missing in the Middle East as a result of air operations on December 5th.

P.O. Pyle was the son of Mrs. M. Pyle, 184, Star Road, and the late Mr. J.R. Pyle, and had been employed in the offices of the London Brick Company at Phorpres House. A fine all-round sportsman, he had been secretary of the Phorpres Athletic Club, and had played rugby for Old Deconians and Nondescripts. His father, a waterworks inspector and captain of Peterborough Football Club, had been killed in the First World War.

P.O. Pyle would later be confirmed as being killed in action on 6th December, aged 25. He is buried in Salerno war Cemetery, Italy.

Another casualty, this time through accident, was A.C.1. Alec Charles Popely, eldest son of Mr. and Mrs. Charles Popely, 25, Hankey Street. A.C.1. Popely died in Ashington Hospital, Northumberland, on Monday 8th December from injuries received in a motor accident. Before joining the RAF he was a clerk for Eastwoods Ltd. The funeral took place at St. Barnabas Church on Saturday 13th.

Also during the middle of December, Mrs. M.E. Stanford, of 1, North Station Road, was anxiously awaiting news of her son, Marine Raymond Denis Stanford, who was serving on the battleship HMS PRINCE OF WALES. The PRINCE OF

WALES was sunk along with HMS REPULSE when they were attacked by Japanese aircraft on December 10th 1941, off the east coast of Malaya.

Marine Stanford was 20, and had been educated at New Road School. He had been a member of Longthorpe church choir, and was employed by John Quality Ltd. before he joined the Navy soon after the outbreak of the war. He was posted to the PRINCE OF WALES in February 1940.

As more than 2,000 survivors had been landed at Singapore from the two ships, Mrs. Stanford was hopeful that her son was safe. On the evening of Monday 14th December, Mrs. Stanford was notified by telegram from the Admiralty that her son had indeed been saved. Singapore fell to the Japanese on Sunday February 15th 1942, and perhaps it comes as no surprise that Marine, PLY/X 3805 Raymond Denis Stanford is recorded as having died on Monday February 16th, aged 21. He has no known grave.

Also serving on board the PRINCE OF WALES was Coder, D.H. Stevenson, son of Mr. and Mrs. H.J. Stevenson, 85, Aldermans Drive. Coder Stevenson was lucky; he was also picked up, and survived the war.

News now reached the city that Sgt. Pilot Ernest Edward Weldon of 36, Silver Street, Fletton, had been killed in action whilst on operations over Germany. The son of Mr. and Mrs. E. Weldon, he was educated at Fletton Secondary School. He joined the RAFVR whilst he was a member of the LNER District's Supt. Staff at Doncaster, and he was reported missing on June 18th and now his death on that date had been confirmed.

Gunner Albert Edward Edis, Royal Artillery, of 30, Highbury Street, was now reported as wounded in action in the Middle East. The son of Mr. and Mrs. A. Edis, he was formerly a van driver for Mr. E.W. Popple, grocer, Lincoln Road.

Christmas 1941
The third wartime Christmas was an understated affair. The Mayor and Mayoress however, endeavoured to make a difference and on Christmas Day visited the Isolation hospital, the Memorial Hospital, St. John's Hospital and Public Assistance Institution, and Westfield Evacuee's Centre. On Boxing Day they entertained some 250 soldiers, drawn from units in the locality, with a dinner at the Town Hall. The food was supplied by the Dujon Café, and the refreshments included plenty of beer.

There was another party on Christmas Day; this had been arranged by Mrs. J.A.J. Atkinson, a repeat of one she had organised the year before. This was held at Woodston Church Hall for 300 soldiers who had been unable to get home or had not been invited elsewhere.

There were no buses at all in the city or district on Christmas Day, although a few firms had made private arrangements for buses to carry staff to factories. No extra buses were put on from Christmas Eve through to Boxing Day by order of the Ministry of Transport.

There were no extra rail services either, with Christmas Day having a Sunday service. The North Station displayed a sign warning people to refrain from travelling long distances during the Christmas period, and explaining that there would be fewer trains than usual running during this time. This was also due to a Ministry of Transport Order.

In the week before Christmas almost all of the trains to and from Peterborough had been packed, even though some had been doubled, and at times there had been as many as 1,000 people waiting on the platform. Christmas leave for servicemen

173

had not been cancelled, although they were forbidden to travel by rail between December 22nd and 28th, in order to ease the burden on the railways. Heavy mails and parcels traffic had added to the transport difficulties, and many of the vacant sidings were used for dispatching and receiving mail.

Turkeys, game and rabbits were very scarce, but ducks and domestic poultry were moderately plentiful.

Undressed turkeys at 2s. 11d., and dressed for cooking, 4s. 2d. was enough to send most people looking in other directions for their Christmas dinner. Roasting chickens, ducks, geese and boiling fowl were all at 1s. 11d. a pound, tame rabbits 1s. 8d. a pound. Brown hares had been fetching 7s. 6d. and mountain hares 4s. Wild rabbits had been extremely scarce, but a number of tame rabbits had been reared in anticipation of the Christmas trade. Hares were not in great demand, and meat joints were of course, on ration.

There were no oranges this Christmas, and a few peanuts at 8d. a pound which were poor consolation for the absence of brazils, almonds and walnuts. Apples were the main fruit, with Cox's and Canadian imports at 1s. 3d. a pound. There were a few small pears at 1s. 6d. a pound, some grapes, but these were not very popular at 7s. 6d. a pound.

Christmas trees however, were plentiful, and ranged from 2s. to 5s. Holly and Chrysanthemums played the main part in decorations due to the moderate price and generous supply.

There had been a shortage of some Christmas pudding ingredients, but the puddings themselves were easily obtainable in the shops and people were snapping them up.

Drink for home consumption was the main disappointment for many. Bottled stout was the easiest to obtain, with beer and cider coming second. Public houses and wine stores however, had already exhausted their meagre supplies of most wines. On Saturday 20th December people queued to receive half a bottle of port or sherry. Spirits were equally scarce, the city's wholesalers having received only 50 per cent of the quantity that had been available in 1939.

The banks were of course closed Christmas Day, as were solicitor's offices, traders, in general were closed both Christmas Day and Boxing Day. Baker Perkins worked Christmas Day but closed on Boxing Day. Brotherhood's closed on Christmas Day only. Newall's Ltd. closed both days, and Perkins Diesel closed from Christmas Eve to the day after Boxing Day.

The various Services Canteens in the city were fairly quiet due to the lack of many Service people travelling, and no special festivities had been arranged.

At the Memorial Hospital the nursing staff did their usual round of carol singing on Christmas morning, the time-honoured turkey however, was missing from the menu, being replaced by veal and pork, accompanied by potatoes and Brussels sprouts. There was also plum pudding and brandy sauce, ale, minerals, and small gifts for every patient. The children's ward had a gigantic Christmas tree, illuminated with fairy lanterns.

Pork from two pigs fattened on the premises, and tinned ham from America figured on the menu at Thorpe Road House and St. John's Hospital. There were 233 inmates of the House, the Hospital, and the Cottage Homes, and everywhere was decorated with red, white and blue and Victory 'V's on the windows.

Twenty patients, mostly children, spent Christmas in the Isolation Hospital, which was decorated with fairy lights, balloons and flowers. There were also two

174

Christmas trees which were hung with presents. They did not miss out on dinner, and feasted on turkey, plum pudding, mince pies and jelly.

Peterborough was the postal distribution centre for five counties, Lincolnshire, Northamptonshire, Cambridgeshire, Huntingdonshire and Rutland. As would be expected, the mail was extremely heavy during this period, however, the service was never in danger of being 'snowed under', and this was in part due to an army of eager volunteers.

To help cope with the Christmas rush, the Post Office had the assistance of around 50 senior King's School boys, 50 senior Deacon's School boys, 12 senior girls from the County School, and 100 men from the Leicestershire and Royal Horse Artillery Regiments, in addition to the large number of women who had been taken on temporarily. The Head Post Office had only 24 members of its original staff of 100. The girls had been used for sorting work and about 40 of the school boys carried out deliveries.

From December 15th, the Corn Exchange was used as an overflow depot, and five 5-ton lorries, hired specially, travelled to and from the old fish sidings at Peterborough North Station which were being used for dispatching and receiving parcels.

Sunday 21st saw the peak of the parcel post, the fish dock was loaded from end to end with an estimated 6,000 bags, another 1,000 were waiting to be loaded at the East Station.

In addition to the Head Post Office, a new parcels office for distribution of parcels to Peterborough and district was opened in the old covered-in market on December 8th. Another step, designed to ease the rush at the Head Post Office was the extension of the counter by about another 20 feet, and this turned out to be a permanent alteration. Registered parcels had jumped at Peterborough from 345 per week, pre-war, to a figure of 10,000 per week.

Spitfire Plaque

On Christmas Day, Councillor Mrs. Bryant, received from the Ministry of Aircraft Production a plaque to commemorate the raising by the city during the time she was Mayor, the sum of £5,600 for a Spitfire. The plaque was of engraved steel mounted on oak, and below the wings of the RAF and the word "Merit" was the inscription:

"In the hour of peril the citizens of Peterborough and District earned the gratitude of the British nations, sustaining the valour of the Royal Air Force and fortifying the cause of freedom, by the gift of a Spitfire aircraft. They shall mount up with wings as eagles."

The plaque was later passed on to the present Mayor at that time, Mr. H.J. Farrow, and was afterwards placed in the Mayor's Parlour.

Shelter Workers

On December 29th, it was announced at a City Council meeting that a force of men, not exceeding 50, would have to be made available for transfer from the City to another area to take part in the construction of air raid shelters. This order came in a letter from the Deputy Principal Officer of the ARP Committee, and was unwelcome news to many in the Council. With a large number of shelters in the city unfinished, condemned, already pulled down or not begun, apparently, so the Council said, due to lack of labour, Alderman Howard asked why this transfer was deemed necessary at all.

175

The City Engineer stated that the city had well over its allocation of men for shelter work. The percentage of shelters required by a city in order to reach the permissible standard of protection was 60 per cent. Peterborough had, including schemes complete or nearing completion, 74 per cent. The protection in the area to which the workmen were being transferred was under 30 per cent, hence the movement of labour.

The point was also made that people were more readily taking to the new Morrison shelters that were on offer, but, countered Alderman Howard, people who were in areas where street shelters were being built for them were not entitled to Morrison shelters. He was informed that although what he was saying was strictly true, the Engineer had received verbal permission to supply Morrison shelters in place of street shelters where they were required.

Salvage
Figures for the salvage sold in November had now been announced: kitchen waste, 33 tons 17 cwts.; tins, 5tons 1cwt.; bottles, 101 dozen.; paper 39tons 2cwts. In six months the tonnage had been 395 tons 10cwts.; which sold for £1,323 19s. 6d. and yielded £188 13s. 9d. as a bonus. This money was paid: £5 to the Foreman, and £4.7s.6d. each to the 42 men. The salvage department was scheduled as "essential work".

Road Accidents
The increasing number of road accidents in the City and District, especially two involving young children, reflected a national trend in which road accidents had soared. A national campaign was started in order to make people aware of the dangers particularly during the black-out. In the last twelve months of peace, road deaths for the country as a whole averaged eighteen per day. In the first year of war, this average had risen to twenty-three, and in the second year it rose to twenty-eight.

In peace time some 2,400 fatal road accidents, or 28 per cent of the total, occurred during the hours of darkness. In the first year of war black-out fatalities were 4,500, 54 per cent of the total, and in the second year, 4,300, 43 per cent of the total.

Too many drivers were driving too fast, and too many pedestrians failed to realise that although they could see the dimmed lights of approaching vehicles, more often than not the drivers of those vehicles could not see them.

During the first two years of war, 5,000 more people were killed on the roads of Britain than in the two preceding peace years. 4,000 of these extra deaths were among pedestrians, including many children. Until the summer of 1940 the number of child pedestrians killed remained at about pre-war level. Afterwards, the situation deteriorated, and in the second year of war the fatalities were 50 per cent above pre-war.

A poster competition for school children was organised as being the best way of getting them to think about the subject of road safety.

A Grand Christmas Day
Through the generous efforts of a number of Peterborough people, some 300 men of the Services who were unable to get Christmas leave and had nothing else to do in the city were wonderfully entertained at Woodston Church Hall on Christmas Day. The wife of the Rector, Mrs. J. A. J. Atkinson, acted as the 'go between' to bring

176

entertainment and Christmas cheer to the men.

There were plentiful supplies of homemade cakes, sausage rolls, mince pies etc. and the men were made to feel at home. Out of forgotten cupboards at the Rectory were unearthed Victorian dresses and with these fancy dress competitions were held, with sausage rolls as prizes. Throughout the afternoon and evening the men played games and were entertained by local artistes.

In addition to all this work, the organizers of the party took hampers of food to camps and were busy distributing them until after night-fall. The party was organized by the church in Woodston, assisted by the WVS.

Away From Home
One of the final sad messages of the year concerned Leading Stoker C.E. Clark, of 67, Padholme Road, who was reported missing. Stoker Clark, who had joined the Navy before the war had started, had been serving on board the cruiser HMS DUNEDIN when she was torpedoed in the Atlantic by a U-boat and sunk between West Africa and Brazil, on November 24th. He would not be home for New Year.

GRAY, Ina Cecil – Section Leader 4281, Auxiliary Territorial Service. Died, aged 25, on the 12th January 1941. The daughter of Capt. Owen Gray and Marion Gray, Peterborough. Buried in Aldershot Military Cemetery. Grave A.34.

RUFF, George William – 200 Palmerston Road, Woodston, Peterborough. A railwayman. Died, aged 37, on the 16th January 1941 at the Peterborough Memorial Hospital as a result of injuries received following an air raid whilst on duty. The husband of A. E. L. Ruff of 200, Palmerston Road, Woodston, Peterborough.

FOSTER, Ronald – Gunner 845057, 2 Battery, 1 LAA Regiment, Royal Artillery. Died, aged 27, on the 2nd February 1941. The son of James and Mary Foster of Darlington, Co. Durham and the husband of Annie Foster of Peterborough. Commemorated at the Cambridge Crematorium. Column 1.

PURDY, Thomas Gordon – Leading Aircraftman 945632, Royal Air Force. Died, aged 23, on the 7th February 1941. The husband of Louisa Purdy of Peterborough. Buried in Eastfield Cemetery, Peterborough. Div. 4. Block 4. Grave 1703.

DOUCY, Charles Arthur – Able Seaman P/JX 167380, HM Submarine Snapper (N39), Royal Navy. Died, aged 21, on the 12th February 1941. The Snapper was lost in home waters after returning from duties in the Mediterranean. The son of Joseph and Lily Doucy of Old Fletton, Peterborough. No known grave he is commemorated on the Portsmouth Naval Memorial, Column 3, Panel 47.

STEADMAN, Harold Francis – 211 New England, Peterborough. Able Seaman P/JX 210207, Royal Navy. Died, aged 24, on the 24th February 1941 when he was a crew member on the SS Linaria that was one of 41 ships in Convoy OB288 that was lost in the North Atlantic. The Linaria was sunk as a result of an attack by U-boat 96. All 31 crew members died. The son of John and Hannah Steadman of New England, Peterborough. He has no known grave and is commemorated on the Portsmouth Naval Memorial, Panel 49, Column 3.

LARKIN, Edward Truman Wyly – Master, Motor Vessel British Strength (London), Merchant Navy. Died, aged 50, on the 15th March 1941. Ship believed sunk by the "Scharnhorst". Only two crew died, the rest were taken prisoner. The son of Matthew and Matilda Truman Larkin and the husband of Ada Larkin of Peterborough. No known grave he is commemorated on the Tower Hill Memorial, London. Panel 21.

STOCKMAN, Douglas Ronald – 18 Williamson Avenue, Peterborough. Leading Airman P/FX 80745, HMS Grebe, Royal Navy. Died, aged 19, on the 19th March 1941 on air operations, as a Telegraphist Air Gunner, in Crete, serving with the Fleet Air Arm. The son of Tom and Violet Lena Stockman. He has no known grave and is commemorated on the Lee-On-Solent Memorial, Bay 2, Panel 2.

BROTHWOOD, John T.V.W. – The 'Horse and Jockey', City Road, Peterborough. Driver 5884053, Royal Engineers, seconded to No 5 Commando's.

Died, aged 22, on the 3rd April 1941. The son of Herbert Bertram John and Margaret Ethel Brothwood of Peterborough. Buried in Eastfield Cemetery, Peterborough, Div. 3, Block 16, Grave 6557.

PRITCHARD, Thomas James – Flying Officer 44422, Royal Air Force. Died, aged 44, on the 5th April 1941. The son of Albert and Sarah Pritchard and the husband of Nora Pritchard of Peterborough. Buried in Kranji War Cemetery, Singapore. 37. C. 13.

HODSON, Bernard Stanley – 28 Oxford Road, Peterborough. Sapper 1947251, Royal Engineers. Died, aged 20, on the 6th April 1941 of Meningitis. The son of Frank and Fanny Hodson of Peterborough. Buried in Eastfield Cemetery, Peterborough, Div. 1, Block 15, Grave 5845.

DAVIES, Anthony John – 77 Huntley Grove, Peterborough. Leading Seaman P/JX 148057, HMS Voltaire, Royal Navy. Died, aged 20, on the 9th April 1941. On the 4th April HMS Voltaire, an armed merchant cruiser, was on isolated patrol in the central Atlantic when at 0615 hours she was spotted by the lookouts of the German raider Thor and the ships headed for each other. At 0645 hours they opened fire and by 0649 hours the Voltaire was ablaze. By 0715 hours only two guns remained in action and by 0800 hours she hoisted the white flag and she sunk shortly after. There were 75 dead and 197 survivors rescued by the Germans. As Davies died on the 9th it can be assumed that it was of wounds received on the 4th. The son of Thomas and Doris Davies of Old Fletton, Peterborough. He has no known grave and is commemorated on the Portsmouth Naval Memorial, Panel 46, Column 3.

THOMPSON, Benjamin – 155 Gladstone Street, Peterborough. A Firewatcher. Died, aged 69, in Priestgate, Peterborough on the 10th May 1941 during an air raid whilst on duty. The husband of Alice Thompson of 155 Gladstone Street, Peterborough.

WYATT, Sidney Everitt – 128 St. Johns Street, Peterborough. A Firewatcher. Died, aged 48, in Priestgate, Peterborough on the 10th May 1941 during an air raid whilst on duty. The son of Edith Mary Wyatt, of 3 Station Road, Sheringham, Norfolk and the husband of Edith Annie Wyatt of 128 St. Johns Street, Peterborough.

ARNOLD, Samuel Arthur – Peterborough. Leading Stoker P/KX 90102, Royal Navy. Died, aged 25, on the 23rd May 1941 when HMS Kashmir was sunk by enemy aircraft bombs in the battle of Crete along with the destroyers Juno, Greyhound and Kelly. The son of George and Hannah Arnold of Peterborough. No known grave he is commemorated on the Portsmouth Naval Memorial, Panel 54, Column 2.

SAMPSON, Leonard – Orton Waterville, Peterborough. Leading Telegraphist C/JX 145023, HMS Kelly, Royal Navy. Died, aged 22, on the 23rd May 1941 when the destroyer HMS Kelly was sunk by aircraft bombs during the battle for Crete along with the destroyers Kashmir, Greyhound and Juno. The son of Ethel Sampson of Orton Waterville, Peterborough. No known grave he is commemorated on the Chatham Naval Memorial, reference 46, 1.

179

GAUTREY, Reginald William – 127 Cromwell Road, Peterborough. Flight Lieutenant 37674, Royal Air Force. Died, aged 27, on the 23rd May 1941 while serving in No 45 Group and whose mission was to ferry Catalina aircraft from America to Britain. It is believed that he was flying Catalina I, AH560 of OADU that went missing between the Azores and Portugal on the 23rd May 1941. The son of Mr and Mrs J. F. Gautrey of Peterborough. No known grave he is commemorated on the Malta Memorial. Panel 1. Column 1.

TOOGOOD, Leslie Bertram – 62 Orton Avenue, Peterborough. Marine PO/X 4878, HMS Hood, Royal Marines. Died, aged 21, on the 24th May 1941 when the Battle Cruiser HMS Hood was sunk by the German Battleship the Bismarck. The son of Bertie and Alice Maud Toogood of Woodston, Peterborough. No known grave he is commemorated on the Portsmouth Naval Memorial, Panel 59, Column 2.

LAYTON, Sidney George – 22 Hampden Road, Peterborough. Marine PO/X 3392, HMS Hood, Royal Marines. Died, aged 19, on the 24th May 1941 when the Battle Cruiser HMS Hood was sunk by the German Battleship the Bismarck. The son of Gladys Mary Layton of Peterborough. No known grave he is commemorated on the Portsmouth Naval Memorial, Panel 59, Column 1.

BINNS, Thomas William – 9 Towler Street, Peterborough. Private 5881824, 5th Northamptonshire Regiment. Died, aged 26, on the 13th June 1941. Next of kin not known. Buried in Eastfield Cemetery, Peterborough, Block 16, Grave 6361.

BERRISFORD, Albert – 13 Windmill Street, Peterborough. Private 4977970, 1st Sherwood Foresters (Nott's & Derby Regiment). Died, aged 27, on the 15th June 1941. Next of kin not known. Buried in Nicosia War Cemetery, Cyprus, Grave 5.A.4.

DAVIS, Joseph William – 15 Bright Street, Peterborough. Trooper 7887555, 6th Royal Tank Regiment, RAC. Died, aged 22, on either the 15th or 16th June 1941. The son of Francis Edward and Elizabeth Davis. No known grave he is commemorated on the Alamein Memorial, Egypt, Column 22.

WELDON, Ernest Edward – 36 Silver Street, Peterborough. Sergeant Pilot 754906, Royal Air Force Volunteer Reserve. Died, aged 23, on the 18th June 1941 when he was 2nd Pilot in an Armstrong – Whitworth Whitley Mk V, Serial No NL462, Code Letters GE – V that took off from Linton – on – Ouse to attack Cologne. His aircraft was shot down by a German night fighter. Four were killed and one was taken prisoner. The son of Horace Edward and Sarah Elizabeth Weldon and the husband of Eileen Mary Weldon of Doncaster. Buried in Eindhoven (Woensel) General Cemetery, Holland. Plot JJ, Grave 22.

HANCOCK, Charles William – St. Margaret's Road, Fletton, Peterborough. Sergeant 909505, Wireless Operator/Air Gunner, Royal Air Force Volunteer Reserve. Died, aged 23, on the 26th June 1941. He was a gunner in a Handley Page Hampden Mk 1, Serial No AD788, code letters EA-V that took off from RAF Scampton to attack Kiel. The Pilot survived and became a POW but the other three crew were killed. The son of John and Mary Hancock and the husband of Ivy Irene

180

Hancock of Old Fletton, Peterborough. Buried in Kiel War Cemetery, Germany. Grave 3.C.2.

ORTON, Ronald Henry – 33 Vere Road, Peterborough. Pilot Officer 62313, 11 Operational Training Unit, Royal Air Force Volunteer Reserve. Died, aged 19, on the 26th June 1941. His aircraft, a Wellington IC R1292, had taken off from Bassingbourn on 21st June 1941 for a night flying detail. While in the circuit, the port engine failed, thus necessitating a forced-landing at 02:15 hours in which the aircraft hit some trees to the West of Wendy, a little over 10 miles SW of Cambridge. Five days after the accident, Pilot Officer Orton died from his injuries. Two others died as well from their wounds. The son of Luke Henry Orton and Eva Ruth Fairchild. Believed to be the Brother in Law of Walter Michael Blom who was also killed. Buried in Eastfield Cemetery, Peterborough. Grave 4198, Div. 1. Block 11.

IVISON, John – Private 4532838, 2nd West Yorkshire Regiment (Prince of Wales Own). Died, aged 33, on the 17th July 1941. The husband of M. Ivison of Peterborough. No known grave he is commemorated on the Athens War Memorial, Greece. Face 5.

RODGERS, George Andrew – 231 Eastfield Road, Peterborough. Fourth Engineer Officer, Merchant Navy. Died, aged 27, on the 22nd October 1941. At 01.42 hours on the 22nd October 1941, the tanker MV Darkdale was torpedoed and sunk by U-68 while anchored in Jamestown harbour, St. Helena, as a storage ship. 37 crew members and four gunners were lost. The husband of Mary Rodgers of Greenock. No known grave he is commemorated on the Tower Hill Memorial, London, Panel 34.

TUCKER, Charles George – Gunner 1576527, 291 Battery, 94 HAA Regiment, Royal Artillery. Died, aged 24, on the 29th October 1941. The son of Charles and Alice Tucker of Stanground, Peterborough. Buried in Heliopolis War Cemetery, Egypt. 1. A. 15.

WHALLEY, Kenneth Edward – 144 Lincoln Road, Peterborough. Pilot Officer 61941, 451 (RAAF) Squadron, Royal Air Force Volunteer Reserve. Died, aged 23, on the 12th November 1941. His Hurricane I, V7353 was shot down by a German BF-109 during reconnaissance at Salum, Egypt. The son of Edward and Mary Whalley of Werrington, Peterborough. No known grave he is commemorated on the Alamein memorial, Egypt. Column 241.

KINGSTON, Edna – Cross Street, Peterborough. A civilian who died, age unknown, on the 14th November 1941 following injuries received in an air raid in Peterborough on the 10th May 1941. The daughter of Frank Kingston who also died.

KINGSTON, Frank – Cross Street, Peterborough. A civilian who died, aged 66, at the Memorial Hospital, Peterborough on the 26th November 1941 following injuries received in an air raid in Peterborough on the 10th May 1941. The father of Edna Kingston who also died.

PYLE, Arthur John – Peterborough. Pilot Officer/Observer 103034, 40 Squadron, Royal Air Force Volunteer Reserve. Died, aged 25, on the 6th December 1941. The son of John and M. M. Pyle of Peterborough and the husband of F. F. Pyle. Buried in Salerno War Cemetery, Italy. Grave II.C.5.

POPELEY, Alec Charles – 25 Hankey Street, Peterborough. Aircraftman 1st Class, 405 (RCAF) Squadron, Royal Air Force Volunteer Reserve. Died, aged 25, on the 8th December 1941. No known next of kin. Buried in Eastfield Cemetery, Peterborough, Div. 1. Block 7. Grave 7377.

KINGSFORD, Edward Cyril – Peterborough. Corporal S/57362, 12 Company, Royal Army Service Corps. Died, aged 23, on the 22nd December 1941 in Hong Kong. The son of the Revd. C. E. B. Kingsford, M.A., and of Mary A. Kingsford of Peterborough. No known grave, he is commemorated on the Sai Wan Memorial, Hong Kong. Column 22.

MANN, A. – Company Quartermaster Sergeant, Royal Army Service Corps. Died, age unknown, on the 22nd December 1941. The husband of Emily Mann of Stanground, Peterborough. No known grave he is commemorated on the Sai Wan Memorial, China. Column 33.

1942

The Year Begins in Gaol

It was a bad start to the year for two men working at the Woodston sugar beet factory. Both men were soldiers and had been released by the army in order to work at the factory and both had been arrested for stealing sugar which was on ration and strictly controlled.

Appearing at the Norman Cross Magistrates on Tuesday 6th January, Lionel Jaffe, aged 23, stated: "we don't call it stealing in the Army; we call it scrounging." Jaffe was accused of stealing 40lb of sugar to the value of 15 shillings, from the factory between October 27th and November 27th 1941. He pleaded not guilty.

Jaffe stated in court that he worked at the factory and had not stolen the sugar. He was allowed to go around the factory "with no questions asked" and there was a room through which the sugar passed and there was always a lot of waste on the floor. He had been told by other employees that it was waste and therefore he occasionally filled a bag and took it home.

After stating that what he had done was called scrounging in the Army the Chairman asked "Do you mean that stealing is not stealing?" To which Jaffe replied' "If you like to take it that way." The Chairman told him he was "casting an aspersion on the people in the Army." After a retirement of 15 minutes the Chairman returned and declared, "There has been too much of this stealing. We are at war and are rationing this stuff, which is much wanted. We are only allowed so much and it was a particularly reprehensible trick to take other people's share. Jaffe's previous good character was taken into consideration, in the Army he had been the company tailor, but he was sent to prison for one month.

The second defendant was Frederick William Rowell, 24, of 3, Durham Road, Peterborough. He was charged with stealing 37lbs of sugar between December 1st and 26th, 1941. Rowell pleaded guilty but told the arresting officer, "I did not bring it out; I won't say who did." The court was told that he had no authority to take the sugar which was of industrial grade.

Asked if there was any question of the sugar being "waste," Mr. William John Greenwood, the factory warehouse keeper, told the court that there was no such thing as waste sugar. It was all cleaned up, melted and remade. Rowell said he was sorry and that it had been his first offence. The Bench stated that they meant to do what they could to stop the stealing as people were being robbed of their rations and Rowell was also sent to prison for one month.

Waste Paper Drive

On a lighter note, a banner had now been hung the length of the Market Place and in letters a foot high stated: "Produce Your Paper and Put Peterborough in the Prize List." This announced the city's part in the National Waste Paper Collection Contest.

The Waste Paper Recovery Association Ltd had given £20,000 to the nation to be distributed to various charities. The allocation would be by way of a contest for the largest amount of waste paper collected per head of population by towns and districts during the month of January. Peterborough was in competition with other towns and urban and rural districts in Huntingdonshire, Hertfordshire, Bedfordshire,

Northamptonshire and the Soke. The area had been allocated £1,000 to be split into five prizes as follows: 1st prize £500, 2nd £250, 3rd £100, and three consolation prizes of £50. The prize money had to be allocated to charities and it had been decided that if Peterborough won it would be divided up equally between Mrs. Churchill's Aid to Russia Fund and the Memorial Hospital. The City Engineer stated the three aims:

1. Meeting the national need for waste paper urgently required in the making of cases for munitions of all kinds.
2. Helping local charities in these difficult times.
3. Peterborough winning the area contest.

"I want every building in the borough ransacked for paper, books, cardboard, etc., during January, and am aiming for a figure of one hundred tons for the month." Businesses were encouraged with a promise that confidential waste would be collected separately, baled in cardboard and sent straight to the mill for pulping.

Mrs. A. H. Mellows, placed the WVS at the disposal of the City Engineer, and 1,000 "cogs" – volunteers from the city's schools enrolled before Christmas – had received folders and pamphlets to deliver to every household. The folder explained what to do with paper and cardboard, bones, metal scrap and food waste, and explained how the various materials could be used to help the war effort. The instructions to the "cogs" contained the note:

"Please see that every house is emptied of all its waste paper during the month of January, and help not only to win a prize for Peterborough, but to win the war."

If required, the "cogs" would also arrange to collect salvaged paper for removal to specially erected booths of wood and canvas which would be emptied regularly. The booths were sited as follows:

1. Werrington Green.
2. Cock Inn, Werrington.
3. Depot No. 4, Mountsteven Avenue.
4. Paston Lane (Shelter 382a).
5. Keeton Road Ambulance Station.
6. Bluebell Corner, Dogsthorpe.
7. Opposite 70, Garton End Road.
8. Opposite 3, Warbon Avenue.
9. Searjeant Street (Shelter 524a).
10. Lime Tree Avenue.
11. Huntley Grove (elastic factory).
12. Broadway Gardens.
13. Newark.
14. Padholme Road Ambulance Station.
15. Bishop's Road (Star Road end).
16. St. John's Street.
17. Church Walk.
18. Westgate (near public shelters).
19. Alderman's Drive (Shelter 1040).
20. At Moorfield and Priory Roads (Shelter 1080).

21. At Thorpe and Thorpe Park Roads.
22. Longthorpe.
23. Palmerston Road, Demontford Terrace.
24. At London Road and Fletton Avenue.

The following schools had their "cogs" enrolled before Christmas:

- Eastholm Senior Boys, Mr. Taylor.
- Eastholm Senior Girls, Miss Lockwood.
- St. Mark's Junior Boys, Mr. Hayes.
- St. Mark's Junior Girls, Miss Pywell.
- Lincoln Road Senior Boys, Mr. Talbutt.
- Lincoln Road Senior Girls, Miss Lever.
- Newark, Miss Paul.
- West Town Junior Mixed, Miss Campbell.
- Walton Senior Mixed, Mr. Avery.
- Werrington, Mr. Martin.
- Woodston Mixed, Mr. Hankins.
- County School for Girls, Miss Vail.
- King's School, Mr. Shearcroft.
- Westwood House School, Miss Mattock.

The booths and refuse freighters were plastered with three slogans, the first being the original one at the Market Place, the other two being; "Turn your cupboards out. We want your waste paper, magazines and old books NOW," and "support your local Hospital by giving your waste paper now." The estimated yield for the first week of January was 30 tons.

In the same edition of the Peterborough Standard that reported the Waste Paper Collection Contest, a letter from Kenneth Murchison of Hargrave Hall was published entitled "Old Documents." The letter was in support of an appeal by the Northamptonshire Record Society who urged that supervision and discrimination should be exercised by everyone responsible for handing over old papers, manuscripts, records, accounts, diaries, etc. for pulping.

The writer warned that there was a real danger that documents of priceless value and writings of the greatest historic interest may be destroyed. Miss Joan Wake, County Hall, Northampton, had stated her desire to go anywhere in the county to inspect potentially important documents before they were pulped.

"For want of thought and discretion," went on Mr. Murchison, "irreparable damage may be done in half a moment." No doubt despite this warning, many important archives were sent to the paper mill throughout the course of the war.

Soke and City Home Guard
A number of changes were now announced regarding the Soke Home Guard. Corporal C. A. Scoble, of the 2nd Northants (Soke) Home Guard, was now promoted Sergeant, and volunteer W. D. Godwin was appointed Lance Corporal. Volunteer F. E. Locke had now been enrolled in 'E' Company, and Volunteer A. W. Garey had been transferred to Baker Perkins' platoon of the City Battalion.

The following promotions were also now notified in the City Battalion:

185

Corporal N.J.C. Donald to Sergeant, Volunteers L.G. Dunham and W.H.S. Stanley to be Corporals. Volunteers R.G. Vale, J. Smith and C. Roberts to be Lance Corporals.

Taken on strength: Volunteers C. Hill, G.C. Winch, F.E. Garnett, R.S. Fletton, D.R. Wakefield, R.E. Webster (from 17th City of London), C.J. Ruderham (from 2nd Northants), L.H. Cheshire, D.G. London, S.C. Puckey, N.V. Critchlow and F.W. Stimpson (from Market Harborough). Twenty-two have been struck off through being called to H.M. Forces at their own request, on transfer or "services no longer required."

Certificates

A total of 134 (City and Fletton) First Aid and Home Nursing awards had now been made as a result of recent examinations by the Peterborough Centre of the St. Johns Ambulance Association. 26 preliminary first aid (Juniors), 67 first aid certificates, 10 vouchers, 5 medallions, 5 labels to medallions, 16 home nursing certificates and three pendants. Home nursing classes, carried out by the St John's Ambulance Brigade would commence at the Trinity Street First Aid Post on January 9th.

Of the 34 members of the Peterborough and District Spotters Club who sat for the national test identification of aircraft by silhouette, 5 gained first class certificates for answers of 100 percent correct and 17 second class certificates for 80 to 99 percent. All first class, and most of the second class winners were school boys. The awards were:

First Class
- D. Greenwood.
- J. Handley.
- N. Rollings.
- P. Sandy.
- R. Tucker.

Second Class
- W. Spreckley.
- P. Gosling.
- F.G. Scarr.
- J. Wilson.
- R. Crosby.
- C. Booker.
- R. Maywood.
- D. Schafer.
- R. Evans.
- A. French.
- R.N. Fox.
- C. Parnell.
- R. Blackman.
- R.J. Hill.
- P. Steels.
- F. Waumsley.
- B. Norwell.

Other Volunteers

The W.V.S. was now asking for more helpers for their canteens. Volunteers were especially needed for the 9am to 11am turn at the Long Causeway canteen on Tuesdays. There was also a continual shortage of night helpers, the turn from 11pm to 7am on Saturday, Sunday and Monday nights were mainly the problem.

Owing to the call-up of women, there was also some difficulty in finding drivers for the mobile canteens – now four in number, three of which ran all day and one at night. Offers for once-a-week duty or even once-a-fortnight were desperately sought and also people for reserve duty.

On January 9th, 334 candidates applied for training as women postal engineers. Of those, 36 were to be trained at a special school at Peterborough. Over 100 were needed in the district but lack of opportunity for training them was holding up recruitment. The G.P.O. department declared that the women were as good as the men.

Police Report for 1941

In the third week of January, the Police Report for 1941 was published, produced by the Chief Constable of Peterborough, Mr. T. Danby, and addressed to the Watch Committee. The Chief Constable stated that the year had been an extremely busy one for the Force. War legislation had very much increased the work, often resulting in greatly increased hours of duty. He mentioned the work of the Special Constabulary and the Warden's Service as rendering very valuable assistance to the Force, and the large number of citizens both male and female who had volunteered for the Fire Guard Service. "I am not sure," he said, "that the loyal and devoted work of these services for the public welfare is fully realised."

The report painted a depressing picture, one which those who believe that crime was considerably less prevalent in times gone by; and that the war years brought people together in a common cause and created good neighbours of all of us, may find themselves abruptly corrected.

The report described the great deal of difficulty which had been experienced with wholesale thefts on the railway; very serious thefts from the General Post Office, and the increase of crime in other ways. During this time the officers of the detective department had performed splendidly.

Scores of cycles had been stolen and it had been necessary to undertake special searches and extensive detective enquiries. Special Constables had helped to stop all cyclists leaving town at key points such as railway and river bridges in order to examine their cycles. All Army camps had been visited and a good many cycles had been recovered.

During the year, 815 indictable offences had been reported to the police. It was found after enquiries that 172 cycles and other articles had been misplaced, lost or taken in error. This left a total of 643, an increase of 143 on the previous year. Offenders in 443 offences were traced. For non-indictable offences 557 persons were proceeded against, a decrease of 36 compared with 1940. Thirty-three persons were dealt with for drunkenness compared with 24 in 1940, 16 were residents, 12 non-residents and 5 vagrants.

The value of property stolen was estimated at £2,368 6s. 9d., and of that recovered at £1,184 15s. 2d. In 1940 the figures were, property stolen £1,336 15s. 7d., value recovered £327 9s. 11d. The value of monies and property obtained by fraud £219 9s. 2d., compared with £20 2s. 10d. the previous year.

During the year 762 persons were reported for offences against sundry statutes and bye-laws, and were warned; 214 of those were for motoring offences. 1,034 persons (including 219 for motoring offences) were dealt with in a similar manner in 1940. Twenty-seven persons were arrested by the City Police for other forces and 57 for the military authorities.

Enquiries had been made and reports submitted to the Coroner in 69 cases of death; 46 inquests were held.

From other forces 2,513 enquiries relating to persons and property wanted and stolen were received for investigation. This work for other forces had created a great burden on the already stretched city force.

Police on night duty found the doors and windows of 140 dwelling houses, 329 lock-up premises and 182 shops insecure.

There were 333 dogs found and placed in the kennels. Delay in tracing owners frequently occurred through their neglect to have their names and addresses inscribed on the dog's collars. It was stated that unless owners took more care in this respect, the police would be compelled to take steps to secure observance of the law on this point. 65 horses, cattle etc. were found straying and restored to their owners.

Of 1,751 articles reported as lost, a large proportion was traced and restored to the owners; 2,348 articles (money, jewellery, etc.), were found and taken charge of by the police; 73 prisoners were conveyed to Leicester, and 7 to Holloway.

There were four registered common lodging houses in the city with a total accommodation for 66 lodgers. All had been regularly visited and found to be satisfactory.

The authorized strength of the Police Force was 56, plus 2 additional, one a policewoman, and 3 civilian clerks. Eleven members of the force were serving with H.M. Forces – 4 in the Army and 7 in the RAF. All members of the force held St. John Ambulance certificates.

The report stated that the increasing number of accidents was a grave concern. There had been 567 accidents involving traffic which had resulted in 7 deaths and 232 people being injured. The accidents were classified as follows:

- Public service vehicles – 40
- Motorcycles – 27
- Private cars 177
- Motor cabs – 14
- Goods vehicles – 129
- Horse drawn vehicles – 15
- Pedal cycles – 97
- Pedestrians – 51
- Dogs killed – 17

Two of the deaths were caused by motorcycles, two by private cars, two by pedal cycles and one by a pedestrian.

The number of street accidents had increased from 539 in 1940 to 569 in 1941, and unsurprisingly drivers of private cars and goods vehicles were responsible for the majority. There had been constant reports made of vehicles speeding and being driven dangerously in crowded streets and on main roads, especially during the hours of darkness. Many appeals had been made through the local press for people to take more care and consider other road users.

A great number of pedal cyclists still did not have efficient lights on their cycles. The report stated that it was especially dangerous to ride without a rear light during the black-out hours and an intensive check was being made by the police. An increasing number of complaints was being received of people being injured by falling over cycles left on footpaths and at the kerbside during the hours of darkness. This was an offence for which owners could be liable for damages to injured persons.

The order enforcing a speed limit of 20 miles an hour in built-up areas during the hours of darkness had served a very useful purpose, but there were still a number of people who considerably exceeded the speed limit, especially, it was stated, if they believed the police were busy elsewhere.

Under the heading "Children and Young Persons," the Chief Constable stated that in 1941, 6 juveniles were proceeded against for house and shop-breaking, 34 for larceny of cycles, from shops, unattended vehicles etc., three for indecent assault and 18 for non-indictable offences, i.e. offences against traffic laws, etc.

In a statement which some would see as being as relevant today as it was during the war, Chief Constable Danby wrote;

"There has been an increase in the number of offences, some of a rather serious character. In nearly every instance a lack of parental care and control was disclosed. Whilst there were a good many cases of damage, the conduct of children generally has been good.

There is always a tendency to speak of children as being worse than those of the preceding generation, but having had experience in a busier industrial town, I have always considered that on the whole they are no worse and, in fact, better behaved than formerly. I do not think there is any cause for alarm so far as Peterborough is concerned."

Casualties

It was reported in the news on January 29th, that Sergeant, 1359941, Wilfred Roy Beeton, RAFVR, of 60, Newark Avenue, Peterborough, had been killed as the result of a flying accident. Sergeant Beeton, who was 29 years of age, was a wireless operator air gunner and had been killed on Saturday 17th January. He was the second son of Mr. and Mrs. W. Beeton, 105, London Road, and formerly of Ramsey. He left a widow, Beatrice Mary Beeton, of East Bergholt, Suffolk, and two children aged 2 and 5 months respectively. After leaving Ramsey Grammar School, he was employed at Manningtree, Essex, until he joined the RAF at the outbreak of war. The funeral took place at St. Margaret's, Fletton, after which he was buried in Old Fletton Cemetery, section 6, grave 128.

At about the same time, Mr. and Mrs. H. Palmer, 11, Princes Gardens, were notified that their only son, Sapper Herbert Reginald Palmer, Royal Engineers, was reported missing after the fall of the garrison in Hong Kong on December 25th, 1941. Before he joined the Army, Spr. Palmer had been a draughtsman with Messrs Peter Brotherhood Ltd. It appears that Sapper Palmer was not killed as he does not feature in any of the casualty lists published at the end of the war.

Mr. and Mrs. G.E. Hillson, 66, Wootton Avenue, Old Fletton, now received bad news regarding their son, Engine Room Artificer, George William Hillson, Royal Navy, (HMS VIMIERA), who was now reported missing. Twenty years of age,

E.R.A. Hillson was their only son and had been apprenticed to Joseph Farrow and Co. Ltd., in the engineering department, before he joined the Navy. He had also been a member of the Woodston Boy Scouts. HMS VIMIERA, under the command of Lieutenant-Commander Angus Alexander Mackenzie, RNR, was sunk by a mine in the Thames estuary off East Spile Buoy on 9 January 1942 with the loss of 96 hands. E.R.A. Hillson is commemorated on the Chatham Naval Memorial.

Two Tier Shelters
To meet demand for an indoor shelter of a larger capacity than the Morrison table type, a two-tier shelter had now been designed and was available for free supply and for sale in the city area. The new shelter was of the same construction as the table shelter but was 4ft 3ins high as against 2ft 5ins. This allowed two beds to be provided one above the other. As it was much higher, the shelter could not be used as a table. The shelter was available for issue to households in exchange for the earlier table type.

So far about 2,000 shelters of the original type had been issued in the city. The council was drawing up plans to recover shelters which had been issued to householders but had not been erected indoors. A number were said to have been seen lying derelict and rusty in front and back gardens.

A further scheme for shelters for Thorpe Road House and the Hospital, estimated to cost £2,124, had been submitted. The scheme included Morrison shelters where convenient.

City Home Guard Changes
Lt. F.A. Errington (HQ) and Lt. T.A. Burnett ('D' Comp), now received permission to resign their Commissions in the 1st Northants (City) Bn. H.G. The latter to re-enroll as a Volunteer and transfer to the 8th West Riding Battalion.

Lt. F.S. Ruald, Sgt. Donald, Sgt. Gooding and Volunteer Burleigh had been on a course of instruction, and Sgt. Ludbrook, Cpl. Booty, L/Cpl Taylor and Sgt. Wittering were on a course of fieldcraft.

The C-in-C Home Forces had now approved the award of a Certificate for Good Service to C/Sgt. R. Collin.

Volunteer A.E.M. Lee had now been promoted to Sergeant and the following Volunteers were taken on the strength of the Battalion:

- S. Kirby Tomlin
- C.W.R.A. Needham
- E.E. Ward
- B.G. Norris
- G.J. Forbes
- F.W. Goodwin
- P.H. Casson
- H.H. Mitchell

The following had now passed an examination of the St. John's Ambulance Association "with high honours":

- Cpl. F.W. Harwell ('A' Comp)

190

- Vol. W.E. Holbrow ('A' Comp)
- Vol. G. Sanderson ('A' Comp)
- L/Cpl B.R.F. Casson ('B')
- Vol. A.C. Fox ('D')
- Vol. C.D. Wickes ('C')
- Vol. A.D. Luff ('C')

In the 2nd Northants (Soke) Battalion H.G., Cpl. C.A. Sable, HQ, Co., was promoted to Sergeant and Volunteer W.D. Godwin, 'E' Comp. to Lance Corporal.

Street Guards

A scheme had now been submitted to Region for the sites of 11 group headquarters for Street Fire Guards. There had been some doubt about the duties of these Street Fire Guards as distinct from those engaged on watching buildings. To resolve this Mr. Rowland Hill, Fire Guard Staff Officer, issued the following directions to street watchers:

1. When on duty, be dressed so that when Alert is sound the section of street concerned can be immediately patrolled
2. During quiet periods, when a watcher may not actually be patrolling the streets, he or she should be in a position to see any bombs that fall. It is desirable to be outside when planes are actually passing over, with due regard for personal protection against H.E. bombs.
3. Should the watcher consider there is imminent danger, the Marshall should be called, and he would use his discretion regarding calling out all other members of the party.
4. Should incendiary bombs actually fall in the vicinity, an immediate warning should be given by short, sharp blasts on whistle, or other effective means.
5. The watcher on first period of duty to rouse his or her successor and pass on information about Alerts, etc.
6. Duties extend over the hours of black-out.

More Casualties

More sad news was reaching the city in February. Gunner Arthur Edward Steels, 885649, Royal Artillery, 135 (The Hertfordshire Yeomanry) Field Regt., of 168, Clarence Road, had now been reported as killed in action in the Far East on 26th January. He was the fifth son of Mr. John Frederick and Mrs. Rose Priscilla Steels. Aged 21 he was a Territorial for several years before the war and was a cleaner on the L.M.S. He is buried in Taiping War Cemetery, Collective Grave 1. A. 1-12.

Gunner Frederick Charles Wright, 905440, Royal Artillery, 135 (The Hertfordshire Yeomanry) Field Regt., of 2, Pipe Lane, Peterborough, was now also reported as killed in action on the 27th January. He was the son of Mr. Charles Horace, and Mrs. Ethel Wright of Intake, Yorkshire, and the adopted son of Mr. and Mrs. Alfred Afford, of 2, Pipe Lane. A Territorial before the war, he was a clerk in Messrs Baker Perkins commercial department. Sgt. Wright was 20 years of age and as a youth was a popular member of Mr. Arthur Ridgway's young Men's Class at Wentworth Street Methodist Church. He is buried in Taiping War Cemetery, Collective Grave 1. A. 1-12.

Gunner Donald Spires, Royal Artillery, The Bakery, New England, Peterborough, had now been reported as seriously ill suffering from burns received in action in the Far East on January 29th. Aged 32, Gunner Spires, who was married, was the eldest son of Mr. and Mrs. Harvey Spires, 284, Dogsthorpe Road, and was associated with the family's bakery business before the war. He served in a Territorial Battery in pre-war days and was to survive the war.

Dr. L.J. Clapham, son of the late Dr. Harold Clapham of Peterborough, was now reported as having been made a prisoner of war in Malaya.

War Savings and HMS Olympus
At the Soke of Peterborough War Savings Committee meeting at the Town Hall on Tuesday 10th February, the City Treasurer, Mr. Frank Smith, reported that since the war started to the end of 1941 the city and district had raised £3,104,553.

In his report he said that in 1941 the amount raised was £1,642,660. The total in War Weapons Week, 1940, was £450,000, and in Warships Week, 1941, £525,000 – an increase of £75,000. The total number of savings groups was now 590. Certificates issued in the last completed year before the war (to March 31st, 1939) were £23,309; in 1940, £286,674; and in 1941, £306,036.

A letter from the Admiralty said that their Lordships learned with pleasure that, as a result of Peterborough's effort, the savings committee had reached their objective and were in a position to adopt HMS OLYMPUS. They would inform the crew of this and hoped a lasting association would be formed between the ship (submarine) and the inhabitants of Peterborough.

Three replicas of the ship's badge were to be made for presentation to the three authorities concerned in the week. If the city desired to give a plaque of their arms to the ship, their Lordships would arrange to have a special celebration to exchange the gifts.

More Home Guard Promotions
Mr. N.J.C. Donald received a Commission as Second Lieutenant, to be Platoon Officer and is posted to HQ, Comp. 1st Northants (City) Battalion., HG. Lieutenant H. Collcott was promoted to Captain, as Battalion chief guide, and posted to 'D' Comp. Second Lieutenant J.G. Lawson was promoted to Lieutenant, as Assistant Adjutant; and Second Lieutenant F.H. Martin to Lieutenant as Platoon Commander, HQ Company. Volunteers F.B.M. Chapman, J.D.T. Lathey and J. Scotney were taken on the strength and posted to 'D' Company. Corporal L.C. Airey and Volunteers W.E. Bruce and G. Knight were called for service in H.M. Forces.

Respirator Tests
The Ministry of Home Security had now become concerned with the importance of keeping respirators in good condition and a perfect fit. In view of the possibility of enemy gas attacks, instructions were issued to local authorities to arrange for testing and overhaul of respirators. At Peterborough, seven Warden's posts would be open from 4 to 9pm from Monday 16th February to the following Saturday, and the public were advised that in the interests of their own safety, they should take their masks for testing. The posts were:

- Showground, Eastfield.
- Paul Pry, Walton.

- St. Paul's Church Hall.
- Corporation Depot, St. John's Street.
- Cobden Street Methodist Church Schoolroom.
- George Street Baptist Church schoolroom.
- The Gaol, Thorpe Road.

Children's respirators would be examined at their schools. Gas masks which were found to be damaged in any way were to be taken to the Old Town Hall (Guildhall) any weekday between 9am and 6pm.

Food Vans

The city had now received two vans from the Ford Emergency Food Vans Trust, which were to be used to distribute food supplies after air raids. They were based at the Corporation Depot and would be brought into use as soon as the projected emergency kitchens were equipped to convey the cooked food. They would also be used if required to supply emergency feeding centres with hot food. The vans were equipped with large containers so that hot meals could be carried long distances and they would be staffed from the City Engineer's Department.

Soldiers Remanded

As if to illustrate Chief Constable Danby's concerns regarding rising crime figures, the court reports published in the 'Standard' on Friday 13th February cover the criminal activities of five soldiers in the city.

Sidney Raybold, Frank Nigel Rice and John Frederick Grogan, soldiers, were charged with breaking and entering the Co-operative Society's grocery branch at Oundle Road, on or about February 10th, and stealing 2 dozen bars of chocolate.

Sidney Raybold (again), John Bland and Granville Sissons, also soldiers, were charged with stealing three mailbags and contents, the property of the Postmaster General, on or about February 5th.

The Chief Constable said that Raybold, Rice and Grogan were arrested only the previous day, and the police had not had time to prepare the case. In the case of Raybold, Hand and Sissons, certain property had been found on them. The men were remanded.

Gas Mask Indifference

At this time there were some 50,000 respirators other than service and Civil Defence types in the city. On the first three days of the week commencing Monday 20th February, only 230 were taken to the seven depots in various parts of the city for the fitting to be tested. On the Monday, several posts had an idle day with only 45 masks been taken in overall. Tuesday's figure rose to 75, and on the Wednesday the number was 110.

Major R. de Gray, the deputy chief warden stated that the response was extremely disappointing in view of the publicity that had been afforded by 500 posters, press advertisements, write-ups and loud speaker reminders. "The public can only blame themselves if the worst happens and they are unprepared," he said. "The Old Town Hall is open every day for the adjustment and repair of respirators, but this week has been one of the slackest we have known."

There was however one ray of sunshine in this depressing response. A Werrington woman, well over 70 years of age, walked to the Paul Pry and back with

193

her respirator, and that of her husband who was too ill to go. The posts would remain open for the rest of the week.

Nursing Cadets

At the St. John Ambulance Nursing Corps enrollment meeting at the Town Hall on Tuesday the 17th, Mrs. Blagden presiding said:

"In one of the blackest hours of the country's history, it is a cheering sight to see so many young people keen and interested in the cadet divisions of the St. John Ambulance Brigade."

Mrs. Blagden added that she had been told that her generation had treated the young wrongly, by making things too easy for them, and she was glad that now they were going to be asked to make a few sacrifices. They must be ready to do these things: Do any job; make sacrifices; and stick to their job.

Lady Corps Superintendent, Mrs. Holmes, said that in every school she had spoken about the Cadets she had been greeted with enthusiasm and offered full support. All the schools had not yet sent in their figures but so far she had 449 volunteers as follows:

- Eastholm – 130
- All Souls – 15
- Woodston – 30
- Cromwell Road – 50
- Orchard Street – 34
- Walton – 41
- Barnack – 17
- Glinton – 14
- Newborough – 12
- Eye – 24
- Helpston – 12
- Castor – 7
- Maxey – 6
- Whittlesey – 3

Explaining the duties of the cadet Mrs., Holmes said that at 14 they could be used on the domestic side, and at 17, when they held their first aid and nursing certificates, they could help in the wards.

Home Guard Changes

From Monday 16th February, resignations from the Home Guard ceased to be optional. Whilst the Home Guard started off as an entirely voluntary organisation, conscription was introduced in January 1942. At that time all men and women between the ages of 18 and 60 were obliged to undertake some form of national service and all available and eligible men between the ages of 18 and 51 were liable to military service of one sort or another including the Home Guard. Service in the latter now precluded the option of resignation.

Colonel Crowden, Commanding the 1st Northants (City) Battalion stated that resignations due to the impending change had been negligible in number. There had been for some time a steady leakage of men who had joined the Forces, and of others who had resigned mainly for medical reasons or advancing years. There had also been some who had dispersed through failing interest.

On the other hand there had been a steady influx, and the Battalion was in good form for all that was required of it. New orders, equipment and instructions were making training very strenuous but all ranks were standing up to it well. There was no lack of enthusiasm and attendances were well maintained.

At the 2nd Northants (Soke) Battalion the situation was much the same, though in scattered country areas it was more difficult for members to put in the required hours of training. Of the latest resignations, fewer than a dozen could be attributed to the new changes and these were mostly amongst the older men. There were some who felt that their age and civilian duties would not allow them to do justice to Home Guard requirements and they retired with regret. The body left was well up to requirements, although there was always room for more.

Casualty Lists
The newspaper reported on the 20th February that Driver Stanley Cooper, Royal Engineers, of Peterborough, was reported missing in the Far East on January 26th. As he does not appear in the casualty lists compiled after the war, we must believe that he did survive the war after all.

Trooper John Butler, Royal Armoured Corps, son of Mr. and Mrs. P. Butler of 23, Silver Street, Peterborough, who had been in the Middle East for seven years, was posted as missing believed killed on November 21st 1941. He was now reported as badly wounded and in hospital in the Middle East. He also survived the war.

Private Harold Stephen (Steve) Stott, second son of Mr. and Mrs. Stephen D. Stott, of 110, Park Road, Peterborough, was now listed as wounded in the Middle East on January 23rd. Private Stott was a monotype operator in civilian life in the printing business of Stott and Sons, Queen Street. He was 26 and voluntarily joined the forces on January 15th, 1940. He was in the Royal Army Ordnance Corps, saw service in France, and was among those who got back home from Brest. He sailed for the Middle East in September 1941. No details were available as to the nature of his wounds although he did survive the war.

Home Guard Now Privates
On Monday 23rd at a City Battalion HQ meeting, Colonel Crowden said that in future the men of the Home Guard would be designated 'Private,' not 'Volunteer,' as in the past. "They were all soldiers now until the end of the war." Additional duties were to be thrown on to the Battalion officers and NCO's in the training of ARP personnel who were expected to join the Guard. In addition they would help to train the boys of the coming Cadet Units.

New Cadet Units
In view of the probability of a long war, Major S.G. Cook now explained that the Army Council had asked the Territorial Association of the Soke of Peterborough and Huntingdonshire to raise a number of Cadet Companies at once to ensure the supply of trained men for the Home Guard and eventually for the Army itself. All boys over 14 years of age would be eligible to be enrolled, and they would receive a three year course of instruction, on the completion of which they would be fit to take their

places at once in the defence of their country.

The Home Guard would provide centres for drill, physical training, scouting exercises, the nature and use of rifles, tommy guns, hand grenades, map reading and all other activities of a soldier. There would be arrangements for weekend camps and the cadets would be supplied with battledress. It was expected that there would be an allotment of three or four hundred cadets for Peterborough and North Hunts.

Tales of Petty Crime

It should be recorded that although the war was now two and a half years old, people in the city still had not learned the importance of the black-out regulations. It was likely that the absence of bombing raids made people complacent but reports from the Peterborough Police Courts continued to cover cases where the regulations were making criminals of local people.

Pauline Elizabeth Humphries of Cowgate was fined £1 for a light at 10.25pm on February 11th. Police Sergeant Gilder said the window had a curtain but it was not up. The defendant, who was a manageress, said it was a store room and the black-out should have been checked by a member of the staff.

Sybil Crane, 273, Eastfield Road, was fined £1 for a like offence at 8.30pm on February 12th. Sergeant Mills said the light was some distance from the window but was reflected by white walls. The Chairman said that neither case was serious.

Mary Iveson, 6, Swans Place, was fined 10 shillings for allowing a chimney to be on fire at 11.50pm on February 15th. P.C. Hubble told the court that the defendant said she could not get a sweep. The Chairman said they appreciated the difficulty of finding a sweep under the present circumstances.

Violet Hilda Parker, 59, Harris Street, was charged with stealing a bottle of coffee, value 4 shillings on or about January 21st and 5s. 6d in cash on or about February 11th, the property of Margaret Mellows and other members of the WVS. Mrs. Parker was a helper at the North Station canteen and sometimes was in charge of the shift.

Constable Unsworth said Parker had admitted that she had been tempted, having seen some fellow helpers helping themselves. She took various small sums at different times and still had them. She asked the constable to give Mrs. Mellows £2 in restitution. The Chief Constable said the defendant and her husband were most respectable people. She had two children and they were in a good position. There was no necessity for her to steal.

The Chairman said the case was "more than distressing." The defendant masqueraded on national service and "pinched" the money. It was sad that "others did it." If so, they ought to be ashamed of it. If they came before the Bench, they would have to do something drastic. The defendant was fined £2 10s on each charge.

Joseph Henry Smith, 153, Cromwell Road, was fined £2 for permitting a car to stand at 10.05pm on February 10th without two white front lights. P.C. Hubble's evidence was that he said he had hardly had time for a pint. The car was outside the Post Office and the defendant came from the direction of the back of the Greyhound.

Eric William Brooks, Queen's Bank, Postland, was fined £1 for allowing a car to cause obstruction on February 7th. P.C. Dobson said the car reduced the traffic in Westgate to a single line and buses had a job to pass.

Jos. Valentine Young, Cromwell Road, was summoned for receiving a quantity of custard powder, cocoa, lard, margarine, dried fruit and tinned tomatoes knowing these to have been stolen. The Chief Constable applied for an adjournment for 14 days.

Fred Stanley Parkinson, a soldier, was charged with stealing a lady's Royal Enfield cycle, value £4 on February 23rd. He pleaded guilty. Arthur Whybrow, employed in Bridge Street, identified the cycle as belonging to Miss Jones who occupied a flat over the shop where he was employed. P.C. Blackwell said he saw the accused with the cycle. He at first said he had borrowed it from a friend and then that he took it from a passage, as he had missed his bus back to the village where he was stationed. Giving the accused some good advice, the Chairman said the case would be dismissed on payment of 17s 6d. costs.

No Prizes for Salvage

Peterborough did not after all get "among the prize money" in the Waste Paper Recovery Association's national competition in connection with paper salvage in January. In Area No. 14, which comprised Bedfordshire, Huntingdonshire, Northamptonshire and Hertfordshire, the cash was allocated as follows:

- £500: Desborough U.D.C.
- £250: Borough of Hemel Hempsted.
- £100: Borough of St. Ives.
- £50 each: Rickmansworth, Watford and Dunstable.

Other prize winners included Area No. 7, £500: Ketton, £250: Oakham U.D.C. Area No. 8, £250: Borough of Wisbech.

Although there was no prize money for the city, they had made a profit of £100 for the month. The Committee's report stated that paper salvaged totaled 221 tons, and that sales in January were:

- Paper: 85 tons.
- Bottles: 73 gross.
- Iron: 19 tons.
- Kitchen Waste: 32 tons.

In appreciation of the work done by the "cogs," the school children who collected the paper under direction of the WVS, the Committee voted £50 for cinema entertainment. The salvage dumps used in January were replaced and divided up into two sections, one for paper and one for scrap iron and rubber.

City P.C. Decorated

P.C. Frederick George Hawkes, of the City Police Force, on Tuesday March 3rd, received from the hands of the King, the British Empire Medal "for brave conduct in civil defence." The citation of the award stated:

"A bomb wrecked a building, and three persons were buried beneath the debris. Hawkes crept through a narrow opening in the wreckage, and, after sawing through wooden joists, was able to release the victims. During this time there was danger of a further collapse of the building but Hawkes continued to work with complete disregard of his own safety."

This incident occurred on the night of May 9th-10th 1941, when a bomb demolished a cottage in Cross Street. The occupants were Mr. and Mrs. Frank Kingston and their invalid daughter, Edna. Mr. Kingston and Edna both died of their injuries in November later that year.

P.C. Hawkes previously possessed the Indian General Service Medal with clasp for his share in the Mohmand operations on the North-West Frontier in 1935, and a certificate signed by General Sir Kenneth Wigram, C-in-C Indian Army, stating "The services of Sig. F.G. Hawkes, 1st Indian Divisional Signals, have been brought to my notice for devotion to duty." P.C. Hawkes had now volunteered for service with the Royal Corps of Signals, and had received orders to report on Thursday 12th March.

Rest Centre Exercises
Rest Centre exercises were now being held at the beginning of March, the intention being that every Centre in the City and Soke would be able to arrange one. The plan was to make these exercises as realistic as possible and to produce conditions such as were likely to arise in an emergency and cause Rest Centres to be opened in order to assist people made homeless by enemy action.

Volunteers (chiefly school children) acted as the "homeless" for practices, and each one was labelled with a particular injury or problem, e.g. fainting, hysteria, general distress, lost relations, lost ration cards, etc. All these problems would be dealt with as far as possible by the Rest Centre staff, which was composed of WVS members who were arranged for duty in a rota of 4-hourly shifts.

It was assumed that many questions would be asked which the helpers would not be able to answer themselves, but information would be available in every Centre as to where it could be sought. The helpers would attend to the immediate needs of their "patients," calm the hysterical and distressed, clothe those who may possibly have rushed in seeking shelter in their night clothes (there was a store of clothes in each Centre), and the ambulance sent for if necessary.

If any serious casualties were unavoidably admitted, a doctor would be summoned (each Centre Leader would be told which doctor had been allocated to their Centre), and an ambulance called for if necessary. Messages might have to be sent by hand if telephones were out of action, and in order to do this each Centre had two messengers on standby.

Warmth and comfort would be provided for all, cups of hot tea, hot water bottles, blankets and "kind and sympathetic helpers waiting to give all the help and assistance they can." Successful practices had so far been held at the following Centres:

- Palmerston Road Church Hall, Woodston, Mrs. Atkinson.
- St. Margaret's Hall, Fairfield Road, Mrs. Laxton and Mrs. Smith.
- King's School, Mrs. Shearcroft.
- Castor, the Hon. Mrs. Pelham.
- Werrington, Mrs. Kirman.

The Methodist Schoolroom, New England Centre, Mrs. Boss and Mrs. Peach Hay, was opened in October 1940, for evacuees from London. It remained open for a week during which about 80 women and children and a few men were housed, fed

198

and looked after.

Missing in the Middle East

Mrs. F. Hoyles, a Woodston woman, whose first husband had been killed in the First World War, was now officially notified that her eldest son was reported missing in the Middle East. At the time she had been anxiously waiting news of her second son who was believed to have been at Singapore.

Mrs. Hoyles and her second husband kept an off-licence and general shop at 49, Palmerston Road. Her first husband, Mr. W. West, was in the Worcestershire Regiment, and died from wounds received in action during the previous war. Her eldest son was Gunner William West, Royal Artillery, who had been employed as a shop assistant by Messrs Trollope, of Westgate, before the war, and afterwards had been a member of the AFS at the Queen's Walk station. He was engaged to Miss Sybil Newport, 65, London Road. Mrs. Hoyle's second son was Private Albert West, who had been employed by the London Brick Company on the presses.

When the communication from the War Office arrived on Wednesday morning (4th), saying that her son had been missing since January 25th, Mrs. Hoyles was serving in the shop. Thinking that the letter was about her second son, she was too distressed to open it, and asked a customer to do so. She had not heard from her eldest son for some time, but in view of the recent happenings at Singapore, she was anxious about her second son.

Mrs. West need not have worried at that time as both of her sons were safe. However, Gunner William West, 1557797, 102 (The Northumberland Hussars) Light A.A./Anti-Tank Regt., R.A. was to die aged 28, on 10th September, 1942. On Wednesday 11th March, Mrs. Hoyle received a telegram saying William was a prisoner of war in an unknown camp in Italy. He subsequently died from unknown causes and is buried in Bari War Cemetery. His brother Albert survived the war.

The Survival of Peterborough United in the Balance

Described by Mr. H.J. Poulter, the secretary as "a last-minute effort to save Peterborough football," a meeting was now organized for anyone who cared to attend at the Rechabite Hall, at 7.45pm on Wednesday 18th March. The question being the future use of the London Road ground.

Peterborough United F.C. rented the ground from the corporation and had asked to be released from the agreement for the period of the war in lieu of the improvements that they, and the Supporters Club had made – shelters, railings, baths and dressing rooms.

The Council's Parks and Recreation Grounds Committee did not see eye to eye with the club's directors and were considering an application from the Newall Engineering Sports Club, who were prepared to pay double the rent that United were paying and take a lease on the ground for a period of years. Because of this, Peterborough United was in danger of having to close down permanently. The improvements that had been made would then become the property of the landlord, (Council).

Teachers in the Home Guard

The position of teachers in the Home Guard on being called for duty had now been considered by the Education Committee. They were put into two categories:

1. To report for duty immediately on mustering and to be stood down when no longer required.
2. To report to headquarters for orders as soon as civil employment permitted – in any case within 48 hours – and be told whether to parade or continue civil employment for a time.

The following were classified in Category 1: Mr. J.G. Avery, Walton; Mr. J.J. Robinson, Walton; Mr. E.W. Macro, Eastholm. Category 2: Mr. R.W. Cowe, Eastholm; Mr. A.H. Taylor, Lincoln Road; Mr. H.C. Child, Fulbridge; Mr. L.C. Ambalino, Education Department.

The following promotions had now been made in the City Battalion, Home Guard: Corporals G.P. Allen, R. Bunyan and P.W. Bayes of 'A' Company to be Sergeants; Lance Corporals J.G. Baldwin and R.A. Wicks of 'C' Company to be Corporals. Appointed Lance Corporals, Privates L.H. Rayment, P. Twomey, A.W.J. Higgins and W.G. Reed 'A' Company, and Private T.E. Stanley 'C' Company.

Lieutenant W.D. Larrett had been Acting Second-in-Command 'C' Company during the absence of Captain A.E. Stewart in hospital. Second Lieutenant N.J.C. Donald had been on a section leading course.

Now taken on battalion strength were Privates A.E. Gutteridge, A.W.J. Higgins, M.E. Walker and A.J. Ward.

Captain C.J. Pilley, Adjutant, City Battalion, was at pains at this time to remind all men who, for whatever reason, had to leave the service, that they were required to return all their clothing and equipment to headquarters, and identity cards for cancellation of Home Guard endorsement.

Billets

Up to the evening of Wednesday 11th March, out of 15,000 billet enquiry forms sent out, only 4,986 had been returned to the Town Hall. People were urged to return these forms at once – or at least by the following Tuesday. The returns would be checked and those who had not returned them were told that action could be taken against them under the Defence Regulations.

Many householders around the country had soldiers billeted with them and these forms asked for information regarding the possibility of people taking in a member of the Services. These were official regulations which people were obliged to follow.

Happy Meeting in Egypt

Happier news was received regarding two sons of Mr. and Mrs. John Hughes, 144, Dogsthorpe Road, who met unexpectedly in Egypt on New Year's Day and spent two days together. They were Corporal John Thomas Hughes, RAF, formerly with Baker Perkins, and Corporal Walter G. Hughes, Royal Marines, who was with Mr. Foster, on Broadway.

Mr. and Mrs. Hughes had two other children in the Forces: Sergeant E.L. Hughes, Royal Artillery, who was believed to be at Singapore, and who in peacetime was at Baker Perkins; and Aircrafts Woman 1st Class, N.J. Hughes, formerly an usherette at the Odeon. It is pleasing to record that all of the Hughes children survived the war.

200

Precinct Shelters

At the ARP Committee on Monday 9th March, a number of announcements were made. Approval was received for the expenditure of £1,900 for demolishing and rebuilding seven air raid shelters in the Cathedral Precincts and contracts were also to be prepared for the repair of damaged houses at 120, Park Road, and 31, Lincoln Road East.

The Ministry of Home Security had now approved an increase in the basic pay of civil defence general services in certain categories. The increases varied from one shilling to four shillings per week for men and from one shilling to five shillings for women. Pay would be graduated from £1 4s. to £3 14s. per week for men, and from £1 1s. to £2 12s. for women.

In respect to a recent case of stealing mineral waters, it was stated that the man concerned had tendered his resignation from the warden's service and the Chief Constable was authorized to fill the vacancy.

Home Guard Compulsion

It was announced at this time that there would be no need to apply compulsory enrolment at present in the Peterborough Battalions of the Home Guard. Civil Defence Regions in which compulsion was going to be enforced included Huntingdonshire, Cambridgeshire, Norfolk, Bedfordshire and the Isle of Ely. New powers of enforcement had been brought in by the government to be used where voluntary enrolment did not bring in enough men.

Lance Corporal F. Pedder of HQ Company, City Home Guard was now promoted to Sergeant, and enrolments in the Battalion were Privates R. Broadhead, G.W. Peters and C. Wilson. Corporal A. Shallcross had been on a course of fieldcraft.

In the 2nd Northants (Soke) Battalion, Home Guard, Lance Corporal P.C. Hill had now been promoted to Corporal and Private S.G. Glover appointed Lance Corporal. Both were in 'B' Company.

Raid Spotters Club

It is probably hardly surprising that aircraft spotting was a very popular pastime during the war, and was also, of course, extremely useful. In the second week of March, the success in the junior section of the Spotters Club, mostly lads under school leaving age, was described as remarkable. Twenty six had obtained the intermediate national spotter's certificate, 46 others had passed the preliminary, and 12 had obtained the second class. Sixty percent of them received full marks.

This encouraged the Secretary to contemplate issuing challenges to the ATC searchlight units, roof spotters clubs in the city, and other raid spotters clubs. The next recognition match had been arranged between Phorpres and Peterborough. On Saturday 7th March, a scratch Peterborough team beat a searchlight battery by 137 points to 49.

619 More Women

On Saturday 7th March, 619 women aged 35, registered at Peterborough Employment Exchange. A large percentage recorded their occupation as domestic responsibilities.

201

Delayed Action Bomb Disposal

An instructional film telling how to deal with delayed action bombs – UXB's – was shown at the City Cinema on the morning of Tuesday 10th. The large audience included members of the city's civil defence services including rescue squads, decontamination squads, first aid personnel, ambulance drivers, Home Guard, firemen, police, wardens and civil and military bomb disposal squads.

The film lasted an hour and showed what to look for when a UXB had buried itself, and precautions which must be taken in the interest of public safety. All types of German bombs, ranging from the 50 to the 1,800 kilo (nicknamed "Satan" and weighing about 2 tons) were dealt with. Defence workers were asked to be especially wary where a small bomb buries itself and explodes underground for it formed a pocket of carbon monoxide which was a deadly gas.

The film also demonstrated the foolishness of inexperienced personnel tampering with fuses and wires which may be attached to a bomb. Lieutenant E. Wakelin, RE Bomb Disposal Section, gave a short talk.

Reported Missing

A steady stream of names was now beginning to appear in the Peterborough Standard of men who had been at Singapore when it fell to the advancing Japanese forces. Captain S. Egar, Royal Artillery, son of Mr. and Mrs. Egar of 'Melrose,' Park Crescent, was officially posted as missing. He had worked at the Milton Estate Office before the war.

Second Lieutenant J. Brian Green, Royal Field Artillery, only son of Canon G.A. Green, of Fletton Rectory, was another missing man. His father being notified by a telegram received from the War Office on March 12th.

Gunner (Driver) Jack Fixter, Royal Artillery, son of Mr. and Mrs. F. Fixter, 10, St Mark's Street, Peterborough, was also missing, believed to have been at Singapore at the time of the capitulation.

Captain Egar and Second Lieutenant Green would return home to see their families again. Gunner, 922763, Francis Jack Fixter, although a prisoner of war at this time did not survive the treatment dished out by the Japanese while in their hands and he died of Beri-Beri on 31st July, 1943. He was 23 years of age and had been attached to H.Q. 18th Indian Division. He is buried, as are so many more city men, in Kanchanaburi War Cemetery, Grave 2. N. 25.

Cuts Begin to Hit Home

Severe cuts and restrictions due to shortages such as foodstuffs and petrol were now announced which would affect the lives of everyone.

No white bread would be baked from Easter Monday, April 6th, until probably the end of the war, or even later than that. The national wheatmeal loaf would take the place of the white loaf, but bakers and confectioners who had stocks of white flour on hand would be allowed to use it in the ratio of 25 parts white to 75 parts wheatmeal. No white flour would be on sale at bakers' and grocers' shops after current supplies were exhausted. There would still be ample flour for home cookery, but it would all be wheatmeal.

Peterborough and District butchers had now completed a scheme to pool their household deliveries of meat, and to save vehicles, fuel and manpower. The grocers still had their plans awaiting approval but many had already made similar arrangements. Some trade groups had failed to reach an understanding so were referred to the Ministry of War Transport for a decision. Butchers whose vans were to be taken off the road were:

- H.S. Hunting
- W. Freeman
- Hand and Son
- W.H. Robinson
- A. Stanyon
- G. Chamberlain
- J.R. Johnson and Sons
- T.R. Crosby
- O. Dawson
- Brown and Son
- Frank Bros.
- S.N. Rumsby
- J. Warr
- J.W. Stocker

Messrs Stocker and Ellwood would have a van off for six months each, and would help each other. In other cases delivery by vans still in use was guaranteed. Three days a week delivery of bread had been in operation since March 1st, and was working well after some teething troubles during the first few weeks.

New restrictions on the delivery of coal to residential premises came into force on Tuesday 17th March. The general effect in the North Midlands Division which included Peterborough was to limit the amount of coal which could be delivered in the following three weeks to residential premises including hotels, clubs and lodging houses to 4cwt, and this amount could only be supplied where existing stocks did not exceed 5cwt. In Fletton Urban Area (Eastern Division) the limit was 5cwt. in three weeks where stocks did not exceed half a ton.

The purpose of the restriction was to check the drain on accumulated reserves occasioned by the recent severe weather. Following this temporary measure, a scheme for rationing coal, electricity and gas for domestic heating and lighting was to be introduced. A cut of at least 25 percent was seen as likely but whatever system was adopted, there would be provision for appeals in cases of hardship such as households with invalids.

Everyone would have to watch the gas and electricity meters when rationing started. Any excess in one quarter's ration would be deducted from the next and persistent over-consumption would lead to the supply being cut off, and to prosecution.

As from Monday 16th March, supplies of daily newspapers would be cut by 10 percent. Mr. S. Stott, of D.H. Stott and Sons, wholesale agents, said: "We have simply knocked 10 percent off the supplies we send to distributors, who have had to work out their own salvation."

Mr. C.H. Barks, of Fulbridge Road, Hon. Secretary of the Newsagent's Federation said: "Where two, or sometimes three papers have gone into one house, only one will be allowed in the future...that will, in our case, account for about half the reduction. Then again, we have been selling up to 500 papers at Brotherhood's and a lot of that will have to be knocked off.

Mr. Jack Bancroft, managing director of the Embassy Theatre, commented on the effect the ban on 'pleasure motoring' would have on attendances. He said if the abolition of basic coupons meant fewer people could motor to the theatre or cinema then the bus facilities ought to be better. "The town services are far from good, and those from the country are worse." Mr. W.J. Stanton, manager of the Odeon pointed out that people who drove their cars to the cinema often came into town to do their shopping at the same time so killing two birds with one stone.

Mr. I. Baker, the Eastern Counties Omnibus Company's traffic superintendent said the loss of basic coupons to motorists would inevitably mean a bigger demand on an already severely strained public transport service. "The question is shall we get extra petrol to cope with the extra demand? Then there is labour to consider – that is one of our biggest problems in Peterborough at present. We are trying now to augment our services, but we do not always find it possible."

A Reprieve for Peterborough United

It was announced on Friday 20th March that the London Road football ground would remain in the tenancy of Peterborough United F.C. for another year at least. Rent of £50 was owed and the city council had given the directors to understand that until it was paid there was no possibility of a new agreement being considered. In the meantime Newall's F.C. offered a rent of £380 a year for a ten year lease.

The United directors could see no way out of the crisis and a meeting was called at the Rechabite Hall at which little progress was made until word was sent to the chairman (Councilor J.E. Swain) that County Councilor W.H. Tebbs, of Eastfield, and his brother, Mr. A.E. Tebbs, of Fulbridge Road, had offered to loan the £50 required. This was accepted with grateful thanks and much relief, and a subscription list was opened immediately with Mr. T.H. Peake, Mr. J.A. Ladds and Mr. J. Blades in charge. Several offers up to £10 were received at the meeting.

Olympus Plaque

The heavy bronze plaque which was to be fixed inside the adopted Royal Navy submarine HMS Olympus had now arrived in the city, ready to be forwarded on to the Admiralty. Beneath the city coat of arms, in bold relief, the plaque carried the inscription:

> "To commemorate the adoption of HMS Olympus by the citizens of Peterborough and District – Peterborough Warship Week, Nov. 27th – Dec. 6th, 1941."

A meeting of group secretaries and district representatives was to be called to receive the gift with fitting ceremony.

Home Guard Motorcycles

At this time many young members of the City Battalion, Home Guard, were being trained as dispatch riders, but a shortage of motorcycles was proving a handicap. An appeal went out to local people to give or loan a motorcycle which was not in use and they were asked to get in touch with the Adjutant, Captain C.L. Pilley.

Other changes were still taking place in the City Battalion, Corporals H.A. Barham and J.H. Goodman, of 'A' Company were now promoted to Sergeants. The following were taken on the strength of the battalion, Privates:

204

- G.H. Coles
- H. Wilson
- R.F. Lyne
- D.R. Tyres
- L.T. James
- G.E. Mayne
- S.A. Collenette
- A.F. Ireson
- T.H. Andrews
- R.A. Farren
- C.F. Ovenall
- A. Robinson
- B.A. Franklin
- R.A. Greenwood
- F.J. Jarvis (from 5th Kesteven)
- L. Webber (from 7th Norfolk)

Fire Guard Personnel
Mr. Rowland Hill, fire guard staff officer, and Mr. Lister Robinson, chief warden, were now on a course for staff officers at Region. Mr. R.P. Palmer, Broadway, had now been appointed fire guard assistant staff officer under Mr. Hill, and Mr. W.J. Banham, Padholme Road, became head fire guard at No.5 Group. Mr. Martin Ball, Fulbridge Road, now succeeded Mr. George Forbear as head of No.8 Group, the latter having gone as Petty Officer in the Navy.

Spotter's Competition
On Friday 13th March, a three-cornered recognition match was held between teams from Phorpres and Electricity Works, King's School and Deacon's and elementary schools. After what were described as "a severe series of tests," (about 75 aircraft), Deacon's and the elementary boys won with 69.7 points. Phorpres and Electricity were second with 66.5, and King's School third with 60.1. Practically all of the planes shown were of enemy air forces.

On Saturday 14th Peterborough met a Searchlight Unit team and scored some 50 percent more points. The teams were entertained afterwards by an E.N.S.A. concert party.

Missing at Singapore
Singapore fell to the Japanese Forces on 15th February, 1942, and a great many local men were in regiments that had been fighting there. The Japanese took 100,000 men prisoner; many had just arrived and had not fired a bullet in anger. The Allied forces were made up of British, Indian and Australian troops and 9,000 of these men died building the Burma-Thailand railway. The garrison surrendered when the situation became hopeless which is why so many men were listed as missing rather than killed. At the time it was impossible to know where individual men were or what had happened to them.

For many weeks the 'Peterborough Standard' published information regarding reports of men missing at Singapore, most of them had been taken prisoner, but many were to die in captivity. On March 13th they reported a number of men from the district missing at Singapore including the following two who were from Peterborough:

Captain Corby Bristow, Royal Corps of Signals, younger son of Mrs. Bristow, 'Medehamsted,' London Road. He had contacted his mother a month before to say he was well.

Private George Allen was the youngest son of Mrs. Allen, St. John's Street. He had been serving in a military hospital in Singapore for about 18 months, and was formerly employed by Montague Burton Ltd., at Sheffield. The War Office stated that there was "a considerable possibility that he is a prisoner of war."

The two men above survived the war, although another man reported in the same issue as wounded, did not. Gunner Reginald Adolphus George Steels had been wounded while serving in the Middle East. Gunner Steels was in the Royal Horse Artillery, 11th (Honourable Artillery Company) Regiment, and was the son of Mr. Robert, and Mrs. Lily Steels, 11, Victoria Street, Fletton. His wife, Doris Evelyn Steels, lived at their home at 50, Palmerston Road, Woodston, and she received a telegram a week previously stating that her husband was in hospital suffering from wounds received on January 25th.

Gunner Steels, who was 26 years of age and before the war had been an agent for the Provident Clothing Club, died on the 23rd January, 1942, and is commemorated on the Alamein Memorial, Column 14. Obviously the news that he had been wounded on the 25th had been wrong.

Closing the Brickyards

It was reported on 20th March that the Committee on the Brick Industry, appointed by the Ministry of Works and Buildings had recommended all steps to be taken to obtain the services of prisoners of war as brick makers. This was due to the decrease in the current national output by twelve and a half percent. Also, they recommended the employment of women in a ratio of 3 women to 2 men to replace men who had been called up, to a total not exceeding 20 percent.

A week later the 'Standard' reported that in accordance with the provisions of the Limitation of Industries Order, the London Brick Company, on Tuesday 31st March, closed their works at Whittlesey, Norman Cross, Dogsthorpe and Eye, to release more men for the war effort. On Thursday 2nd April, a substantial number of men who had been released from the Army, rejoined their regiments. The older employees left were being absorbed in the Fletton brick yards.

More War Cases

Cases brought before General Strong and other Magistrates at the Peterborough Police Court on Wednesday 1st April, included that of Charles Davy, 41, Eastfield Grove, who was charged with stealing 10 tins of bully beef on 26th March, property of the Ministry of Food, from a shed which had been taken over as a food store. Also being charged was Victor Gerald Hornsby, 5, Palmerston Road, for receiving five of the tins knowing them to be stolen.

Both men worked on the railway and had previously good characters, Davy, aged 46, had served in the First World War until being wounded and discharged in 1917, and Hornsby, aged 23, was fighting in the rearguard at Dunkirk before being rescued and returned to England to rejoin the Railway Company. Both men admitted temptation and the defence asked the Bench to exercise clemency and deal with the accused as first offenders. The Chairman said it was lamentable that men with such characters should cramp the people who were trying to provide for the country in the event of an emergency. They were fined £10 each.

Also in court were Barrons (Tailors) Ltd., Market Place, who were being summoned for supplying Leslie Peter Cope, Minnie Elizabeth Tarratt and George Stafford Evans with rationed goods against the surrender of coupons without requiring the production of the ration document on February 5th.

Mr. Dale, prosecuting, said it was illegal for a shopkeeper to supply rationed goods except on surrender of the ration document (ration book). The tradesman must then detach the coupons from the document. On February 5th, three customers at the defendant's shop purchased goods in ten minutes and each handed over loose coupons. Mr. Cope bought a tie and the salesman said "I suppose you know you should produce the ration book?" Mr. Evans also bought a tie, and Miss Tarratt, a blue collar. Mr. Evans tendered loose coupons and Miss Tarratt part of a document with the owner's name removed.

These three customers were in fact employees of the Board of Trade and were making test purchases. They went back to the shop together later and Mr. Dunham, the chief director, admitted that he should not have done what he did, and, having done it, he regretted it. There was a great deal of illicit trading in loose coupons and the Board of Trade asked Justices to stamp it out, and to see that ration documents and coupons were used only by the persons to whom they were issued.

Mr. Hunt said he had to rely to a great extent on the honesty of his customers and he had to employ inexperienced assistants. He asked the Bench to believe that this was no case of black market or fraud, but a simple omission to do the proper thing. The Chairman said if it gets to be known that at one particular shop people are not bothered if they don't do everything they ought to do about producing their ration books, that shop, with a certain class of people, is likely to get more custom than it otherwise would, so that actually, though perhaps without knowing it, you may be taking an unfair advantage of your competitors who do strictly observe the regulations. This is the first case we have had of this sort, and in future heavier penalties will be put on. There will be a fine of £1 on each of these cases.

Also facing the magistrates that day was William Frederick Martin, 5, Burmer Road, who was summoned for attempting to obtain 10s. 7d. by false pretences on March 14th, and for disobeying a lawful order given to him in the course of his employment as an air raid warden on the same date. Martin had been instructed to clean up the ARP post where he worked but he said it was in such a state and he wasn't able to find the key so he decided to leave it, and return on his day off with his wife to do it. He said he didn't do it when instructed because he had a daytime job at Marks and Spencer and had to wait until his day off. However, because he was going to be doing the work on his day off, he did book the time on his timesheet for the day he was supposed to do the work which was the reason for the first summons.

Defending, Dr. Hunt said it was all a storm in a teacup. At most, disciplinary action should have been taken – not criminal proceedings. The first summons was dismissed and on the second he was fined £3. The Chairman said it was most disquieting to find a permanent warden working in the daytime.

More Singapore Names

On 3rd April, the 'Standard' printed further news of Peterborough and District soldiers posted as missing, following the capitulation of Singapore. The following were from Peterborough and I have indicated those men who did not survive:

Sergeant Robert Cooke, 839740, 135 (The Hertfordshire Yeomanry) Field Regiment, Royal Artillery, 5, Park Terrace, Garton-End Road. Son of Mr. Robert and Mrs. Millis Cooke and husband of Mrs. Rosina Cooke, Peterborough. Sergeant Cooke was married in 1939 and his wife gave birth to a son the day after receiving the official notification that he was missing. Sergeant Cooke would not return home, instead he would die on 8th May 1944, aged 26, of Dysentery in a Japanese prisoner of war camp in Thailand. He is buried in Kanchanaburi War Cemetery, Thailand.

Lance Sergeant John Thomas Meeds, Royal Artillery, of 277, Longthorpe, was missing. He was the only son of Mr. and Mrs. G.H. Meeds, aged 30; he had been stationed at Singapore for four years.

Lance Bombardier John William Thompson, Royal Artillery, Dairy Cottages, Gunthorpe, was the son of Mr. and Mrs. W. Thompson, and was married with a child of two years old. Before the war he had worked at Read's of Stone Lane.

Driver Douglas Walter Gray, Royal Artillery, 3, Albert Place, Peterborough, was the eldest son of Mr. and Mrs. W. Gray, 41, Norfolk Street. He was 24 years old and married with two children. Before the war he had worked with Mr. H. Gaunt, butcher, in Long Causeway.

Driver W.R. Wilson, Royal Engineers, 735, Lincoln Road, aged 24 years old, was the son of Mr. and Mrs. A. Wilson. Before the war he had been a butcher with Mr. R.W. North, Midgate. His father served with the Northamptonshire Regiment from April 10th, 1912, to March 4th, 1919, and enlisted again when the Second World War broke out. He was invalided out of the Royal Army Ordnance Corps on September 4th, 1941.

Gunner James Frisby Gilbert, Royal Artillery, 326, Longthorpe. Gunner Gilbert, who was married, was the son of Mr. W. Gilbert, Hall Farm, Longthorpe.

Gunner Russell Alfred Norman, Royal Artillery, 351, Longthorpe, was the only son of Mr. and Mrs. S. Norman. He had just turned 22 years of age, and before the war had been an upholsterer with the Fairway Supply Co.

Gunner Thomas Henry Bishop, Royal Artillery, 24, Summerfield Road, Peterborough, was the fourth son of Mr. and Mrs. T.H. Bishop. He was 20 years old and before the war had been employed at Marks and Spencer.

Gunner Donald Robinson, Royal Artillery, 48, Saxon Road, was the eldest son of Mrs. Mortimer, 30, Saxon Road. Aged 28 years old, he was married to Elsie Cavender of Newborough and had one son. Gunner Robinson was at Peter Brotherhood's before the war. His father, Private J. Robinson, was killed in the First World War. There were three other brothers in the services.

Gunner Sidney Biggs, Royal Artillery, 242, Cromwell Road, was the son of Mr. and Mrs. Biggs. He was 22 years old and before the war was with Reads furniture removers, Stone Lane.

Lieutenant D.G. Viney, Royal Artillery, was the younger son of Councilor A.W. Viney, MBE., of Charwood, Park Road. He had been educated at King's School and trained as an engineer at Brotherhood's where his father was works manager. He preferred the law and became a pupil of Dr. Hunt, passing his final examination to qualify as a solicitor three years earlier.

Gunner William Neville, 915812, 135 (The Hertfordshire Yeomanry) Field Regiment, Royal Artillery, aged 21, was the son of Mr. and Mrs. E. Neville, and husband of Mrs. Jane Neville. Before the war he had been an electrical engineer with Mr. J.H. Prescott, Bishops Road. Gunner Neville would not return home, he was reported to have died in a Japanese prisoner of war camp sometime between 11th and 14th February, 1942, almost two months before news reached home that he was missing. He is buried in Kranji War Cemetery, Singapore. His brother, Edward, would also be killed in action in 1944, serving as an Air Gunner in the RAFVR.

Gunner Alfred Jones, Royal Artillery, 13, Eastleigh Road, Peterborough, was 24 years old and the son of Mrs. E.A. Biggin. He had worked at the brickyards before the war and had four brothers in the Army.

Private Vincent Stanley Venn, 5830532, 1st Cambridgeshire Regiment, 12, Alma Road, Peterborough, was the son of Mr. Stanley, and Mrs. Elsie Venn and husband of Ann Lillian Venn of Woodston. Aged 23 and married in 1941, Private Venn had worked as a hairdresser with Mr. C. Henson of Fulbridge Road before the war and had been a member of Walton Cycling Club. Private Venn died of dysentery on the 8th November, 1943, in a Japanese prisoner of war camp and is buried in Chungkai War Cemetery, Thailand.

City and Soke Army Cadet Force
Back in the city, Major S.G. Cook, OBE, TD, DL, Director of Education for Huntingdonshire, was now confirmed as County Cadet Colonel Commandant for the Hunts., and Soke of Peterborough Cadet Unit.

Recruiting for the Cadet Force was going on well, and it was expected that by the end of the second week of April, the authorized strength of 600 would be reached. It was then probable that the authorization for a larger number would be sought. The present, official strength of 292 Cadets in the companies already in being was as made up as follows:

- King's School   92
- Deacon's School   66
- Fletton and Stanground   54
- Fletton Secondary School   47
- Walton   33

In addition there was a company in the course of enrolment at New Road, consisting mainly of boys and old boys of New Road and Eastholm schools. This was expected to add two companies, or 200 boys, to the strength. Also, a company was to be formed at Stamford, which, although mainly in Lincolnshire, was included in the Soke for Cadets, as it was for Home Guard purposes. Enrolments for Walton and New Road companies were taking place at Mountsteven Avenue and Eastholm Senior Boys School respectively.

Uniforms would be issued for boys of 14 to 17, and would consist of full battle-dress, with field service caps, badges and web anklets. The badges would be that of the Northamptonshire Regiment for the boys of the Soke, and in the Hunts., it would be the badge which had been adopted by the Home Guard, the rampant stag of the old Huntingdonshire Cyclists Battalion.

At 17 a boy could join the Home Guard, still keeping his membership of the Cadets if he wished. The headquarters of the Hunts., and Soke Cadet Force was at Swanspool House, Midgate, Peterborough.

Waste Paper Drive Danger

Concern was still being raised by Miss Joan Wake, Hon. secretary and custodian of the Northamptonshire Record Society, regarding historical records being given over to salvage.

"It appears," she said, "that lately some of these civil records (parish records and church registers) have been turned out for salvage. This has undoubtedly been done with the best intentions but I would respectfully point out that not only are these records of the parish officers of value for village history, but that they form an important source for the social and economic history of the county at large, and that it is not in the national interest that any further destruction should take place.

Moreover, together with other civil records in our churches, they have been committed to the care of the incumbents and churchwardens (who are jointly responsible for their safe custody) by a series of Acts of Parliament, which so far from having been repealed, have been confirmed by Statute as recently as in 1933."

RAF Casualties

It was reported on Friday 10th April that Sergeant Air Gunner, 1379450, Reginald Thomas Ward, 22, Queens Gardens, Peterborough, was missing believed killed following a recent flight. The son of Reginald Thomas Ward and Lilian Ward, and husband of Winifred Victoria Ward, he had been a salesman for Alexander Thomson Ltd., before joining the RAFVR 18 months previously. Sergeant Ward's death is recorded as having taken place on 25th March, 1942, and he is commemorated on the Runnymede Memorial.

Aircraftman First Class, 122472, Edward Jack Dorman, only son of Mr. Edward and Mrs. Martha Dorman, 44, South Street, Stanground, had now returned home from Oklahoma, United States, where he had gained his wings and been gazetted Pilot Officer. He had been educated at Fletton Secondary School and was employed at the GPO as a sorting clerk and telegraphist. He was now on 14 days leave. Flying Officer (Pilot) Dorman, 28 Squadron, would be killed in action on the 10th October, 1943. He is buried in the Imphal War Cemetery.

Railings

Still no information had been received regarding removal of railings in the city for salvage. Work on the clearance of Huntingdon's iron railings which had been scheduled for removal, was to commence shortly. The contract for the work was held by Mr. W. Scott, of St. Ives, and experience in that borough and the St. Ives Rural District had shown almost unanimous co-operation in the removal of the railings to aid the war effort.

City Home Guard

Lieutenant L.T. Howlett and Second Lieutenant C.H. Saunders, both of 'D' Company were now permitted to resign their commissions. Lance Corporal A.B. Bowering, HQ, Company, had been promoted to Corporal, and the following had been taken on strength: Privates C. Baker, S.J. Crawley, A.R. Wright, A.T. Boyson, H.L. Bridgefoot and J.W. Calder.

In the 2nd Northants Battalion (Soke of Peterborough) Home Guard, promotions and appointments were also being announced. CSM J.J. Robinson became Second Lieutenant in 'D' Company, Private H. le P. Grimwade, Lieutenant and Platoon Officer; and Second Lieutenant E. Hicks, Lieutenant and Platoon Commander.

Major J.W. Goddard, MC, was transferred as Second in Command to No.1 Platoon, 'A' Company; Captain E.W. Canham, became Battalion Contact Officer, and Captain H.H. Senior, Battalion Gas Officer. Promotions were Private H.F.V. Barton to be Corporal; and Private H.J. Goodliffe to be Sergeant.

Girls Leisure Hours

The 366 registration cards filled in on March 28th by 17 year old girls in the Soke of Peterborough had now been handed over to the Youth Organiser. Only 6 percent of the girls were concerned with any youth organization or Civil Defence work, but it was felt that when interviewing started the girls would be found as eager and enthusiastic as the boys to give up some of their leisure time to help their country. It was hoped the majority would be able to spare the time to join a youth club to meet and mix with other young people for recreation.

Many More Missing at Singapore

A third list of names of men missing after the capitulation of Singapore was published on 10th April, and the news was horrific. I have indicated those who did not survive captivity:

Lance Sergeant Richard Beales, Suffolk Regiment, 3, Keeton Road, Peterborough. He was the son of Mr. and Mrs. R. Beales, 92, Fulbridge Road. Aged 23, L/Sgt Beales, who before the war was with Mr. Bratley, builder, of Fulbridge Road, married Miss O. Walden three years earlier, they had one child.

Corporal C.W. Palmer, Royal Norfolk Regiment, 55, Tower Street, Fletton. He was married with five children and they had come to the city five years earlier.

Acting Corporal James Gordon Garn, 5831197, 2nd Battalion, Cambridgeshire Regiment, 72, New Road, Peterborough. Aged 24, he was the youngest son of Mr. Robert F. Garn and Mrs. Florence Ellen Garn, of Eastfield, Peterborough. Corporal Garn had been killed in action two months earlier on the 9th February, 1942, and is buried in Kranji War Cemetery.

Lance Corporal Harry Hornsby, 5833551, 2nd Battalion, Cambridgeshire Regiment, 307, Clarence Road. Aged 30, he was the youngest son of Mr. C.T. and the late Mrs. Hornsby. He married Miss Marjorie Hurst of 76, Clarence Road, and before the war served his apprenticeship with Jellings Builders as a painter and decorator. He died of Beri-Beri in captivity on 27th August, 1943, and is buried in Chungkai War Cemetery, Thailand.

Lance Corporal Phillip Montague Casburn, 7690231, Corps of Military Police, 18th Divisional Provost Coy, 87, Grange Road, Peterborough. Aged 32, he was the son of Mr. Montague and Mrs. Catherine Casburn, and husband of Doris Louisa Casburn of Towler Street. Before the war he worked in the Co-operative butchery department, Park Road. Lance Corporal Casburn died of a tropical ulcer on the 9th August 1943, in a Japanese prisoner of war camp and is buried in Thanbyuzayat War Cemetery, Burma (now Myanmar).

Lance Corporal Edward Alphonso Lane, Suffolk Regiment, of 47, Dogsthorpe Road was now posted as missing at Singapore. He was the son of Mr. and Mrs. E. Lane, 19, Milton Street.

Lance Corporal Albert Edward Brains, Royal Norfolk Regiment, 50, Saxon Road, was missing. Aged 22 years old, he was the eldest son of Mr. and Mrs. A.E. Brains, and before the war had been with the London Brick Company. He had played both football and cricket for Phorpres.

211

Lance Corporal Alec George Bussey, 5832504, Cambridgeshire Regiment, 86, South Street, Stanground, Peterborough. At 28 years old, he was the youngest son of Mrs. S. Bussey, and the husband of Miss K.W.J. Marriott , originally of Westcott. Before the war he had been with the London Brick Company. Lance Corporal Bussey died on the 12th September 1944, aged 31, on board the Japanese transport ship RAKUYO MARU after it had been torpedoed and sunk by the US Submarine SEALION. He is commemorated on the Singapore Memorial, Singapore. Column 57.

Lance Corporal E.A. Davis, Suffolk Regiment, 27, Midland Road was now missing. He was the son of Mr. Alfred E. Davis and before the war had been with the Eastern Counties Omnibus Co. His father, who served under Major H.H. Staton in the First World War, and had been awarded the DCM, had also had his left leg amputated owing to wounds. Lance Corporal Davis' eldest sister had been a member of the ATS since August, 1941.

Gunner Walter John Harry Casbon, 940900, 135 (The Hertfordshire Yeomanry) Field Regiment, Royal Artillery, 32, St. John's Street, Peterborough, was the youngest son of Mr. and Mrs. W. Casbon. Before the war he had been employed in the Co-operative Society's butchery department in Park Road. Gunner Casbon died on the 14th June 1943, aged 23, in a Japanese prisoner of war camp. He is buried in Kanchanaburi War Cemetery, Thailand. Coll. Grave 6. B. 75-78.

Gunner Frederick Thomas Elliott, 922904, 135 (Hertfordshire Yeomanry), Royal Artillery, 8, St. Marin's Street, Peterborough. Although listed as missing in April, Gunner Elliott died of wounds on the 26th January 1942, aged 21, and is buried in Kranji War Cemetery.

Private George Leslie Dolby, 5832971, 4th Suffolk Regiment, 7, Hereward Road, Peterborough, was the youngest son of Mr. and Mrs. G.E. Dolby. Private Dolby was unmarried and before the war had been employed by Ellis and Everard Ltd. He died in a Japanese prisoner of war camp on the 25th June 1943, aged 28, and is buried in Chungkai War Cemetery, Thailand.

Gunner Thomas Phillips, 1557762, 125 Anti-Tank Regiment, Royal Artillery, of 137, Gladstone Street, was the son of Son of Mr. John Thomas and Mrs. Florence Emma Phillips, of Peterborough. Before the war he had been employed as Assistant Sales Manager at the Fifty Shillings Tailors, Bedford Branch. Gunner Phillips died on the 12th September 1944, aged 28, as a Japanese prisoner of war following the sinking of a Japanese transport vessel en route to Japan. He is commemorated on the Singapore Memorial, Singapore.

Gunner Bernard Cecil Yarrow, 1787274, 7 Coast Regiment, Royal Artillery, 68, All Saint's Road, Peterborough, was the second son of Mr. and Mrs. William Owen Yarrow and husband of Sarah Ann Yarrow, of Peterborough. Gunner Yarrow, who was 35 years old, was a postman before the war. He would die on the 5th March 1943, aged 36, in a Japanese prisoner of war camp. He is commemorated on the Singapore Memorial, Singapore. Column 34.

Private Hector MacDonald Hart, 212, New England, Peterborough, was the youngest son of Mr. and Mrs. C.H. Hart, 207, New England. He was married with a son aged three and a daughter aged four. Before the war he had been a district salesman for Kleen-e-zee Brush Co. and later a parcels porter at the North Station.

Private William Alfred Tyler, 5833147, 4th Suffolk Regiment, 23, Wood Street, was 23 years of age and before the war had been with Ellis and Everard. Private Tyler died on the 21st September 1944, aged 24, on the Japanese transport ship the

HOFUKU MARU (also known as the TOYOFUKU MARU), when it was sunk by aircraft from a United States aircraft carrier, while on the way to Formosa (now Taiwan). Of the 1,289 Allied prisoners on board, 1,047 were lost. He is commemorated on the Singapore Memorial, Singapore. Column 56.

Private James Arthur Brown, 5830899, 5th Suffolk Regiment, 67, Tower Street, New Fletton, Peterborough, was the only son of James and Annie Brown. Aged 24, he had been a greaser on the LMS before the war. Private Brown died on the 13th August 1943, aged 24, in a Japanese prisoner of war camp. Buried in Sai Wan War Cemetery, Hong Kong.

Private Frederick Steels, 5830917, 5th Suffolk Regiment, 52, Hunting Avenue, Fletton, Peterborough, was the son of Mr. and Mrs. Jack Steels, Chapel Street, Stanground, Peterborough, and husband of Vera Steels. Before the war he had been employed at the Central brickyards. Private Steels died on the 22nd August 1943, aged 25, in a Japanese prisoner of war camp and is buried in Thanbyuzayat War Cemetery, Myanmar (previously Burma).

Private Jonathan (Jack) Nichols, Royal Norfolk Regiment, 30, Celta Road, Woodston, Peterborough, was now posted as missing. He was the son of Mr. John Nichols and the late Mrs. Nichols, and before the war had been a drawer at the London Brick Company.

Private Cyril Longfoot, Royal Norfolk Regiment, 20, George Street, Woodston, Peterborough, was missing. Aged 29 he was the son of Mr. and Mrs. W. Longfoot, and husband of Mrs. Violet Longfoot of Saxon Road. Before the war he was in the electrical department of the LNER.

Driver Frank Button, 5th Battalion, Royal Norfolk Regiment, 20, Bamber Street, was the youngest son of Mrs. W. Button. Aged 25 he was engaged to Miss Dorothy Lenigar, of Northwich. Before the war he was a Salvation Army insurance agent.

Private Donald Charles Poole, Cambridgeshire Regiment, 171, High Street, Fletton, was the only son of Mr. P.J. Poole, hairdresser, and Mrs. Poole. Aged 24, he assisted his father in the family business.

Private Fred Stallebrass, Cambridgeshire Regiment, 31, North Street, Stanground, Peterborough, was the second son of Mr. and Mrs. C. Stallebrass. Aged 29, before the war he had been at Carlton Mills.

Private Harold Peach, Cambridgeshire Regiment, 206, Walpole Street, was the only son of Mr. and Mrs. H. Peach. At 23 years of age, he had been employed at Baker Perkins prior to the war.

Private Leslie William Lane, 5830971, 1st Cambridgeshire Regiment, Suffolk Regiment, 12, Marne Avenue, Peterborough, was the son of Charles and Ethel May Lane and had been a locomotive driver for the East Midlands Gravel Co. before the war. He died on the 21st September 1944, aged 27, on the Japanese transport ship the HOFUKU MARU (also known as the TOYOFUKU MARU), when it was sunk by aircraft from a United States aircraft carrier, while on the way to Formosa (now Taiwan). Of the 1,289 Allied prisoners on board, 1,047 were lost. He is commemorated on the Singapore Memorial, Singapore. Column 59.

Private Albert V. K. Smart, Suffolk Regiment, 67, Clarence Road, Peterborough, was the youngest son of Mr. and Mrs. J. Smart. Aged 28, before the war he had been a porter on the LNER.

Private Len Carnell, Suffolk Regiment, 13, Russell Street, Peterborough, was the son of Mrs. Carnell, and before the war had been employed at the London Brick Company.

Private Albert West, Cambridgeshire Regiment, 49, Palmerston Road, Woodston, Peterborough, was the second son of Mrs. F. Hoyles. At 24 years of age, he had formerly been employed at the London Brick Company. Mrs. Hoyles' eldest son, Gunner William West, Royal Artillery, was a prisoner of war in Italy at this time and would die in captivity.

Private Alfred George Nightingale, Cambridgeshire Regiment, 156, Belsize Avenue, Woodston, Peterborough, was 26, and before the war had been employed at the London Brick Company.

Private James Arthur Brown, 5830899, 5th Suffolk Regiment, 67, Tower Street, Fletton, was the only son of Mr. and Mrs. J. Brown. He was 23 years of age and before the war had been employed on the LMS. Private Brown died on the 13th August, 1943, aged 24, in a Japanese prisoner of war camp and is buried in Sai Wan War Cemetery, Hong Kong.

Private George Herbert Nightingale, 5830908, 5th Suffolk Regiment, 41, Wootton Avenue, Old Fletton, Peterborough, was the eldest son of Mr. Herbert Nightingale and the late Mrs. Nightingale. He was 22 years of age and was with Flettons Ltd before the war. Private Nightingale died on the 26th July, 1943, of Cholera while in a Japanese prisoner of war camp. He is commemorated on the Singapore Memorial, Singapore, column 56.

These were just the Peterborough men, there were many more men on this list from the outlying district including Whittlesey, Coates, Farcet, Yaxley, Bourne, Thorney and Ramsey. This was the biggest tragedy to hit the city since Dunkirk.

Fletton Home Guard

'A' Company (Fletton) of the 1st Hunts. Battalion, Home Guard, had now organized a special casualty service, but at that moment there was a shortage of personnel and a further 20 recruits were required. Any man with elementary first aid training, or who was prepared to undergo such training, was asked to send in his details to the Officer Commanding 'A' Company, Drill Hall, Peterborough. Men who were prepared to undertake the duty, would in many cases be releasing younger men for more active and combatant work.

A Battalion mortar team led by Corporal B. Allen from No. 2 (Railway) platoon of 'A' Company did extremely well at a demonstration of Home Guard weapons. A very accurate and impressive performance was much applauded by the audience of Home Guard and Regular military officers of high rank.

The following men had now been taken on the strength of 'A' Company:

H.Q.
- Private J.P. Bristow

No. 1 Platoon
- W. Fowles
- D.T. Dean

No. 2
- L. Dutton

No. 3
- C.G. Rowlett

No. 4
- A.E. Mason
- W.S. Berry

214

- J.T. Bunkley
- S.F. Castle
- V.R. Hull
- G. Kelly
- T. Morris
- A. Redhead
- J. Studdard
- R.A. Williams
- H.F. Draper
- J.W. Pell
- W.E. Radbourne
- P.G. Wilkins

No. 6
- I.A.L. Cox
- V. Nuttall
- R.G. Bedford

Recent promotions were:
- No. 1 Platoon, Private Snow to Sergeant, Lance Corporals Groom and G. Johnson to Corporals.
- No. 2 Platoon, Privates H.J. Caines to Sergeant Clerk at Company Headquarters, D. Crick Sergeant in charge of first aid arrangements, Elliot and Godfrey to Lance Corporals, Corporal B. Allen to Sergeant in charge of the Company spigot mortar teams, Private Tiplady to Corporal in charge of No. 2 spigot teams.
- No. 4 Platoon, Private Jeffrey to Lance Corporal, Lance Corporal Woolfson to Corporal, Corporals Wilkinson and Thompson to Sergeants.
- No. 5 Platoon, Corporals Askew and Hurrall to Sergeants, Lance Corporal Blake and Lance Corporal Brown to Corporals.
- No. 6 Platoon, Private Holmes to Lance Corporal.

Soldiers in Trouble
Two stories relating to soldiers in the city were reported on 17th April. Lance Corporal Joseph Alfred Lee, Royal Engineers, aged 29, of 31, Huntley Grove, was sentenced to three months imprisonment at Bootle, having pleaded guilty to stealing 42 bottles of whiskey and 42 bottles of wine from a railway wagon.

At the other end of the scale, Gunner Livingstone, Royal Artillery, was knocked off his bicycle in Burghley Square at 11.15 pm on Saturday 11th April by a car which did not stop. He was taken to the hospital suffering from head injuries and a fractured radius. The car was believed to have a damaged windscreen and front lamp, and the police were asking for help in tracing the owner.

Fourth List of Missing at Singapore
A fourth list of servicemen from Peterborough and District who were reported missing at Singapore was published on Friday 17th April:

Captain John Marcus Neal, Royal Artillery, was in the list of missing. He was the eldest son of Mr. A. Marcus Neal, J.P. chairman of directors of Peter Brotherhood Ltd, and Mrs. Neal, Lathbury House, Lincoln Road. Captain Neal was a solicitor at Buckle and Sons. His wife, Mrs. J.M. Neal, formerly Miss May Walker, daughter of Dr. Alec Walker, J.P. and Mrs. Walker, gave birth to a son on January 21st.

Sergeant Douglas Herbert Smith, 5830916, 5th Suffolk Regiment, 23, Warbon Avenue, Clare Estate, Peterborough, was the youngest son of Frederic Ernest and Martha Jane Smith, and husband of Margaret Smith (nee Hay) of 35, Westfield Road, who he had married in April 1941, and who was now in the ATS. Sergeant Smith, who had been a footman valet before the war, died on the 16th July, 1943, aged 24, in a Japanese prisoner of war camp and is commemorated on the Singapore Memorial, Singapore. Column 53.

Corporal George Rowland Todd, 5828758, 1st Cambridgeshire Regiment, Suffolk Regiment, 575, Lincoln Road, Peterborough, was the son of Mrs. E. Wright. He was 23 years of age and before the war had been in service with Lady Craven of Newbury. Corporal Todd died on the 21st September 1944, aged 26, on the Japanese transport ship the HOFUKU MARU (also known as the TOYOFUKU MARU), when it was sunk by aircraft from a United States aircraft carrier, while on the way to Formosa (now Taiwan). Of the 1,289 Allied prisoners on board, 1,047 were lost. He is commemorated on the Singapore Memorial, Singapore. Column 57.

Bombardier, Harry Neave, Royal Artillery, School Place, Albert Place, Peterborough, was the son of Mrs. Neave and before the war had been a clerk at the Westwood Works.

Sapper Victor Wallace Beech, 1888803, 287 Field Company, Royal Engineers, Vere Road, Peterborough, was the son of William Headey Beech and Mary Beech, and husband of Dorothy Beech, of Bishop's Stortford, Hertfordshire. Sapper Beech died on the 8th July, 1943, aged 28, in a Japanese prisoner of war camp and is buried in Thanbyuzayat War Cemetery, Myanmar.

Private Thomas Harbour, Cambridgeshire Regiment, 163, New England, Peterborough, was the eldest son of Mr. and Mrs. S. Harbour. Aged 22 years, before the war he had been with Mr. E. Climpson, butcher, of New England.

Private Sidney Harbour, Suffolk Regiment, 163, New England, Peterborough, was the second son of Mr. and Mrs. S. Harbour. Aged 21, before the war he had been a rope maker for Messrs Snowdens between leaving school and joining the Army.

Private W.A. Bridges, Suffolk Regiment, 2, St John's Street, Peterborough, was the only son of Mr. and Mrs. D.H. Bridges. He was 29 years of age and before the war had been employed at the London Brick Company. News would later be received that he was a prisoner of war.

Private William Jenkins, 5777117, 5th Royal Norfolk Regiment, Flag Fen, Newark, Peterborough, was the fifth son of Mr. and Mrs. C. Jenkins. He died on the 21st September, 1944, aged 27, on the Japanese transport ship the HOFUKU MARU (also known as the TOYOFUKU MARU), when it was sunk by aircraft from a United States aircraft carrier, while on the way to Formosa (now Taiwan). Of the 1,289 Allied prisoners on board, 1,047 were lost. He is commemorated on the Singapore Memorial, Singapore.

Private Ernest Stanley Bucknell, 5777217, 5th Royal Norfolk Regiment, 79, Montague Road, Peterborough, was the son of John Thomas Bucknell and Louisa Bucknell, of Peterborough, and husband of Grace J. Bucknell, of Walton, Peterborough, and was employed at the Westwood Works before joining the Army. Private Bucknell died on the 1st February 1944, aged 29, of Avitaminosis (the chronic or long-term deficiency of one or more vitamins) in a Japanese prisoner of war camp and is buried in Chungkai War Cemetery, Thailand.

Private Charles Benjamin Hill, 5777114, 5th Royal Norfolk Regiment 35, High Street, Fletton, Peterborough, was the second son of Mr. and Mrs. A. Hill, 10, South Street, Peterborough. He was 26 years of age and married with one son and was with Mac Fisheries before the war. Private Hill died on the 15th February, 1942, in Singapore, and is buried in Kranji War Cemetery, Singapore.

Private Leonard Henry Fishpool, 5945841, 5th Bedfordshire and Hertfordshire Regiment, 87, Wellington Street, Peterborough, was the son of John Henry Fishpool, and Mary Elizabeth Fishpool, of Peterborough. Before the war he worked on the LNER. Private Fishpool died on the 15th August, 1945, aged 42, in a Japanese prisoner of war camp and is buried in Sai Wan War Cemetery, Hong Kong.

Private Horace Jones, Bedfordshire and Hertfordshire Regiment, 72, Cromwell Road, Peterborough, formerly cellarman at the Bull Hotel, was the husband of Mrs. Rene Jones, attendant in the Bull Market Bar.

Private Leslie George Preston, 12, London Road, Peterborough, aged 26, was married and had been in the employ of Ellis and Everard Ltd., before the war.

Private Arthur Wilfred Yarrow, 5834849, 5th Suffolk Regiment, 30, South Street, Eastgate, Peterborough, husband of Mrs. F.A. Yarrow, was aged 31 and had three children. Before the war he was employed at the Whittlesey brick yards. Private Yarrow died on the 18th July, 1943, of Cholera in a Japanese prisoner of war camp and is commemorated on the Singapore Memorial, Singapore.

Private Charles Ernest Yarrow, Suffolk Regiment, 30, South Street, Peterborough, who was listed as missing, also worked at the Whittlesey brickyards.

Private George Bruce, Royal Norfolk Regiment, 16 Fulbridge Road, Peterborough, was the only son of Mr. J.E. Bruce, and the late Mrs. Bruce.

Private Reginald Mitchell, 5779614, 5th Royal Norfolk Regiment, Shortacres Road, Fletton, Peterborough, had been a partner in the Peterborough Window Cleaning Company before the war. He died on the 21st September 1944, aged 31, on the Japanese transport ship the HOFUKU MARU (also known as the TOYOFUKU MARU), when it was sunk by aircraft from a United States aircraft carrier, while on the way to Formosa (now Taiwan). Of the 1,289 Allied prisoners on board, 1,047 were lost. He is commemorated on the Singapore Memorial, Singapore, Column 51.

Private Albert Harold Wright, Suffolk Regiment, 70, Alexandra Road, Peterborough, was the adopted nephew of Mr. and Mrs. J.T. Wright, and before the war was on the staff of the Great Northern Hotel.

Private George William Thompson, 5833660, 1st Cambridgeshire Regiment, Suffolk Regiment, 19, Star Road, Peterborough, was one of the four sons of Mrs. Isabella Thompson who were serving in the Army. Mrs. Thompson lost her first husband in the First World War. Before the present war Private Thompson had been employed at Hicks No. 1 yard at the brickyards. He died on the 21st September, 1944, aged 24, on the Japanese transport ship the HOFUKU MARU (also known as the TOYOFUKU MARU), when it was sunk by aircraft from a United States aircraft carrier, while on the way to Formosa (now Taiwan). Of the 1,289 Allied prisoners on board, 1,047 were lost. He is commemorated on the Singapore Memorial, Singapore, Column 61.

Many more men from other parts of the district were listed including; Conington, Whittlesey, Thorney, Coates, Warboys, Ramsey, Holme, Kings Cliffe and Somersham.

Gas 'Released' in City Streets

A series of practical gas exercises commenced on the city streets on Monday 20th April. The first concerned three groups who took part in six different incidents and continued the next day. Although slightly different each of the exercises followed a similar theme, that being an explosion which denoted the dropping of a bomb and the resultant discharge of gas. Wardens, rescue and first aid parties then made their way to the scene to deal with the casualties.

Valuable experience was gained during these exercises, not least in the wearing and correct adjustment of the various types of gas masks and other protective clothing and equipment. Some of the spectators who had gathered to watch the practice were of the opinion that although the wardens were on the scene rather too early to be realistic - well before the bomb had dropped – the first aid and rescue parties were rather slow in appearing. This resulted in casualties not being removed from the scene for up to three quarters of an hour in some cases.

Some of the public gave the demonstration a wide berth, but others, particularly small boys and girls, kept on the scene and gained a lot of experience in the protracted wearing of respirators. Among those directing operations at different points were Mr. Lister Robinson and Major de Gray (chief and deputy chief Wardens); Dr. J.H. Davis (identification officer); Dr. W. Johnstone (city medical officer); Major J.A. Mollison (ARP officer); Major Dr. Holmes (Home Guard); Mrs. Holmes (lady superintendent of first aid parties); Mr. H. Thorpe (deputy city engineer). Instructors in charge of operations at the different centres were:

- Trinity Street, N.A. Brewin ARPS
- Star Road, W. Torode LARP
- Wharf Road, H. Lyon LARP
- Queens Walk, T.W. Blake ARPS
- River Lane, J.B. Fosbrooke LARP
- Westwood Playing Fields, H.V. Shepherd LARP
- Lincoln Road East, W.C. Hubble LARP (and later H.V. Shepherd)
- Bedford Street, T.F. Sewell LARP
- Saxon Road, J.B. Fosbrooke

Further exercises were planned for the following week.

'Bring Out Your Salvage'

Saturday May 2nd was to see the commencement of Peterborough's 14-day drive to achieve the collection of 137 tons of salvage. This target was more than double the amount that would normally be collected in a fortnight and to achieve success, householders would need to turn out every ounce of paper, metal, bone, rubber, rag and kitchen waste they could lay their hands on. All of these materials were vital for the war effort.

During the two weeks a campaign would be in place which included visiting every house and business in the city so that the need of the nation could be explained. In addition to 170 WVS stewards – one in every street – wardens, fire watchers, tradesmen and the 1,400 school children enrolled in the "cog" scheme would provide support. "Salvage" was to be in everyone's mind from May 2nd to May 16th – and onwards until the end of the war. Processions, films, talks, exhibitions, loudspeaker cars, photographic and window displays, banners and leaflets would all be pressed into service to produce the greatest effect. The target was to be made up as follows:

- Paper: 60 tons, material for
    - 2,000 anti-aircraft 4.5 shell containers
    - 3,000 mortar shell carriers
    - 4,000 3 inch H.E. mortar bomb carriers
    - 5,000 cases for 40mm shells
    - 75,000 gun fuses
- Metal: 40 tons, material for
    - One cruiser tank
    - One 4 inch naval gun
    - Two Bofors guns
    - One naval mine
    - 1,000 Bren guns
- Bones: 5 tons, material for
    - 12cwts glycerine for explosives
    - 12cwts glue for aircraft construction
    - Fertilisers etc.
- Rags: One ton
- Kitchen Waste: 28 tons
- Rubber: Two tons
- Bottles: One ton

Organising the drive were Mr. F.J. Smith, the city engineer and Alderman R.C. Howard, chairman of the Highways Committee. The opening Saturday would see a procession starting at the Town Hall headed by the Home Guard band. It would include units of three battalions of the Home Guard, City, Soke and Hunts., Civil Defence personnel, National Fire Service, WVS, Salvage Stewards and Cogs, the ATC and Boy Scouts and Girl Guides.

The Chamber of Trade, through their ARP Committee would canvas the centre of the city for salvage. The WVS Stewards and the Cogs would be responsible for all other streets. In the course of the fortnight 36 three minute speeches would be made at places of entertainment, the Embassy, Empire, Broadway, Odeon, City, Princess and Savoy cinemas. One hundred and twenty posters would be placed on shelters, vehicles, hoardings and windows. There would be talks to wardens at their posts, fire watchers, civil defence workers and others.

Three indicators, at the Market Place, New England Triangle and the South Ward, would show the daily progress of the drive. The Ministry of Supply would arrange photographic displays at 35, Bridge Street, Barrett's shop, Long Causeway; and the Triangle and St. Paul's Road branches of the Co-operative Society. Also window displays at Thomson's, Queen Street; and the gas showroom on Westgate.

Large street banners were to be put up at the Market Place and in the main approaches to the city, Westgate, Midgate, Broadway and Church Street. Two short films about salvage would be shown at places of entertainment and there would be a Ministry of Information travelling film. Other films would be shown at various halls in the city and loudspeaker cars and display vans would tour the area. Head teachers would give talks at school on salvage and the subject would form the theme for essays to be written by the children.

Fifteen thousand leaflets had been received from the Ministry of Supply to be distributed to every household which carried "appealing" cartoons and slogans such as: "Just an old bone, but it helps to bring down Heinkels." "That old tin will help to make a tank." Your old rags will make equipment for the troops."

Salvage dumps in the city would be increased from 22 to 50 and the Peterborough Road Haulier's Association and Co-operative Society's transport department were ready to keep the dumps clear at their own expense by taking the salvage to the Corporation, St. John's Street, depot. The railway companies, who had their own efficient systems of salvage, were also co-operating. They would receive posters, etc., direct from their own headquarters.

At a council meeting it was decided that the money raised by the sale of the salvage would go to the rates. It was also decided however that the matter of giving some of the proceeds to charity would be discussed at a later date.

Fifth list of Singapore Names
Another list of city men reported missing at Singapore was published on Friday 24th April.

Lieutenant Gilbert Crick, 135th Field Regiment, Royal Artillery, youngest son of Mr. G.A.S. Crick, Springfield, Thorpe Road, was missing. His wife, Mrs. Dorothy Crick, was the sister of Mr. Arthur Mellows. Lt Crick was living in Harpenden.

Lieutenant Lionel E. Schofield, Sherwood Foresters, 36, Peveril Road, who was reported missing in the first list of casualties was now unofficially reported as wounded and a prisoner of war. His parents, Mr. A. Schofield, French master at Deacon's School, and Mrs. Schofield, had received news from a brother officer that Lt. Schofield was wounded in the arm and in hospital.

Corporal Kenneth Smith, Cambridgeshire Regiment, 130, Walpole Street, youngest son of Mrs. Smith and the late Mr. T. Smith, was 22 years old. He had been with Barber and Ross of Long Causeway before the war and had played football for Rob Roy and cricket for West Town.

Private G.E. Cottom, Suffolk Regiment, 158, Star Road, was now missing. He was the eldest son of Mr. and Mrs. G. Cottom, and before the war had worked in the LNER Goods Department.

Private Dennis Albert Briggs, 5779703, 5th Royal Norfolk Regiment, 54, Queens Road, was aged 28 and married. He had been Manager of the Co-operative Society's butchery branch in Stanground. Private Briggs died on the 25th June 1943, aged 29, in a Japanese prisoner of war camp and is buried in Kanchanaburi War Cemetery, Thailand.

Private Charles Albert Duggan, 5830936, 1st The Cambridgeshire Regiment, Suffolk Regiment, 86, Padholme Road, was the eldest son of Mr. and Mrs. George Duggan. He was 23 years old and had been with Dyson Brothers, printers, in Gladstone Street. Private Duggan died on the 21st September 1944, aged 25, when the Japanese transport ship the HOFUKU MARU, in which he was being taken from Thailand to Japan, was sunk by planes from an American aircraft carrier. He is commemorated on the Singapore Memorial, Singapore.

Private Harry Mills, 5959684, 5th Bedfordshire and Hertfordshire Regiment, 118, Eastgate. Aged 37 and married, he had been a corporation employee before the war. Private Mills died of avitaminosis (deficiency of vitamins) on the 1st January

1944, in a Japanese prisoner of war camp while working on the Burma-Thailand railway, and is buried in Chungkai War Cemetery, Thailand.

Private Edgar Herbert Newell, 5959689, 5th Bedfordshire and Hertfordshire Regiment, 60, St. Martin's Street, was the only son of John Thomas Newell and Frances Elizabeth Ann Newell, and husband of Florence Newell, of Peterborough. Private Newell died on the 10th September 1943, aged 37, in a Japanese prisoner of war camp while working on the Burma-Thailand railway, and is buried in Chungkai War Cemetery, Thailand.

Marine Raymond Dennis Stanford, PLY/X, HMS PRINCE OF WALES, Royal Navy, 1, North Station Road, Peterborough, was the son of Ernest William Stanford, and Maud Ethel Stanford, of Peterborough. He had been rescued when HMS Prince of Wales was sunk on 10th December, 1941, and was subsequently attached to a wireless station at Singapore. Marine Stanford died on the 16th February, 1942, and is commemorated on the Plymouth Naval Memorial, Panel 103. Column 2.

Other Casualties
Friends who feared for the safety of Sergeant Leslie Fulbourn, of 92, Westwood Street, were now relieved to learn that his wife had received news that he was safe and well in India. He had been a Private when she last heard from him and before the war had been a painter at the wagon repair works.

Mrs. Marjorie Stephens, 3, South View, London Road, had now received a telegram informing her that her husband, Leading Seaman, Albert E.M. Stephens, was a survivor of the sinking of HMS DORSETSHIRE which had been sunk by Japanese dive bombers in the Indian Ocean on the 5th April, 1942. Leading Seaman Stephens, who was 25 years old, had been in the Navy since he was 15. His wife was the only daughter of Mr. and Mrs. Arthur Shedd, 3, South View.

Oranges for Children
Mr. George Baker, secretary of the local Committee for Imported Fruit Distribution now stated that fresh supplies of oranges were to be available in the shops in the Peterborough district and would be reserved for a period of five days for issue at the rate of 1lb per head to children in possession of the green ration book. Retailers were required to record the sale by cancelling the necessary coupon in the grid at the bottom of page 15 of the yellow supplementary ration book, R.B.9., with a mark that could not be erased.

After the five days reservation period had elapsed, surplus oranges could be sold to other customers but retailers were asked to give priority to children (whether holding a green ration book or not), schools, hospitals and invalids.

Street Fighting in the Home Guard
On the evening of Tuesday 21st April, Lieutenant Colonel C.W.D. Rowe, Battalion Commander, 1st Hunts Battalion Home Guard, delivered a lecture on "Street Fighting" at Fletton Secondary School. The lecture formed part of the training programme of 'A' Company, and visiting officers from other Battalions included Colonel A.H. Mellows (Battalion Commander 2nd Northants Battalion) and a number of officers from the 1st Northants (City of Peterborough) Battalion.

Lt. Col. Rowe emphasized the importance of every member of the Home Guard having some knowledge of the tactics of fighting in streets and houses, and after dealing with the weapons which would be used, outlined the tactical operations

221

involved in an attack upon a building held by an enemy force.

One of the points made by Colonel Rowe was that those taking part in street fighting must be able to move quickly, surely and silently. He suggested that the ordinary Army boot was not suitable for this type of fighting and urged that efforts should be made to equip all street fighting patrols with some form of light rubber shoe. Any patriotic citizen with an old pair of rubber tennis shoes or plimsolls would help the Home Guard if they were prepared to hand them over for this purpose. An advertisement had been inserted in the 'Peterborough Standard' giving details of this request.

A number of promotions were now published at this time. Sergeant H.J. Caines (No. 2 Platoon) was now promoted to Second Lieutenant and was to carry out the duties of Company Intelligence Officer. P.S.M. Smith, Warrant Officer in charge of No. 3 (Sugar Beet Factory) Platoon, 'A' Company, had returned from a course at the Eastern Command Weapon Training School, passing out as Instructor, Grade 1.

Additional recruits were still required in 'A' Company and vacancies remained in the Company Casualty Service for men willing to undergo Red Cross training. Applicants were asked to contact the officer commanding 'A' Company, at the Drill Hall, London Road, or 31, Priestgate, Peterborough.

Other promotions appearing in Part 2 Orders of the 1st Northants (C.P.) Home Guard were, to be Corporals: Privates J. Adkins and T.H. Breadon ('HQ' Company) and Lance Corporal D.B. Johnson ('A' Company). The following were taken on the strength of the Battalion and posted to the Companies denoted: Privates H.J. Birkbeck and C.G. Williamson ('D'), W.B. Elmer and C.R. Goose ('C'), J.W.H. Sharpe ('A'), P.J. Dunham, W.L. Martin, A. Joyce, R.B. Brammall, F. Meakin and T. Bennett ('HQ').

The following were recent promotions in the 2nd Northants (Soke) Battalion: Private R. Hodgkinson to Corporal, Lance Corporals W. Lunn, C.W. Guymer and W.A. Crowson to Sergeants, (all 'C' Company). Sergeant A.J. Jarrett to be Company Sergeant Major, 'D' Company. Lance Corporal Long to be Corporal 'D' Company, Private N.F. Cherry to be Corporal 'B' Company.

Other appointments were Privates B. Butler, G. Wann, J. Read, F. Cavender and T.D. Sismore to be Lance Corporals, all 'D' Company.

More Missing at Singapore

Two more city men could now be found in the lists of the missing at Singapore.

Lieutenant T.R. Miles, Cambridgeshire Regiment, 'Rockbourne,' Oundle Road, Orton Longueville. Eldest son of Mr. and Mrs. W. Miles, before the war he had been woodwork instructor for the Huntingdonshire Education Committee.

Listed as "Missing at Sea" was, Lieutenant Colonel, Augustus Harry Ives, 70684, Royal Army Ordnance Corps, Commanding '10' Section. Aged 47, he was the son of Captain J. Foster Ives M.C., and Mrs. Ives, Queen Street, Peterborough. He had joined the Royal Artillery as a Gunner when he was 18 years old and was later transferred to the Ordnance Corps. His wife was evacuated to India after five years at Singapore, and he had two sons in the Army – one in the Artillery at Aden and the other on Home Service in the RAOC. Lieutenant Colonel Ives, is listed as having died on 2nd March, 1942, and is commemorated on the Singapore Memorial, Column 107.

Bernard James Balchin	Ronald Beales	Claude Howard Bee
Victor Wallace Beech	James Arthur Bonsor	Herbert Michael Bradley
William E.K. Brown	Stanley Burbage	Lewis William Chapman

Stanley Cole

Henry Oswald Collin

Kevin Sean Dodrill

Christopher Elmer

John Evans

Anthony C. Evans-Evans

Roland G. Evans-Evans

Francis Jack Fixter

John Watson Gage

Reginald William Gautrey	Charles William Hancock	Bertram Sidney Hills
George Fred Hornsby	Tom Roland Hutchings	Nebojsa Kujundzik
Leslie William Lane	George Martin	Thomas A. Mellows

George Albert Meredith

Edgar Herbert Newell

Ronald Henry Orton

Percy Ambrose Partridge

Leslie J.L. Reynolds

William Ruff

Cecil Charles Rusdale

Frederick G. Scarr

Trevor Setchfield

Frederick L. Steels

Leslie B. Toogood

William A. Underwood

Vincent Stanley Venn

Douglas H. Wakeling

Ezra Wardle

William West

Frank Woodward

John Henry Wyborn

'Gas' in City Streets

Gas exercises continued in the city on the evenings of Monday 27th and Tuesday 28th April, in order to test the efficiency of the Civil Defence services. Wardens, casualty and ambulance services, decontamination squads, rescue parties and special constables took part in the four incidents on the Monday, and three on the Tuesday.

Thunder flashes marked the discharge of the gas – tear and G.2.D., a substitute for mustard gas. The wardens, on detecting the gas warned householders in the locality to shut their windows; in an actual raid, houses in the gas concentration area would have been evacuated. Affected streets were closed and traffic diverted by special constables and wardens, and casualties were taken by ambulances to the nearest first aid posts. Decontamination squads then cleared the streets with neutralizing agents.

The incidents were umpired by head wardens and their deputies from other groups. The Vice Chairman of the ARP Committee Councillor E. Ross, Head Warden Lister Robinson, Deputy Head Warden Major R. de Gray, Doctor Johnstone, Inspector Stokes and Mr. D. Patterson (casualty staff officer) visited all the exercises. Major de Gray would summarise the umpires' reports and "friendly criticism" would be sent to the posts.

The incidents were staged at the following locations and the gas was discharged by the people named:

Monday
- Newark Schools – Mr. H. Lyon.
- Burrows Garage, Dogsthorpe Road – Mr. N.A. Brewin.
- Grange Avenue – Mr. W.E. Hubble.
- Stone Lane – Mr. F.H. Sewell.

Tuesday
- Burmer Road – Mr. Sewell.
- Itter Crescent – Mr. H. Shepherd and Mr. E. Smedley.
- Junction of South View, Croyland Road and Churchfield Road – Mr. J.V. Fosbroke and Mr. R. Rutherford.

Registrations

Girls aged 16, who registered at the Employment Exchange on Saturday 25th April (and also through the post) numbered 712. Those who were not attached to any youth organization would be interviewed with a view to "some suitable interest" being found for them.

Two weeks later over 250 girls in the 17-year-old age group had been interviewed following their registration. A very large percentage asked to train with the St. John Ambulance Brigade. Others wished to do canteen work, gardening or pre-service training for the WRENS, WAAFS or ATS. Nearly all of these girls wanted to join some club or youth organization, where they could develop their talents and learn the way to future citizenship.

Home Guard

Sergeant J.C. Ingledew 'C' Company, City Battalion Home Guard, was now promoted to Company Sergeant Major (Warrant Officer Class 2). Private R.P. Sergeant, 'HQ' Company was appointed Lance Corporal. The following were now taken on strength of the Battalion: Privates I.S. Hayward, J.H. West, K. Wiggins,

A.J.W. Hills and J.H. Wood.

Suicide at Orton Longueville
Gunner Richard Bertram Crowe, age 39, was found in bed at Orton Longueville Rectory with gunshot wounds in the head on Friday 1st May. The police also found a note addressed to Crowe's wife. Crowe, a married man with five children, came from Lavendon, Buckinghamshire, and was stationed at the rectory with four other men, all officers' servants.

At the inquest which was held the next day it was stated that he was found in the morning lying in bed with a bullet entry wound above his right eye, an exit wound above his left ear and the bullet itself embedded in the wall. A revolver was found lying beside him. Gunner Crowe was taken to the Memorial Hospital where he died a few hours later of laceration of the brain. The note which was found was not read out in court.

Salvage Piles Up
Up to the night of Wednesday 6th May, 40 tons 17cwts. of salvage had been collected in the city's great drive. This was made up as follows:

- Paper 20 tons.
- Rags 11 cwts.
- Metal 10 tons.
- Rubber nearly 2 tons.
- Bottles 2 tons.
- Bones 6 cwts.
- Kitchen waste 6 tons.

The campaign opened on Saturday 2nd with a procession and public meeting. Grouped with the city in Northamptonshire's effort were Peterborough, Barnack, Oundle and Thrapston's rural districts, and Oundle urban district. Other drives were taking place in Nottinghamshire, Derbyshire and Leicestershire.

Casualties
Mrs. Smith of 94, Alexandra Road, received news from the Royal Navy Welfare Office at this time that her younger son, Petty Officer Stanley Smith, was in hospital slightly wounded. P.O. Smith was the grandson of Mr. W.H. Hadman, district secretary of the Foresters Friendly Society.

Private Kenneth Church, 5827913, 1st, Cambridgeshire Regiment, of 24, New Road, Woodston, was now reported missing at Singapore. He was Captain of the Clarion Cycling Club and a member of Rob Roy Swimming Club. Private Church would be later reported as having died on 28th June, 1943, aged 23. He was the son of Kenneth and Ellen Brown Church, and husband of Winifred May Church, of Eye, Northamptonshire, and died of cholera at Kinsaiyok, Thailand. He is commemorated on the Singapore Memorial, Column 58.

Fire Guard Exercises
The first exercise of the local authority fire guard was now due to commence on Monday 11th April. Bomb flashes heard and seen would denote scenes of incidents

and whistles would be sounded. It was hoped that as many fire guards as possible would see the exercise. Householders were asked to place two buckets of water outside their door facing the street for this exercise and always do so. In case of an Alert the exercise in progress would be discontinued.

Also at this time a new series of siren tests was being held in the city at 11 am from Thursday 7th April for the following seven days. The siren switch being depressed for one second only.

Soke Battalion Home Guard

In the 2nd Northants (Soke) Battalion many promotions were notified in orders at this time. Private L.H. Elcombe, 'A' Company and Corporal Bonser, 'E' (Stamford) Company were now commissioned Lieutenants to act as Intelligence Officers in their respective companies.

The following NCO promotions were also now made: Lance Corporal M. Leeder to be Sergeant; Lance Corporal S.W. Catmul, Corporal; Lance Corporal J.H. Cooper, Corporal; Corporal C. Gray to Sergeant; Lance Corporal Headland to Corporal; Corporal J.T. Oliver to Sergeant; Private F. Smith to Sergeant; Corporal A. Parker to Sergeant; Lance Corporal L. Goddard to Corporal.

The following were also now appointed to Lance Corporals: Privates H. Harvey, J. Fairweather, W.J. Holloway, J.S. Phillips and P.E. Charles.

Full Scale Invasion Exercise

Just when it seemed that the Home Guard were concentrating on little more than internal promotions, a combined military and Civil Defence invasion exercise was now planned to take place in Fletton and Stanground from 11 o'clock on Saturday 23rd May until the early morning on Sunday 24th May. It was to be assumed that German landings had taken place on the South and East coasts and that advanced elements, breaking through Whittlesey, were attempting to capture Peterborough. Dive bombing attacks were said to have destroyed the main road bridge over the Nene and parachute troops had landed west and south of Fletton. How strange it seems to read this now, but how real the probability was to the people of the city in those uncertain times.

Warning was given that during the exercise all civilians should remain indoors and in particular should keep off the roads, which at certain times may be closed to traffic. Any civilian who leaves their house, should carry their identity card and gas mask. Aircraft may be taking part and (unless an Alert has been sounded) no alarm should be felt at the sound of low-flying aircraft and the noise of what appeared to be bomb explosions.

Military units engaged would include 'A,' 'B,' 'D' and 'E' Companies of the 1st Hunts Battalion Home Guard, and substantial contingents from the Isle of Ely Battalion. One feature would be the prior training and use of a number of senior boys from local Cadet units to act as messengers. All Civil Defence services would be co-operating in order to make the scheme a real test of the district invasion preparations.

Salvage Tops 138 Tons

By the night of Wednesday 13th May, the city salvage drive had reached 138 tons 1 cwt. Therefore the target of 137 tons had been topped and there were still three more days to go. The total was made up in the following way:

CITY

	Tons	cwts	qrs	Target Tons
Paper	53	17	1	60
Metal	53	3	1	40
Bottles	8	5	2	1
Rags	2	18	1	1
Rubber	3	4	0	2
Kitchen Waste	15	2	3	28
Bones	1	10	1	5

PETERBOROUGH RURAL

	Tons	cwts	Target Tons	Target cwts
Paper	5	0	7	0
Metal	10	0	6	0
Bones		11		5
Rags		8		5
Rubber		4		5
Sundries		7		5

BARNACK DISTRICT

	Tons	cwts	Target Tons	Target cwts
Paper	2	0	2	10
Metal	3	0	2	10
Bones		2		2
Rags		2		2
Rubber		4		2

Wardens came across a big quantity of high grade steel, brass, copper and other metals on the dump alongside Mr. C. Cash's house on Thorpe Road on Sunday 10th May. Thirty-two wardens were kept busy from 10 am to 1 pm and 2.30 to 6, with Mr. Lister Robinson and his deputy Major R. de Gray directing operations. Salvaging the metals was slow because the ground had to be dug and raked over. The day's yield was about 2 tons and it was hoped that they would find more on the following Sunday.

The City Engineer expressed great satisfaction with the quality of the metal received. Most of it had been carted some years ago from engineering works and had not weathered to any great degree.

Criminal Assaults
While great things were happening all around the city to bring people closer together in adversity, the sad fact was that crime was still ever present. Two cases of assault were reported in the 'Standard' on Friday 15th May, 1942. A Foreman at Brotherhood's factory, Kenneth David Hodson was found guilty of punching 17 year old Thomas Clifford Marshall twice in the face on the 17th April. He was ordered to pay £2. 2s. in damages, for causing the boy's eye and lip to bleed. Hodgson said that he thought Marshall was going to pick up a spanner and hit him with it, so he "dotted him one." After listening to the details of the case, the Judge

said that although the boy was possibly "an excessively irritating person to have to deal with," there was no excuse for the assault.

Two Woodston boys, one aged 15 and the other 14 were charged at a special Norman Cross Court on Wednesday 13th May, before Mr. C.G. Argles, with assaulting with intent to rob Miss Constance Barber, shopkeeper of Orton Waterville, on Tuesday 12th. The case against them was that they went into Orton Waterville with the intent of robbing Miss Barber's till. The police produced two pieces of wood and said that Miss Barber was struck on the left side of the head whilst she was stooping.

Mr. Argles asked the boys whether they thought their action was a very British thing to do. It was bad enough to strike a man, but there was nothing more contemptible than striking a woman. The boys said they were sorry for what they had done. They were remanded until the following Tuesday but were allowed bail of £10 each. Mr. Argles commented that "the pictures" were leading boys astray. They were the worst things ever invented.

Home Guard Funeral

No. 4 Platoon, 'C' Company, Home Guard, paid their last tribute to a comrade, Corporal Raymond Arthur Wicks, 4, Keeton Road, Peterborough, who died on the 7th May, 1942, by forming a guard of honour at the funeral at St. Paul's on Monday 11th.

Corporal Wicks was 27 years old and had been a member of the Home Guard since it was raised as the LDV. He had been ill about nine weeks and died as a result of bronchial catarrh and heart failure. He had been an expert with the Lewis gun, and a keen footballer, taking much interest in No. 4 Platoon's team. He gave considerable help to 'C' Companies Entertainment Committee.

Corporal Wicks left Barford and Perkins, where he was apprenticed, when he was 16, and joined the Reparco Wagon Repair Co. at the East Station. He was with them for over 10 years. His brother, Signaller Wicks had been taken prisoner at Singapore.

The guard of honour, which preceded the hearse to the church, was under the command of Lieutenant L. Bichener, and other officers present were: Major H.J. Farrow, Major H.A. Goodacre, officer commanding 'C' Company; Captain H. Collcott, Lieutenant W.D. Larrett and Company Sergeant Major Ingledew.

Ration Cards Rush

An inordinate rush for the new clothing and personal ration cards set in on Monday 18th May. In spite of the official announcement that a large number of stations would be open at specified places in all localities at stated hours, people flocked straight away to the headquarters in Priestgate. To deal with the situation that developed, the large lecture room at the museum was hired and staffed. Even so, queues sometimes reached to the museum gates on the street.

"It is as though people have got in the habit of queuing, and love doing it," said one official. People were told how unnecessary it was and that in any case, the books could not be used until June 1st, but still they came. The result was that in the first three days of the week, 10,000 books were exchanged. The total to be dealt with in the whole area was about 75,000.

All Night "Attack" on City

"Casualties" were ferried across the Nene from Wharf Road to a point near the old bathing sheds in the course of the big combined Home Guard and Civil Defence exercise in the Fletton district on the night of Saturday 23rd May. This was because the river bridge was assumed to have been demolished in an air attack heralding a land assault on the city from the south and south east. Over 500 people had their allotted duties in an exercise skillfully planned and enthusiastically carried out from the word go at 11 o'clock until Cease Fire at 6 am an hour earlier than was arranged.

A German invasion was assumed to have been in progress for five days and landings had been affected on the South and East Coasts. Heavy fighting was taking place at Wisbech, and the enemy, in an effort to prevent British reinforcements arriving from the west, had decided to attempt the capture of Peterborough as an important communication centre.

'A' Company, 1st Hunts Battalion, Home Guard, had the all important job of defending the bridge approaches. At zero hour the officer commanding the defenders, Major C. Greenwood, was advised that light enemy armoured units had captured Whittlesey and that an estimated force of 200 men had landed by parachute west of St. Botolph's Bridge and east of Yaxley. These forces were, in reality, the 1st Isle of Ely Company, and 'B,' 'D' and 'E' Companies of the 1st Hunts Battalion, and the odds in their favour were two to one.

Soon after 11 o'clock news came through that the enemy had begun their attack with air raids. The Civil Defence at once got busy and in less than 25 minutes attention was being given to eight incidents involving fire, rescue, first aid and traffic diversion. These were devised by the City Engineer, and went on throughout the night in weather conditions that were in themselves a test of endurance.

A 'Standard' reporter, who joined the attackers near Horsey Toll, found that they had copied the Commandos and had blackened their faces and teeth with burnt cork. The first clash came about midnight, near Stanground, when a large enemy force was taken by surprise by a defence patrol, which crept up and threw bombs. The umpire awarded 50 casualties, and described this as an excellent piece of work.

Police and specials were kept busy looking for fifth columnists, and caught 6 out of 15. Several persons not carrying their identity cards were taken to Police H.Q. and put to some inconvenience. A cycle outside a house was confiscated.

The 'Standard' reporter found the "Keep" – the combined military and civilian headquarters – near the East Station, comprised three shelters surrounded by barbed wire and wagons, and two sentries and a special constable were on guard. He was challenged and in spite of his official armband, identity card and other papers, he had much difficulty in getting in. Inside, Major Greenwood was directing defence operations and working in close co-operation with Mr. J.E. Clarke (ARP sub-controller) and Mr. F.H. Ashton. Mr. F.L. Bloodworth (chairman of the Invasion Committee) was also there. Messages were coming in rapidly and quick decisions were called for. Major Greenwood was busy sending out fighter patrols to meet the enemy.

At 1.10 a message was received that two persons were trapped in a loft in Park Street, and the reporter went out with the rescue party. They had to make a detour owing to roads being blocked by craters, and return by another route to Wharf Road, where, because the bridge had been blown up, a ferry had been established. An ambulance waiting on the opposite bank took the casualties to an emergency hospital.

By 5 o'clock the enemy had come within close range of the "Keep" and they were reinforced by a large bombing force (represented by a Blenheim bomber), which dive-bombed the "Keep" and bridgeheads. Before a final assault could be made Colonel Rowe fired the green Verey lights which brought operations to an end.

At a conference of umpires at the Angel Hotel a few hours before the attack, Colonel C.W.D. Rowe, Group Commander, who had devised the exercise, explained all the intricacies of it. The whole purpose, he said, was not to see which side won the battle, but to test Home Guard and Civil Defence precautions and the co-operation between the two in the urban area south of the river.

Colonel M.D. Barkley, Zone Commander, who watched the whole of the exercise, said that he thought it had gone off very well. He was especially enthusiastic about the success of the messenger service as for the purposes of the exercise it had been assumed that all telephone communications had been disrupted, and all messages had to be carried by 8 dispatch riders and 20 Cadets aged between 14 and 16.

The men themselves had been very grateful for the services of the WVS mobile canteens throughout the night, and for the substantial hot breakfast provided at Westgate, British Restaurant. Captain Shaw, the chief umpire had his headquarters at Farrow's factory. Other umpires were Colonel Berridge, Captain Plaistowe and Captain Belville (Attacking Force A); Captain D.C. Banks and Lieutenant A.P. Allen (Force B); Major Naylor and Captain P. Gurney Coombes (Force C); Major L. Farley and Lieutenant A.W. Ruddle (Force D); Captain W.B. Buckle and Lieutenant Daking (The Keep); Colonel A.H. Mellows and Major W.K. Yarnold (Central Defence); Colonel MacDonald and Lieutenant Anderson (East Defence); Major Stanyon and Captain Senescall (West Defence).

Ration Books
Up to Thursday 28th May, about 40,000 of the 75,000 new ration books for the Peterborough area had been issued. It was hoped that the rest would be cleared by the weekend. An advertisement in the "Standard" gave particulars of the schools which would be open for the purpose, and the hours on Saturday. These would save a journey to the food office in a large number of instances.

Olympus Plaque
The shield to mark the city's purchase of HMS OLYMPUS had now been received. It was about two feet wide and bore the arms of the ship with the symbolic lightning flashes. It was expected that other plaques would be sent to Peterborough and Barnack Rural District Councils. Documents relating to the history of the ship would also be received. Gifts of books and games for the men of the crew were being asked for and taken to the Town Hall.

Home Guard
Movement within the Home Guard went on unabated, and at the City Battalion there were further promotions: Private J.K. Bellamy, 'A' Company had been promoted to Lance Corporal. Privates R.T. Winch, F.R. Saberton, C.R. Walkington and A.E. Coulson had been taken on strength.

In the Soke Battalion, Sergeant A.H. Taylor, 2nd Northants had been promoted to Lieutenant and seconded for duty with the Hunts and Northants Cadets. Privates H.

Measures, J.G. Coulson and Ransome, all 'A' Company, were promoted to Corporals. Corporals P.C. Hill and G. Squires, both 'B' Company to Sergeants. Appointments to Lance Corporal were Privates Gathercole 'A' Company, T.W. Smith 'B,' J.W. Pauley 'E' and B.R. Downes and P.R. Johnson.

Cogs

On the morning of Saturday 23rd May, 1,000 of the city's salvage cogs were treated to a film show at the Broadway Kinema, arranged by the City Engineer in appreciation of their work during the salvage campaign. They saw a comedy "Ride 'em Cowboy," featuring Bud Abbott and Lou Costello; a picture entitled "The Watchers," depicting the work of the coastguards, the news, and a Ministry of Information film.

Fire Guard Practices

In the Fire Guard exercises which took place between May 11th and 22nd, at least 100 "incidents" were arranged and it was estimated that around 3,000 guards took part. There was an umpire present at each incident, and for the greater part of those the proceedings were under the personal observation of Mr. Rowland Hill, Staff Officer, his deputy Mr. R.P. Palmer, or Inspector Stokes.

Practice incendiary bombs were used and nearly all were effectively dealt with. Mr. J.C. Webster, senior training officer from Region, saw some of the tests and was very satisfied with progress. Thanks were expressed afterwards to Mr. P. Crowson, of the Ladder Co., Messrs Elliotts of Lincoln Road, and Mr. W.B. Jellings, of Westwood, for shavings and other materials which helped to make the exercises more realistic.

Home Guard killed on Duty

The first death on duty of a member of the City Home Guard took place on the night of Wednesday 3rd June. George John Austin Taylor, aged 28, of 159, Queens Walk, Fletton, was a dispatch rider in the 1st Hunts Battalion, Home Guard. His motorcycle came into collision with a three ton lorry driven by George Henry Chambers, 308, Oundle Road, Woodston, on London Road.

Mr. Taylor, an A.I.D. inspector at Newall's, was the only son of Mr. and Mrs. G. Taylor, 80, Silver Street. Five years earlier he had married Miss Hilda Brown of St. Mary's Street, Peterborough. He is buried in Old Fletton Cemetery, Sec. 6. Grave 231.

At an inquest held at the Memorial Hospital on Friday 5th May, it was revealed that Private Taylor had only recently acquired his motorcycle and that it was the first time he had ridden it on duty. It was also stated that although he had lost the sight of his left eye four years earlier in an accident at work, he had excellent sight in the other eye.

The driver of the lorry, Mr. Chambers, stated that it was about 10.15 pm on the Wednesday night when he was driving along the London Road coming towards Peterborough at a speed of about 30 miles per hour. He saw the motorcyclist coming towards him and taking a bend at about 60 to 70 miles per hour. The motorcycle came over the white line and the rider then appeared to lose control and hit the nearside wing and bumper of the lorry.

The rider was taken to hospital in an ambulance from a military camp; he was deeply unconscious, and bleeding from both ears and nostrils. He had fractures of both femurs and compound fractures of the tibia and fibula. He died at 11.45, cause of death being a fracture of the base of the skull and multiple fractures of his legs.

Ration Books

Up to the night of Saturday 30th May, culminating in a rush at the out-stations, 70,999 new ration books had been issued. On Monday 1st June, 960 more had gone out, on Tuesday about 500, and on Wednesday another 500 so that approximately 73,000 had been issued. There were still many absentees and people who had moved to take into account which made up for the total to be issued of 75,000. Issues were still being made at the Food Control Office.

Home Guard

Promotions, appointments, training and recruiting continued to gather pace at the various Home Guard Battalions. Also, the new Cadet Force was increasing its numbers daily. In the Society of Miniature Rifle Clubs Wartime League, Baker Perkins Home Guard was competing against 11 other Home Guard Battalions, they were runners up and took the Bronze Medal. The Lieutenant for Cambridge and the Isle of Ely, Major C.W.R. Adeane, was asking employers of youths in the Cadet Force to release them for at least seven days in the summer so that they could attend camp. Because many of the lads worked on farms, the camps were being arranged for times when their absence would cause the farmers least inconvenience.

On the 11th June, No. 2 Platoon of 'D' (Railways) Company, City Home Guard, won for the second time, the cup given by Councillor J.A. Bartram for all round efficiency. The competition which took place on King's School ground in the presence of a very large assembly, included gas, Lewis gun, bombing, Northover Projector and arms drill. The result was as follows:

Platoon	Officer	Points
No. 2	Lt. C. Brewer	71½
No. 1	Lt. F. Dent	68½
No. 3	Lt. J. Booker	66

"Reassuring News" from Singapore

A strange story was published in the 'Standard' on Friday 12th June, regarding the treatment of prisoners in Singapore. From what we now know about the treatment that the Japanese Forces dished out, this naïve letter was far off the mark.

The news took the form of a letter sent to Dr. A.M. Pilcher, of Broadway, Peterborough. The letter was sent by a Mrs. Ormiston, daughter of Mr. Hugh Pilcher, who was Toc H Warden at Lille, and was captured by the Germans when France fell. Mrs. Ormiston received it from a "very influential prisoner in Singapore," who managed to successfully get it away from the island.

The writer described the Japanese Commander as a Christian who was behaving very well. The writer stated that the island was being policed by the British, and that life was going on "extraordinarily normally," even to playing tennis. Europeans, he added, are prisoners only to the extent that they are not allowed to leave the island.

The actual source of this fairytale remains unknown, however, if it gave some comfort to those who had loved ones on the island, then perhaps it had its uses, at least for a short while.

Airman Missing

Flight Sergeant, 963850, Percy Hudson Thimblebee, Royal Air Force Volunteer Reserve, 214, Palmerston Road, only son of Mrs. J. Thimblebee, 204, Palmerston Road, and husband of Margaret Annie Thimblebee, was now reported as missing in action on May 29th. Formerly at the LNER Accountant's office, he was an old Deaconian and won many athletic prizes at school. He married Miss. Margaret Pettit, only daughter of Mr. and Mrs. J.W. Pettit, 204, Palmerston Road.

Flight Sergeant Thimblebee, was officially reported as having been killed in action on 27th May, 1942, aged 23 years old. He is commemorated on the Runnymede Memorial, Surrey. Panel 76.

City Submarine Lost

At the end of May the city received the shield commemorating the money it raised during "Warship Week" in order to 'buy' a submarine, HMS OLYMPUS. Little did they know at the time that the submarine had already been sunk. An Admiralty communiqué issued on the night of Saturday 13th June, stated: "The board of Admiralty regrets to announce that HM Submarine Olympus (Lieut. Cmdr H.G. Dymott, RN) has been lost. The next of kin have been informed."

The OLYMPUS had been adopted by the Soke and City of Peterborough as a result of the raising of £523,000 in Warship Week. Arrangements had been made for Admiralty representatives and Lt. Cdr. Dymott to come to Peterborough for a ceremonial exchange of the plaques. One in the shape of a shield, a gift from the Admiralty to the city, commemorating its adoption of the vessel, and one from the city intended to be fixed to the deck plates of the submarine. It was thought that the first plaque would probably still be placed on the wall in the main entrance of the Town Hall. Schoolchildren in the city had been collecting books to send to the crew, and the Mayor wrote to the Admiralty offering the deep sympathy of the citizens to the relatives and friends of the officers and men who had lost their lives in the cause of freedom.

"I think it is up to everyone," wrote the Mayor in a letter to the 'Standard,' "to endeavour to save as much as possible in order to replace this ship."

HMS OLYMPUS had been built by William Beardmore & Co., Dalmuir, Scotland. Launched on the 11th December, 1928, she was commissioned on 14th June, 1930. On the 8th May, 1942, HMS OLYMPUS was mined and sunk off Malta in approximate position 35°55'N, 14°35'E. She had just left Malta on passage to Gibraltar with personnel including many of the crews of the sunken submarines HMS PANDORA, HMS P36 and HMS P39. There were only 9 survivors out of 98 on board. They had to swim 7 miles back to Malta. 89 crew and passengers were lost with the ship.

It didn't take the Admiralty long to find a replacement submarine, and on Thursday 25th June, the Savings Group secretaries, meeting at the Town Hall were told that the Admiralty had allocated the submarine HMS P512 to Peterborough in place of the lost Olympus. Books, games and other gifts intended for the crew of Olympus would instead be sent to the P512.

In a ten week's savings drive beginning on July 20th, the Soke and City were now asked to increase savings by 50 per cent, over the corresponding period the previous year, to enable five tanks to be named after the area.

The secretary referred to the loss of HMS OLYMPUS and to the new savings drive, "Tanks for Attack." It was the committee's aim to get five tanks to be named

237

after Peterborough during the ten weeks from July 20th. To qualify, the Soke and City must show a 20 per cent increase in small savings over the corresponding period the previous year in which £231,000 was raised. The average weekly savings must be increased from £25,000 to £28,000. A 20 per cent increase would qualify for five Valentine tanks, 25 per cent, five Matildas, and 30 per cent, five Churchills. Any tank could bear not more than three names of groups which had done exceptionally well, in addition to the name of the town.

The secretary said that it was "timid" of the committee to ask for only a 20 per cent increase, he would like to see 50 per cent, and he knew it could be done. At the same time the committee wanted Peterborough to hit back and replace the Olympus. Statistics showed that 35 per cent of the city's population were savers; that was not enough. A hundred per cent increase in membership, with a 50 per cent increase in savings, should be the new goal.

The secretary also said that Mrs. Whyman had made a free gift of £5 4s., raised by a competition for a cushion cover, won by Mrs. Long, of Orton Avenue. (*From small acorns giant oak trees grow!*)

For those readers who may be concerned for the safety of the crew of HMS P512, considering the fate of the earlier ship and the long years of war yet to come, I can reveal that the submarine survived the war, (just). She started out in life in the United States Navy as United States Submarine R-17, built by the Union Iron Works, San Francisco, California, U.S.A., and was launched on 24th December, 1917. The 'old lady' was transferred to the Royal Navy and commissioned as HMS P512 on 9th March, 1942. She never left American waters, being stationed at Halifax (1942-43) and Bermuda (1943-44) for anti-submarine warfare training. She was refitted at Philadelphia. HMS P512 was handed back to the United States Navy on 6 September 1944 and sold for scrap to the North American Smelting Co., Philadelphia, shortly after the end of the war on 16 November 1945.

HMS P512 does have one claim to fame, she was a movie star! She starred as an extra in a propaganda film that featured HMS P512 and a Corvette. It was called Corvette K225 which was released in the USA in 1943, starring Randolph Scott. In the UK the film was called "The Nelson Touch". Some of the crew had to dress in German uniforms and then undertake gun action against the Flower Class Warship. The men drew lots to see who would "star" in the film, and operate the deck gun. Dummy rounds were no use as the resultant splash was too puny. Instead they were required to use live ammo. The skipper had a serious word and impressed upon them that they were not under any circumstances to hit the Corvette with live rounds! They fired well over the ship's masts and afterwards when ashore, the Canadian crew of the corvette ribbed them with the chant "the Limeys' can't even hit a barn door at ten paces."

Sixth Raid

There had been a break in air raids over the city, the last being in May the previous year. The next one took place on 30th June 1942, and in this one many incendiary bombs were dropped in the area of the North Station and St. Leonards Street. Among the buildings damaged were the Northern Hotel, George Hotel and the Pony's Head public house. There was only one casualty, Mr. Sidney Hope, who was taken to hospital after having received burns to his legs when a bomb fell on his house.

238

The constant Civil Defence training paid dividends as much work was done by the fire services, householders and many others who tackled the bombs immediately they fell. The few fires which were started were got under control within a short time after the raid was over. Only one was of any size, in a store in one of the shopping streets.

At one of the public houses there were a number of guests and Miss Martin, the licensee's daughter said: "The firemen did marvellous work. Working in relays they moved every bit of furniture that could be carried, and when the fire was well under control they set to and brought everything back." The owner of another business premises said: "I have nothing but praise for my fire watchers and the people who live round about. They did amazingly good work, and I cannot thank them sufficiently."

A damaged garage had a board out the next morning: "Down but not out. Business as usual." Of eleven cars on the ground floor, and ten in adjoining lock-ups, only one was slightly damaged.

Home Guard Damage

Not all of the Civil Defence services were being praised at this time. At the Property Owner's Association meeting on Wednesday 1st July, it was stated that damage had been done to property and gardens when the Home Guard had held their exercises. Mr. T. Christian asked whether anything could be done about this damage as instead of going around the fences, the Home Guard soldiers went through and over the gardens. "If you spoke to them about the damage they just told you where to get off, and said they were doing it for your benefit."

The Secretary, Mr. J.C. Bessell, and President, Mr. D.H. Ruff, said they had received similar complaints and that the Home Guard had no right to cause damage unless there was a direct threat of invasion. The Association could not tolerate the present situation and would make a strong protest. They stated that they would do all they could to support the local government in anything, but would not tolerate damage done by "a gang of men." They would take it up with the local Home Guard officers.

Mr. E.O. Daking said that if Mr. Christian wanted to visit the Home Guard he would be able to obtain a form to fill in to enable him to claim for the damages. Mrs. Daking said she thought the Commanding Officers of the Home Guard were very nice gentlemen. She did not think that they knew their men had done any damage. If they did, she was sure they would forbid the men to do it. The damage could be stopped by a nice word.

Mr. Andrew Gordon said it was all very well telling them to get a form; he thought a strong letter would do more good. Mr. T.L. Huetson suggested that the Secretary should write to the National Federation about the matter. Mrs. Daking was unhappy with all the talk about people's rights and involving officials in a matter which she thought was easily solved. "You do not want that with your Home Guard," she said. "Send your letter (if you like) worded nicely. The Home Guard are us – our boys and brothers. We are not dealing with the Germans."

It was decided that a "nice letter" be sent to the Commanding Officer of the Home Guard.

More Casualties

Group Captain Philip Reginald Barwell, 22062, Group Captain, Royal Air Force, DFC., was now reported to have been killed in action. As a Flying Officer in May 1930 he married Miss Mary Elizabeth Peach Hay in St. Paul's Church. Aged 35 years old, he was the father of two sons aged 11 and 4. He was listed as missing on air operations on 1st July, 1942, while flying Spitfire Mk Vb, Serial no AB806, and is buried in Calais Canadian War Cemetery, Leubringhen, Pas de Calais, France.

Barwell, of Peterborough, was born in 1907, commissioned into the RAF in September 1925, and posted to 19 Squadron at Duxford, under instruction. On 9th September, 1929 he went to a staff appointment at CFS, Upavon and on 5th August, 1930, he was posted to the Home Aircraft Depot, Henlow for an engineering course. With this completed he went to the Aircraft Depot, Hinaidi, Iraq. On 1st June, 1933, Barwell moved to the engineer section at Hinaidi, on the staff of Iraq Command. He returned to Britain in late 1934 and on 7th January, 1935, was posted to Central Flying School, Upavon as an instructor. Barwell took command of 46 Squadron at Digby on 4th January, 1937, and led it until late October 1939.

He was awarded the DFC (28.11.39) for leading a flight of six aircraft on October 21 over the North Sea to intercept enemy bombers approaching a British convoy about thirty miles out. He shot down one enemy aircraft and shared in the destruction of another. Whilst commanding RAF Coltishall in October 1940, Barwell flew three operational sorties with 242 Squadron on the 5th of the month, in Hurricane R 4115, thus qualifying for the Battle of Britain clasp. He took command of RAF Biggin Hill in June 1941, and sometimes flew as No 2 to Sailor Malan on fighter sweeps. On 4th July, 1941, he shared a probable Bf 109 with Malan and a week later he destroyed a Bf 109. One day in early 1942 Barwell's engine cut out on take-off and he crash-landed just beyond the runway and broke his back. He still took part in operations and flew for several months encased in plaster, which made it difficult for him to turn his head.

On 1st July, 1942, Barwell, accompanied by Squadron Leader R.W. Oxspring, took off from Biggin Hill an hour before sunset on a standing patrol between Dungeness and Beachy Head. Control at Biggin Hill warned of unidentified aircraft in the area, which proved later to be two Spitfires from Tangmere flown by inexperienced pilots. Barwell, apparently oblivious to the warning, was attacked by one and shot down in flames into the sea. Although Oxspring saw him trying to open his hood Barwell did not bale out, perhaps being too hampered by his plaster cast. Despite intensive searches no trace of him was found. His body was eventually found later, washed up on the French coast.

Pilot Officer Kenneth Edward Whalley, 61941, 451 (R.A.A.F.) Squadron, Royal Air Force Volunteer Reserve, 144, Lincoln Road, who had originally been reported missing in the Middle East in November 1941, was now reported as having been killed in action on 12th November, 1941, aged 23. He is commemorated on the Alamein Memorial, Egypt, column 241. The records show that Hurricane I, V7353, in which he was flying, was shot down by a Messerschmitt Bf-109 fighter during a reconnaissance flight at Salûm, Egypt. P.O. Whalley was the only son of Mr. and Mrs. E.H. Whalley and on leaving King's School he had become an aeronautical engineer with the De Havilland Company.

Private Eric John Sandy, 5884354, 1st Leicestershire Regiment, of Britannia Studios, Long Causeway, Peterborough, was now reported as missing in Malaya. He was last heard of as being in Singapore. Private Sandy would die on the 18th

November, 1943, aged 25, in Japanese prisoner of war camp and is commemorated on the Singapore Memorial, Singapore. Column 66.

Day Nurseries Open

The city's first two wartime day nurseries – one in Caverstede Road and the other in London Road – opened for the reception of children on Monday 6th, July. In the morning, two children were taken to Caverstede and ten to London Road. The children immediately settled down well and many more were expected as the service became better known.

The nurseries, which were identical, had pegs and lockers for coats, hats, shoes and gas masks. There was a large bathroom, laundry and rest room and weighing scales for babies. Meals were served in rest rooms and there were play pens and collapsible beds. There was a stove at each end of the room and a fully staffed kitchen where mugs, plates and baby's feeding bottles were kept. Toys were being collected and there was a sandpit and seesaw in each garden. The Matron at Caverstede, Miss Cooper, said that she had received several enquiries from mothers who had not yet taken war jobs but would do so if they found that the nursery came up to their expectations.

The WVS promised to make special nursery clothes which the children would put on as soon as they arrived. The mothers paid a shilling a day for each child which covered everything, including any special food that a child might require. Each nursery could accommodate up to forty children aged up to five years. Women in full time work would be given preference and the children could come in at 7.30 am and stay until 8 pm.

At London Road, where the youngest child was seven weeks old, the Matron, Miss Folker, said there had been a few tears at first, but the children had soon settled down. When the 'Standard' reporter visited, he found the children in the bathroom being washed before their lunch – stewed steak, mashed potatoes, greens, and a milk pudding.

Perilous Souvenirs

Still with children, the police now issued a notice in the city stating that a number of unexploded incendiary bombs had been picked up by children and kept as souvenirs. The police pointed out that in their unexploded state, these bombs were extremely dangerous. A proportion of them contained an explosive charge sufficient to kill any person who is unprotected and close to the bomb if it explodes. Anyone who possessed one of these bombs was urged to contact the police so arrangements could be made to collect them.

The police had also been informed by the City Engineer's department that a number of tin water containers which had been placed in the streets were being emptied and taken away. Also, that bags of sand were being thrown about and wasted. The police tried to impress upon the children that these were a means of fire fighting and were very valuable in the early stages of a fire, and that it was the duty of everyone to ensure that they were not damaged in any way.

Another Home Guard Cup Win

Contests for the 'B' Company, City Home Guard Cup took place during the second week of July. The Post Office Company of the 13th Leicesters (formerly part of 'B' Company), invited to take part with other platoons, won the cup.

Contests were between platoons, and were divided into sections. One was for rifle handling, grenades, bombs and other specialist weapons; another for field exercise in attack and defence; and a third for general field work – map reading, fire control, etc. The contests were very close, so much so that although some 1,400 points were awarded, only 12 separated the first team. The final placings were:

1. Post Office (Lieutenant Watson).
2. Baker Perkins (Captain Plaistowe).
3. Perkins Diesel (Lieutenant Pailing).

Women's Land Army
It was now announced that there were 110 volunteers for the Women's Land Army in the Soke. Of these, 106 were employed, and four were receiving training. The Barnack and Newborough hostels each housed 26 women, and 54 were employed privately, living on the farms. During June, six new volunteers were enrolled.

Compulsion
The first batch of men compulsorily enrolled in the City Home Guard reported for training on July 18th. A large number of men had anticipated calling-up and had enrolled voluntarily.

Regulations were also expected shortly for the compulsory training of fireguards. The training was likely to take place during the ordinary period of fire watch duty, and would apply to guards both in residential and business premises. Regular members of the National Fire Service (NFS) would co-operate, and instruction would include the use of appliances and the study of the locality and premises guarded.

Registration
Women born in 1900 who registered for National Service at the employment exchange on Saturday 4th July, numbered 564.

More Missing
Mrs. E.W. Slater of Beamsley House, 87, Lincoln Road, Peterborough, was now hoping that her younger son, Acting Captain, W.A. Roy Slater, RAOC, was safe, after having been reported missing in the Middle East.

Mrs. Slater had originally received official news in the second week of July that her son was posted as missing. On 16th July, she received by airmail from Egypt a letter from Captain Slater dated July 9th – after the date on which official notification had been received. Mr. John Slater, Captain Slater's brother, said: "In view of this development we are very hopeful that he is safe. In fact, we think it is a hundred to one that he is." Captain Slater was partner in the firm of Slater and Sons, corn merchants.

At this time Battery Quartermaster Sergeant (BQMS) Hubert George Keeble, Royal Artillery, was also posted as missing in the Middle East. He was the eldest son of Mrs. Keeble, 241, Park Road, Peterborough, and the late Mr. J.Y. Keeble. He volunteered for service on the day war broke out, and was posted to a light anti-aircraft unit of the Royal Artillery. He had been in the Middle East for some time and was last heard of at Tobruk, Libya. At the beginning of September, news would reach his home that he was a prisoner of war in Italy. A brother, Oliver, also a BQMS was believed to be in the Middle East as well.

Another missing man was Driver Jack Parrott, Royal Army Service Corps, of 24, Grove Street, New Fletton, Peterborough. Now reported missing at Tobruk, he was a married man, and was employed by the builder, Mr. B. Stokeley before the war.

Home Guard Anti-Aircraft Defences

In common with towns in other parts of the country, Peterborough was now to have its own Home Guard Battery to man anti-aircraft defences. Already preliminary arrangements had been made and during the weeks of July, hundreds of men would be required to build the Battery up to full strength.

After initial training with a regular Anti-Aircraft Battery, the Home Guard would take over operational night duty. Each man would then be on duty one night a week at least. This was the first A.A. Battery, Home Guard, to be formed in Northamptonshire and provided a great opportunity for local men to serve in an operational role under active service conditions.

Men between the ages of 17 and 60, interested in gunnery, and keen to "have a go at the Hun," were asked to apply at the Battery H.Q., Unity Hall, Northfields Road, Peterborough. It was understood that transfers from existing Home Guard units would not be sanctioned except under special circumstances. All ranks of the Home Guard A.A. Batteries would wear the "flash" of the local A.A. Division.

Sea Cadet Corps Started

As a result of a meeting held in the Mayor's Parlour on Friday 10th July, more than 100 boys had now applied for admission to the newly raised Sea Cadet Corps. The Parlour had been packed to overflowing with boys aged 13½ to 16½ and the boys were given a motto by Rear Admiral A.H. Alington, which was on the quarter deck of many ships, "Fear God; Honour the King."

The membership of the Sea Cadets was limited to 100 and all of the boys were interviewed over the following days by the Commanding Officer, Mr. J.W. Henson (Local Food Controller) who had served in the Navy in the previous war, and members of the committee. The training quarters were the N.F.S. hut at the Bishop's Road car park, which had been loaned for certain evenings each week.

Raid Spotters Club

The annual meeting of the Raid Spotter's Club was held at the City Museum on Friday 10th July. Mr. C.C. Bains (Chairman), was supported by Mr. R.B. Garratt (Vice Chairman), Mr. R. Maywood (Secretary), and Mr. J. Earnshaw (Treasurer).

Mr. Bains, in his report, said that the club's activities had been chiefly competitions in making model aircraft and tests in identifying all types of planes from silhouettes. The club met the Observer Corps twice, and were beaten on both occasions by a narrow margin of points. They had also met and defeated Phorpres Spotters Club, an Observer unit. A competition for a cup given by the Vice-Chairman for the best model aircraft made by a member had been won by R. Blackman, a schoolboy, with a Macchi 202.

Mr. Bains regretted that there was not enough keenness among senior spotters in the works. The Ministry of Home Security had asked them to take advantage of facilities offered by Spotters Clubs, which were equipped with a fine set of models, as well as the silhouettes of British, American and German types of aircraft.

More Casualties

Sergeant George Frederick Clarke, 5886012, 5th Battalion, Northamptonshire Regiment, 298, Lincoln Road, Peterborough, was injured in a bomb explosion in Scotland on Monday 20th July, and died a few hours later. Sergeant Clarke was the son of Mr. and Mrs. G. Clarke, 298, Lincoln Road, and on February 7th had married Private A.M. Essom, ATS, of 21, Fulbridge Road. Before entering the Army, Sergeant Clarke had been an apprentice turner at Brotherhood's, and a member of the Coronation Boxing Club.

His funeral took place on Friday 24th July, at St. Paul's Church, with full military honours. Major W.V. Hart, MC. was in charge of a party from the Northamptonshire Regiment. Sergeants of the battalion carried the coffin and a guard of honour was formed by members of the 1st Northamptonshire Home Guard. Sergeant Clarke was buried in Peterborough (Eastfield) Cemetery.

Now reported missing in Egypt since June 20th was Corporal George (Dick) Burroughs, Expeditionary Force Institute, 17, Harris Street, Peterborough. He was the son of Mrs. L. Burroughs, 52, Tower Street, New Fletton, and was formerly an assistant to Mr. E. Chappell, grocer, of Bridge Street. Corporal Burroughs, who had a young daughter, was a member of Wentworth Street Young Men's Fellowship and married Miss Doris Langsley, daughter of Mr. and Mrs. D. Langsley, 17, Harris Street.

Also missing in the Middle East was Driver Richard Biggs, Royal Artillery, 242, Cromwell Road, Peterborough. Aged 21 years old, he was the son of Mr. and Mrs. C.J. Biggs, and had been in the Middle East for around 18 months. Before joining the Army he was with Hunting, Orland, Ltd., of Westgate. He would later be reported as a prisoner of war in Italian hands.

Another missing man, now reported a prisoner of war in Italy, was Able Seaman Thomas A.W. Field, Royal Navy, 17, Westwood Row, Peterborough. A.B. Field was the second son of Leading Signalman George Field R.N. and Mrs. Field, who were now at Aberdeen. He was 23 years of age and joined the Navy in March 1939. After 12 months on a minesweeper sloop, he was transferred to the destroyer HMS BEDOUIN which was sunk by the combined action of Italian cruisers Montecuccoli and Eugenio di Savoia and SM.70 torpedo bombers on 15 June 1942. She was hit by at least 12 six-inch rounds and near-misses from the cruisers and an aerial torpedo before sinking. She managed to shoot down the torpedo bomber which delivered the coup de grace to her. 28 men from her complement were killed in action and 213 were taken as prisoners of war by the Italian Navy.

In civilian life, A.B. Field worked first for Mr. W. Sallabanks, Builder, and after that for Messrs Barber and Ross. In August 1941 he married Miss L. Coles, of 18, Barr Street, Whittlesey. His father, a pensioner with service in the last war, was now in the navy again.

Driver William James Lake, Royal Army Service Corps, was missing in the Middle East. He joined up when war broke out and was with Reads of Peterborough, removal contractors. Aged 26 years old and married, he was the son of Mr. and Mrs. H. Lake, 149, Alexandra Road.

Trooper Charles Springthorpe, Royal Tank Regiment, was now reported wounded on active service in the Middle East. He had been in the Army four years and was previously with A.B. Woodcock, Ltd. He was the brother of Mrs. Whitehead, 27, Abbey Road, Walton, Peterborough.

Finally news had come regarding a city man who had been posted as missing in action more than two years earlier. Gunner Harry Bernard Johnson, 1531762, 43 Battery, 101 Lt. A.A./Anti-Tank Regiment, Royal Artillery, died of wounds in France on 7th June, 1940, aged 19. He had been the eldest of four sons of Harry and Florence Gertrude Johnson, 259, St. Paul's Road. Before joining the Army he had been a goods porter on the LNER. Gunner Johnson is buried in St. Valery-En-Caux Franco-British Cemetery, Seine-Maritime, France.

Sapper Reginald Palmer, Royal Engineers, the only son of Mr. and Mrs. Bert Palmer, 11, Princes Gardens, was now reported as being a prisoner of war in Japanese hands. Aged 22, he was serving at Hong Kong with the 22nd Fortress Company, Royal Engineers and before the war had been a draughtsman at Brotherhoods.

Brothers Win Distinguished Service Medals
It was now reported that two of the three sons of Mr. and Mrs. John Hughes, 144, Dogsthorpe Road, Peterborough, had been awarded the DSM. At the beginning of July, their eldest son, Corporal John Thomas Hughes, RAF, serving at that time in the Middle East, had received the award. At the end of the month they heard that their second son, Corporal Walter G. Hughes, Royal Marine Commandos, had been similarly decorated for gallantry at Malta.

The third son, Sergeant Llewellyn Hughes, Royal Artillery, was reported missing at Singapore. Their only daughter, Joyce, was a Leading Aircraftwoman in the WAAF. In civil life Thomas and Llewellyn had been at Westwood Works, Walter was with Mr. R. Foster, Fruiterer, Broadway, and Joyce was an usherette at the Odeon.

Shelter Work Stopped
In the first week of August the City Engineer reported to the ARP Committee that all labour had been withdrawn from the construction of communal domestic shelters. The Engineer said that he was allowed to finish shelters under construction but many were waiting for doors and bunks to be fitted and lighting installed. About 300 would be lit but the remainder would not because the Government had withdrawn permission to use electric cable which was wanted for more urgent purposes.

The Engineer explained that for the construction of the shelters they had called in the aid of 40 firms of builders, whose labour had now been withdrawn. That did not prevent his department from putting the bunks into position, but his staff had been reduced and was hopelessly overworked. He had 1,500 bunks to be put in, and that work would be completed in the course of time. The lighting question was entirely out of his hands.

The Engineer also explained that all available seating would be put into shelters not yet fitted with bunks, but he was afraid it would not go very far.

Wardens to have Uniforms
The whole of the effective strength of the Civil Defence personnel in the city was now to be provided with uniforms at a cost of £10,096, all of which, except for £3,500, would rank for a grant.

Alderman Snowden, Chairman of the ARP Committee said that the Wardens were the oldest Civil Defence services and had been the least costly. Some part-time volunteers in other services already had full uniform but all the Wardens had were macs and dungarees, which were now showing signs of wear and ought to be renewed. The Committee thought that all services ought to be on the same footing. Firemen, Special Police and the Casualty, Rescue and Repair services all had uniforms. On the military side, so had the Home Guard and Cadet Force.

No wonder the Wardens felt that theirs was the Cinderella of the services. Why should they have to wear out their own clothes and boots in these days of coupons? It might be argued that the Wardens wanted uniforms only for ceremonial parades, but those who knew the Wardens knew that the argument did not hold water. They had given this city service second to none in the country.

More Home Guard Matters

The 101 Northamptonshire Home Guard 'Z' Ack Ack Battery, Royal Artillery, was now proving to be a popular attraction for recruits. Its number was growing rapidly and training had begun. There were still openings with the Battery for people doing light work in the orderly room and stores. Also the Battery could take boys of 16-17 for certain duties if they had their parent's consent.

The Secretary of the Property Owner's Association had now written to Colonel Crowden regarding damage to property and crops in gardens caused by some members of the Home Guard when engaged on exercises. The Colonel replied that he was very much distressed to receive the letter and asked for full particulars so that he could carry out a full investigation. "In the meantime," he said. "I have given instructions that, during exercises in future, property is to be more respected. I am very sorry to have received this complaint, and will take appropriate action on receipt of further details."

Airman Missing

Sergeant Pilot Cyril Spencer, RAF, was now reported missing from operational duties on the night of July 31st. He was the son of Mr. Charles M. Spencer, 39, Huntley Grove, Peterborough, Art Master at Deacon's School, and was an Old Deconian. Before joining the RAF in October 1940, he was an art student at Leicester College of Art.

Sergeant Pilot Spencer had been on operational duties since September 1941, and on the night he was posted as missing, the RAF carried out a heavy bombing raid on Dusseldorf, from which 30 bombers failed to return.

Bomb on Bonfire

A soldier staying with his wife at an address in Peterborough was injured when an incendiary bomb, which he threw onto a bonfire, exploded.

P.C. Bush was in Eastfield Road on the evening of Monday 10th August, when he heard a loud bang and saw a piece of burning timber land on the roof of a bungalow in a neighbouring street. He and Fireman Long investigated and found smouldering debris scattered in a nearby garden. Near the fire was a Corporal, injured, and in the debris were three pieces of an incendiary bomb.

Mrs. Russell, a nurse, of Princes Gardens, gave first aid until Dr. Michael arrived and the injured man was taken to hospital and detained suffering from severe burns on the face and left forearm. The soldier subsequently made a statement to the police in which he said that when he was coming home on leave, another soldier on the train gave him an incendiary bomb, which he put into his pack. He showed it to his wife, who became nervous of having it in the house, and he decided to destroy it by burning it.

New Grouping of Home Guard
The local battalions of the Home Guard were now being reorganized to enhance co-operation and as a result the Hunts. and Soke of Peterborough Operational Group would supersede the former Zone.

The Group would comprise the 1st, 2nd and 3rd Battalions of the Hunts. Home Guard, and the 1st (City) and 2nd (Soke) Northants. Battalions. The whole would be under the Group Commander, Colonel C.W.D. Rowe, MBE, TD., and the battalions would be commanded as follows:

- 1st Northants – Lieutenant Colonel R.J.C. Crowden, MC.
- 2nd Northants – Lieutenant Colonel A.H. Mellows, TD.
- 1st Hunts. – Lieutenant Colonel – W.T. Cook.
- 2nd Hunts. – Lieutenant Colonel – E. Wilson, DSO.
- 3rd Hunts. – Lieutenant Colonel J. Macdonell, MC.

The designations and areas of battalions and their badges and flashes remained unchanged. N.N. denoted Northants, and H.D.S. Hunts. the figure indicated the particular battalion.

More Casualties
Gunner (Driver Mechanic) John William Darlow, 880055, 3, Field Regiment, Royal Artillery, was the only son of Mr. Frederick T. and Mrs. Mary Darlow, 20, Eastleigh Road, Peterborough. Aged 25, he was an old boy of New Road School, and was once a baker, leaving the Co-operative Society to join the Royal Artillery in March 1938. In July 1939 he sailed with his unit for India, and had not been home since. Gunner Darlow died on the 15th July 1942, in the Middle East, and is buried in El Alamein War Cemetery, Egypt.

Driver J. Essom, 105, Westwood Street, Peterborough, was now reported a prisoner of war in the Middle East. Before the war he had been in the London Brick Company Transport Department.

Officer's Cook, Colin James Bryan, Royal Navy, was reported as having injured his back in an accident and was having to have an operation. Aged 18, he was the eldest son of Mr. A.J. Bryan, 723, Lincoln Road, and the late Mrs. Bryan. His father received an airmail letter on July 10th 1942 written by his son's friend saying that he was on a hospital ship. The postmark was Freetown, Sierra Leone. O.C. Bryan had been living with his aunt, Mrs. E.A. Butler, of 35, Allen Road, for ten years and had worked as a confectioner with A.B. Woodcock Ltd., before he volunteered for the Navy.

Private Cyril John Annis, Essex Regiment, 103, Wootton Avenue, Fletton, was reported as missing in the Middle East since July 1st. Aged 28 years old, he married Miss F. Webb of St. Margaret's Road, Fletton, four years earlier. He was the third son of Mr. and Mrs. J. Annis, 206, New England, Peterborough, and before the war was with J.R. Johnson and Sons, Westgate. After a period with the AFS at Fletton, he was called up for the Army.

Another Incendiary Explosion
An incendiary bomb which it was believed had been dropped during an earlier raid on the city, exploded in the back yard of a house on Wednesday 19th August. Mr.

Frank Britten, of 3, Globe Street, told police that he had been repainting a bicycle in his kitchen in the afternoon, when he heard a bang and saw a fire in the yard. He went to put it out with a sandbag and his trousers caught alight, with the result that his left leg was burned and his hair was singed. He received treatment at a first aid post and at the hospital. Mr. Britten had been in the yard several times since the raid but had not seen an incendiary bomb.

Mr. F. Andrews, 41, Oxford Road, who was employed at the electricity works, was cycling along Albert Place at the time the bomb exploded and Mr. Britten ran to him for assistance in getting it under control. After helping to put it out, Mr. Andrews took possession of the remains. The explosion created several piles of debris in the yard and knocked a number of heavy tiles from the roof.

More Problems with Shelters

More discussion was taking place at Fletton Urban District Council, regarding the closed or incomplete shelters in the city. The Clerk said people who had no domestic shelters provided could apply for Morrison shelters (steel structures that could be assembled inside houses), which were in good supply.

The surveyor said he had not completed his list of domestic shelters. Those who did not need Morrisons were asked to give way to those who did. Fletton had an allocation of 90 Morrison shelters from the Peterborough City Council and were delivering them as fast as transport would allow. Some people had refused Morrisons but there were 400 others still waiting for them. Mr. Peake said there was nothing stopping people from using the unfinished shelters, but these were more dangerous than their houses during a raid.

Mr. Kendrick referred to people who had Morrison shelters and left them standing against a wall to rust, and also to people who had them, but went out to the public shelters. The Chairman could not understand people who had Morrisons but did not use them. They could not stop people going into the public shelters. He supposed some people intended to rush out and erect their Morrisons when the Alert sounded!

Casualties Continue

Leading Aircraftman C.W. Toyne, RAF, son of Mr. and Mrs. W. Toyne, of 403, Lincoln Road, Peterborough, was in Hospital in Lanarkshire after falling out of an aeroplane while it was on the ground. He was an instrument maker and was working on the aircraft when he fell from it, twisting his back, which resulted in him needing an operation. Before the war L/AC Toyne was trained as a linotype operator on the "Standard" staff. His younger brother, Driver Bernard J. Toyne, Royal Artillery, was serving in the Middle East.

Driver Christopher Noel Pickersgill, T/103921, 550 General Transport Company, Royal Army Service Corps, was now unofficially reported as killed in the Middle East. Aged 22, he was the eldest son of Mr. and Mrs. Pickersgill, 313, Walpole Street, Peterborough. His parents were informed on Monday 17th August, that, in an airmail letter to his wife, Driver E.A. Orchard, 57, Churchfield Road, Walton, had said that one of his friends, Driver Pickersgill, had been killed by a shell on August 2nd. Driver Pickersgill was formerly with Messrs English Brothers, and was Secretary of Harris Street, Baptist Young People's Institute, and Clubmaster of the church's pack. He had been in the Army almost three years, and took part in the evacuation from Dunkirk. Driver Pickersgill actually died on the

248

30th July 1942, in the Middle East and is buried in El Alamein War Cemetery, Egypt. Mr. and Mrs. Pickersgill's second son, A/C 1 Ronald Pickersgill was serving in the RAF.

Lance Corporal Frederick Cobley, Sherwood Foresters, only son of Mr. and Mrs. E. Cobley, 108, Cromwell Road, Peterborough, originally reported missing, was now reported as being a prisoner of war in Italy. He had been in the Army for eight years and had been captured at Tobruk.

Petty Officer F.K. Adams, Royal Navy, son of Mr. and Mrs. W.H. Adams, of 62, Dogsthorpe Road, Peterborough, was now reported dangerously ill with Pneumonia in a military hospital in Gibraltar. He had been at sea for some time, serving on board an aircraft carrier. His parents received the news in a letter from the hospital matron, after that another letter arrived stating that his condition was showing some improvement.

Private Frank Mucklin, Royal Army Service Corps, 130, St. John's Street, Peterborough, was now reported as missing in the Middle East since June 20th.

Private H. Woods, Gloucester Regiment, son of Mr. and Mrs. Woods, Council Houses, High Street, Stanground, was now reported as seriously ill with malaria in Assam.

Private Roy Albert James Mitchem, 6094576, 2nd Queen's Own Royal West Kent Regiment, 342, Fulbridge Road, Paston, Peterborough, was now reported wounded by enemy action in Malta. Private Mitchem was the only son of Mr. Francis Albert and Mrs. Emily Victoria Mitchem, and had been in Malta for more than two years. He attended King's School and was a Cathedral chorister. Before the war he was in the Co-operative Society's outfitting department at Park Road. Private Mitchem died on the 16th November, 1943, aged 26, on the island of Leros, and is buried in Leros War Cemetery, Greece.

Driver Jack Parrott, Royal Army Service Corps, who was reported missing on June 20th, was now stated to be a prisoner of war in Italy. Driver Parrott had been married for five years and lived at 24, Grove Street, Fletton. He was the only son of Mrs. R. Parrott, 60, Tower Street, and the late Mr. Parrott. He was a sign writer and decorator with Mr. B. Stokeley, builder, Henry Street, before the war.

Gunner Arthur James Nutt, Royal Artillery, was now reported as having been wounded while serving in the Middle East on June 26th. Gunner Nutt, who lived at 12, Chester Road, Peterborough, was married with three children, and was formerly with the Corporation electricity department.

Good Advice
Good advice was being offered to city people at the end of August.

"If you go to your shelter during an Alert, leaving the house entirely unoccupied, every light should be switched off, every window uncovered, every fire in grates put out. If fire bombs are falling, and you are in the house, you should uncover blacked out windows in all unoccupied rooms. The object is to prevent undetected fire bombs from causing preventable damage."

Unsurprisingly the police were also drawing people's attention to the fact that it was illegal to retain any objects which may be dropped from the air, whether they are enemy planes or of defence origin.

"There have been instances lately, of unignited incendiary bombs being retained, and in at least one case serious injury resulted. Anything found must be handed to the police, who will pass the articles on to the military or RAF authorities."

Murder in the City

After the body of a man shot through the stomach had been found in a communal air raid shelter in Northfield Road on the night of Sunday 30th August, a young soldier was arrested.

The sound of a rifle being fired was heard at about 8.50pm, and on investigation, the body of a man was found lying in the shelter. A telephone call was received by the police from a phone box and a short time later War Reserve Sergeant Jones took a soldier into custody.

At the police station on the Monday morning, Dennis Victor Edgeley, aged 21, of Doddington, Cambridgeshire, was charged with feloniously killing and slaying one William Edward Beach, of the US Army Air Corps, with malice aforethought at Peterborough on August 30th. The Chief Constable applied for the accused to be remanded to Leicester Gaol until the Petty Sessions on Wednesday 16th September.

The accused, a native of Doddington, who was seen by a doctor, was the son of Mr. and Mrs. J.W. Edgeley, of Newgate Street. On December the 11th, 1941, he was married at Peterborough Registry Office to Miss Vera Maud Atkin, daughter of Mr. and Mrs. G. Atkin of Eye.

Boy Shot in Face

In another shooting in the city a boy was shot in the face during an invasion practice in Victoria Street, on the morning of Sunday 30th, August. The practice was being carried out by members of a detachment of the 1st Northants. Battalion, Home Guard, when the boy was hit on the side of his face and head by splinters from a blank cartridge.

The boy was Brian Crowson, aged 7, elder son of Mr. and Mrs. A. Crowson, St. Martin's Street, Peterborough. The splinters caused the loss of a quantity of blood and he was taken to the hospital for treatment, but was not detained.

Brian, who was just recovering from an attack of mumps, was with other children in Victoria Street, watching the exercise. A whistle was blown by a Home Guard to indicate that the street was to be cleared as the men were going to fire blank cartridges. Brian was standing with his little brother, Derek, near the wall of a house at the St. Martin's Street end of Victoria Street when a shot was fired by a Home Guard from a garden. A neighbour called to Mrs. Crowson that her son had been hit. He was taken to the St. Martin's Street, First Aid Post for treatment for shock, and from there to the hospital.

Survivor of the Eagle

First Class Stoker, Richard Bird, Royal Navy, of 15, New Road, Woodston, Peterborough, was now reported as a survivor of the sinking of the aircraft carrier HMS EAGLE in the Mediterranean.

He was back in the city at the beginning of September and spoke of his experiences during the sinking. They were with a convoy half way to Malta, about 500 miles out to sea, when the EAGLE turned into the wind to allow four aircraft to take off. As she turned back she was hit by four torpedoes and at once began to list.

Stoker Bird described how he crawled up the flight deck and jumped overboard from the boat deck. The EAGLE was hit at around 1.15pm and sank within seven minutes. Along with many other members of the crew, Stoker Bird was in the water for about 1¾ hours before he was picked up by a destroyer.

For the first three quarters of an hour his lifebelt kept him afloat, then, he and 15 others climbed onto a cork float. "We could see other chaps going past clinging to bits of wood or anything they could get hold of," he said. "I saw no lifeboats because as they were lowering them, the EAGLE turned over."

"The men on the destroyer were fine; as we drifted up to them they even jumped overboard to bring the survivors in."

The survivors were taken to Gibraltar, where they remained for a week before sailing home. Stoker Bird was the son of Mr. and Mrs. J. Bird of Woodston, and attended the Fletton Council School. Before the war he had been employed at the London Brick Company.

HMS EAGLE had been involved in the famous August 1942 convoy (Operation 'Pedestal') when 41 warships fought a running battle to get just five merchantmen through out of a total of fourteen that started to lift the siege of Malta. On 11 August 1942 whilst still in the Malta bound convoy HMS EAGLE (Capt. Lachlan Donald Mackintosh, RN) was hit by 4 torpedoes from the German submarine U-73 and sank in position 38°05'N, 03°02'E. Two officers and 158 ratings were lost but 927 of her ship's company including Captain Mackintosh were picked up by the British destroyers HMS LAFOREY, HMS LOOKOUT and the British tug, HMS JAUNTY.

Able Seaman John Douglas Chapman, Fleet Air Arm, second son of Mr. and Mrs. J.D. Chapman, 638, Lincoln Road, Peterborough, was also home on survivors leave. His ship was also damaged in the attack on the Malta convoy. Able Seaman Chapman was 24 years of age and had been in the Navy for nine years, serving in HMS ARK ROYAL for 18 months, being transferred six months before she was sunk. He had also taken part in the Abyssinian battles and the Spanish Civil War.

Battle of the Desert Fort
Lance Corporal J. Wilson, attached 9th Army Headquarters, son of Mr. and Mrs. John Wilson, 54, Welland Road, Peterborough, had been having a lively time of it in the Middle Eastern desert and sent home a graphic account of a battle for a desert fort.

He wrote, "We went in with fixed bayonets between our tanks and Bren carriers. We had crept in during the night and waited for first light. Isolated machine gun nests tried to stop us, but we soon had them bolting from their hideouts. It seemed that the smart guys had already made their getaway leaving the slow witted type to shift for themselves. Without their armour, these Nazis seemed very much in the dumps. Only a party with a machine gun in the high tower in the centre of the fort kept up any resistance.

My section passed through a litter of burnt out enemy tanks and lorries and was enlivened by occasional incidents when some enemy went to ground in odd corners but we winkled them out. About half a mile north of the position, we halted in readiness for a counter attack, but the ground was very rocky and all we could do was to pile up little heaps of stone for cover.

At 8pm the enemy came straight across our front, firing high explosive shells, tracer and incendiary bullets while his artillery laid down a creeping barrage. Our tanks were in a defensive circle behind us all around the fort, and our field guns and anti-tank 2 pounders banged back shell for shell with interest. Most of the enemy's hits were scored on his own abandoned lorries and dump. For two hours they hammered away but got nowhere, and during the night they suddenly withdrew.

At dawn the enemy made another counter attack but our tanks gave them such a reception that they soon got out of it. Suddenly we spotted four German tanks, 400 yards away, coming straight for us. Our chaps were heavily armed with Bren guns and grenades, anti-tank grenades, daggers and rifles, so we were confident of giving them a hot welcome. The tanks stopped, opening fire on a British tank about forty yards behind us. Their first shell struck the turret and the next three were direct hits broadside.

No sound came from our tanks. We settled down to wait for the main effort by the German infantry. To our astonishment, our tank opened up with all he had. The Germans started to withdraw, but our tank stopped two retreating enemy machines and at 900 yards scored a direct hit on a third, setting it alight. We saw the German crews scrambling out of their helpless tanks and opened fire. Our tank suffered no serious damage and all the crew were unharmed. In the wrecked German tanks we found two of the crew dead."

Lance Corporal Wilson added, "Even out here we hear a bit of what some people are talking about at home, such as the inferiority of our weapons to those of the Germans. Having seen so many of our present day weapons and handled quite a few in action in this war in the Western Desert, I would like the people at home to know and realise that we are a match for the Boche when met any time on anything like equal terms."

Missing

At the beginning of September, Signaller B.C.P. Allen, Royal Corps of Signals, of Peterborough, was reported missing in Malaya when Singapore fell. He was 21 years of age and nephew of the late Mr. Ben Goodly of 40, Whalley Street, and of Mr. J. Goodley, 13, Vergette Street. An old Deaconian, he had been in the Army for two years, and was formerly in Messrs Dakings and Wright's offices.

Street Attack

After the entry into the war of the United States, there became a worrying number of attacks on American soldiers in the city. It will be remembered that Dennis Victor Edgeley had murdered William Edward Beach, a Sergeant Air Gunner in the US Army Air Corps, in an air raid shelter in Northfield Road the previous August.

Cecil Alec Turner, of Padholme Road, was now at the Police Court on Wednesday 9th September, where he was committed for trial on a charge of maliciously inflicting grievous bodily harm upon Stanley Bennett, a US serviceman, on August 23rd.

The siren had sounded about 10.40pm and Private Bennett was making his way towards an air-raid shelter in Bishop's Road car park when he was struck a severe blow from behind. Another soldier, Private Devillier, saw Turner strike the blow. A complaint was made to the police and Turner was arrested. It was ascertained that Bennett's jaw had been broken, possibly by a fist, but more likely a knuckle-duster well padded with a handkerchief.

Private Adam Horace Devillier, US Army, said that Bennett and a young lady were going into the shelter and three men followed them. One man, Turner, struck Bennett in the entrance to the shelter, and then he and his two companions went towards a US Sergeant who was standing next to a lorry, the Sergeant called out for help.

Sergeant Constantine Sidorak, US Army Medical Corps, said the three men came towards him and he began to walk away, but they then surrounded him and he called out to one of the lorry drivers. Corporal Charles Boyce Hines, US Military Police, saw the men and approached the group who then dispersed. Turner was picked out by a number of people later at an identity parade and was committed for trial.

Missing

The list of city men missing in action grew by the week. Pilot Officer Leslie Cox, only son of Mr. and Mrs. D. Cox, 111, Scotney Street, Peterborough, was now reported missing in the Middle East. The previous June, P/O Cox had married Miss Daphne Hopper, eldest daughter of Mr. and Mrs. B.C. Hopper, 83, Peveril Road, Peterborough. An old Deaconian, he was formerly in the City Treasurer's department. P/O Cox and Mrs. Cox were members of the Harris Street Baptist Young People's Institute, and P/O Cox was assistant offertory secretary at the church. On Friday 2nd October, it was reported in the 'Standard' that P/O Cox had become a prisoner of war when his aircraft had to make a forced landing in Egypt.

Corporal Robert Frank Howard, of The Green Howards, son of Mrs. Howard, 22, Flag Fen Road, Peterborough, was reported as missing in the Middle East since June 4th. Corporal Howard, who was aged 24, had been in the Middle East 18 months and had seen fighting around Tobruk. He joined the Army in 1939 seeing service in France, and was one of the last to leave Dunkirk.

Bombardier Jack Leaman, Royal Artillery, All Saint's Road, Peterborough, was reported missing in the Near East on June 20th and was now reported to be a prisoner of war.

Gunner J. Smith, Royal Artillery, 12a, St. Mary's Street, Peterborough, and Gunner Dennis Derry, Royal Artillery, 807, Lincoln Road, Peterborough, both previously reported missing in the Middle East, were now reported as being prisoners of war in Italy. Gunner Derry, who was 21, was the youngest son of Mr. and Mrs. H. Derry. He had attended Gladstone Street School and worked at the East Station before he was called up with the Territorials at the outbreak of war.

Not Enough Air Raid Shelters

Air raid shelters were again the subject of discussion at the Old Fletton Urban District Council on Monday 21st September. Domestic shelters built under Scheme 1 were now to be taken down, and those constructed under Scheme 2 were to be strengthened. About 700 Morrison shelters had been delivered and there were 250 applications to be dealt with.

Mr. Wright stated that a number of houses were not large enough to take Morrison shelters, and as no more public shelters were to be provided, what form of protection could be given to these small houses? The Clerk said that in most cases there were public shelters near the small cottages, and Woodston Hill people could use those at the sugar works. Public shelters were primarily for those people caught in the streets but people living near could use them.

Mr. Wright said many small houses were occupied by old people who wanted protection most, and got it least. St. Margaret's Road was given as an example. The City Surveyor said that people in St. Margaret's Road could use the shelter at the Secondary School.

Mr. Ibbott said that some of the shelters were 100 or 150 yards away, how could people get there? Mr. Peake said that it was started all over the country that no more public shelters would be built; it did not only apply to Old Fletton.

It was hoped that more Anderson shelters would find their way to the city and an application would be made to the County Council for a new public shelter to be built on Oundle Road, near New Road.

More Casualties

Driver William James Lake, Royal Army Service Corps, 149, Alexandra Road, Peterborough, reported missing in the Middle East in June, was now reported to be a prisoner of war in Italian hands.

Trooper George Stanley Meadows, 7945696, 9th Armoured Division, Royal Armoured Corps, eldest son of Mr. and Mrs. E.S. Meadows, 22, Exeter Road, Peterborough, was now reported as having been killed in an accident on 22nd September, 1942. Aged 19, he had been an old Deaconian and went from school to the staff of Barclay's Bank at Thrapston, later being transferred to Kettering. Details of the accident, which took place in England, were sketchy, but it was understood that a tank was involved. Trooper Meadows was buried in Eastfield Cemetery, Peterborough, Division 1. Main Avenue, Grave 54.

Diver Christopher Noel Pickersgill, T/ 103921, 550 General Transport Company, Royal Army Service Corps, eldest son of Mr. Edward and Mrs. Gertrude Elizabeth Pickersgill, 313, Walpole Street, Peterborough, was now reported as having been killed in action in the Middle East on 30th June, 1942. His parents were informed on August 17th that, in an airmail letter to his wife, Driver E.A. Orchard, 57, Churchfield Road, Peterborough, had said that one of his friends, Driver Pickersgill, had been killed by a shell. His death had now been confirmed by the War Office. Driver Pickersgill was formerly with English Brothers, and was secretary of Harris Street Baptist Young People's Institute, and Cubmaster of the church's pack. A memorial service was held at Harris Street on Sunday 4th October. Driver Pickersgill is buried in El Alamein War Cemetery, Egypt.

Private Cedric Purton, Essex Regiment, only son of Mr. C.W. Purton, Manager of the American Red Cross Club at St. Peter's College, was now reported as being a prisoner of war in Italy. On July 1st, Mr. Purton heard that his son was missing believed killed, and since then all enquiries had failed to bring any news. It was now officially confirmed that there were only eleven survivors of the unit of the regiment to which Sergeant Purton was attached, and Mr. Purton was so grateful that his son had been one of the eleven that he donated £5 5s. to the Red Cross.

Torpedoed Twice in One Year

Torpedoed twice within a year and losing all his belongings each time, Cadet Navigation Officer Peter W.F. Holmes, son of Doctor Arthur and Mrs. Holmes, of Glebe House, Paston, Peterborough, was determined to go to sea again.

"Jerry is a bit of a nuisance, but he won't stop me going back," he stated to the 'Standard.' "If this has got to happen, it will, and I don't mind so long as I get away with my life."

Cadet Officer Holmes was 18, and an only son. He went from King's School to Rossall, and then joined the Merchant Navy as a cadet. In September 1941 his ship was torpedoed 70 miles from land and he was rescued after drifting on a raft for more than an hour.

Describing his latest adventure he said' "We had been in the Middle East and in August were returning un-laden in convoy. When we were in the Caribbean one morning about four o'clock, I had just been relieved on the bridge and was tumbling into my bunk when there was a crash that rocked the ship. I didn't need telling what that was, and I joined the rest of the crew in a dash for the lifeboats."

"With an un-laden boat you never know whether she's going to break her back and go down right away, so there's no time to lose. Our ship kept afloat for several hours, and we had plenty of time to get clear. I had no chance however, to get my things together, and for the second time everything I had went to the bottom."

"We were picked up within half an hour by a boat from one of the naval escort vessels, transferred to another merchantman, and landed at a port in Florida. From there we went by train to New York, and then on to Canada. Finally we sailed for home in a passenger boat and had an uneventful crossing. We later learned that the torpedo was one of two fired from a submarine. The first went across our bows and the second struck just forward of our engine room."

Cadet Officer Holmes arrived home on Friday 25th September on survivor's leave.

The Railings Come Down

The compulsory removal of iron railings for salvage created a 'row' in the city council chambers on Friday 25th September. Contractors removing the railings were being accused of a lack of care with demolition by Alderman Fletcher.

He alleged that for every ton of iron removed, and for which 25 shillings was payable, £35 worth of damage was being done which had to be borne by the property owner. He was told that the removal of the railings was not the concern of the council and was purely the responsibility of the Ministry of Works.

Alderman Fletcher was not satisfied with the council washing its hands of the whole business. He had seen in two other towns appalling damage done to the disadvantage of the owners, in many cases he stated, working men whose life savings had gone into the purchase of the property.

The railings had been hammered and slashed away and copings broken until the streets looked as if they had had a very heavy blitz. There was no equality of sacrifice when 25 shillings a ton was offered for the iron and for every ton, damage to the extent of £35 had to be borne by the property owner. He proposed that the City Engineer be instructed to press for the removal to be done in a different fashion.

"I know Peterborough well enough to know there will be a terrible row if more care is not taken," he said. "It is said that the railings are necessary to the war effort, but is it necessary to take them when there are still untouched dumps of iron that have been lying neglected for years?"

Mr. Viney replied' "Alderman Fletcher talks of equality of sacrifice. Is there any comparison between the sacrifices we are making and sacrifices the flower of our young manhood is being called to make, and the sacrifices the defenders of Stalingrad are making?"

"The whole thing is potty and absurd. I don't think Alderman Fletcher has made any sacrifice; I don't think any of us has really made any sacrifice. We are fighting to prevent the enslavement of Britain, not to keep our railings at the right height."

Alderman Fletcher explained that he meant equality of sacrifice among the ratepayers themselves. Some had wooden fences and were losing nothing; others had iron and were losing everything.

The Engineer said he had discussed the matter with a Ministry of Works official on the lines suggested by Alderman Fletcher, and the official said the Ministry were quite prepared to see that a wall was restored to decent condition.

Singapore Postcards

It was now announced that eleven hundred postcard messages for relatives of men taken prisoner at Singapore had arrived at Lourenco Marques (now called Maputo, in Mozambique), en route to the UK. The names of the senders had been cabled to the British Red Cross Society headquarters in London and the War Office were letting relatives know. The cards would follow in due course, but it was expected that they would take some time to arrive.

There was no news of any message having been received locally, but the Mayor had written to the Red Cross asking if any men from Peterborough and District were among the senders of the postcards.

More Casualties Reported in October

Able Seaman Stanley John Frost, Royal Navy, of Peterborough, was now reported missing since the sinking of the Destroyer HMS SIKH, off Tobruk on the 14th September 1942. Seaman Frost, who was 18 years of age, was the youngest son of Mr. and Mrs. J.A. Frost, 11, Mayor's Walk, Peterborough. He had been on HMS MALAYA when she was torpedoed in 1941, and also on HMS PENELOPE which withstood bombardment from the air for 17 days as she lay in Malta Harbour. He was taken off this ship suffering from nervous exhaustion, and from Easter 1942, to August was in hospital in Malta, and since then he had been on HMS SIKH. His father and elder brother were both in the Navy.

Private Cyril John Annis, Essex Regiment, of 103, Wootton Avenue, Old Fletton, reported missing in the Middle East, was now reported as a prisoner of war. Private Annis was married, and before the war was with Messrs J.R. Johnson and Son. He was also a member of Old Fletton Fire Brigade.

Trooper Joseph William Davis, 7887555, 6th, Royal Tank Regiment, Royal Armoured Corps, son of Mr. Francis Edward and Mrs. Elizabeth Davis, of Peterborough, was now reported as killed in action between the 15th and 16th June, 1941. Aged 22 years old at the time of his death, Trooper Davis is commemorated on the Alamein Memorial. Trooper Davis had been a railwayman before he joined the Army six years earlier, and had made his home with his brother and sister-in-law, Mr. and Mrs. S.C. Davis, 15, Bright Street, Peterborough. He was the son of the late Mr. F.E. Davis, Farrier, of New Road.

Also reported at the beginning of October was the very sad death of Edna May Bussey, of 86, South Street, Stanground, Peterborough. Edna, aged 26, had been the fiancée of Leading Aircraftman Alex James Smith, RAF, who had been killed in an air raid on Gosport in 1940. Being in poor health since receiving the shock of his death, Edna passed away on Sunday 27th September, 1942.

Sergeant Pilot, George Rae, 1179958, 112 Squadron, Royal Air Force Volunteer Reserve, son of Mr. George, and Mrs. Sophie Lillian Rae, of 111, Northfield Road, Peterborough, was now reported to have lost his life as the result of an aircraft accident in the Middle East on 2nd October, 1942. Sgt. Pilot Rae, who was 20 years of age, was killed when his Curtis Kittyhawk I fighter aircraft, AL192, dived into the ground after take-off in Egypt due to an engine fire. Educated at Leamington College, and King's School, Peterborough, he became head of the school in 1940, and was house captain of St. Chad's in that year, when they won the school shield.

He obtained his Oxford School Certificate in 1937 and the Oxford Higher in 1939, and won a Hulme exhibition scholarship at Brazenose College, Oxford, but as he was keen to join the RAF, he deferred the scholarship and enlisted on August

28th, 1940. He received his training in England, gaining his wings in October 1941, as a fighter pilot. He went to the Middle East on active service early in 1942.

Sergeant Pilot Rae had been a keen sportsman and obtained his colours for cricket, rugby and hockey. He captained the first eleven at cricket in 1940. His father was an inspector in the Post Office Engineering Department. Sgt. Pilot Rae is buried in El Alamein War Cemetery, Egypt.

Money for Three Tanks

The Soke of Peterborough Tanks for Attack campaign figures now showed a net increase of £29,459, or 13.56%. Mr. Frank Smith, Hon. Secretary, presented the figures to the Soke Savings Committee on Tuesday 6th October, mentioning that the target was a minimum increase of 20%. This would have given them the right to name five light tanks; the increase actually achieved gave the right to name three.

The three names suggested for the tanks were 'Peterborough W.V.S. Street Groups.' 'Peterborough Schools,' and 'Soke of Peterborough.' The chairman, the secretary and Mrs. W.D. Larrett and M. Bailley were appointed to arrange a schools savings drive.

The secretary mentioned that the bronze plaque intended for HMS OLYMPUS had been handed to the museum as an object of historic interest. He had sent two parcels of books to the city's new adopted submarine, HMS P512.

Fire Watching Registration

By the beginning of October 1942, about 65 percent of the women, and about 90 percent of the men who had registered in the city for fire-watching duties, were claiming exemption. The official view was that there was no reason to believe that the claims were invalid. Women between the ages of 20 and 45, and men of 18 to 60, not previously registered, had been called upon to enrol, and the final figures were:

Women – 8,935

Men – 786

Men and women who were unable to register at the centres open on September 26th had to attend at the Town Hall. There, more than 3,000 were interviewed by WVS helpers and members of the Town Hall staff under supervision of the Fire Prevention Officer, Mr. A. Wilson. On Saturday 3rd October, at least 700 people registered and were dealt with so efficiently that at no time were there more than twenty waiting.

Mr. Wilson said that most of the women claimed exemption on the grounds that they had to take care of children under the age of 14. In these cases they were required to give the children's national registration number. Others gave as their reason long working hours, and some stated that they were already undertaking fire watching duties.

"All these claims will be investigated," Mr. Wilson said. He added that the men's grounds for exemption were almost in every case long working hours.

Gunner Shot in Shelter

At Peterborough Magistrates Court on Wednesday 7th October, Dennis Victor Edgeley was committed for trial at Northampton Assizes on a charge of murdering William Edward Beach, a Sergeant Air Gunner in the US Army Air Corps, at Peterborough on August 30th. Beach's body was found in an air raid shelter in

Northfield Road, with bullet wounds in the abdomen and head injuries. A British Army rifle was found nearby.

Edgeley was seen leaving the shelter in a hysterical state and was unsteady on his feet. The only remark he made to a policeman at the time was "My wife, my wife." It was known that the murdered man had been friends with Edgeley's wife.

When brought before the court, Edgeley had to be assisted into the dock, and during the brief proceedings he took no interest in anything that went on. He fidgeted about with head bent and cleared his throat incessantly. The judge told the jury that they could see for themselves the demeanour of the accused and that he was probably unfit to plead.

Dr. G.W. Taylor, of Leicester Prison said the accused was admitted to prison on August 31st in a state of mania. He had since quietened down, but was incapable of understanding anything that was said to him, or even of repeating a sentence except perhaps for the last word. He did not think the accused would know what was going on in court.

The judge, Mr. Justice Lawrence, ordered that Edgeley be kept in strict custody during His Majesty's pleasure, after the jury found the defendant insane, and unfit to plead.

Home Guard in Court

At the Peterborough Police Court on Wednesday 14th October, General Strong addressed Arthur Edward Coulson, of 135, New England, Peterborough, who was on a charge of absenting himself from Guard duty at the 1st Battalion, Northants, Home Guard Headquarters on August 3rd. He told him:

"You do not seem to realise the position. You are practically a soldier to whom we looked for defence. It would be a nice state of things if the whole of the guard one night 'went on the jolly,' and that was the particular night Hitler sent paratroops across! We have had no trouble but a few bombs. You do not seem to realise that you were practically on active service, and active service men who are absent get shot. You are not going to get shot this time, but you must pay a fine of £3."

Another Home Guard soldier, Frederick William Griffiths, of 21, Lincoln Road, Peterborough, was also summoned for absenting himself from Home Guard parades on July 14th and August 13th at the East Station, and on July 26th at London Road Drill Hall. Griffiths was also charged with 'stealing as bailee' a pair of Army boots and an Army haversack, being items of kit that had been issued to him but that he had sold. As Griffiths had recently received his call-up into the Regular Army, the Chairman said that he would not saddle him with a fine. The first charges of absenteeism would be adjourned for three months to see if he behaved himself in the Army. If he did, the Bench might dismiss them. For the theft of equipment he would be bound over for 12 months.

Sea Cadet Corps

The Peterborough Sea Cadet Corps was affiliated to the Navy League on July 17th 1942 with a membership of between seventy and eighty cadets whose ages ranged between 14 and 17 years.

The commanding officer of the unit, appointed by the Admiral Commanding Reserves, was the chief of the local Food Office, Sub-Lieut. J.W. Henson, RNVR, (S), who had served in the Royal Navy during the First World War. He was assisted by a number of officers and chief petty officers nearly all of who had served in the

258

Navy or Merchant Service. It was said that they were creating in Peterborough a very efficient body of lads, all eager to fit themselves for national service.

Permission was granted by the Regional Commissioner NFS, for the cadets to use the NFS recreational hut in the car park on two evenings each week provided it was not required by the fire services. Unfortunately, just as training was about to begin the hut was not available and alternative accommodation was found at St. Mary's Hall. Shortly after however, this was also needed for other purposes and the Local Education Authority then allowed them the use of the Brook Street School as a temporary measure.

Negotiations had been ongoing for some time to acquire the Old Customs House on Bridge Street as permanent headquarters, and owing to the 'public spirited action' of the tenant, Mr. Fowler (Sturton & Sons), who had been using the premises as a store, but vacated it at no little inconvenience to himself, this was made possible. The owners, Milton Estates, willingly accepted the Sea Cadets as tenants, and the building, which was scheduled as an ancient monument, would be put into a good state of repair and equipped as a pre-naval training centre.

City Combed for Metals
The City Engineer (Mr. F.J. Smith) had now arranged a comb-out of the city for the non-ferrous metals salvage drive which commenced on Monday 19th October, and which would continue until October 31st.

WVS Salvage Stewards under the direction of Mrs. A.H. Mellows, were carrying out a house-to-house canvass. Schoolchildren "Cogs" were following up with a collection of unwanted metalware, other than iron and aluminium, and the metal was being accumulated at special salvage dumps which had been set up at all schools.

The dumps were cleared daily by the City Engineer's department, and as the recovered articles were mostly complete and of value, every care was taken to ensure that they were disposed of for re-melting, rather than finding their way to second-hand dealers. The metal was kept under close observation at the schools, and immediately on arrival at the corporation depots, articles such as ornaments were smashed in order that they lost any resale value.

The City Engineer suggested that the public may be able to give up some of the following articles:

Ash trays, badges and brooches, bedstead fittings, candlesticks, coal-scuttles, curtain rings and rods, door handles, dinner bells, gongs, hinges and hooks, picture hooks, clothes hooks, lamp brackets and stands, letter weights, metal tops of bottles, ornaments, picture wire, paper weights and desk fittings, scales, stair rods, toothpaste tubes, belt buckles, brass bowls, zinc buckets, cigarette cases, chandeliers, door knockers, drawing pins, fire irons, garden syringes, insides of old clocks, letter boxes, lighters, lead or brass piping, nameplates, propelling pencils, personal jewellery, paper clips, spectacle frames and trays. It was officially stated that the initial public response was "not over-whelming."

Missing at Sea
Ordinary Telegraphist, C/JX233636, Charles Wilkinson Hall, aged 29, of 282, Lincoln Road, Peterborough, was now reported missing at sea. He was the youngest son of Mr. John and Mrs. Louisa Hall, and husband of Irene Mary Hall and before the war had been a Prudential Insurance agent.

Ord. Tel. Hall had been serving on board the anti-aircraft cruiser HMS

CURACOA which was lost on 2nd October, 1942, in a collision with the SS Queen Mary while on escort duties off the coast of Donegal in the North Western Approaches. He is commemorated on the Chatham Naval Memorial.

News from Peterborough's Submarine
Mr. Frank Smith, as secretary of the Soke Savings Committee had now received a letter from Lieutenant J.C. Ogle, commanding officer of HM Submarine P512, thanking him for a letter and a parcel of books.

In reply to a question Lt. Ogle said the only things the crew really lacked were English papers, magazines, books and illustrated papers. The public were asked to note the request and the items asked for would be gladly received at room 54 of the Town Hall. These would be forwarded to the City's new "foundling" – as the officer called it.

City's Air Defences
The city's air defences would now soon be manned by citizens of Peterborough who had enrolled in the Home Guard, Anti-Aircraft 'Z' Battery. The majority of the men were already carrying out work of national importance during the day and although they were provided with basic necessities while on night duty, additional comforts were being asked for. A fund was set up to provide amenities and a little extra comfort for Home Guard gunners carrying out their duties on cold winter nights. All contributions were requested to be sent to the Home Guard Gunners Welfare Fund, Home Guard A.A. 'Z' Battery, Unity Hall, Northfields Road, Peterborough.

Awards for City Men
Commander Trevor George Payne Crick, Royal Navy, eldest son of Mr. Charles W. Crick, 101, Lincoln Road, Peterborough, was now awarded the Distinguished Service Cross for his part in the action which led to the capture by British Forces of Diego Suarez, Madagascar, in May.

Also, Mentioned in Despatches, was Petty Officer (Air Artificer, 4th Class), F.K. Adams, Fleet Air Arm, son of Mr. and Mrs. W.H. Adams, 62, Dogsthorpe Road, Peterborough. The citation read "For bravery and enterprise while serving with the Royal Fleet Auxiliary in the successful operations which led to the surrender of Diego Suarez, Madagascar."

In addition to this action, Petty Officer Adams had taken part in another naval epic. He sailed in one of the escort vessels on the famous convoy to Malta, Operation Pedestal, which was attacked for two days and nights. His ship was hit and he suffered a leg injury and shock. Pneumonia intervened, and after a period in a naval hospital in Gibraltar, he came home on leave.

More casualties
Sergeant Air Gunner, Stanley Victor Price, 1427176, Royal Air Force, aged 22, only son of Mr. and Mrs. A.V. Price, of 39, Grange Road, Peterborough, and formerly a clerk at the Co-operative Society's Wagon Works, was now reported missing following an operational flight. Price was a gunner in Short Stirling Mk I, Serial No R9184, code letters HA-U, which took off at 18:35 on the 23rd October 1942 from Downham Market to bomb Nuremburg and failed to return. All eight crew were killed and he is buried in Abbeville Communal Cemetery Extension, Somme, France. Plot 6. Row T. Grave 2.

Corporal James Gordon Garn, 5831197, 1st Battalion, Cambridgeshire Regiment, youngest son of Mr. and Mrs. R.F. Garn, 72, New Road, Peterborough, had been reported missing in Malaya and news now reached home that he had been wounded prior to the fall of Singapore. It would be revealed later that Corporal Garn had been killed in action at Singapore on 9th February 1942, aged 24. He is buried in Kranji War Cemetery, Singapore.

Sergeant William David Judson, 35, Thistlemoor Road, Peterborough, and Private V.F. Mucklin, Royal Army Service Corps, of 120, St. John's Street, Peterborough, both reported missing in the Middle East on June 20th were both now reported as being prisoners of war in Italian hands.

Private C.E. Parker, Royal Army Service Corps, of 10, Allen Road, Peterborough, was now reported as being seriously ill in hospital in India with a fractured pelvis, bacillary dysentery and the effects of malaria. Aged 26, Private Parker was the youngest son of Mr. and Mrs. E. Parker. Before the war he had been a motor mechanic at Donald's Garage, Lincoln Road East, and joined the Army two days before war broke out. He served in France until the capitulation and sailed for India about a year before becoming ill. The telegram conveying the news that he was ill arrived on Monday 26th October, 1942, two days after an airgraph letter, dated a month previously, in which he said that although he had been ill with malaria, he had been able to sit an examination and had passed out as a First Class Mechanic.

Bombardier J. Leaman, Royal Artillery, of All Saint's Road, Peterborough, was now also reported as being a prisoner of war in Italian hands in the Middle East.

Church Bells as Scrap
An alarming and somewhat extreme suggestion was made by Mr. W.J. Coates at the City Council on Friday 30th October, when he said that bells should be given up for scrap. He said bells in churches, chapels and public places contained valuable alloy, and weighed from 5cwt to a ton each. The brass alloy bells on National Fire Service vehicles should also be given up.

Well meaning but misguided people were often suggesting, and in some cases sending in, the most inappropriate items for salvage. As we have already seen, a number of pleas had been made asking people not to send ancient and historical documents in for paper salvage.

Alderman Howard said that if church wardens and deacons cared to give the bells they would be gladly received. The Mayor said church bells were reserved for use in invasion, and the City Engineer said that they were earmarked for a special occasion when 'Jerry' announces his arrival to our Home Guard. There was no further discussion.

Killed at Dover
Gunner John William Abbott, 11426750, 218 Battery, 73 Lt. A.A. Regiment, Royal Artillery, 'Acacia,' Peterborough Road, Stanground, Peterborough, was now reported to have been killed while on active service at Dover on 9th November, 1942. Aged 35, he was the son of the late Mr. and Mrs. Abbott of New England, Peterborough. Before he joined the Army six months earlier he had been with the London Brick Company. He married Miss Carpenter, of Kirton, and had two children aged 4 and 14 months. He is buried in Stanground South Cemetery, Grave 146.

Exercise 'Delta'

If Peterborough were to suffer a heavy air attack followed by an attempted invasion, how would the military and civil defence services and the public react? This was the question that Exercise Delta was designed to answer. The exercise was carried out with "keenness and enthusiasm" by all the services on the weekend of $21^{st}/22^{nd}$ November, 1942.

In the main it was a military exercise but the first phase was purely civilian, bringing in the hospital, ambulance, first aid, rest centre, fire, rescue, warden's and messenger services. The second was military and civil combined.

The exercise commenced with the sounding of the sirens at 4.30pm on the Saturday, and closed, so far as outside events were concerned at 1pm on Sunday. The initial air attack was carried out by fewer planes than some people expected, but it provided plenty of 'incidents' to give all units a sound try-out in the following five hours.

On Sunday at 9am invasion operations began, and by mid-morning practically the whole of the centre of the city was in enemy hands. Then there was a great rally and when hostilities ceased, the 'enemy' were in full retreat. The 'Standard' reporter wrote that the exercise demonstrated that Peterborough's civil defence services compared favourably with those of any London borough. Certain defects were found, but these could, and would be rectified. Particularly noteworthy was the "hearty" co-operation between the public and the services.

The general picture of the weekend's incidents, operational and assumed, went as follows. Saturday's raids started fires and interrupted gas and electricity services. Thousands were homeless, and the National Fire Service was depleted. Sunday morning found the main thoroughfares pitted with bomb craters, the hospital demolished, several bridges wrecked, all the rest centres packed with homeless and special trains taking thousands of refugees to Huntingdon.

All of the time the 'enemy' was infiltrating by many routes towards the city centre, driving before them the Home Guard defenders and civilian services. Rest centres were crowded, and houses, cinemas, churches and any other buildings still standing were taken over for the homeless, and mobile canteens were operating at full pressure. Rest centres actually functioning were those at St. Margaret's Hall, Fairfield Road, St. Mary's Hall, King's School, and New England Methodist Schoolroom.

From the civil defence angle everything worked out according to plan. The centre of the town had incidents a few minutes after the sounding of the siren. In Westgate incendiaries dropped on buildings including the Congregational Church, and while they were still falling, women fire guards worked with stirrup pumps. Two soldiers on a flat roof were labelled as serious casualties. They became bored and cold, so they were brought down for a cup of tea before returning to await rescue! The injured were rushed to Trinity Street first aid post and the hospital.

The gas works was later involved, but danger was averted by the prompt action of firemen. Just as darkness fell a hangar and other buildings were set alight, and there the NFS had realistic practice in which about 12,000 gallons of water were used.

The wardens were given a useful lesson in adaptability. Several posts were destroyed, and headquarters were established in private houses on the phone. No sooner was this done than the telephone exchange went out of action and total reliance had to be placed on the messenger service based at King's School, Eastholm

School (Padholme Road), and Lincoln Road School (York Road). The service worked moderately well. There were delays because some of the boys were not thoroughly conversant with the geography of the city.

A big incident on Sunday morning occurred in the Midland Road district. The Memorial Hospital was demolished, bomb craters blocked the roads, and Crescent Bridge and Spital Bridge were down. Such was the situation when the Co-operative bakery caught fire in many places. Wardens and fire guards did all they could, but six houses became involved, 30 people were rendered homeless and many were injured, one fatally. Three people trapped on a roof had to be rescued by wardens, the fire service being unable to cope with all the calls.

The first phase of the air attack was assumed to involve the use of 2,750 incendiary bombs, which caused fires in 17 places, destroyed 17 houses, damaged 206, and rendered 385 people homeless. Then 141 high explosive bomb incidents were packed into 50 minutes. These were assumed to have caused 780 casualties (246 fatal), demolished 773 houses, and damaged 4,894, rendering 11,565 people homeless.

When the military forces had penetrated into the city on Sunday morning, several attempts were made to capture the police station, but the police and Home Guard resisted so fiercely that the invaders beat a retreat. This force had approached from the west. Meanwhile a second column approached via Lincoln Road, Lincoln Road East and Park Road. At the corner of Fitzwilliam Street they walked into a trap. Turning aside to attempt the capture of the cattle market, many were wiped out by fire from a machine gun behind a wall. The few who survived suffered losses from snipers and camouflaged defenders with automatic rifles.

Some of the hardest fighting was seen around the North Station, which although isolated, remained in the defenders' hands. In Bridge Street, attackers took advantage of every scrap of cover as they crept forward foot by foot, until they rushed the defences at the foot of the bridge and won the day. Simultaneously an armoured force converged from Bishop's Road and cornered all the survivors of the civil defence services in the car park.

At 2.30 the emergency committee met to hear confidential reports from officials as to how the organizations had coped with the overload problems. The Deputy Regional Commissioner (Principal H.A.S. Wortley), who presided, congratulated the emergency and the Invasion Committees on difficult work well carried out. There were many gaps revealed in the services, but when the reports came to be sorted out and compiled, it was thought possible to remedy the defects.

Colonel O.G. Body, military director, said that from the military point of view the exercise had been a great success. The Home Guard had found they had many lessons to learn, but they entered into the exercise with splendid spirit.

Colonel C.W.D. Rowe, Group Commander, Home Guard, expressed pleasure at the splendid way in which the civil defence subordinated to military requirements. The defenders had 160 killed, 220 seriously wounded and 310 walking injured; enemy losses were considerably higher.

The Town Clerk, who was Controller and Coordinating Officer, remarked: "Far too many visitors came to my room, which was more like a reception room. In such circumstances one could not do one's job."

Mrs. A.H. Mellows, WVS County Organiser, reported upon action taken to care for the homeless. The Chairman said that in a real raid every cinema and church would be commandeered, and the homeless could even be put five or eight in a room of any house left standing. Another point was that some civil defence personnel stood quite calmly only a few yards from the enemy. They had a lot to learn in backing up and supporting the military.

The Chairman also commended the "yeoman work" of the City Engineer (Mr. F.J. Smith) as local promoter and deputy controller. The Chief Constable (Mr. T. Danby) said he found the messenger service most efficient.

Column Officer Ridge, NFS, said his experience suggested that many more messengers were necessary, but it was very difficult to get them. The service of the Control was very good.

Some of the theoretical casualties in the 'Delta' exercise became real and required treatment at the Memorial Hospital. They were confined to military personnel, and most of the injuries were minor. One man, however, was badly hurt on the face, dangerously close to an eye although his sight was not impaired. The discharge of a blank cartridge was said to be the cause of the injury. Others were treated at first aid posts, mainly for cuts on the hands and face.

Men in Enemy Prison Camps
Information supplied by the Red Cross at this time showed that by November 1942, there were 85 men from Peterborough in enemy prison camps. Some had been in captivity since the early days of the war, others for no more than a few months.

"Although their lot is unenviable" it was said, "we know that they endure hardship and monotony uncomplainingly, even cheerfully. Their letters, as any next-of-kin will tell you, are invariably cheery and optimistic. Their tails, in short, are still up"

For this, much of the credit must go to the Red Cross and to 11 million contributors to the Red Cross, Penny-a-Week Fund. The regular supply of parcels of food, tobacco, and other comforts – a vast undertaking and one of great difficulty – did much to keep up the prisoners' health and spirits. The supply of games, sports equipment and musical instruments also helped greatly, whilst the work of the educational books section of the Red Cross was of great practical value. This work was costing the Red Cross approximately £4,500,000 a year.

Captain Crick Killed
It was reported on 4th December, 1942, that Captain Peter Charles Crick, 62714, 104 (The Essex Yeomanry) Regiment, Royal Horse Artillery, had been killed in action in the Middle East, on the 28th October. Captain Crick, who was 32 years of age, was the second son of Mr. Charles Crick and the late Mrs. Crick, of Dryden House, Lincoln Road, Peterborough. He had previously been reported as having been wounded.

Captain Crick served as a Territorial for several years before war broke out, and joined up immediately. He spent some time in Peterborough and Norfolk, and in March 1941, left the country. He first went to India and then Iran, later heading for the Middle East. He had three brothers still serving, one in the Navy, another reported missing at Singapore and the other an Accountant Officer in the RAF, at Aden.

He was educated at King's School, Maidenhead and Oundle. After leaving school he joined the Peterborough Rugby F.C. and was a regular player and supporter. He played forward and three-quarter, and turned out for the club regularly for many seasons. For part of the time he was vice-captain, and one season he played for Northampton (The Saints) and for Leicester (The Tigers). He also played golf and squash, and was a member of the City and Counties Club.

Most of his business life was spent in insurance, but he was with Messrs. Kodak, Ltd. in London and Glasgow for about two years. Before the war he was an inspector for the Employers' Liability Assurance Corporation, Ltd. and travelled in a wide area. Captain Crick is buried in Alamein War Cemetery, Egypt.

Railings Removed

Peterborough's collection of iron railings for munitions began in the second week of December. It was carried out by Messrs. John Lucas (Peterborough) Ltd., Dogsthorpe Road, and Mr. B. Stokely, Henry Street, Peterborough, who were the official contractors.

As far as possible, the clearance of the iron was being made street by street, Mr. Stokely being responsible for one part of the city and Messrs. Lucas for the other. The collectors had begun by taking railings from the East Ward and the centre of the city.

Loss of HMS AVENGER

Leading Air Mechanic, Frederick John Samuel Davis, 79879, Fleet Air Arm HMS AVENGER, Royal Navy, was now reported killed in action on 15th November, 1942. Aged 24 and married, he was the only son of Mr. and Mrs. J.S. Davis, 45, Taverner's Road, Peterborough. Educated at Deacon's School, he trained at Winchester for the teaching profession. Before the war he held a post at St. Mark's boy's school. He was a keen rugby player for the school and for the Old Boys. Volunteering for the Fleet Air Arm, he was called to service in June 1940.

After taking part in the Operation Torch landings of North Africa in November 1942, HMS AVENGER departed Gibraltar with convoy MKF 1 on the 14th November, heading home to the Clyde in the UK. At 0305 on the 15th November, HMS AVENGER was torpedoed by U-155. She was hit on the port side amidships, which in turn ignited her bomb room, blowing out the centre section of the ship. Her bow and stern sections rose in the air and sunk within 2 minutes in position 36°15'N, 07°45'W, leaving only 12 survivors.

Leading Air Mechanic Davis is commemorated on the Lee-On-Solent Memorial, Hampshire. Bay 3. Panel 4.

Official News of Singapore Officers

On the 18th December, 1942, it was announced that official notification had been received that several Royal Artillery officers from the Peterborough area, who were reported missing at the time of the fall of Singapore, were now prisoners of war. The news was received in a War Office telegram from the Under-Secretary for War. Notifications included the following men from the city:

Captain Sam Egar, only son of Mr. S. Murley Egar, C.C. and Mrs. Egar, Melrose, Park Crescent, Peterborough. Capt. Egar was in the Milton Estate office before the war.

Lieutenant Maurice Crick, third son of Mr. Charles W. Crick, Dryden House, Lincoln Road, Peterborough. His twin brother, Captain Peter Crick, had been reported killed in action just two weeks earlier.

News was still awaited for Captain John Marcus Neal, Royal Artillery, Lathbury House, Lincoln Road, Peterborough. Son of Mr. A. Marcus Neal, J.P. chairman of directors of Peter Brotherhood Ltd.

Captain Corby Bristow, son of Mrs. F.A. Bristow, Medehamsted, London Road.

Lieutenant Gilbert Crick, of Harpenden, son of Mr. G.A.S. Crick, Springfield, Thorpe Road, Peterborough.

Lieutenant Lionel Schofield, Sherwood Foresters, son of Mr. and Mrs. A. Schofield, 36, Peveril Road, Peterborough.

Lieutenant Douglas G. Viney, son of Councillor A.W. Viney, MBE, Charnwood, Park Road, Peterborough.

Second Lieutenant J. Brian Green, Royal Artillery, son of Canon G.A. Green, Fletton Rectory. Only the day before, Canon Green had a letter returned to him that he had sent to his son on October 1941.

More Attacks on American Soldiers

A special sitting of Peterborough Magistrates was now arranged for Tuesday 22nd December to hear charges of assault by British soldiers who were alleged to have attacked and robbed Americans. On Monday the 14th the following had appeared before A.J. Dillingham Esq.

Richard Walsh for being concerned with Thomas Weston in assaulting and robbing Dennis Holland Connell of £11; and for being concerned with Weston, Albert Quigley and Thomas Donahae, in assaulting and robbing David Burkett of a pocket knife and one shilling.

Thomas Weston was charged with being concerned with Walsh in assaulting Connell and robbing him of a wallet containing £11 and other property; with being concerned with Walsh in assaulting Burkett; and with stealing a wallet containing £2. 10s. belonging to Mr. H. Purton, manager of the American Red Cross Club.

John Axon was charged with being concerned with Thomas Donahae and another man named Hamlet in assaulting and robbing Clifford Bazimore of £1 and a pocket knife.

Lance Bombardier Thomas Donahae was charged with being concerned with Axon and Hamlet in robbing Bazimore; and with using personal violence and stealing property.

Albert Quigley was charged with being concerned with Weston, Walsh and Donahae in assaulting and robbing Burkett.

The Chief Constable said the prisoners were apprehended by Detective Inspector Frost and Detective Sergeant Beal, near Peterborough, and he asked that they be remanded in custody to Leicester Gaol until Tuesday 22nd.

Tobruk Casualty

Trooper Walter Gerald Hitchborn, 6294215, 5th Battalion, Royal Tank Regiment, Royal Armoured Corps, eldest son of Mr. W. Hitchborn, 78, New Road, Peterborough, was now reported to have died of wounds in the Middle East on 29th November, 1942.

Trooper Hitchborn, who was 30, was born in Woodston, and on leaving Woodston School was employed by the Eastern Counties Omnibus Company. He later left for London where he married Miss Widner. Trooper Hitchborn is buried in the Tobruk War Cemetery, Libya.

A Submariner Returns Home

On the 18th December, 1942, it was announced that Leading Signalman Jack

William Smith, of Star Road, had arrived back in Peterborough after having been on a two and a half year cruise in the submarine HMS TRUANT, which had been waging warfare over half the globe.

During her 80,000 miles of travel, this submarine, under the command of Lieutenant Commander H.A.V. Haggard, sank or damaged more than 20 vessels. Ldg. Sig. Smith was 30 years of age and while away had grown a beard.

"When he opened the door and I saw it was Jack," said his mother, "I did not bother about his whiskers. I kissed them all over."

Ldg. Sig, Smith had been in the Royal Navy for fifteen years, joining at the age of fifteen. About ten years earlier he had been transferred to the submarine service and had served in various parts of the world in HMS SEAWOLF and another submarine in the China Seas. In January 1940, he went to HMS TRUANT and did service in the Mediterranean, Adriatic, Indian Ocean, Surabaya, Java, Sunda Straits and the Malacca Straits. He possessed a certificate from the First Lord of the Admiralty which stated:

"By the King's Order the name of Leading Signalman John William Smith was published in the 'London Gazette' on March 17th 1942, as Mentioned in Despatches for distinguished service. I am charged to record His Majesty's high appreciation.- A.V. Alexander, First Lord of the Admiralty."

Ldg. Sig. Smith did not know for which incident amongst a list of many that he had been awarded this honour. In one action connected with the sinking of an enemy vessel he received 34 pieces of shrapnel in his body. He still had some of them left in his right arm and chest, but they caused him no trouble.

Amongst some of HMS TRUANT's exploits was blowing to pieces an enemy ammunition ship whilst under fire from shore batteries. They were caught in the glare of a searchlight one night and crash dived. Twenty depth charges exploded around the submarine but it got away safely.

It once grounded in only a few feet of water and when a destroyer passed over it, "it sounded like an express train going through a station." During this incident the Captain called to his crew, "Hold your hats on men," and they waited for death which did not come.

The crew heard on the Japanese radio twice that their submarine had been sunk. "Our Captain was the coolest man I ever met," said Jack.

Ldg. Sig, Smith's father had died about three years earlier. There was a family of six – four sons and two daughters. One brother, Ted, was in the RAF, out East, and another brother, Joe, was in the National Fire Service at Fletton.

Peterborough Man Hanged in Canada

It was reported in the 'Standard' on 18th December 1942, that Sergeant Tom Roland Hutchings, Royal Air Force, a native of Peterborough, had been hanged at St. Andrews, New Brunswick, Canada, early on the morning of Wednesday 16th.

Sergeant Hutchings had been convicted of the rape and murder of nineteen year old Bernice Connors while he was stationed at Pennfield Ridge, Air Station. The 'St. Croix Courier' carried the following story in its December 17th edition:

"Tom Roland Hutchings of Peterborough, England, paid the penalty for the murder of Bernice Connors at Black's Harbour last June when he was hanged at St. Andrews early yesterday morning. He went to his death calmly, preserving to the end the silence and poise which had characterized his conduct since he was arrested

267

at the Pennfield air station last summer while serving as a sergeant armourer with the Royal Air Force. The sentence of death was carried out at 1:50 a.m. Wednesday morning, and he was pronounced dead at 2:02 o'clock.

Thus the book was closed on one of the most gruesome crimes in the history of Charlotte County. The body of Bernice Connors, covered with moss to form an inconspicuous mound, was discovered on Sunday, June 7, near the Deadman's Harbor road in Black's Harbor, not far from the Community dance hall where she had attended a dance the previous Friday evening. She was not seen alive after that night. The body was about 300 yards from the hall in a field.

Arrested June 10

Hutchings was arrested Wednesday, June 10, and arraigned in the magistrate's court at Black's Harbor the same day before Ellis A. Nason where he was charged with murder. Preliminary hearing followed, and he was tried in St. Andrews early in October when the Crown called 38 witnesses. Mr. Justice Richards presided. The trial was completed on October 6, when the jury after deliberating 3 1/2 hours found him guilty with a recommendation for mercy, and the death sentence was pronounced late that night.

Evidence of the witnesses was that Hutchings was in the company of Bernice Connors when she was last seen walking up the Deadman's Harbor road the night of June 5, and that he later appeared at the dance hall with blood on his face and clothing.

Hutchings himself made no statement at any time, and no witnesses were called by the defence.

Remained Unshaken

While in solitary confinement at the county jail since his conviction, Hutchings for most of the time retained the cool, detached attitude which he had shown ever since his arrest, although as time went by with no news to indicate that Ottawa might act on the recommendation for mercy there were times when he was depressed and morose. He ate heartily and evinced considerable interest in what went on about him. Special guards maintained constant watch outside his cell.

On Monday of this week it became certain that the death penalty would be carried out when officials of the remission branch of the Secretary of State at Ottawa announced that "the law was to take its course". All the arrangements had already been completed by Sheriff C.W. Mallory. A scaffold had been erected in the yard of the courthouse, and Camille Blanchaud, official hangman for the Province of Quebec, was already on hand to carry out the execution.

Last Moments

Hutchings last visitors, at 1:30 a.m., were a chaplain and a doctor from the Pennfield station, Squadron Leader Mann and Squadron Leader Stewart, respectively. When the time came to leave his cell, Hutchings walked out unaided, but outside turned, walked back deliberately and switched out the light, then rejoined the official party and walked with firm steps to the courtyard and up the 18 steps to the gallows. He wore a beltless R.A.F. tunic with his sergeant's stripes on the arms, and slacks. Accompanying him were Squadron Leader Stewart, his two prison guards, and the hangman. The trap was sprung at 1:50 a.m. Twelve minutes later he was pronounced dead. The execution was the first to take place in Charlotte County in 65 years.

The only spectators were the official group. The scene was screened from outside view by a temporary fence and a covering over the top. Medical men in attendance were Dr. H.P. O'Neill of St. Andrews and Dr. R.A. Massie of St. George. The body was buried in the Rural Cemetery at St. Andrews. The official record was completed Wednesday morning when the formal inquest was held before Dr. F.V. Maxwell of St. George." Sergeant Hutchings left a wife and child in Peterborough.

Killed in Action in Tunisia
In the Christmas Day edition of the 'Standard' it was announced that official news had been received of the death in action in Tunisia on November 28th of Major William Victor Hart, M.C. 5th Battalion, Northamptonshire Regiment, son of Mrs. Hart and the late Mr. G. Hart, of 'Charnwood' London Road, Peterborough.

Major Hart was 30, and married with a four month old daughter. His wife was Miss Enid Mary Moresby, of Leicester, and they were married at Leicester on 23rd September, 1939.

As a boy Major Hart attended King's School. He served his apprenticeship with Mr. Calcutt, chemist, of the old Narrow Bridge Street, and was later with Mr. W.E.H. Barnes, and finally Messrs. Timothy White and Taylor Ltd. For a time he captained the Town Rugby Football Club and University College, Leicester, rugby team.

Joining the Territorials soon after leaving school, he took an officer's course at Sandhurst, and was Captain Hart when war broke out. His regiment was part of the B.E.F. in France, and in the retreat to Dunkirk he was awarded the Military Cross for conspicuous gallantry. He was also Mentioned in Despatches several times.

Captain Hart received his decoration from the hands of the King at Buckingham Palace on 7th August, 1940, and was promoted Major before going abroad again.

The "Major in a South Midlands regiment" whose exploits in Northern Tunisia had recently been featured in the daily press was believed to be Major Hart. A report from Reuter's special correspondent in Tunisia had stated:

"A small force from a South Midlands regiment fought its way back to British lines with only one casualty – after waging a guerrilla campaign in a desert part of Northern Tunisia.

After having been cut off by some German tanks near Mateur, 30 men, led by a Major from Peterborough, in peacetime a chemist, decided to make themselves as big a nuisance as possible. They first attacked some supply wagons, and quickly making off, they began wandering without means of knowing where they were until an Arab peasant gave them a pocket motoring guide.

They halted German motor transport going to the front by shooting at the back tyres. They sowed mines on the road in front of some tanks, and 'beating it' as fast as possible, heard the mines exploding. They ambushed and knocked to pieces a lorry load of German paratroops. They lived on tea, bread and eggs obtained from

269

Arabs by trading clothing. Having tramped 100 miles, they regained the British lines, many wearing only gym shoes with no socks." Major Hart is buried in Massicault War Cemetery, Tunisia.

More Singapore Prisoners

More official news now reached the city that the following were prisoners of war in Singapore:

Captain Corby Bristow, Royal Corps of Signals, was the younger son of Mrs. Bristow, of 'Medehamsted,' London Road, Peterborough. He had been in Malaya for more than a year and the last letter from him, dated February, and sent from Singapore stated that he was well. He was in the volunteer force which fought in Finland in 1939, and made an adventurous escape from that country.

Lieutenant Gilbert Crick, Royal Artillery, was the youngest son of Mr. G.A.S. Crick, 'Springfield,' Thorpe Road, Peterborough. Until the outbreak of war he was with the Shell-Mex company. Some years earlier he had been in business with his father and uncle (Mr. C.W. Crick) in the family corn merchants' business. He and Lieutenant Maurice Crick, who was also a prisoner, were in the same Battery.

Lieutenant Douglas G. Viney, Royal Artillery, was the younger son of Councillor A.W. Viney, MBE, 'Charnwood,' Park Road, Peterborough. After apprenticeship as an engineer at Peter Brotherhood's he decided to study law. He was articled to Dr. J. Hunt, and became a solicitor in 1938. He remained with Dr. Hunt until the outbreak of war. An old boy from King's School, he was a member and ex-captain of the Town Rugby Club. His father received a cable from him from Malaya and another from Singapore just before the capture. Councillor Viney's other son, Brevet-Colonel W.J.K. Viney, had been in charge of important work at Quetta, India, and had now been posted to Colombo, Ceylon.

Lieutenant Lionel Schofield, Sherwood Foresters, was the elder son of Mr. and Mrs. A. Schofield, 36, Peveril Road, Peterborough, and was 23 years of age. He went to Deacon's School and then to University College, Nottingham, and was studying for his B.Sc (Econ.) when war broke out. He was at that time in the Officer's Training Corps (OTC) and was gazetted Second Lieutenant in the Sherwood Foresters. His father was senior master at Deacon's School, and an Inspector in the Special Constabulary. Lieutenant Schofield was reported missing in the first Singapore casualty list, and later his father received a letter from a brother officer saying he had an arm wound and was in hospital.

Second Lieutenant T.R. Miles, Suffolk Regiment, was the eldest son of Mr. and Mrs. W. Miles, of 'Rockbourne,' Oundle Road, Peterborough, and was 25 years of age. His father was an engineer's draughtsman at J.P. Hall and Son's. Second Lieutenant Miles was educated at Fletton Secondary School, and after three years training at Loughborough College, became woodwork instructor to Hunts. Education Authority.

ROLL OF HONOUR 1942

HILLSON, George William – Wootton Avenue, Peterborough. Engine Room Artificer 5th Class, C/MX 76798, H.M.S. Vimiera, Royal Navy. Died, age not known, on the 9th January 1942. The destroyer HMS Vimiera was sunk by a mine in the Thames estuary off East Spile Buoy. No known grave, he is commemorated on the Chatham Naval Memorial, Reference 60, 2.

BAKER, Leonard Alec – Sergeant 526668, 113 Squadron, Royal Air Force. Died, aged 24, on the 11th January 1942. The son of William and Elsie Baker of Woodston, Peterborough. Buried in Moascar War Cemetery, Egypt. Grave 1. A. 10.

BEETON, Wilfred Roy – Newark Avenue, Peterborough. Sergeant (W.Op./Air Gnr.), 1359941, Royal Air Force Volunteer Reserve. Died, aged 29, on the 17th January 1942. The son of Wilfred Beeton and Elsie Amelia Beeton (nee Carter) and husband of Beatrice Mary Beeton, of East Bergholt, Suffolk. Buried in the Old Fletton Cemetery, Peterborough. Grave 128, Section 6.

STEELS, Reginald Adolphus George – Palmerston Road, Peterborough. Gunner 975258, (Honourable Artillery Company), Royal Horse Artillery. Died, aged 26, on the 23rd January 1942. The son of Robert and Lily Steels and the husband of Doris Evelyn Steels of Woodston, Peterborough. No known grave he is commemorated on the Alamein Memorial, Egypt. Column 14.

CHAMBERS, Leslie Charles – Private 5832948, 2nd Cambridgeshire Regiment. Died, aged 26, on the 24th January 1942. Killed in action at Sengarrang, Malaya. The son of Arthur and Martha Chambers of Peterborough. No known grave he is commemorated on the Singapore Memorial. Column 58.

GILBY, William Clarence – 48 Shakespeare Avenue, Peterborough. Gunner 920975, 135 (Hertfordshire Yeomanry) Field Regt, Royal Artillery. Died, aged 21, on the 25th January 1942. The son of John and Lillian Gilby of Peterborough. No known grave, he is commemorated on the Singapore Memorial. Column 36.

ELLIOTT, Frederick Thomas – 8 St. Martins Street, Peterborough. Gunner 922904, 135 (Hertfordshire Yeomanry) Field Regt, Royal Artillery. Died, aged 21, on the 26th January 1942. Next of kin not known. Buried in Kranji War Cemetery, Singapore. Grave 36.A.2.

STEELS, Arthur Edward – 168 Clarence Road, Peterborough. Gunner 885649, 135 (Hertfordshire Yeomanry) Field Regt, Royal Artillery. Died, aged 21, on the 26th January 1942. The son of John Frederick and Rose Priscilla Steels of Peterborough. Buried in Taiping War Cemetery, Malaysia. Collective Grave, 1.A.1-12.

BELT, Harry – 7 Fengate Close, Peterborough. Sergeant 848960, 135 (Hertfordshire Yeomanry) Field Regt, Royal Artillery. Died, aged 22, on the 27th January 1942. The son of John Belt and Mary Belt (nee Cooper) of Peterborough. Buried in Kranji War Cemetery, Singapore, Grave 17.E.8.

WRIGHT, Frederick Charles – 2 Pipe Lane, Peterborough. Gunner 905440, 135 (Hertfordshire Yeomanry) Field Regt, Royal Artillery. Died, age not known, on the 27th January 1942. The son of Charles Horace and Ethel Wright, of Intake, Yorkshire. Buried in Taiping War Cemetery, Malaysia. Collective Grave, 1.A.1-12.

CASWELL, Richard William – Sergeant 914347, 336 Battery, 135 (Hertfordshire Yeomanry) Field Regiment, Royal Artillery. Died, aged 27, on the 27th January 1942 during the Japanese invasion of Malaya and Singapore. The son of Albert and Lottie Caswell and the husband of Mary Caswell of Peterborough. No known grave he is commemorated on the Singapore Memorial. Column 35.

GARN, James Gordon – 40 Ashcroft Gardens, Peterborough. Corporal 5831197, 1st Cambridgeshire Regiment. Died, aged 24, on the 9th February 1942. The son of Robert and Florence Ellen Garn of Eastfield, Peterborough. Buried in Kranji War Cemetery, Singapore. Collective Grave, 18.B.1-4.

POPPLE, Herbert William – 131, Northfield Road, Private 5779637, 4th Royal Norfolk Regiment. Died, aged 29, on the 11th February 1942. The son of Herbert and Lily Popple and the husband of Dorothy Popple of Peterborough. No known grave he is commemorated on the Singapore Memorial. Column 52.

NEVILLE, William – 13 Gladstone Street, Peterborough. Gunner 915812, 135 (Hertfordshire Yeomanry) Field Regt, Royal Artillery. Died, aged 21, between the 11th and 14th February 1942. The son of Ernest and Emily Neville of Peterborough and the husband of Jane Neville. His brother Edward also died, in 1944, on active service. Buried in Kranji War Cemetery, Singapore. Special Memorial, 31. A. 10.

PRYKE, Lawrence – 35 Peveril Road, Peterborough. Gunner 885407, 135 (Hertfordshire Yeomanry) Field Regt, Royal Artillery. Died, aged 21, on the 13th or 14th February 1942. The son of William and Gertrude Pryke of Peterborough. Buried in Kranji War Cemetery, Singapore. Grave 14.D.16.

CHAPMAN, Walter Harry – 1 Morris Street, Peterborough. Gunner 922770, 135 (Hertfordshire Yeomanry) Field Regt, Royal Artillery. Died, aged 21, on the 14th February 1942. The son of W. W. and Kate Chapman, of Peterborough. Buried in Kranji War Cemetery, Singapore. Grave 18.C.18.

NUNN, Alderman James – Lance Corporal 2037561, 41 Fortress Company, Royal Engineers. Died, aged 25, on the 14th February 1942. The foster-son of Mrs A. J. Newland of New England, Peterborough. No known grave he is commemorated on the Singapore Memorial. Column 39.

HILL, Charles Benjamin – 10 South Street, Peterborough. Private 5777114, 5th Royal Norfolk Regiment. Died, aged 26, on the 15th February 1942. Next of kin not known. Buried in Kranji War Cemetery, Singapore. Collective Grave 17.E.9-12.

POUNTNEY, Howard Owen – 66 Vere Road, Peterborough. Private 5833629, 1st Cambridgeshire Regiment. Died, aged 21, on the 15th February 1942. The son of

Albert and Edith Annie Pountney of Peterborough. No known grave, he is commemorated on the Singapore Memorial. Column 60.

STANFORD, Raymond Dennis – 1 North Station Road, Peterborough. Marine PLY/X 3805, Royal Marines. Died, aged 21, on the 16th February 1942. He was a crew member of the Battleship HMS Prince of Wales that was sunk, along with HMS Repulse, by Japanese dive bombers on the 10th December 1941 with the loss of 327 crew members. Having been rescued he was killed in the area of HMS Sultan, the naval base at Singapore. The son of Ernest and Maud Ethel Stanford of Peterborough. He has no known grave and is commemorated on the Plymouth Naval Memorial. Panel 103, Column 2.

LEWIS, William – Peterborough. Gunner 1545095, 55 (The Suffolk Yeomanry) Anti-Tank Regt. Died, age unknown, on the 21st February 1942. The son of Sophia Bird of Peterborough. Buried in Eastfield Cemetery, Peterborough. Grave 6960, Div. 4. Block 17.

IVES, Augustus Harry – Peterborough. Lieutenant Colonel 70684, Royal Army Ordnance Corps. Died, age unknown, on the 2nd March 1942. Next of kin not known. No known grave, commemorated on the Singapore Memorial. Column 107.

DOUGHTY, George Harold – Warrant Officer Class II 7583192 (Armt. Q.M.S.), Royal Army Ordnance Corps. Died, aged 42, on the 5th March 1942. The son of George and Amy Doughty and the husband of Ethel Doughty of Peterborough. Buried in Shrewsbury General Cemetery. Grave Extension. Plot 10. 382.

WARD, Reginald Thomas – 22 Queens Gardens, Peterborough. Sergeant 1379450, Royal Air Force Volunteer Reserve. Died, age unknown, on the 25th March 1942. The son of Reginald and Lilian Ward and the husband of Winifred Victoria Ward. No known grave he is commemorated on the Runnymede Memorial, Panel 96.

WATSON, Claude Bernard Bunnage – Sick Berth Attendant, P/MX 82575, HMS Lanka, Royal Navy. Died of illness, aged 33, on the 8th April 1942. The son of Arthur and Elizabeth Watson of Peterborough and the husband of Nellie Watson of Peterborough. Buried in Colombo General Cemetery, Sri Lanka. Plot 6B. Row P. Grave 6.

FARROW, Mary Jane – 60 Huntley Grove, Peterborough. Died, aged 66, on the 29th April 1942 in an air raid on York at 55 Chatsworth Terrace. The daughter of William and Mary Corney of West Cottingwith and the widow of Richard Farrow. Buried in the York City and County Borough Cemetery.

THIMBLEBEE, Percy Hudson – 214 Palmerston Road, Peterborough. Flight Sergeant 963850, Royal Air Force Volunteer Reserve. Died, aged 23, on the 27th May 1942. The son of Joseph and Sarah Thimblebee and the husband of Margaret Annie Thimblebee of Farcet, Peterborough. No known grave he is commemorated on the Runnymede Memorial, Panel 76.

TAYLOR, George John Austin – 159 Queens Walk, Fletton, Peterborough. Private, Dispatch Rider, 1st Huntingdonshire Home Guard. Died, aged 28, on the 3rd June 1942. Whilst on duty his motorcycle collided with a lorry on the London Road, near Yaxley, Peterborough. The son of Mr & Mrs G. Taylor of 80, Silver Street, Peterborough. Buried in the Old Fletton Cemetery, Peterborough. Section 6, Grave 231.

ULYATT, David Sidney – 96 Newark Avenue, Peterborough. Lance Corporal 179818, Royal Army Service Corps. Died, age unknown, on the 9th June 1942, believed in a road accident. Next of kin not known. Buried in Eastfield Cemetery, Peterborough. Div. 3. Block 16. Grave 6549.

WADSLEY, Eric – Peterborough. Gunner 1766825, Royal Artillery. Died, aged 34, on the 20th June 1942. The husband of Ellen Nora Wadsley of Peterborough. Buried in Woodston Cemetery, Peterborough. Sec. 6, Grave 9.

NUTT, Arthur James – Chester Road, Peterborough. Gunner 1102117, 74 Field Regiment, Royal Artillery. Died, aged 32, on the 26th June 1942. The son of John and Elizabeth Nutt and the husband of Edith Annie Nutt of Peterborough. Commemorated on the Alamein Memorial, Egypt, Column 36.

BARWELL, Philip Reginald – Peterborough. Group Captain 22062, Royal Air Force, DFC. Died, aged 35, on the 1st July 1942 when Barwell, accompanied by Squadron Leader Oxspring, took off from Biggin Hill an hour before sunset on a standing patrol between Dungeness and Beachy Head. Control at Biggin Hill warned of unidentified aircraft in the area, which proved later to be two Spitfires from Tangmere flown by inexperienced pilots. Barwell, apparently oblivious to the warning, was attacked by one and shot down in flames into the sea. Although Oxspring saw him trying to open his hood Barwell did not bale out. Despite intensive searches no trace of him was found. His body was washed up on the French coast and he is buried in Calais Canadian War Cemetery, Grave 5.G.1. The son of Reginald and Alice Barwell and the husband of Mary Elizabeth Barwell of Peterborough.

MEARS, Walter Alec – 110 Cromwell Road, Peterborough. Bombardier 914345, 135 (The Hertfordshire Yeomanry) Field Regt, Royal Artillery. Died, aged 25, on the 6th July 1942. Next of kin not known. Buried in Kuala Lumpur Civil Cemetery, Malaysia. Grave 827.

DARLOW, John William – 20 Eastleigh Road, Peterborough. Gunner 880055, 3rd Field Regiment, Royal Artillery. Died, aged 25, on the 15th July 1942. The son of Frederick and Mary Darlow of Peterborough. Buried in El Alamein War Cemetery, Egypt. Grave IV.C.11.

CLARKE, George Frederick – 298 Lincoln Road, Peterborough. Sergeant 5886012, 5th Northamptonshire Regiment. Died, aged 21, on the 20th July 1942, of wounds received in a bomb explosion in Scotland. Next of kin not known. Buried in Eastfield Cemetery, Peterborough. Grave 3579, Div. 1. Block 11.

BLACKADDER, William Smith – Pilot Officer (Wireless Op / Air Gunner) 134028, 18 Squadron, Royal Air Force Volunteer Reserve. Died, aged 21, on the 24th July 1942. He was the Pilot Officer in a Blenheim, Serial No Z7428 that took off from Wattisham for an Intruder operation to Vechta airfield. The cause of loss was not established. The son of John and Maggie Blackadder and the husband of Rita Blackadder of Woodston, Peterborough. All three crew died. Buried in Sage War Cemetery, Oldenberg, Germany. Grave 14. C. 1.

RUSDALE, Jack Kirby – Peterborough. Gunner 1531192, 128 H.A.A. Regiment, Royal Artillery. Died, aged 25, on the 28th July 1942. The son of George and Daisy Rusdale of Old Fletton, Peterborough. Buried in the Old Fletton Cemetery, Peterborough. Sec 6, Grave 147. His brother Cecil was also killed in 1944.

PICKERSGILL, Christopher Noel – 313 Walpole Street, Peterborough. Driver T/103921, 550 General Transport Company, Royal Army Service Corps. Died, aged 22, on the 30th July 1942. The son of Edward and Gertrude Pickersgill of Peterborough. Buried in El Alamein War Cemetery, Egypt, Joint Grave X.C.24-25.

HIRST, Tom William – 21 Balmoral Road, Walton, Peterborough. Sergeant 567589, Flight Engineer, Transport Command, Royal Air Force. Died, aged 23, on the 13th August 1942. The son of William and Mary Hirst and the husband of Muriel Hirst of Walton, Peterborough. Buried in Habbaniya War Cemetery, Iraq. Grave 2.E.1.

SHARP, Frederick Leslie – Lance Bombardier 5882270, 28 Field Regiment, Royal Artillery. Died, aged 28, on the 29th August 1942. The son of Herbert and Alice Sharp of Peterborough. Buried in Tripoli War Cemetery, Libya. Grave 7. F. 17.

WEST, William – 49 Palmerston Road, Peterborough. Gunner 1557797, 102 (The Northumberland Hussars) Lt. A.A./Anti-Tank Regiment, Royal Artillery. Died, aged 28, on the 10th September 1942. The son of William and Eliza West of Woodston, Peterborough. Buried in Bari War Cemetery, Italy. Grave XIV.D.2.

IGGULDEN, Humphrey Vint – 88 London Road, Peterborough. Pilot Officer 129056, Royal Air Force Volunteer Reserve. Died, aged 19, on the 12th September 1942. He had been flying training in South Africa when he was returning on the HMT Laconia that was sunk by the German submarine U-156. The son of Henry Vint and Ellen Iggulden of Peterborough. No known grave he is commemorated on the Alamein Memorial, Column 248.

MEADOWS, George S. – 22 Exeter Road, Peterborough. Trooper 7945696, 9th Armoured Division, Royal Armoured Corps. Died, aged 19, on the 22nd September 1942 in an accident in England. No known next of kin. Buried in Eastfield Cemetery, Peterborough. Grave 54.

BOX, Eli – Peterborough. Sapper 1911131, 694 Works Company, Royal Engineers. Died, aged 44, on the 26th September 1942. The husband of Phyllis Box of Peterborough. Buried in Eastfield Cemetery, Peterborough. Div.4, Block 16, Joint Grave 6360.

RAE, George – 111 Northfield Road, Peterborough. Flight Sergeant (Pilot) 1179958, Royal Air Force Volunteer Reserve. Died, aged 20, on the 2nd October 1942 when his Kittyhawk aircraft AL192 dived into the ground after take-off due to an engine fire. The son of George and Sophie Rae of Peterborough. Buried in Alamein War Cemetery, Egypt. Grave XXXIII.D.7.

HALL, Charles Wilkinson – Lincoln Road, Peterborough. Ordinary Telegraphist C/JX 233636, Royal Navy. Died, aged 29, on the 2nd October 1942, when the cruiser HMS Curacoa was lost after a collision with the SS Queen Mary while on escort duties off the coast of Donegal in the North Western Approaches. The son of John and Louisa Hall and the husband of Irene Mary Hall of Peterborough. No known grave he is commemorated on the Chatham Naval Memorial, Reference 59.3.

PRICE, Stanley Victor – Peterborough. Sergeant (Air Gunner) 1427176, 218 Squadron, Royal Air Force Volunteer Reserve. Died, aged 22, on the 23rd October 1942. He was a gunner in Short Stirling Mk 1, Serial No R9184, code letters HA-U that took off from Downham Market to bomb Nuremburg. All eight crew members were killed. The son of Albert and Dorothy Price of Peterborough. Buried in Abbeville Communal Cemetery Extension, Somme, France. Plot 6, Row T, Grave 2.

CRICK, Peter Charles – 101 Lincoln Road, Peterborough. Captain 62714, 104 (Essex Yeomanry) Regiment, Royal Horse Artillery. Died, aged 32, on the 28th October 1942. The son of Charles and Ettie Crick of Peterborough. Buried in Alamein War Cemetery, Egypt. Grave V.G.25.

ILETT, Charles Edward – 168 New England, Peterborough. Lance Bombardier 1647743, Royal Artillery, attached 3 Battery, 1st Lt. A.A. Regt, Royal Indian Artillery. Died, aged 31, on the 30th October 1942. The son of Charles and Emily Ilett and the husband of Lucy Ilett of New England, Peterborough. Buried in Rangoon War Cemetery, Myanmar, Grave 5.F.3.

MEREDITH, George Albert – Star Road, Peterborough. Assistant Steward, SS Reynolds, Merchant Navy. Died, aged 19, on the 31st October 1942 when the unescorted SS Reynolds was hit by two torpedoes from U-504 about 210 miles east of Durban. She was hit amidships and in the stern, capsized and sank within seconds. The ship was en route from Durban to India with general cargo. No survivors were ever found. The son of Mr and Mrs G. H. Meredith of Peterborough. No known grave he is commemorated on the Tower Hill Memorial, London, Panel 86.

ABBOTT, John William – Stanground, Peterborough. Gunner 11426750, 218 Battery, 73 Lt. A.A. Regiment, Royal Artillery. Died, aged 35, on the 9th November 1942. The son of Albert and Emma Abbott and the husband of Phyllis Abbott of Peterborough. Buried in Stanground South Cemetery, Peterborough, Grave 146.

MUCKLIN, Ronald Eric – Stoker 1st Class C/KX 110191, HMS Karanja, Royal Navy. Died, aged 20, on the 12th November 1942. HMS Karanja, Landing Ship Infantry, was bombed and sunk by German aircraft off Bougie, Algeria. The son of

John and Sarah Mucklin of Peterborough. No known grave he is commemorated on the Chatham Naval Memorial. Panel 62, 2.

DAVIS, Frederick John Samuel – 45 Taverners Road, Peterborough. Leading Air Mechanic FAA/FX 79879, HMS Avenger, Royal Navy. Died, aged 24, on the 15th November 1942. After taking part in the Operation Torch landings of North Africa in November 1942, HMS Avenger departed Gibraltar with Convoy MKF 1 on the 14th November, heading home to the Clyde in the UK. At 0305 on the 15th November HMS Avenger was torpedoed by U-155. HMS Avenger was hit on the port side amidships, which in turn ignited her bomb room, blowing out the centre section of the ship. Her bow and stern sections rose in the air and she sank within two minutes leaving only twelve survivors. The son of John and Annie Davis and the husband of Gladys Davis of St. Julian's, Malta. He has no known grave and is commemorated on the Lee-On-Solent Memorial, Hampshire. Bay 3, Panel 4.

WEBB, Windsor Francis Richard – Peterborough. Sergeant 1320645, 207 Squadron, Royal Air Force Volunteer Reserve. Died, aged 19, on the 25th November 1942. The son of Leslie and Florence Webb of Peterborough. No known grave he is commemorated on the Runnymede Memorial, Panel 96.

HART, William Victor – "Charnwood", 80 London Road, Peterborough. Major 64774, 5th Northamptonshire Regiment. Died, aged 30, on the 28th November 1942. Next of kin not known. Buried in Massicault War Cemetery, Tunisia. Grave IV.D.13.

HITCHBORN, Walter Gerald – Woodston, Peterborough. Trooper 6294215, 5th Royal Tank Regiment, Royal Armoured Corps. Died, aged 30, on the 29th November 1942. Next of kin not known. Buried in the Tobruk War Cemetery, Libya. Grave 1.F.8.

HENSON, George William Thomas – Private 6100261, 6th Queens Own Royal West Kent Regiment. Died, aged 22, on the 30th November 1942. The son of William and Phoebe Henson of New Fletton, Peterborough. No known grave he is commemorated on the Medjez-el-bab Memorial. Face 26.

REGAN, Charles – 58 Garton End Road, Peterborough. Aircraftman 2nd Class 1079339, Royal Air Force Volunteer Reserve. Died, aged 22, on the 1st December 1942 in a Japanese prisoner of war camp. The son of John and Elizabeth Regan of Peterborough. Buried in Yokohama War Cemetery, Japan. Grave Sec. C.C.4.

JOHNSON, Edward Ellis – Eastfield Road, Peterborough. Lieutenant 226244, Coast Regiment, Royal Artillery. Died, aged 25, on the 7th December 1942. Believed lost at sea. The son of William and Ethel Johnson of Peterborough. No known grave, he is commemorated on the Brookwood Memorial, Surrey. Panel 2, Column 2.

HODGKINSON, Edward – Peterborough. Engine Room Artificer 4th Class C/MX 62562, HMS Partridge, Royal Navy. Died, aged 23, on the 18th December 1942 when HMS Partridge, on an anti – submarine sweep with Force 'H' was hit by one torpedo from U-565 and sank west of Oran, Algeria. Three officers and thirty - five ratings were lost. The son of Leonard and Mary Hodgkinson of Peterborough. No known grave he is commemorated on the Chatham Naval Memorial, Panel 60, Column 2.

O'DELL, Austin Roy – Flight Sergeant (Air Gunner) R/101932, 428 Squadron, Royal Canadian Air Force. Died, aged 21, on the 20th December 1942. He was a crew member in a Halifax, Serial No DT570 of 76 Squadron that took off from Linton-on-Ouse. The cause of loss was not established. The plane crashed near Weeze, 6 km from Goch. All seven crew members died. The son of Mr and Mrs Charles O'Dell and the husband of Annie O'Dell of Dogsthorpe, Peterborough. Buried in the Reichswald War Cemetery, Germany. Grave 2.G.9.

CUFFE, Eric Edward George – 9 School Place, Peterborough. Private 5890848, 5th Northamptonshire Regiment. Died, aged 20, on the 24th December 1942. The son of Reginald and Mildred Cuffe of Shaftesbury, Dorsetshire. Buried in the Medjez-El- Bab War Cemetery, Tunisia. Grave 18.C.5.

1943

Two More Wounded

The January 1st edition of the 'Standard' began where it left off the previous year, with another list of men. This time they were killed and wounded from the area. There were two men from Peterborough on the list who had been wounded:

Private P.S. Swiffen, Northamptonshire Regiment, 28, Fulham Road, Peterborough, son of Mr. W.E. Swiffen, coal merchant, New Road, Woodston, Peterborough, with whom he was in business before the war. Private Swiffen was mobilised with the Territorials in 1939, and was safely evacuated from Dunkirk after serving in France. Private Swiffen would find his way to a hospital in Scotland before the end of the month where it would be recorded that he was suffering from wounds to the head, face, left arm and hand, right hand and left thigh.

Private C. Gayler, Northamptonshire Regiment, 32, St. James's Avenue, Peterborough, was the youngest son of Mr. R. Gayler, 1, Parliament Street, Peterborough. Private Gayler was formerly at Messrs. Shaw and Allen's tannery, Fengate, Peterborough, and was in the Territorials for more than three years.

The lists went on; on January 8th RQMS Gerald Beardsall, Northamptonshire Regiment, of 109, Granville Street, Peterborough, was reported as being in hospital in North Africa suffering from a broken arm among other injuries. An accountant in civil life, he had joined the Northamptonshire Territorials a few years before the war and had served in France and was evacuated from Dunkirk. His wife received a letter from him on December 24th giving details of his recent injuries. RQMS Beardsall would have six more months to live.

Someone who had most certainly been killed was Assistant Steward, George Albert Meredith, SS REYNOLDS, Mercantile Marine, who was now being reported in the 'Standard' as missing at sea. He was the only son of Mr. and Mrs. G. Meredith, 177, Star Road, Peterborough. Aged 19 he was formerly at Peter Brotherhood's, and had joined the Merchant Navy some fifteen months earlier. In December 1942 his employers had written that his ship had been missing for some time, and that there was no news of the crew. Just before Christmas a further letter was received, stating that there was still no news. Steward Meredith was an old boy of Brook Street School, and also a member of the drum and fife band of the 5th Northamptonshire Territorials.

At 17.18 hours on 31 Oct, 1942, the unescorted SS REYNOLDS was hit by two torpedoes from U-504 about 210 miles east of Durban. She was hit amidships and in the stern and capsized and sank within seconds. The ship was en route from Durban to India with general cargo. No survivors were ever found.

Widespread regret was reported on January 15th on the death in Tidmouth Military Hospital of Corporal Denis John Urwin, 2nd Glider Pilot's Regiment, Army Air Corps, son of Edwin George and Kathleen Urwin, of 106, Broadway, Peterborough; and husband of Vera May Urwin, of Longthorpe, Peterborough. Aged 25 years old, he had died of injuries received in the course of war service.

Educated at Deacon's school, before the war he had been garage proprietor at Longthorpe, and was in the Territorial Artillery before war broke out. Keen on games he was a cricketer with his school and with the Town Club, he also played in Army matches. He was also a very successful table tennis player locally, twice

279

winning the local singles championship. With his wife he won the mixed doubles championship in 1938-39. They had similar success in the Spalding League. He left a wife and small son aged nearly two, and is buried in St. Botolph's Churchyard, Longthorpe.

Pilot Officer Neil Fairbairn Home

P/O Fairbairn, of 15, St. Mark's Street, Peterborough, was now home on leave after two year's service in Canada. Formerly a sergeant in the pay accounts department, he entered the Royal Canadian Air Force Navigation School at London, Ontario, and graduated as an air navigator in early December, receiving his wings and commission at that time. In recognition of having gained first place in his class he was presented with a bronze trophy.

Later promoted, Flying Officer Fairbairn, 50478, Bomber Command, 622 Squadron, Royal Air Force, died on the 25th April, 1944, aged 21. He was a Navigator in Avro Lancaster Mk I, Serial No ME693, code letters GI-F, which took off from Mildenhall at 22:10hrs to attack Karlsruhe and failed to return, all seven crew were killed. He is buried in Rheinberg War Cemetery, Germany

Youths Register for Service

On Saturday 9th January, 301 youths born between 1st October, 1924, and 31st March, 1925, registered at the Employment Exchange. Of these, 106 stated a preference for the Army, 95 for the RAF (flying and ground crew), and 93 for the Navy or Marines. Applications were made for deferment of call-up on behalf of 7 boys still at school,

More Casualties in North Africa

1943 had started off badly, with a never ending list of casualties both wounded, killed and missing being reported with each issue of the 'Standard.'

Private J.A. Parkinson, Northamptonshire Regiment, of 18, Pipe Lane, Peterborough, was now reported wounded in North Africa. He was the youngest son of Mr. and Mrs. W. Parkinson, 1, Silver Street, Fletton, Peterborough, and was married. Before the war he had been employed by the Co-operative Society in their dairy department.

Private Langley Lane, Northamptonshire Regiment, fourth son of Mr. and Mrs. E. Lane, Milton Street, Peterborough, who was married and lived at 88, London Road, Peterborough, was now reported missing in North Africa since 24th December. A Territorial, he served in France and was evacuated from Dunkirk. His brother was missing in the Far East. News would be received at the beginning of February that Private Lane was a prisoner of war at Stalag 9c, in Germany.

Gunner A. Dolby, Royal Artillery, eldest son of Mr. and Mrs. G.E. Dolby, 7, Hereward Road, Peterborough, was now reported wounded in North Africa on January 13th. His youngest brother, Leslie, was a prisoner of war in the Far East after the fall of Singapore, which is where he would die on the 25th June that year.

Lance Corporal Thomas C. Dickens, youngest son of Mr. and Mrs. J.W. Dickens, 18, Wellington Street, Peterborough, had been posted as missing in Libya towards the end of 1942, and still no more news had been forthcoming. Like his brother, Private A. Dickens, who was in India, he had served in France in 1940, and came home safely through the Dunkirk evacuation.

Sergeant Pilot (Len) Langdale Francis Simpson, Royal Air Force Volunteer Reserve, eldest son of Mr. and Mrs. J.W. Simpson, 29, Hunting Avenue, Woodston, Peterborough, was now reported as having been killed on active service. His parents received a telegram on the night of Wednesday 27th January, which read, "Deeply regret to inform you your son lost his life on Wednesday, Jan. 27th." Sgt. Pilot Simpson would have been 21 in May. He was home on leave just before Christmas, when his engagement was announced to Miss Beryl Elliott, of Burmer Road, Peterborough, He returned from Canada the previous August, having gained his wings. He was formerly a clerk on the LNER, and is buried in Old Fletton Cemetery, Peterborough.

Lance Sergeant William Layton, 774560, 5th Battalion, Northamptonshire Regiment, only son of Mrs. Layton, 25, Flag Fen Road, Peterborough, was now reported severely wounded in the left side of the chest, in action in North Africa. He had been working as a plasterer in Ireland before the war broke out, and being on reserve, was recalled to the Colours. He fought in France and took part in the withdrawal to Dunkirk. L/S Layton would recover from his injuries but would lose his life, aged 38, fighting in Italy on the 30th October, 1943. He is buried in Cassino War Cemetery.

Wings for Victory
It was announced at the end of January that the Wings for Victory campaign in the city would commence on May 6th. The target would be £480,000, the cost of a squadron of Lancasters. On Tuesday 19th January, the Soke Savings Committee stated that this was the highest objective that Peterborough had ever set itself.

Mr. A. Tibbitts, Deputy Regional Commissioner, Lincoln, said Peterborough had done remarkable things in the savings movement. It held a top position in the area for street groups' efforts and for selling centre results. He hoped Peterborough would be able to provide sufficient to buy a squadron of Lancasters. If Peterborough gained its target it would be granted Victory Wings, in the form of a plaque, and the committee could present to the Air Ministry special log books recording the operations of aircraft provided.

Following the Tanks for Attack campaign, Peterborough had been allocated seven tanks. One was to be named 'Peterborough W.V.S. Street Groups,' another 'Peterborough Schools Groups,' and the remaining five 'Soke and City of Peterborough Savings Groups.'

The secretary (Mr. Frank Smith) reported that savings in the area in 1940 were £1,262,000, in 1941 £1,642,700, and in 1942 £1,237,154. The 1940 figure included £450,000 for War Weapons Week, and 1941 £525,000 for Warships Week. Since the beginning of the campaign the Soke had raised £4,141,707. W.V.S. Street Groups had in 18 months subscribed £115,995, a remarkable effort.

The secretary also read a letter of thanks from the Commander of the submarine P512 for the third parcel of magazines and books.

Fatal Fall
An inquest was held at the Peterborough Memorial Hospital on Friday 22nd January, 1943, into the death of Thomas Hayes, aged 62, of 16, Monument Street, Peterborough. Mr. Hayes had fallen from the roof of a boiler house at the Newall Engineering Works at Fletton, on Sunday 17th. It was stated that he had gone up the fire-spotter's ladder on the bottom of which was a notice saying, "No unauthorised

person is allowed on this roof." Mrs. Mary Conway of Dublin identified the deceased, her stepfather. He had come to England on 4th September, 1942. Most of his life had been spent at sea as a stoker.

Mr. John Dupont, the plant engineer, said the deceased's duty was stoking in the boiler house and he had no authority to go onto the roof. If the firing was excessive there was a possibility of flames and sparks coming out of the chimneys and the deceased had been told to prevent this from happening. It was during the black-out hours that the incident occurred but it was not necessary to go onto the roof to look for sparks as they could be clearly seen from the yard.

Henry Stocks, 19, St. Margaret's Road, Old Fletton, a roof spotter at the works, said he was in the crow's nest roof spotting on the Sunday at about 7am and had seen the deceased lying in the yard. The deceased had come on to the roof to see him at about 4 minutes to 7 and he had seen him twice before on the roof. Ernest Davey, of 250, Clarence Road, Peterborough, also a roof spotter, said he had also seen the deceased on the roof before. P.C. Overton said the distance from the roof to the ground was 19ft 10ins. From the mark of a shoe on part of the guttering it appeared that the deceased had fallen from the roof.

Thomas Hayes' body was taken back to his previous home in Dublin where he was buried.

Missing at Sea

Lieutenant Edward Ellis Johnson, 226244, 456 Coastal Regiment, Royal Artillery, eldest son of Mr. William and Mrs. Ethel Johnson, 169, Eastfield Road, Peterborough, was reported missing at sea. His father, who was chief clerk in the Gas Company's office, received official notification on January 9th that his son was missing.

Lieutenant Johnson was articled for five years to Mr. Norman B. Hart, BA, LL.B, FSAA, a partner in the firm of Stephenson, Smart and Co., accountants. Afterwards he became an audit assistant at the firm's Peterborough office, and he was there until January 1940, when he joined the RASC. On receiving a commission he was transferred to the Royal Artillery. While he was with Stephenson, Smart and Co. he passed the intermediate examination of the Society of Incorporated Accountants and Auditors. He was studying for the final examination when he was called-up. Lt. Johnson is officially recorded as being lost at sea on the 7th December 1942, aged 25, and is commemorated on the Brookwood Memorial, Surrey.

Another city man missing at sea was Ordinary Seaman George William Peet, C/JX 317771, HMS WELSHMAN, Royal Navy. He was the elder son of Mr. Sidney Baden Peet, and Mrs. Millicent Peet, of 66, Padholme Road, Peterborough. On Monday 8th February, he was reported in a letter from the Admiralty as missing, and it was stated that it was feared there was no hope of him being alive. Mrs. Peet had only received a letter from her son on Saturday 6th February, dated January 28th. Seaman Peet, who was 20 years old, had formerly lived with his parents at Eye. He had first worked in the brickyards, but just before joining the Navy was with the LMSR, qualifying as a fireman. In the Navy he had lately been serving on a minelayer. His younger brother, who was also in the Navy, was now home on leave.

At 17.45 hours on the 1st of February, 1943, U-617 fired a spread of four torpedoes at a vessel identified as a cruiser of the Dido class and observed two hits and a boiler explosion. At 17.55 hours, the ship capsized and sank by the stern after two hours. The victim was the minelayer HMS WELSHMAN (M 84) which sank 35 miles east-northeast off Tobruk, Libya. Nine officers and 139 ratings were lost, also an unknown number of military passengers (among them two civilians and four aircrew members that had been badly burnt in a plane crash on Malta). Only a few survivors were rescued by HMS TETCOTT (L 99) and HMS BELVOIR (L 32). Seaman Peet is commemorated on the Chatham Naval Memorial, Kent.

Another casualty reported at this time was a soldier, Private Eric Edward George Cuffe, 5890848, 5th Battalion, Northamptonshire Regiment, son of Mr. Reginald Albert and Mrs. Mildred Dorothy Cuffe, of Shaftsbury, Dorset, and grandson of Mrs. Mace, 9, School Place, Peterborough, was now reported as killed in action in North Africa on the 24th December, 1942. Aged 21, Private Cuffe had been brought up by his grandmother, who had received greetings from him in a cablegram on 12th January. He is buried in the Medjez-El-Bab War Cemetery, Tunisia.

News of Prisoners

Two city men were now reported as being prisoners of war in Japanese hands. CSM Alec Porter, Argyle and Sutherland Highlanders, was brother of Mr. William (Jock) Porter, licensee of the Elephant and Castle public house, and old Peterborough United footballer. CSM Porter was reported missing after the gallant rearguard action in Malaya.

Bombardier Harry Neave, 336 Battery, 135 Field Regiment, Royal Artillery, was the son of Mrs. Neave, of School Place, Peterborough, who received the official information from the War Office. Bombardier Neave had previously been reported missing in Malaya, but it was now stated he was a prisoner of war in Japanese hands in a camp in Malaya.

The trials and tribulations ahead of CSM Porter and Bdr. Neave in Japanese hands can only be imagined. Sometimes the Japanese treatment of Allied prisoners was beyond even imagination. Contrast this then with the contents of a letter sent home to his parents, Mr. and Mrs. F.C. Doughty, 23, Queens Walk, Fletton, Peterborough, by their son, Private Frank Edward Doughty, taken prisoner of war by the Germans during the Battle of Crete, and now residing in Stalag XVIII D. Private Doughty, who was in the Co-operative Society butchery department before the war wrote:

"We had a very good Christmas indeed. Christmas Day was fairly quiet. We went to the farms and had an excellent dinner – roast pork and chicken and lovely soup. On Boxing Day we had a lot better time. We had breakfast in the Laager – a very good one – and dinner at the farm, and when we came back we had a bit of fun singing and card playing. A little later we pulled the big table into the middle of the room, put two blankets on it, and set it for a late dinner. We cooked the tinned meat and the plum pudding in the copper and also cooked some apples. We set the table with two bottles of wine at each end, and all 11 of us sat down together. I received my fifth parcel five days before Christmas, so that was very good."

This incredible description of life in a German prisoner of war camp was written either by the luckiest POW in the war, or a son who did not want to worry his parents. We can only surmise that in the years of captivity and privation yet to come, Private Doughty would find things getting a whole lot tougher.

Two More Killed

Flight Sergeant Francis William Gurney, 932499, Royal Air Force Volunteer Reserve, aged 22, only son of Mr. and Mrs. W.H. Gurney, 5, Fletton Avenue,

Peterborough, was now reported killed on active service on 15th February, 1943. Flt/Sgt Gurney was a wireless operator/air gunner and before the war had been a clerk with Cadge and Coleman Ltd. He is buried in Old Fletton Cemetery.

Corporal Edward Cyril Kingsford, S/57362, Royal Army Service Corps, eldest son of the Rev. C.E.B. Kingsford and Mrs. Kingsford, of Rishworth School, Yorkshire, was now reported as having been killed in action at Hong Kong on the 22nd December, 1941, aged 23. His father was formerly a curate at St. John's church, Peterborough, and his mother was the daughter of Mr. G.A.S. Crick, of Thorpe Road. Corporal Kingsford joined the Army on leaving school, and volunteering for service in the Far East, was in Hong Kong before the war. His younger brother was a prisoner of war in Italy. Corporal Kingsford is commemorated on the Sai Wan Memorial, Hong Kong. Column 22.

Rifleman A.R. Holmes, Rifle Brigade, aged 27, the eldest son of Mr. and Mrs. A. Holmes, 680, Lincoln Road, Peterborough, was now reported as being a prisoner of war in Italy, having been captured 12 months earlier. He had been an Old Deaconian and before the war was an auditor at the London Brick Company.

Prisoner Broadcasts Message

In March, Bandsman L.H. Cousins, Northamptonshire Regiment, second son of Mr. and Mrs. Cousins, 44, Hunting Avenue, Peterborough, and whose wife and three children lived at 42, London Road, Peterborough, was reported as having been missing in North Africa since 19th February. Before the war he had been with the London Brick Company. A Territorial, he was mobilized in 1939, and, after the fighting in France, came safely through the Dunkirk evacuation.

Later that month, Bandsman Cousins was officially reported as being a prisoner of war in German hands in Tunis. In a broadcast message to his wife on Friday 19th March, he said:

"Hello, Hello, this is Bandsman L.W. Cousins of 42, London Road, Peterborough, calling his wife Beryl. Hello Beryl, darling, this is Laurie speaking, I am alright and a prisoner of war. The Germans are treating me very nice. There is nothing to worry about, I am ok. Keep smiling darling."

Also in March, news was received regarding Private James Houghton, Northamptonshire Regiment, husband of Mrs. Houghton of 128, Palmerston Road, Woodston, Peterborough. The news was that he had been wounded in action in North Africa on February 22nd and was now in hospital with both arms fractured.

Worse news was received regarding Lance Corporal Dennis Hammond, 2661704, 2nd Battalion, Coldstream Guards, son of Mr. William and Mrs. Annie Hammond, of Peterborough, and husband of Gladys Kathleen Hammond, also of Peterborough. Aged 27, L/Cpl Hammond was killed in action in North Africa on the 28th February, 1943, and is buried in the Medjez-El-Bab War Cemetery.

The wife of Gunner Frederick Sidebotham, 1827679, 48 Light. A.A. Regiment, Royal Artillery, of Peterborough, had not heard news of him for 14 months until Saturday 13th of March, 1943, when she heard that he was a prisoner of war in Japanese hands in Borneo. Before the war he had worked in the LNER Chief Accountant's office in Cowgate.

Gunner Sidebotham would suffer the many privations accorded to prisoners of war by their Japanese captors but would not return home. He died in a Japanese prisoner of war camp only a few months before the end of the war on the 28th April, 1945, aged 28, and is buried in Labuan War Cemetery, Malaysia.

Flight Sergeant Newman Missing

On 2nd April, 1943, a report appeared in the 'Standard' stating that Peterborough airman, Flight Sergeant Charles Hugh Newman, was now missing following a raid on Berlin on the night of Monday 29th March, in which 21 aircraft were lost.

Flt/Sgt Newman, who lived at 28, Eastgate, Peterborough, was a pilot with 77 Squadron, Royal Air Force Volunteer Reserve. He was an Old Boy of King's School and the son of Mrs. A.E. Newman, and brother of Miss Phyllis Newman, a well-known contralto. In civil life he was a music salesman with Messrs. J. Claypole and Son., Bridge Street, and a member of the Choral and Orchestral Society.

He married Miss Dorothy Pick, formerly secretary to Mr. J.O. Ladds, general secretary to the Co-operative Society. Mrs. C.H. Newman's parents were Mr. W. Pick, Verger of St, John's church, and Mrs. Pick, 6, Kent Road, Peterborough. Flt/Sgt. Newman had a two month old baby and had been home for the christening on Sunday, 21st March, 1943.

On the Saturday night he had piloted a Halifax bomber, and this flight was his second over the German capital, bringing his number of operational trips close to fifty. Most of these had been over Germany, but he had also bombed Milan and other Italian targets. His first visit was on 17th January, the night before his wife's birthday. After his safe return from the raid on Saturday he gave an account of his experiences:

"At first I thought we were not going to see the city – the clouds were so thick all the way. Then, when we were almost on top of it, the clouds began to split up. It was just like looking down into a great arena, with Berlin in the middle. Just before we got into clear sky we saw the defences starting.

It looked just like those night films of raids. We watched other bombers – Halifaxes, Lancasters and Stirlings – going in and out in the starlight. I counted eight big cones of searchlights, with about eight beams in each. It was pretty exciting trying to dodge them. When we had bombed we could see straight lines of fire, as if marking out streets. Once I saw three Lancasters silhouetted below me against the fires of Berlin."

Flt/Sgt. Newman had been the pilot of Handley Page Halifax Mk II, Serial No JB842, code letters KN-E, which took off from Elvington at 22:06hrs to bomb Berlin. The aircraft was shot down in the early hours of Tuesday 30th March, 1943, and all seven crew were killed. Four are buried in Berlin, one in Denmark, and two are remembered at Runnymede. Flt/Sgt. Newman is buried in Berlin 1939-1945 War Cemetery.

"Calling Gibraltar"

On Tuesday 6th April, Mrs. Edward Redmore, 90, Wellington Street, Peterborough, had the pleasure of sending a message by wireless to her husband. Private Redmore had been in the Army for just over three years, and for ten months had been at Gibraltar. The talk was arranged in the programme "Calling Gibraltar" and Mrs. Redmore went to London to speak from the Criterion Theatre. She said:

"Hello Ned, Ruth speaking. Richard is fine dear; I would love you to see him. We are all waiting to see you here again soon, so keep smiling dear. All my love."

She took their little boy with her, a youngster of 18 months, but he declined to speak into the microphone. May the 18th was the third anniversary of Mr. and Mrs. Redmore's wedding and Mrs. Redmore hoped to hear that her husband had received her greeting. She was formerly Miss Ruth May Saberton.

Fire Duty in the Future

New fire prevention orders, due very soon, would state that men would cease to be liable for compulsory fire prevention duties, either at business premises, or in street parties, at age 63, and that women would cease to be liable at 45. Men volunteers would be able to carry on until 70 and women until 60.

No boy volunteers would be accepted below the age of 15, and no girl volunteers below 18. Boys between 15 and 16 would still be accepted as volunteers only with written consent of their parent or guardian, only at premises at which they worked or were taught, and only if the appropriate authority was satisfied that the boys were really needed.

More Missing

As April continued, news of more missing men was eagerly awaited by their families and friends.

Bombardier Alfred Jones, Royal Artillery, third son of Mrs. T. Biggin, 13, Eastleigh Road, Peterborough, and the late Mr. F. Jones, was now reported a prisoner of war in Japanese hands, interned at Taiwan Camp. Bombardier Jones had been with the London Brick Company before the war and had been missing since 15th February, 1942.

Gunner Bernard Redman, Royal Artillery, youngest son of Mrs. Redman and the late Mr. A. Redman, 'Allways' Thorpe Park Road, Peterborough, was reported as missing in North Africa since February. He had two brothers serving – Lance Corporal Jack Redman, of the Royal Tank Regiment, and Corporal Leslie Redman, RAF. Lance Corporal Redman was reported missing a year earlier but was rescued later during the advance from El Alamein.

Private J. Crofts, Cambridgeshire Regiment, Burton Street, Peterborough, was now reported as being a prisoner of war in Japanese hands in a camp in Malaya.

4,800 Clothing Books Stolen

Nearly 4,800 complete books of clothing coupons, some with supplementary coupons attached, and nearly 1,575 loose sheets of supplementary coupons, were stolen from the Food Office in Priestgate during the night of Monday 12th April.

On the same night the office of Mr. W.J. Adnitt, accountant, in New Road, Peterborough, was entered, and an unsuccessful attempt was made to open a safe. Marks on the windows indicated that the same instrument was used to force an entry in each case.

The Food Office was locked up at 8:30 on the Monday night and the discovery that there had been a burglary was made at around 7am the next morning. A first floor window at the rear had been forced open, and all the rooms had been ransacked. Steel filing cabinets were open, and in some cases the fronts had been wrenched off. Candlegrease, matches and burnt papers were found in all the offices.

A check soon revealed that the clothing coupon books and supplementary sheets were missing. £18 7s. 8d. in notes and silver, taken from cash boxes, and 40 half-crown savings stamps had also been taken.

Wings Week Exhibitions

It was now announced that Air Chief Marshall Sir Robert M. Brooke-Popham,

286

GCVO, KCB, DSO, AFC, would be the principal speaker for the opening of Wings Week at the Embassy, Peterborough, beginning the 6th of May. Among other activities the week would consist of many exhibitions, one staged by the RAF at the Corn Exchange. Model aircraft would be displayed at the Co-operative Hall with a portrait gallery of local men and women in the RAF, and photographs were being asked for.

Kings School was organising an exhibition illustrating the life and activities in the USSR and the instruction school for the RAF in Kings Street would be open. Another exhibition staged at the Mayor's Parlour, by bird artist Mr. Roland Green, a personal friend of Mr. Rowland Hill, manager of Barclays Bank.

Registration Surprise
So many more nurses and midwives than were expected registered under the State Registration Order on Saturday 10th April that the Peterborough Employment Exchange ran out of forms. The shortage was so marked that registration of nurses at the Memorial Hospital was deferred.

The total number who did register was 397, of these, 232 were employed in nursing or midwifery, or had been during the previous twelve months; 158 had nursing experience but had not practiced during the past year. The numbers far exceeded those expected, and postal registrations were yet to come in.

At the annual meeting in February of the Memorial Hospital governors, it was stated that the hospital had a matron and nursing staff of 64, of whom 17 were sisters and 46 nurses. This would bring the total to 462, without the postal registrations.

The women seemed eager to register, and although the majority wished to remain in Peterborough, quite a few stated that they did not mind where they were sent.

Bravery in Walpole Street
While playing with his little friends on the afternoon of Monday, 12th April, five year old Terence Barry Rose, of 431, Gladstone Street, Peterborough, was pushed into a static water basin and drowned. The basin was in a field at the corner of Walpole Street and Westwood Bridge.

At the inquest on the following Wednesday it was stated that the children Terence had been playing with had been traced, but they were so young that their evidence would be inadmissible in court.

It was said that there were hurdle sections fastened by wire to the main chain link fence around the tank which made it very easy to gain access. However, there was nothing more permanent that could have been devised considering the urgent need for getting fire pumps to the basin with the least possible delay.

The verdict was Accidental Death but the jury added a rider that some means of strengthening the existing fence should be found along with a method of securely fastening the gates.

Terence was the son of Mrs. Gwendoline Rose, an employee at the Westwood Works, and the late Mr. Isaac T. Rose, who had been a railway porter.

Mrs. Edith Winifred Glitheroe, 50, Walpole Street, a machine operator at Westwood Works said she had seen the children playing around the basin; they were very close to the water and seemed very young. She hurried to get to them and said one of the boys was standing on the edge of the tank with his back to the water when another boy gave him a playful push, the first boy threw up his arms and he fell backwards into the water. Mrs. Glitheroe ran into Walpole Street and stopped Partridge's coal lorry. Mr. Partridge and Edward Smith jumped out of the lorry and ran with her to the basin, by which time the other children had run away.

There was a lifebelt on the fence but it could not be used as the knot couldn't be untied. Although he was unable to swim, Edward Smith slid into the water and waded out towards the boy who was four or five yards out from the edge. The water was up to his neck by the time he reached the boy but he managed to grab hold of him and bring him to the bank where they started artificial respiration. An ambulance arrived twenty minutes later but the boy did not breathe again.

The Coroner stated: "I am sure the jury would wish me to say that this witness (Edward Smith) kept his head and performed a very gallant action." The jury heartily agreed. "On behalf of the widow I must say that I am satisfied that Smith did his utmost to save the little lad. It was extremely plucky to go into the water, not being able to swim, and not knowing the depth."

The Coroner ended by saying that the fencing was not very secure judging by pre-war standards, but unclimbable 10ft fences that would have been required were no longer obtainable. The fence complied with official requirements and was inspected regularly so it was doubtful whether one could say anyone was to blame for the accident. The chief problem was how to keep children away from something attractive to them, and he could imagine nothing more attractive than a pool of water.

More Casualties

Major G.O. Gauld, Royal Army Medical Corps, previously reported missing at Singapore was now reported as being a prisoner of war. Major Gauld had married the eldest daughter of Mrs. Tebbs, 189, Thorpe Road, Peterborough, a Squadron Officer in the WAAF.

Lance Sergeant Sidney Roland Ayres, Irish Guards, was now reported wounded in North Africa. He was the son of Mr. and Mrs. F. Ayres, of 45, North Street, Stanground, Peterborough. In civil life he had been a clerk with J.W. Barber Ltd., Builders, Stanground.

At the end of April 1943, it was announced that Sergeant Alan Smithdale, 1293011, 57 Squadron, Royal Air Force Volunteer Reserve, was missing from air operations over Germany. Sergeant Smithdale, a Wireless Operator/Air Gunner, was the eldest son of Mr. and Mrs. A.E. Smithdale, 11, Fulham Road, Peterborough. On 17th December 1942, he married Miss Christine Isherwood, of Salford, and before joining the Air Force he had been with J.P. Hall and Sons, Ltd. Sergeant Smithdale died on 20th April, 1943. He was in the crew of Avro Lancaster Mk I, Serial No ED770, which took off on that date at 21:44hrs from RAF Scampton to bomb the German town of Stettin. The aircraft was shot down and all seven crew were killed. Sergeant Smithdale is buried in Poznan Old Garrison Cemetery, Poland.

In Japanese Hands

On April 30th the 'Standard' announced the names of four city men who were now confirmed as being prisoners of war in Japanese hands. Better news than if they had been reported killed in action it is true; however, none of them survived the terrible treatment that they were subjected to in captivity.

Lance Corporal Philip Casburn, 7600231, 18th Divisional Provost Company,

Corps of Military Police, of 87, Grange Road, Peterborough, son of Montague and Catherine Casburn, died in a Japanese prisoner of war camp on the 9th of August, 1943, aged 32. Originally reported as being a prisoner of war in a Malayan camp, he is buried in Thanbyuzayat War Cemetery, Myanmar (Burma).

Lance Corporal Alec George Bussey, 5832504, 1st Battalion, Cambridgeshire Regiment, Suffolk Regiment, 86, South Street, Stanground, Peterborough, also reported a prisoner of war in Malaya, died on 12th September, 1944, and is commemorated on the Singapore Memorial, Singapore.

Private James Brown, 5830899, 5th Suffolk Regiment, the only son of Mr. and Mrs. J. Brown, of 67, Tower Street, Fletton, Peterborough, was now reported as being a prisoner of war in a camp in Taiwan. Missing since the fall of Singapore, he died on the 13th August, 1943, aged 24, and is buried in Sai Wan War Cemetery, Hong Kong.

Private Kenneth Church, 5827913, 1st Battalion, Cambridgeshire Regiment, Suffolk Regiment, husband of Winifred Church, 24, New Road, Woodston, Peterborough, was now reported as a prisoner of war in a camp in Malaya after having been missing at Singapore since February 1942. Before the war he had been with C.A. Barlow and Sons, and was captain of the Clarion Cycling Club and a member of Rob Roy Football Club. Private Church died in a Japanese prisoner of war camp on the 28th June, 1943, aged 23. He is commemorated on the Singapore Memorial, Singapore.

Easter 1943

The feature of the Easter weekend in Peterborough was the very large congregations at all churches and many of the men and women were in uniform. There were fewer weddings than in Easters pre-war, and many of the brides and grooms also wore uniform. Rail traffic was light, there were no complications and no Special trains were running.

Buses, however, were very busy, most passengers being carried into town in the afternoon and early evening in time for indoor entertainments. Easter always saw stage shows and films playing to capacity and Good Friday was a heavy day with houses full.

Twelve hundred people saw a team of League footballers, now resident in Peterborough, beat the Czechoslovakian Army XI 10-2 at London Road on Monday morning. In the afternoon, 400 people watched the City Police v Wardens and Fire Guards match, raising funds for the Merchant Navy Comforts Service.

City Prisoners Repatriated

On the 30th April it was reported that two Peterborough men were known to be among a number of British prisoners of war repatriated in exchange for Italian prisoners; they were Corporal George (Dick) Burroughs, Royal Army Service Corps, of 17, Harris Street, and Able Seaman John Frost, of 11, Mayor's Walk.

Corporal Burroughs was one of 450 men who reached England on the Good Friday in the ship SS NEWFOUNDLAND, and Mrs. Burroughs had received a telegram informing her that he would be arriving on that day. Cpl. Burroughs, who had been wounded and captured in the Middle East on 20th June, 1941, wrote in a letter that he was well and "getting very fat." He attributed this to the quantity of Italian macaroni he had eaten and added that he did not wish to see any more of it!

He confessed to his wife he escaped death by the skin of his teeth when all those with him had been killed. He had been in the Army for about two years and had been on NAAFI work. He was formerly with Mr. E. Chappell, grocer, Bridge Street, Peterborough, and was the son of Mrs. L. Burroughs, 52, Tower Street, Fletton, Peterborough. At present he was in hospital in the South of England and expected to be home in a few days.

The SS NEWFOUNDLAND, became the British hospital ship HMHS NEWFOUNDLAND shortly after this repatriation, and painted white with large red crosses along her side and deck she was duly sunk in the Mediterranean by German aircraft on 13th September, 1943. This was hardly a mistake as they had tried to sink her twice the day before. Thankfully there were only two patients on board, but six of the British nurses and all of the Medical Officers were killed. Another example to go with the murder of prisoners in Japanese camps of why the war was being fought.

The other prisoner to be repatriated was Able Seaman Frost, Royal Navy, who was the youngest son of Mr. and Mrs. J.A. Frost, 11, Mayor's Walk, Peterborough. Aged 19, AB Frost had been taken prisoner the previous September when his ship, HMS SIKH, was sunk off Tobruk. Educated at St. John's school, he was a member of the St. John's Scouts troop. He joined the Navy when he was 15. He was at Cairo when he wrote home and said he was well treated by the Italians but he had to work hard. All his letters were very cheerful.

Casualties Rise Again
Corporal Stanley Burbage, 5827909, 9th Battalion, Durham Light Infantry, youngest son of Mrs. E. Trowell, 15, Westwood Row, Peterborough, was now reported to be a prisoner of war in Italian hands. At around the time of the Italian surrender in 1943, Corporal Burbage must have been transferred into German hands as he would later die on the 18th January, 1944, aged 26, in a prisoner of war camp, and be buried in Klagenfurt War Cemetery, Austria. Before the war Corporal Burbage had been with the London Brick Company. Mrs. Trowell had four other sons in the Forces.

Lieutenant F.A. Goodenough, Green Howards, youngest son of Mr. and Mrs. A.J. Goodenough, 33, Glebe Road, Peterborough, was now reported to have been wounded in action in North Africa on April 6th. An old boy of Fletton Secondary School, he was in the offices of the National Deposit Friendly Society before he joined the Army. News had been received that he was making good progress.

Sergeant George William Goodman, Northamptonshire Regiment, eldest son of Mr. and Mrs. F. Goodman, 107, Bishop's Road, Peterborough, was reported missing, believed to be a prisoner of war on April 14th in North Africa. In the previous June he had married Miss Joyce Haddon, only daughter of Mr. and Mrs. A. Haddon, 30, Silverwood Road, Peterborough. Before the war he had been a printer with D.H. Stott and Sons. Sergeant Goodman would later be confirmed in June as being a prisoner of war in Campo 66, Italy.

Craftsman Cyril Ernest Parker, Royal Electrical and Mechanical Engineers, youngest son of Mr. and Mrs. E. Parker, 10, Allen Road, Peterborough, had now been placed on the seriously ill list whilst serving in the Indian theatre of war. His parents received a telegram from the War Office telling them of their son's condition. He was said to be suffering from face and chest burns and malaria. Towards the end of 1942 he was in hospital with a fractured pelvis, dysentery and malaria, and made a good recovery. He was formerly a motor mechanic with Mr. N.J.C. Donald, Lincoln Road East, Peterborough.

Private George Platt, Suffolk Regiment, was now reported a prisoner of war in a camp in Thailand. Only son of Mr. and Mrs. G.W. Platt, 21, Grange Road, Peterborough, before he joined the Army he was at the New England Loco sheds.

Gunner Bernard Redman, Royal Artillery, youngest son of Mrs. Redman and the late Mr. A. Redman, 'Allways' Thorpe Park Road, Peterborough, who was earlier reported missing in North Africa since February, was now confirmed as being a prisoner of war in Italy.

More Blackout Charges

Dorothy Wood, 14, Broadway Gardens, Peterborough, was summoned before the Peterborough Police Court on Wednesday 28th April, for permitting an unobscured light at 9.45 pm on April 15th. Special Constable A.J. Ball said there was a very vivid light from a bedroom at 10 o'clock. He asked to see the room and there was no blackout. Mrs. Wood said that she put the children to bed and left the window open as it was so hot. The children must have got up and put the light on (this they admitted). She was fined £2, the Chairman noting it was not long after blackout.

These minor infringements of the blackout went on all of the time, they were all caused by carelessness, probably brought about by the fact that the last air raid had been back in August 1942. There would be no more raids on the city for the rest of the war.

Evelyn May Hill, 91, Clarence Road, Peterborough, was summoned for a light in a building at 10.55 pm on April 14th. PC Hubble said he saw a bright light coming from the premises of Perkins Ltd. in Priestgate. This was a lamp burning in an unscreened window. Sergeant Ward said he was told by the defendant that she cleaned the office and she put the light on to do her work and had not put it out as was her usual custom. She was fined £3.

Home Guard is Three Years Old

On Sunday 9th May, local battalions of the Home Guard, in common with those all across the country, celebrated the third anniversary of the formation of the Home Guard, formerly the Local Defence Volunteers, in May 1940.

The City Battalion carried out a display of Home Guard training and weapons in King's School field which included bayonet fighting, Lewis guns, Smith guns, unarmed combat, Northover projectors, spigot mortars, Sten guns, foot drill and rifle drill. Specialist officers commanded teams demonstrating bombs, signalling, stretchers and first aid, camouflage and gas squads.

Units of the Soke Battalion carried out demonstrations at the following locations:
'A' Company, Longthorpe and Castor platoons were at Thorpe Park carrying out weapons and battle drill.
'B' Platoon, battle drill and weapons at Uffington, Barnack and Helpston.
'C' Platoon, demonstration of strength and weapons at Brown's field, Werrington. Including Dispersal: showing how 100 men can disappear; demonstration of camouflage, demonstration of battery of Northover projectors; Sten gunners, demonstration of light machine gun and spigot mortar teams, rifles, bayonet fighting and platoon attacks.
'D' Platoon, demonstration of all platoon weapons at the Dogsthorpe range.
'E' Platoon, demonstration of weapon firing, spigot mortar, grenade throwing, platoon in the attack, and bayonet fighting in Burghley Park.

'A' and 'C' Companies of the 1st Hunts Battalion combined for a display in the evening in the fields adjoining The Glen, between Fletton and Stanground.

Conscientious Objector to be Dismissed

On May 7th it was reported that Mr. R.E. Groom, a conscientious objector, who was a teacher at Walton Junior Mixed School, was to be dismissed by the City Education Committee because he declined to give an undertaking that in future he would carry out all instructions of the head teacher during school hours.

Mr. Groom was reported to have refused to obey an instruction to supervise a class preparing posters for the 'Wings for Victory Week' competition. The matter was put before the Schools Management Committee who presented to the Education Committee their recommendation that Mr. Groom be given one month's notice if he refused to sign the undertaking.

There was no reference to any decision yet taken by the Education Committee but at a meeting of the City Council, Mr. Swain said he believed there was a Government order that when a man was a genuine conscientious objector he was to be protected by law. This man was asked to do something which was, Mr. Swain understood, contrary to his convictions and beliefs, and he refused to do it. Was it fair to put an obstacle or test before a man who had convictions? Mr. Swain added that he was not saying he had sympathy with the man's attitude, but the Council was there to administer the law and see that it is carried into effect with proper conditions and treatment. He referred the decision back to the Education Committee for them to deal with further.

Paston Railings Removed

The removal of iron railings from the Paston Estate was spoken of at the City Council at the beginning of May. The Town Clerk had found that the railings had been removed without the knowledge of any official of the Council.

The Highways Committee authorized the Town Clerk to point out to the Ministry of Works and Planning that in the Committee's opinion, when an owner of railings objected to their removal, the objection should be looked into and the owner notified of the decision before the railings were removed.

Mr. Coates asked at the committee meeting if there was any instance of "ordinary individuals" having obtained permission from the Ministry to retain their gates or railings. The City Engineer said he knew of none. Mr. Coates said it seemed rather strange that some people were making such a fuss about their gates being taken, while others were having their own flesh and blood taken at 18 and had no opportunity of objecting.

The Engineer said the railings were scheduled to be removed and the contractors went to remove them. The owner got on the phone with a Corporation official and asked him to stay his hand. The official replied that the matter was out of the Corporation's hands, but that a Ministry official was coming on the following day. Unbeknown to the local official or the Government official, another Government official came on the scene and immediately instructed the contractors to remove the railings. The owner of the railings was very indignant at that.

'Wings for Victory Week' Target Smashed

On Friday 14th May, still with collections over the weekend ahead of them, Frank Smith, the City Treasurer announced that the city's target of £480,000, enough to purchase 12 Lancaster bombers, had been reached. "This does not mean we are going to shut up shop and take our ease," he said. "We have the weekend in hand; there are many promises still to harvest; and enthusiasm in all ranks is still soaring.

A situation like that must be turned to our country's account, so the Committee is now out for another £120,000 – the price of 12 Spitfires to serve as an escort for the Lancasters. This will make the City and Soke total £600,000. It is not a case of if we get the further £120,000; the Committee is going to get it."

"In this way we shall show in 'striking' fashion our gratitude to the RAF," was how Mr. Smith put it on the Thursday evening. "The most satisfactory aspect," he said, "is that small savers have rallied round wonderfully. A very big part of the great sum will be from small savings." Mr. Smith could not speak too highly of the work of the savings groups and their officers, calling them "The gallant 600." Another feature was the great success of the Savings Shop in Church Street. By the Wednesday night it had collected £34,000. The larger sums were contributed by the following organisations:

Royal Insurance Co.	£5,000
Liverpool, London and Globe Insurance Co.	£5,000
Joseph Farrow & Sons	£2,500
Crawley & Sons	£1,000
Mr. H.B. Hartley	£500
Mrs. H.B. Hartley	£500
General Accident Fire and Life Assurance Corporation	£500
Barclays Bank Ltd.	£15,000
Lloyds Bank	£15,000
Midland Bank	£15,000
National Provincial Bank	£15,000
Westminster Bank	£15,000
Peterborough Trustee Savings Bank	£20,000
Marks & Spencer	£1,000
Norwich Union Insurance	£2,500
Co-operative Insurance Co.	£10,000
Peterborough Building Society	£10,000
Pearl Insurance	£5,000
County Fire Office Ltd and Alliance Assurance Corporation	£2,500
Yorkshire Insurance Co. Ltd.	£2,000
Eagle Star Insurance Co. Ltd.	£2,500

The following gifts to the Wings fund also showed the generous spirit sweeping through the city:

Mrs. Wilkinson, Westwood Club, whist drive: £3 10s.

D. Northrop, from sale of eggs: £2 15s.

Mr. Anthony Payen, magic lantern show: £10 6s.

Mrs. Simms, concert, Eastholm School: £18 15s.

Mr. and Mrs. Lenton: £2.

Mr. Walter Smith and Bryan: £4. 9s. 6d.

Mrs. G.E. Cox: £2.18s.

'A Pensioner': £1.

Comb Out of Scrap Metal

The Ministry of Works drive for scrap metal visited Northamptonshire in the middle of May and was to last eleven or twelve weeks. The reason was that the United

States had long ceased to send scrap metal to the UK and therefore Britain had to depend entirely on her own resources. Steel from raid damaged buildings, hundreds of thousands of tons of iron from gates and railings, steel and iron from the demolition of derelict buildings, old plant and machinery, unwanted bridges, war relics such as guns, and many thousands of tons of scrap from farms and business yards found their way back to the foundries.

The Ministry of Works' team consisted entirely of women. There were eight locators under a section leader, with a press and publicity officer attached. The locators called on farmers, builders, merchants and anyone from whom quantities of metal, irrespective of the tonnage, and whether it was intended as a national gift or offered for sale, may be obtained and removed while the drive was on. The team would clear Northamptonshire area by area, and shift the dumps that had been lying around for some time.

Long Casualty Lists

The casualty lists containing information about men from Peterborough were now becoming longer and more frequent as indicated by those published on May 14th.

Sergeant R.E. Hemsworth, Royal Air Force, was now reported missing from an operational flight over Germany. Son of Mr. and Mrs. E.E. Hemsworth, of New England, Peterborough, he married Miss Lathey, daughter of Mr. and Mrs. C. Lathey, 656, Lincoln Road, Peterborough.

Sergeant George William Bines, 852698, 135 (The Hertfordshire Yeomanry) Field Regiment, Royal Artillery, eldest son of Mr. and Mrs. William Bines, 40, Westwood Street, Peterborough, was now reported as being a Japanese prisoner of war in a camp in Thailand. Originally reported missing after the fall of Singapore, he was formerly in the LNER Engineer's department, Westwood Street. Sergeant Bines would die on the 1st April 1944, aged 26, of dysentery and malaria in a Japanese prisoner of war camp in Thailand, and is buried in Chungkai War Cemetery, Thailand. Two of his brothers were also in the Forces – Gunner Edward Bines, Royal Artillery, and 1st Class Stoker Robert Bines, Royal Navy. A third, Private Reginald Bines, was in the City Battalion, Home Guard; while two more, Arthur and Roy, were Army Cadets.

Lance Sergeant R.A. Smith, Royal Artillery, 46, Shakespeare Avenue, Peterborough, was another now reported as being a prisoner of war in Japanese hands in a camp in Thailand.

Lance Corporal John William Frederick Hardy, Royal Armoured Corps, of 45, Gladstone Street, Peterborough, elder son of Mr. and Mrs. F. Hardy, 34, Scotney Street, Peterborough, was reported as being wounded in North Africa on April 21st. His wife had been informed that his wounds were on his right wrist, right thigh and left fore-finger. When Lance Corporal Hardy received his wounds, the driver of his tank, Trooper Kenneth Stimpson, of Eye, was killed. Lance Corporal Hardy was formerly a painter and decorator with the City Council.

Private Frederick Leslie Curtis, Northamptonshire Regiment, 141, Huntley Grove, Peterborough, was reported missing in North Africa since April 14th. Married with three children, Private Curtis was an old Territorial, and had served in France with the Northamptonshires. Before the war he had been with the London Brick Company at Eye Green. Mrs. Curtis had heard unofficially that her husband's name had been included in a list of prisoners in Italian hands, broadcast over Vatican Radio.

294

Gunner Lawrence William Ruff, Royal Artillery, youngest son of Mr. and Mrs. T. Ruff, 41, St. Paul's Road, Peterborough, was now reported as being a prisoner of war in Japanese hands. Before the war he had been a printer with Barron and Co., Bridge Street, Peterborough.

More bad news was published the following week on May 21st. Captain Anthony Emery, Northamptonshire Regiment, brother of the Mayoress of Peterborough and son-in-law of the Deputy Mayoress, was now believed to be a prisoner of war in Italy.

Reverend Rupert Godfrey, Chaplain to the Forces, second son of Rev. and Mrs. G. Godfrey of All Saint's Vicarage, Peterborough, was now reported as being a prisoner of war in Japanese hands. Rupert Godfrey left his parish of St George's in Birmingham to join the 48th Light Anti-Aircraft Regiment as chaplain, embarking for Singapore in 1941. When they reached the Far East his regiment was put ashore in Java and he was captured by the Japanese and imprisoned in Java and then Japan. He kept a diary before and after his capture and kept 25 sermons that he preached while chaplain at Zentsuji and Fukuoka POW camps. He recorded events in tiny script in a series of small notebooks from which he drew together his accounts after the war. He was to write of the deaths of many comrades and included such details as night-time air raid alerts, Red Cross supplies getting through, the cold from snow, illness, death and British officers viciously beaten for complaints about shortage of rations.

Sergeant Taylor, Royal Artillery, with the First Army in Tunisia, of 33, Belsize Avenue, Woodston, Peterborough, was reported wounded in North Africa. He had been a London Brick Company employee before the war and had 17 years as a Territorial.

Sergeant Sidney Tinkler, 1320307, Royal Air Force Volunteer Reserve, son of Mr. and Mrs. Tinkler, 174, Belsize Avenue, Woodston, Peterborough, was now reported missing following a raid on enemy territory. He had been a butcher before joining the RAFVR. Sergeant Tinkler was killed in action on 14th May, 1943, he had been a gunner in Short Stirling Mk I, Serial No R9242, code letters BU-O, which took off at 00:01hrs from Chedburgh to bomb Bochum. The aircraft was shot down by a night-fighter and crashed near Heerlen in Holland. Four of the crew were killed, and three became prisoners of war. Sergeant Tinkler is commemorated on the Runnymede Memorial, Surrey.

Corporal James Gordon Garn, 5831197, 1st Battalion, the Cambridgeshire Regiment, youngest son of Mr. and Mrs. R.F. Garn, 72, New Road, Peterborough, was now reported killed in action on the 9th February, 1942, before the fall of Singapore, he was 24 years old. Before the war he was with C. and J. Peck, Ltd., ironmongers, of Ely. Corporal Garn is buried in Kranji War Cemetery, Singapore.

Signaller Bruce C.P. Allen, Royal Corps of Signals, nephew of Mr. and Mrs. J.T. Goodley, of 13, Vergette Street, Peterborough, was now reported to be a prisoner of war in Japanese hands in a camp in Thailand. Before the war he had been a clerk with Messrs. Daking and Wright after leaving Deacon's School.

Trooper Arthur Thomas Greenaway, 5832623, 142nd Regiment, (7th Suffolks), Royal Armoured Corps, second son of Mrs. A. Tee, 14, Eastleigh Road, Peterborough, and the late Mr. F. Greenaway, was now reported killed in action in North Africa on April 24th, he was 29 years old. Before the war he was employed at the London Brick Company. Trooper Greenaway is buried in Medjez-El-Bab War Cemetery, Tunisia.

Bandsman Charles Harold Dewberry, Northamptonshire Regiment, of 1, Pipe Lane, Peterborough, was now reported missing in North Africa, believed to be a prisoner of war. He was the son of Mrs. B. Dewberry, of 9, Grace Close, Corby, and before the war had been with the London Brick Company.

Fusilier George Rusdale, third son of Mr. and Mrs. G. Rusdale, 71, High Street, Fletton, Peterborough, was now reported to be a prisoner of war in Italy. Aged 21, he was educated at Stanground, and until he joined the Army in April 1943, was employed by Messrs. Foster, Fruiterers, Broadway, Peterborough. He had also been a member of the Hunts Home Guard. His name was included in a list of prisoners broadcast by Vatican Radio on May 15th. Mr. and Mrs. Rusdale have two other sons in the Army.

Private Cyril W. Longfoot, Royal Norfolk Regiment, who was married, and the son of Mr. and Mrs. Longfoot, 29, George Street, Peterborough, was now reported as being a Japanese prisoner of war in a camp in Malaya. Before the war, Private Longfoot, who was 30 years old, was in the LNER Electrical Department.

Private Charles Knight, 5832683, 5th Suffolk Regiment, 30, South Street, Stanground, Peterborough, son of Mr. and Mrs. Knight of Fletton, Peterborough, was now reported as being a prisoner of war in Japanese hands. He had been well known in the Toc H, and was with Brown, Son and Co., of Peterborough before war broke out. Private Knight would die in the prison camp little more than two months later on 30th July, 1943, aged 29. He is buried in Thanbyuzayat War Cemetery, Myanmar (Burma).

Private Cyril Gray, of Orton Waterville was now reported as being a prisoner of war in Japanese hands in Malaya.

Postcards from Japanese Camps
Towards the end of May, Mrs. F.A. Bristow, of Broadway Gardens, Peterborough, received a postcard from her son, Captain Corby Bristow, who was a prisoner of war in Japanese hands. The card was believed to be the first to reach the district, it was printed, and the sender crossed out the words which were not applicable. Captain Bristow's message read: "Imperial Japanese Army. I am interned in Taiwan, My health is excellent. I am working for health ("pay" crossed out). Please see that you, the family and Phyllis are taken care. My love to you – Corby."

The card was addressed to Mrs. Bristow at Medehamsted, London Road, Peterborough, which indicated that he had not received any of his mother's letters as she had moved to Broadway Gardens more than a year earlier. Captain Bristow had been on the Thai border when the Japanese invaded and fought the length of Malaya before he was captured.

On Wednesday 19th May – the day before his 24th birthday – Mr. and Mrs. H. Palmer, 11, Princes Gardens, Peterborough, received a card from their son, Sapper Herbert R. Palmer, Royal Engineers, who was captured at Hong Kong at Christmas 1941, and was reported in August 1942 as being a prisoner of war. Sapper Palmer was a draughtsman at Brotherhood's before he joined the Army. The card he sent was headed: "Imperial Nipponese Army," and read, "I am interned in Osaka Prisoner of War Camp, Kobe sub-camp. My health is usual. I am working for pay. Please see that mother and father are taken care of. My love to you."

Jimmy the Donkey is Dead

It was announced on 21st May that Jimmy the Donkey was dead and had been interred in the Children's Corner at the town park. Mrs. Heath, his devoted owner and custodian, planned to erect a stone to his memory.

The story went that Jimmy was born in the trenches on the Somme in 1916 and "had a trace of the mule in his blood." He was brought to England with spare Army horses in 1919 and was in a lot purchased at Southampton by a Peterborough man. Coming to Peterborough market, Jimmy was auctioned, and although Sanger's Circus ran up his price, Mrs. Heath became the purchaser. Since then his chief missions in life were to amuse the children and to collect for the RSPCA and other good causes on many flag days. Children loved him and he raised large sums of money for charity. He died of senile decay, though he was by no means old for a donkey.

Wings for Victory Week Final Figure

The final figure for the City and Soke Wings for Victory Week was £617,245. This was easily the highest amount yet reached locally in a special savings effort. It worked out at £10 9s. 3d. per head of the population. The amount raised was equivalent to the cost of 12 Lancaster bombers and an escort of 27 Spitfire fighters.

Speaking at a meeting of the Soke Savings Committee at the Town Hall on 20th May, the Hon. Secretary, Mr. Frank Smith, said that three weeks ago he asked for £200,000 from savings groups and savings bank depositors. He thought he was asking the impossible, but small savers had actually contributed more than £420,000. It was through the efforts of the group secretaries that the target had been so comfortably surpassed and Mr. Smith doubted if any other town had so high a percentage of small savings. The fact that there were 1,000 new group members proved that the enthusiasm was infectious.

The industrial groups special mention was made of the splendid work of Perkins Diesels Ltd., whose group raised £32,000; of Baker Perkins with £30,254; Peter Brotherhood's with £15,021; and LNER with £6,000. "I dare not pick out any of the other groups because street, schools, shop and office groups have been without exception, miles above anything even I could have dared to ask, and have been simply grand," Mr. Smith added.

Tremendous work had been put in by the WVS, especially at head office and the savings shop. These "grand people" had worked at least 12 hours a day and had taken over £50,000 across the counter, mostly in very small sums. The savings shop was the only one in the region exclusively manned by a voluntary staff and no paid staff could have been more efficient. The Mayor, as chairman of the Soke Savings Committee, received a telegram of congratulations from Lord Kindersley, president of the National Savings Association. A similar message was received from the Chancellor of the Exchequer.

Casualty List

On the 28th May, another list of casualties appeared, the majority were men who were confirmed as prisoners of war but inevitably others were killed in action.

Sergeant Douglas W. Creevy, 1330741, 12 Squadron, Royal Air Force Volunteer Reserve, Bomber Command, eldest son of Mr. and Mrs. W. Creevy, 292, Dogsthorpe Road, Peterborough, was now reported missing from air operations over enemy territory. Sergeant Creevy, who had carried out his flying training in Canada, was an old Deaconian and before the war had been very interested in the Scout movement and Toc H. It would later be confirmed that Sergeant Creevy had been killed in action on 26th May, 1943, aged 22. He was an Air Bomber in Avro Lancaster Mk III, Serial No ED967; code letters PH-F, which took off from RAF Wickenby at 00:37hrs, to attack Dusseldorf. The aircraft crashed at Ratingen and all seven crew were killed. Sergeant Creevy is buried in Reichswald Forest War Cemetery, Germany.

Lance Sergeant Eric Knight, 5830969, 1st Battalion, Cambridgeshire Regiment, second son of Mr. and Mrs. F.C. Knight, 206, Lincoln Road, Walton, Peterborough, was now reported as being a Japanese prisoner of war in a camp in Malaya. Before the war he had worked at the Westwood Works. Lance Sergeant Knight would die in captivity later that year on 28th October, aged 25, and is buried in Chungkai War Cemetery, Thailand.

Corporal Charles William Palmer, Royal Norfolk Regiment, 55, Tower Street, New Fletton, Peterborough, had been missing since the fall of Singapore. He was now reported as being a Japanese prisoner of war in Malaya. Corporal Palmer was married with five children and before the outbreak of the war had worked for the local council.

Driver Douglas Walter Gray, Royal Engineers, eldest son of Mrs. Gray, 41, Norfolk Street, Peterborough, was also now reported as being a prisoner of war in Malaya. He had been with Mr. G. Gaunt, Butcher, Long Causeway, Peterborough, before joining the Army three years earlier. His wife was Miss Levine of Peterborough, and they had two children, aged 5 and 3.

Trooper William Edward Lucy, 5834702, 142nd Regiment (7th Suffolks), Royal Armoured Corps, only son of Mrs. and the late Mr. Lucy, was 30 years old and married. Before joining the Forces he was with Messrs. Elliot Bros., of Gladstone Street, Peterborough. Trooper Lucy had now been reported as having been killed in action in North Africa on 28th April, he is buried in Medjez-El-Bab War Cemetery, Tunisia.

Private Hector Macdonald Hart, Royal Norfolk Regiment, youngest son of Mr. and Mrs. B. Hart, 207, GNR Cottages, New England, Peterborough, was another now reported to be a prisoner of war in Malaya.

Private Thomas (Pat) Honeyball, 5828943, 5th Battalion, Suffolk Regiment, son of Mr. and Mrs. Alfred Honeyball, 138, Newark Avenue, Peterborough, was now reported as being a prisoner of war in a camp in Taiwan. Private Honeyball, who before the war was a printer with Mr. Hector Pickering, in Church Street, Peterborough, would not see the end of the war, instead he would die in a Japanese prisoner of war camp in Thailand and is buried in Yokohama War Cemetery, Japan.

More Lists in June

Sergeant Observer Ronald George Hands, Royal Air Force, of 92, Harris Street, Peterborough, was now reported as missing from an operational flight over enemy territory. No more news was forthcoming.

Sergeant R.E. Hemsworth, originally reported as missing, was now believed to be a prisoner of war in Germany. Sergeant Hemsworth's name had been heard included in a list of British prisoners of war given on the German wireless. His wife, Mrs. Vera Hemsworth, 656, Lincoln Road, Peterborough, had heard her husband's name read out but had not received any official news from the Air Ministry that he was a prisoner.

Gunner Donald Robinson, Royal Artillery, 48, Saxon Road, Peterborough, was now reported to be a prisoner of war in Japanese hands in Malaya. Married with two children, he was the son of Mrs. Mortimer of 30, Saxon Road. Before the war he had worked at Peter Brotherhood's Ltd. His father, Private John Robinson, had been killed during the First World War.

Private A.E. Butler, Northamptonshire Regiment, youngest son of Mr. and Mrs. L. Butler, 249, St. Paul's Road, Peterborough, was reported wounded in North Africa at around Christmas time and was now in a hospital in England. He was formerly a conductor with the Eastern Counties Omnibus Company.

Private Jack Nichols, Royal Norfolk Regiment, second son of Mr. Jonathan Nichols, 30, Celta Road, Peterborough, was now reported as being a Japanese prisoner of war in Malaya. Before he joined the Army three years earlier he had been with the London Brick Company. He had one brother serving in Scotland and another in the Middle East Forces.

Sergeant Eric Charles Pammenter, Royal Artillery, only son of Mr. and Mrs. Frederick Pammenter, 9, Cavendish Street, Peterborough, was another now reported to be a Japanese prisoner of war in Malaya. His wife and baby son lived at 16, St. Margaret's Place, and before the war he had been with Blood and Kendrick, Builders.

Corporal Henry Johnston Brown, 5883580, 2/5th Battalion, Leicestershire Regiment, 14, Walpole Street, Peterborough, was now reported missing believed wounded in North Africa. He used to work at the Westwood Works before the war and played in the Territorial Band and the PSA Orchestra. Corporal Brown died 22nd March, 1943, in North Africa, almost three months before the news that he was missing was published, and is commemorated on the Medjez-El-Bab Memorial, Tunisia.

Gunner Thomas Phillips, 1557762, 125th Anti-Tank Regiment, Royal Artillery, son of Mrs. Phillips, 137, Gladstone Street, Peterborough, was now reported as being a prisoner of the Japanese in Malaya. Before the war he had worked at the Fifty Shilling Tailors in Bridge Street. Gunner Phillips died 12th September, 1944, aged 28, as a Japanese prisoner of war and is commemorated on the Singapore Memorial, Singapore.

Private Bernard Westwood, 5835556, 4th Battalion, Suffolk Regiment, of 26, Cobden Street, Peterborough, was another man on a seemingly never ending list of Japanese prisoners of war. Private Westwood was married with two children, Barbara and Bryan, and before the war had been at the Westwood Works, playing regularly for the football team. He died on 27th December, 1944, aged 28, in a Japanese prisoner of war camp and is buried in Yokohama War Cemetery, Japan.

Airman's Death in Combat
The death on active service of Sergeant, Wireless Operator/Air Gunner, Philip George Spreckley, 51 Squadron, Royal Air Force Volunteer Reserve, was now announced. Just turned 19 years old, he was the elder son of soldier Mr. T.G. Spreckley, DCM, an Old Contemptible and a Lieutenant in the City Battalion, Home Guard. The family lived at 11, New Road, Peterborough.

Sergeant Spreckley was one of the crew of a Halifax bomber aircraft on which he was mortally wounded and another crew member was badly injured. The body was brought back to Peterborough on Wednesday 16th June and was placed before the high altar of All Souls' Catholic Church ready for the last rites and the homage of his friends and fellow servicemen.

Sergeant Spreckley had been a scholar of All Souls' School where he had been a very able pupil. He had been a Scout and had several trophies indicating his skill as a boxer. A leading figure in play productions at school, he kept up his interest in later years as a Playgoer, and occasionally as a Court Player at the Empire. He also made an appearance at the Little Theatre, Citizen House, Bath.

He and his brother and sisters were Chums of Auntie Rhona (a newspaper club for children) and the 'Standard' had many records of their efforts on behalf of good causes. "One can recall," a report stated, "seeing two little boys in white sailor suits, collecting for the lifeboats, and with other members of the family helping on other flag days." He was an alter server at his church and a guild member. On leaving school he worked for a short time in Messrs. Fox and Vergette's office.

He had a passion for flying and when only eleven years old he had several flights in the Gorlestone British Empire Jubilee Air Display, one of which was awarded free for his skill in estimating height. On its formation he joined the 114 Squadron of the Air Cadet Training Corps. He had also been in the Messenger Service at the Town Hall ARP centre, and he had enrolled in the City Home Guard on reaching the required age, serving in 'A' Company under Major Hassall.

He eventually joined the RAFVR and in September 1942, completed his service training and passed out as a Sergeant Wireless Operator/Air Gunner. Although his time in the service had been brief, he had already completed 20 operational flights. He had been home recently on 48 hours leave and returned to duty only a few days before his death.

What the newspaper report did not describe were the circumstances of Sergeant Spreckley's death. He was part of the crew of Handley Page Halifax Mk II, Serial No DT742, code letters MH-Y, which took off on 11th June, at 23:25hrs from RAF Snaith to attack Dusseldorf. The aircraft returned safely until it was hit and shot down on the 12th June by anti-aircraft fire from a British convoy in the North Sea, roughly 10 miles north east of Sheringham, Norfolk. The crew was rescued by lifeboat but Sergeant Spreckley died and another man was injured. Philip Spreckley is buried in Peterborough (Eastfield) Cemetery.

Casualties Increase

Sergeant William Alexander (Alec) Underwood, Indian Army Ordnance Corps, eldest son of Mr. and Mrs. A. Underwood, Aboyne Lodge, Palmerston Road, Woodston, Peterborough, was another on the list of men confirmed as being Japanese prisoners of war. Born in Ireland, he came to Peterborough where he worked for the Newall Engineering Company. On the outbreak of the war he was called up to the Peterborough Battery in Lincoln Road, eventually being transferred to the Indian Army. He was at Singapore from October 1940 until its fall in the following February, when he was posted missing.

Corporal Edgar George Bellars, Reconnaissance Corps, 9, Muswell Road, Peterborough, had now been reported as seriously ill in hospital with a compound fracture of the right femur after being wounded in action in North Africa. He was the son of Mr. and Mrs. Bellars, 243, Gladstone Street, Peterborough, and his wife was Miss Churchill. He was at the Co-operative Society Dairy before he joined the Army at the outbreak of the war, and came safely through the evacuation from Dunkirk.

Private Eric Edward Clarke, 4867365, 2nd Battalion, Bedfordshire and Hertfordshire Regiment, second son of Mr. and Mrs. Arthur Clarke, 48, Westfield

Road, Peterborough, was now reported killed in action in North Africa on 6th May, aged 20. Before the war he had been with the London Brick Company. His father was in the Corps of Military Police, his elder brother, Private Arthur Clarke, was in the Durham Light Infantry in India, and another brother, Private Roy Clarke, was in the Royal Electrical and Mechanical Engineers. Private Clarke is buried in Massicault War Cemetery, Tunisia.

Gunner Donald Harvey Spires, Royal Artillery, The Bakery, New England, Peterborough, was another man now reported as a Japanese prisoner of war in Malaya. He was wounded in January 1942 and was reported missing after the fall of Singapore the following month. He was the eldest son of Mr. and Mrs. Harvey Spires, The Cedars, Dogsthorpe Road, Peterborough, and was formerly a confectioner in his father's business. His wife was Miss Winifred Ground of Spalding.

Private Walter Leslie Munton, 5831528, 2/5th The Queen's Royal Regiment (West Surrey), Old Fletton, Peterborough, was now confirmed as having died of wounds on 22nd May, 1943, aged 27, whilst on active service with the Middle East Forces. He was married and the son of Mrs. A. Munton, of Station Road, Nassington. Before the war he had been with Messrs. George Mason Ltd., grocers, Westgate, Peterborough. Private Munton is buried in Enfidaville War Cemetery, Tunisia.

Sergeant Edgar (Bob) Cadmore, 1331075, 76 Squadron, Royal Air Force Volunteer Reserve, youngest son of Mr. and Mrs. S.C. Cadmore, 234, Gladstone Street, Peterborough, was now reported missing after operations over enemy territory. Sergeant Cadmore had volunteered for flying duties in the RAF at the end of 1940, and passed out as a Sergeant Air Gunner around the middle of 1942. Since then he had taken part in many operational flights. Before he joined the RAF he had been in the Co-operative Society's grocery department. Sergeant Cadmore would later be confirmed as having been killed in action on 12th June, 1943, aged 21, and is buried in Reichswald Forest War Cemetery, Germany. He was a Gunner in Handley Page Halifax Mk V Serial No DK200, code letters MP-L, which took off at 22:54hrs from Linton-on-Ouse to bomb Dusseldorf. The aircraft crashed at Scherlebeck near Recklinghausen. Two others in the crew were killed and four became prisoners of war.

Sergeant Cyril Frederick Broughton, 5886089, 4th Regiment, Reconnaissance Corps, Royal Armoured Corps, 516, Gladstone Street, Peterborough, husband of Miss Maisie Gaff, and son of Mr. and Mrs. Frederick Broughton who lived next door, was now reported as having been killed in action in North Africa on 6th May, 1943. A volunteer for the Northamptonshire Regiment, he was transferred to the Reconnaissance Corps after the capitulation of France. Before the war he was in the Co-operative Society's grocery department at Belham Road, Peterborough. Sergeant Broughton is buried in Massicault War Cemetery, Tunisia.

Private Don Poole, Cambridgeshire Regiment, only son of Mr. and Mrs. P.J. Poole, 171, High Street, Fletton, Peterborough, was another man now reported to be a Japanese prisoner of war. No official notification had been received from the War Office, but Mr. and Mrs. Poole received a postcard from him on Thursday 24th June. Before joining the Army he helped his father in his hairdressing business.

Home from Malta
Royal Navy Telegraphist, Ronald Laxton, youngest son of Mr. and Mrs. T.W.

Laxton, 14, Glebe Road, Peterborough, came home at the beginning of July after service in Egypt, Palestine and South Africa. Previously he spent eight months in Malta, from October, 1941, to June, 1942.

Tel. Laxton said that he was in Malta during the most severe bombing. "It was the most bombed place on earth," he said, "Tobruk was second and we kept records of which had the most raids. The anti-aircraft barrage was terrific. For three months we had an average of six big raids a day. The air raid shelters are the best in the world, cut in the sandstone rock for which Malta is famous. We should hand the laurels to the gunners at Malta, the ships in the harbour, and the RAF fighters who, although outnumbered and seemingly fighting a losing battle, won through."

Asked about the Maltese people, Tel. Laxton said, "They struck me as being very religious, devout Roman Catholics. They were very cheerful and friendly." He mentioned the cowardly behaviour of Italians there. "They would completely lose their heads and start screaming during the raids," he said.

Tel. Laxton joined the Navy three years previously and before then was at the College of St. Mark and St. John, Chelsea. He is an Old Petriburgian (former pupil of King's School, Peterborough), and a member of the Town Cricket Club and the Operatic Society.

Home Guard Muster

'B' Company, 1st Hunts. Battalion, Home Guard (Company Commander Major Maurice Garrett), held a mustering exercise on the last weekend of June. On the Saturday afternoon men were called from their homes and gardens – one from a cinema – the final muster, after allowing for sickness, amounted to nearly 100 per cent.

Guards were posted, observation posts manned, patrols operated by day and night, and the whole of the administration as well as the operational role of the company was practiced. Each platoon accepted responsibility for cooking its own meals and it was said that samples of the evening meal tasted by inspecting officers made them regret that they had arrived after the meal had been served.

Visitors included the Battalion Commander (Colonel W.T. Cook) Sector Training Officer (Major Queckett), Battalion Second in Command (Major Charles Greenwood) and Battalion Quartermaster (Captain Gilboy). Great keenness was displayed by all ranks and valuable lessons were learned. The Battalion series of training camps was continuing, and 'B' and 'F' Companies would be under canvas for the following four weeks.

July Casualty Lists

Not specifically a casualty, Lieutenant R.A. Roberts, Reconnaissance Corps, youngest son of Mr. and Mrs. W. Roberts, 83, Park Road, Peterborough, was now reported as being in hospital suffering from fibrositis. Lt. Roberts had been in the Army almost four years and was in the evacuation from Dunkirk. He later joined the Commandos and took part in a raid on the Norwegian coast. His parents received a letter from him describing the thanksgiving service at Carthage. An old Deaconian (former pupil at Deacons School, Peterborough), he was formerly at the Post Office.

Sergeant Observer Ronald George Hands, RAF, of 92, Harris Street, Peterborough, earlier reported as missing on air operations, was now confirmed as being a prisoner of war. His wife heard him speak over the German wireless on 24th June. His message was, "Am quite ok, do not worry. Landed by parachute quite unharmed. Give Celia (his only child) my love. Hope it will not be long before I am with you again. Tell Dad I am ok."

As a postscript Sergeant Hands asked for his pipe and tobacco. Mrs. Hands had received over 100 letters and had numerous callers informing her of the broadcast. Sergeant Hands was reported missing five weeks previously after his 33rd operational flight. An Old Deaconian, he was a schoolteacher at Hayes, Middlesex, and formerly at Lincoln Road, Senior Boy's School.

Lance Bombardier Frederick Smith, 4, Burns Close, New England, Peterborough, was now confirmed as a Japanese prisoner of war. He was a gardener at the park before he joined the Army.

Private R.C. Butler, Royal Norfolk Regiment, 104, Walpole Street, Peterborough, was also now reported as being in Japanese hands. He was the fourth son of Mr. and Mrs. W. Butler, 121, Wellington Street, Peterborough. His wife had received a typewritten card from him saying that he was quite well. Before the war he had been in the Co-operative Society Dairy.

Another prisoner of war, this time in Italy, was Private William Arthur Stocks, son of Mr. and Mrs. F. Stocks, 22, Fengate Close, Peterborough. Private Stocks had originally been reported missing on 22nd February.

Private Leslie Preston, Royal Norfolk Regiment, 12, London Road, Fletton, Peterborough, had now written to his wife from a Japanese prisoner of war camp. He said, "Don't worry, I am quite safe and well." His parents lived at 33, St. Margaret's Road, Fletton, Peterborough. He married Miss Nelson, of 12, London Road, only five weeks before he embarked for the Far East.

Gave His Life to Save Village
It was reported on 9th July that in recognition of the gallantry of the pilot of a Lancaster bomber who gave his life in a successful effort to prevent his machine from crashing on a Huntingdonshire village, the villagers sent a donation to the RAF Benevolent Fund. Wartime restrictions prevented the publication of the name of the village but I can reveal it was Yaxley.

On the morning of the 4th March, 1943, Flying Officer Nebojsa Kujundzic and crew boarded Lancaster W4333 PM-B for a training flight from RAF Elsham Wolds. During this flight one of the Lancaster's engines caught fire causing serious damage and 'Neb' gave the order for his crew to bale out. All did so successfully. Flying Officer Kujundzic remained at the controls and the aircraft crashed near Peterborough. It is thought that he stayed with his aircraft to prevent it crashing onto houses in the area below. The aircraft crashed in an orchard at Yaxley near Peterborough. Flying Officer Kujundzic was sadly killed and is buried at Peterborough (Eastfield) Cemetery.

Nebojsa "Neb" Kujundzic was born in Belgrade, Yugoslavia, and came to England to study Engineering at Leeds University before the war. He spoke excellent English, was a talented musician and a popular student. In 1941 he was one of the first group of students to be trained at the newly formed Leeds University Air Squadron. On completion of his course he sailed for Florida in the USA to undertake further pilot training and returned to England in 1942, where he converted to bombers at Operational Training and Heavy Conversion Units. He was posted from 1656 HCU at RAF Lindholme to 103 Squadron at RAF Elsham Wolds on the 3rd March 1943. Tragically he was killed, aged 24, on the daylight cross country flight the next day.

303

More Prisoners

Gunner James Wright, Royal Artillery, 38, Cobden Street, Peterborough, was now reported as being a Japanese prisoner of war in Java. Before the war he had been in Messrs. Paten and Co.'s bottling stores in Mayor's Walk, Peterborough. No news had been heard from him since he was drafted to the Far East at the end of 1941.

Private Frederick Freemantle, Royal Norfolk Regiment, 102, Russell Street, Peterborough, was also now confirmed as a prisoner in Japanese hands.

Private G.L. Dolby, youngest son of Mr. and Mrs. Dolby, 7, Hereward Road, Peterborough, was now confirmed as a Japanese prisoner of war. Before the war he had been with Messrs. Ellis and Everard.

Trooper John Alfred Smart, Royal Tank Regiment, eldest son of Mr. and Mrs. Smart, 67, Clarence Road, Peterborough, was reported as being in hospital in North Africa. He was aged 33, and before he joined the Army he had been with the Eastern Counties Omnibus Company. He married Miss Anthony of Whittlesey and had a baby daughter.

Postcards from the Missing Begin to Arrive

It was now reported on 16th July that postcards just received from prisoners of war in Japanese hands had now brought good news to many Peterborough homes. Nothing had been heard of some of the men since they were reported missing 16 months earlier.

The cards had the recipient's name and address, along with some Japanese words on one side, and the message, in hand-written capital letters on the other. Only one of the cards carried a date, that of June, 1942, 13 months earlier, and it had to be assumed that much could have happened to the men since they had written their messages.

Captain John Neal, Royal Artillery, wrote that living conditions were good and that he was pleased to have had news of his son, whom he had not yet seen. He was the elder son of Mr. A. Marcus Neal, Chairman of Peter Brotherhood's, and husband of Miss May Walker, daughter of Dr. R. Alec Walker.

Captain Sam Egar, Royal Artillery, wrote, "Am well and doing a lot of gardening, agricultural lecturing, reading, climate not bad. Food, clothing, accommodation adequate. Remember me to all my friends. Lots of love, Sam." He was the only son of Mr. S.M. Egar, Melrose, Park Crescent.

Captain Douglas Viney, Royal Artillery, said, "I am very well and being well treated. Food and billets are good. My love to all." He was the younger son of Councillor A.W. Viney MBE, of Charnwood, Park Road.

Lieutenant Maurice Crick, Royal Artillery, said he was fit and well and hoped all at home were. He was the son of Mr. C.W. Crick, 101, Lincoln Road.

Lieutenant J. Brian Green, Royal Artillery, sent a message to his father, Canon Green, Rector of Fletton, "Unwounded and well. No illness at any time. Food and treatment alright."

Sergeant George William Bines, Royal Artillery, son of Mr. and Mrs. W. Bines, 40, Westwood Street, wrote, "My darling mother. I am a prisoner of war, but am fit and well. Food, clothing, accommodation are good. Hope you are well. Fondest love to all, George." Conditions changed rapidly as Sergeant Bines would die of dysentery and malaria in April 1944.

304

Lance Sergeant Beales, 5th Suffolk Regiment, 3, Keeton Road, wrote, "I am a prisoner of war. I am well treated and in good health. Please tell mother and folks at home. Love, Dick." He was the son of Mr. and Mrs. R. Beales, 92, Fulbridge Road.

Lance Bombardier William Baxter, Royal Artillery, 1, South View, Westwood Street, wrote to his wife, "I am safe and well. We are treated very well. No need to worry. Keep smiling. Love to all. Lots of love, Bill." He was the eldest son of Mr. and Mrs. W. Baxter, 285, Gladstone Street, and before the war had been a bricklayer with Messrs. Bagley and Cooper.

Gunner Francis Jack Fixter, Royal Artillery, 10, St. Mark's Street, wrote to his parents, Mr. and Mrs. F. Fixter, "I am a prisoner but safe and well, so do not worry. Always thinking of you and hoping you are well. Keep smiling. All my love, Jack." He had been a painter and decorator with Mr. L.S. Folker, Bright Street, Peterborough. Gunner Fixter's circumstances would change as he would die on the 31st July, 1943, aged 23, of Beri-Beri in a Japanese prisoner of war camp, Thailand. He is buried in Kanchanaburi War Cemetery, Thailand.

Gunner Kenneth William Wood, Royal Artillery, son of Mr. and Mrs. W. Wood, 146, Mountsteven Avenue, wrote, "Dear mother, I am in best of health and spirits. I received no injuries. I am getting well fed. I hope that Kath and Ted are happily married, and in the best of health. Love Ken." Gunner Wood was 22 years of age and had been a turner at Brotherhood's.

Gunner R.J. Bull, Royal Artillery, wrote to his parents, Mr. and Mrs. H. Bull, 18, Nicholls Avenue, "I am well and in good health. We are being well treated. The food is good and we have a canteen. I received no injuries in action. I hope you are all well. See you soon. Your loving son, Bob." Before the war he was a fitter at Baker Perkins where his father was employed.

Gunner J. Gilbert, Royal Artillery, wrote to his wife at 326, Longthorpe, "Dear wife: I am a prisoner of war, keeping fit and well. Hope you and all at home are the same. Love to you all. So please don't worry. From your loving husband, Jim."

Gunner L.W. Ruff, Royal Artillery, wrote to his parents, Mr. and Mrs. J.F. Ruff, 41, St. Paul's Road, saying he was well and cheerful and the food and accommodation were good. He added that they were not to worry.

Corporal Edward Alphonso Lane, 4th Suffolk Regiment, wrote to his wife at 47, Dogsthorpe Road, saying that he was well. He was the eldest son of Mr. and Mrs. E. Lane, of Milton Street.

Lance Corporal W.L. Sharpe, Army Catering Corps, attached Royal Artillery, told his parents, Mr. and Mrs. F. Sharpe, 95, New England, "I am quite well, and being well looked after. Hope all at home are well. No need to worry. Please let everybody know I am safe and sound."

Private Harold Peach, Cambridgeshire Regiment, only son of Mr. and Mrs. H. Peach, 206, Walpole Street, wrote, "Dear mum and dad. Hope you are both well. I am safe and well, and have had no illness. Remember me to Lottie and Perce and all at home. There is no need to worry. Love to you all. Harold." Before the war he had been employed in the plate shop at the Westwood Works.

Private William Alfred Tyler, 4th Suffolk Regiment, 23, Wood Street, wrote to his sister, Mrs. Broom, "Am a prisoner of war and in good health. Please inform all. Your loving brother, Alf." Before the war he had been a coalman with Messrs. Ellis and Everard Ltd. Private Tyler would be killed on the 21st September 1944, aged 24, on board a Japanese transport ship when it was sunk by aircraft from an American aircraft carrier.

Private John Dewberry, 197, Gladstone Street, wrote to his parents, Mr. and Mrs. G. Dewberry, that he was being treated well and was in good health. Before the war he had been a coalman with the Co-operative Society.

Private Harry Revell, Suffolk Regiment, Alwalton, third son of Mr. and Mrs. T. Revell, Water End, wrote, "Am prisoner of war, safe and well. Hope you are all keeping the same. Best love to all." He had been a gardener for Mr. and Mrs. J.B. Laurance, Alwalton.

Private W. Gripton, Royal Norfolk Regiment, wrote to his wife at 52, Star Road, that he was safe and well in No. 2 Camp, Thailand.

Gunner C.A. Finch, Royal Artillery, wrote to his wife at 3, Harris Street, to say he was safe and well as a prisoner of war in Japanese hands. His parents were Mr. and Mrs. A.F. Finch, 212, St. Paul's Road.

Gunner T. Bishop, Royal Artillery, fourth son of Mr. and Mrs. T.H. Bishop, 24, Summerfield Road, wrote, "I am safe and in good health. Food is good and we are well-treated. So please don't worry. Love to all at home and all friends. Take care of yourself, mother. Am thinking of you always and will be with you soon. Keep smiling. All my love, Tom." He had been missing since the fall of Singapore, and before the war had worked at Marks and Spencer Ltd.

Private Arthur Wilfred Yarrow, 5th Battalion, Suffolk Regiment, South Street, Eastgate, wrote to his wife, "This is your darling husband writing to say that I am quite ok, although I have had the misfortune to become a prisoner of war. Hope you are all right, and also our darling kiddies, Val, Trev, and Syl." Private Yarrow was formerly employed by the London Brick Company and was a keen boxer. Unbeknown to Private Yarrow, his second child, Trevor, had died in the previous April, but the others were all well. Private Yarrow's family would not see him again; he died on the 18th July, 1943, aged 31, of Cholera in a Japanese prisoner of war camp, just two days after his postcard appeared in the 'Standard.' He is commemorated on the Singapore Memorial.

Private George Anker, 4th Battalion, Suffolk Regiment, 143, Northfield Road, wrote to his wife, "My dear wife and son. I am fit and quite comfortable. Love to all, George." He was formerly an electrician with Messrs. Crussell, ironmongers, Lincoln Road. Private Anker would not live to see his family again; he died two weeks later on the 2nd August, 1943, aged 30, in a Japanese prisoner of war camp, and is commemorated in Kanchanaburi War Cemetery.

Gunner William James Hall, Royal Artillery, son of Mr. and Mrs. A.L. Hall, 201, Fletton Avenue, wrote to his parents to say, "Dear mum and dad. I am very well indeed. Am in good billets, and having good food. Hope you are all well. Your loving son, Bill." Gunner Hall, who was 23 years old, had been with Frank Perkins Ltd. before the war.

Most of these men had been prisoners of the Japanese for sixteen months or more and the circumstances of their captivity would have been appalling by the time these postcards were received, as the deaths of many of them testify. If they had been sent around June 1942, as indicated by the one card that carried a date, then it is not credible to believe that after four months of captivity in Japanese camps, their circumstances could have been much better. It is likely that these cards, which appear to be similar, were worded in order not to worry their loved ones at home. Indeed, it is very possible that the British officers with them had told the men what to write. For example, the use and frequency of the word "accommodation" seems a little out of place in these short messages, and suggests an official line rather than a personal one. The final arbiter of what they were allowed to write was of course the Japanese Forces.

Cards were received from many other men at this time but what they wrote is not revealed, possibly because they all carried the same message. The following men were included in this group:

Sergeant T.W. Haskayne, Royal Artillery, who married Miss Kathleen Judd of Walton.

Sergeant J. Graham Freeman, Royal Artillery, of Barclays Bank, who married Miss Marjorie Harbour, only daughter of Mr. and Mrs. Harbour, 34, Westwood Park Road.

Gunner Alan Morton, Royal Artillery, only son of Mr. and Mrs. F. Morton, 64, Gilpin Street. He was in the Sanitary Inspector's department before the war.

Gunner Frederick Sidebotham, 48 Lt. Anti-Aircraft Regiment, Royal Artillery, who was in the LNER Chief Accountant's office before the war. Gunner Sidebotham would die on the 20th April, 1945, aged 28, in a Japanese prisoner of war camp. He is buried in Labuan War Cemetery, Malaysia.

Gunner Fred Norris, 336 Battery, 135 (The Hertfordshire Yeomanry) Field Regiment, Royal Artillery, son of Mr. and Mrs. A. Norris, 22, Fulham Road. Gunner Norris would return to Peterborough after the war but would die on the 25th March 1946, aged 24, after ill treatment as a Japanese prisoner of war. He is buried in Peterborough (Eastfield) Cemetery.

Gunner Jack Henry Walker, Royal Artillery, eldest son of Mr. and Mrs. W.H. Walker, 13, Eastfield Road.

Gunner C.A. Finch, Royal Artillery, 3, Harris Street, son of Mr. and Mrs. A.F. Finch, 212, St. Paul's Road. Formerly a sorting clerk, he was a member of Peterborough Swimming Club.

Private George Edward Cottom, Suffolk Regiment, eldest son of Mr. and Mrs. Cottom, 158, Star Road, He had been in the LNER Goods department.

Private Alfred Oliver Davis, 5th Royal Norfolk Regiment, 64, Shakespeare Avenue. He had a daughter aged a year and eleven months old and had been a railway porter for seven years. Private Davis would die on the 14th September, 1944, aged 28, in a Japanese prisoner of war camp. He is commemorated on the Singapore Memorial, Singapore.

Corporal Harry Mills, 5th Battalion, Bedfordshire and Hertfordshire Regiment, 118, Eastgate. He worked for the Corporation before the war and his wife was a Postwoman. Corporal Mills would die on the 1st January, 1944, aged 37, in a Japanese prisoner of war camp and is buried in Chungkai War Cemetery, Thailand.

Private Walter Richard Colbert, 5th Royal Norfolk Regiment, of Eastfield. He married Miss Kathleen Emery, daughter of Mr. and Mrs. R. Emery, of Bowberry Road, Eye. Private Colbert would die on the 25th July, 1943, aged 26, in a Japanese prisoner of war camp, only a month after his wife received the postcard. He is buried in Kanchanaburi War Cemetery, Thailand.

Private Albert Victor Kitchener Smart, Suffolk Regiment, youngest son of Mr. and Mrs, J. Smart, 67, Clarence Road. Before the war he had been a porter on the LNER and was a member of the Coronation Cycling Club. He was engaged to be married to Miss Stanley, 13, Marholm Road.

Private Dennis Briggs, 5th Battalion, Royal Norfolk Regiment, 92, Russell Street. Aged 29, he was married to Miss Rose Matthews, 54, Queen's Road, and was the son of Mr. and Mrs. Briggs, 114, Dogsthorpe Road. Before the war he was manager of the Stanground branch of the Co-operative Society. Private Briggs would die on the 25th June, 1943, in a Japanese prisoner of war camp, a month before his postcard reached his wife, and is buried in Kanchanaburi War Cemetery, Thailand.

Private Cyril Longfoot, Royal Norfolk Regiment, 20, George Street, Woodston, told his parents that he was as well as could be expected.

Private Len Carnall, Suffolk Regiment, youngest son of Mrs. G. Carnall, 13, Russell Street. He was formerly in the Co-operative Society's furnishing department.

Lance Corporal E.A. Davis, 5th Battalion, Suffolk Regiment, of 27, Midland Road.

Gunner H.R. Topham, Royal Artillery, of 18, Dryden Road.

Women Win Fire Guard Test

Miss N. Wright (Captain), Miss J. Relph and Miss V. Johnson, representing Group 5 (East Ward) won the Coney Fire Guard Cup at the town park on Saturday 9th July. Their instructor was Mr. H.V. Shepherd. Runners up were Group 8, another all-female team. The final tests took place at the training hut at the park and were judged by Mr. G.H. Keeble, Fire Guard Staff Officer and members of his staff.

Mr. Keeble said he had come to test the cream of the city's Fire Guard. The Fire Guard throughout the country numbered 5,000,000, and was the largest department of Civil Defence. There never was a time when it was wanted more, and he claimed that it was keeping the German planes away. They had defeated the air menace, and he thought the Germans would think twice before they tried again. He was proposing to award marks for attack from cover; final attack after explosion; smoke and heat crawl; methods adopted and skill in using them; first aid (diagnosis and treatment).

There were seven teams of three, and part of the test had to be performed in the smoke-filled hut. Here the teams tackled a fire using a stirrup pump. They also had to rescue a "casualty" made insensible by smoke, and give first aid, and finally escape from a burning building by means of a first floor window. The tests took more than two and a half hours to complete.

Mr. Hill said the public had done handsomely to turn up well to see the contests on such an uninviting afternoon. Group 5 had won because of good training, and he congratulated Mr. Shepherd, the trainer. It was a great achievement for three young ladies to win the cup, especially as the standard attained was so high. Mr. Hill handed the cup, given by Mr. B.R. Coney, the former Staff Officer, to Miss Wright, who expressed her thanks.

Serious Theft of Ration Books

Thieves were about in the city again as a very serious theft of ration books and other important documents was carried out at the Food Control Office (the old Vicarage) in Priestgate in the early hours of Tuesday 13th July. A policeman on duty found a forced window at the back which opened out towards Cowgate.

Inside there was little disorder, but plenty of evidence of the visit. A drawer had been forced and the items stolen. The ration books were awaiting issue and had some details already filled in. In addition, a number of blank identity cards had gone and other items it was said that were "calculated to help in the fraudulent use of the stolen goods." It was thought that the thefts took place somewhere between 1am and

3am when there appeared to be more movement about the streets than usual. Many similar thefts had been reported from all parts of the country.

Bedside Screens Donated to the Hospital

In the middle of July, 42 bedside screens donated by the Wardens and Fire Guard services, were delivered to the Memorial Hospital. Mr. Frank A.C. Taylor, Secretary and House Governor at the hospital expressed great thanks and the screens were put into immediate use.

The screens cost about £250 and every penny was raised in the spring and early summer by donations and social events organised by the two services. The screens comprised of four hinged folds, standing on spread feet with rubber castors so that they could be easily and silently moved and adjusted. The frame was light tubular metal, black japanned, and the covering, which was in one piece so there were no gaps, was a blue material for the men's wards and fawn for the women's. They were 6ft high and each section was 2ft wide.

Each screen had a tablet on it inscribed "Presented by Wardens and Fire Guards, City of Peterborough, 1943." I am sure it is too much to hope that any of these screens survive today, but who knows, somewhere in an old cupboard at the Memorial Hospital (soon to be demolished as I write this), there may still be lurking one of these screens bearing the proud inscription upon it.

Postcards Translated

The Rev. S.C. Woodward, Vicar of St, Mark's and formerly of Japan, was now translating into English the Japanese wording on the postcards that were still being received in the city from local prisoners of war in Japan. Mr. Woodward had been able to tell all those who had brought him cards that they were sent from Malai Camp. Mr. Woodward said, "If anyone would like to know what the writing is, I may be able to read it." More cards had been received in the third week of July from the following;

Sergeant Douglas Herbert Smith, 5th Battalion, Suffolk Regiment, Warbon Avenue. Before the war he had been a footman for Earl and Countess Spencer. Sergeant Smith would die on the 16th July 1943, aged 24, in a Japanese prisoner of war camp.

Sergeant Robert Cooke, 135 (The Hertfordshire Yeomanry) Field Regiment, Royal Artillery, 79, GNR Cottages. Sergeant Cooke would die on the 8th May 1944, aged 26, of Dysentery in a Japanese prisoner of war camp in Thailand.

Lance Sergeant Ronald A. Smith, son of Mr. and Mrs. Smith, 46, Shakespeare Avenue.

Corporal Kenneth Smith, Cambridgeshire Regiment, son of Mrs. R.E. Smith, 130, Walpole Street. He was with Messrs. Barber and Ross, before joining the Army in 1940.

Bombardier Gordon D. Austin, Royal Artillery, son of Mr. and Mrs. Austin, 34, Westwood Street. Before the war he was in Messrs. Paten and Co's., bottling stores in Mayor's Walk.

Lance Bombardier F.E. Roy Phillips, Royal Artillery, son of Mr. and Mrs. G.E. Phillips, 22, Charles Street.

Lance Bombardier Charles Edward Ilett, attached 3rd Battery, 1st Lt. Anti-Aircraft Regiment, Royal Indian Artillery, 168, GNR Cottages, who before the war was with the LNER. L/Bd Ilett died on the 30th October 1942, aged 31, in a Japanese prisoner of war camp and is buried in Rangoon War Cemetery, Myanmar (Burma).

Gunner D.H. Spires, Royal Artillery, New England Bakery. He wrote that he was in the best of health and that two of his friends, Jim Goodwin and Walter Sharpe, were well.

Gunner William J. Wadsley, Royal Artillery, 17, Milton Terrace, Peterborough. Before he joined the Army he had been with Jellings Builders Ltd.

Gunner Bernard Cecil Yarrow, 7th Coast Regiment, Royal Artillery, second son of Mrs. S.A. Yarrow, 68, All Saint's Road. Gunner Yarrow, who had been a postman before the war, would die on the 30th October 1942, aged 31, in a Japanese prisoner of war camp and is buried in Rangoon War Cemetery, Myanmar (Burma).

Gunner Albert Smith, Royal Artillery, 22, Arundle Road, Walton, Peterborough. Before the war he had worked at Peter Brotherhood's.

Driver Walter R. Wilson, Royal Engineers, son of Mr. A. Wilson, 735, Lincoln Road, Peterborough. Aged 24, before the war he was a butcher with Mr. R.W. North, Midgate.

Private George William Thompson, 1st Battalion, Cambridgeshire Regiment, son of Mr. and Mrs. Thompson, 19, Star Road. He was with the London Brick Company before the war. Gunner Thompson was killed on the 21st September 1944, aged 24, when the Japanese transport ship in which he was being taken from Thailand to Japan, was sunk by American aircraft. He is commemorated on the Singapore Memorial, Singapore.

Private Edgar Herbert Newell, 5th Battalion, Bedfordshire and Hertfordshire Regiment, 60, St. Martin's Street, Peterborough. Private Newell died on the 10th September 1943, aged 37, in Japanese prisoner of war camp and is buried in Chungkai War Cemetery, Thailand.

Private George Bruce, 16, Fulbridge Road, Peterborough.

Private R.W. Mills, Royal Norfolk Regiment, 14, Gloucester Road, Fletton, Peterborough. He was married and had a daughter of fifteen months and before the war had worked on the LMS Railway.

Private George Charles Atton Brown, 118 Field Regiment, Royal Artillery, 105, Lincoln Road, Peterborough. Private Brown would die on the 24th June 1943, aged 24, in a Japanese prisoner of war camp and is buried in Kanchanaburi War Cemetery, Thailand.

Private John Howard, 29, Silver Street, Peterborough.

Private Albert William Mills, 6th Battalion, Royal Norfolk Regiment, St. Paul's Road, only son of Mr. and Mrs. Mills, Star Cottages, King's Dyke. Private Mills would die on the 17th October 1943, aged 26, in a Japanese prisoner of war camp and is buried in Kanchanaburi War Cemetery, Thailand.

Private Frederick Leslie Steels, 5th Battalion, Suffolk Regiment, 52, Hunting Avenue, Fletton, Peterborough. Private Steels would die on the 22nd August 1943, aged 25, in a Japanese prisoner of war camp and is buried in Thanbyuzayat War Cemetery, Myanmar (Burma).

At the end of July, Lance Bombardier Charles Rouse, Royal Artillery, and Private Vincent Francis Button, Royal Norfolk Regiment, both of Peterborough, would be confirmed as being Japanese prisoners of war, after being posted as missing for many months.

"Gas Attack" on the City

An object found by a boy, and fired in his backyard, produced a miniature gas attack in the city on the afternoon of Wednesday 11th August. From 2:15 onwards the police received numerous telephone reports of a strong smell of gas in the centre of the city; the messages indicating that the effect was strongest in the vicinity of the railway around Westwood Street and St. Leonard's Street. The effects produced were mainly sharp irritation of the chest, coughing, and sickness in some cases.

Police made enquiries and questioned a boy aged 12. The boy admitted that with three other boys he had been on a site recently vacated by military authorities and found an object in a scrap heap. He took it home, and on the Wednesday afternoon he lit it in the backyard. It gave off dense clouds of chemical smoke, but the only ill effects the boy received were stinging of the throat and coughing. Another boy who was said to have buried a similar object in his back garden was later traced by the police.

It was stated that no one complained of more than temporary effects, and no one had cause to seek medical aid. Slight effects of the smoke were reported as far away as Bridge Street. Eventually, the police recovered four containers – the two mentioned and two more from the site. They were tins similar in size to respirator containers, but somewhat longer. They had a hole in the top through which it was thought a fuse would protrude.

The police asked the 'Standard' again to stress the danger of children and others interfering with strange objects which may be found. It was essential that such finds should be reported promptly to the police or a warden.

RAF Casualty

On the 13th August it was reported that Sergeant (rear-gunner), Wilfred Marlow, 57 Squadron, Royal Air Force Volunteer Reserve, was missing from air operations over enemy territory. Aged 23, he was the eldest son of Mr. and Mrs. William Marlow, 15, George Street, Woodston, Peterborough, and had joined the RAF three years earlier. Before the war he had been a driver and salesman for the Standard Yeast Company. He married Miss Elfreda Mary Webb, and had one child. Sergeant Marlow had been a Gunner in Avro Lancaster Mk III, Serial No JA696, code letters DX-J, which took off from RAF Scampton at 00:07hrs on the 3rd August 1943, to bomb Hamburg. The aircraft failed to return and all seven crew were killed. Sergeant Marlow is buried in Becklingen War Cemetery, Germany.

Plane Crashes in Priory Road

At 9 o'clock on the morning of Wednesday 18th August, 1943, an aeroplane crashed in Priory Road, off Mayor's Walk, and several houses were damaged. No one was injured, not even the pilot, although a number of people had miraculous escapes.

The plane, a Miles Master Training aircraft, T8659, was from the nearby RAF Westwood airfield. It developed engine trouble while over the north end of the city, and the pupil pilot baled out. The aircraft carried on and lost height, just passing over the grocery shop belonging to Mr. M.G. Garey, at 44, Priory Road, and slightly damaging the roof.

The plane then crashed on the pavement on the opposite side of the road and struck the front of No. 37, the home of Mr. and Mrs. C.W. Wilson. No. 39, occupied by Mr. and Mrs. Robert Shelton, was also hit, and debris broke windows at No. 41, where Mr. and Mrs. E.A. Livesley lived. Not one of the occupants of the three houses was injured.

Mrs. S.A. Garey, was in her shop and had just finished serving a customer when the smash occurred. "Suddenly I heard a loud bang," she said, "and I thought a bomb had hit the shop. I waited to see if there were any more coming and then went out into the road and saw the damage at Mrs. Wilson's." One side of the roof of the shop was damaged.

Mrs. Cyril Garey, who managed the shop for her mother-in-law, was in town at Messrs. Barber and Ross when the accident occurred. "All the assistants went out to see the plane crashing, and I watched it as well," she said. "I didn't know until I got home that the shop had been hit."

Where the plane struck the edge of the pavement it caused a large dent, and then bounced through the front fence of No. 37 completely smashing it, making a crater in the garden, and hitting the front of the house and the side of No. 39.

Mrs. Wilson had just gone upstairs, and was in the back part of the house at the time. The porch and stairs were smashed, and Mrs. Wilson was assisted down by the rescue workers who were soon on the scene. She was suffering from severe shock. Mr. Wilson had left for work earlier. The front room of the house was badly damaged, but as the plane had approached almost at ground level, the damage did not reach very high. Petrol was splashed out over the front of the house, and nearby residents were instructed not to use their gas. The plane itself was smashed to pieces, with its remains scattered all over the place. The side of No. 39 was badly grazed, and bushes in the garden were thrown several yards. No one in the house was injured, and very little of the inside damaged.

No. 41 suffered from flying debris. It had four windows broken and the front garden ploughed up. Mrs. Livesley was in the front room bathing her baby at the time. "I was just washing baby's head," she said, "so I didn't see anything. The first I knew about it was that glass from the windows came flying into the room and went all over. I got down from the chair on to the floor in case anything else came. Soon after a friend came and took the baby away. Neither of us was injured."

ARP services, NFS and police were soon on the job, helping to clear up. No fires were started and the pilot was unhurt.

August Casualty List

Lieutenant Arnold Gerald Beardsall, 5th Battalion, Northamptonshire Regiment, 109, Granville Street, was now reported killed in action in Sicily. He joined the army before war broke out and had formerly been with Messrs. Yarnold and Gilbert. He had been with the Northamptonshires in North Africa and only a few weeks earlier had been granted a Commission, having previously been a Sergeant.

His wife, Annie Evelyn Beardsall, received the news of his death on Tuesday 10th August, in a letter from his Commanding Officer, who said that one of seven enemy bombers dropped a bomb on the truck in which Lt. Beardsall and others were travelling. He was killed instantly along with all his staff. The writer described the spot where he was buried.

The Colonel said, "Our loss is great, yours is inestimable, and the whole battalion extend their heartfelt sympathy to you in your deep loss... He was a great and loyal friend, and we feel his loss tremendously. We were very pleased when he got his Commission, and are deeply sorry that he did not enjoy the position longer."

Besides his bereaved wife, Lt. Beardsall, who had been a Stamford School boy, left two little sons, the second born just a few weeks earlier.

Lt. Beardsall was killed in action in Sicily on the 30th July 1943, aged 32, and is commemorated on the Cassino Memorial, Italy.

Regimental Quartermaster Sergeant, Walter Ralph Stedman, 5th Battalion, Northamptonshire Regiment, son of Mr. and Mrs. E.W. Stedman, 9, Padholme Road, Peterborough, was also now reported killed in action in Sicily on 30th July. An old Deaconian, he chose journalism as his profession and served in various offices in Sir Richard Winfrey's series of newspapers, eventually coming to Peterborough.

He joined the Northamptonshire Territorials around the time of Munich and was mobilised in 1939, after which he went to France and was evacuated from Dunkirk. After a period at home he went with the First Army to Tunisia, and was killed on 30th July (the same date as Lt. Beardsall).

RQMS Stedman's wife, a Kettering woman serving in the Women's Land Army at Lamport, Northamptonshire, received a letter from his Colonel stating that her husband had been killed in the same truck as Lt. Beardsall. RQMS Stedman, who was 30 years of age, is commemorated on the Cassino Memorial, Italy.

Private E.R. Elliot, DCM, Black Watch, Peterborough, was now reported wounded in North Africa, and Private John Marlow, Cambridgeshire Regiment, Peterborough, was now reported as being a Japanese prisoner of war.

More Postcards from Japanese Prisoners

More postcards bringing news of Japanese prisoners of war were received from the following men at the end of August. All had originally been posted as missing in action.

Battery Sergeant Major H.H. Hawkins, Royal Artillery, Peterborough. He had formerly been an inspector for the Yorkshire Insurance Co. at Peterborough, and had been missing since the fall of Singapore.

Sergeant E.L. Hughes, Royal Artillery, third son of Mr. and Mrs. J. Hughes, 144, Dogsthorpe Road. Also missing since Singapore, his parents received the card on the 12th August which read, "I am in excellent health and the food and living quarters are good. Inform everyone of receipt of this card and let Irene (Miss Irene Spires, Vere Road, Peterborough) know immediately. You are always in my thoughts and I am quite happy. Fondest regards." Sergeant Hughes was formerly at Westwood Works. There were three other sons and a daughter serving.

Lance Sergeant William Edward Gripton, Royal Artillery, youngest son of Mr. and Mrs. G.F. Gripton, 218, Clarence Road, was apprenticed with Baker Perkins Ltd. before the war and was also in the Peterborough Territorials. He was sent out East and was last heard of 17 months earlier. In his postcard he said he was fit and well and the food was good. He asked his parents to tell his friends.

Bombardier Jack Truss, Royal Artillery, 20, Granville Street, Peterborough. His wife received a postcard from him on Friday 13th August. Formerly a coalman with the Co-operative Society, he had been missing since the fall of Singapore. His father lived at 162, Garton End Road.

Gunner Frederick George William Watson, 135 (The Hertfordshire Yeomanry) Field Regiment, Royal Artillery, was the eldest son of Mr. and Mrs. W. Watson, 82, Russell Street, Peterborough, and before the war had been employed at Smith's Garage, Granville Street. He had been missing since Singapore and wrote, "I am safe and well, conditions good. Will be seeing you all soon. Don't worry. Am always thinking of you." Gunner Watson would not see his family again; instead he would die of black water fever on the 4th June 1945, aged 24, in a Japanese prisoner of war camp and is buried in Kanchanaburi War Cemetery, Thailand.

Gunner R.A.E. Walker, Royal Artillery, eldest son of Mr. and Mrs. A.E. Walker, 51, Silver Street, Peterborough. Aged 22, he wrote saying he was safe and well and not wounded in action, and that conditions were good. Gunner Walker had been a locomotive driver with the East Midland Gravel Company, and was taken prisoner at Singapore.

Sergeant Major Arthur Johnson, B.S.M. 135 (The Hertfordshire Yeomanry) Field Regiment, Royal Artillery, wrote to his wife Mrs. Lily Johnson, at 80, Walpole Street, Peterborough, "My darling wife. I am safe and well; food and billets are good. Hope you and the babies are well. Remember me to all. Don't worry, still keep smiling. Your ever loving husband, Arthur." Sgt. Major Johnson had worked in the machine shop at Baker Perkins Ltd. before the war, and saw many years of service with the Territorials. He was the son of Mr. Arthur Johnson, Mountsteven Avenue, Peterborough. Sergeant Major Johnson would not return to his family again, instead, after spending many years in captivity, he would die just before the end of the war on the 20th April 1945, aged 33, in a Japanese prisoner of war camp and is buried in Yokohama War Cemetery, Japan.

Lance Corporal Albert Edwin West, Cambridgeshire Regiment, aged 25; he was the second son of Mrs. F. Hoyles, 49, Palmerston Road. He wrote to his mother, "My darling mother. Please don't worry, I am all right and in the best of health. Hope you are the same. Give my love to all and to Winnie, please. I shall soon be seeing you, dear, so keep your chin up. I am being well fed and looked after, so cheerio, God bless you my love, your ever loving son, Albert." L/Cpl. West was with the London Brick Company and played football for Phorpres. He was engaged to Miss Winnie Canham, St. John's Street.

Lance Corporal Harry Hornsby, 2nd Battalion, Cambridgeshire Regiment, 76, Clarence Road, Peterborough, youngest son of Mr. C. Hornsby, 307, Clarence Road. He wrote to his wife, "Don't worry about me, as I am well and in good spirits. We are being fed ok – that's the main thing. Remember me to all at home and take care of yourself. It will not be long before we are all back again." L/Cpl. Hornsby was formerly a painter and decorator at Croxley Green, Watford. He would not return as he said he would, but would die on the 27th August 1943, (the exact same date his postcard was published in the 'Standard') aged 30, in a Japanese prisoner of war camp and is buried in Chungkai War Cemetery, Thailand.

Private Charles Albert Duggan, 1st Cambridgeshire Regiment, elder son of Mr. and Mrs. G. Duggan, 86, Padholme Road, Peterborough, sent a postcard which had become damaged in transit however what he wrote was still legible. "I am quite well and safe – hope you are the same. We are being treated well and the food is good. Please do not worry. Lots of love to all at home." Private Duggan died on the 21st September 1944, aged 25, when the Japanese transport ship in which he was being taken from Thailand to Japan, was sunk by American aircraft. He is commemorated on the Singapore Memorial, Singapore.

Gunner A.B. Cook, Royal Artillery, eldest son of Mr. and Mrs. A. Cook, 29, Glenton Street, Peterborough, wrote that he was safe and well. He was on the LNER before his call-up, and on 15th October, 1941, he married Miss J. Waite, of Earlstoun, Scotland.

Sailor Died of Burns

Able Seaman, Granville B.C.F. Burgess, HMS ARROW, Royal Navy, son of Charles and Alice Burgess, and husband of Phyllis K. Burgess, of Peterborough, was reported in the 'Standard' on 27th August, as having died of burns, as a result of endeavouring to extinguish a fire in a merchant ship.

On the 4th August, 1943, the merchant ship SS FORT LA MONTEE caught fire at Algiers. It was towed into the bay and the forepart blew up, damaging the destroyer HMS ARROW. The aft section of the merchant ship had to be sunk by gunfire from a Royal Navy submarine to stop it blowing up, and the remains of the forward section burned for several days. HMS ARROW sustained major damage which caused many casualties and disabled the destroyer. She was eventually towed to Gibraltar for repair. A.B. Burgess died the next day on the 5th and is buried in Dely Ibrahim War Cemetery, Algeria.

Sicily Soldier Mystery

Mr. and Mrs. A. Ilett, of 43, Grove Street, Peterborough, were now anxiously awaiting official news of the fate of their third son, Private William David Ilett, 1st Battalion, Dorsetshire Regiment. On Monday 30th August, they received a communication from the War Office stating that Private Ilett had been killed in action in Sicily on August 2nd. The next day a cheerful letter arrived from Private Ilett himself, saying he was safe and well and "chasing the Nazis across Sicily." There was no date on this letter, but the field postmark was August 26th – four days before the letter was delivered. Mr. and Mrs. Ilett felt they had every reason to hope that the War Office had made a mistake in announcing their son's death.

The War Office of course, had not made a mistake, and William was one of two sons that the Iletts would lose to the war. Private William David Ilett was indeed killed in action in Sicily on 2nd August, 1943, aged 28, and is buried in Catania War Cemetery, Sicily. Private Ilett volunteered for the Army in November 1939, and was previously at Peter Brotherhood's.

Mr. and Mrs. Ilett had two other sons in the Army; Lance Bombardier Charles Ilett, Royal Artillery, who had been missing since the evacuation of Burma and unbeknown to his parents at this time, had died in a Japanese prisoner of war camp nearly a year earlier on 30th October, 1942, and Private A. Ilett, who was in North Africa.

More Casualties

At the beginning of September another list of casualties was published. Sergeant Frederick George Scarr, Flight Engineer, 90 Squadron, Royal Air Force Volunteer Reserve, son of Mr. and Mrs. W.J. Scarr, 1, Hereward Close, Peterborough, was now reported missing from air operations over Germany. Sergeant Scarr died on the 28th August 1943, aged 20, and is buried in Durnbach War Cemetery, Bayern, Germany. He was a Flight Engineer in Short Stirling Mk III, Serial No EF439, code letters WP-H, which took off at 21:46hrs from RAF Wratting Common to bomb Nuremburg. The aircraft failed to return and six crew were killed, one became a prisoner of war.

Bombardier J.H.P. Ellis, Royal Artillery, 9, North Bank Road, Peterborough, was now reported to be a prisoner of war in Japanese hands.

Private Leslie William Lane, 1st Battalion Cambridgeshire Regiment, fourth son of Mr. and Mrs. C. Lane, 12, Marne Avenue, Walton, Peterborough, was also now reported to be a Japanese prisoner of war. Until this time he had simply been reported as missing in action, however he would eventually die in captivity on 21st September, 1944.

Private Isaac Ambrose, 1st Battalion, Gordon Highlanders, fourth son of Mrs. Lucy Ambrose, and the late Mr. John William Ambrose, 11, Globe Street, Peterborough, was now reported killed in action in Sicily during July. He was only 18 years old and before joining the Army had been a waiter in a hotel in Preston, Lancs. His brother was in the King's Royal Rifle Corps in North Africa. Private Ambrose was actually killed on 23rd July, 1943, and is buried in Catania War Cemetery, Sicily.

Gunner Russell Norman, Royal Artillery, of Longthorpe, Peterborough, was now reported to be a Japanese prisoner of war. He wrote that he was well and happy and added that food and conditions were good. Before the war he had been with Fairways Ltd. Broadway, Peterborough.

Sapper Alfred Brown, 994 Docks Operating Company, Royal Engineers, son of Caroline Brown and stepson of John William Kilby, of 14, Brookdale, Stanground, Peterborough, was now reported missing, presumed drowned. He had joined the Army two years previously and had been with the Post Office before the war. He was posted missing in June and his mother heard at the end of August that he must be presumed drowned. Sapper Brown is recorded as having drowned on the 17th June, 1943, and is commemorated on the Brookwood Memorial.

Pilot Officer Lawrence Alan Walker, Royal Air Force, only son of Mr. L A Walker, 51, Huntley Grove, Peterborough, was now reported as having been killed during an operational flight in North Wales on the 4th September 1943. He had returned to his station a week earlier after coming home on leave. Aged 21, he was educated at Deacon's School and was apprenticed with the Newall Engineering Company as a draughtsman. He had joined the RAF two years earlier and received his training in America. He received his wings there and in May 1942 he returned to Britain as an instructor. Four months earlier he had been promoted to Flight Sergeant and a few weeks after that had attained his commissioned rank. The funeral took place at Llanbelig, Carnarvon, on Wednesday 8th September.

Italy Surrenders

At six o'clock on Wednesday 8th September people throughout the city turned the wireless on to listen to the news. Seconds later the atmosphere was electrified with the announcement of Italy's unconditional surrender. Although the Italian capitulation had been anticipated, it still came as a great surprise as it had not been expected so soon.

Mr. H. W. Kelley, chairman of the Peterborough Labour Party and Mayor-elect of the city said: "There are tremendous possibilities now that the Adriatic can be opened up, but the full value of the capitulation cannot be gauged until it is seen what sort of fight the Germans remaining in Italy are prepared to put up. In any case, now that the weakest link in the Axis chain has snapped, the end of the war is nearer than we dared to hope up to a few weeks ago.

The achievements of the Eighth Army with the Canadians and their American Allies must never be forgotten. Their successes in North West Africa and Sicily and the pounding of the Italian cities and ports by the magnificent RAF and American Air Force have undoubtedly been a factor which has now got rid of the first of the hard-pressed Axis powers."

316

At the Service canteens in the city during the evening it was said that there were "great scenes of hilarity." At the Allied Officer's Club there was a great crowd with many Americans joining in the celebrations. At the canteen in Long Causeway there was an even bigger crowd consisting mainly of servicemen passing through the city.

The news of the surrender had not officially been made known to the Italian prisoners at the camp close to Peterborough on the Wednesday night. One of several employed at a local dairy who spoke English was told the news the following day. He was delighted and lost no time in telling his compatriots who all greeted the news enthusiastically.

On the Thursday morning flags of the Allied nations appeared in the centre of the city by order of the Mayor. The Union Jack flew above the Town Hall, the American flag was broken out at the south end and the Soviet flag flew from the north block. A strange flag was also hoisted above the old Town Hall (Guildhall) in Cathedral Square and many people walked up the stairs to the ARP offices inside to ask what it was. They were told it was the flag of the Chinese Republic. China had been fighting the war against the Axis powers longer than any other nation so their flag was flying above the city's oldest public building.

There were many Peterborough men amongst the 70,000 Allied prisoners of war in Italian hands and their relatives were anxiously waiting for news of their early return. The Geneva Convention stated that when belligerents concluded an armistice they should begin repatriation of prisoners.

Group Captain Receives DSO

In August 1943 Acting Group Captain John Henry Searby, DFC, of Cambridge Avenue, Peterborough, had played an important role as 'Master Bomber' during a bombing raid on the German target of Peenemunde, a Nazi radio research and development station which was also experimenting with 'V' weapons. It was now announced in the 'Standard' that he had been awarded the DSO. The citation read: "Night fighters were extremely active over the target but in spite of this he executed his task with consummate skill and faultless leadership, great courage and resolution throughout."

The first use of what was to become known as the 'Master Bomber' technique was carried out by Guy Gibson during the Dams Raid in May 1943, but it was Gibson's replacement as CO of No 106 Sqn who was to develop the technique on a large scale. John Searby had been a Flight Commander on 106 Sqn, under Gibson and when Gibson was posted to form 617 Sqn, Searby took over the reins. However, within a couple of months he had been promoted to Group Captain and appointed CO of No 83 Sqn. It was the Peenemunde Raid of August 1943 that Searby first employed the 'Master Bomber' role when he flew over the German research station in the Baltic directing and redirecting the bombers of the Main Force in order to maintain an accurate aiming point.

John Searby however, was not a product of Cranwell; he had joined the RAF in 1929 as an Aircraft Apprentice in the 19th Entry at Halton. Six years later he had qualified as a pilot and was promoted to Sergeant. Following commissioning in 1939, he attended the Specialist Navigation School after which he became an instructor flying Blenheims. A spell ferrying aircraft across the Atlantic and then a staff post was followed by promotion to Squadron Leader as a Group Navigation Officer before undertaking his first full operational tour as a Flight Commander with No 106 Sqn at Coningsby and later Swinderby. For his work on the night of 17/18

August 1943 over Peenemunde he was awarded an immediate DSO and remained in command of 83 Sqn until November when he moved to RAF Upwood as OC. However, his replacement at 83 Sqn was shot down shortly after taking command and Searby returned to command the squadron for a further two weeks before resuming command of Upwood. His final posting before the end of the war was Command Navigation Officer at HQ Bomber Command.

At 30 years of age, he had already taken part in many heavy raids on Germany and Italy including Berlin, Cologne, Nuremberg, Bremen, Essen and Lorient.

Killed in the North Atlantic
Leading Supply Assistant, Bertram Sydney Hills, HMS POLYANTHUS, Royal Navy, was now reported missing, presumed killed in the North Atlantic. Aged 22, he was the son of Walter and Annie Hills and lived at 15, Allen Road, Peterborough. He had volunteered four years earlier and was formerly a clerk with the CWS wagon works. A keen member of St. Pauls, he was also a Patrol Leader of Paston Church Scouts Troop. He was engaged to Miss Audrey Allen, 94, Cobden Street. Home on leave only two weeks earlier, he had just returned to his ship.

At 0022 hours on 21 September 1943, the German submarine U-952 fired a Gnat torpedo at an escort of the convoy ON-202 and heard after three minutes a detonation, followed by sinking noises. HMS POLYANTHUS was hit and sank immediately. The British frigate HMS ITCHEN picked up one survivor, but he died when the frigate was torpedoed and sunk two days later by U-666.

Airmen Casualties
Flying Officer Edward Jack Dorman, Royal Air Force, was now reported killed in action in India on 10th October 1943. Aged 22, he was the only son of Mr. and Mrs. E. Dorman, 44, South Street, Stanground, Peterborough. Educated at Fletton Secondary School he was employed at the GPO until he joined the RAF two years previously. He had trained in America and had been in India for about a year. He is buried in Imphal War Cemetery, India.

Sergeant Edward Sydney Taylor, Royal Air Force, was now reported missing following an operational flight over the Aegean Sea on 20th September 1943. Aged 21, he was the second son of Mrs. E. Taylor, 117, Cromwell Road, Peterborough. He joined the RAF direct from Deacon's School as an apprentice clerk at the age of 16. He has no known grave and is commemorated on the Alamein Memorial, Egypt.

Aircraftman 2nd Class Charles Regan, Royal Air Force, was now reported as having died whilst a prisoner of war in Japanese hands. He was the youngest son of Mr. and Mrs. J.R. Regan, 58, Garton End Road, Peterborough, and had been reported missing about a year earlier. His parents had heard nothing from him until a telegram arrived in the middle of October 1943 informing them that the Air Council had received news through the International Red Cross of their son's death. Before he joined the RAF he had been a fitter at the Westwood Works. He is buried in Yokohama War Cemetery, Japan.

Wings for Victory Plaques Presented
The plaques won by Peterborough City Council, Peterborough Rural Council and Barnack Rural Council by raising £617,000 in Wings for Victory Week were presented at the Town Hall on Thursday 21st October by Group Captain Council, the new Commanding Officer from a nearby air station on behalf of the Air Ministry.

Afterwards the Mayor presented log books to Group Captain Council, these would go to the Lancasters which the £617,000 had provided and would be returned to the Soke Committee after the war.

Sir Theodore Chambers, Vice Chairman of the National Savings Committee, said that when he had seen Peterborough's figures he thought there must be some mysterious secret about the place which enabled it to produce such astonishing results. At the beginning of the war Peterborough had 65 groups; now there were 600, saving £25,000 a week. The Mayor said that having known Peterborough for 40 years, he knew there was not a more generous hearted lot of people anywhere.

Group Captain Council said the RAF could provide the air crews, men of matchless courage and grim determination, but they could not do the job without the tools. He presented the certificate of merit to the Mayor and the Mayor presented the log books. Each was inscribed: 'This log book which will record the operational activities of an aircraft, is a tribute to the success achieved by Soke of Peterborough Savings Committee in the Wings for Victory National Savings Campaign, 1943. Target £480,000; achievement £617,000, representing the cost of 12 Lancaster bombers and 27 Spitfires.'

News of Prisoners
Three years earlier Leading Aircraftman W. Eric Smith had been made a prisoner of war in Lybia by the Italians. He was incarcerated in Sulmona prison camp, Italy, until the Allied offensive began, when he was transferred to Campo Bologna, Northern Italy. Then, when the Germans took control of Northern Italy his parents, Mr. and Mrs. C. Smith, 1, Geneva Street, Peterborough, heard no more of their son. They did not know whether he had been transferred to Germany, whether he had escaped with others and was in Switzerland, or fighting with the guerrillas.

On Wednesday 20th October they were listening to a German broadcast in English, and were delighted to hear the last announcement: "Here is a message from Leading Aircraftman Eric Smith, of Peterborough, to his parents: Dear Mum – I am in Bavaria, Southern Germany, keeping well. Hope you are the same, love, Eric."

The next day Mr. and Mrs. Smith received a telegram from the Air Ministry confirming that the broadcast had been picked up in this country and that the camp address had not yet been notified. L/Ac Smith joined the RAF five years earlier and was in Egypt when war broke out. He was previously a motor engineer with Burrows Brothers, Dogsthorpe Road.

Better news was received regarding Bandsman George Arthur Wilkinson, Northamptonshire Regiment. His parents, Mr. and Mrs. H. C. Wilkinson, 143, High Street, Fletton, had now heard that their 24 year old son was expected to be home on the 29th or 30th of October as part of a group of prisoners being repatriated from Germany. A number of other local men from Oundle and Barnack were also among this group.

Sure enough, Bandsman Wilkinson returned to a home decorated with Union Jacks after three years and five months in captivity. Educated at Fletton Council School, before joining the Territorial Band in 1937 he was employed by G. Meadows, fruiterer, of Cowgate. He went to France in 1939 and was taken prisoner in May 1940 when he was in hospital in Belgium.

Speaking about his treatment he said that it was "sometimes good and sometimes bad. I was attached to the medical staff and was luckier than most because many are working their fingers to the bone." Asked what he thought of Germany, he replied, in the words of many other prisoners when asked the question: "Not much." The guards were more sociable of late, but were sometimes very arrogant. As he played the trumpet in a prisoners' band when in Stalag VIII (b), and went on tour to entertain other captive troops, he saw something of Germany.

Nine Days Adrift in a Lifeboat
It was now announced in the news that after nine days in a lifeboat, Second Officer Ivor Rose, son of Mr. and Mrs. P.F. Rose, 109, Park Road, Peterborough, landed 23 survivors from his torpedoed ship on an island off the coast of West Africa. Some native fishermen saw the party land but they ran away when they were approached. An hour later a little procession came out of the bush, headed by a native policeman who could speak a little English. He took the seamen to a primitive village five miles away, the natives carrying all their gear.

At the village they were well treated and the next day they crossed a river in dugout canoes to a larger village where they were well fed and housed by the head-man until the District Commissioner came with a launch to take them away.

Second Officer Rose, who was serving in a Federal Steam Navigation Company ship, had been awarded the MBE and Lloyd's Medal. He and Fireman Albert Kale, who came from Essex, saved the life of an engineer trapped in the flooded boiler room when the ship was torpedoed.

Killed in a Jeep
An Ailesworth ATS Private coming home on leave met her death on the Great North Road on Saturday 23rd October. She was Private Maisie Rachel Hill, aged 19, only daughter of Mr. and Mrs. Cardinal Hill, Main Street, Ailesworth. The accident happened a quarter of a mile north of Thornhaugh. Miss Hill was walking and accepted a lift in a jeep driven by a Technical Sergeant in the American Army. There was a collision between the jeep and a stationary Army lorry and Miss Hill was thrown out. She received terrible injuries and died almost at once. The sergeant was not hurt.

Miss Hill had been in the ATS nearly two years. After leaving Castor School she worked on a farm and later went to the London Brick Company. Her father was Farm Foreman for Captain W. B. Feeny, of Ailesworth, and there were two sons, Gunner Reginald Hill, Royal Artillery, and Mr. Stanley Hill. She was buried in Castor (St Kyneburgha) churchyard.

Twenty One Days Adrift in a Lifeboat
Senior Engineer Officer Walter Smith, Merchant Navy, of Peterborough was now home on six weeks' survivor's leave after spending twenty one days adrift in a lifeboat in the Indian Ocean. He was on watch when his ship, an oil tanker belonging to the Eagle Oil and Shipping Company, was torpedoed, and though injured and suffering from the effects of blast, he made a miraculous escape from the engine room.

Senior Engineer Smith was the youngest son of Mr. and Mrs. E. Smith, 149, Crown Street, Peterborough, and had married Miss Ivy Papworth of Bowberry Road, Eye. He had been in the Merchant Navy for four years and before that had been an apprentice with Messrs Peter Brotherhood, Ltd.

With Senior Engineer Smith at the time when the first torpedo struck were the Junior Engineer who was killed, and the greaser who was badly wounded. Smith himself was knocked over in the engine room when the water came rushing in but eventually reached the companion way and was carried to a lifeboat. Snr. Eng. Smith continued: "When we got in the lifeboat we pulled away, dropped the sea anchor and waited around to see what would happen. We thought that if the submarine had gone we could go back to the ship and collect various things. Suddenly the submarine sent a torpedo into the midships. The magazine blew up, and the last we saw of it, it was blazing and smoking away. We didn't see the submarine at all.

There were two lifeboats, and we had 18 in the one I was in. Later, four of the fellows volunteered to go to the other boat to give more room for the rest of us. Both boats managed to keep together for three days, and then we didn't see the other fellows any more until we got to civilisation. The lifeboats are only about five feet long, which meant we had no means of exercise. They were strong and stocked fairly well. We had one biscuit, a small cube of chocolate, four Horlicks tablets and three ounces of water in the morning and the same at night.

The climate varied, we had a monsoon one day, just like that in the film at the Odeon this week, 'The Rains Came.' It started at two o'clock one Saturday afternoon and didn't stop until well into the next day. Sometimes we leaned over the side of the boat to keep cool, and then at night time it became very cool.

You can imagine our feelings when Junior Engineer Harrison saw land. We felt as though we wanted to jump for joy, but could do little more than cheer. Well, we sailed towards it, and when we got fairly near, we found the current taking us away. The land was surrounded by coral reef, and we became anxious in case we shouldn't get in. We saw some boats leaving the land and tried to attract the attention of the men inside, but didn't succeed. Later another boat sailed away and we waved a yellow flag to attract their attention. This time we succeeded and they took us to the island where we landed.

The islands were called the Maldive Islands, just south west of Ceylon. The natives couldn't speak English, but they made us welcome and we slept in mud huts, lying on a floor of leaves. They kept us there about ten days and then took us to the governor island called Male. We were travelling about one and a half days in an Indian dhow. On this island we lived in a bungalow and for the first time for about a month we were sleeping in proper beds. We were there about eight days, and then we had another journey in a dhow, this time to Colombo, Ceylon. Here we had some food from the Australian Red Cross. Previously we had lived on curry, rice and coconuts.

All the natives were really good to us, giving up their rice ration for us. You really should have seen us when we landed in Colombo. We all wore sarongs. It was a good thing we were given them because our own clothes were all tattered and torn. From Colombo we had a three and a half days' train journey to Bombay. We travelled first class, but first class there is just about like our third class."

Sen. Eng. Smith had already had three weeks leave and had another three to come before returning for duty.

Casualties

At the beginning of November it was announced that Sub-Lt. (E) Ian Donald Leverett, HMS CHARYBDIS, Royal Navy, was reported missing at sea. He was the grandson of Mrs. S. Smith, 83, New England, Peterborough, with whom he had

321

made his home since the death of his parents. He was serving on board the cruiser HMS CHARYBDIS.

On 21 October 1943, CHARYBDIS and destroyers HMS Grenville, Rocket and four Hunt class destroyers (HMS Limbourne, Wensleydale, Talybont and Stevenstone) intercepted the German ship Münsterland off Ushant, Brittany. The force was attacked at night by the German 4th Torpedo Boat Flotilla (five Elbing Class torpedo boats), which was escorting the blockade runner.

CHARYBDIS was almost immediately torpedoed by the German torpedo boats T-23 and T-27. HMS Limbourne was also hit during this action and had to be sunk by HMS Rocket. The German force escaped unharmed. Charybdis sank, with the loss of 30 officers and 432 ratings just off the North Coast of Brittany. The Münsterland was eventually forced ashore and destroyed west of Cap Blanc Nez by fire from British coastal artillery on 21 January 1944.

Soon after the sinking, the bodies of 21 Royal Navy and Royal Marine men were washed up on the island of Guernsey. The German occupation authorities buried them with full military honours. The funerals became an opportunity for some of the islanders to demonstrate their loyalty to Britain and their opposition to the Nazi occupiers, with around 5,000 islanders attending the funeral, laying some 900 wreaths. This was enough of a demonstration against the Nazi occupation for subsequent military funerals to be closed to civilians by the German occupiers.

Previously Sub-Lt. Leverett had served on the Ark Royal from the outbreak of the war and was mentioned in dispatches for devotion to duty on that ship. He is commemorated on the Plymouth Naval Memorial, Devon.

Gunner H. Ellis, Royal Artillery, son of Mr. and Mrs. H. Ellis, 11, Chapel Street, Stanground, Peterborough, was now reported as being in hospital suffering from a nervous breakdown. He had seen service in Sicily and before the war had been with Marks and Spencer until called up in March 1940.

On November 12th it was reported that Sergeant Pilot Peter Coxell, RAF, was missing from air operations. Aged 20, he was the son of Mr. and Mrs. H. Coxell, 197, Fletton Avenue, Peterborough. He joined the RAF in September 1941 and went in January 1942 for training in South Africa. Before the war he had been a clerk with the London Brick Company and was a member of Phorpres swimming club. On November 26th it was reported that his parents had been informed by the Air Ministry that it was believed that their son had made a forced landing and was probably a prisoner of war. He was known to be uninjured. It turned out that Sergeant Coxell had indeed been captured and he survived the war.

On the same day, Sergeant Air Gunner Joseph Edward Owen, RAF, was also posted as missing from air operations. Sgt. Owen was 29 and the eldest son of the late Mr. and Mrs. D. Owen, 14, Clifton Avenue, Peterborough. He had been in the RAF for more than two years and previously had been in charge of the Prudential agency in Grantham. He married Miss Agnes Pizer and they had a three year old son. A keen sportsman, he specialised in running and swimming. His mother and father died within eight days of each other in March 1943, and his brother-in-law, an officer in the RAF, was a prisoner of war. Sgt Owen was a Wireless Operator / Air Gunner in 434 (RCAF) Squadron, Royal Air Force Volunteer Reserve. He died on the 3rd November 1943 in Halifax Mk V, Serial No EB257, code letters IP-E that took off from Tholthorpe to bomb Dusseldorf. Four of the crew died and Sgt. Owen is buried in Rheinberg War Cemetery, Germany.

Also at this time, Private Barry Riseley, Northamptonshire Regiment, was reported as being in hospital with malaria. He was the only child of the late Mr. and Mrs. Fred Riseley, 4, Phorpres Houses, London Road, Peterborough. He went overseas in November and was in the victory parade in Tunis.

More Transfers from Italy
Three Peterborough mothers learned during the second week of November that their sons had been transferred to German prison camps from Italy. The men were: Lance Corporal C. Dickens, Northamptonshire Regiment, 18, Wellington Street; Private V.F. Mucklin, 130, St. John's Street, and Private Plumb, 118, Star Road. Private Plumb had been captured at Derna and was a prisoner at Benghazi for ten months, being moved three days before the town was re-captured. The three men were taken prisoner in 1942 and were together in Campo PG53, PM3300.

Girl Slept in Shelter
The sad tale of a nineteen year old girl was told at the Magistrate's Court on Wednesday 10th November, when Beryl Constance Grindley, of no fixed address, was charged with sleeping out on November 10th and with being unable to give a good account of herself – she pleaded guilty.

PC Dobson said that at 1.30am that day he found the prisoner in an (air raid) shelter, between the car park and the river. She was wrapped in sacking, which was used to black-out the shelter entrance. She told him she would be 19 next week and lived in a caravan in Westwood. He told her that he had reason to believe she had been sleeping in shelters for some weeks, and that she associated with American soldiers at all hours of the day and night. He told her that if she did not go home she was liable to be arrested as an idle and disorderly person.

At 3.30 she was still in the shelter, and she told him then that she lived at Wansford, and it was too far to walk. He had warned her several times about sleeping out. She had lately become very untidy and unclean, and her arms and legs were covered in sores. When she was taken into custody she had 3d. in her possession.

Inspector Frost said the girl had travelled from London to March in 1942 and had obtained employment on a milk round. She absconded with some money and in September she was fined ten shillings for travelling from March to Peterborough without a railway ticket. For ten weeks she had been sleeping in shelters, and she was greatly in need of care and supervision, and of medical attention. She had been living on money received from American soldiers, and was in grave moral danger.

Beryl was sent to prison for two months. The Chairman of the Magistrates told her that her health would be properly looked after.

Czechs Remember Peterborough
Readers of this book will have learned by the time they reach this page that the people of Peterborough had much to be proud of by this stage of the war. I am sure pride in Peterborough will have been raised another few notches after reading the following article.

A Czech officer wrote in the 'Standard' on November 26th: "When I remember Peterborough it is more to me and to many of my countrymen than just a town somewhere in England. Our unit was the first to arrive and the first to leave, so we must logically be responsible for much of the feeling in this town towards us. When

I first arrived, I dare say I was a bit afraid. The places we had been to before were small and the population took great interest in us – but Peterborough presented a much bigger problem, being quite a large and active town, and therefore seeing more of the forces.

Our situation is so much different from that of Dominion and American troops. Many of us have lost our homes, and our families shot out of hand, and have not heard from home for over four years – long years of fighting and suspense with our only hope that England would fight on and that England would win. Sympathy to men in this position means much more than to those who have got families to go back to, a home and a future, and Peterborough really surprised us all. After expecting nothing, to get so much from the Mayor to the bus driver. I felt again to be a fellow-fighter and fellow citizen of another democracy, which will never forget what England and Peterborough has done for us...

Many of us may never return to Czechoslovakia but those who do will have Peterborough in mind. The mass at Peterborough Cathedral; the bus driver who overlooked us when it came to pay the fare the day before pay day, the owner of the Fox and Hounds who kept bottle beer especially for us because we liked it, and many other very little but very kind things and thoughts. England means decency and democracy to us and Peterborough had more than a good share to improve this feeling and make it a good and lasting friendship."

More City Men Killed

Reports on November 26th recorded the deaths of three more city men. Flying Officer Leslie Harold Lister, RAF, was reported as having been killed in a flying accident. F.O. Lister was a Wireless Operator/Air Gunner in 53 Squadron, Royal Air Force. He died, aged 23, on the 15th November 1943 when a Coastal Command Liberator, BZ817, crashed after take-off two miles from Beaulieu, Hampshire. The son of Christopher and Edith Lister and the husband of Joan Lister of Peterborough, he is buried in Eastfield Cemetery, Peterborough.

Sergeant (Flight Engineer) Arthur Ernest Sly, RAF, was now reported missing from operations over Germany. He was the younger son of Mr. and Mrs. C.W. Sly, 46, Exeter Road, Peterborough, and had just celebrated his 20th birthday. Before the war he had been in the LNER Signal and Telegraph Department. Sgt. Sly was in 622 Squadron, Royal Air Force Volunteer Reserve, and died, aged 20, on the 18th November 1943. He was the Flight Engineer in Short Stirling Mk III, Serial No EF128, code letters GI-D. The aircraft took off from Mildenhall to bomb Mannheim, Germany. Seven crew died and are buried in Lachalade Churchyard, Meuse, France.

Gunner Arthur James Nutt, Royal Artillery, son of John and Elizabeth Nutt, and husband of Edith Annie Nutt, 12, Chester Road, Peterborough, was now reported as having died of wounds received in action in the Middle East on June 26th. Aged 34, he left a widow and three children, the youngest of whom he had never seen. Before the war he had been in the Corporation Electricity Department and joined the Army in October 1940. He is commemorated on the Alamein Memorial, Egypt.

Explosion

Just before midnight on Tuesday 14th December, an explosion occurred and a sailor was injured. This did not take place, as might be supposed, on the high seas as the result of enemy action, but on Barratt's Corner, Long Causeway, when a traffic control box exploded.

Shop windows were broken when the metal box containing the traffic light controls exploded at twenty-five minutes to midnight. A gas main at the junction of Long Causeway and Midgate had become slightly fractured, probably due to the low temperatures, causing gas to escape. Some of this gas was thought to have found it's way along a street drain and into the base of the control box where it eventually ignited.

Large fragments of the box were thrown through a number of shop windows including Barratt's, and one piece grazed the leg of a passing sailor who was hurrying by to catch a train. The City Engineer, ARP services, Electricity Company and Gas Company operatives all attended the scene, and early the following morning work was under way to repair the gas main. The traffic control box took a little longer to replace and police officers carried out point duty at the junction for a number of days afterwards.

More Cards from Missing Men

A number of city homes had a better than expected Christmas in 1943 when they received cards from loved ones who were prisoners of war in Japanese hands. Some men had been posted as missing at Singapore in February 1942 and this was the first news that had been heard of them.

Mr. and Mrs. Eason, 112, Church Street, Werrington, had a card from their son, Gunner F.W. Crombleholme, Royal Artillery, the first since he was reported missing. He wrote that he was in good health and spirits, and was dearly longing to see all at home. This card, which brought much cheer to the family at Christmas, had a tragic secret. Gunner Francis William Crombleholme had died a month earlier aged 24, on the 12th November, while a Japanese prisoner of war, he is buried in Kanchanaburi War Cemetery, Thailand.

Mr. J.T. Wright, 70, Alexandra Road, Peterborough, received the news that his nephew, Private Harold Wright, Suffolk Regiment, formerly employed at the Great Northern Hotel, was a prisoner in No. 1 Camp, Thailand, and was in excellent health.

Mrs. Gray, of 3, Albert Place, Peterborough, received a postcard dated February 1943, from her husband, Driver Douglas W. Gray, who was reported missing in the Far East in 1942. He wrote: "Dear Peg. In best of health. Hope you and the children are the same. Remember me to all at home. All my love, Doug."

Another sender was Dispatch Rider, Private Ernest Bucknell, Royal Norfolk Regiment. His wife lived at 79, Montague Road, Walton, Peterborough, and he was the youngest son of Mr. and Mrs. Bucknell, Eastgate. He had been missing since the fall of Singapore, and his wife had heard nothing from him until Christmas Eve when she received a card on which he said he was quite well. He was at Westwood Works before he joined the Army. His wife was formerly Miss Grace Parkinson, 572, Fulbridge Road, and they had one daughter, Veronica. Private Bucknell died of avitaminosis less than two months later aged 29, on the 1st February 1944 while a Japanese prisoner of war. He is buried in Chungkai War Cemetery, Thailand.

Private F.A.W. Reynolds had sent a card to his mother, Mrs. A.V. Reynolds, 5, Haddon Road, Peterborough. His brother, Private Eric Reynolds, was a prisoner of war in Germany and both were at Westwood Works before the War.

Private A. Smart wrote to his mother, Mrs. E. Smart, 67, Clarence Road, Peterborough: "I am all right so far. Hope you are the same. Tell Anne to keep the old chin up. Hope to be home soon." This was the second card Mrs. Smart had received; the first arrived on July 10th.

Private Sydney Harbour, Suffolk Regiment, second son of Mr. and Mrs. S. Harbour, 163, New England, Peterborough, had written to his parents. He was formerly with Messrs. Snowden, Exchange Street.

More Casualties

The edition of the 'Standard' published on the last day of 1943 contained news of two more city men killed in action.

Lance Sergeant William Layton, 5th Battalion Northamptonshire Regiment, was reported as being killed in the Central Mediterranean theatre of war on October 30th. He was the son of Mrs. Layton, Flag Fen Road, Peterborough, and had married a Scottish girl, Agnes, from Throsk, Stirlingshire, four days before he was sent abroad. A Reservist, he was called up when war broke out. He fought in France and was evacuated from Dunkirk. His next operational theatre of war was North Africa, where he was severely wounded. L/Sgt. Layton is buried in Cassino War Cemetery, Italy.

Private Roy Albert James Mitchem, 2nd Battalion Queen's Own Royal West Kent Regiment, 342, Fulbridge Road, Werrington, was now reported missing in the Middle East. Private Mitchem died aged 26, on the 16th November 1943. He was the son of Francis and Emily Mitchem of Paston, Peterborough, and is buried in Leros War Cemetery, Greece.

URWIN, Denis John – Longthorpe, Peterborough. Corporal 916615, 2nd The Glider Pilot Regiment, A.A.C. Died, aged 25, on the 10th January 1943. The son of Edwin and Kathleen Urwin of Peterborough and the husband of Vera Urwin of Longthorpe, Peterborough. Buried in Longthorpe Churchyard, Peterborough.

SIMPSON, Langdale Francis – 29 Hunting Avenue, Peterborough. Sergeant (Pilot) 1319895, 550 Squadron, Bomber Command, Royal Air Force Volunteer Reserve. Died, aged 20, on the 27th January 1943. The son of John and Lily Simpson of Peterborough. Buried in the Old Fletton Cemetery, Peterborough. Section 7, Grave 28.

PEET, George William – 66 Padholme Road, Peterborough. Ordinary Seaman C/JX 317771, HMS Welshman, Royal Navy. Died, age unknown, on the 1st February 1943. At 17.45 hours on 1st February 1943, U-617 fired a spread of four torpedoes at HMS Welshman and observed two hits and a boiler explosion. At 17.55 hours the ship capsized and sank by the stern after two hours. HMS Welshman (M84) sank 35 miles off Tobruk, Libya. Nine officers and 139 ratings were lost, also an unknown number of military passengers. Only a few survivors were rescued. The son of Sidney Baden and Millicent Peet of Peterborough. No known grave he is commemorated on the Chatham Naval Memorial, reference 70, 2.

GURNEY, Francis William – Peterborough. Sergeant (Wireless Operator / Air Gunner), 932499, Royal Air Force Volunteer Reserve. Died, aged 22, on the 15th February 1943. The son of William and Florence Gurney of Peterborough. Buried in the Old Fletton Cemetery, Peterborough. Section 6, Grave 166.

BUTT, Thomas Alfred George – Peterborough. Sergeant 801506, 90 Squadron, Royal Air Force (Auxiliary Air Force). Died, aged 25, on the 15th February 1943. He was in a Stirling bomber, Serial No BF438 that took off from Ridgewell to attack Cologne, Germany. The aircraft was lost without trace. All seven crew died. The son of George and Myra Butt and the husband of Celia Butt of Old Fletton, Peterborough. No known grave he is commemorated on the Runnymede Memorial, Panel 144.

HAMMOND, Dennis – Peterborough. Lance Corporal, 2nd Coldstream Guards. Died, aged 27, on the 28th February 1943 in North Africa. The son of William and Annie Hammond of Peterborough and the husband of Gladys Hammond of Peterborough. Buried in Medjez- El-Bab War Cemetery, Tunisia. Grave 8.E.17.

YARROW, Bernard Cecil – 68 All Saints Road, Peterborough. Gunner 1787274, 7th Coast Regiment, Royal Artillery. Died, aged 36, on the 5th March 1943 while a Japanese prisoner of war. It is believed he was one of 600 'Gunners' moved from a camp in Changi. The POW's were taken to Singapore Docks where they boarded a ship believed to be the "Masta Maru" and endured horrendous conditions. On the 5th November 1942 the ship docked at Rabaul on the island of New Britain in Papua New Guinea where the men were unloaded and marched along dusty tracks ankle deep with volcanic ash despite many being without footwear. During this period the men were made to work in the tropical sun with many beatings. At the end of November the prisoners were gathered and the fittest 517 were told that they were to be taken to build an airfield for the Japanese. 82 men did not go with the party as they were not deemed fit enough. The 517 were taken by another "hell ship" on the two day journey to the small island of Ballale which is approximately 4 miles in diameter to build an air strip. In time, probably on completion of the air strip and the news being received by the Japanese that the Allies were closing in, orders were given that the POW's were to be disposed of. As a result, on 5 March 1943, those who were still alive, some having died of illness and others as a result of Allied bombing, were massacred in cold blood and not one of those taken to Ballale survived. In 1946 the remains of 438 of these British servicemen were recovered on Ballale and were finally interred in graves in the Bomana Commonwealth War Cemetery at Port Moresby. He was the son of Mr and Mrs William Yarrow and the husband of Sarah Ann Yarrow of Peterborough. No known grave he is commemorated on the Singapore Memorial, Column 34.

BROWN, Henry Johnston – 14 Walpole Street, Peterborough. Corporal 5883580, 2/5th Leicestershire Regiment. Died, age unknown, on the 22nd March 1943 in North Africa. The husband of Winifred Brown of Peterborough. Commemorated on the Medjez – El – Bab Memorial, Tunisia, Face 17.

NEWMAN, Charles Hugh – 82 Eastgate, Peterborough. Flight Sergeant (Pilot) 1201836, 77 Squadron, Royal Air Force Volunteer Reserve. Died, age unknown, on the 30th March 1943. He was the pilot of Handley Page Halifax Mk II, Serial No JB842, code letters KN-E. The aircraft took off from Elvington in North Yorkshire, part of a bomber force of 329, to bomb Berlin. During the operation 21 aircraft were lost. This aircraft crashed in the Fehmarn Belt in Denmark, the cause of which was never established. All seven crew died. Next of kin unknown. Buried in Berlin 1939-45 War Cemetery. Collective Grave 2.L.12-16.

MCINNERNY, John Leslie – Sergeant 806086, 19 Field Regiment, Royal Artillery. Died, aged 28, on the 31st March 1943. The son of Mr and Mrs John McInnerny and the husband of Ida McInnerny of Peterborough. Buried in Medjez-El-Bab War Cemetery, Tunisia. Grave 15.C.9.

HARBOTTLE, George Raymond – Sergeant 538409, 57 Squadron, Royal Air Force. Died, aged 25, on the 5th April 1943. He was in Lancaster, Serial No W4252 that took off from Scampton to attack Kiel. All seven crew died. The son of George and Florence Harbottle and the husband of Dora Harbottle of Peterborough. He has no known grave and is commemorated on the Runnymede Memorial, Panel 152.

SMITHDALE, Alan – 11 Fulham Road, Peterborough. Sergeant (Wireless Operator / Air Gunner) 1293011, 57 Squadron, Royal Air Force Volunteer Reserve. Died, aged 23, on the 20th April 1943. He was the Wireless Operator in Avro Lancaster Mk I, Serial No ED770, code letters DX-E. The aircraft took off from RAF Scampton to bomb Stettin. All seven crew died. The son of Alfred and Agnes Smithdale and the husband of Christine Smithdale of Salford. He is buried in Poznan Old Garrison Cemetery, Poland. Collective Grave 6.A.3-5.

GREENAWAY, Arthur Thomas– 14 Eastleigh Road, Peterborough. Trooper 5832623, 142nd Regiment, 7th Suffolk's, Royal Armoured Corps. Died, aged 29, on the 24th April 1943 in North Africa. The son of James and Amy Greenaway of Peterborough. Buried in Medjez- El-Bab War Cemetery, Tunisia. Collective Grave 8.E.4.

LUCY, William Edward – 396 Gladstone Street, Peterborough. Trooper 5834702, 142nd Regiment, 7th Suffolk's, Royal Armoured Corps. Died, aged 30, on the 28th April 1943 in North Africa. The son of William and Gertrude Lucy of Peterborough and the husband of Kathleen Lucy of Peterborough. Buried in Medjez- El-Bab War Cemetery, Tunisia. Grave 11.F.9.

BROUGHTON, Cyril Frederick– 516 Gladstone Street, Peterborough. Sergeant 5886089, 4th Regiment, Reconnaissance Corps, Royal Armoured Corps. Died, aged 30, on the 6th May 1943 in North Africa. The son of Mr and Mrs F. Broughton and the husband of M. A. M. Broughton of Peterborough. Buried in Massicault War Cemetery, Tunisia. Grave I.N.17.

CLARKE, Eric Edward – Westfield Road, Peterborough. Private 4867365, 2nd Beds & Herts Regiment. Died, aged 20, on the 6th May 1943 in North Africa. The son of Arthur and Fanny Clarke of Peterborough. Buried in Massicault War Cemetery, Tunisia. Grave IV.D.7.

TINKLER, Sidney Richard – Belsize Avenue, Peterborough. Sergeant 1320307, 214 (F.M.S.) Squadron, Royal Air Force Volunteer Reserve. Died, aged 21, on the 14th May 1943. He was a gunner in a Short Stirling Mk I, Serial No R9242, code letters BU-O. The aircraft took off from Chedburgh to bomb Bochum when it was shot down by a night – fighter and crashed near Heerlen in Holland. Four crew died while three were taken prisoner. The son of Albert and Fanny Tinkler of Woodston, Peterborough. No known grave he is commemorated on the Runnymede Memorial, Panel 167.

MUNTON, Walter Leslie– Old Fletton, Peterborough. Private 5831528, 2/5th The Queens Royal Regiment (West Surrey). Died, aged 27, on the 22nd May 1943 in North Africa. The son of Arthur and Annie Munton and the husband of Ivy Munton of Old Fletton, Peterborough. Buried in Enfidaville War Cemetery, Tunisia. Grave I.D.25.

CREEVY, Douglas William – 292 Dogsthorpe Road, Peterborough. Sergeant 1330741, 12 Squadron, Bomber Command, Royal Air Force Volunteer Reserve. Died, aged 22, on the 26th May 1943. He was an air bomber in Avro Lancaster Mk III, Serial No ED967, code letters PH-F that took off from Wickenby to attack Dusseldorf. The aircraft crashed at Ratingen where all seven crew died. The son of William and Katie Creevy of Peterborough. Buried in Reichswald Forest War Cemetery, Germany. Grave 5.D.13.

SPRECKLY, Philip George – Probate Court, New Road, Peterborough. Sergeant (Wireless Operator / Air Gunner) 1271792, 51 Squadron, Royal Air Force Volunteer Reserve. Died, age unknown, on the 12th June 1943. He was a Wireless Operator in

Handley Page Halifax Mk II, Serial No DT742, code letters MH-Y. The aircraft took off from Snaith to attack Dusseldorf. The aircraft returned safely but was hit and shot down by anti – aircraft fire from a British convoy in the North Sea roughly 10 miles from Sheringham, Norfolk. The crew were rescued but Spreckly died. The son of Thomas Spreckly, D.C.M., and Norah Spreckly of Peterborough. Buried in the Eastfield Cemetery, Peterborough, Grave 42, Div. 3. Block 9.R.C.

CADMORE, Edgar – 234 Gladstone Street, Peterborough. Sergeant (Air Gunner) 1331075, 76 Squadron, Royal Air Force Volunteer Reserve. Died, aged 21, on the 12th June 1943. He was a gunner in Handley Page Halifax Mk V, Serial No DK200, code letters MP-L. The aircraft took off from Linton – on – Ouse to bomb Dusseldorf when it crashed at Scherlebeck near Recklinghausen. Three died and four became prisoners. The son of Sidney and Ethel Cadmore of Peterborough. Buried in Reichswald Forest War Cemetery, Germany, Grave 18.B.8.

CASBON, Walter John Harry – St. John's Street, Peterborough. Gunner 940900, 135 (The Hertfordshire Yeomanry) Field Regiment, Royal Artillery. Died, aged 23, on the 14th June 1943 while a Japanese prisoner of war. The son of William and Elisabeth Casbon of Peterborough. Buried in Kanchanaburi War Cemetery, Thailand, Collective Grave 6.B.75-78.

BROWN, Alfred – 14 Brookdale, Stanground, Peterborough. Sapper 5834555, 994 Docks Operating Company, Royal Engineers. Died, aged 30, on the 17th June 1943. The 994 Docks Operating Company was on the SS Yoma on the 17th June 1943. The SS Yoma was a liner of the British & Burmese Steam Navigation Company that was serving in the Mediterranean as an Auxiliary Transport ship. She was sunk by U-boat 81 en route from Sfax to Alexandria. There were 1670 on board with 451 lost. The son of Caroline Brown, and stepson of John William Kilby. No known grave he is commemorated on the Brookwood Memorial, Surrey. Panel 5. Column 3.

HICKLING, Norman Victor – Sergeant (Wireless Operator / Air Gunner) 1272101, Royal Air Force Volunteer Reserve. Died, aged 21, on the 22nd June 1943. He was a crew member of a Halifax bomber, Serial No JB852, which was shot down by flak crashing onto a German artillery range in Holland. The son of Albert and Elsie Hickling of Watford. Buried in Ede General Cemetery, Holland. Collective Grave H. 7-11.

BROWN, George Charles Atton – 105 Lincoln Road, Peterborough. Gunner 944677, 118 Field Regiment, Royal Artillery. Died, aged 24, on the 24th June 1943 while a Japanese prisoner of war. The son of George and Charlotte Brown of Barnsbury, London. Buried in Kanchanaburi War Cemetery, Thailand, Grave 6.A.9.

BRIGGS, Dennis Albert – 92 Russell Street, Peterborough. Private 5779703, 5th Royal Norfolk Regiment. Died, aged 29, on the 25th June 1943 while a Japanese prisoner of war. Next of kin not known. Buried in Kanchanaburi War Cemetery, Thailand, Grave 2.M.62.

DOLBY, George Leslie – 7 Hereward Road, Peterborough. Private 5832971, 4th Suffolk Regiment. Died, Aged 28, on the 25th June 1943 while a Japanese prisoner of war. The son of Mr and Mrs G. E. Dolby of Peterborough. Buried in Chungkai War Cemetery, Thailand, Grave 4.N.9.

CHURCH, Kenneth Sidney James – 24 New Road, Woodston, Peterborough. Private 5827913, 1st Cambridgeshire Regiment. Died, aged 23, on the 28th June 1943 while a Japanese prisoner of war. The son of Kenneth and Ellen Church and the husband of Winifred Church of Eye, near Peterborough. No known grave he is commemorated on the Singapore Memorial, Column 58.

NICHOLLS, Charles Ernest – 10 Milton Street, Peterborough. Gunner 849383, 135 (The Hertfordshire Yeomanry) Field Regiment, Royal Artillery. Died, aged 23, on the 29th June 1943 while a Japanese prisoner of war. The son of George and Florence Nicholls of Peterborough. No known grave he is commemorated on the Singapore Memorial, Column 36.

BEECH, Victor Wallace – 43 Vere Road, Peterborough. Sapper 1888803, 287 Field Company, Royal Engineers. Died, aged 28, on the 8th July 1943 while a Japanese prisoner of war. The son of William and Mary Beech and the husband of Dorothy Beech of Bishop's Stortford. Buried in Thanbyuzayat War Cemetery, Myanmar, Grave B3.K.4.

SMITH, Douglas Herbert – Warbon Avenue, Peterborough. Sergeant 5830916, 5th Suffolk Regiment. Died, aged 24, on the 16th July 1943 while a Japanese prisoner of war. The son of Frederick and Martha Smith and the husband of Margaret Smith of Peterborough. No known grave he is commemorated on the Singapore Memorial, Column53.

YARROW, Arthur Wilfred – 19 South Street, Peterborough. Private 5834849, 5th Suffolk Regiment. Died, aged 31, on the 18th July 1943 while a Japanese prisoner of war. The husband of F. A. Yarrow, of Peterborough. No known grave he is commemorated on the Singapore Memorial, Column 56.

AMBROSE, Isaac – Globe Street, Peterborough. Private 14206964, 1st Gordon Highlanders. Died, aged 18, on the 23rd July 1943 in Sicily. The son of John and Lucy Ambrose of Peterborough. Buried in Catania War Cemetery, Sicily, Grave IV.B.14.

COLBERT, Walter Richard – Eastfield, Peterborough. Private 5777225, 5th Royal Norfolk Regiment. Died, aged 26, on the 25th July 1943 while a Japanese prisoner of war. Next of kin not known. Buried in Kanchanaburi War Cemetery, Thailand, Collective Grave 10.F.L.4. 2-10.

NIGHTINGALE, George Herbert – 41 Wootton Avenue, Peterborough. Private 5830908, 5th Suffolk Regiment. Died, aged 24, on the 26th July 1943 while a Japanese prisoner of war. The son of Mr and Mrs Herbert Nightingale of Old Fletton, Peterborough. No known grave he is commemorated on the Singapore Memorial, Column 56.

BEARDSALL, Arnold Gerald – 111 Granville Street, Peterborough. Lieutenant (Quartermaster) 294290, 5th Northamptonshire Regiment. Died, aged 32, on the 30th July 1943. The son of Frank and Annie Beardsall and the husband of Annie Beardsall of Peterborough. No known grave he is commemorated on the Cassino Memorial, Italy, Panel 9.

KNIGHT, Charles Frank– 30 South Street, Stanground, Peterborough. Private 5832683, 5th Suffolk Regiment. Died, aged 29, on the 30th July 1943 while a Japanese prisoner of war. Next of kin not known. Buried in Thanbyuzayat War Cemetery, Myanmar, Grave B4.A.16.

STEDMAN, Walter Ralph– 9 Padholme Road, Peterborough. Warrant Officer Class II, R.Q.M.S., 5886160, 5th Northamptonshire Regiment. Died, aged 30, on the 30th July 1943. The son of Mr and Mrs E. W. Stedman of Peterborough and the husband of Ethel Stedman of Kettering. No known grave he is commemorated on the Cassino Memorial, Italy, Panel 9.

VERGETTE, Robert Sidney Webster– 37 Paston Lane, Peterborough. Private 5886243, 5th Northamptonshire Regiment. Died, aged 23, on the 30th July 1943. The son of Lucas and of H. M. B. Vergette of Walton, Peterborough. No known grave he is commemorated on the Cassino Memorial, Italy, Panel 9.

FIXTER, Francis Jack – 10 St. Marks Street, Peterborough. Gunner 922763, Royal Artillery, attached H.Q. 18th Indian Division. Died, aged 23, on the 31st July 1943, believed of Beri – Beri while working on the Thailand to Burma railway as a Japanese prisoner of war. The son of Francis and Annie Fixter of Peterborough. Buried in Kanchanaburi War Cemetery, Thailand, Grave 2.N.25.

ANKER, George – 143 Northfield Road, Peterborough. Private 5832910, 4th Suffolk Regiment. Died, aged 30, on the 2nd August 1943 while a Japanese prisoner of war. The son of George and Marie Anker and the husband of Florence Anker of Peterborough. No known grave he is commemorated in the Kanchanaburi War Cemetery, Special Memorial 9.M.4.

BEE, Claude Howard – Driver 1890012, 560 Field Company, Royal Engineers. Died, aged 24, on the 2nd August 1943. The son of Walter and Katherine Bee of Peterborough. No known grave he is commemorated in Kanchanaburi War Cemetery, Thailand. Special Memorial 9.M.9.

ILETT, William David – 43 Grove Street, Peterborough. Private 5886672, 1st Dorsetshire Regiment. Died, aged 28, on the 2nd August 1943. The son of Arthur and Emily Ilett of New Fletton, Peterborough. Buried in Cantania War Cemetery, Sicily, Grave I.J.33.

MARLOW, Wilfred – 15 George Street, Peterborough. Sergeant, Air Gunner, 1177760, Bomber Command, 57 Squadron, Royal Air Force Volunteer Reserve. Died, aged 23, on the 2nd August 1943. He was a gunner in Avro Lancaster Mk III, Serial No JA696, Code Letters DX-J. The aircraft took off from Scampton to bomb Hamburg. All seven crew died. The son of William and Ida Marlow of Peterborough and the husband of Freda Mary Marlow of Peterborough. Buried in Becklingen War Cemetery, Germany, Grave 11.F.5.

BURGESS, Granville B.C.F. – Whitsed Street, Peterborough. Able Seaman P/JX 214671, HMS Arrow, Royal Navy. Died, Aged 23, on the 5th August 1943. Died of wounds following an explosion. The son of Charles and Alice Burgess and the husband of Phyllis Burgess of Peterborough. Buried in Dely Ibrahim War Cemetery, Algeria. Grave 4.K.16.

FAULKNER, Job – Peterborough. Gunner 1097186, 64 Medium Regiment, Royal Artillery. Died, aged 33, on the 7th August 1943. The son of Thomas and Margaret Faulkner and the husband of Edith Faulkner of Peterborough. Buried in Cantania War Cemetery, Sicily. Grave IV.E.42.

CASBURN, Philip Montague – Grange Road, Peterborough. Lance Corporal 7690231, 18th Divisional Provost Company, Corps of Military Police. Died, aged 32, on the 9th August 1943 while a Japanese prisoner of war. The son of Montague and Catherine Casburn and the husband of Doris Casburn of Edmonton, Middlesex. Buried in Thanbyuzayat War Cemetery, Myanmar. Grave B4.C.9.

TOKENS, Albert Edward – 11 G.E.R. Cottages, Peterborough. Gunner 895162, 135 (The Hertfordshire Yeomanry) Field Regiment, Royal Artillery. Died, aged 27, on the 10th August 1943 while a Japanese prisoner of war. Next of kin not known. Buried in Kanchanaburi War Cemetery, Thailand. Grave 2.Q.67.

BROWN, James Arthur – Tower Street, Fletton, Peterborough. Private 5830899, 5th Suffolk Regiment. Died, aged 24, on the 13th August 1943 while a Japanese prisoner of war. The son of James and Annie Brown of New Fletton, Peterborough. Buried in Sai Wan War Cemetery, Hong Kong. Grave VII.F.23.

CLAXTON, John Alfred – Private 10554999, 18 Div. Workshops, Royal Army Ordnance Corps. Died, aged 28, on the 13th August 1943 while a Japanese prisoner of war. The son of John and Emma Claxton of Dogsthorpe, Peterborough. He is buried in Chungkai War Cemetery, Thailand. Grave 2.K.2.

SMITH, Harold – 77 Church Street, Werrington, Peterborough. Trooper 5884676, 61st Regiment, Reconnaissance Corps. Died, aged 23, on the 18th August 1943. The son of Helena Smith and the husband of Daisy Smith of Werrington, Peterborough. Commemorated in the Werrington Churchyard, Peterborough.

CROOKS, Leslie – 221 Lincoln Road, Peterborough. Wing Commander (Pilot), 44054, DSO, DFC, 426 (RCAF) Squadron, Royal Air Force. He died, aged 33, on the 18th August 1943. He was the pilot of Avro Lancaster Mk II, Serial No DS681, Code Letters OW-. The aircraft took off at 2132 on 17th from Linton-on-Ouse to attack the V1 & V2 research facility at Peenemunde. Crooks was the Commanding Officer of 426 Squadron and was killed on the eighth operation of his second tour. Probably shot down by a night-fighter. One member of the crew survived. The son of Arthur and Bertha Crooks and the husband of Flora Crooks of Peterborough.

Buried in Berlin 1939-45 War Cemetery, Brandenburg, Germany. Collected Grave 7.Z.11-13.

STEELS, Frederick Leslie – Hunting Avenue, Fletton, Peterborough. Private 5830917, 5th Suffolk Regiment. Died, aged 25, on the 22nd August 1943 while a Japanese prisoner of war. The son of Mr and Mrs Jack Steels of Peterborough and the husband of Vera Steels of Woodston, Peterborough. Buried in Thanbyuzayat War Cemetery, Myanmar, Grave G.9.

HORNSBY, Harry – Clarence Road, Peterborough. Lance Corporal 5833591, 2nd Cambridgeshire Regiment. Died, aged 30, on the 27th August 1943 while a Japanese prisoner of war. No known next of kin. Buried in Chungkai War Cemetery, Thailand. Grave 5.H.6.

SCARR, Frederick George – 1 Hereward Close, Peterborough. Sergeant, Flight Engineer, 1624092, 90 Squadron, Royal Air Force Volunteer Reserve. Died, aged 20, on the 28th August 1943. He was the Flight Engineer in a Short Stirling Mk III, Serial No EF439, code letters WP-H. The aircraft took off from Wratting Common to bomb Nuremburg. Six of the seven man crew died. The son of William and Catherine Scarr of Peterborough. Buried in Durnbach War Cemetery, Bayern, Germany. Grave II.J.21.

THORPE, Leslie John – 483 Fulbridge Road, Peterborough. Sergeant, Wireless Operator / Air Gunner, 1389321, Royal Air Force Volunteer Reserve. Died, aged 21, on the 3rd September 1943. The son of Joseph and Sarah Thorpe of Werrington, Peterborough. Commemorated in Werrington Churchyard, Peterborough.

WALKER, Lawrence Alan – 51 Huntley Grove, Peterborough. Pilot Officer, 148702, Royal Air Force Volunteer Reserve. Died, aged 21, on the 4th September 1943 during an operational flight in North Wales. The only son of Mr L. A. Walker of 51 Huntley Grove, Peterborough. Buried in Llanbeblig Public Cemetery, Caernarvon. Grave 2216.

DOWSE, Stanley – Peterborough. Driver T/155545, R.A.S.C. Died, aged 27, on the 8th September 1943. Dowse was one of three soldiers who were killed in an explosion at Hexham Railway Station in Northumberland as they were unloading ammunition from a train. The son of Mr and Mrs Willie Dowse and the husband of N. Dowse, of Peterborough. Buried in Eastfield Cemetery, Peterborough. Grave 6362, Div. 4, Block 16.

HOWARD, John Thomas Alfred – 29 Silver Street, Peterborough. Private 5830955, 4th Suffolk Regiment. Died, aged 25, on the 8th September 1943 while a Japanese prisoner of war. No known next of kin. Buried in Kanchanaburi War Cemetery, Thailand. Grave 2.N.59.

NEWELL, Edgar Herbert – St. Martin's Street, Peterborough. Private 5959689, 5th Beds & Herts Regiment. Died, aged 37, on the 10th September 1943 while a Japanese prisoner of war. The son of John and Frances Newell and the husband of

Florence Newell of Peterborough. Buried in Chungkai War Cemetery, Thailand. Grave 5.C.4.

NICHOLLS, Frederick Walter – 38 Milton Street, Peterborough. Warrant Officer Class II (BSM), 813817, 135 (The Hertfordshire Yeomanry) Field Regiment, Royal Artillery. Died, aged 29, on the 13th September 1943 while a Japanese prisoner of war. The son of George and Florence Nicholls of Peterborough and the husband of Mary Nicholls of Peterborough. Buried in Kanchanaburi War Cemetery, Thailand. Collective Grave 6.C.62-67.

HILLS, Bertram Sidney – 15 Allen Road, Peterborough. Leading Supply Assistant P/MX 61120, HMS Polyanthus, Royal Navy. Died, aged 22, on the 20th September 1943. At 00.22 hours on the 20th September 1943 the German U-952 fired a Gnat torpedo at an escort of the convoy ON-202 and heard, after three minutes, a detonation followed by sinking noises. HMS Polyanthus, a Flower Class Corvette, was hit and sank immediately. The son of Walter and Annie Hills of Peterborough. No known grave he is commemorated on the Portsmouth Naval Memorial, Panel 79, Column 1.

TAYLOR, Edward Sidney – 117 Cromwell Road, Peterborough. Flight Sergeant 591419, 227 Squadron, Royal Air Force. Died, aged 20, on the 20th September 1943 believed while on an operational flight over the Aegean Sea. The son of E. S. and Elsie Taylor of Peterborough. No known grave he is commemorated on the Alamein Memorial, Egypt. Column 270.

ROSE, William Henry – Private 5836721, 233 Company, Pioneer Corps. Died, aged 42, on the 25th September 1943. The son of John and Nellie Rose of Peterborough. Buried in Catania War Cemetery, Sicily. Grave I. A. 35.

SHARMAN, Alec James – Sergeant 1620530, 5007 Airfield Construction Squadron, Royal Air Force Volunteer Reserve. Died, aged 39, on the 27th September 1943. The son of James and Emma Sharman of Peterborough and the husband of Elsie Sharman of Peterborough. Buried in Eastfield Cemetery, Peterborough. Grave 7437. Div. 1. Block 17.

LOBLEY, Harold Christopher - 2nd Northamptonshire (Soke of Peterborough) Battalion, Home Guard. Died, aged 35, on the 10th October 1943. The son of George and Annie Lobley and the husband of Elizabeth Lobley (nee Jeffries) of Peterborough. Buried in Eye Cemetery, Peterborough. Grave 29. Sec 1.

DORMAN, Edward Jack – 44 South Street, Stanground, Peterborough. Flying Officer (Pilot) 122472, 28 Squadron, Royal Air Force. Died, aged 22, on the 10th October 1943 believed in a flying accident in India. The son of Edward and Martha Dorman of Stanground, Peterborough. Buried in Imphal War Cemetery, India. Grave 6.D.4.

MILLS, Albert William – St. Paul's Road, New England, Peterborough. Private 5775731, 6th Royal Norfolk Regiment. Died, aged 26, on the 17th October 1943 while a Japanese prisoner of war. The son of Albert and Mary Mills and the husband of Joyce Mills of New England, Peterborough. Buried in Kanchanaburi War Cemetery, Thailand. Grave 4.C.3.

LEVERETT, Ian Donald – 83 New England, Peterborough. Lieutenant (E), HMS Charybdis, Royal Navy. Died, aged 24, on the 23rd October 1943 when the Charybdis was hit in the English Channel by 2 torpedoes from the German torpedo boats T-23 and T-27. 464 died and 107 survived. The son of Donald and Lily Leverett. No known grave he is commemorated on the Plymouth Naval Memorial, Panel 78, Column 1.

KNIGHT, Eric – 206 Lincoln Road, Walton, Peterborough. Lance Sergeant 5830969, 1st Cambridgeshire Regiment. Died, aged 25, on the 28th October 1943 while a Japanese prisoner of war. No known next of kin. Buried in Chungkai War Cemetery, Thailand. Grave 6.N.12.

LAYTON, William – Flag Fen, Peterborough. Lance Sergeant 774560, 5th Northamptonshire Regiment. Died, aged 38, on the 30th October 1943. The son of Charles and Susan Layton (nee Harbour) and the husband of Agnes Layton of Throsk, Stirlingshire. Buried in Cassino War Cemetery, Italy. Grave VII.A.9.

OWEN, Joseph Edward – 14 Clifton Avenue, Peterborough. Sergeant (Wireless Operator / Air Gunner), 1223682, 434 (RCAF) Squadron, Royal Air Force Volunteer Reserve. Died, aged 29, on the 3rd November 1943. He was in a Halifax Mk V, Serial No EB257, code letters IP-E that took off from Tholthorpe to bomb Dusseldorf. Four of the crew died. The son of David and Caroline Owen and the husband of Agnes Owen of Grantham. Buried in Rheinberg War Cemetery, Germany. Grave 2.H.15.

VENN, Vincent Stanley – Alma Road, Peterborough. Private 5830532, 1st Cambridgeshire Regiment. Died, aged 24, on the 8th November 1943 while a Japanese prisoner of war. The son of Stanley and Elsie Venn and the husband of Anne Venn. Buried in Chungkai War Cemetery, Thailand. Grave 6.H.12.

LENTON, Albert Edward – 34 Craig Terrace, Peterborough. Guardsman 2623073, 6th Grenadier Guards. Died, aged 20, on the 10th November 1943. The son of Mr and Mrs Frank Lenton and the husband of Doris Lenton, of Peterborough. No known grave he is commemorated on the Cassino Memorial, Italy. Panel 3.

CROMBLEHOLME, Francis William – 12 Church Street, Werrington, Peterborough. Gunner 894851, 135 (The Hertfordshire Yeomanry) Field Regiment, Royal Artillery. Died, aged 24, on the 12th November 1943 while a Japanese prisoner of war. The Nephew of Mary Eason of Werrington, Peterborough. Buried in Kanchanaburi War Cemetery, Thailand. Grave 2.B.40.

LISTER, Leslie Harold – Peterborough. Flying Officer (Wireless Operator / Air Gunner) 49790, 53 Squadron, Royal Air Force. Died, aged 23, on the 15th November 1943 when a Coastal Command Liberator, BZ817, crashed after take-off two miles from Beaulieu, Hampshire. The son of Christopher and Edith Lister and the husband of Joan Lister of Peterborough. Buried in Eastfield Cemetery, Peterborough. Grave 6671. Div.1. Block 17.

MITCHEM, Roy Albert James – 342 Fulbridge Road, Peterborough. Private 6094576, 2nd Queens Own Royal West Kent Regiment. Died, aged 26, on the 16th November 1943. The son of Francis and Emily Mitchem of Paston, Peterborough. Buried in Leros War Cemetery, Greece. Grave 2.D.11.

SANDY, Eric John – Long Causeway, Peterborough. Private 5884354, 1st Leicestershire Regiment. Died, aged 25, on the 18th November 1943 while a Japanese prisoner of war. The son of Mr and Mrs J. Sandy of Peterborough. No known grave he is commemorated on the Singapore Memorial. Column 66.

SLY, Arthur Ernest – 46 Exeter Road, Peterborough. Sergeant (Flight Engineer) 1632077, 622 Squadron, Royal Air Force Volunteer Reserve. Died, aged 20, on the 18th November 1943. He was the Flight Engineer in Short Stirling Mk III, Serial No EF128, code letters GI-D. The aircraft took off from Mildenhall to bomb Mannheim, Germany. Seven crew died. Buried in Lachalade Churchyard, Meuse, France. Collected Grave 2-4.

YOUNG, Arthur – 410 Gladstone Street, Peterborough. Private S/238931, Royal Army Service Corps. Died, aged 37, on the 28th November 1943. The son of Thomas and Lavina Young, of Peterborough. Buried in Eastfield Cemetery, Peterborough. Grave6316, Div. 4. Block 16.

BROADHURST, James – Sergeant 522691, Royal Air Force. Died, aged 29, on the 29th November 1943 while a Japanese prisoner of war. He was on a Japanese transport ship, the Suez Maru, which was taking a number of sick prisoners of war and sick Japanese to Java. The ship was torpedoed by the American submarine the USS Bonefish in the Java Sea. Many drowned but a large number managed to swim away from the sinking ship. A Japanese mine sweeper, acting as an escort, opened fire on the survivors and rammed lifeboats and rafts. All prisoners were murdered in the water. The escort saved as many Japanese survivors as it could before leaving. The son of Henry and May Broadhurst of Atherton, Lancashire and the husband of Gladys Broadhurst of Dogsthorpe, Peterborough. No known grave he is commemorated on the Singapore Memorial. Column 425.

FULLER, Frederick Charles – Able Seaman P/JX 330664, HMS Holcombe, Royal Navy. Died, aged 20, on the 12th December 1943. HMS Holcombe, an escort Destroyer, was hit by a Gnat torpedo from the German submarine U-593 and sank north-east of Bougie, Algeria. 83 members of her crew went down with the ship. The survivors were picked up by a US destroyer. The son of Frederick and Edith Fuller of Peterborough. No known grave he is commemorated on the Portsmouth Naval Memorial. Panel 74, Column 2.

CASS, Alec Cyril – Orton Waterville, Peterborough. Trooper 14301052, 2nd Northamptonshire Yeomanry, Royal Armoured Corps. Died, aged 20, on the 25th December 1943. The son of Marjorie Cass of Northborough, near Peterborough. Commemorated in Orton Waterville Churchyard, Peterborough.

1944

More Cards in January

Cards from prisoners of war were arriving fast in the city in the first week of January bringing great relief to many families. Some were the first cards to be received; others were the second to arrive. The cards were mostly from the Japanese theatre and were the type on which the sender filled in blank spaces or crossed out non-applicable phrases. However, some prisoners managed to send further information.

Captain Corby Bristow, son of Mr. and Mrs. F.A. Bristow, Broadway Gardens, Peterborough, wrote on a card dated July 15th: "My health is fair, now nearly 9st. I am working. I have received letters dated 1941 from Hilda, Phyllis and Mother. Don't worry. I am ok. Take care of yourselves." Captain Bristow was in Taiwan Camp; the majority of the others were in Thailand 1 and 2 camps.

Mrs. Rosina Cooke, 5, Park Terrace, Garton End, Peterborough, was relieved to hear news that her husband Sergeant Robert Cooke, Royal Artillery, had received at least one of her letters, because on his card he said: "See that Patrick is taken care of." Patrick was born after Sgt. Cooke sailed for the Far East. Sergeant Cooke's request to his wife seems somewhat fatalistic, and indeed he would never return home to see his son, but instead would die aged 26, on the 8th May 1944 while a Japanese prisoner of war. He was the son of Robert and Millis Cooke of Peterborough, and is buried in Kanchanaburi War Cemetery, Thailand.

Sapper H. Reginald Palmer, Royal Artillery, 11, Princes Gardens, Peterborough, sent his parents a typed card dated June 26th on which he said he was feeling fit. He had sent cards from Hong Kong (where he was captured on Christmas Day 1941) and from Kobe, and was now in a prisoner of war camp in Osaka. He added: "I haven't yet had a letter from you, but am hoping for one soon, and for the day of reunion."

Another who had sent a card was Private William Jenkins, 5th Battalion Royal Norfolk Regiment, fifth and twin son of Mrs. A. Jenkins, 5, St. Mary's Street, Peterborough, and one of seven brothers in the Forces. Private Jenkins was another man who would not return home. He would die aged 27, on the 21st September 1944 while a Japanese prisoner of war. He was on board a Japanese transport ship, the TOYOFUKU MARU, that was attacked by planes from an American aircraft carrier about 80 miles north of Corregidor. The Americans were not aware that the ship was carrying prisoners of war. He is commemorated on the Singapore Memorial.

A card also arrived from Private Charles Albert Duggan, 2nd Battalion, Cambridgeshire Regiment, on his mother's birthday, Mrs. C. Duggan, 86, Padholme Road, Peterborough. Private Duggan would not see his mother again; instead he would also die on the TOYOFUKU MARU, aged 25.

There were the names of approximately one hundred other prisoners of war from the city and district published from whom cards had been received. Many of those would surely never return home.

Airman Killed

At the end of the first week of the New Year it was reported that Flying Officer (Navigator) John Watson Gage, 463 Squadron, (RAAF) RAFVR, was missing from air operations. F.O. Gage, 23 years old, was the elder son of Mr. Harry Gage, chief clerk and cashier with the London Brick Company and Mrs. Minnie Gage, 169, Fletton Avenue, Peterborough. Educated at Fletton Secondary School, he matriculated at 15 and was training as a designer-draughtsman at Baker Perkins when he volunteered for the Air Force. He trained in Canada and when he was awarded his commission he was top of his class and received the Starratt Memorial Watch, given to the man receiving the highest percentage by a Mr. Starratt in memory of his own son. F.O. Gage returned to England in February 1943. He was nephew of Miss B. Chapman, head teacher of Woodston Junior School, and of Lt. C.E. Martin, RNVR, and Mrs. Martin, 3, St. Margaret's Road, Peterborough.

F.O. Gage died aged 24, on the 3rd January 1944. He was a Navigator in Avro Lancaster Mk III, Serial No JA902, code letters JO-D that took off from RAF Waddington to bomb Berlin. The aircraft crashed into water which has since been reclaimed to form the Noor-Oost-Polder in Holland. All seven crew died, four were buried on various dates in Holland. The others, including F.O. Gage, have no known grave and are commemorated on the Runnymede Memorial.

Also at this time it was reported that Able Seaman Gordon Tee was in a Sicilian hospital suffering from hand injuries. He was the eldest son of Mr. and Mrs. E.J. Tee, 72, Welland Road, Peterborough, and was a Naval Commando. He had been in hospital since September 7th.

Respirator Checks
At the beginning of January, the Town Clerk, as ARP Controller for the City and Soke, and Mr. A. Lister Robinson, chief warden, were responsible for the local arrangements in connection with a nationwide check-up of respirators which was to be completed by the end of February.

Wardens were set to visit every house, and the public were asked to have their respirators handy to help expedite the work. Up to and including February 29th replacements would be made, and repairs done, free of charge. After that date, payment would have to be made.

Prisoners of War
Mrs. Wakefield, of 45, Charles Street, Peterborough, now received news that her husband, Sergeant C.T. Wakefield, RASC, was another local man who had been transferred from an Italian prison camp to Germany.

Another man, Bombardier Jack Leaman, Royal Artillery, second son of Mr. and Mrs. A.J. Leaman, 9, All Saint's Road, Peterborough, had been captured during the fighting at Tobruk, and was taken to an Italian prison camp. News was now received that he had escaped from this camp and had been at liberty for fourteen days until he was unfortunately re-captured.

In a card to his wife Edna, he said: "I was re-captured in Italy on September 25th after 14 days liberty and have been here (a German prison camp) for three weeks. I am well and will be leaving for another camp very shortly, having completed registration today. Rations are better here and we have had issues of Red Cross parcels since arrival. Love to everyone. Do not worry."

Bombardier Leaman was at one time a linotype operator with a local newspaper. Mr. and Mrs. Leaman had two other sons in the Forces – Bombardier Alec Leaman, Royal Artillery, and L/ac. Ralph Leaman, RAF.

Special Operations Airman Killed

Sergeant Thomas Samuel Howlett, 138 Squadron, Royal Air Force Volunteer Reserve, was now reported killed whilst returning from operations. He was 22 years of age and the eldest son of Mr. and Mrs. George Howlett, 206, St. Paul's Road, Peterborough. He joined the RAF about 18 months earlier after a period in the offices at Brotherhood's Works, and was home on leave the previous Christmas.

Sergeant Howlett died, on the 8th January 1944. He was the Flight Engineer in Handley Page Halifax Mk V, Serial No LK743, code letters NF-J that took off from RAF Tempsford on the 7th January. 138 Squadron was a Special Duties (SD) Squadron, its role was to drop and pick up agents of the Special Operations Executive in occupied Europe and also to drop supplies by parachute. On this operation the Halifax was returning from Belgium with three Belgian agents on board. The aircraft crashed at Tetworth Hill near Bedford. All seven crew and the three agents were killed and Sergeant Howlett is buried in Eastfield Cemetery, Peterborough.

Also in January, Corporal F.W. Lewis, Queen's Royal Regiment, 44, Silverwood Road, Peterborough, was reported missing in the Middle East since November 16th (1943). Corporal Lewis had been in the Army for four years and all except for six months of his service had been abroad. Before the war he had been a hairdresser with Mr. W. Slaughter, Eastfield Road. His wife was L/Acw. Lewis, WAAF. Cpl. Lewis would later be confirmed as a prisoner of war in Germany.

Food Office Thefts Arrest

A man who admitted two break-ins at Peterborough Food Office was now sentenced to three years in prison at Worcester Quarter Sessions. Douglas Atkinson, aged 54, described as an engineer of Grimsby, pleaded guilty to two charges of burglary from Great Malvern Food Office, Worcestershire, and asked for six other offences to be taken into consideration. These included two at Peterborough, which were:

Breaking and entering Peterborough Food Office on the night of April 12th-13th, 1943, and stealing 4,789 clothing coupon books, 1,575 sheets of supplementary green coupons and a quantity of cash and savings stamps.

Breaking and entering Peterborough Food Office on the night of July 12th-13th, 1943, and stealing ration books and blank identity cards. In each case a window at the rear had been forced and cupboards and drawers broken open. It was stated that evidence obtained by the Peterborough City Police materially assisted in establishing Atkinson's identity.

Atkinson's downfall came about after he had broken into the Great Malvern Food Office. He had been disturbed by the police who had been watching the office and made his escape bizarrely leaving behind a pair of plus-four trousers. The next morning Detective Cook was on Great Malvern Station when he saw Atkinson wearing a pair of plus-fours identical to those in the possession of the police. Atkinson tried to bluff his way out but the officer held on to him.

Passing sentence, the Chairman said he understood that Atkinson had been "In and out of prison for 20 years."

Vandalism in Shelters

Much attention was being given in the daily Press at this time to the problem of the enormous damage that was being done all over the country to air raid shelters and static water tanks (which held water to put out fires during bombing raids). Yes, throw away those rose-tinted spectacles; vandalism was common during the war, just as it is today. What was Peterborough's record regarding this sort of damage?

Chief Warden Lister Robinson said that in air raid shelters, the chief problem was people wrenching off and stealing electric lamps, and tearing down cable. Another problem was the use of the shelters as toilets and for acts of indecency. The majority of the places were now kept locked and the trouble had abated.

Major De Gray, deputy chief, told a similar story, and said in addition that in some of the underground shelters stones were thrown down the steps and manhole covers had been removed and sometimes broken. Forms (benches), had been placed in the centre of the shelters and turned over in such a way that people might fall over them.

A police official said that some irresponsible members of the public, he was sure, did not realise how vital it was in their own interests to keep the shelters and water tanks in first class condition. Regarding the shelters, the police were constantly receiving complaints of lights broken or stolen, doors smashed, and places fouled in numerous ways. Supervision of the shelters was a constant job for the police. While they were satisfied that a lot of minor damage was done by children, some was obviously the work of youths and young men. Fouling the shelters was an offence covered by bye-laws, and, if the police could obtain concrete evidence of any person being responsible, they would not hesitate to take proceedings.

An officer of the National Fire Service said that he had heard of "extensive mischief" being done at static tanks in some parts of the district. If it was not as bad at Peterborough, it was still very annoying and senseless. There were "loads of bricks" found in the water, also old wire netting and other rubbish involving a need to empty the tanks, so causing a serious waste of water.

Wire netting erected to keep children from falling into the water had actually been broken down by the weight of rubbish thrown in. In one case a thief discarded the evidence of his theft by throwing it into the water. In another instance part of a pram was found in a tank.

One or two of the lighter concrete tanks had been found broken, but it was thought that this might have been the result of accidents. Other officials told of minor "finds" in the water, but nothing to rival the Norwich list of a 10 cwt garden roller, a barrage balloon cable, two pig food bins, a perambulator and a Bren gun and ammunition. Another town had salvaged a hearse from its tanks!

George Medal for Woodston Man

It was now announced that the George Medal had been awarded to Woodston man, Leading Aircraftman Frederick Arthur Withers, RAFVR, for rescuing a soldier who lay wounded in a minefield.

L/Ac Withers was born at 213, Belsize Avenue, Woodston, Peterborough, in 1921, and spent two years at Orton Longueville School, the family eventually moving to Coventry. His grandparents were Mr. and Mrs. R. Fowler, 25, Wootton Avenue, Peterborough.

In August 1943, four soldiers entered a minefield somewhere in England. Three were killed instantly and a fourth lay seriously wounded. L/Ac Withers, who was a driver, accompanied by two nursing orderlies, Corporal N. Goulden, BEM, and Corporal R. North, waded through a canal, crossed barbed wire entanglements, and penetrated 16 feet into the minefield to give first aid. They carried the injured man on a stretcher across the canal, with water up to their armpits. The official citation stated that throughout the entire incident, they showed great fortitude and initiative, and complete disregard for their own safety.

A relative in the city said of L/Ac Withers that: "He never knew the meaning of fear." During the big air raid on Coventry in November 1940, when he was in his teens, he saved his mother's house from destruction by dragging an incendiary bomb down the stairs.

Before he joined the RAF three years earlier, he had been a van driver for the Coventry Co-operative Bakery. In August 1942, he married Miss Betty Thompson, and they made their home at Coventry. L/Ac Withers' late father, Mr. Edward Withers, served in the Middle East and India throughout the First World War.

Airman's DFM

Another man to be awarded a medal at this time was Sergeant Lewis William Chapman, 244 Squadron, Coastal Command, RAFVR, only son of Mr. and Mrs. Frank Chapman, Spital Bridge Inn.

The citation for his Distinguished Flying Medal reads: "On October 16th 1943 the above mentioned NCO Pilot was on patrol in the Gulf of Oman when he sighted a submarine on the surface. He carried out a brilliant attack which resulted in the damaging and possible sinking of the U-Boat. Confirmation is awaited. Although Sgt Chapman has only been in 244 Squadron for a period of two months and is new to the job, he showed great initiative and clear-headedness in a situation that could have been ruined by the slightest error or delay." Records show that U-533 was sunk on 16th October 1943 in the Gulf of Oman by depth charges from a British Bisley (Blenheim) aircraft of 244 Squadron, so Sgt. Lewis did indeed sink the submarine.

Sgt. Chapman was attached to the Persia and Iraq Force. His parents did not know the circumstances of the incident in which he won his award, and in a letter home, referring to the incident, he said: "I am not going to tell you any more about it." Born in 1922, Sgt. Chapman was educated at Deacon's School, and afterwards was a clerk with the British Sugar Corporation for nine months before he enlisted in the RAF in 1941. By the time this news was reported he had been promoted to the rank of Pilot Officer.

P.O. Chapman was killed on the 31st July 1944, when a 44 Squadron Dakota, Serial No KG690, which was transporting 244 Squadron personnel from Riyan to Salalah, crashed into a mountain 30 miles from Salalah. Apparently the approach was very difficult and should only have been undertaken in good visibility. In this instance there was heavy cloud. Five South African crew were killed along with twenty-seven passengers of whom P/O. Chapman was one. He is commemorated on the Alamein Memorial, Egypt.

Killed in London Air Raid

A son, daughter-in-law and grand-daughter of Mr. and Mrs. J.R. Sharpe, 95, New England, Peterborough, were killed by a direct hit during a Luftwaffe air raid on their house in London on the night of Saturday, 29th January.

They were Mr. Charles William Sharpe, aged 31, his wife, Doris, aged 28, and their five months old daughter, Jennifer. Mrs. Sharpe's parents, Mr. and Mrs. Morgan, and her sister, Miss Morgan, also lost their lives. Mr. and Mrs. Sharpe occupied the top of the house, and his wife's family lived on the ground floor. The house was demolished, as was an adjoining house, the three occupants of which were also killed. Eight people were seriously injured. Mr. Charles William Sharpe, a fitter on the LNER, had served his apprenticeship at the New England Loco sheds. The funerals took place in London.

Bad News from the Far East

A statement made by the Foreign Secretary, Anthony Eden, in the House of Commons on the treatment of British and other prisoners of war and civilian internees in Japanese hands now came as a great shock to families in the district. An exceptionally large proportion of local servicemen were known to have fallen into Japanese hands on the collapse of the Allied front in Malaya and elsewhere.

Only the previous Christmas, a very large number of postcards arrived in the city from these prisoners, the majority with the message, "My health is good, I am working for my pay." Naturally the hopes of the families receiving these cards were raised as it appeared that their loved ones were being treated well. However, Mr. Eden's statement appears to have altered that perception and some of the true barbarity dished out by the Japanese was beginning to be known.

Unfortunately nothing could be done to alleviate this new anxiety and suspense. The latest news was that the International Red Cross was seeking permission from the Tokyo Government to conduct immediate investigations in Japan and Japanese occupied territories.

Four Bevin Boys Selected

Bevin Boys, named after Ernest Bevin, the Minister of Labour and National Service, were young British men conscripted to work in the coal mines of the United Kingdom, from December 1943 until 1948. Chosen at random from conscripts but also including volunteers, nearly 48,000 Bevin Boys performed vital but largely unrecognised service in the mines, many of them were not released until years after the Second World War ended. Ten percent of those conscripted aged 18–25 were selected for this service. The following four youths from the city had now been conscripted as Bevin Boys for service in the mines:

Roland (Roger) Ward, son of Mr. and Mrs. E. Ward, 332, Lincoln Road, had been sent to Askern Colliery, near Doncaster. For four and a half years he had been with Baker Perkins as an engineer's apprentice.

Raymond Tempest Beales, younger son of Mr. and Mrs. R. Beales, 92, Fulbridge Road, had been in the Co-operative Society's boot department for four years and was waiting for instructions to go to a training centre at Doncaster.

Peter Knight, only son of Mr. and Mrs. A.J. Knight, 5, Dickens Street, had been sent to Stoke-on-Trent. An old Petriburgian, he was at the income tax office in Priestgate.

George Hinch, son of Mr. and Mrs. S. Hinch, 6, Nene Street, was sent to Cresswell Colliery, Derbyshire. After leaving Deacon's School, he had worked in the City Treasurer's office.

Two More Casualties

Pivate John Towers, MM, Queens Royal Regiment, 26, Pipe Lane, Peterborough, was now reported killed in action on January 26th aged 28. He was awarded the Military Medal for bravery on December 16th and is buried in Minturno War Cemetery, Italy.

Sapper Sidney Arthur Ellender, Royal Engineers, son of Mr. Arthur and Mrs. Annie Ellender, 31, Gordon Avenue, Woodston, Peterborough, was now reported as having been killed in Italy on January 20th aged 20 years old. He joined the Army two years previously and was formerly with Jellings Builders Ltd. as a carpenter. He is also buried in Minturno War Cemetery, Italy.

Crime Report for 1943

The first annual crime report from the new Chief Constable, Mr. F.G. Markin, covering 1943 was now published. The report was generally reassuring regarding the serious and minor crime statistics although there had been a marked increase in cases of female drunkenness, (a problem that many today believe is something particular only to our modern society). A new photographic department had been set up and the Chief Constable stressed its importance in up to date methods of crime detection. The report also showed that there had been a fall in the number of traffic accidents, but the records indicated that there was further scope for lorry and van drivers and cyclists to exercise a great deal more care.

During the year 983 indictable offences were reported, but in 268 cases, cycles and other things reported stolen were found to have been misplaced, lost or taken in error. This left 715 cases, an increase of six on the year. Offenders in connection with 393 cases were traced, and proceedings were taken against 171. Of these 150 were summarily dealt with, 133 being convicted. Of 322 offences undetected, 159 were thefts of pedal cycles, and during the year 191 cycles were stolen in total.

"The prevalent habit of carelessly leaving cycles unattended has caused a very great increase in this particular offence, and a corresponding increase in the work of the police," said the report.

The following table indicates comparative figures for robberies;

	1943	1942
Number reported	633	638
Detected	321	372
Value	£5,210	£2,510
Recovered	£1,972	£772

There were 32 cases of fraud, involving £213 17s. 6d., and in all cases the offender was traced.

For non-indictable offences, 307 persons were proceeded against; a decrease of 228 compared with 1942, and 286 convictions were obtained. The 33 persons proceeded against for drunkenness included 13 females. The police received 2,631 pieces of information regarding persons wanted by other forces and 106 arrests were made. The year saw 79 juveniles brought to court, an increase of eight on 1942. Premises found insecure numbered 683 comprising of 68 houses, 401 lock-up premises, and 214 shops.

The number of adult aliens registered as resident in the city at the end of the year was 117. This figure did not include a large number of workers from Eire who, after a change in the law, became subject to registration with the police in 1944.

Dealing with vehicles for public hire, the Chief said: "Complaints were received by the police during the year from local residents who were unable to obtain taxis for catching trains etc. and in most instances the police were able to assist. The position however is not entirely satisfactory, and further efforts are being made to ensure that this limited type of transport is as far as possible fairly distributed." It seems inconceivable to us today that the police were being used as a free to call taxi service and were doing their best to meet demand!

344

The number of articles found and taken charge of by the police was 2,600, while a large proportion of the 2,133 items reported lost was found and returned to the losers. The amount of found and lost property dealt with by the police during 1943 exceeded that of any previous year. A noticeable feature had again been that sums of money, sometimes fairly large, had been handed to the police, and yet no report had been made of the loss.

The street accidents total, 344, again showed a decrease. They involved three fatalities, 28 people seriously injured and 110 slightly hurt. "As in former years," said the Chief, "drivers of lorries, vans etc. have been responsible for the largest number of accidents (139), and pedal cyclists (85), again show up prominently in this respect." Street accident numbers over the past five years had been: 1943: 344, 1942: 397, 1941: 567, 1940: 539, 1939: 736.

On December 31st the authorised strength of the force was 56, with five reserves, 45 war reserves, two WAPCs, (Auxilliary Police Constables) and three junior civilian clerks. The actual strength was 39 in the Force, one reserve, 31 war reserves, three WAPCs, and an acting inspector detached for ARP duties. The number of days lost through sickness was 630, compared with 474 in 1942. One inspector, two sergeants and seven constables were commended for zeal and efficiency in the execution of their duties.

More Casualties

News was now received that Chief Petty Officer R.D. Curtis, Royal Navy, was a prisoner of war in Germany. CPO Curtis was the son of Mr. and Mrs. F. Curtis, Percival Street, Peterborough, and was educated at Deacon's School. He served his apprenticeship at Brotherhood's and later joined the technical staff at the power station. He became assistant control engineer at Dundee power station and joined the Navy three years ago.

Private Frederick Shaw, Northamptonshire Regiment, was now reported as having been wounded in the left leg in the Central Mediterranean theatre. Private Shaw was the youngest son of Mrs. M.A. Shaw, 38, Crawthorne Road, Peterborough, and his wife and daughter lived in Kettering. Before the war he had been a bricklayer and he had been in the Army eight months.

Flight Engineer Eon Arthur Cairns, Coastal Command, Royal Air Force, was now reported missing. Aged 21, he was the youngest son of Mr. and Mrs. R.N. Cairns, Exeter Road, Peterborough. Before the war he had been an engineer with Frank Perkins Ltd., a member of Toc H and a member of the St. John's choir since boyhood. He had been expected home at the end of February to celebrate his 22nd birthday. Eon Arthur Cairns was killed in action on the 17th February 1944; he has no known grave and is commemorated on the Runnymede Memorial.

Private Ernest Afford, 1st Battalion, Northamptonshire Regiment, was now reported as having been killed in action in Burma on January 18th. Private Afford was a twin son of Mr. George Afford and the late Mrs. Afford, 239, Clarence Road, Peterborough, and had been abroad nearly two years. He had been wounded twice and in civilian life had been with the London Brick Company. Private Afford has no known grave he is commemorated on the Rangoon Memorial, Myanmar (Burma).

Dispatch Rider Killed in City

An Army dispatch rider who "went over the top" of a taxi after a head-on-collision, died in Peterborough Memorial Hospital on Monday 21st February, six days after the

345

accident, never having regained consciousness. The dead man was Gunner John James Snowden, aged 19, of Newcastle-on-Tyne. The taxi was driven by Arthur Roughton, 103, Alexandra Road, Peterborough, and the accident happened on Spital Bridge just after 2pm on Tuesday February 15th. A verdict of accidental death was returned by the coroner.

Doctor Marshall, Hon. Surgeon at the hospital, said Snowden was admitted deeply unconscious. His crash helmet had been forced hard onto his head, and was removed with difficulty. There was bleeding from the nose and right eyelid, and indications of a fracture to the base of the skull and injury to the brain. A witness said that as the taxi was approaching the crown of the road, the motor cyclist came from the opposite direction, in the centre of the road and collided with the car's bumper and radiator. The speed of the motorcycle was 15 to 20 miles per hour; the rider went over the top of the taxi, falling on the road behind it.

War Reserve Police Constable Ruff, who was in Mayor's Walk, said the motorcycle was wedged into the front of the taxi, and a soldier lay behind the taxi. The witness recognised the soldier as a dispatch rider who had passed him, travelling at 35 to 40 miles per hour, in the centre of the road because of the air raid shelters.

The taxi driver had tried to pull to one side in order to avoid a collision but the motorcycle was in the middle of the road and it had been impossible to get out of the way in time.

City Nurse in Front Line
Mr. and Mrs. J.W. Feild, 74, Huntley Grove, Peterborough, had a pleasant surprise when they opened their morning paper on Tuesday 22nd February, and read that their daughter, Miss D.M. Feild was serving as matron on the Arakan front in Burma.

Miss Feild had lived in Peterborough nearly all her life. She was educated at All Saint's School, and received her nursing training at Northampton General Hospital and at Edinburgh Royal Hospital. She had seen seven years nursing in Burma and had also been in Mandalay. Miss Feild was a sister of Police Inspector J. Feild, of All Saint's Road.

Writing on Saturday 19th February, a daily newspaper reporter said: "When the Seventh Indian Division on the far side of the Mayu Ridge is relieved, the wounded will find British nurses waiting to tend them. These nurses – there are only five of them so far – are the first women to serve right up at the Arakan front in this campaign or any other. And they are the only white women within 120 miles of Chittagong, whence they arrived last night, aching with weariness after bumping over hot, dusty roads.

Early this morning they were at work in casualty clearing stations in the neighbourhood of Bawii Bazaar, a village a few miles north of the Ngakyedauk Pass, over which the wounded will be brought out. From down the road came the thud of mortar bombs and the crash of shells. The nurses took no notice; they just carried on, living up to the name they have already given themselves, 'the most forward women in Arakan.'

They were just sitting down to a meal of bully and beans in their hill-top mess tent, overlooking the Naaf River, when I met them. Their matron, Miss D.M. Feild, of Peterborough, spent seven years nursing in Burma, and marched out the hard way with our troops and the refugees when we withdrew to India. Now, with three pips on her shoulders, she has returned to nurse the men on the Arakan front, because she thinks it will help our wounded if they have a woman's care and attention, immediately they come back from the line."

Died in Prison Camp
Mrs. E. Trowell, 15, Westwood Row, Peterborough, now received news that her son, Private Stanley Burbage, had died of polyneuritis (nerve damage which can be caused by diabetes, vitamin deficiency and blood disorders), on January 18th in a German prisoner of war camp to which he had been transferred from Italy. Private Burbage had been serving with the Durham Light Infantry when he was taken prisoner. He was 26 years of age and the youngest son of Mrs. Trowell and the late Mr. J. Burbage, and is buried in Klagenfurt War Cemetery, Austria.

Missing Over Germany
At the beginning of March, Sergeant (wireless operator/air gunner) Leonard Charles Barrett, 12 Squadron, RAFVR, was reported missing from air operations. He was the second son of the four sons of Mr. and Mrs. S.L. Barrett, of the Beehive Inn, Albert Place, Peterborough, and the husband of Mrs. Gladys Barrett. A native of Peterborough, he went to London with his parents, and returned to the city with them in the early days of the bombing. In Peterborough he was employed by the Co-operative Society, and was well known through his association with George Fovargue's band. He had been married exactly two years on the day he was reported missing.

Sergeant Barrett died on the 26th February 1944; he was the wireless operator in Avro Lancaster Mk I, Serial No ME632, code letters PH-P that took off from RAF Wickenby to attack Augsburg. All seven crew died and he is buried in Choloy War Cemetery, Meurthe- et- Moselle, France.

'Wild West' Chase in the City
The city experienced a chase with a 'Wild West' touch about it on the morning of Sunday 27th February, when an American military policeman in a jeep sped through the streets after a runaway horse, ridden bareback by a boy.

Police Sergeant. D. Ward was in Westgate, near the Bull Hotel, at twenty minutes to one, when the horse came galloping out of Midgate, with its young rider, Trevor Greeves, aged ten, of 19, Granby Street, hanging grimly onto a rope halter, and screaming for help. The sergeant was unable to divert the horse; for fear that it might swerve into a shop window and seriously injure the rider.

As the horse passed the end of Park Road, an American military police jeep was turning into Westgate. The driver immediately gave chase along Westgate and into Westwood Street. Near Westwood Bridge the boy was thrown, and almost at once the driver pulled the jeep alongside the horse. Leaning out, Sergeant Young seized the trailing halter and brought the horse to a standstill.

Meanwhile, Sergeant Ward had requisitioned Mr. Don Collier's car, and had also gone in pursuit. The boy was picked up unconscious, and the Americans took him to the hospital, where he was detained suffering from concussion. Police Sergeant Ward took the horse to the pound at the Bull Hotel.

Later it transpired that Greeves had been given permission by his grandfather, Mr. Harry Jenkins, horse dealer, of City Road, to take the horse out for exercise. He fetched it from the Bull stables at 12.15 and was riding it bareback, with no harness other than a rope halter, when it apparently took fright, turned, and galloped back the way it had come. There was little road traffic about, and few pedestrians. The boy's father, Mr. William Greeves, was a turner at Brotherhood's.

Manoeuvres Accident
Whilst on duty on Monday 28th February, Sergeant Instructor Colin Archie Sewter, of Peterborough, was killed by a bullet. At an inquest held on the following Wednesday a verdict of Accidental Death was recorded. Evidence was given that the deceased was an instructor and assisted in training soldiers at a depot. He was on manoeuvres when the accident occurred. The inquest was attended by his widow and his uncle, Mr. Bert Crowson.

Sergeant Sewter was the only son of Mr. and Mrs. A. Sewter, of 184, Alexandra Road, Peterborough. He was an old Deaconian, and before enlisting four years previously, had been employed as a salesman by the Peterborough Gas Company. He was 25 years of age and lived with his wife at 22, Charles Street, Peterborough. He is buried in Eastfield Cemetery, Peterborough.

Another Airman Killed
Sergeant Frank Woodward, 460 Squadron (RAAF) RAFVR, was now reported missing from air operations. He was the son of Mr. and Mrs. A.N.H. Woodward, Hicks Lane, Fletton, Peterborough, and had been in the Air Force since the outbreak of war. In civilian life he had worked at the London Brick Company.

Sergeant Woodward died aged 37, on the 25th February 1944. He was a mid-upper gunner in Avro Lancaster Mk III, Serial No JB742, code letters AR-D that took off from RAF Binbrook to attack Augsburg. The aircraft crashed near Rotweill, a town on the River Neckar, and all seven crew were killed. He is buried in Durnbach War Cemetery, Bayern, Germany.

Singapore Prisoner
Mrs. Florence Newell, 60, St. Martin's Street, Peterborough, received news from the Red Cross in the middle of March that her husband, Private Edgar Herbert Newell, 5th Battalion, Bedfordshire and Hertfordshire Regiment, was a prisoner of war in Singapore. This was the first official news she had received since he was reported missing more than two years earlier.

What Mrs. Newell could not yet know was that her husband had already died aged 37, on the 10th September 1943 while a Japanese prisoner of war. He is buried in Chungkai War Cemetery, Thailand.

Terrible Tragedy at Sea
Other news was received in the city at this time that Sister Roberta Alice Warwick, Queen Alexandra's Imperial Military Nursing Service Reserve, had been reported missing at sea on February 18th. Sister Warwick was the elder daughter of the late Mr. and Mrs. C.J. Warwick, of Queen's Walk, Peterborough, and had for many years been surgery nurse with Doctor Walker before joining the Nursing Service Reserve in February, 1943.

Sister Warwick was sailing on the troopship SS KHEDIVE ISMAIL in Convoy KR8 in February, 1944, which was sunk under terrible circumstances. No less than 1,297 people lost their lives in the space of the two minutes it took to sink the ship, including seventy-seven women (the single worst loss of female service personnel in the history of the British Commonwealth). Carrying 1,511 personnel from the Army and the Royal and Merchant Navies, the KHEDIVE ISMAIL sank on Saturday 12th February 1944, torpedoed by Japanese submarine *I-27* in the Indian Ocean. Only 208 men and 6 women survived the ordeal.

As survivors floundered in the sea, *I-27* submerged and hid beneath them. While HMS PALADIN lowered boats over her side to begin rescuing survivors, HMS PETARD raced in to release depth charges. The destruction of an enemy submarine that might sink more ships took precedence over the lives of the survivors, and *I-27* under Commander Fukumura had a history of machine-gunning survivors of ships she had sunk. On PETARD's third run, her depth charges forced *I-27* to the surface. PALADIN rammed the submarine, in the process causing considerable damage to herself, and finally a torpedo from PETARD destroyed the *I-27*. Sister Warwick is commemorated on the Brookwood Memorial.

More Airmen Casualties

At the end of March Mrs. Dodrill, 1, The Crescent, Woodston, Peterborough, received the news that her husband, Flight Lieutenant Kevin Sean Dodrill, 107 Squadron, RAFVR, had been killed on active service. F/L Dodrill, came from Dublin to join the RAF and married Miss Dorita Angela Margaret O'Dell. He is buried in Woodston Cemetery, Peterborough.

Flight Lieutenant Bernard James Balchin, Royal Air Force, was now reported as having been killed in a flying accident in England on March 22nd. Aged 27, he was the son of Mr. and Mrs. G. Balchin, of Chiddingfold, Surrey, and had been in the RAF since 1935. He was engaged on Transport Command duties when he met his death. Some three and a half years earlier he married Miss Gladys Donnelly, youngest daughter of Mr. and Mrs. H. Donnelly, 160, Garton End Road, Peterborough. Later he went to Canada for a while as an instructor and his wife joined him there, returning in October 1943. Mrs. Balchin was cashier at the Princess Cinema, then moving to the Trustee Savings Bank and finally to Brotherhood's. F/L Balchin is buried in Eastfield Cemetery, Peterborough.

Another airman, Flying Officer John Henry Wyborn, 7 Squadron, RAFVR, had now been reported missing from recent air operations. He was the first member of the City Police Force to become a war casualty. F/O Wyborn, who was married and lived in Sallows Road, Peterborough, died, aged 28, on the 22nd March 1944. He was the navigator in Lancaster Mk III, Serial No JA964, code letters MG-P that took off from RAF Oakington to attack Frankfurt. Four of the seven man crew died. F/O Wyborn joined the RAFVR and trained at Carlstrom Field in Florida, U.S.A. as a pilot and qualified for his wings, although he flew with the Lancaster on this raid as a navigator. The son of Frederick and Jessie Wyborn and the husband of Elizabeth Wyborn of Wolverton, Buckinghamshire, he is buried in Rheinberg War Cemetery, Germany.

Trooper Charles Wright, 1st Recce Regiment, Reconnaisance Corps, Royal Armoured Corps, was now reported killed in action in Italy. He was the third son of Mr. John William and Mrs. Sarah Wright, 3, Hurn Road, Werrington, and left a wife and three daughters at Newton in Nottinghamshire. He was formerly with the London Brick Company at Eye Green. Trooper Wright was killed on the 10th March, and is buried in Beach Head War Cemetery, Anzio, Italy.

Home Guard Exercise

An exercise involving the Home Guard in an area extending from Peterborough to South Bedfordshire was held from Saturday 1st April at 6.15pm to Sunday at 7am.

The exercise tested signals communications and administration, and it was said that many lessons were learned. Battalions taking part included the 1st and 2nd Northants, and 1st Hunts. It was assumed that paratroops (Home Guard from other areas) had been dropped and were dealt with by the defenders. Regular soldiers dressed as Germans were also "dropped" and when captured spoke German all the time. Their captors had to detect from their uniforms and papers the particular units of the German forces to which they were attached. During the exercise the City was theoretically "flattened out" making conditions even more difficult for defenders.

The G.O.C. Eastern Central District and the Sector Commander (Colonel C.W.D. Rowe) were present at various stations and battle points during the exercise.

RAF Sergeant Missing

Sergeant John Ellis, 50 Squadron, Bomber Command, Royal Air Force Volunteer Reserve, son of Mr. Frank and Mrs. Lillian Ellis, 95, Taverners Road, Peterborough, and husband of Betty Ellis, was now reported as missing from a recent raid on enemy territory. An old King's School boy, he had later worked in the Income Tax collection department. His father was an organist at Wentworth Street Methodist Church and was proprietor of a music shop in Westgate.

Sergeant Ellis died, aged 22, on the 19th March 1944. He was the air bomber in Lancaster Mk I, Serial No ED308, code letters VN-J that took off from RAF Skellingthorpe to attack Frankfurt. Three of the seven man crew died and he is buried in Durnbach War Cemetery, Bayern, Germany.

Boy Shot Dead in City

An inquest was held on Friday 14th April on the death of a boy from Walton, Peterborough, who was shot and mortally injured whilst playing with another boy on the afternoon of Wednesday 12th April. The dead boy was Roland Trevor Dixon, aged 9, the only child of Mr. and Mrs. Dixon, 57, Montague Road. He was playing with the boy from next door, Raymond Scoble, only son of Mr. and Mrs. C.A. Scoble, 59, Montague Road, who was about three years older than Roland.

For a time the boys had been running around the gardens of both houses, between which there was no separating fence. Mrs. Dixon, the dead boy's mother, was downstairs at the back of her house, and at about 2.15pm she heard a bang and her boy shout out. She found he had gunshot injuries and Mr. Young, of the Post Office, rang Doctor Holmes. In the meantime Mrs. Dixon went to Paston Lane first aid post, and returned with two personnel. When she got back Dr. Holmes was there, but the boy was dead.

The body was taken to the Memorial Hospital. Raymond Scoble's father was a Captain in the Home Guard, and it it was his revolver that the boys had been playing with when Roland was shot.

Danger of Bows and Arrows

In April there had been four cases that had come to the notice of the police of children suffering serious injuries to their eyes as a result of playing with home-made bows and arrows. Instigated, no doubt, by the popular 'Western' movies that were being shown at the time. One boy had an eye so badly damaged that it had to be removed. Two other children each lost the sight of one eye and a fourth suffered a very painful injury. In addition there had been other less serious casualties, all receiving hospital treatment. One boy had a knee bone damaged.

A police official said: "We do appeal to parents to do all they can to prevent children playing with these dangerous toys. All school teachers have been asked to do the same, and we have received the co-operation of Mr. W.J. Stanton, who last Saturday (22nd April), warned the members of the Odeon Children's Club of the dangers they were running."

The police had received a number of complaints of children damaging bushes and shrubs in public and private gardens in the search for wood to make the bows and arrows. An arrow picked up in a Dogsthorpe garden was so dangerous as to be "almost lethal." The nose of the arrow, made from willow, had been weighted with a four-inch nail driven into the end of it.

Flying Officer Missing

On April 28th, it was reported that Flying Officer Neil Joseph Fairbairn, 622 Squadron, Royal Air Force, son of Mr. Walter and Mrs. Bernice Fairbairn, 15, St. Mark's Street, Peterborough, was missing from an operational flight over enemy territory. He was an old boy of All Souls and Deacons School.

F/O Fairbairn died aged 21, on the 25th April 1944. He was the navigator in Avro Lancaster Mk I, Serial No ME693, code letters GI-F that took off from RAF Mildenhall to attack Karlsruhe. All seven crew died, he is buried in Rheinberg War Cemetery, Germany.

City Pilot's "Bag"

Another city airman was to have much better luck; news had now reached the city about Sergeant Geoffrey Bird, RAF, of Vere Road, Peterborough, who had shot down two Messerschmitts in four minutes, near Rome on Monday 8th April. Sergeant Bird was in a squadron of Spitfires flying back from a sweep when 18 Messerschmitts, all carrying long range fuel tanks, were seen flying below them. The Spitfires dived from 11,000 feet and within four minutes there were many blazing wrecks in a wood overlooking Lake Bracciano. The Squadron Leader said later that they were low enough to see the German planes blow up as they hit the ground. Only one pilot had time to bale out.

Sergeant Bird, who was 23 years old, was the eldest son of Mr. and Mrs. Bird, Vere Road. He was born in Uppingham but came to Peterborough with his parents when he was nine. He was educated at Deacon's School, and before the war had worked at Baker Perkins. He had been in the RAF two years and had served in South Africa, the Middle East and Italy. He was engaged to a South African girl.

Fourth "War Week"

Salute the Soldier week opened on Thursday 11th May, and was Peterborough's fourth big savings effort of the war. In 1940 the Soke and City War Weapons Week target was £350,000, and the total raised was £450,000. The following year the Savings Committee set out to raise £425,000 for Warship Week, and again the target was topped by £100,000. Then there was a break until 1943 when the Wings for Victory target was £480,000, and the result was a magnificent £620,000. Now the Committee was asking for a "Half Million Salute," but they were pushing for £750,000!

The money was to be raised in a number of ways, including the many savings groups set up by people in and around the city. Some of the main events were to include, band concerts, War Office exhibitions, Home Guard displays, and Civil Defence and military parades.

On Friday 19th May, it was announced that the original target of £500,000 had been reached the day before, and there were still two days to go. A good deal more money was expected through donations, for example, from large engineering firms in the city, so there was still room for improvement. Small, individual savers had contributed around £20,000 which wasn't bad for seven days. Local companies had made generous contributions, for example:

Peterborough Co-operative Society - £30,000
Barclays Bank - £15,000
Lloyds Bank - £15,000
Midland Bank - £15,000
National Provincial Bank - £15,000
Westminster Bank - £15,000
Peterborough Trustee Savings Bank - £20,000
Norwich Union Life and Fire Insurance Society - £2,000
Pearl Assurance - £5,000

Many other firms and businesses contributed as did the local people, who raised money in every possible way they could think of. On May 26th, the final target was announced, £627,015, which was £127,015 above the original target. Telegrams of congratulation were received from the Chancellor of the Exchequer and the chairman of the National Savings Committee on the "magnificent effort." Individual savings groups accounted for £328,905, which on a population basis (59,000) worked out at £5 11s. 6d. per head. The biggest total for any savings group was that of Baker Perkins which contributed £40,710.

Evacuation Charges
On Saturday 13th May, the Town Clerk, Mr. W.B. Buckle told Peterborough Rural District Council that "a rather amusing position had arisen regarding evacuation."

When in 1939, about 496 evacuees came into the area, the Council were good enough to say that he could have a certain salary for dealing with them. Now the number had dwindled to about one tenth and the Minister of Health had woken up to the fact that he was still being charged for the same number as in 1939. He thought that it was "just a little bit too thick."

Mr. Buckle stated that he had "left the thing well alone," because whatever he got, his Majesty's Government took most of it back again by way of taxation. Reduction of the amount payable by 75 per cent would meet expenses as there was still a certain amount of work to be done. Mr. Neaverson asked: "What has become of the money that the Clerk has been collecting?" Mr. Buckle replied: "The proportion I receive would not buy me much more than 100 cigarettes."

Mr. Buckle would not know it, but he would shortly be finding himself having to deal with a great and unexpected influx of evacuees later in the year.

Nazi Submarine Sunk
It was now reported that Petty Officer Clifford A. Vines, aged 22, of 102, Lincoln Road, Walton, Peterborough, had been the rear gunner in a Fleet Air Arm Swordfish

aircraft which had destroyed a German U-boat in Arctic waters. The aircraft had been on convoy protection duties at the time. The pilot, Lieutenant E.B. Bennett, RNVR, of Westcliffe-on-Sea, told a reporter: "It was bitterly cold when we saw a U-boat on the surface about 12 miles away and heading straight for the convoy. We quickly took a bearing and climbed into the clouds. We flew for five minutes, then dived through a gap and saw the submarine immediately below. I got her fixed in my bomb sights and attacked with bombs. She was taken completely by surprise and I saw the bombs hit.

As we climbed away to port, Vines gave her 50 rounds from the machine-gun in her conning tower. The U-boat was by now zigzagging out of control. About two minutes later she turned hard to starboard, her stern rose some 60 degrees, and she sank.

P/O Vines was the second son of Mrs. E. Vines, 102, Lincoln Road, Walton, and the late Mr. Vines, and had been in the Fleet Air Arm about three years. He was formerly at the Co-operative Society's New England grocery branch, and was a member of Walton Cycling Club. His brother, P/O Harry J. Vines, R.N. was awarded the B.E.M. on July 20th, 1943. He had been in charge of a ship's boat for 39 days after being sunk by enemy action in the South Atlantic.

At the Anzio Bridgehead
Private J. Edwards, 89, Wootton Avenue, Fletton, Peterborough, now told of his recent experiences in the front line when he was out repairing the main signal line forward from Headquarters in the Anzio bridgehead, Italy.

"We started about 7 o'clock, just after last light, and mended no less than 12 separate breaks before we got to the nearest company. There was the usual machine-gun tracer whistling overhead, and several mortar 'stonks.' We got soaked to the skin taking cover in a flooded ditch. At midnight we were still on the job, and had to come right back for more cable. We took out two drums and relayed to the furthest company, but already the line had gone 'dis' again behind us.

Tracing it back we mended several more breaks. Once half a dozen mortar bombs fell almost on top of us, and on the lateral road, the blast of one shell sent us sprawling, though neither of us was hit. The rain was coming down solid by the time we got back to the Command Post, about 3am – to find that the line had gone again. We'd been out eight hours, and there was really nothing to report."

Two Soldiers Killed
The deaths of two city soldiers were reported at the beginning of June. Lance Corporal Leslie Walter Wenlock, 2nd Bedfordshire and Hertfordshire Regiment, son of Mr. Walter and Mrs. Grace Wenlock, 64, Granville Street, Peterborough, was reported as having died of wounds received on active service in Italy on 18th May 1944. L/Cpl Wenlock, who was aged 28, is buried in Naples War Cemetery, Italy.

Private George Ernest Towers, 1st Northamptonshire Regiment, son of Mr. Ernest and Mrs. Mabel Towers, 269, Cromwell Road, Peterborough, was reported killed in action in Burma on April 17th. He was actually killed on April 16th, aged 27, and is buried in Imphal War Cemetery, India.

Duel with the Japs
A Bofors gun team including a Peterborough man, Gunner F.W. Adams, of Lincoln Road, had been in action on the Imphal front on May 24th and beat off a determined

Japanese assault on their gun site, killing one Japanese officer, two warrant officers, nine other ranks and taking two prisoners, together with a medium machine-gun, a battalion flag and two swords. They followed this up at daybreak by firing forty rounds with the Bofors at the remaining Japanese troops hiding in bunkers below them.

The bunkers collapsed on top of their occupants after which a platoon of Sikhs of the Frontier Force Regiment put in an attack and mopped up the remaining enemy troops as they tried to escape. So close was the action that scores of troops sat on a hill watching the Japanese being dug out of the bunkers, "like rabbits out of a warren."

INVASION

The news of the D-Day invasion as it spread on the morning of Tuesday 6th June did not cause any great outpourings of excitement or emotion in the city. This greatest of news, which had long been foretold, long been prepared for and long been proclaimed as imminent, was now actually happening: that was the plain, stupendous fact.

The lack of excitement in the streets however, was not an indication that people were unaware of this momentous happening. Every scrap of news was avidly awaited, wireless sets were kept busy and demand for all editions of the evening newspapers was greater than at any time since the war had begun.

A notice was put up at the Cathedral gates: "Invasion of Europe. Prayers for those who are fighting will be offered in the Cathedral each week-day evening at 8pm."

All places of entertainment reported that houses in the late evening on that Tuesday were below normal. The reason was believed to be that people were anxious to hear the King's Speech on the wireless at 9 o'clock. At the Embassy Theatre and the Broadway Kinema the programmes were interrupted so that the audience could hear the speech.

News was now received from Airborne Divisional Composite that Arthur Holmes of the RASC (airborne) was reported missing as from 7th June. He was the youngest son of Mr. and Mrs. Arthur Holmes, 680, Lincoln Road, New England, Peterborough, and before the war had been a driver for the Petroleum Board. His eldest brother, Alec Richard Holmes, was a prisoner of war in Germany. It might be deduced that Arthur Holmes could have been the first man from the city to be killed in action at the beginning of the invasion of Europe. Fortunately he does not appear in the casualty lists and we can therefore assume that he was a prisoner of war.

Decorations for Two City Airmen

Two city airmen were awarded decorations during the second week of June. Pilot Officer Charles Ralph Barford Everard, RAFVR, was awarded the Distinguished Flying Medal; and Pilot Officer Bernard Ernest Patrick, RAFVR, the Distinguished Flying Cross.

P/O Everard was the youngest son of Mr. and Mrs. Everard, of Werrington Hall, and the official citation stated that he had completed a tour of operational duty during which he took part in attacks on the enemy's major targets, including Berlin, Hamburg, Hanover and Nuremberg. He also participated in the Battle of the Ruhr.

The official communiqué stated: "As an air gunner he always maintained a high standard of vigilance and courage. In July 1943, his aircraft was attacked by an enemy night-fighter while illuminated by numerous searchlights. By the quick and skilful directions he gave his captain the attack was frustrated, but not before severe damage had been inflicted on the enemy by Flight Sergeant Everard's accurate return of fire."

P/O Patrick, was the youngest son of Mr. and Mrs. A. Patrick, 103, Granville Street, Peterborough. His award came as a wedding present as he was married in Wisbech on the 27th May, to Miss Joan Lillian Pollock, of Wisbech. He was attached to No. 109 Squadron, and was awarded the DFC for high skill, fortitude, and devotion to duty in many successful operations against the enemy. He received the gilt wings of the Pathfinders Force (Bomber Command) and had operated in Wellingtons, Lancasters and Mosquitoes. He had taken part in a total of 79 operational flights.

Born in Peterborough in 1922, he was educated at Deacon's School. A member of the Peterborough Salvation Army Band, in civilian life he had been and agent for the Salvation Army Assurance Society.

Invasion Front Casualties

Inevitably, news now began to come in regarding casualties from the invasion front. A long list was published in the 'Standard' on June 16th containing the names of many men from the Peterborough area, only three were from the city.

Private Cyril Goodwin, 1st Suffolk Regiment, only son of Mr. Stanley and Mrs. Marjorie Goodwin, 27, Clifton Avenue, Peterborough, actually died in hospital in England on 8th June, aged 26, from wounds received in action in Normandy. Before the war he had been in the Co-operative Society's bakery department, and was at one time captain of West Town Cricket Club. The funeral took place at St. John's on Wednesday 14th June, and he is buried in Eastfield Cemetery, Peterborough.

Gunner George Hazell, Royal Artillery, 123, South Street, Stanground, Peterborough, was reported to have lost part of his right leg during the fighting in Normandy, and was stated to be in a serious condition. He was 34 and married with one child. He joined the Army two years previously and had been with the London Brick Company.

Lance Corporal Charles Jepson, Suffolk Regiment, Stanground, Peterborough, was reported wounded in the leg by the accidental explosion of a hand grenade. He was the second son of Mrs. E. Barnes, Peterborough Road, Farcet, and was married with three children. He was in hospital in the north of England.

It was also now reported that Pilot Officer Humphrey Iggulden, RAFVR, only son of Mrs. and the late Mr. H.V. Iggulden, 88, London Road, Peterborough, had been killed on the 12th September, 1942. Aged only 19, he had been flying training in South Africa when he was returning on the HMT Laconia that was sunk by the German submarine U-156. He has no known grave and is commemorated on the Alamein Memorial, Egypt.

More invasion front casualties were reported the following week on June 23rd. Private Herbert Lawrence Ladds, 1st Suffolk Regiment, second son of Mr. Ernest and Mrs. Emma Ladds, 101, Church Street, Werrington, Peterborough, and husband of Edith Ladds, 72, Church Street, Werrington, was reported as having died of wounds received in action in Normandy on the 10th June. He was 26 years old and had a six year old son. In civil life he was a butcher with Mr. T.W. Cook, New England, and later Mr. A.E. Pepper, Millfield. Private Ladds is buried in Hermanville War Cemetery, Calvados, France.

355

Driver Frank Samworth, RASC, 14, South Street, Stanground, Peterborough, had been wounded in the head and burned. He was 31 years old and the younger son of the late Mr. and Mrs. Samworth, of South Street. His wife was Miss C. Elsom and they had three children. Driver Samworth joined the Army two years earlier after working for the London Brick Company and was in hospital somewhere in England.

Another casualty, this time in Italy, was Lance Corporal George Ernest Shaw, 'A' Sqn, 4th Regiment, Reconnaissance Corps, Royal Armoured Corps, eldest son of Mr. and Mrs. Ernest Shaw, 185, Padholme Road, Peterborough. L/Cpl. Shaw died of wounds in Italy aged 26 on 6th June, 1944. He had been a greengrocer before the war; and had joined the Territorials. He was in the withdrawal from Dunkirk and had seen action in Tunis, Africa and Italy. His sister Joyce was in the ATS and his brother Ronald was in the Marines. L/Cpl. Shaw is buried in Cassino War Cemetery, Italy.

On June 30th it was announced that Sub Lieutenant (A) Alan Horstead, RNVR, Fleet Air Arm, HMS Daedalus, 131, Cromwell Road, Peterborough, had been killed on active service on June 25th following a raid on Cherbourg while on air operations with 886 Squadron. Sub-Lt. Horstead, who was 21, married Miss Peggy Elaine Williamson, the previous August. He is buried in Eastfield Cemetery, Peterborough.

On the 7th July two more casualties were reported, this time fortunately neither had been killed. Private Cyril Parkinson Chapman, 18-year-old son of Mr. William Chapman, 28, Crawthorne Street, Peterborough, and the late Mrs. Chapman, had been wounded in the left arm and left leg by shrapnel sustained in action in France on June 19th. He was in hospital in Derby. Private Chapman had formerly been with the Patent Safety Ladder Company, and was a messenger with the N.F.S. His father had been parcels porter at the North Station for 38 years.

Private James Alfred McManus, Northamptonshire Regiment, younger son of Mr. and Mrs. M. McManus, 96, Wharf Road, Woodston, Peterborough, was now reported missing believed prisoner of war in the Central Mediterranean Theatre. Private McManus, who was 19, joined the Northamptonshire Regiment a year earlier and had gone abroad almost immediately. He was with Cadge and Coleman Ltd. His brother Malcolm was in the RAF.

More Cards from the Far East
More prisoner of war postcards had now found their way to the homes of missing men right across the city. After almost two years' silence, Mrs. F.W. Nicholls had now received word from her husband, BSM Frederick Walter Nicholls, that he was a prisoner of war in Japanese hands. He sent greetings to his son and daughter, Michael and Marlene, who lived with their mother at 38, Milton Street, Peterborough. Mrs. Nicholls had received news that her husband had been wounded, later news came through that he had been killed. On the card he said he was well and working for pay. BSM Nicholls, whose parents, George and Florence Nicholls, lived at 10, Milton Street, had been a machinist with John Thompson & Co., Cromwell Road, Peterborough. His brother Ernest, also in the Royal Artillery, was a Japanese prisoner too. BSM Nicholls, 135 (The Hertfordshire Yeomanry) Field Regiment, Royal Artillery, died, aged 29, on the 13th September 1943, about ten months before his wife received the postcard. He is buried in Kanchanaburi War Cemetery, Thailand.

Mrs. Palmer of 55, Tower Street, New Fletton, Peterborough, had now received a card from her husband, Corporal Charles C.W. Palmer, Royal Norfolk Regiment. He wrote: "Your mails are received with thanks. My health is good. I am working for pay." The card arrived just in time for the birthday of his daughter Sheila.

Mr. J.T. Wright, 70, Alexandra Road, Peterborough, had now received a third card from his nephew, Private Albert Harold Wright, 5th Suffolk Regiment, dated December 31st, 1943. Private Wright had been a waiter at the Great Northern Hotel.

Private Thomas William Honeyball, 5th Suffolk Regiment, son of Mr. Alfred and Mrs. Beatrice A. Honeyball, 138, Newark Avenue, Peterborough, was in Taiwan Camp, and had written to tell his family and friends that he was well. Private Honeyball would die of acute enteritis the following year, aged 25, on the 25th March 1945 while a Japanese prisoner of war at the Fukuoka No 24 Branch Camp, Senryu Coal Mine. He is buried in Yokohama War Cemetery, Japan.

Mock Fire Raid on the City

Back in the city, Peterborough citizens had now shown that should Hitler decide to launch a fire bomb attack against their homes, they could take comfort from the fact that the local fire services would prove equal to any emergency.

2,000 regular firemen, messengers and volunteer fireguards demonstrated their qualities when they dealt with a mock fire attack on the city on the night of Friday 30th June. Some of the most up to date fire-fighting equipment and life saving devices were brought into action and fire chiefs from Region and the surrounding districts watched the operations. It was later to be reported that the tests were very successful.

Shortly after 8pm the first shower of incendiary bombs straddled the city at points ranging from Werrington to Fletton. Those that fell in the streets or on open spaces were speedily dealt with by volunteer fireguards manning stirrup pumps.

About 20 bombs were assumed to have penetrated to the ground floor of the Co-operative Society premises in Park Road. A small trailer pump, manned by National Fire Service men, was brought into action, and it was then discovered that people were trapped on the top floor. A call was put through for assistance, and in a very short time one of the city's newest pieces of equipment, a turntable ladder, was on the scene. This ladder was mounted on a revolving platform, and could rise to 100ft. With the aid of this ladder, the people were soon rescued.

Meanwhile a major incident from the centre of the city had been reported. A fire that had broken out at Woolworth's was assumed to have spread to Marks and Spencer's, the Grand Hotel and Wentworth Street Chapel. To deal with this, zone control was set up under Column Officer R. Craggs, and water was relayed by many lengths of hose from the River Nene. The umpires agreed that the flames were soon under control.

Added diversions with which fireguards had to cope were attacks by phosphorous bombs and "Butterfly" anti-personnel bombs. In one case it was assumed that the Party Officer was killed, and his second in command took over. The bombs were encased with sandbags, and the police and wardens notified. Bomb disposal squads were then brought into action.

The Memorial Hospital also came in for its quota of incendiaries, but the staff fireguard and others from the locality dealt successfully with them. The umpires praised their work, especially the handling of the hospital's trailer pump.

The final 'genuine' bomb to fall on Peterborough during the war was dropped almost two years earlier on the 10th August, 1942. The people of the city were not to

357

know this, of course, and the threat was taken seriously right up until the end of the war with Germany.

New Influx of Evacuees

Peterborough may have already seen the last of Hitler's bombs, but London and the South East were now facing a new threat, the V1 flying bomb (Doodlebug), and the V2 rocket. These "Revenge" weapons were now being fired indiscriminately from occupied Europe across the Channel to England. They were extremely inaccurate and could only be aimed at targets as large as cities. They were however, lethal, the V2 carried a one ton warhead and could not be stopped or intercepted once it had been launched. The only way to prevent these weapons being fired was for the Allied advance in Normandy to move inland and overrun their launch sites one by one.

By the middle of July, Peterborough and its neighbourhood had received several thousand evacuees from London and Southern England. The great majority had come to private billets arranged with relatives and friends, but others travelled on the off-chance of finding accommodation and had imposed a considerable strain on the billeting authorities and the W.V.S. helpers. (It may be assumed that the Town Clerk, Mr. W.B. Buckle, mentioned earlier, was now really earning the extra salary he had been taking for looking after the 'non-existent' evacuees during the previous few years).

On one Saturday afternoon and evening a number of evacuees had arrived in the city on various trains. The Town Hall was closed, and the evacuees tried their luck at the police station, from where they were directed to the Public Assistance Institution. There they stayed until the following Monday, when it was found necessary to open Woodston Church Hall in Palmerston Road, as a rest centre.

Mrs. J.A.J. Atkinson was in charge of the W.V.S. staffing arrangements, with Mrs. Day as her deputy. A rota of volunteers was arranged to staff the hall 24 hours a day for a week, and the work they did in difficult circumstances was said to be beyond praise. The evacuees had a midday dinner at the British Restaurant, and the W.V.S. prepared all other meals for them.

Other W.V.S. people scoured the district in the unenviable task of finding accommodation. But the job was done, and the centre at Woodston was then closed. Some of the evacuees were sent to other parts of the country. The billeting authorities had found it extremely difficult to find billets for mothers who refused to have their five or six children split up.

At this time it was confirmed that there was not one empty house in the city. The position in other parts of Northamptonshire was much the same. To illustrate the problem there was the case of three hundred evacuee boys from London who were still in need of billets at Kettering at this time. When a survey was made, the majority of householders who volunteered to take evacuees expressed a wish for girls.

Huntingdonshire had found homes for a fair number of unaccompanied schoolchildren, mainly from the East End of London. First arrivals at Huntingdon were a trainload of 190, of whom 82 remained in the borough and 108 went to Spaldwick, Brampton, Hamerton, Abbots Ripton, Woodwalton, Sawtry and Molesworth. St. Ives urban and rural districts accommodated 139 children on Saturday 7th July, and St. Neots 140.

"Close Shave" in Normandy

Private John Thomas Hunter, a member of the Airborne division who had gone to Normandy, was now back home with his parents, Sergeant and Mrs. Samuel Hunter, 45, Glenton Street, Peterborough. He was their eldest son and had returned with a bullet wound through the upper left arm. Aged 20 at this time, he had once been an apprentice at the Westwood Works. He had joined the Army aged 15 and when the war started was in the R.A.S.C. Afterwards he "got among the parachuters," and with nearly a dozen descents in his training record, he went to Normandy in the first flight. He was back in an English hospital four days later.

Private Hunter had the misfortune to drop close to a German machine gun post, and was treated to a burst of fire, one bullet going through his arm. He lay motionless hoping the Germans would think him dead as he didn't want another burst of fire in his direction. Then a British fighter plane came over and, when the enemy gunner's attention was diverted, he was able to hit back with a weapon he had in his pocket (probably a grenade), and the enemy gunners gave him no further trouble.

He was able to deal with his wound, and was then taken back to base and shipped to England, where he was recovering after a term in hospital. It was stated that the double wound he suffered was almost healed but he still had a stiff muscle. Private Hunter found that he had had an even narrower escape. In the breast pocket of his overall blouse was a tin tobacco box; this was pierced back and front by a bullet and the contents were "knocked to pieces."

In the inside pocket of the jacket was a metal portion of a weapon he carried, and this too showed signs of having been hit. It may have been this that diverted the bullet.

Private Hunter believed that he had been hit by two successive bullets but had no recollection of being struck in the breast. In view of the direction of his wound, he did not believe that one bullet glanced off and caused the arm injury. It was a narrow squeak indeed. Sergeant Hunter's father, Samuel, was a Sergeant in the Royal Artillery, serving in Egypt.

Escaped Prisoners

Mrs. Lake of 149, Alexandra Road, Peterborough, had now heard from her husband, Driver W.J. Lake, R.A.S.C., an escaped prisoner of war, that he was waiting for a ship to take him to England. He had been taken prisoner two years previously at Mersa Matruh, Egypt. When the fall of Italy came he was to have been transferred with other prisoners to Germany. He escaped, and ever since had been in hiding. Mrs. Lake received the news on Wednesday 12th July, after nine months silence. Driver Lake was the elder son of Mr. and Mrs. H. Lake, 149, Alexandra Road, and was formerly a driver for Read's Removals Ltd. He had a five year old son.

Good news was also received now by Mrs. Fovargue, of the Eight Bells, Lincoln Road, Peterborough. After two years in captivity, her husband, Private Frank Fovargue, had escaped from a German prison camp and had reached Allied lines in Italy. He was now awaiting transport home.

Casualties Continue

News now reached Mr. Harold and Mrs. Minnie Mallett, of 84, New England, Peterborough, that their son, Trooper Harold Mallett, 'A' Sqn, 2nd Lothian and Border Horse, Royal Armoured Corps, had been killed on 20th June in Italy, aged 21.

Trooper Mallett had joined the Army two years earlier and had seen 16 months service abroad. Formerly with S.G. Howes, Ltd., outfitters, Cowgate, he is buried in Assisi War Cemetery, Italy.

News had also been received now that Gunner George Robert Mason, Royal Artillery, had been wounded in the chest, arms and one leg in Normandy. He was the son of Mrs. Dingle, 18, Goodyer's Yard, Bridge Street, Peterborough, and had made his home with his sister, Mrs. Smith, 22, Goodyer's Yard. He had been with Ellis and Everard Ltd., coal merchants.

On July 21st it was announced that Flight Sergeant (Engineer) D. Sharpe, Royal Air Force, was missing from an operational flight during May. He was the son of Mr. and Mrs. E.A. Sharpe, 4, Haddon Road, Peterborough.

Driver William West Thompson, 13 Field Squadron, Royal Engineers, 148, Wellington Street, Peterborough, was now reported killed in action in Normandy on the 28th June. He was 35 years of age and had been a Pavior for the City Corporation before joining the Army two years earlier. Driver Thompson is buried in St. Manvieu War Cemetery, Calvados, France.

Private Peter O'Dell, 1, The Crescent, Woodston, Peterborough, who had been wounded in Normandy, was now back in England recovering from his wounds which consisted of fractures of both arms and both legs. Before the war he had been an inspector of gauges with the Newall Engineering Co., and joined the Army a year previously.

More Far East Cards

After almost two and a half years without news, Mr. Thomas and Mrs. Laura Harlock, 210, St. Paul's Road, Peterborough, had now received three cards from their son, Private Thomas Harlock, 2nd Cambridgeshire Regiment. Before the war he had been on the staff of Baker Perkins Ltd. The news, although extremely welcome, was bittersweet. Private Harlock died aged 25, on the 23rd July 1945, at Nakon Pathom, of tuberculosis and exhaustion while a Japanese prisoner of war. He is buried in Kanchanaburi War Cemetery, Thailand.

Mr. Charles and Mrs. Ethel Lane, 12, Marne Avenue, Walton, Peterborough, had now received two cards within three months from their son Private Leslie William Lane, 2nd Cambridgeshire Regiment. They had been without news of him since August 1943, when after 19 months silence since the fall of Singapore, they learned that he was a prisoner. He was in No. 2 Camp, Thailand, and said his health was excellent. Private Lane would be dead two months later, losing his life on the Japanese transport TOYOFUKU MARU which was sunk on the 21st September.

After two and a half years of suspense, news was now received by Mrs. C.E. Stallabrass, widow of Mr. H. Stallabrass, North Street, Stanground, Peterborough, from her son, Private Frederick Stallabrass, who had been taken prisoner in Malaya, after the fall of Singapore. No previous communication had been received from him. Her youngest son, Private R. Stallabrass, was in Italy, and her eldest, Private H. Stallabrass, was in training in England.

Mr. and Mrs. H. Wilson, 30, Monument Street, Peterborough, had also now received the news that their son, Stanley Frank Wilson, was a prisoner in Thailand Camp. It was also two and a half years since they had heard news that he had arrived at Singapore. He was formerly in the Co-operative grocery department, Park Road.

Missing Officer

Mr. and Mrs. W. Stimpson, 9, Council Street, Walton, Peterborough, were still waiting at this time for definite news of their son, Lieutenant John Stimpson, who had been reported missing in Normandy. Lt. Stimpson's name had been read out in a German broadcast in a list of prisoners taken by the Germans, but no official confirmation had been received. Aged 26, Lt. Stimpson was an old Deaconian, and was on the teaching staff of New Road School.

Killed in Plane Crash

When the plane in which the Prime Minister's son, Major Randolph Churchill was travelling crashed in Yugoslavia on July 16th, his batman, Corporal Douglas John Sowman, Suffolk Regiment, attached Special Operations Executive, of Woodston, lost his life.

Corporal Sowman was 24 years of age, and the elder son of Mr. Robert, and Mrs. Lydia Sowman, 22, Orton Avenue, Woodston, Peterborough. He married Miss Joan Watson, of 33, Tower Street, Peterborough. When he left school he went to the London Brick Company, transport department, and he joined the Suffolk Regiment four years previously, later transferring to the Signals, and then becoming a Paratroop Commando. He took part in a number of raids, and went through the African campaign, gaining the Africa Star. In Africa he joined Major Churchill's staff and was his batman for 18 months.

Corporal Sowman's widow received a telegram from the Prime Minister, Winston Churchill, stating: "Deeply regret to inform you that your husband was killed when aircraft in which he was flying crashed in Yugoslavia.. Accept my deepest sympathy and that of my son in this cruel misfortune."

Shortly afterwards Mrs. Sowman received a letter from Mrs. Churchill: "Dear Mrs. Sowman – I want you to know how grieved Mr. Churchill and I feel at the news of your husband's death, and how deeply we feel for you in your sorrow. I know that our son was much attached to him, and we had the pleasure of meeting him when he was in London for a few hours on his way to join you in Peterborough. Our son has asked us by telegram to send you his deepest sympathy, in which we join. My thoughts and prayers are with you in your grief – Yours sincerely, Clementine S. Churchill.

Corporal Sowman, who was in Force 123, Special Operations Executive, is buried in the Belgrade War Cemetery, Serbia and Montenegro.

Casualties Increase

It seemed that the more success the Allies had, the more casualties there were. Second Lieutenant Ronald John Sydney Hicks, 147 (The Essex Yeomanry), Field Regiment, Royal Artillery, was now reported as having been killed in action in Normandy on the 29th June. He was the son of Mr. and Mrs. S.J. Hicks, of Dartford, and formerly of Huntley Grove, Peterborough, where Mr. Hicks had a builders business. Second Lieutenant Hicks and his brother, Tony, now a Sub-Lieutenant in the Navy, were both educated at Deacon's School. Second Lieutenant Hicks is buried in Tilly-sur-Seulles War Cemetery, France.

Petty Officer Christopher Frank Elmer, (Airman) Fleet Air Arm, HMS SHRIKE, (a shore station), Royal Navy, was now reported missing, presumed killed. P/O Elmer was 20 years old and the second son of Mr. Frank and Mrs. Susannah Elmer, 29, Taverners Road, Peterborough. He joined the Navy in June 1942, and was transferred to the Fleet Air Arm soon afterwards. In civilian life he was on the staff of Mr. R.H. Miller, Midgate, and was a Home Guard. His fiancée was Miss Aurea Hobbs, of Oundle Road, Woodston, Peterborough. P/O Elmer was killed in an air crash on the 21st July, 1944, and has no known grave. He is commemorated on the Lee-on-Solent Memorial.

Private William Ernest Kenneth Brown, 2nd Lincolnshire Regiment, was now also reported killed in action on the 8th July in Normandy. Aged 20 years old, he was the son or Mr. Ernest and Mrs. Kathleen Brown, of 64, Paston Lane, Peterborough. His parents had first heard the news of his death a week earlier from a Corporal in his unit, and later from his Lieutenant who wrote: "He was a grand soldier, very popular, and he met his death during an attack, fighting by the side of his pals." Private Brown had been in the Army three years, following employment with the Newall Engineering Company. He was educated at Walton School, and was a keen footballer and boxer. He is buried in Ranville War Cemetery, Calvados, France.

Lieutenant George Terry, eldest son of Mr. and Mrs. W. Terry, 109, Padholme Road, Peterborough, who had been wounded in Italy, was now reported as progressing satisfactorily. Before the war he had been with Baxter and Guion Ltd., and later was a civilian clerk at the police station before he joined the Birmingham Police Force.

Corporal Maurice Sims, eldest son of Mr. and Mrs. A. Sims, 68, Burmer Road, Peterborough, who had been wounded in the leg, was now in hospital in the North of England. This was the second time he had been wounded; the first was on June 29th but he was able to remain on duty. He had been with Mr. Bert Hales, butcher, Lincoln Road, and joined the Army four years previously.

Mr. and Mrs. Sims had also received news that their second son, Able Seaman Joe Sims, was in hospital suffering from pneumonia after arriving in England from the USA. He had been in the Navy over two years and had seen service with Russian convoys before going to the States. He had been with Paten & Co.

Driver J. McBean, Royal Artillery, was now reported wounded in Italy, his wife lived at Stanground and his mother at Farcet, and both were notified on Saturday 21st June. Driver McBean had been in the North Africa campaign, and had received the Africa Star.

Private L.J. Hall, Belsize Avenue, Woodston, Peterborough, was now in hospital in England recovering from wounds received in Normandy. He went from the Corporation Electricity Company to the Army four years previously.

Trooper J. Measures, eldest son of Mr. and Mrs. J.S. Measures, 74, Dickens Street, Peterborough, was now reported wounded in Normandy where he landed on the first day of the invasion. He had bullet wounds on his right side, wrist and buttock, and burns on his left hand. Aged 20 years old, he joined the Army two years previously after an apprenticeship as a plumber with J. Cracknell Ltd. He was making satisfactory progress in a Glasgow hospital.

Driver Eric Harvey, Royal Artillery, only son of Mr. and Mrs. W.E. Harvey, 126, Queens Walk, Fletton, Peterborough, was now in hospital with hand and arm wounds received in France.

Life on Board a Rescue Vessel
The variety of war work carried out by Peterborough people was increasingly varied. Mr. J.M. Sneath, builder's merchant, 236, Lincoln Road, had now just returned after spending a month in the Navy under the Admiralty yachtsmen's

emergency service scheme. He had been on a motor fishing vessel engaged on Red Cross work, rescuing survivors and injured people from boats.

Mr. Sneath went on June 27th and returned on Saturday 29th July. There were six men on his boat, on which he was an Able Seaman. The skipper had been invalided after Dunkirk, the Mate was a Master Mariner, and another member of the crew was a Brigadier and a cousin of Winston Churchill.

Mr. Sneath said: "I found life aboard the vessel an interesting experience, even under war conditions. Most of the days were eventful, and I particularly remember July 10th, it was pretty rough, and we had great difficulty in manoeuvring alongside and taking patients off a battleship. Three days later we were called to a 10,000 ton Liberty Ship which had been mined amidships; despite this, only three men were missing. The ship was beached and we had to fetch a body found floating in the engine room after ten days immersion.

The next day we had survivors who had been 30 hours on a raft. On another occasion we fetched the body of a Chinaman who had died on a cargo vessel. Once it took us four hours to find a ship which was in our area, as visibility was poor. Two days before I returned we rescued 14 survivors from a motor torpedo boat which had been lost in action." Mr. Sneath had his yachtsman's master ticket, and was a member of the Nene Boating Club.

City Soldier's Military Medal

Lance Corporal John William Edwards, 14th Sherwood Foresters (Nott's & Derby) Regiment, son of Mr. John and Mrs. Mabel Edwards, 89, Wootton Avenue, Fletton, Peterborough, had now been awarded the Military Medal for outstanding courage and devotion to duty in the Anzio beach-head during the period March 10th – 25th, and April 1st – 10th.

Aged 20, L/Cpl Edwards was one of the youngest soldiers in his unit, and was a signaller at battalion headquarters. Direct communication with forward companies was not possible by day as the route was under observation by the enemy. It was therefore essential that line communication be maintained whenever possible.

Every night throughout the period during which the battalion was in the line, Edwards went forward at last light, and worked throughout the night, maintaining existing telephone lines and carrying new lines, often under intense enemy fire from mortars, artillery and machine-guns. His courage and determination not to take cover until his task was complete resulted in communications being maintained at a time when they were most needed.

On the night of April 5th/6th the enemy sent three patrols to attack the forward company of this unit, and the attacks were accompanied by intense and sustained mortar fire and shell fire for two and a half hours. Edwards went forward as usual to repair the line, and for two hours he worked in the open under incessant enemy fire. With complete contempt for the danger he was in, he eventually established communication, an achievement which made it possible for the forward company commander to call for fire to harass the enemy who had meanwhile been beaten off. Edwards' dogged perseverance and complete disregard for his own safety were a constant inspiration and example to his fellow signallers.

Lance Corporal Edwards died in hospital in Italy on 26th August, just two weeks after this report appeared, from multiple injuries received in an accident. He is buried in Ancona War Cemetery, Italy.

More Normandy Casualties

Driver Mechanic, George William Barber, 76 Field Regiment, Royal Artillery, had now been reported killed in Normandy on the 28th June. He was the son of Mr. Christopher and Mrs. Lily Barber, 43, Palmerston Road, Woodston, Peterborough, and was 34 years of age. He joined the Army in December 1942, after working as a plasterer in Cambridge, where his wife and one son, aged five lived. Up to 1930 he was Captain of Paston Athletic Football Club. He is buried in Ranville War Cemetery, France.

Lance Corporal John William Bellamy, 56, Lincoln Road, Werrington, Peterborough, was now in hospital in England after being wounded in both legs by shrapnel in Normandy in July. He was the only son of Mr. and Mrs. H. Bellamy, of Oakham.

Lance Corporal E.G.E. Church, son of Mrs. Shrive, 40, St. Mary's Street, Peterborough, was now reported wounded in the right leg in action in Normandy. He was in a Guards Regiment and was at Peter Brotherhood's before the war.

Private Kenneth Wright, son of Battery Sergeant Major C.W. Wright and Mrs. Wright, 287, Dogsthorpe Road, Peterborough, had now been wounded in action in Normandy and was in a hospital at Warwick. After attending Lincoln Road School, he became a bricklayer for Mr. W.S. Read, Princes Street.

Lance Sergeant Stanley La Barte Quibell, 7th Royal Norfolk Regiment, of 20, Eastfield Grove, Peterborough, had now been killed in action in Normandy on 8th August. Aged 32 years old and married to Stella Kathleen Quibell, he was the son of James and Isabella Quibell of Crown Street. He had served four years with the Norfolk Regiment and had formerly been with Messrs. Barber and Ross at their Towler Street branch. He is buried in Bayeux War Cemetery, Calvados, France.

Private Frank Ernest Lawlor, Dispatch Rider, 7th Royal Norfolk Regiment, had been killed in action in North West Europe on 7th August. He was the only son of Mr. and Mrs. E.J. Lawlor, 16, Fulham Road, and was 21 years old. On leaving the New England Boy's School he was in the Park Road butchery department of the Co-operative Society. He is buried in Bayeux War Cemetery, Calvados, France.

Another Normandy victim was Private George Frederick Cocker, 7th Royal Norfolk Regiment, who had also been killed in action on 7th August. Private Cocker was only 19 years of age and was the fourth son of Mr. and Mrs. J. Cocker, 11, The Crescent, Woodston, Peterborough. He joined the Army in 1943 and before that had been employed by the London Brick Company. He was also a member of the Peterborough Boys Club. He is buried in Bayeux War Cemetery, Calvados, France.

Prisoners of War

Sergeant Lawrence S. Fisher, Royal Air Force, originally reported missing following an operational flight over Germany during July was now known to be a prisoner of war. Sergeant Fisher was the son of Mr. W.S. Fisher, 198, Dogsthorpe Road, Peterborough, and was based in the Central Mediterranean area.

Lance Corporal Walter Galley was now known to be a prisoner of war at Stalag 7a. Lance Corporal Galley was 22 years old and the second son of Mr. and Mrs. A. Galley, 36, Orchard Street, Woodston, Peterborough. The official news that he was a prisoner followed an announcement to that effect on the German radio. He joined the Army in 1941 and served in the African campaign and was taken prisoner in Italy. He used to be a bricklayer for Mr. W.L. Russel, Park Street, London Road, Peterborough.

364

In August, two Peterborough soldiers returned home after spending many months as prisoners of war in Italy and wandering about after escape from captivity. Driver W.J. Lake, R.A.S.C. of 149, Alexandra Road, and driver R.W. Biggs, R.H.A. of 242, Cromwell Road, were both captured in North Africa and taken to Italy. Both escaped after the Italian surrender, and wandering through the strange countryside they eventually reached the Allied lines. They did not meet in Italy, but both arrived in England on Friday 11th August. They were now at their homes, making the most of 30 days' leave.

Fletton Family Lose Two Sons

Mr. and Mrs. G.W. Rusdale, 71, High Street, Fletton, Peterborough, had now suffered a further bereavement by the death in Normandy on August 19th of their fourth son, Private Cecil Charles Rusdale, of The Parachute Regiment. Private Rusdale was 19 and was with the first paratroops to land in Normandy on D-Day. He joined the Tank Corps nearly two years previously and volunteered for the paratroops. Employed at Reed's Garage in his civilian days, he is buried in Putot-en-Auge, Calvados, France.

This was not the first time that tragedy had struck the family, and Mrs. Rusdale said: "We thought we had given enough to this war." Two years earlier, Gunner Jack Rusdale, another son, died in a military hospital in England. Then in April 1943, Fusilier George Rusdale was taken prisoner, and was now in a prison camp in Germany.

A fourth son, Commando Alfred Rusdale, who had been serving since the outbreak of the war, was in India. The fifth son, Bernard, was at present at Reed's Garage, and would shortly register with the 17 year-olds for service. The father, Mr. G.W. Rusdale, saw three and a half years service with the 2nd Bedfordshire Regiment in the First World War.

Wartime Regulations Relaxed

Peterborough was happy to take its share in the relaxation of wartime restrictions and regulations announced by the Government on the night of Wednesday 6th September. These were:

- Black-out to be relaxed and modified street lighting to be introduced on and from 17th September, when British Double Summer Time ended.
- Fire watching, day and night, to be suspended from Tuesday 12th September (except at night in London and South East England).
- Whole time Civil Defence personnel to be released for other war work.
- Home Guard to be on a voluntary basis from Monday 11th September.

Orders were already being issued to the Fire Guard to stand down as from Tuesday 12th. Improved street lighting would be introduced stage by stage but a special master-switch could now be used to turn them all off together if a raid was to occur. "Peace time curtains" could now be used, as an order went out stating that windows other than skylights would only need to be curtained sufficiently to prevent objects inside the buildings being distinguishable from the outside. This meant that people could use ordinary curtains through which a diffused light was visible in the street.

Compulsory Home Guard drills and training were to be discontinued and operational duties would be carried out only on a voluntary basis. The call-up for further entrants was suspended. The Force had become a stand-by service but with a contingent liability to recall to full discipline and activity should the need arise.

Casualties Continue to Mount in Europe

Private E. Bines, second son of Mr. and Mrs. W. Bines, 40, Westwood Street, Peterborough, had found himself in a hospital in Italy, although strangely he had been wounded in France. He enlisted in 1940 after working in Hick's brickyard.

Private William Alfred Coles, 2nd/5th Leicestershire Regiment, was killed in action in Italy on the 31st August. Aged 30, he lived with his wife and four children at 62, Wellington Street, Peterborough. Born in Yaxley, he was formerly employed at the Eastwood Brick Company. He is buried in Montecchio War Cemetery, Italy.

Sapper Samuel Thorogood, Royal Engineers, had now been killed in action in Italy on the 1st September. He was the son of Mr. and Mrs. G.S. Thorogood, 21, Sergeant Street, Peterborough, and was 32 years of age. He had been in the Eighth Army throughout the campaigns in North Africa and Sicily. Before joining the Army in 1940, he had been a moulder at Brotherhood's and had a great interest in sport. He is buried in Florence War Cemetery, Italy.

Private Arthur William Butler, eldest son of Mr. and Mrs. F.E. Butler, 8, Great Eastern Terrace, Peterborough, was now reported missing in North Western Europe since August 21st. Aged 20 years old; he was formerly with English Brothers.

Sergeant Air Gunner Frederick Arbon, 51 Squadron, Bomber Command, RAFVR, previously reported missing on his first operational flight, was now confirmed as having been killed on 2nd May. He was buried in Belgium and his grave was found by Allied troops as they advanced. Aged 20, he was the son of Mr. A. Arbon, caretaker at the food office, and Mrs. Arbon, of 45, Hankey Street, Peterborough. Before the war he had been a fitter at Peter Brotherhood's.

Sergeant Arbon was the Rear Gunner in a Handley Page Halifax Mk III, Serial No MZ593, code letters MH-Z. The aircraft took off from RAF Snaith to bomb rail installations at Mechelen and was shot down by a night fighter. Four of the seven man crew died. Sergeant Arbon is buried in Wevelgem Communal Cemetery, West Vlaanderen, Belgium.

Trooper V.C. Matthews, Royal Tank Regiment, 28, Clarence Road, Peterborough, son of Mr. and Mrs. Matthews, 1, Park Street, London Road, Peterborough, had now been missing in France since the 7th September. He had been a clerk in the Corporation service in his civilian days. In his four years in the Army he had seen much active service, fighting in all the big battles from El Alamein to Tunisia, and on to Sicily and Italy. Going to France on the first day of the invasion, he fought at Caen and Falaise. He was wounded at one point but remained at his post. Trooper Matthews was married and had a son, Terrence aged six. They would be reunited at the end of the war.

Private Kenneth Gordon Cunnington, 1st Battalion, Suffolk Regiment, formerly of Fletton, Peterborough, was killed in action in France on 13th August. He was the youngest son of Mr. and Mrs. R. Cunnington, who left Peterborough five years earlier and moved to Buckinghamshire. Private Cunnington, who was 21 years old, was educated at Fletton Council School, and until he joined the Army in January 1944, was with Burchnall's Battery Service. He is buried in St. Charles de Percy War Cemetery, Calvados, France.

Lance Bombardier A.S. Lovell, Royal Artillery, of Peterborough, had been wounded in action near the Albert Canal in Belgium. He was flown to England after spending a night in a Brussels hospital and was now in an emergency hospital at Newport. He was a director of Lovell's Garage Ltd., Westgate, and in one more month would have been in the Forces five years. He spent a short period in France before the capitulation, followed by 10 months at Dover during the Battle of Britain.

Private Arthur Allen, 7th Battalion, Black Watch, youngest son of Mr. and Mrs. J.W. Allen, 11, Craig Street, Peterborough, was now reported killed in action in France on the 13th September; he had just turned 19 years old. He volunteered for the Army in May 1943, and had previously been a clerk with Williams and Co., solicitors. He is buried in Ste. Marie Cemetery, Le Havre, France.

Private Percy Ellis, third son of Mr. and Mrs. J.W. Ellis, 11, Chapel Street, Stanground, Peterborough, was now in a military hospital in England recovering from shell shock and exhaustion received while fighting in France. Aged 20 years old, before the war he had been with the London Brick Company.

Killed on the Way to Arnhem
Sapper John Evans, 9th (Airborne) Field Company, Royal Engineers, youngest son of Mrs. J. Evans, 35, Glenton Street, Peterborough, was now reported killed in a glider accident in Somerset on the 17th September. Aged 25, Sapper Evans had been a fitter with the Gas Company, and was a member of St. Mary's branch of the Anglican Young People's Association. In his four years and four months in the Army he saw service in Africa, Sicily and Italy, and received the Africa Star.

Just after 10.00 hours on Sunday 17th September 1944, sixteen glider and tug combinations took off from RAF Keevil for Arnhem as part of Operation Market Garden. Horsa Glider RJ113 (Chalk 389) was in this group of aircraft and contained 21 men, including Sapper Evans, from No 1 Platoon, 9th (Airborne) Field Company, Royal Engineers. The tugs and gliders took a course north-west towards Gloucester to pick up Squadrons from RAF Fairford and then headed out over the Severn and Bristol Channels to form up. Here they took a turn south-west down the Bristol Channel with other aircraft and gliders, and made a turn east over Weston-Super-Mare and headed for Arnhem. While over the village of Farrington Gurney an explosion occurred in RJ113 splitting the glider in two. With no tail section the glider lost lift, broke its tow line and crashed into the Double Hills meadow near Paulton killing all occupants. Sapper Evans is buried in Weston-Super-Mare Cemetery.

1,000 Letters Home
Lance Corporal T. Thornthwaite, 22, Alma Road, Peterborough, wrote to the editor of the Standard from his R.A.S.C unit in the South East Asia Command in September saying: "Sir, I have been receiving the Standard more or less regularly now for the past five years, and I very much appreciate the local news that keeps me in touch with happenings at home.

In the last five years, up to September 1st, 1944, I have written exactly 1,000 letters to my wife. I numbered all my letters right from September 1st, 1939, my first day in the Army. I wonder if this number is anywhere near a record for letter writing?

I spent nine months in France 1939-40, and have been in India and on the Indo-Burma front for the last two and a half years. I am looking forward to the time when I can read the Standard in front of my own fireside.

Among the Peterborough chaps I have met out here are Driver George Hutchinson, 66, Orchard Street, Joe Frith, Woodston, C/Sgt. Partridge (Royal Norfolks). L/Cpl. Frank Crisp, of the Paul Pry, two brothers, Willie and Johnny Goodacre, Cpl. Tommy Appleyard – he was an L.B.C. driver – and several others whose names I can't recall.

Some of these chaps are in the same unit as myself and are glad to have the Standard handed on to them." Sergeant Partridge would later be killed in action in Burma in April 1945. The rest, including L/Cpl. Thornthwaite, would survive the war.

Civil Defence Defined

It was now October and the Home Guard had just been reduced to a voluntary force and the roles of the rest of the Civil Defence organisation were defined. Personnel were being released and paid staff was reduced drastically, but people were told to keep their uniforms and basic equipment in case they were called back in an emergency.

Wardens and Messenger Service – Instead of a long rota of duties which had been carried out over the past few years, posts were being manned only from 9pm to 10.30pm daily. Some jobs still needed doing, and the volunteers of the service wanted to stay till the bitter end. Wardens were required to collect respirators from the public and equipment from men and women of the service, which would take some time.

Fire Guards – All training and duties in the Fire Guard were stopped, although they stood by ready to be called upon if required. People were asked to ensure that private stirrup pumps and other equipment were kept in good order in case they were suddenly needed. At the high point, in Peterborough and Old Fletton, there had been more than 10,000 Fire Guards carrying out regular training and ready for action.

First Aid and Ambulance Posts – This had been a fully paid service and was still in operation but reductions were beginning to take effect. First aid posts had been reduced from 23 to 5, and shortly afterwards, of those left, No. 1. Trinity Street; No. 2. Mayor's Walk; No. 4. Keeton Road; and No. 5. Mountsteven Avenue, were closed. This left only No. 3. St. Martin's Street, open. There had once been three ambulance stations but these had been reduced to two for some time, No. 1. Station, Padholme Road (Miss Coles), and No. 3. Paston Lane (Miss Josephine Farrow), and now it was expected that one more would close.

De-contamination and Rescue – These services were under the City Engineer and it seemed obvious that they had already become surplus to requirements. The Rescue Service had been reduced from 25 people to 3, Mr. G. Townsin (superintendent), Mr. H. Gibson and Mr. R. Williams.

Waterworks – The seven patrolmen who had been employed at the waterworks which supplied the city were to be dispensed with.

Report and Control – this was reduced from 6 to 2, Miss H.M. Pledger and Mrs. F. Whittome.

National Fire Service – Part demobilisation of the NFS had already begun in the area. Personnel released would come under the direction of the Ministry of Labour and National Service, and could be drafted to the Armed Forces or industry according to age category.

I was at Arnhem

At least one Peterborough soldier was able to say he was at Arnhem, that was Signaller William Larman, Royal Signals, son of Mr. and Mrs. Ernest Larman, 89, Garton End Road, Peterborough. In peacetime he had been a compositor at the 'Standard' printing works. Signaller Larman reached England by air on Friday 29th September, following the withdrawal of the Arnhem survivors, and came home on Tuesday 3rd on 14 days leave.

"We were in the second lift," he said, "which went over on Monday September 18th, and we were put down at Oosterbeek, just outside Arnhem. A fair bit of small arms fire greeted us, and there was more when we moved off to join the rest of the party.

Things were reasonably quiet for the first day or so, and we established divisional headquarters in a hotel, occupying practically all the rooms. Then Jerry started his shelling, and he let us have it every morning – from six until eleven. We had to beat a hurried retreat to the cellars, where headquarters remained until the time came to pack up and go. While we were 20ft below ground Jerry registered a few hits on the hotel, but we were safe. Our main difficulty was water, because our only supply was a well which was continually covered by a sniper. The only people who could get water were the R.A.M.C. chaps. They showed their Red Cross and the firing ceased until they had drawn the water.

We had to make the best of the little water we had. It was impossible to wash and shave, and we soon had beards and plenty of dirt. The food position was not too bad, but we could never cook, because as soon as we made a start, over would come a shell and we had to leave it. In the end though things got a bit short and we had to ration ourselves pretty severely. There was little or no rest for any of us for the nine days we were there. The noise was terrific all the time. Italy was bad enough, but compared with Arnhem it was a picnic.

Things gradually got worse, and eventually we had orders to move out. As it happened we were one of the first parties to go. With our faces blacked with boot polish and our feet muffled, we moved down to the Rhine beaches about ten o'clock at night. There was a lot of firing going on, and I was knocked off my feet twice by shell blast before we broke camp.

The din then was indescribable, but it was good to know that most of the noise came from the terrific barrage our Second Army was laying down. When we were down by the river there was little enemy fire in our direction, because Jerry had not realised what was happening. We queued for our turn to cross, and Second Army men ferried us over the Rhine in flat-bottomed boats. Over the other side I was separated from my little party, but I managed to get in with a few stragglers, and then everything in the garden was lovely."

Another Peterborough man who had returned to England following the withdrawal from Arnhem was Lieutenant K.A. Hall, younger son of Mr. and Mrs. I. Hall, 114, Alexandra Road. Lt. Hall was in the 1st Airborne Division, Royal Engineers, and was an Old Petriburgian (Kings School boy).

Missing at Arnhem

Lance Bombardier Stanley Cole, 1st Airborne Division, Royal Artillery, had now been reported missing since the withdrawal from Arnhem. Aged 21, he was the son of Mr. R.A. Cole and the late Mrs. Cole, 4, East Station Road, Peterborough. He worked for the London Brick Company, transport department, before the war and joined the Army two years previously. He saw service in North Africa and Italy before being parachuted into Holland.

In a letter to Mr. Cole, an officer wrote: "I am very sorry to say that your son did not manage to get back across the River Rhine, and I sympathise with you; it is a great loss, but perhaps only temporary. There is every possible chance of him being alive and a prisoner of war. He was alive and well at the time the evacuation was ordered. But on the way down to the river he lost touch with us.

He was, however, reported to have been seen on the river bank, and with many others he had to surrender, as daylight made further resistance and the crossing of the river impossible. We are very sorry to lose him, as he is a very nice boy, and worked extremely well for us."

On 24th November, the 'Standard' carried a small report stating that L/Bdr. Cole was confirmed as being a prisoner of war in Germany, and he had written to say that he was safe and well.

Place Names Return

On Tuesday 10th October, the Home Secretary made an order revoking the Removal of Direction Signs Order. From that date all emergency restrictions on the exhibition of place names came to an end throughout Great Britain. Railway station name boards were also to be reinstated as quickly as the provision of labour permitted.

The Casualty Lists Continue to Grow

Sergeant Air Gunner Edward Neville, 50 Squadron, Bomber Command, RAFVR, was now missing from an operational flight. Aged 20, he was the second son of Mr. and Mrs. E. Neville, 11, Kent Road, Peterborough. Their only other child, Gunner William Neville, Royal Artillery, had died in a Japanese prisoner of war camp in February 1942. Sgt. Neville had been an L.N.E.R. fireman and joined the RAF a year previously. He died on the 12th September 1944 while flying as a gunner in a Lancaster Mk I, Serial No PD294, code letters VN-A which took off from RAF Skellingthorpe to attack Darmstadt. Four of the seven man crew died, he is buried in Durnbach War Cemetery, Bayern Germany.

Lance Corporal John Travers Dixon, 6th Battalion, Lincolnshire Regiment, had been killed in action in Italy on the 17th September. He was 28 years old and the only son of the late Mr. and Mrs. H. Dixon, of Fairfield Road, Fletton, Peterborough. He married Miss D.M. Hill, of 163, Oundle Road, Peterborough, and had a son aged three. Educated at Deacon's School, he became a clerk with Aveling-Barford Ltd., Grantham, and joined the Army in 1939. He is buried in Forli War Cemetery, Italy. A memorial service was held for him at St. Augustine's Church on the evening of Monday 9th October, and a requiem mass on the following Tuesday morning.

Private William Ruff, 1st Battalion, Duke of Wellington's (West Riding) Regiment, was now reported as having been killed in action in Italy on the 14th September. Aged 25, he was the son of Mr. William and Mrs. Hannah Ruff, 52, Eastgate, Peterborough, and is buried in Florence War Cemetery, Italy.

RAF Regiment Hero

News was now received in the city of the death in action of Flight Lieutenant Roland Gwynne Evans-Evans, 2804 Squadron, RAF Regiment. Aged 30, he was the youngest son of Mr. Anthony Arthur and Mrs. Margaret Ann Evans-Evans, of

Peterborough, and husband of Hilda Evans-Evans. He was killed in armoured car action in Belgium on the 2nd October, and is buried in Leopoldsburg War Cemetery, Belgium.

Flt. Lt. Evans-Evans was, like his three officer brothers, educated at King's School, where he was a boarder for ten years. In 1938 he married Miss H. Spink, of Eastfield. In civilian life he was in partnership with one of his brothers in a garage business at Stilton, which was now run by his widow.

In a letter to his widow, Flt. Lt. Evans-Evans' Colonel wrote: "I am writing to try to express in some small way my sympathy in the loss of your husband. He came to me on a course when I commanded the battle school, and he was always so unfailingly cheerful and hardworking that it was a pleasure to have him. I have been down to see his flight, who were quite lost without him.

I am more than sympathetic with you as I lost my own wife at the Guards Chapel. From our own points of view these are just inevitable disasters. I feel that there is nothing for us but to realise that we are just two among hundreds of thousands who are suffering some kind of loss.

From a personal look at the ground I feel sure that he carried out a very gallant little patrol. By seeing that his armoured cars did not close up, and were ready to move off, after being already turned round, he saved many more losses.

As I see it, what happened was as follows: The unit had just moved to a new position, actually in the front line, and your husband, with a troop of A.F.V.s (armoured fighting vehicles) and two rifle flights from another squadron, had been detailed for their protection. In view of the tricky situation in front, your husband moved to go out with a patrol to try to clear it up, and find out exactly where the enemy were.

Just before getting to a crossroads overlooked by buildings on the far side of a canal, he appears to have become suspicious, and halted his three armoured vehicles under cover. He had been told that the enemy were in this vicinity. He himself dismounted and went forward alone to investigate more closely, and it was at this point that the enemy opened fire. He was hit with the first shot, but returned the fire. The enemy then brought very heavy mortar fire to bear on the whole patrol. It was by one of these mortar shells that your husband was hit. He is buried nearby a little shrine."

The padre and other officers also wrote letters of consolation and to praise Flt.-Lt. Evans-Evans' courage and leadership. One officer wrote: "In the presence of his men, he was buried at the foot of a wayside Calvary."

Old Soldier

Warrant Officer Class I, H.J. Wood, M.S.M., R.A.S.C., of 70, Windmill Street, Peterborough, was now about to receive his discharge from the Army as a volunteer, after nearly five years service in the war. He served for two years on the Gold Coast, assisting in the raising and training of the West African Army in mechanism and general motor transport duties. Leaving the Gold Coast towards he end of 1942, he had a brief spell at home prior to being detailed for the North African campaign, for which he received the Africa Star.

Warrant Officer Wood also served in the First World War. He enlisted in the Royal Naval Air Service in January 1915, later transferring to the Army Service Corps, mechanical transport. In this he served in France, Egypt, Palestine and Syria; and was awarded the general service medal and victory medals.

But that was not his first experience of war, as he fought in the Boer War of 1901-02, and was for a time attached to Colonel Fortescue's flying column. He was in possession of the Queen's South African Medal, with four clasps, and there could be few men who were entitled to wear both that medal and the Africa Star.

More Reports of Casualties

The sad roll of the dead continued. Soon after his return to duty after 21 day's leave, in which he became engaged to Miss Jean Bowen of Malvern, Leading Stoker Leslie Harry Woods, H.M.L.S.T. 413 (His Majesty's Landing Ship 'Tank'), Royal Navy, 23, Huntley Grove, met his death by drowning on 20th October.

He was the fourth son of Mr. and Mrs. O.C. Woods, who received a telegram from the Admiralty on Sunday 22nd. Leading Stoker Woods, who was 20, was educated at St. John's School, and later worked for Mr. F.W. Brown, butcher, Long Causeway. He volunteered for the Navy two years previously and served in the Mediterranean and in the Normandy invasion. His younger brother, Reg, was also in the Navy, and another brother, Charles, was a Sergeant in the Royal Artillery somewhere in Europe. Leading Stoker Woods was buried in Broadway Cemetery, Peterborough, on Wednesday 25th, after a service at Wentworth Street Methodist Church.

Sergeant Patrick Noel Gent, Bomber Command, R.A.F.V.R., 212, Cromwell Road, Peterborough, was now reported killed in a flying accident on 12th October, a few days before his 22nd birthday. An old Deaconian, he was the younger son of Mr. Arthur and Mrs. Mabel Gent, and before the war had been a railway clerk, volunteering for the RAF in August 1942. His elder brother, Corporal Donald Gent, was also in the RAF. Sergeant Gent is buried in Chester (Blacon) Cemetery.

Lance Corporal George Frederick Papworth, 1st Battalion, Kings Liverpool Regiment, 77 Indian Infantry Brigade, 45, South View Road, Walton, Peterborough, was now officially reported missing in Burma since 23rd May. In a letter to his mother, Mrs. F. Papworth, his Colonel wrote that he was killed instantly. L/Cpl. Papworth was 23 years of age and had been a Territorial before the war. Soon after the outbreak of hostilities he went to Brotherhood's as an electric welder but was later recalled to the Colours. He had been overseas since the beginning of 1944 and had two brothers in the Forces, with 14 and 10 years service respectively.

L/Cpl. Papworth was later officially recorded as having been killed on the 24th May 1944. He was part of the 2nd Chindit operation in Burma in 1944, one of 'Wingate's Chindits'. He has no known grave and is commemorated on the Rangoon Memorial, Myanmar (Burma).

Captain John Norton Lowe, Essex Regiment, attached Nigeria Regiment, R.W.A.F.F., was killed in action on 7th October in action in Burma. He was the elder son of Captain A.E. and the late Mrs. Lowe, of The Orchard, Orton Longueville, Peterborough. He was educated at Kimbolton School, and served his articles as a solicitor with Messrs. R.Y. Norris and Sons, of Priestgate. He then went to Messrs. Elewes Turner and Smith, solicitors, Colchester.

Captain Lowe joined up immediately on the outbreak of war, with the Territorials and was commissioned with the Essex Regiment in 1941, and served with the 2nd Battalion until 1943, when he went to British West Africa. After about three months there, he was sent to India, and then on to Burma where he was serving with the 4th Battalion, Nigeria Regiment.

Captain Lowe, who was 30 years of age, was well-known and very popular in Peterborough and district. He was a keen member of the Peterborough Debating Society, and an enthusiastic player at the Peterborough Tennis Club. He has no known grave and is commemorated on the Rangoon Memorial, Myanmar (Burma).

Sergeant Kenneth Johnson, 81st Anti-Tank Regiment, Royal Artillery, of 49, Parliament Street, Peterborough, was killed in action in Italy on 11th October, aged 25. He was the younger son of Mr. and Mrs. W.J. Johnson, and had been in the Army almost five years. Before the war he had been with Mr. L.A. Wells, estate agent and auctioneer, Bridge Street. He was a server at St. Paul's Church and as a member of Toc H, assisted at the Market Place Services Canteen. A requiem mass was held at St. Paul's on Wednesday 25th. Sergeant Johnson is buried in Faenza Cemetery, Italy.

Corporal Leslie Jack Lane Reynolds, 1st Battalion, Royal Norfolk Regiment, 10, Hankey Street, Peterborough, was now reported killed in action in Holland on the 15th October. Aged 27, he was the only son of Mrs. C.A. Reynolds, his father, Mr. Ted Reynolds, lost his life in the First World War. Corporal Reynolds is buried in Overloon War Cemetery, Holland.

Private Richard Wilkins, 188, Oundle Road, Woodston Peterborough, was now reported missing in action in Italy on 2nd October. Aged 20, he was the eldest son of Mr. and Mrs. D. Wilkins. He had been wounded on 4th September and had just returned to the line when he was reported missing. He joined the Army in April 1939 when he was fifteen, and was formerly in the Woodston Scouts.

Private Raymond Larrington, Old Fletton, was now reported wounded in both ankles in Holland on 6th October. He was 18 years old and the younger son of Mr. and Mrs. P. Larrington, 31, Milton Road, Peterborough. He joined the Army in February, and was formerly a baker with Messrs. Smith, Oundle Road. His elder brother, Gunner Percy Larrington, was also on the Continent.

Private C.A. Swetman, Lincolnshire Regiment, 28, Milton Street, Peterborough, was now in hospital in England suffering from shrapnel wounds in the left side and arm, a fractured scapula and fractured ribs, sustained in action in Holland.

Salute the Soldier Plaques Presented
The Army was now represented on the walls of the Town Hall by a plaque alongside mementoes of earlier savings weeks for the RAF and Navy. The War Office Plaque, which was presented by Colonel C.W.D. Rowe representing the Secretary of State for War, to the City Council on Friday 3rd November, commemorated the raising of £627,000 in Salute the Soldier Week. Members of the Soke Savings Committee, their wives and a few guests, first enjoyed a cocktail party in the Mayor's Parlour.

Back Broken Twice
Flight Sergeant John Gerrard of Broadway Gardens, Peterborough, pilot of a rocket-firing Typhoon aircraft, was now recovering from a broken back for the second time in his flying career. He was a member of the Typhoon squadrons which had accounted for 135 enemy tanks when the Germans had made a big attempt to break through the Allied lines at Avranches. Later, he was one of the pilots who strafed the German convoys so successfully in their retreat through the 'Falaise Gap.'

"We couldn't go wrong," he said. "We shot up the leading vehicles, and, having blocked the roads, flew up and down blazing away at our leisure. The main problem was from our own aircraft, for every plane that could be spared was in the air. It was just like target practice."

On the evening of the third day, Flight Sergeant Gerrard's Typhoon was hit by anti-aircraft fire and he was forced to crash land. It was the second time he had broken his back, the first occasion being when flying a Master aircraft during training at Christmas 1942. In civilian life he was employed by Brotherhood's, of which his father was company secretary. He was educated at Deacon's School.

Flight Sergeant Gerrard was already out of bed by 10th November and was rapidly getting used to his second spell in a plaster jacket.

Home Guard Stand-Down Directive
Definite notice had now been received from the authorities stating exactly what items of clothing members of the Home Guard would be able to retain when they were finally disbanded. Members would be allowed to retain boots, anklets, battle-dress, greatcoat, cap and badge, shoulder titles, Mark III spectacles, proficiency and service badges and anti-gas cape. Until the Home Guard was finally disbanded, these articles were to be held on trust only and should not be disposed of. Gas masks would also be retained, and notification would be given when these were to be returned. Web equipment and belts would be returned after the final parade on 3rd December.

Any other equipment had to be returned at once to their company stores. No article of clothing or equipment issued by the Home Guard was allowed to be bought or sold. Ammunition was not supposed to be in the possession of any member of the Home Guard, but it was stated that if by any legal or illegal means they had any, it was earnestly requested that it should be returned at once (no questions asked)! This was really important as carelessness with ammunition had frequently resulted in accidents to children.

Soldier Saved by Bible
A new testament, one of the official copies issued to the Forces, had just saved the life of a Peterborough soldier – Private Kenneth Wright, son of B.S.M. and Mrs. C.W. Wright, 287, Dogsthorpe Road.

Private Wright was fighting in France during August, and a bullet struck him in the chest in the area of his heart. Fortunately he carried his New Testament in the left breast pocket of his tunic, and this lay in the path of the bullet, which ploughed across the width of the Testament, glanced across to Private Wright's upper left arm, and tore a muscle.

Private Wright, who was 22 years of age, was an old boy of Lincoln Road School, and had been with Mr. W. Read, builder, of Princes Street. He was at present convalescing in a hospital in England.

Gun Action
Gunner J. Hall, of 17, Walpole Street, Peterborough, was now named in dispatches for his role in an incident on the Western Front. He assisted with others to man-handle a gun under heavy fire to cover a German gun position. As they rounded a corner by a house, they saw a German self-propelled gun only 400 yards away, moving into a new position. They got their own gun into action, fired one shot, and the German gun "brewed up." In all, the troop destroyed one S.P. gun, blew up a

house containing several Germans, and shot several more with Bren guns, helping considerably to disperse a counter-attack.

U.S. Thanksgiving Day at the Cathedral

On Thursday 23rd November, the 'Stars and Stripes' flew from the Cathedral flagstaff in honour of America's Thanksgiving Day. In the afternoon, some 600 men of the United States Army attended a service there. Assembled behind the Embassy Theatre, they marched to the Cathedral led by the Air Training Corps Band, a contingent of the RAF numbering about 100, and 50 members of the Women's Auxiliary Air Force. The RAF units included Australians, New Zealanders and Canadians. One half of the nave was filled with the general public, including American Red Cross personnel.

When the troops had taken their places in the trancepts and nave, the civic procession arrived with a guard of honour of four American Military Police. Next came the Bishop, Dean and choir. The Dean, receiving the 'Stars and Stripes' from three American soldiers, laid it upon the altar, where it remained throughout the service. The Bishop extended a hearty welcome to the troops, after which Chaplain Thomas B. Richards, U.S. Army, read the Presidential Address and said:

"We have had not only an abundant harvest of grain, but also an overwhelming harvest of ships, planes and guns; an overwhelming harvest of men and materials with which to ensure victory against the enemies of freedom. In the face of this superiority in men and materials we were in danger of adopting an attitude of superiority. This would be inappropriate to Thanksgiving Day. The attitude of humility was the only attitude we dare assume on this day."

Chaplain Richards said the time had come when we must make our America and our Britain. We had fought well together because we shared the same tradition, and he hoped we might work as well together in peace. He was confident that the harvest of future years would be plentiful; that it would be a harvest of better homes, better schools and churches, and he hoped, of better people.

After the singing of the National Anthems of the United States and Great Britain, the service was brought to a close with the Blessing given by the Bishop.

Life in an Italian Prison Camp

A Peterborough man who had spent 14 months in an Italian prisoner of war camp had now returned home and spoke of, with some feeling, about the difference between the treatment he received and the way Italian POWs were treated in England. He was Corporal W.M. Holdich, R.A.S.C., elder son of Mrs. E. Holdich, and the late Mr. W. Holdich, 179, St. Paul's Road, Peterborough. Corporal Holdich said he took: "vigorous exception to the Italians being allowed to walk around how they like and be given such treatment. There is a definite contrast between the treatment they get and the treatment we received. The people of the North of Italy treated us very well but all prisoners here are southerners."

In the Italian camp they were not ill-treated, he said, but the food was terrible. Most of the time they had thin soup, which sometimes contained rice or macaroni. "We got the Red Cross parcels when the Italians didn't eat them," he said. Corporal Holdich was captured by the Germans at Tobruk on 21st June, 1942 and handed over to the Italians. He was then taken to an Italian prisoner of war camp and remained there for 14 months. He told his story as follows:

"When the fall of Mussolini came on 8th September, 1943, the Italian commandant told us we should be released the following morning. Everybody rejoiced and took off their prisoner of war patches. About three o'clock on the following day, Germans surrounded our camp and our spirits sank. A German commandant took over and we later got the best food we had had for months.

About eleven days later they started moving everybody to Germany. We were packed into box cars, about 40 of us in each, with the sliding doors locked. We looked around, noticed that the back of the truck was slightly damaged, and with the aid of a jack-knife, hacked a hole in it. We managed to squeeze ourselves through this hole feet first, pushed by those inside.

We had arranged beforehand that we should act individually when we got out. When I jumped off I landed on the signal wires at the side of the track and started walking along the road by the side of the line. I passed two men and nearly jumped into a hedge but thought better of it and walked past unnoticed. I heard a clock striking and walked towards its direction but couldn't find it. I found a cow shed in which I spent the night, having milk for breakfast in the morning!

I walked along the road and met a man on a bike who asked me if I wanted a change of clothes (I was still in uniform). I jumped at the chance and he took me to a railway station and then to a mountain cafe where I was received by a mother and her daughter, who gave me wine, food and clothes. I stayed there for about three weeks until it became a bit too hot, with too many Germans popping in.

It was decided that I should make for the Swiss frontier and after five day's walking over the mountains, guided by the daughter from the cafe, I was left at the top of the mountain from where we could see the Swiss frontier. Some four hours later I got down and met a Swiss soldier, who thought I was a German."

Corporal Holdich was treated with great kindness and stayed there for about a year. He arrived on the French-Swiss border on 9th October, 1944, and travelled across France by express train. From Marseilles he went by an American boat to Naples and after a short stay there, went by British boat to Gibraltar, and then back to England, where he arrived on 2nd November.

More News of Casualties

Aircraftman 2nd Class, (Wireless Operator) John Leonard Pearson, RAFVR, 75, South Street, Stanground, Peterborough, was now reported killed in an accident in Greece on 14th November. He was married to Joyce Pearson and his parents, Mr. John and Mrs. Ivy Pearson, lived at 90, High Street, Fletton, Peterborough. In civilian life he had been a railway telegraph clerk at Kings Cross, and joined the RAF in 1941. His two years service abroad entitled him to the Africa Star. A/C Pearson was aged 23 when he died and is buried in Phaleron War Cemetery, Greece.

Better news was received regarding Trooper Victor Matthews, Royal Tank Regiment, 28, Clarence Road, Peterborough, who had been missing in North West Europe since 7th September. He was now reported to be a prisoner in a transit camp in Germany.

Driver Arthur Holmes, R.A.S.C., (Airborne), missing since the first day of the invasion of France was now reported as a prisoner of war in Stalag IVB in Germany. His brother, Rifleman A.R. Holmes, Rifle Brigade, who had been taken prisoner in Italy, was in Stalag IVD. They were the sons of Mr. and Mrs. Arthur Holmes, 680, Lincoln Road, New England, Peterborough.

Warrant Officer (fighter pilot) Ronald Arthur Hawkins, 177 Squadron, RAFVR, 19, Princes Road, Fletton, Peterborough, was now reported missing from air operations over India. He joined the RAF in June 1941 after service as a clerk with the London Brick Company. He was trained in Rhodesia and saw service with Ferry Command and Coastal Command, and was a fighter pilot at Gibraltar, Malta, Cairo, the Middle East, Madagascar, Ceylon and India. He had seen 33 months of foreign service and when he came home on leave in March 1943, he married Miss Doreen Sylvia Butler, of Wellington Street. In civilian life he was well known locally as a dance band leader and athlete. Little more is known about his fate, he is recorded as having been killed in action on 1st December, 1944, and is commemorated on the Singapore Memorial.

Private Isaac Henry Ulyatt, 1st Battalion, Manchester Regiment, 44, Aldermans Drive, Peterborough, had now been reported killed in action in Holland on 27th November, aged 34. Private Ulyatt had been assistant relieving officer for the Soke Guardians Committee from May 1932, and joined the Army in January 1944, going abroad in September. In 1939 he married Miss Edith Steiner, a Czechoslovakian, whom he met on holiday; they had one daughter, Eva Jane, aged four and a half.

He was the only surviving son of the late Mr. and Mrs. H.R. Ulyatt, 234, Cromwell Road, Peterborough. His eldest brother was killed in the Battle of Jutland in the First World War, and the youngest, David, had been killed in a motor accident in 1942. Private Ulyatt was at one time secretary of the Junior Imperial League and was a keen churchman, being a server at St. Barnabas' and for some time a member of St. Mark's Club. He is buried in Groesbeek Canadian War Cemetery, Holland.

News reached Peterborough now that Private James Arthur Brown, 5th Battalion, Suffolk Regiment, son of Mr. James and Mrs. Annie Brown, 67, Tower Street, New Fletton, Peterborough, had died aged 24, on the 13th August, 1943, in a Japanese prisoner of war camp. He had formerly been a greaser on the L.M.S. and he joined the Army in October 1939. He is buried in Sai Wan War Cemetery, Hong Kong.

The Tragedy of HMS LST 420

Two airmen from the city were now reported as having been killed on 7th November but no further news of the circumstances of their deaths was published at the time. One was Aircraftman 2nd Class, William Percy Gill, Base Signals Radar Unit, RAFVR. A/C Gill, of 15, Marholm Road, Walton, Peterborough, was reported missing at sea on 7th November. Aged 38, he was formerly the manager of the Gas Company's show-rooms in Westgate. He was married with one son aged 11, and is commemorated on the Runnymede Memorial,

The second man was Leading Aircraftman, Horace Lightfoot, Base Signals Radar Unit, RAFVR, of 'Racedale,' St. Botolph's Lane, Orton Longueville, Peterborough, he was also reported lost at sea on that date. Before joining the RAF three years previously, he had been a gardener-porter at the Isolation Hospital, Fengate, Peterborough. He was the husband of Alice Lightfoot, and the son of Mr. Edward and Mrs. Helen Lightfoot. Aged 38 when he died, L/Ac Lightfoot is buried in Ostend New Communal Cemetery, Ostend, Belgium.

The date, 7th November, the identity of the unit, 'Base Signals Radar Unit,' and the fact that L/Ac Lightfoot was buried at Ostend, gives us sufficient clues to identify the ship on which they were sailing when they were killed.

HMS LST (Landing Ship 'Tank') 420, was built at Bethlehem-Fairfield Shipyard Inc., Baltimore, Maryland, U.S.A. The ship was launched on 5th December, 1942, and went straight into service with the Royal Navy. The RAF Base Signals Radar Unit (B.S.R.U.) was called forward for service on the Continent after spending eighteen months in England training, and carrying out the training of other radar units. They embarked with their equipment and vehicles on HMS LST 420 on the morning of the 7th November, 1944, and set out for Ostend.

The weather at this time had been atrocious, and the ship had waited for a number of days hoping that conditions would improve. When they did eventually sail the weather began to deteriorate steadily and by the time they were off Ostend, a storm had arisen and a heavy sea was running. Due to these conditions, the Captain decided it was not safe enough to attempt a landing and ordered the ship to return to England. It was on this return voyage at about 3 o'clock in the afternoon and still in sight of the Belgian coast that the ship struck a mine amidships, was blown in two, and sank in a very short space of time.

In addition to the damaging effect of the mine, the galley fires that were on in preparation of an evening meal for the ship's compliment, set fire to the petrol running out of the damaged vehicle's fuel tanks, and the whole stern section of the ship was rapidly enveloped in flames. The heavy seas made it impossible for all but the larger vessels in the vicinity to go to the rescue, and out of 263 officers and men on board, only 32 were saved.

There were many examples of bravery taking place during the sinking and the stories of many would never be told. Several of those who had found some measure of safety on life rafts, abandoned them to swim out to their comrades who were drowning, but then found that they were unable to get back due to the heavy seas. The beaches upon which many of the bodies were washed up were still mined, and the task of retrieving them was fraught with danger.

This sinking, in which 13 officers and 218 other ranks lost their lives, is thought to have been the worst disaster suffered by RAF Signals during the whole European war.

Boy Injured by a Bullet
Back in the city, children were still playing with ammunition that had not been handed in. Raymond Baker aged 11, of 28, North Street, Stanground, Peterborough, was in the Memorial Hospital with severe shock and injuries received when he was playing in the street with a bullet on Tuesday 28th November. Raymond and another boy found the bullet, a .303, and placed it in a small hole in the fence round Stanground recreation ground. They then hit the bullet with a brick and it exploded. The brick hit Raymond heavily on the temple. The police warned children and adults yet again, not to touch any objects they found in the streets, but to report them to the police station.

The Home Guard's Final Parade
Nearly fourteen hundred men of the Home Guard of Peterborough, the Soke and North Huntingdonshire marched past the Deputy Adjutant General of the Forces, Major General the Viscount Bridgeman, in the great Stand Down parade on Sunday 3rd December.

Mustering at four points, they had marched to the town cricket ground for inspection by the Deputy Adjutant General, who was accompanied by Colonel C.W.D. Rowe, Sector Commander, Lt. Col. W. Marsh, 16 Anti-Aircraft Regiment, Royal Artillery, Lt. Col. E.W. Bromidge, 10th H.G. Anti-Aircraft Regiment, the

Mayors of Peterborough, Huntingdon, Godmanchester and St. Ives, as well as other dignitaries and representatives of the N.F.S., A.R.P. and W.V.S.

Colonel Rowe welcomed the visitors and read the King's message to the Home Guard. Lord Bridgeman made an address in which he thanked the Home Guard for the great service it rendered in the country's hour of need. The military and civic parties then travelled by car to the Embassy steps, and the Home Guard marched by way of Crawthorne Road and Broadway. Lord Bridgeman took the Salute, and the parade took 25 minutes to pass him. The Band of the 1st Northants Battalion, which had led the parade, played all the units past the base.

Returning to their several assembly points, the Battalions were addressed by their own Commanding Officers before the last dismiss was ordered.

Soldier Shoots at Wife

A soldier who was stated to have been given compassionate leave from Italy because of trouble in the home was bound over for 12 months at the Magistrate's Court on Wednesday 20th December, on a summons for being drunk on 16th December, and for being in unlawful possession of a firearm. The defendant was Arthur William Ilett, Bayne's Yard, Wood Street, Peterborough. It was stated in court that he was arrested on a charge of shooting at his wife with intent to do her grievous bodily harm. Dr. Hunt, for the defendant, pleaded guilty to the summons.

Detective Constable Dobson said he saw the defendant and told him his wife complained that he had shot at her with a pistol. The defendant showed him two dueling pistols, and later an automatic pistol and two rounds of ammunition. He was in the Northamptonshire Regiment and was home on compassionate leave. The defendant made a statement that he had differences with his wife, and had some drink. He came home and struck her, and then fired the pistol out of the door after she had gone away. He would not have done it had he not had drink. He said he brought the revolver and ammunition from Italy, and had no licence. Dr. Hunt said that there had been trouble over domestic affairs.

The defendant, a former corporation employee, joined the Army in 1939 and came through Dunkirk. He landed with the First Army in Africa, and served with them until he got compassionate leave owing to trouble at home. His wife wrote to him and said she had taken up with an Allied soldier, and was "in a certain condition." The defendant had made her an allowance and sent three sums amounting to £25. He was a good husband and citizen and it was a great shock to him.

He arrived at Peterborough on 5th December and found that although he had sent his wife money, she had got rid of a proportion of the home. He was dissatisfied with the way the children were kept. He hoped for reconciliation, but the wife said she still loved the Allied soldier. They could understand, Dr. Hunt said, the effect such a position would have on a respectable man. He brought the revolver home from Italy. He was in a drunken condition and fired it to frighten his wife. Unfortunately such cases were not singular in these times. He asked the bench to deal leniently with the defendant, who was willing to hand in the revolver and ammunition, and understood now that such conduct could not be permitted.

The Clerk said that on the charge on which the defendant had been arrested – shooting at his wife with intent to do grievous bodily harm – the Chief Constable would offer no evidence. The Chairman said the defendant very nearly got into a very serious charge. They realised that the man's provocation was very great, and were going to bind him over for 12 months. He must not take the law into his own hands. Dr. Hunt said the defendant would hand in the revolver.

Some More Casualties

Corporal Lawrence Ward, 2nd Queens Royal Regiment (West Surrey), 16th Brigade, 26, Church Street, Stanground, Peterborough, was now reported as having died in India of head injuries received in an accident on 16th December. He was 29 years of age and attached to the 1944 Special Forces 'Chindits' operation. Cpl. Ward joined the Army in 1939 after employment with Frank Perkins Ltd. He left a widow and two children, Laurel aged 6 and Gloria aged 2. He is buried in Kirkee War Cemetery, India.

Private (Craftsman) Clive Feetham, R.E.M.E. (attached Royal Scots Greys), son of Mr. and Mrs. H. Feetham, 65, Queen's Road, Fletton, Peterborough, had injured his knee in an accident in Holland. Pte. Feetham had been in the Army nearly two years and had formerly been with the London Brick Company.

Private George William Jackson, Parachute Regiment, son of Mr. and Mrs. G. Jackson, 12, Allen Road, Peterborough, originally reported missing at Arnhem, was now stated as having been wounded in the left shoulder before contact with him was lost on 20th September, three days after he landed with the first airborne troops. News would be received a few weeks later that he was a prisoner of war in Appledorn.

Private B. Hitchborn, Essex Regiment, 30, Westwood Row, Peterborough, originally reported as wounded and missing, was now stated to be safe and well, and awaiting repatriation.

Lance Corporal Gordon Baxter, youngest son of Mr. and Mrs. J.R. Baxter, 571, Fulbridge Road, Werrington, Peterborough, reported missing in Italy, was now known to be a prisoner of war. Corporal Baxter's family came to Peterborough from Emneth. At first he worked at the Co-operative Society's, Park Road, grocery branch, and he later joined the City Police Force.

Guardsman Sydney Ryan, Grenadier Guards, only son of Mr. and Mrs. J. Ryan, 18, Marne Avenue, Walton, Peterborough, had been wounded in the shoulder and legs in Italy early in December. He had served nearly five years in the Army, and served in North Africa before going to Italy.

Cards and Letters from the Far East

Christmas in many homes in the city and district was brightened now by the receipt of letters and postcards from prisoners in Japanese hands. Most bore the dates of the previous January. Mrs. F. Hoyles, 49, Palmerston Road, Woodston, Peterborough, received a postcard from her son, Privates Albert Edwin West. The card, which was posted in February, stated he was receiving mail, was in good health and was working for pay. Private West joined the Army in 1939 after employment with the London Brick Company and was taken prisoner at Singapore.

A card had been received by the parents of Lance Corporal E.A. Davis, 5th Battalion, Suffolk Regiment, who said he too had received mail, for which he was very grateful. L/Cpl. Davis, whose home was at 27, Midland Road, Peterborough, had been with the Eastern Counties Bus Company and joined the Army in 1939. His two sisters were also serving. The eldest, Mollie, was in the A.T.S. with over three years service, and Margery had been in the N.F.S. for more than two years as a driver, one year of which had been in one of the most heavily raided areas in the country. Mr. A. Davis, his father, had served under Major Staton in the First World War. He had lost his left leg owing to wounds received and had been awarded the D.C.M.

Mr. and Mrs. H. Palmer, 11, Princes Gardens, Peterborough, had received a letter from their only son, Sapper H.R. Palmer, Royal Engineers, who was in Osaka Camp, Japan. In the letter, which was dated 27th October, Sapper Palmer said: "I am glad to say I am being well treated and that I am in good health. Give my best wishes to all our friends." Mr. and Mrs. Palmer had received several cards from their son, but this was the first letter. He was captured at Hong Kong three years previously, and was formerly a draughtsman with Peter Brotherhoods Ltd.

City Officer Wins Military Cross

The Military Cross was now awarded to Lieutenant Frederick Turrall Ashby, Army Air Corps, of Peterborough, for services on the Italian front. The citation stated:

"On June 1st 1944, Lt. Ashby was a member of a parachute force dropped near Avezzano behind the enemy lines with orders to operate on the road Sora-Avezzano and force the enemy to withdraw with such speed as to be unable to implement their demolition plan. The enemy reacted quickly and attacked the party on June 2nd. Lt. Ashby however managed to disengage and succeeded in mining the road that night.

On the night of June 3rd he again reached the road and attacked a German convoy, two vehicles and passengers being destroyed. The area was by now full of Germans, and Lt. Ashby found that he was unable to reach the supplies dropped to him. The advance of the Allied relieving troops had moreover stopped, and he had no wireless. Lt. Ashby kept his party together, and continued to operate until he picked up a leaflet dropped by aircraft ordering him to return on June 7th.

This officer is a most determined and courageous fighter, and will not be diverted from his objective. He returned with his complete party except for one man killed and three captured."

Gunner Receives Military Medal

It was now announced that the Military Medal had been awarded to Gunner John Carey Hargreaves, of Whittlesey Road, Stanground, Peterborough, for services on the Italian front. The citation read:

"Gunner Hargreaves is the signaller at the Command Post of his battery. On May 30th he went forward with his party to reconnoitre a gun area. The area was thickly strewn with tellermines (German land mines), and under sporadic shell fire. An infantry carrier went up on a mine and the driver was severely injured. Gunner Hargreaves at once ran to his assistance and staunched his bleeding with shell dressings. He took charge of the situation and made two journeys through the mined area to fetch coats and a stretcher. He then took the driver to the regimental aid post. His coolness and quiet resource were an object lesson to all.

On June 2nd Gunner Hargreaves was again on a forward reconnaissance in the Alatri area. The gun area was heavily shelled during the whole afternoon. The party took cover in a bank and an ammunition lorry which was parked just outside was hit and caught fire. At the same time a dump of 4.2 mortar bombs caught fire on the other side of the bank. An officer of the Kensingtons was hit by a shell splinter in his shoulder. Amid an inferno of bursting shells and enemy shell fire which was now playing on the burning lorry, Gunner Hargreaves ran unhesitatingly to the assistance of the wounded officer. He helped him to some scant cover and quickly and calmly applied shell dressings and stopped all bleeding.

During these two acts of gallantry, Gunner Hargreaves showed splendid unselfishness and disregard for his own safety, which drew the unconcealed admiration of all around."

MILLS, Harry – 118 Eastgate, Peterborough. Private 5959684, 5th Beds & Herts Regiment. Died, aged 37, on the 1st January 1944 while a Japanese prisoner of war. Believed to be the brother of Edwin Mills, of 118 Eastgate, who was killed in the First World War Battle of the Somme in 1916. Buried in Chungkai War Cemetery, Thailand. Grave 3.G.11.

GAGE, John Watson – 169 Fletton Avenue, Peterborough. Flying Officer 151085, 463 (RAAF) Squadron, Royal Air Force Volunteer Reserve. Died, aged 24, on the 3rd January 1944. He was a Navigator in Avro Lancaster Mk III, Serial No JA902, code letters JO-D that took off from Waddington to bomb Berlin. The aircraft crashed into water which has since been reclaimed to form the Noor-Oost-Polder in Holland. All seven crew died. Four were buried on various dates in Holland. The others have no known grave and are commemorated on the Runnymede Memorial. The son of Harry and Minnie Gage of Peterborough. He was one who has no known grave and is therefore commemorated on the Runnymede Memorial, Panel 206.

HOWLETT, Thomas Samuel– 206 St. Pauls Road, Peterborough. Sergeant (Flight Engineer) 1614728, 138 Squadron, Royal Air Force Volunteer Reserve. Died, aged 22, on the 8th January 1944. He was the Flight Engineer in Handley Page Halifax Mk V, Serial No LK743, code letters NF-J that took off from Tempsford on the 7th January. 138 was a Special Duties (SD) Squadron, its role was to drop and pick up agents of the Special Operations Executive in occupied Europe and also to drop supplies by parachute. On this operation the Halifax was returning from Belgium with three Belgian agents on board. The aircraft crashed at Tetworth Hill near Bedford. All seven crew and the three agents were killed. The son of George and Lucy Howlett of Peterborough. Buried in Eastfield Cemetery, Peterborough. Div. 3. Block 6. Grave 2662.

AFFORD, Ernest – Clarence Road, Peterborough. Private 5889395, 1st Northamptonshire Regiment. Died, aged 29, on the 18th January 1944 in Burma. The son of George and Ada Afford of Peterborough. No known grave he is commemorated on the Rangoon Memorial, Myanmar. Face 15.

BURBAGE, Stanley – 15 Westwood Row, Peterborough. Corporal 5827909, 9th Durham Light Infantry. Died, aged 26, on the 18th January 1944, believed in a prisoner of war camp. The son of Elizabeth Burbage of Peterborough and the husband of Hilda Burbage of Peterborough. Buried in Klagenfurt War Cemetery, Austria. Grave 7.B.14.

ELLENDER, Sidney Arthur – 31 Gordon Avenue, Peterborough. Sapper 5784432, 252 Field Company, Royal Engineers. Died, aged 20, on the 20th January 1944 in Italy. The son of Arthur and Annie Ellender of Woodston, Peterborough. Buried in Minturno War Cemetery, Italy. Grave II.C.17.

TOWERS, John Alexander – 61 Pipe Lane, Peterborough. Private 5831597, 2/5th The Queens Royal Regiment (West Surrey). Died, aged 28, on the 26th January

1944. The recipient of the Military Medal. No known next of kin. Buried in Minturno War Cemetery, Italy. Grave VIII. F. 24.

WAKELING, Douglas Henry – 26 Glenton Street, Peterborough. Private 5830902, 2nd Northamptonshire Regiment. Died, aged 25, on the 29th January 1944. The son of William and Nellie Wakeling of Peterborough. Buried in Minturno War Cemetery, Italy. Grave III.C.7.

SHARPE, Charles William – 31 Cranley Drive, London. Home Guard. Died, aged 31, on the 29th January 1944 along with his wife Doris and daughter Jennifer at 31 Cranley Drive as a result of a German bombing raid. The son of John and Fanny Sharpe of 95 New England, Peterborough. Buried in the Municipal Borough Cemetery, Ilford.

BUCKNELL, Ernest Stanley – Montague Road, Peterborough. Private 5777217, 5th Royal Norfolk Regiment. Died, aged 29, on the 1st February 1944 while a Japanese prisoner of war. The son of John and Louisa Bucknell of Peterborough and the husband of Grace Bucknell of Walton, Peterborough. Buried in Chungkai War Cemetery, Thailand. Grave 1.D.2.

HALL, Albert – 10 South View Road, Walton, Peterborough. Gunner 1823204, 129 H.A.A. Regiment, Royal Artillery. Died, aged 34, on the 9th February 1944. The son of Joseph and Harriet Hall of Peterborough and the husband of Mary Hall of Walton, Peterborough. Buried in Paston Churchyard, Peterborough. Grave D.1.

WARWICK, Roberta Alice – Queens Walk, Peterborough. Sister 266463, Queen Alexandra's Imperial Military Nursing Service. Died, aged 40, on the 12th February 1944. The daughter of Charles Joseph and Anne Warwick of Queens Walk, Peterborough. No known grave she is commemorated on the Brookwood Memorial. Panel 22, Column 3.

CAIRNS, Eon Arthur – 47 Exeter Road, Peterborough. 1614727 Sergeant, Air Gunner, Coastal Command, Royal Air Force Volunteer Reserve. Died, aged 21, on the 17th February 1944. The son of Robert and Mary Cairns of Whiteley Village, Surrey. No known grave he is commemorated on the Runnymede Memorial, Panel 226.

KENDALL, Victor – Ordinary Seaman P/JX 522060, HMS Penelope, Royal Navy. Died, aged 18, on the 18th February 1944 when the unescorted HMS Penelope was hit in the engine room by one torpedo from U-boat 410 when 35 miles west of Naples, Italy. The light cruiser sank immediately when the commander, 24 officers, 368 ratings and 24 Marines were lost. The son of Mr and Mrs F. W. Kendall of Peterborough. No known grave he is commemorated on the Portsmouth Naval Memorial. Panel 84, Column 1.

WOODWARD, Frank – Hicks Lane, Old Fletton, Peterborough. Sergeant 960435, 460 (R.A.A.F.) Squadron, Royal Air Force Volunteer Reserve. Died, aged 37, on the 25th February 1944. He was a mid-upper gunner in Avro Lancaster Mk III, Serial No JB742, Code Letters AR-D that took off from Binbrook to attack Augsburg. The aircraft crashed near Rotweill, a town on the River Neckar. All seven crew died. The son of Harry and Alice Woodward of Old Fletton, Peterborough. Buried in Durnbach War Cemetery, Bayern, Germany. Grave 11.B.18.

WALKER, Harold George – Orton Waterville, Peterborough. Sergeant 6022143, 5th Essex Regiment. Died, aged 27, on the 26th February 1944. The son of Maurice and Annie Walker of Orton Waterville, Peterborough. Buried in the Sangro War Cemetery, Italy. Grave XVII.A.19.

BARRETT, Leonard Charles – Albert Place, Peterborough. Sergeant, Wireless Operator / Air Gunner, 1467119, 12 Squadron, Royal Air Force Volunteer Reserve. Died, age unknown, on the 26th February 1944. He was the Wireless Operator in Avro Lancaster Mk I, Serial No ME632, Code Letters PH-P that took off from Wickenby to attack Augsburg. All seven crew died. The son of Stanley and Beatrice Barrett and the husband of Gladys Barrett. Buried in Choloy War Cemetery, Meurthe- et- Moselle, France. Collective Grave 4.D.1-6.

SEWTER, Colin Archie – 184 Alexandra Road, Peterborough. Sergeant 5830498, 8th Suffolk Regiment. Died, aged 25, on the 28th February 1944. The husband of Hilda Sewter of Peterborough. Buried in Eastfield Cemetery, Peterborough. Grave 6312. Div. 1. Block 16.

WRIGHT, Charles – Trooper 10602937, 1st Recce Regiment, Royal Armoured Corps. Died, aged 28, on the 10th March 1944. The son of John and Sarah Wright of 3 Hurn Road, Werrington, Peterborough and the husband of Edna Wright of Shelford, Nottinghamshire. Buried in Beach Head War Cemetery, Anzio, Italy. Grave VII.F.5.

DODRILL, Kevin Sean – 1 The Crescent, Woodston, Peterborough. Flight Lieutenant 49027, DFC, 107 Squadron, Royal Air Force Volunteer Reserve. Died, age unknown, on the 17th March 1944. The son of George and Margaret Dodrill from Dublin and the husband of Dorita Angela Dodrill (nee O'Dell) of Woodston, Peterborough. Buried in Woodston Cemetery, Peterborough. Section 7, Grave 57.

ELLIS, John Robert – 95 Taverners Road, Peterborough. Sergeant, Air Bomber, 50 Squadron, Bomber Command, Royal Air Force Volunteer Reserve. Died, aged 22, on the 19th March 1944. He was the air Bomber in Lancaster Mk I, Serial No ED308, Code Letters VN-J that took off from Skellingthorpe to attack Frankfurt. Three of the seven man crew died. The son of Frank and Lillian Ellis of Peterborough and the husband of Betty Ellis of Peterborough. Buried in Durnbach War Cemetery, Bayern, Germany. Grave 1.H.16.

WYBORN, John Henry – Sallows Road, Peterborough. Flying Officer, Navigator, 124519, 7 Squadron, Royal Air Force Volunteer Reserve. Died, aged 28, on the 22nd March 1944. He was the navigator in Lancaster Mk III, Serial No JA964, Code Letters MG-P that took off from Oakington to attack Frankfurt. Four of the seven man crew died. John Wyborn was a former policeman stationed in Peterborough. He joined the R.A.F.V.R. and trained at Carlstrom Field in Florida, U.S.A. as a pilot and qualified for his wings, although he flew with the Lancaster on this raid as a navigator. The son of Frederick and Jessie Wyborn and the husband of Elizabeth Wyborn of Wolverton, Buckinghamshire. Buried in Rheinberg War Cemetery, Germany. Grave 8.A.14.

BALCHIN, Bernard James – Flight Lieutenant (Pilot), 46515, Royal Air Force. Died, aged 27, on the 22nd March 1944. The son of George and Lily Balchin and the husband of Gladys Balchin of Peterborough. Buried in Eastfield Cemetery, Peterborough. Div. 1. Block 17. Grave 7449.

JENKINS, Alfryn James – Pilot Officer 161735, 100 Squadron, Royal Air Force Volunteer Reserve. Died, aged 31, on the 24th March 1944. The son of William and Mary Jenkins of Penclawdd, Glamorgan and the husband of Mary Jenkins of Penclawdd. Pilot Officer Jenkins was a serving Police Officer with the Peterborough Police Force. Buried in the Berlin War Cemetery. Grave 1.Z.3.

SELKIRK, Neil Alexander – Major 72906, 9th Royal Sussex Regiment. Died, aged 32, on the 24th March 1944. The son of David and Helen Selkirk and the husband of Barbara Selkirk of Peterborough. Buried in Taukkyan War Cemetery, Myanmar. Grave 4. E. 18.

BINES, George William – 40 Westwood Street, Peterborough. Sergeant 852698, 135 (The Hertfordshire Yeomanry) Field Regiment, Royal Artillery. Died, aged 26, between the 1st April 1944 and the 31st May 1944 while a Japanese prisoner of war. The cause of death believed to be dysentery and malaria. The son of George and Florence Bines of Peterborough. Buried in Chungkai War Cemetery, Thailand. Grave 2.B.2.

TOWERS, George Ernest – 269 Cromwell Road, Peterborough. Private 5954183, 1st Northamptonshire Regiment. Died, aged 27, on the 16th April 1944. The son of Ernest and Mabel Towers, of Peterborough. Buried in Imphal War Cemetery, India. Grave 5.A.6.

MANN, Alexander Leonard – Private, Hong Kong Dockyard Defence Corps. Died, aged 27, on the 19th April 1944 while a Japanese prisoner of war. The son of Alexander and Emily Mann of Old Fletton, Peterborough and the husband of Violet Mann of Bath. Buried in the Yokohama War Cemetery, Japan. Brit. Sec. B. D. 10.

FAIRBAIRN, Neil Joseph – 15 St. Mark's Street, Peterborough. Flying Officer 50478, Bomber Command, 622 Squadron, Royal Air Force. Died, aged 21, on the 25th April 1944. He was the navigator in Avro Lancaster Mk I, Serial No ME693, Code Letters GI-F that took off from Mildenhall to attack Karlsruhe. All seven crew died. The son of Walter and Bernice Fairbairn of Peterborough. Buried in Rheinberg War Cemetery, Germany. Collected grave 20.A.23-25.

ARBON, Frederick James – 45 Hankey Street, Peterborough. Sergeant (Air Gunner) 1869934, Bomber Command, 51 Squadron, Royal Air Force Volunteer Reserve. Died, aged 20, on the 2nd May 1944. He was the Rear Gunner in a Handley Page Halifax Mk III, Serial No MZ593, Code Letters MH-Z. The aircraft took off from Snaith to bomb rail installations at Mechelen. The plane was shot down by a night fighter. Four of the seven man crew died. The son of Mr and Mrs A. Arbon of Peterborough and the grandson of Mr and Mrs Alfred Arbon of Peterborough. Buried in Wevelgem Communal Cemetery, West Vlaanderen, Belgium. Grave E.454.

COOKE, Robert – 5 Park Terrace, Garton End Road, Peterborough. Sergeant 839740, 135 (The Hertfordshire Yeomanry) Field Regiment, Royal Artillery. Died, aged 26, on the 8th May 1944 while a Japanese prisoner of war. The son of Robert and Millis Cooke of Peterborough and the husband of Rosina Cooke of Peterborough. Buried in Kanchanaburi War Cemetery, Thailand. Grave 8.A.11.

WENLOCK, Leslie Walter – 64 Granville Street, Peterborough. Lance Corporal 5954203, 2nd Beds & Herts Regiment. Died, aged 28, on the 18th May 1944. The son of Walter and Grace Wenlock of Peterborough. Buried in Naples War Cemetery, Italy. Grave II.B.3.

PAPWORTH, George Frederick – 45 South View Road, Walton, Peterborough. Private 5884463, 1st The Kings (Liverpool) Regiment, (77 Indian Infantry Brigade). Died, aged 23, on the 24th May 1944. He was part of the 2nd Chindit operation in Burma in 1944, one of 'Wingate's Chindits'. No known next of kin. No known grave he is commemorated on the Rangoon Memorial, Myanmar. Face 6.

BIGGS, Alfred Henry George – 26 Brownlow Road, Peterborough. Pilot Officer 169653, 219 Squadron, Royal Air Force Volunteer Reserve. Died, aged 34, on the 24th May 1944. The son of Alfred and Elizabeth Biggs and the husband of Dora Biggs of Harrogate. No known grave he is commemorated on the Runnymede Memorial, Panel 210.

THORPE, Derrick Gordon Cobley – Flight Sergeant 132343, 576 Squadron, Royal Air Force Volunteer Reserve. Died, aged 22, on the 25th May 1944. He was a crew member of Avro Lancaster, Serial No NE171 that took off from Elsham Wolds. The aircraft was shot down by a night- fighter and crashed near Aachen, Germany. The son of James and Laura Thorpe of Peterborough. No known grave he is commemorated on the Runnymede Memorial. Panel 222.

SHAW, George Ernest – 185 Padholme Road, Peterborough. Lance Corporal 5886057, 'A' Sqn, 4th Regiment, Reconnaissance Corps, R.A.C. Died, aged 26, on the 6th June 1944 in Italy. The son of Ernest and Mildred Shaw of Peterborough. Buried in Cassino War Cemetery, Italy. Grave II.J.5.

GOODWIN, Cyril Albert – 27 Clifton Avenue, Peterborough. Private 5830570, 1st Suffolk Regiment. Died, aged 26, on the 8th June 1944 in hospital in England of wounds received at Normandy. The son of Stanley and Marjorie Goodwin of Peterborough. Buried in Eastfield Cemetery, Peterborough. Grave 6487. Block 6. Div.1.

HARKNESS, Robert William – Private 3190558, 8th Kings Own Scottish Borderers. Died, aged 26, on the 10th June 1944. The son of William and Mary

Harkness and the husband of Edith Harkness of Walton, Peterborough. Buried in Castleton Churchyard, Roxburghshire. Grave 930.

LADDS, Herbert Lawrence – 72 Church Street, Werrington, Peterborough. Private 6020034, 1st Suffolk Regiment. Died, aged 26, on the 10th June 1944. The son of Ernest and Emma Ladds of Werrington, Peterborough and the husband of Edith Ladds of Werrington, Peterborough. Buried in Hermanville War Cemetery, Calvados, France. Grave 1.H.6.

MALLET, Harold – 84 New England, Peterborough. Trooper 7963159, 'A' Sqn, 2nd Lothian and Border Horse, R.A.C. Died, aged 21, on the 20th June in Italy. The son of Harold and Minnie Mallett of Peterborough. Buried in Assisi War Cemetery, Italy. Grave IV.G.11.

WRIGHT, James – 310 Gladstone Street, Peterborough. Gunner 1735786, 21 Lt A.A. Regiment, Royal Artillery. Died, aged 37, on the 24th June 1944 while a Japanese prisoner of war. The son of Albert and Edith Wright and the husband of Mary Wright of Heanor, Derbyshire. No known grave he is commemorated on the Singapore Memorial, Column 34.

HORSTEAD, Alan – 131 Cromwell Road, Peterborough. Sub – Lieutenant (A), Fleet Air Arm, HMS Daedalus, Royal Naval Volunteer Reserve. Died, aged 21, on the 25th June 1944 while on air operations with 886 Squadron. The son of Herbert and Marie Horstead and the husband of Peggy Horstead of Peterborough. Buried in Eastfield Cemetery, Peterborough. Grave 7451. Div. 1. Block 17.

SMART, Robert William – Sergeant (Wireless Operator/Air Gunner), 1294239, 212 Squadron, Royal Air Force Volunteer Reserve. Died, age unknown, on the 27th June 1944. The son of George and Ethel Smart and the husband of Winifred Smart of Peterborough. Buried in Madras War Cemetery, Chennai, India. Grave 6.D.3.

THOMPSON, William West – 148 Wellington Street, Peterborough. Driver 14240839, 13 Field Squadron, Royal Engineers. Died, aged 35, on the 28th June 1944. No known next of kin. Buried in St. Manvieu War Cemetery, Calvados, France. Grave VI.G.3.

BENSTEAD, Wallace George – Driver T/10703360, Royal Army Service Corps. Died, aged 42, on the 28th June 1944. The son of John and Elizabeth Benstead of Peterborough, and the husband of Laura Benstead of Carisbrooke, Isle of Wight. Buried in Bari War Cemetery, Italy. Grave XIV.C.24.

BARBER, George William – Gunner 14370690, 76 Field Regiment, Royal Artillery. Died, aged 34, on the 28th June 1944. The son of Christopher and Lily Barber of Peterborough and the husband of Kathleen Barber of Cambridge. Buried in Ranville War Cemetery, France. VIII. D. 19.

HICKS, Ronald John Sydney – Peterborough. 2nd Lieutenant 304946, 147 (The Essex Yeomanry) Field Regiment, Royal Artillery. Died, age unknown, on the 29th

June 1944 in Normandy. No known next of kin. Buried in Tilly Sur Seulles War Cemetery, France. Grave II. A. 13.

BROWN, William Ernest Kenneth – 64 Paston Lane, Peterborough. Private 5892035, 2nd Lincolnshire Regiment. Died, aged 20, on the 8th July 1944. The son of Ernest and Kathleen Brown of Walton, Peterborough. Buried in Ranville War Cemetery, Calvados, France. Grave II.B.9.

SETCHFIELD, Trevor – 263 Clarence Road, Peterborough. Sergeant 1429948, Bomber Command, 550 Squadron, Royal Air Force Volunteer Reserve. Died, aged 22, on the 13th July 1944. He was the Air Gunner in Lancaster Mk I, Serial No LL796, Code Letters BQ-O that took off from North Killingholme to attack rail facilities at Revigny. The plane collided in the air with a 103 Squadron Lancaster. All seven crew died. The son of Walter and Pearl Setchfield of Woodston, Peterborough. Buried in Perreuse Chateau Franco-British National Cemetery, Seine-et-Marne, France. Collected Grave 20-23. Plot 2. Row B.

SOWMAN, Douglas John – Peterborough. Private 5833127, Suffolk Regiment. Died, aged 24, on the 16th July 1944. He was attached to the Special Operations Executive, Force 133 and died in Yugoslavia. The son of Robert and Lydia Sowman of Peterborough and the husband of Joan Sowman of New Fletton, Peterborough. Buried in the Belgrade War Cemetery, Serbia and Montenegro. Collected Grave 2-9.10.B.

BERGSTROM, Alfred William – Rifleman 6970133, 7th (1st Bn. London Rifle Brigade). Died, aged 25, on the 18th July 1944. The son of John and Mary Bergstrom and the husband of Maud Bergstrom of Stanground, Peterborough. Buried in Arezzo War Cemetery, Italy. Grave V.C.17.

ARISS, Edward John George – Trooper 305650, Royal Horse Guards. Died, aged 24, on the 19th July 1944. The son of Arthur and Violet Ariss and the husband of Mrs Ariss of Woodston, Peterborough. Buried in Hermanville War Cemetery, Calvados, France. Grave 2. B. 12.

HILSON, John Thomas Henry – Belle Vue, Stanground, Peterborough. Lance Corporal 5945674, 5th Beds & Herts Regiment. Died, aged 38, on the 20th July 1944 while a Japanese prisoner of war. The son of Joseph Thomas Henry and Ellen Hilson and the husband of Ada Hilson of Stanground, Peterborough. Buried in Kanchanaburi War Cemetery, Thailand. Grave 8.A.54.

ELMER, Christopher Frank – 29 Taverners Road, Peterborough. Petty Officer (Airman) FAA/FX, 607659, HMS Shrike, Royal Navy. Died, aged 20, on the 21st July 1944 in a plane crash serving with the Fleet Air Arm. The son of Frank and Susannah Elmer of Peterborough. No known grave he is commemorated on the Lee-On-Solent Memorial, Panel 2, Bay 5.

CHAPMAN, Lewis William – The Spital Bridge, Westwood Street, Peterborough. Pilot Officer 179798, DFM, Coastal Command, 244 Squadron, Royal Air Force Volunteer Reserve. Died, age unknown, on the 31st July 1944. P/O Chapman was killed when a 44 Squadron Dakota, Serial No KG690, was transporting 244 Squadron personnel from Riyan to Salalah when it crashed into a mountain 30 miles from Salalah. Apparently the approach was very difficult and should only have been undertaken in good visibility. In this instance there was heavy cloud. Five South African crew were killed along with twenty-seven passengers of whom P/O. Chapman was one. Chapman received his DFM in January 1944. The citation reads; On October 16th 1943 the above mentioned NCO Pilot was on patrol in the Gulf of Oman when he sighted a submarine on the surface. He carried out a brilliant attack which resulted in the damaging and possible sinking of the U-Boat. Confirmation is awaited. Although Sgt Chapman has only been in 244 Squadron for a period of two months and is new to the job, he showed great initiative and clear-headedness in a situation that could have been ruined by the slightest error or delay. Nb. U-533 was sunk 16 October 1943 in the Gulf of Oman by depth charges from a British Bisley (Blenheim) aircraft (244 Squadron). The son of Frank and Emily Chapman of Bournemouth. No known grave he is commemorated on the Alamein Memorial, Egypt. Column 279.

COCKER, George Frederick – 11 The Crescent, Woodston, Peterborough. Private 1459141, 7th Royal Norfolk Regiment. Died, aged 19, on the 7th August 1944 in Normandy. The son of Joseph and Edith Cocker of Woodston, Peterborough. Buried in Bayeux War Cemetery, Calvados, France. Grave XXIII.E.8.

LAWLOR, Frank Ernest – 16 Fulham Road, Peterborough. Private 5783974, 7th Royal Norfolk Regiment. Died, aged 21, on the 7th August 1944 in Normandy. The son of Ernest and Edna Lawlor of Peterborough. Buried in Bayeux War Cemetery, Calvados, France. Grave XXIII.E.20.

QUIBELL, Stanley La Barte – 20 Eastfield Grove, Peterborough. Lance Sergeant 5780965, 7th Royal Norfolk Regiment. Died, aged 32, on the 8th August 1944 in Normandy. The son of James and Isabella Quibell and the husband of Stella Quibell of Gosport, Hampshire. Buried in Bayeux War Cemetery, Calvados, France. Grave XXII.D.4.

CUNNINGTON, Kenneth Gordon – Peterborough. Private 14698188, 1st Suffolk Regiment. The son of Robert and Lillie Cunnington of Calvert, Buckinghamshire. Died, aged 21, on the 13th August 1944. Buried in St Charles de Percy War Cemetery, Calvados, France. I.A.12.

BARBER, Anthony Levoir – 40 Norfolk Street, Peterborough. Able Seaman P/JX 354529, H.M.L.C.F. (L) 1, Royal Navy. Died, aged 21, on the 17th August 1944. His Majesty's Landing Craft Flak (Large) No.1. was taking part in Operation Neptune, the cross-channel operations involved in the D-Day landings, when it blew up and sank. The son of Bertram and Annie Barber and the husband of Doris Barber of Peterborough. No known grave he is commemorated on Portsmouth Naval Memorial, Hampshire. Panel 81. Column 3.

RUSDALE, Cecil Charles – Fletton, Peterborough. Private 14370768, The Parachute Regiment. Died, aged 19, on the 19th August 1944. The son of George and

Daisy Rusdale of Old Fletton, Peterborough. His brother Jack was killed in action in 1942. Buried in Putot-en-Auge, Calvados, France. Grave A.1.

STURGESS, Francis Arthur – Corporal 1084398, Royal Air Force Volunteer Reserve. Died, aged 34, on the 20th August 1944. The son of Ernest and Lizzie Sturgess and the husband of Doris Sturgess of Eastgate, Peterborough. Buried in Eastfield Cemetery, Peterborough. Div. 4. Block 20. Grave 8655.

MELLOWS, Thomas Anthony – The Vineyard, Minster Precincts, Peterborough. Captain 166686, 27th Lancers, Royal Armoured Corps (seconded to Special Forces). Died of wounds, aged 24, on the 21st August 1944 with a Jedburgh Team, part of the Special Operations Executive, in Mont de Marsan, France. They were fighting with the French Resistance. The son of William Thomas Mellows, M.B.E and Beatrice Mellows, of Peterborough. Buried in Mont-De-Marsan Communal Cemetery, Landes, France. Grave 23. Plot 3. Row 5.

HART, John Rodney – The Vineyard, Minster Precincts, Peterborough. Lieutenant Commander (E), HMS Southdown, Royal Navy. Died, aged 31, on the 26th August 1944 of cardiac failure on board ship. The son of Charles and Muriel Hart (nee Pitt) and the husband of Ursula Hart of Peterborough. Buried in Shotley Royal Naval Cemetery, Suffolk. Grave 2.B.2.

EDWARDS, John William – 89 Wootton Avenue, Fletton, Peterborough. Lance Corporal 4982567, Military Medal, 14th Sherwood Foresters (Nott's & Derby) Regiment. Died, aged 20, on the 26th August 1944 in hospital in Italy from multiple injuries received in an accident. The son of John and Mabel Edwards of Peterborough. Buried in Ancona War Cemetery, Italy. Grave IV.A.4.

COLES, William – 62 Wellington Street, Peterborough. Private 5883930, 2/5th Leicestershire Regiment. Died, aged 30, on the 31st August 1944. No known next of kin. Buried in Montecchio War Cemetery, Italy. Grave IV.C.11.

THOROGOOD, Samuel – 21 Searjeant Street, Peterborough. Sapper 1943953, 626 Field Squadron, Royal Engineers. Died, aged 32, on the 1st September 1944. The son of George and Emma Thorogood of Peterborough. Buried in Florence War Cemetery, Italy. Grave II.D.5.

PHILLIPS, Thomas – 137 Gladstone Street, Peterborough. Gunner 1557762, 125 Anti – Tank Regiment, Royal Artillery. Died, aged 28, on the 12th September 1944. As a Japanese prisoner of war he was being transported on a Japanese transport ship, the Rakuyo Maru, when it was sunk by the American submarine USS Sealion. The son of John and Florence Phillips of Peterborough. No known grave he is commemorated on the Singapore Memorial, Column 27.

BUSSEY, Alec George – 86, South Street, Stanground, Peterborough. Lance Corporal 5832504, 1st Cambridgeshire Regiment. Died, aged 31, on the 12th September 1944. Son of Mrs. S. Bussey and Husband of Miss K.W.J. Marriott. As a Japanese prisoner of war he was being transported on a Japanese transport ship, the

Rakuyo Maru, when it was sunk by the American submarine USS Sealion. No known grave he is commemorated on the Singapore Memorial, Column 57.

NEVILLE, Edward – 13 Gladstone Street, Peterborough. Sergeant (Air Gunner) 1880703, Bomber Command, 50 Squadron, Royal Air Force Volunteer Reserve. Died, aged 20, on the 12th September 1944. He was a gunner in a Lancaster Mk I, Serial No PD294, Code Letters VN-A which took off from Skellingthorpe to attack Darmstadt. Four of the seven man crew died. The son of Ernest and Emily Neville of Peterborough. His brother William also died, in 1942, on active service. Buried in Durnbach War Cemetery, Bayern Germany. Grave 1.C.2.

ALLEN, Arthur – 11 Craig Street, Peterborough. Private 14428084, 7th Black Watch (Royal Highlanders). Died, aged 19, on the 13th September 1944 at Le Havre in France. The son of John and Ethel Allen of Peterborough. Buried in Ste. Marie Cemetery, Le Havre, France. Grave 13.67.O.

DAVIS, Alfred Oliver – Shakespeare Avenue, Peterborough. Private 5777228, 5th Royal Norfolk Regiment. Died, aged 28, on the 14th September 1944 while a Japanese prisoner of war. No known next of kin. No known grave he is commemorated on the Singapore Memorial, Column 50.

RUFF, William – 52 Eastgate, Peterborough. Private 11413695, 1st Duke of Wellington's (West Riding) Regiment. Died, aged 25, on the 14th September 1944. The son of William and Hannah Ruff of Peterborough. Buried in Florence War Cemetery, Italy. Grave IV.C.2.

EMMINGTON, Leonard – 46 St Leonards Street, Peterborough. Sergeant 749032, 99 Squadron, Royal Air Force Volunteer Reserve. Before the war he was employed as a fitter's labourer at the Newall Engineering Company in Peterborough. Joined the R.A.F. just before the outbreak of war and had been stationed in Ceylon (Sri Lanka) for three years. Died, aged 41, on the 14th September 1944 in the India Command Hospital at Bombay, following a short illness from toxic hepatitus. The son of George and Louise Emmington and the husband of Edith Emmington of Peterborough. Buried in Kandy War Cemetery, Sri Lanka. Grave 6.B.4.

CHAPMAN, Raymond Henry – Eversden, Marholm Road, Peterborough. Flight Sergeant (Flight Engineer) 1615749, 356 Squadron, Royal Air Force Volunteer Reserve. Awarded the French Croix de Guerre. Died, aged 21, on the 16th September 1944. He was a crew member in a Mk VI Liberator bomber that collided with another Liberator while flying in formation at 1,000 feet during a bombing operation to Maymyo Railway Station, Burma. Seventeen others also lost their lives. The son of Horace and Emma Chapman of Peterborough. Buried in Taukkyan War Cemetery, Myanmar. Collected Grave 28.F.8-17.

DIXON, John Travers – 38 Fairfield Road, Peterborough. Lance Corporal 4803464, 6th Lincolnshire Regiment. Died, aged 28, on the 17th September 1944. No known next of kin. Buried in Forli War Cemetery, Italy. Grave I.B.4.

EVANS, John – Peterborough. Sapper 1572485, 9th (Airborne) Field Company, Royal Engineers. Died, aged 25, on the 17th September 1944. Just after 10.00 hours on Sunday 17 September 1944 sixteen glider and tug combinations took off from RAF Keevil for Arnhem as part of Operation Market Garden. Horsa Glider RJ113 (Chalk 389) was in this group of aircraft and contained 21 men, including Sapper Evans, from No 1 Platoon 9th (Airborne) Field Company, Royal Engineers. The tugs and gliders took a course north-west towards Gloucester to pick up Squadrons from Fairford and then headed out over the Severn and Bristol Channels to form up. Here they took a turn south-west down the Bristol Channel with other aircraft and gliders, and made a turn east over Weston-Super-Mare and headed for Arnhem. While over the village of Farrington Gurney an explosion occurred in RJ113 splitting the glider in two. With no tail section the glider lost lift, broke its tow line and crashed into the Double Hills meadow near Paulton killing all occupants. The son of John and Ann Evans of Peterborough. Buried in Weston-Super-Mare Cemetery, Section Y. Grave 281.

DRAYCOTT, William Frederick (Roy) – 15 Springfield Road, Peterborough. Lance Sergeant 2619077, 1st Grenadier Guards. Died, aged 30, on the 20th September 1944 in action during the battle of Nijmegen, Holland. The son of Henry and Sarah Draycott and the husband of Hilda Draycott of Bedford. Buried in Jonkerbos War Cemetery, Netherlands. Grave 22. G. 1.

BEAN, Roy Francis – Private 5833205, 4th Suffolk Regiment. Died, aged 31, on the 21st September 1944 while a Japanese prisoner of war. He was on board a Japanese transport ship, the Toyofuku Maru, that was attacked by planes from an American aircraft carrier about 80 miles north of Corregidor. The Americans not knowing she carried prisoners. The husband of E. Bean of Westwood, Peterborough. No known grave he is commemorated on the Singapore Memorial, Column 54.

DUGGAN, Charles Albert – 86 Padholme Road, Peterborough. Private 5830936, 2nd Cambridgeshire Regiment. Died, aged 25, on the 21st September 1944 while a Japanese prisoner of war. He was on board a Japanese transport ship, the Toyofuku Maru, that was attacked by planes from an American aircraft carrier about 80 miles north of Corregidor. The Americans not knowing she carried prisoners. The son of Mr and Mrs G. Duggan, of Peterborough. No known grave he is commemorated on the Singapore Memorial, Column 58.

JENKINS, William – 5 St. Mary's Street, Peterborough. Private 5777117, 5th Royal Norfolk Regiment. Died, aged 27, on the 21st September 1944 while a Japanese prisoner of war. He was on board a Japanese transport ship, the Toyofuku Maru, that was attacked by planes from an American aircraft carrier about 80 miles north of Corregidor. The Americans not knowing she carried prisoners. The son of Mrs A. Jenkins of 5 St. Mary's Street, Peterborough. No known grave he is commemorated on the Singapore Memorial, Column 51.

LANE, Leslie William – 12 Marne Avenue, Walton, Peterborough. Private 5830971, 2nd Cambridgeshire Regiment. Died, aged 27, on the 21st September 1944 while a Japanese prisoner of war. He was on board a Japanese transport ship, the Toyofuku Maru, that was attacked by planes from an American aircraft carrier about

80 miles north of Corregidor. The Americans not knowing she carried prisoners. The son of Charles and Ethel Lane of Walton, Peterborough. No known grave he is commemorated on the Singapore Memorial, Column 59.

MITCHELL, Reginald – 7 Fengate Close, Peterborough. Private 5779614, 5th Royal Norfolk Regiment. Died, aged 31, on the 21st September 1944 while a Japanese prisoner of war. He was on board a Japanese transport ship, the Toyofuku Maru, that was attacked by planes from an American aircraft carrier about 80 miles north of Corregidor. The Americans not knowing she carried prisoners. No known next of kin. No known grave he is commemorated on the Singapore Memorial, Column 51.

THOMPSON, George William – 19 Star Road, Peterborough. Private 5833660, 1st Cambridgeshire Regiment. Died, aged 24, on the 21st September 1944 while a Japanese prisoner of war. He was on board a Japanese transport ship, the Toyofuku Maru, that was attacked by planes from an American aircraft carrier about 80 miles north of Corregidor. The Americans not knowing she carried prisoners. The son of William George and Isabella Thompson of Peterborough. No known grave he is commemorated on the Singapore Memorial, Column 61.

TODD, George Roland – Lincoln Road, Peterborough. Corporal 5828758, 2nd Cambridgeshire Regiment. Died, aged 26, on the 21st September 1944 while a Japanese prisoner of war. He was on board a Japanese transport ship, the Toyofuku Maru, that was attacked by planes from an American aircraft carrier about 80 miles north of Corregidor. The Americans not knowing she carried prisoners. The son of Mrs E. Wright of Peterborough. No known grave he is commemorated on the Singapore Memorial, Column 57.

TYLER, William Alfred – 23 Wood Street, Peterborough. Private 5833147, 4th Suffolk Regiment. Died, aged 24, on the 21st September 1944 while a Japanese prisoner of war. He was on board a Japanese transport ship, the Toyofuku Maru, that was attacked by planes from an American aircraft carrier about 80 miles north of Corregidor. The Americans not knowing she carried prisoners. No known next of kin. No known grave he is commemorated on the Singapore Memorial, Column 56.

HARDY, Desmond George – Pilot Officer (Navigator) 195329, 48 Squadron, Royal Air Force Volunteer Reserve. Died, aged 24, on the 21st September 1944. It is believed that all crew died when their Dakota aircraft crashed during a supply mission in support of Operation Market Garden. The son of George and Annie Hardy of Peterborough. Buried in Arnhem Oosterbeek War Cemetery, Holland. Collective Grave 4.C.2.

PARKINSON, Tom Joseph William – 572 Fulbridge Road, Peterborough. Private 14684691, 2nd Highland Light Infantry (City of Glasgow) Regiment. Died, aged 19, on the 24th September 1944. The son of James and Elizabeth Parkinson of Peterborough. Buried in Mierlo War Cemetery, Holland. Grave IV.C.8.

FOX, Kenneth David – Warrant Officer 751873, 206 Squadron, Royal Air Force Volunteer Reserve. Died, aged 24, on the 28th September 1944. The son of Bertram and Frances Fox and the husband of Jean Fox of Peterborough. No known grave he is commemorated on the Runnymede Memorial, Panel 213.

EVANS-EVANS, Roland Gwynne – Peterborough. Flight Lieutenant 123750, 2804 Squadron, Royal Air Force. Died, aged 30, on the 2nd October 1944. The son of Anthony and Margaret Evans-Evans of Peterborough and the husband of Hilda Evans-Evans of Stilton, near Peterborough. His brother Anthony Caron Evans-Evans also died in 1945. Buried in Leopoldsburg War Cemetery, Belgium. Grave VI.D.16.

ARCHER, Stanley George – Corporal T/185340, Royal Army Service Corps. Died, aged 31, on the 2nd October 1944. The son of John and Lillian Archer and the husband of Lydia Archer of Peterborough. Buried in Brussels Town Cemetery, Belgium. Grave X. 22. 43.

LOWE, John Norton – Orton Longueville, Peterborough. Captain 176280, Essex Regiment, attached Nigeria Regiment, R.W.A.F.F. Died, aged 30, on the 7th October 1944. Mentioned in Despatches. The son of Alfred and Eleanor Lowe of Orton Longueville, Peterborough. No known grave he is commemorated on the Rangoon Memorial, Myanmar, Face 15.

JOHNSON, Kenneth – 49 Parliament Street, Peterborough. Sergeant 1545103, 81st Anti-Tank Regiment, Royal Artillery. Died, aged 25, on the 11th October 1944. The son of William and Hannah Johnson of Peterborough. Buried in Faenza War Cemetery, Italy. Grave V.G.6.

GENT, Patrick Noel – 212 Cromwell Road, Peterborough. Sergeant (Pilot) 1615002, Bomber Command, Royal Air Force Volunteer Reserve. Died, aged 21, on the 12th October 1941 in a flying accident. The son of Arthur and Mabel Gent of Peterborough. Buried in Chester (Blacon) Cemetery. Grave 1029. Sec.A.

REYNOLDS, Leslie Jack Lane – 10 Hankey Street, Peterborough. Corporal 5777273, 1st Royal Norfolk Regiment. Died, aged 27, on the 15th October 1944. The son of Edward and Edith Reynolds of Peterborough. Buried in Overloon War Cemetery, Holland. Grave III.E.2.

WOODS, Leslie Harry – 23 Huntley Grove, Peterborough. Leading Stoker P/KX 158595, H.M.L.S.T. 413, Royal Navy. Died, age unknown, on the 20th October 1944. Believed drowned. No known next of kin. Buried in Broadway Cemetery, Peterborough. Grave 314.

GARN, Dorothy – 40 Ashcroft Gardens, Peterborough. Sister 266193, Queen Alexandra's Imperial Military Nursing Service. Died, age unknown, on the 24th October 1944. No known next of kin. She was trained at the Peterborough Memorial Hospital and did private nursing. She was a night staff nurse at Addenbrooke's hospital in Cambridge before being appointed as Sister to the Queen Alexandra's Imperial Military Nursing Service. Died in Northampton on the 24th October 1944, the cause of death is not known. Buried in Peterborough Old Cemetery. Grave 246.

BIRCH, Albert George – Sergeant 7912202, 2nd County of London Yeomanry (Westminster Dragoons) Royal Armoured Corps. Died, aged 30, on the 3rd November 1944. The son of Albert and Lettie Birch and the husband of Edith Birch of Peterborough. Buried in Mierlo War Cemetery, Holland. Grave V.D.6.

GILL, William Percy – 15 Marholm Road, Peterborough. Aircraftman 2nd Class 1633962, Base Signals and Radar Unit, Royal Air Force Volunteer Reserve. Died, age unknown, on the 7th November 1944. No known next of kin. No known grave he is commemorated on the Runnymede Memorial, Panel 243.

LIGHTFOOT, Horace – Orton Longueville, Peterborough. Leading Aircraftman 1467078, Base Signals and Radar Unit, Royal Air Force Volunteer Reserve. Died, aged 38, on the 7th November 1944. The son of Edward and Helen Lightfoot and the husband of Alice Lightfoot of Orton Longueville, Peterborough. Buried in Oostende New Communal Cemetery, Oostende, Belgium. Grave 21.Plot 9. Row 2.

PEARSON, John Leonard – 90 High Street, Fletton, Peterborough. Aircraftman 2nd Class 1462173, Royal Air Force Volunteer Reserve. Died, aged 23, on the 14th November 1944. The cause of death believed to have been an accident in Greece. The son of John and Ivy Pearson of Peterborough and the husband of Joyce Pearson of Stanground, Peterborough. Buried in Phaleron War Cemetery, Greece. Grave 15.A.17.

KILBY, Ronald – 15 Hunting Avenue, Fletton, Peterborough. Private 14714600, 5th Duke of Cornwall's Light Infantry. Died, aged 19, on the 25th November 1944 of wounds while in a German Field Hospital. The son of Thomas and Emily Kilby of Peterborough. Buried in the Reichswald Forest War Cemetery, Germany. Grave 62.B.5.

ULYATT, Isaac Henry – 44 Alderman's Drive, Peterborough. Private 14703340, 1st Manchester Regiment. Died, aged 34, on the 27th November 1944. The son of Henry and Caroline Ulyatt and the husband of Edith Ulyatt of Peterborough. Buried in Groesbeek Canadian War Cemetery, Holland. Grave XII.D.10.

HAWKINS, Ronald Arthur – 19 Princes Road, Fletton, Peterborough. Warrant Officer 1333580, 177 Squadron, Royal Air Force Volunteer Reserve. Died, age unknown, on the 1st December 1944. No known grave he is commemorated on the Singapore Memorial, Column 433.

SUTTON, Frederick – Petty Officer Stoker C/K8305, HMS Monck, Royal Navy. Died of illness, aged 54, on the 1st December 1944. The husband of Francis Sutton of Peterborough. Buried in Eastfield Cemetery, Peterborough. Div. 1. Block 16. Grave 6069.

WARD, Lawrence – 22 Church Street, Stanground, Peterborough. Corporal 5779343, 2nd The Queens Royal Regiment (West Surrey), 16 Brigade. Was attached to the 1944 Special Forces Chindits operation. Died, aged 29, on the 16th December 1944. Cause of death believed to be head injuries as a result of an accident in India. No known next of kin. Buried in Kirkee War Cemetery, India. Grave 3.C.9.

AKASS, Charles Richard – Corporal 930476, 2757 Squadron, RAF Regiment, Royal Air Force Volunteer Reserve. Died, aged 25, on the 16th December 1944. Believed killed when a V2 rocket hit a cinema in Antwerp. The son of Francis and Ethel Akass and the husband of Vera Akass of Peterborough. Buried in Schoonselhof Cemetery, Antwerp, Belgium. Grave V. D. 73.

WATSON, Ronald Henry – 1 Granville Street, Peterborough. Lieutenant 134474, 77 Field Regiment, Royal Artillery. Died, aged 26, on the 26th December 1944. The son of Arnold and Grace Watson of Peterborough. Buried in Phaleron War Cemetery, Greece. Grave 18.B.4.

WESTWOOD, Bernard – 26 Cobden Street, Peterborough. Private 5835556, 4th Suffolk Regiment. Died, aged 28, on the 27th December 1944 while a Japanese prisoner of war in the POW camp known as Matsushima or Tokyo Camp 2 –D. The cause of death being cardiac beri – beri. The son of John and Annie Westwood of Goldthorpe, Yorkshire and the husband of Edith Westwood of Peterborough. Buried in Yokohama War Cemetery, Japan. Grave L.C.16.

1945

New Year Shortages

It had been a very cold Christmas and New Year which was now compounded by a serious countrywide shortage of fuel. Traffic, cooking and lighting were all affected. Mr. Frank Smith, the Fuel Controller, said that the coal situation had got steadily worse and there would have to be a great economy if there was to be enough to go around over the winter period. The biggest problem though was transport, "We are in the hands of the railways and other operators," he said, "and they in turn are in the hands of the national authorities and in the grip of war conditions." He was satisfied that the dealers were doing their best in difficult circumstances. Works and industrial concerns of vital importance were getting fuel and causing the severe rationing of orders.

The Ministry of Fuel was appealing to people to economise in the use of electricity, especially between the hours of 8am and 10am. If the load became too great, the Central Electricity Board – under whom the Peterborough power station operated – could cut off consumers to ease the burden. This had already happened in some areas.

Mr. Smith said that although some people in the city had tried to economise, others seemed determined to keep up their central heating and big coal grates as well. The quality of the coal was generally poor, but this is all there was available. People were advised to try to secure loads of wood instead of coal, and the supply of coke was under national control and could not be relied upon either.

The problem of supply of electricity was not so much a scarcity of fuel; rather it was a shortage of plant. During the previous five years of war the stations had not been given any new plant due to increased demand from other industries and the power stations were suffering because of it. Ironically, Peterborough had more plant than was necessary to supply its own area, but being part of the national grid, they had to supply that as well, which drained what they had.

Mr. Raymond Prince, director, manager and engineer of the Peterborough Gas Company said that their present stocks of coal and coke were adequate. Their chief problem was a shortage of labour. Consumers must economise, but there was no fear of the company having to cut off the gas. The shortage of labour affected both production and maintenance. Before the war they had 22 fitters, now they had only 9, and some were regularly on other national work.

The beer problem, always more pronounced at holiday time, had now become acute. At the Christmas weekend, the closing down of the factories and influx of visitors made quick inroads on the local supply. The result was that a number of public houses ran out on Christmas Day. There had been a breakdown in transport so that several breweries failed to get stocks through and a number of pubs did not open until the New Year weekend. It had been one of the 'driest' weeks for a long time.

On Leave from the German Front

The first D-Day man to arrive home on leave locally was Lance Corporal James Frederick Rothery, eldest son of Mr. and Mrs. F. Rothery, 39, South Street,

Stanground, Peterborough, arriving by train on the final leg of his journey from Kings Cross on Tuesday 2nd January.

"It was Friday, and near Bastogne, when I first heard I was to have leave," he said. "And was I surprised? I should say I was, for I had previously written home to say that I was one of the unlucky ones."

L/Cpl. Rothery was a Signaller, and one of the men who made the initial landings on D-Day. Since then he had travelled hundreds of miles across Holland, France and Belgium, right to the German border. With him all this time had been his friend, Corporal Len Cooper from Peterborough. "I have been very lucky," he said. "Once I got burnt on a cheek and hit in a leg when a soldier who lay beside me was killed."

He told how his work as a Signaller took him right up to the front line with the infantry, and how, when they captured a certain place, they did not realise that there was a German patrol operating within 20 yards of them each night. Throughout his travels L/Cpl. Rothery received great hospitality from the French, Belgians and Dutch. "We were especially welcome in Holland and Belgium," he said.

Lance Corporal Rothery, who was 24 years of age, was with the Highland Division in Africa, where he received the Africa Star. He was also with the Allies when they invaded Sicily. After that he went into Italy, and was there only a few days before he was drafted home for D-Day. He had two brothers, one serving in the Navy in South Africa, and the other, a Corporal, with the Army in Holland. L/Cpl. Rothery was formerly employed by the London Brick Company.

Girls without Cards

Even though war restrictions were now being relaxed in many areas, three Peterborough girls now found themselves being fined at the Magistrates' Court for failing to produce their identity cards to police officers in uniform. The girls were, Eileen Winfield, Montague Road, Walton, on 9th December; fined 10s., and Ivy and Violet Ferris, St. John's Street, on 8th December, fined 5s. each.

Police had been checking the cards of girls at the American Red Cross club and Eileen Winfield had not got hers with her. She was given two days in order to produce it at the police station but was late in doing so. On being fined, the Magistrate said that she had caused a number of people unnecessary trouble.

Ivy and Violet Ferris had been in an American lorry when it was stopped by police for checks. They were also given two days in which to produce their cards but were four days late. Violet told the court that she was sorry, Ivy did not turn up.

Mediterranean Casualties

The first news of casualties in 1945 now began to appear. Captain Charles W.H. Aldridge, elder son of Mr. and Mrs. Charles Aldridge, 79, All Saint's Road, Peterborough, was now reported missing in Athens. Captain Aldridge had been an apprentice journalist with the "Peterborough Advertiser." He volunteered when war broke out and was soon commissioned. He went right through the North Africa campaign, and saw service in Italy before going to Greece.

Lieutenant Ronald (Mac) Watson, 77 Field Regiment, Royal Artillery, son of Mr. and Mrs. A. Watson, 1, Granville Street, Peterborough, had been reported killed in action during December in the Mediterranean theatre. Lt. Watson joined the Army after receiving his education at King's School. In his civilian days he was with J. Claypole and Son, Bridge Street. Five days after receiving a War Office telegram carrying the news of their son's death, Mr. and Mrs. Watson had a letter from him, written from Greece in December. In the letter Lt. Watson described conditions in Greece, and his pleasure at seeing Athens. Lt. Watson, who was 26 years old, died on 26th December, 1944, and is buried in Phaleron War Cemetery, Greece.

Lance Sergeant Douglas Richard Templeman had now been wounded in the left arm and thigh whilst serving in the Mediterranean theatre of war. Aged 24, he was the only son of Mr. and Mrs. Templeman, 179, Mountsteven Avenue, Walton, Peterborough. He had been abroad for three and a half years, serving in Iraq, Egypt, North Africa, Syria, Cyprus and Italy. Before joining the forces at the outbreak of the war he was in the offices of Baker Perkins Ltd.

Mrs. George Feetham, Senior V.A.D., Royal Navy, wife of Bombardier Feetham, 16, Huntley Road, Woodston, Peterborough, had now been invalided home from Malta, after having contracted Typhoid. She had served in the Royal Navy hospitals in various parts of Britain and in Malta for five years.

Only ten days before he was due for leave, Sapper Arthur William Macer, Royal Engineers, of Orton Waterville, died of head injuries received in the course of his duties on the Shetland Isles. He was the only son of Mr. and Mrs. E.B. Macer, late of Fletton, Peterborough, and was married. Aged 31, he joined the Royal Engineers in 1942, and three months later was attached to the Scottish Command. He had served in the Shetlands for 16 months and his last leave had been in October. Sapper Macer was educated at Fletton Council School. He is buried in Woodston Cemetery.

A Messerschmitt Kill
Flight Sergeant Alan John Griffen, son of Mr. and Mrs. J.L. Griffen, 12, Scotney Street, Peterborough, a former L.M.S. fireman, was an RAF pilot in a Spitfire fighter-bomber squadron, Second Tactical Air Force, on the Western Front. News had now come through that he had shared in the destruction of a Messerschmitt Me 109 fighter over Germany.

"This was the first time I had actually contacted a German aircraft," he said. "Number Four was fired upon by a Me 109 after leaving the target area. I turned and started on the 109 immediately, making a head-on attack. I broke away and resumed the attack from the rear. During this time Number Two got in a burst.

Then I manoeuvred into a position line astern of the enemy aircraft, closed in from 300 yards' range, and opened fire again. I saw strikes on both wings and on the fuselage, and followed the Messerschmitt down through the cloud and saw it burst into flames and crash."

Educated at Walton School, Flt. Sgt. Griffen joined the RAF in October 1941. His early training was done in the United States, and he returned in March 1943, being stationed at the Tactical Exercise Unit before joining his squadron on 3rd June. Flt. Sgt. Griffen had flown on 90 operations by the time of his success, bombing and strafing enemy strong-points, cutting railway lines and bombing factories and bridges.

Another Military Medal Awarded
The Military Medal had now been awarded to Private Herbert Cecil Wright, Royal Norfolk Regiment, of Peterborough, for services in North West Europe. The citation stated: "On August 7th, 1944, Private Wright was travelling on the lead carrier which was the first to cross the bridge over the River Orne in the battalion group of essential vehicles. He was sitting high up on the back of the carrier. On reaching a

point about 600 yards over the bridge the road was heavily mortared, and one man on the carrier was wounded. Private Wright immediately dressed the man's wounds, refusing to take cover from the mortaring. Five Germans opened fire from the roadside.

Private Wright, still sitting on the carrier, at once replied and killed at least one German and the others withdrew. The vehicles next came under heavy Spandau (machine-gun) and rifle fire from 40 yards range. Private Wright again engaged the enemy, still remaining on top of the carrier until the wireless operator in the carrier was wounded. Private Wright then dressed this man's wounds still completely exposed to heavy fire.

Private Wright then manned the wireless set and kept the vehicle group in touch with battalion H.Q., until the vehicles arrived in the battalion bridgehead. Throughout this action Private Wright showed a degree of courage and devotion to duty which has rarely been surpassed while his actions were largely instrumental in getting the vehicles safely through to the battalion."

U.S. General gives Thanks to the City
Although there had been a few minor problems in the city during the war relating to American service personnel, whether they were being robbed or beaten up in the city centre, or having relationships with the wives of city men away serving in the Armed Forces, these were only ever very exceptional incidents when compared to the great multitude of U.S. servicemen who passed through Peterborough during the war years.

The American Armed Services now thanked the people of the city for their great hospitality in the form of a letter to the Mayor from Lieutenant General John C.H. Lee, U.S. Army. The Lt. General wrote: "Dear Mayor Farrow, Our necessitated operational departure from the United Kingdom prevented me from personally thanking you in the name of General Eisenhower, and indeed each man and woman in the United States Forces, who was privileged in visiting your city.

The hospitality and helpfulness of your people on so many occasions has enabled us to administer these Forces, building with your own the team necessary for the Allied liberation of Europe. Through such understanding and natural kindness I believe we have more firmly moulded the friendly relations of our two nations.

As I write this, some of our Army are still in Great Britain and I know would also wish to share in these expressions. In grateful appreciation of all that has been done to make our stay in the United Kingdom such an unforgettably happy experience, and with abiding best wishes always, I remain, ever gratefully yours, John C.H. Lee, Lieutenant General, U.S. Army."

Chaplain Takes Germans Prisoner
In the middle of January it was reported that after landing in Normandy with the vanguard of the invasion forces, the Rev. R.E. Cox, C.F., vicar of St. Barnabas', Peterborough, wandered away from his unit in search of a burial ground. Turning a corner he found himself confronted by 16 German soldiers. A Chaplain goes unarmed but the Germans did not seem to care. They immediately surrendered and the surprised Chaplain had to take them in as his prisoners.

This was one of several stories Mr. Cox told when he came home on leave in the middle of the month. Another story concerned the first hours of the invasion. The sight of the colossal fleet of invasion ships crossing the Channel on D-Day was evidently too much for one German soldier. He got absolutely "tight," and as the ships arrived and the troops poured off, this German stood on the beach directing them like a traffic policeman. He caused so much amusement that the British troops left him to it.

Mr. Cox next described something that he said was just typical of the British Army. A German shell landed near a British slit trench occupied by a sentry. Suddenly a head popped out of the trench, with a tin hat perched to one side and a cigarette dangling from a corner of a mouth. The Tommy said. "Silly ------, missed again!"

City Officer Awarded Military Cross

The King had now awarded the Military Cross to Lieutenant (temporary Captain) Herbert Selwyn Nundy, Reconnaissance Corps, Royal Armoured Corps, second son of Mrs. S.M. Nundy, 1, Alderman's Drive Peterborough. The decoration was awarded to the ex-Kings School boy in recognition of gallant and distinguished service in North West Europe.

The citation stated: "On August 9th, 1944, Lieutenant Nundy was ordered to patrol with his armoured car troop down the road Vire-Tenchbray. Contact was gained and the troop came under very heavy fire from mortars and 75mm S.P. (self-propelled) gun, and one armoured car was knocked out. A patrol consisting of Lt. Nundy's and one other car, continued to keep the enemy under observation at the same time passing back much valuable information.

Later, Captain A.S. Gardner, the acting Squadron Commander, came forward to carry out a reconnaissance on foot, and was severely wounded by a hand grenade. Although aware that the enemy was within 50 yards, Lt. Nundy immediately dismounted from his armoured car, and in doing so, he himself was wounded in the head. Without any thought for himself, he went to the assistance of Captain Gardner, and succeeded in evacuating him on his armoured car. Later he returned, and still in the face of the enemy, succeeded in recovering the damaged armoured car. This he had to do by means of towing. Throughout this action, in which at least 15 enemy were killed, Lt. Nundy displayed courage and leadership of a very high order."

Lieutenant Nundy, who was 28 years old, was mobilized with the Territorials at the outbreak of war, going with the 5th Battalion, Queen's Royal Regiment, to France in March 1940, and was evacuated at Dunkirk. He was commissioned in the Reconnaissance Corps in July 1941, and landed in Normandy soon after D-Day. He had seen action in France, Holland and Belgium. Since September 1944 he had been in hospital in Scotland following an accident.

Casualties

Sergeant Peter Stimpson, Wireless Operator/Air Gunner, RAFVR, son of Mr. and Mrs. Stimpson, 60, Hall Lane, Werrington, Peterborough, was now reported missing, believed drowned, when his plane crashed into the sea off the coast of Scotland, immediately after taking off. Sgt. Stimpson, who was 19 years old, had been in the Air Force for about eighteen months, and was formerly at Reed's Garage. He left a wife, Alice Stimpson, and one child aged seven months. Sgt. Stimpson died on 11th January, 1945, and is commemorated in Werrington churchyard.

Corporal Elsie Kathleen Norris, A.T.S., attached 139 (mixed) H.A.A. Regiment, Royal Artillery, daughter of Mr. and the late Mrs. R.H. Norris, 295, Oundle Road,

Peterborough, had now died in hospital in Belgium from accidental injuries. Cpl. Norris, who was 24 years of age, died on 13th January, 1945, and is buried in Heverlee War Cemetery, Leuven, Belgium.

Lance Corporal Alec George Bussey, 1st Battalion, Cambridgeshire Regiment, son of Mrs. and the late Mr. Bussey, 86, South Street, Stanground, Peterborough, had been a prisoner of war of the Japanese for some time. He was now reported missing while being transported by ship to another camp. L/Cpl. Bussey, who was 31 years of age, died on the 12th September 1944. He was being transported on a Japanese transport ship, the RAKUYO MARU, when it was sunk by the American submarine USS SEALION. He is commemorated on the Singapore Memorial.

Lance Corporal John Barber (Jack) Shelton, 5th Battalion, Seaforth Highlanders, second son of Mr. and Mrs. C.W. Shelton, Barton House, 73, Garton End Road, Peterborough, was now reported killed in action in France on 11th February, 1945. L/Cpl. Shelton, who was 31 years of age, was educated at Fletton Secondary School, and was in business with his brother, Mr. C.W. Shelton, junior, building contractor. L/Cpl. Shelton is buried in Reichswald Forest War Cemetery, Germany.

Private W. Friend, youngest son of Mr. and Mrs. Friend, 54, Taverner's Road, Peterborough, reported missing since October 26th, was now known to be a prisoner of war in Germany. He joined the Army from the London Brick Company Ltd., and served in Sicily and Italy, where he was captured. He had two brothers in the Army, Stanley, in Greece, and Edgar, in Holland.

Two local men were killed in a plane crash whilst returning from an operational flight on 6th February, 1945. They were Flight Sergeant John Coleman, Transport Command, RAFVR, aged 21 years old, son of Mr. and Mrs. C. Coleman, 91, All Saint's Road, Peterborough, and Warrant Officer Donald Francis Barber, from Oundle.

F/Sgt. Coleman, an Old Petriburgian, was formerly at the food office. His brother was a Bevin Boy, and he had a sister in the Forces. The two airmen, who had been friends, were both buried in Oundle Cemetery.

Death from Heart Failure

The deepest sympathy was now extended to Mr. Rowland Hill, MBE, and Mrs. Hill, of Princes Gate, Peterborough, on the sudden death of their elder son, Flying Officer John William Rowland Hill, DFC, at the age of 22.

F/O. Hill died at Rauceby RAF Hospital from cardiac failure following an operation for appendicitis on 22nd January, 1945. He had played football for the RAF station a few days before the operation and everything appeared to be normal as it progressed. However, a few minutes afterwards, he passed away.

At Repton, F/O. Hill represented his school at tennis, and on leaving was apprenticed as a brewery pupil with Soames and Co. Ltd., Spalding. Before he had finished his apprenticeship he volunteered for the RAF and underwent flying training in Canada. He flew 30 operational flights, including six over the Alps, and his plane was only ever damaged twice by enemy flak. In 1944 he was gazetted the award for the Distinguished Flying Cross, and was waiting for the command to receive it from the King when he died.

His father, Mr. Rowland Hill, retired from the position of manager of Barclay's Bank at Peterborough, at the end of 1944, and at the same time relinquished the honorary post of Chief Fire Guard. Mr. and Mrs. Hill had another son, Paul, at Repton, and a daughter, Mary. The family moved home to Wroxham, near Norwich, at the end of the war, which is why F/O. Hill is buried in Wroxham (St. Mary) Churchyard.

Two More RAF Awards

Two Peterborough RAF officers now appeared in the latest list of awards published by the Air Ministry. Station Commander, Group Captain Anthony Caron Evans-Evans, son of Lt. Colonel A.A. Evans-Evans, of Peterborough, received the D.F.C., and Acting Flight Lieutenant Bernard E. Patrick, RAFVR, of Granville Street, Peterborough, received a bar to his D.F.C.

Group Captain Evans-Evans had taken part in action over many heavily defended targets during his wartime career and was Station Commander at RAF Coningsby. On one mission he had been forced to parachute out of his crippled bomber, and as Station Commander had set a great example to the operational crews of 83 Squadron. His leadership had been chiefly responsible for the outstanding successes achieved by the squadrons at the station.

Born in Cardiff, Group Captain Evans-Evans, now aged 43, was educated at the Fletton Secondary School and King's School, Peterborough, and the University College, Nottingham. From 1921 to 1922 he was a Private in the Royal Army Ordnance Corps, and in 1924 he was commissioned in the RAF. He spent the next 15 years on flight and signal duties. In April 1942, he went to Canada, where he commanded No. 34 Operational Training Unit, and returned to Britain in 1943, when he was given command of RAF Coningsby. He attained the rank of Group Captain in June 1942, and was Mentioned in Despatches in June 1944.

An old boy of Deacon's School, Flight Lt. Patrick served in the ranks before being commissioned in 1944, when he won his D.F.C. Since then he had completed numerous operational sorties, displaying outstanding keenness for operational flying, and achieving considerable success. He continued to display courage and devotion to duty of a high order, which, combined with his unfailing determination to complete his allotted task, had set an excellent example to all pilots.

Crime Report for 1944

The Chief Constable, Mr. F.G. Markin, paid a great deal of attention to street accidents in his annual report for 1944, when 352 accidents in which vehicles were involved were reported to the police. There were 7 fatalities, 13 people were seriously injured and 92 slightly injured. He said that indiscriminate parking of vehicles in the streets added to the dangers on the road, and a scheme for building car parks in the town centre should be addressed immediately after hostilities ceased.

During 1944 there were 835 indictable offences reported, but it was ascertained that 287 cycles and other articles reported stolen had either been misplaced, lost, or taken in error. This left 597, a decrease of 118 compared with 1943. The offenders in 330 cases were traced, and 116 were proceeded against, a decrease of 55.

Of 267 offences undetected, 206 were pedal cycle thefts. "The prevalent habit of carelessly leaving pedal cycles unattended has again caused a very great increase in this particular offence, and a corresponding increase in the work of the police.

Robberies reported were 533, a hundred fewer than in 1943. Property stolen was valued at £5,372, and that recovered £869. Of the total value of property unrecovered (£4,503), £2,796 represented the proceeds of two big robberies.

Three hundred and thirty offences were detected, compared with 321 out of a total of 633 in 1943. There were 272 prosecutions for non-indictable offences, and 25 for drunkenness, while 345 cautions were issued for minor offences.

Persons apprehended for other forces, or as military absentees were 142, against 106. In addition 286 Allied soldiers were temporarily lodged in the police station cells. Fifty-five children and young persons were brought before the court, a decrease of 22.

No fewer than 787 premises were found insecure at night – 111 houses, 435 lock-up premises, and 241 shops. The Chief Constable stated this total exceeded the 1943 figure by 104. The increase, he said, could perhaps be accounted for by the cancellation of fire-watching duties, as many businesses had been occupied during the hours of darkness.

Members of the Police Force serving in the Armed Forces numbered 22, and 5 held commissioned ranks. There were 13 commendations issued to officers, two men receiving two each.

The authorised strength of the Special Constabulary was 160 although the actual strength was 107, and they worked 23,508 hours. Twenty-eight police messengers had been recruited from past and present boys of secondary schools.

Dogs found straying and placed in the police station kennels numbered 237. Many were unclaimed and were subsequently sold to new owners. The report concluded with thanks to the members of the Watch Committee, to the personnel of the force, and to British and Allied military authorities for their co-operation.

Prisoners Rescued

Mr. and Mrs. J. Smart, 67, Clarence Road, Peterborough, now received news that their son, Private A.V.K. Smart, Suffolk Regiment, had been rescued after a Japanese transport ship taking prisoners from Thailand to Tokyo, was sunk on 12th September, 1944. Formerly a goods porter on the L.N.E.R., he was captured in Malaya. The last message his parents had from him was sent in June 1944.

Mrs. Gray, 3, Albert Place, Peterborough, had heard that her husband, Driver D.W. Gray, Royal Engineers, had also been rescued, apparently from the same transport. He had been with Mr. George Gaunt, butcher, Long Causeway.

Two Japanese transport ships carrying prisoners were sunk on the 12th September, 1944. The RAKUYO MARU (1,317 pows), sunk by the United States submarine USS SEALION, and the KACHIDOKI MARU (900 pows), sunk by the United States submarine USS PAMPANITO. Both ships had sailed with convoy HI-72 from Singapore, and the Japanese did stop to rescue some men in the water which is probably how these two men survived.

When they realised that the two ships were carrying Allied prisoners of war, the US submarines began their own search for survivors, picking up 63 men from the RAKUYO MARU. Of these, 4 died after being rescued. The RAKUYO MARU lost 1,159 prisoners to the sea after they were in the water for up to 4 days.

Two Wounded

In the middle of February it was announced that Captain J.W.O. Elliot, 3rd Scots Guards, son of Mr. and Mrs. Hubert Elliot, Longthorpe House, Peterborough, had been wounded in North West Europe. Captain Elliot had been wounded in the leg and it was hoped that he would be brought back to England shortly.

Sapper Frank Dewey, Royal Engineers, son of Mrs. Dewey, 23, Milton Street, Peterborough, had been wounded in the right leg after the explosion of a land mine in North West Europe, and was now in hospital in Scotland. Before the war he had been with Messrs. Bull, plumbers, North Street, and joined the Army in 1941. He landed in France with the early invasion forces.

Group Captain Evans-Evans Missing

Just a week after being awarded the D.F.C., Group Captain Anthony Caron Evans-Evans, was now reported missing believed killed, from an operational flight over Germany on 21st February, 1945. Group Captain Evans-Evans married Miss Joyce Emerton, daughter of Mrs. G. Emerton, 107a, Lincoln Road, Peterborough, they had two children.

Group Capt. Evans-Evans was the pilot of an Avro Lancaster Mk III, Serial No NE165, code letters OL-Y, which took off from RAF Coningsby to mark the Mittelland Canal near Gravenhorst in Germany for bombers from Number 5 Group to attack. This was a very experienced crew, four of whom were decorated. Evans-Evans had the DFC, which was announced on 16th February, five days previously. The aircraft was shot down by a night-fighter and crashed in Holland. All seven crew died. At 43 years of age, he was one of the oldest senior officers to die on bombing operations during the war. He was, at the time, also Station Commander of RAF Coningsby. He is buried in Mierlo War Cemetery, Holland.

The Group Captain's brother, Roland Gwynne Evans-Evans, was killed in action in 1944.

Casualties Reports Rise in March

The casualty lists lengthened in March, not just for Western Europe, but the Far East was still claiming men who had been killed up to a year earlier.

Sergeant John Derek Hall, 186 Squadron, RAFVR, was now posted as missing on air operations on the night of 13th and 14th February, 1945. He was the eldest son of Mr. and Mrs. E. Hall, 4, Williamson Avenue, Peterborough, and joined the RAF 18 months previously. He had been an old Deaconian and before the war was employed at the drawing office at the electricity works. Sergeant Hall died, aged 20, on 14th February 1945. He was the Flight Engineer in Avro Lancaster Mk I, Serial No NG353, code letters AP-X that took off from RAF Stradishall as part of operation Thunderclap to attack Dresden. All seven crew died. He is buried in Berlin 1939-45 War Cemetery, Germany.

Gunner James Wright, Royal Artillery, was still missing at sea following the sinking of a Japanese transport ship carrying prisoners of war from Java to Japan on 24th June, 1944. Gunner Wright's wife lived at Castor, and he was the son of Mrs. Wright, 310, Gladstone Street, Peterborough. Before the war he had been with Messrs. Paten and Co's wine stores. Gunner Wright has no known grave and is commemorated on the Singapore Memorial.

Private George Sexton, Army Catering Corps, Royal Artillery, youngest son of Mr. and Mrs. S. Sexton, Rose Cottage, Church Street, Werrington, Peterborough, was now reported killed on the Burma front. Private Sexton was 23 years of age and worked at Provender Mill, Fenbridge Street, Werrington, and joined the Army three years previously. He is buried in Taukkyan War Cemetery, Myanmar.

Private Walter Frederick Reynolds, 5th Black Watch, (Royal Highlanders), 84, Mayor's Walk, Peterborough, had been reported killed in action in Western Europe. Son of Mr. George and Mrs. Emily Reynolds, he left a wife, Mrs. Eva Reynolds, and two children. Private Reynolds died, aged 32, on 25th February, 1945, and before the war had been employed at the G.P.O. He is buried in Rheinberg War Cemetery, Germany.

Private Frank (Ted) Creed, son of Mr. and Mrs. F.E. Creed, Muswell Road, Peterborough, had now been wounded with shrapnel in Western Europe. He had written a cheerful letter home. Before the war he had been in the office of Mr. W. Granger, buyer for the Co-operative Society, and was the organiser of the Co-operative Youth Club. Formerly at Lincoln Road Boy's School, he was not yet 19 years old.

Private Edward Perkins, youngest son of Mr. and Mrs. H. Perkins, 19, Henry Street, Peterborough, had now been reported wounded while serving with the 14th Army in Burma.

Corporal Gordon Victor Peach, Royal Corps of Signals, 33, Exeter Road, Peterborough, was in hospital in Italy suffering from sciatica.

Another man who was sick in hospital was Lance Corporal M.H. Calvert, 117, New England, Peterborough. He was in Connaught Hospital suffering from malaria contracted in India, where he had been on service as a Military Policeman. He won the Military Medal for courageous conduct at Tobruk in 1941. His parents, Mr. and Mrs. M. Calvert, lived at 1, Crown Street, Peterborough.

Driver J.W. Creamer, K.S.L.I. of Fletton, Peterborough, had been seriously wounded while serving in Western Europe. He had gone over on D-Day, and had recently met his step-brother, Leading Aircraftman Eric Wilson.

City Airman's C.G.M.

Sergeant Derrick J. Allen, RAFVR, of No. 467 (RAAF) Squadron, a former Peterborough carpenter, had now been awarded the Conspicuous Gallantry Medal. He stayed behind in a blazing bomber to free a trapped comrade and was still in the aircraft when it broke in two. He fell clear and landed by parachute. He was a mid-upper gunner aboard the bomber which attacked Dusseldorf one night in November 1944, when the plane was attacked by an enemy fighter and set on fire.

With complete disregard for his own safety, Sergeant Allen promptly went to the assistance of a comrade. "The aircraft was now on fire and falling rapidly," said the official report. "Nevertheless, this gallant airman hacked away at the turret doors with an axe and finally succeeded in freeing his comrade. Just as Sergeant Allen got ready to jump, the aircraft broke in two. He fell clear however, pulled the ripcord of his parachute, and descended safely. In the face of extreme danger, this airman displayed conduct in keeping with the best traditions of the Royal Air Force."

Sergeant Allen was born at Peterborough in 1924, and lived in the district. He enlisted in the RAF in 1943.

Meeting in Calcutta

Gunner Alfred Rusdale, son of Mr. and Mrs. Rusdale, High Street, Fletton, Peterborough, who joined up in September 1939, and volunteered for the Commandos, saw service in Tunisia and Italy, and was wounded in the Akyab landing south of Mandalay. He was taken to Calcutta Hospital, where he was surprised to meet a peacetime friend with whom he had worked for a number of years at Messrs. Fairways, Broadway – Private James Bonsor, Fengate Close, Peterborough.

Private Bonsor was in the Northamptonshire Regiment, and had also been wounded on the road to Mandalay. They had not seen each other for four years, and the coincidence of being taken to the same hospital after fighting hundreds of miles apart, caused them great pleasure and surprise.

Another Water Tank Incident

Archibald Hill, aged six, of 14, Milton Terrace, Peterborough, owed his life to Mr. Walter J. Deacon, Clerk of the Peace and Clerk of the Soke County Council. Mr. Deacon rescued the boy from a static water tank in Priestgate on the afternoon of Sunday, 18th March.

Entering his yard from Priestgate at five minutes past three, Mr. Deacon saw Archibald's brother, Charles, aged five, running about, crying and pointing to the water tank. Mr. Deacon then saw the other boy floating face downwards in the water, and pulled him out. The boy was barely conscious. Mr. Deacon carried the boy into his house and telephoned for the police and an ambulance. The boy was undressed and wrapped in blankets before he was taken to the hospital, where he was detained, suffering from shock and the effects of his emersion. The father of the two boys had been discharged from the Army on medical grounds and was in Scotland.

The tank was six feet deep, and was constructed from the cellars of a block of offices demolished by a bomb in 1941. It was approached from Priestgate through a high wooden gate, and between it and Mr. Deacon's property were a sapling and a wire fence.

Prisoner Released

News was now received by the wife of Private George Fincham, 27, St. Margaret's Road, Fletton, Peterborough, that he had been released from Stalag XXB by the Russians, and was expected to arrive in England very soon. He had been a prisoner for almost five years.

City Tank Driver

Corporal Don Gale, 44, South Street, Peterborough, was the driver of a tank called "Ballinamallard," which had seen heavy action on the Western Front. "Ballina-mallard" was one of the few surviving original tanks of the battalion, and the only one of the squadron to last the course since the Normandy landings. Twice during the campaign it was hit, once so seriously that a complete new engine had to be installed.

In a recent action the 17-pounder gun with which the tank was armed was used to blast a pocket of stubbornly resisting enemy out of a group of houses at a range of 2,000 yards. The troop, of which "Ballinamallard" was a member, scored direct hits on a Spandau post and German anti-tank gun. The large number of German dead counted later, testified to the accuracy of the shooting.

Corporal Gale formerly worked with his father on a farm. His brother John was a Sergeant Pilot in the RAF, and another brother, Leslie, was also in the RAF, in England.

High Praise

"He did a really magnificent job," said a Battery Commander of 89 Light Anti-Aircraft Regiment, speaking of the courage and efficiency displayed by Signaller Lance Corporal P.R. King, of 276, Lincoln Road, Peterborough.

"At the time," said the officer, "we were operating on the flank of the Division, and to carry out the task we had been given it was necessary for some of the guns to be brought up under cover of darkness to concealed positions in front of the infantry. With these guns went Lance Corporal King, his job being to maintain contact with Battery H.Q. by radio.

The following day, the Boche (Germans), reacting to the pressure that was being put on to him, started to shell and mortar our gun area. This went on for nearly 36 hours without stopping. In my opinion, Lance Corporal King deserves the very highest credit, as, during the entire period, despite the stress, and dangerous conditions under which he was working, he never failed to keep contact with us at Battery Headquarters, and much of the success of that operation must be attributed to the splendid work which he did."

More Casualties Reported in March

Flight Lieutenant Bernard Chapman Brooker, D.F.C. and Bar, 156 Squadron, RAFVR, had now been killed in a flying accident on 11th March. He was the husband of Mrs. Joan M. Brooker, second daughter of Mrs. S. Kirby, 1, Vergette Street, Peterborough.

Flt. Lt. Brooker was a Pathfinder and joined the service six months after the evacuation from Dunkirk, in which he took part as a soldier. He was popular at his station and had been recommended for promotion. Mrs. Brooker was formerly at the Co-operative Society's hairdressing department, and she served for four years in the A.T.S.

Flt. Lt. Brooker was the Navigator in Avro Lancaster Mk III, Serial No PB669 that took off on a training flight from RAF Warboys. At the time he was attached to the Pathfinder Force Navigation Training Unit. The aircraft crashed at high speed at Old Weston near Spaldwick, Huntingdonshire. All eight crew died. He received his DFC in May 1944 as an acting Warrant Officer and the Bar in October 1944 as an acting Flight Lieutenant. Both were awarded while serving with 35 Squadron. He is buried in Eastfield Cemetery, Peterborough.

Private Benjamin Bollard, 2nd Welch Regiment, 2, Fengate Close, Peterborough, had now been killed in action in Burma. Aged 35 years old, he was killed on 22nd February, 1945. Before the war he had been with Luke Turner and Co., Princes Street, and played in the British Legion and Home Guard Bands. He has no known grave and is commemorated on the Rangoon Memorial, Myanmar (Burma).

Private Raymond Parbles, only son of Mr. and Mrs. A. Parbles, 3, Hereward Close, Peterborough, was now reported wounded in action in Northwest Europe. Aged 22, this was the second time he had been wounded, the first was in Holland the previous November. Private Parbles was with Mr. J.C. Perkins, tobacconist, Midgate, and joined the Army three years earlier.

Flying Officer Neil Joseph Fairbairn, 622 Squadron, Bomber Command, RAF, 15, St. Mark's Street, Peterborough, son of Mr. Walter and Mrs. Bernice Fairbairn, had been reported missing from air operations on 25th April, 1944, and was now presumed to have been killed on that date. He was the navigator in Avro Lancaster Mk I, Serial No ME693, code letters GI-F that took off from RAF Mildenhall to attack Karlsruhe. All seven crew died and are buried in Rheinberg War Cemetery, Germany.

Private Clifford Church, youngest son of Mr. and Mrs. H. Church, 30, Scotney Street, Peterborough, had now been reported wounded in the back in Western Europe. He had been serving overseas since D-Day.

Private Eric Cyril Herson, Army Catering Corps, eldest son of Mrs. Herson, 21, Wellington Street, Peterborough, had now died aged 28, of injuries received in an accident on 13th March, 1945, in the Central Mediterranean theatre of war. He joined the A.C.C. five years previously and before then had been with the London Brick Company. His widow lived at 200, Walpole Street, with his little daughter, Pam, whom he had never seen. He is buried in Bologna War Cemetery, Italy.

A Soldier's Courage

Mrs. Savidge, 6, Coneygree Road, Stanground, Peterborough, wife of Corporal C.F. Savidge, Royal Norfolk Regiment, now received a glowing account of her husband's courage and devotion to duty under heavy shell and mortar fire whilst serving in France on 8th July, 1944.

She received the citation from the Adjutant of her husband's battalion. "On July 8th, Corporal Savidge was N.C.O. in charge of a mine clearance detachment. This task was successfully completed by this N.C.O.'s detachment. Later, heavy counter-shelling commenced, and a member of his platoon was badly wounded. Stretcher-bearers were at a premium and this N.C.O. applied first aid and moved the wounded officer into a shell hole to await aid.

Two stretcher-bearers arrived but both were hit, so the N.C.O. applied dressings to their wounds and got them under cover. Four members of the platoon were then hit, and Corporal Savidge dealt with them, and made them comfortable and went in search of stretcher-bearers. He got back through heavy shelling, collected stretchers and men, as the stretcher-bearers were already working overtime, and returned to where he had left the casualties.

On arrival he found they had been collected, so he dismissed his men and awaited further orders. This N.C.O. worked throughout under heavy shell and mortar fire and was instrumental in saving the lives of one officer and six other ranks. He showed a great sense of duty and courage when his own task of clearing mines had been successfully completed."

Corporal Savidge, who had a six year old son, had been in the Army for almost five years and was formerly a lorry driver for Ellis and Everard, Ltd. He left England on D-Day and by March 1945 was in Germany.

Nearly Shot by Mistake

Private George Fincham, 27, St. Margaret's Road, Old Fletton, Peterborough, arrived home on Wednesday 4th April, 1944, after nearly five years as a prisoner of war in German hands. He told of how a Polish girl had saved him along with a number of other British POW's from being shot by Russian soldiers who had not recognised them as Allies.

Private Fincham was in Stalag XXIB, in Poland, and on January 23rd, 1945, was out as usual with a party working on the land. "One day the Russian tanks came along the road," he said. "We weren't expecting them, and they didn't know who we were. They opened fire and we were lucky to escape. A young Polish girl, whom none of us had seen before or have seen since, ran down the road towards the tanks in face of their fire. They stopped shooting and she explained to the Russians that we were British prisoners. They then sat down and played cards with us in their own way!"

Private Fincham was one of more than 1,300 soldiers, sailors and airmen released from German and Polish prison camps by the advancing Red Army. They disembarked on Saturday 31st March, at a port in Scotland, and after going to a transit camp, were sent home on 42 days leave, after which they could be sent to fight in any part of the world.

Speaking of camp conditions Private Fincham said that for the first 18 months they were almost intolerable, but later, thanks to the Geneva Convention, there was a very definite improvement. "It was only the Red Cross food that pulled us through," he said. "None of us will live long enough to repay them for what they did and are doing."

Casualties Reported in April

Sergeant Gunner Henry (Harry) Oswald Collin, 207 Squadron, RAFVR, aged 23, only son of Mr. and Mrs. Arthur Collin, 211, Dogsthorpe Road, Peterborough, had now been reported missing from air operations over Germany on March 20th, 1945. He had been educated at Orchard Street School, and before joining the RAF had been employed at Peter Brotherhood Ltd. He played football for the works team.

Sergeant Collin died on the 21st March 1945. He was the Mid Upper Gunner in Avro Lancaster Mk I, Serial No PA196, code letters EM-D that took off from RAF Spilsby to attack a synthetic oil plant at Bohlen. The aircraft was lost without trace. All seven crew died and he has no known grave and is therefore commemorated on the Runnymede Memorial.

Gunner Lawrence Pryke, Royal Artillery, 39, Peveril Road, Peterborough, who had originally been reported missing at Singapore, was now known to have been killed when a shell hit his dugout on February 13th, 1942. Aged 21, he was the eldest son of Mr. William and Mrs. Gertrude Pryke, and is buried in Kranji War Cemetery, Singapore.

News was now received that Private Arthur Cranfield, Parachute Regiment, eldest son of Mr. and Mrs. Cranfield, Orton Avenue, Woodston, Peterborough, had received a gunshot wound in the right thigh on March 24th while serving in Western Europe. Private Cranfield was married and his wife was formerly Miss Jeffries, of High Street, Fletton.

Private Ronald Kilby, Duke of Cornwall's Light Infantry, youngest son of Mr. and Mrs. T. Kilby, 15, Hunting Avenue, Fletton, Peterborough, was now reported as having died of wounds on March 25th, two days after being taken prisoner by the Germans in Holland. Private Kilby was 18 years of age, and was formerly with Mr. A.J.E. Stanyon, butcher, Bridge Street. He was engaged to Miss Iris Winterton, of Belsize Farm, Marholm. Private Kilby's father, Mr. T. Kilby, was a prisoner of war in Germany for two years in the First World War. Private Kilby died of wounds while in a German Field Hospital and is buried in the Reichswald Forest War Cemetery, Germany.

Private Ebenezer Allen Cole, son of Mr. and Mrs. Allen Cole, 68, Russell Street, Peterborough, was now reported missing since March 24th in Western Europe. There was some hope that he may have been taken prisoner. Aged 19, he had been in the Army for nine months and overseas for three months. He was first in the Royal

411

Norfolk Regiment and later the Argyll and Sutherland Highlanders. Before joining up he had been with John Lucas, Ltd., Builders.

Private Stephen Williamson, son of Mr. and Mrs. T. Williamson, 164, Palmerston Road, Woodston, Peterborough, had now been severely wounded in action in the right arm in Western Europe. He was now in hospital in England.

Driver Frank Leach, Royal Army Service Corps, only son of Mr. Alec and Mrs. Minnie Leach, 32, Park Street, Peterborough, had died in the Middle East on March 7th. Before joining up he had been with the Halford Cycle Co., Bridge Street. He is buried in Aleppo War Cemetery, Syria.

Evacuees Soon to Return

A scheme for the return of official evacuees to their homes had now been issued to local authorities. However, it was not to be carried out until instructions were received to do so. It gave details of trains and other arrangements to come into operation when the time came. Numbers of evacuees in this district were approximately as follows:

- City of Peterborough   671
- Old Fletton Urban   65
- Peterborough Rural   60 to 70
- Norman Cross Rural   146

War Not Over Yet

British soldiers fighting in Germany did not expect the war on the Continent to be over before the end of August according to a letter received by Mr. Arthur Johnson, of Pembroke House, Eastfield, Peterborough, a Director of Arthur E. Craig & Co. Ltd., from his son, Private A.R. Johnson, Wiltshire Regiment.

Private Johnson, who was 19 years old, was attached to the 43rd Division, and had been with the forward troops in Northwest Europe since August 1944. Before the war he had been on the staff of the Midland Bank at Peterborough. Private Johnson wrote, "I am afraid the war seems over bar the shouting to you in England and for you perhaps it is, but not for us. I still give it until August, and this opinion is shared by most of the lads, many of whom are even less optimistic. It tends to make us rather annoyed to read the papers, for they make it look rather like a walk-over. Believe me, it isn't that by any means yet. Still, we are all keeping our fingers crossed and hoping for the best.

The resistance we have met so far has been very patchy and we have seen few Jerries, which makes us wonder where they are all pulling out to. So far we have not had any trouble from the civilians. We have met many types – the cowed, arrogant, and snivelling and we have even had some who have waved to us as we have gone through. We have seen some very pretty and attractive girls, but the order is 'No Fraternising,' although I think it is going to be very difficult to stop it.

Many of the people seem sure we are going to shoot them, whilst others seem glad to help us. Even so, they are a crafty lot, and believe me, I never have my rifle far from my side. They all try to make out they are Poles, French or Russians, and never seem to like to admit they are members of the alleged master race."

Home from German POW Camps

With the overtaking of the prisoner of war camps in Germany as the Allied armies advanced, many Peterborough men had now been liberated from captivity. As quickly as possible they were being transferred to centres in Allied hands far behind the scenes of front line operations. Then, they were being sent to Great Britain, and every day, numbers were reaching their final destination – Home.

Driver George Drake, Royal Army Service Corps, son of Mr. George Drake and the late Mrs. Drake, 170, Dogsthorpe Road, a prisoner since June 1st, 1941, reached home on Friday 20th April. Driver Drake, who had been in the butchery business before the war, left England for the Middle East in 1940, and was taken prisoner in Crete. He was sent to Berlin and later to Middle Germany; then to Elzdorf, in Saxony, near to the city of Halle. He was there from November 1943, until he was rescued by the American Third Army.

After they had given him a good time, he was flown in transport planes to Nordhausen, and then to Brussels by American aircraft. The Red Cross brought him home; he was fitted out with clothing and was now on six weeks leave, fully appreciative that "England is the best country in the world!"

His treatment as a prisoner was "none too good," but, "much depended on the man who happened to be in charge." They did not have enough to eat, and without Red Cross parcels "a lot of us would not be here," he said. Thanks to medical supplies, again from the Red Cross, he never actually went sick. The work was rough labouring and the hours did not leave much time for recreation, but while in Berlin they did play some football. They had indoor games and plenty of reading, again, thanks to the Red Cross. The only Peterborough man he knew of in the same camp as himself was Private W.D. Judson, Royal Corps of Signals, whose home was at Thistlemoor Road.

A good piece of news waiting for him at home was that his brother, Trooper Robert Drake, Royal Tank Corps, who was captured in Belgium in May 1940, had also been rescued and was on his way home. All he knew of him was that he was a prisoner in Marienburg, East Prussia.

Trooper Robert Drake, of the 15/19 Hussars, who served with the Armoured Division, arrived home on the evening of Tuesday 24th April, and was the younger brother of Driver George Drake. A serving soldier, Trooper Drake went to France in October 1939, and was captured near Brussels on May 17th, 1940. He had been wounded and after being in hospital in Holland, was taken to Thome, Poland. Most of the rest of his imprisonment was in West Prussia, working on farms.

He was released on April 18th by General Montgomery's Army. The Allies had overrun his prison village near Marienburg, and the prisoners were being marched to near Hanover when British Forces came through – and they were free! They were about 600 in number, mostly English, but including some Americans, Poles and French. "Then everything was good." They first went to a German barracks in Celle, then to Brussels and home, all by plane. He reached Peterborough at 8 o'clock on the Tuesday night. He had heard that his brother George had been liberated, and was highly delighted to meet him.

The first year in prison was not very good, he said. Clothing was scanty and the food poor. This was improved when they started receiving Red Cross parcels early in 1941. Some of his work had been in towns when the food was not so good, but on the farms it was better. They were closely supervised but they had chances to play football with other Stalags. Some of their marching had been in snow, and they had some rough quarters. The civilians in Germany would sometimes be good to them, but the Army would not allow it.

413

Asked if he saw much change in Peterborough, Trooper Drake remarked on the missing railings and the air raid shelters, but he saw in England nothing of the things which the Germans had told them of, in their (German produced) camp paper. He saw much destruction in Germany and plenty of starvation among the people but, here again, the best off were those people nearest farms.

Signalman William David Judson, Royal Corps of Signals, aged 26, whose home address was 35, Thistlemoor Road, arrived home on Sunday 22nd April, after being a prisoner of war for 28 months. He was taken at Tobruk on June 20th, 1942, and after being in a prison camp in Italy, was moved to Stalag IVB in Germany. From there he was transferred to Stalag IVD, a small working camp.

He regained his freedom thanks to the Americans on Friday 13th April, and said that at this camp they were treated fairly well, although the food allotted to them was very poor, consisting mainly of watery soup, ersatz coffee (made from ground acorns), and a loaf of bread between seven. He said they practically lived on Red Cross parcels. The prisoners were compelled to work 10 hours a day, and 12 hours on alternate Sundays.

Mrs. D. Garner, 68, Saxon Road, received a telegram on the afternoon of Tuesday 24th April, saying that her husband, Lance Corporal W. Garner, 5th Northamptonshire Regiment, had arrived in England. He had been a prisoner of war since Dunkirk and was now in hospital in Derby. He was expected home in a few days.

Flags were out in Clarence Road, to welcome the arrival of Private John Stamper, second son of Mr. and Mrs. Joseph H. Stamper, 232, Clarence Road. On the morning of Wednesday 25th April, Mrs. Stamper received a telegram saying, "Arrived safely. See you soon. John." Since then she had been busy cleaning, dusting and generally preparing for the long awaited moment. Neighbours had contributed to the welcome by taking various "tit-bits" to Mrs. Stamper.

Private Stamper, who was in the 2nd Northamptonshire Regiment, had been taken prisoner in May 1940, in France, and was held at Stalag XXA. He had attended Lincoln Road School, and before the war had been in the battalion band. Mr. and Mrs. Stamper had four sons and three daughters. All of the sons were in the Forces. One daughter was in the A.T.S. before her marriage, the youngest had now joined it. The other daughter was a bus conductress.

Gunner Leonard Sydney Roberts, Royal Artillery, youngest son of Mr. and Mrs. E.T. Roberts, 180, New England, arrived home on Tuesday 24th April, after five years imprisonment in Stalag XXA. He was taken prisoner when France surrendered and one of the hardships he had to undergo was a march lasting 14 weeks. Like many others, he said that the Red Cross parcels kept the prisoners going. Gunner Roberts used to be in the Co-operative Society's general offices.

Signalman E.H. James, Royal Corps of Signals, younger son of Mrs. James, 81, Northfield Road, and the late Mr. T.H. James, was freed by the Americans at the beginning of April. He was taken prisoner in June 1942, at Tobruk, sent to Italy, and when that country capitulated, transferred to Germany. His camp was Stalag XIB.

Sig. James' treatment was said to have been not as bad as that of some prisoners. He spoke about the Red Cross parcels, and like many other men, said that but for them, they would not have survived. In peacetime he had been a civil servant in London. Mrs. James had been living in London but had been blasted out of her home three times by air raids and had come to live with her elder son, Mr. L.T.

James, in Northfield Road, who had reported at an Army depot three weeks previously.

Driver F. Gant, brother of Mrs. Mould, 33, Stone Lane, was in hospital in Surrey suffering from the privations endured on a 700 mile march from Stalag 344, Lansdorff, to a camp near Frankfurt. In his civilian days he was with Read's Transport, Ltd., Stone Lane. Joining the Army, he went abroad five years previously and was taken prisoner at Crete.

Private C.H. Lightfoot, 17, Celta Road, Fletton, Peterborough, arrived home on Friday 27th April, after spending nearly five years in a German prison camp. Speaking about a march of 900 miles to Germany from Congress, Poland, he said that sugar beet pulp, raw potatoes, mangolds, and Swedes were their food. Before the war he had been employed at the London Brick Company.

Casualties Continue

Along with the good news there was always the bad, and more casualties were announced in the month of April. C.S.M. Percy Ambrose Partridge, 2nd Royal Norfolk Regiment, had now died of wounds in Burma on April 2nd, 1945. Aged 35, he was one of two soldier sons of Mr. and Mrs. Charles Partridge, 39, Hankey Street, Peterborough. His wife, Maud Somme Partridge, lived at 32, Old Westwood Row, Peterborough, with their three year old son, whom his father had never seen.

The child was born ten days after his father left England for the last time. C.S.M. Partridge had over 14 year's service in the Army, much of it in Egypt and Palestine. He was in the Dunkirk evacuation, and over three years ago again went to the East. Before joining the forces he had been a postman driver at Peterborough. It was reported that, "he behaved with great gallantry in the fighting near the Burmese village of Saye. A company of his regiment, after the village had fallen, moved up to consolidate the position and ran into a post held by a number of Japanese. C.S.M. Partridge took a leading part in the resulting attack which eliminated the danger spot." C.S.M. Partridge was posthumously awarded the Distinguished Conduct Medal for action in Burma; the following citation records the incident:

"On February 20th, 1945, during the battalion's assault on the village of Saye, near Mandalay, the reserve company, while mopping up, ran into a strongly entrenched machine gun post. The leading platoon commander was wounded attempting to knock out the post. A troop of tanks returning to harbour was passing the scene of this encounter at the time and C.S.M. Partridge immediately signalled them to the platoon's assistance, and then reorganised the platoon.

Covered by fire from the tanks, he then approached three times the mound on which the bunker was and threw several grenades over the top, rushing over the top at the third approach. His Sten gun jammed, and showing complete disregard for his personal safety, he changed magazines. The gun again failed to fire. C.S.M. Partridge became so infuriated at this that he rushed back from the slope, threw away his Sten gun, grabbed a rifle and bayonet, and again went over the top.

He bayoneted two Japs, and shot one, his grenades having previously silenced two others. Two L.M.G.'s were captured in the position, which was wiped out, largely due to the determination and speed of C.S.M. Partridge's assault, which was a great inspiration to the men of the platoon." C.S.M. Partridge is buried in Taukkyan War Cemetery, Myanmar.

Corporal Gordon Wilson, King's Royal Hussars, son of Mr. and Mrs. C. Wilson, 74, Lincoln Road, Walton, Peterborough, was now reported wounded in the forehead and in hospital in Belgium, but wrote home that he was, "going on well." Before the war he had been in the Walton branch of the Co-operative Society.

Private William Martin Rimes, Army Air Corps, aged 24, eldest son of Mrs. Rimes, 27, Glenton Street, Peterborough, and the late Mr. C. Rimes, previously reported missing, was now known to have been wounded in the right hand. He was in No. 9 General Hospital overseas. He was a moulder with Baker Perkins Ltd., when war broke out, and was mobilised with the Territorials. Two days before he was to have been married at Sheffield, he was recalled from leave to take part in the airborne operation in which he was wounded.

Lance Sergeant James Durham, 8th Parachute Regiment, Army Air Corps, younger son of Mr. and Mrs. J. Durham, 22, Seargeant Street, Peterborough, was now reported killed in action in Germany on March 24th. L/Sgt. Durham was 28, and left a widow, formerly Miss Brenda Woods, of Priestgate, whom he married the previous December. Formerly employed at Brotherhood's Works, he joined the Army nine years previously and spent six years abroad, first in India, then in Eritrea, and later in Egypt. In Egypt he met his brother, Lieutenant Alfred Durham, Royal Artillery, their first sight of each other for ten years. Lt. Durham was now in hospital in Italy, recovering from wounds.

L/Sgt. Durham returned to England in April 1944, and was transferred from the 1st Northamptonshire Regiment to the Parachute Regiment. He went to Western Europe in December and came home for a short leave after he was wounded. L/Sgt. Durham is buried in Reichswald Forest War Cemetery, Germany.

Lance Corporal William (Bill) Harry Wilson, 1st Royal Dragoons, Royal Armoured Corps, had now been killed in action in Western Europe, on April 1st, 1945, aged 35 years. He had served in the Middle East with the Eighth Army. He was the eldest son of Mrs. H. Wilson, 5, Manor House Street, Peterborough, and the late Mr. H. Wilson, and was mentioned in dispatches a short time before his death. Before joining the Forces, he was with Mac Fisheries, Long Causeway. His father, Mr. Harry Edgar Wilson, lost his life in the First World War; his brother was still serving in the Middle East. L/Cpl. Wilson is buried in Diepenheim General Cemetery, Holland.

Death Camp Horrors on Screen

In the first week of May, the three principle cinemas in the city were showing a newsreel entitled, "Horror in Our Time," which told the barbaric story of the German concentration camps, principally those at Buchenwald and Belsen. A 'Standard' reporter wrote, "Nobody moved, and in the long sequences when the commentator's voice is silent, the only sounds were gasps from the packed audience when the shambling, skeleton-like forms of the Buchenwald survivors were seen, and when there was a glimpse of the decomposing bodies where they had fallen in the camp near Liepzig." Some members of the audience were stopped as they left and spoke about what they had seen.

An Airborne soldier said: "We have known what we have been fighting. Now *you* know."

A young woman: "It is appalling, but it is a picture that everybody should steel themselves to see."

A middle-aged woman: "I must confess I didn't believe these things until I saw them. Now I think there ought to have been more of it, to make people realise that such dreadful things are possible."

Another woman: "Every boy old enough to understand should be made to see it, to make them realise what war means."

An elderly man who stopped and heard the previous lady added: "Never mind about our people. Make the Germans see it and keep on seeing it until it makes them sick."

Casualties Reported in May

The death in action of Sergeant John William Earl, 53rd Heavy Regiment, Royal Artillery, had now been reported. Killed in Western Europe, aged 30, on April 19th, Sergeant Earl had been in the Army since 1935, serving in Africa and India. In March 1945 he received a certificate from Field Marshal Montgomery for outstanding devotion to duty. His widow was a teacher at New Road Boy's School, and he had a daughter, Christine, aged two. Sergeant Earl is buried in Reichswald Forest Cemetery, Germany.

Corporal George Robert Martin, 1st East Surrey Regiment, eldest son of Mr. and Mrs. S. Martin, 20, South Street, Stanground, Peterborough, was now reported killed in action in Italy on April 17th. Corporal Martin, who was 25 years of age, sang in the parish church choir and worked for the London Brick Company at Fletton. He joined the Forces five years earlier and left a widow, Ada Martin, and two sons. Corporal Martin is buried in Faenza War Cemetery, Italy.

Private Raymond Clifford Parker, Middlesex Regiment, 15, Fengate Close, Peterborough, was now in hospital with a broken jaw received in an accident in Western Europe on April 16th. The second son of Mr. and Mrs. E. Parker, 10, Allen Road, Peterborough, he had been a conductor with the Eastern Counties Omnibus Company, and had six year's Army service. He was married to Miss Doris Woods, third daughter of Mr. and Mrs. William Woods, Star Road, and was home on leave a month previously. His elder brother, George, was in the Royal Artillery, and his younger brother, Cyril, had seen more than three year's service in the R.E.M.E. in Burma.

Private Kenneth George (Tim) Elliott, Dorsetshire Regiment, third son of Mr. and Mrs. G.E. Elliott, 76, Clarence Road, Peterborough, had now been killed in action in Western Europe on April 20th. He was called up on July 20th, 1944. His eldest brother, Gunner E.C. Elliott, Royal Artillery, had been serving in India and with the South East Asia Command, for four years, and another brother, Private E.R. Elliott, D.C.M., The Black Watch, was now in India after fighting through the North African campaign. He was wounded in Sicily on July 18th, 1943, and was awarded the D.C.M. for his service at Wadi Akarit. Private Elliott, who was aged 19 years old, is buried in Hanover War Cemetery, Germany.

GERMANY SURRENDERS

It was at 3 o'clock on Tuesday 8th May that the Prime Minister, Winston Churchill, announced that Germany's act of unconditional surrender was signed at 2.41am on Monday 7th, and was to be ratified in Berlin on the Tuesday. That night the King broadcast a victory tribute to his people, testifying to their faith and unity in the cause of world freedom.

The unofficial tidings of the capitulation of Germany to the Allies which came through on Monday 7th cut across the official announcement. The city had awaited the cessation of hostilities and authority to "knock-off" early for the remainder of the day and the next one. The first news had come through other channels. At 2

417

o'clock there had been a hint of something to come, and at 3 o'clock news came of total capitulation via German radio. Then at 7.30pm a special announcement was made informing people that at 3pm on the Tuesday, Mr. Churchill would broadcast official tidings; and this was followed at 9 o'clock with a statement that Tuesday was to be VE Day (Victory in Europe Day), and that day, and Wednesday were to be general holidays.

Germany's unconfirmed statement at 3pm was enough for many. Up to that hour the Union Jack, the Stars and Stripes and the flag of China had reigned in solitary glory above the Town Hall, and the Red Flag above the Guildhall. Suddenly Bridge Street became alive with colour. The facade of the Angel Hotel was covered in a matter of minutes, and flags and bunting appeared everywhere.

Throughout the evening men were busy erecting streamers across the principle streets and by nightfall, "the city presented the gayest picture its citizens had seen for years." The Union Jack was predominant, but there were dozens of tributes to the United States, to Russia and to the Dominions. The part also played by the Merchant Navy in the war was represented by a great quantity of Red Ensigns. Polish paratroops eagerly picked out their own national flag, and also seen were the flags of China, France (some with the Cross of Lorraine of Fighting France), Czechoslovakia, Belgium and Holland.

In the evening a holiday atmosphere reigned, and places of entertainment were filled to capacity. After the shows, many people strolled around town and family groups stood at their front gates eagerly discussing the great news. On the Tuesday a great many people were out and about early, but not to celebrate. They were making for good places in the queues awaiting the opening of the fish shops at 8 o'clock; by 9 o'clock the stocks had gone. Bakers and some grocers' shops opened for a few hours in the morning. At first there was a rush, but later things reverted to normal. A pleasantly warm morning brought many people to the town centre, there to stand and chat, or to stroll about admiring the decorations.

Some of the best were to be seen in out-of-the-way places. For instance, Milton Terrace, near the police station was almost hidden behind flags and streamers, while across the fronts of the houses were the words' "Victory and Peace," in 2ft. high letters, made of red, white and blue crepe paper.

In the afternoon the Market Place was filled with people, listening to the broadcast of the Prime Minister's speech, relayed from loudspeakers in the attic windows on either side of the Guildhall clock. Mr. Churchill's words were listened to attentively and greeted with great applause. Then followed the ceremonial sounding of "Cease Fire" by buglers of the Scots Guards, and the National Anthem. Simultaneous with the first bars came the last "All Clear," a steady note for ten minutes on the Town Hall siren.

Broadcast dance music kept big crowds around the Market Place all that afternoon, with many couples dancing on the cobbles. The completed portion of the new riverside embankment – a length of some 300 yards – attracted thousands in search of a cool and restful rendezvous. The town park was full, with many children in the paddling pool, and people on the bowling greens and in the tennis courts. St. John's Church had a capacity congregation for the 4 o'clock special service of thanksgiving – an hour after the formal announcement of the cessation of hostilities. The Cathedral and nearly all the other places of worship held services. Thousands of people had flocked to the Market Place and at times it became impossible to move.

418

Members of the 'Standard' staff made a life-size effigy of Hitler, and pinned a notice on it, "The Standard, always first – we've found him!" French sailors of the Fleet Air Arm seized the 'corpse' and carried it in triumph to the Market Place. There it was strung up on one of the poles supporting the decorations and burnt.

A very exuberant American G.I. climbed nearly to the top of the big lamp-post between the Market Place and the Minster Foregate. Civilian youth, not to be outdone, followed him, reached the top, removed his hat and bowed to the cheering crowd. Where they could move, people linked arms and sang and danced in the streets. There was dancing in the Market Place until one o'clock on the following Wednesday morning, and it was overwhelmingly good humoured.

The flood lighting of the Cathedral West Front shone out brightly, and was the same system used at the Coronation in 1937; the apparatus was renovated after being carefully stored. Twenty-eight projectors were used, each with a 300 watt lamp so that a total flood of 8,400 watts was directed onto the building and could be seen for miles around.

Bugle calls were sounded from the lantern tower of the Cathedral by massed buglers from the three pre-service training units under command of Chief Petty Officer A.D. Barber. At 10pm, the bugles sounded 'Sunset,' and the Colours on the tower were slowly hauled down by Leading Seaman Weiss, according to Service custom. This was followed by the sounding of "Last Post" and "Reveille." The bugles ceased and the flood-lights went up.

Many people produced thunder-flashes and fire-crackers. Some of these were thrown from the rooftops of tall buildings around the Market Place. When a vehicle tried to edge its way through the mob, as many people as possible tried to cling on to it. So great was the press of people trying to enter the precincts to see the flood-lighting that the police had to institute one-way traffic. Full street lighting was on, and the illuminations included the lantern towers of the Town Hall and the old Customs House. A huge Union Jack above Frank Perkins works in Queen Street was floodlit.

Tuesday night's scenes of rejoicing were repeated on Wednesday. The crowd in and around the Market Place reached tremendous proportions, estimated by the police to number at least 10,000. Once more there were fireworks, singing and dancing. The big event was the ceremonial burning of another effigy of Hitler, complete with his Iron Cross, but for some not very evident reason, equipped with an umbrella and shopping bag. Liberally stuffed with fireworks, he was strung up on the lamp-post at the entrance to Bridge Street, and burnt above the heads of the cheering crowd. There was another lamp-post climbing contest; first a Polish paratrooper reached the top, and then two RAF men went up, hauling a Union Jack, which they tied to the top.

The Great Thanksgiving Parade

Sunday 13th May saw a thanksgiving parade and service at the Cathedral, followed by a march-past at the front of the Town Hall, where the Marquess of Exeter took the Salute.

Nearly 3,000 took part in the parade under about thirty groupings. They assembled at the cricket ground and moved off at 10.30am. Led by the Home Guard Band, the route was Broadway, Long Causeway and the Minster Foregate. The sun shone and the streets were deeply lined on both sides by brightly dressed people. The victory bunting still waved cheerfully in the soft wind. Big as it was, the

Cathedral could not accommodate everyone, and many of the procession were diverted to the cloister where they heard the service on loudspeakers.

After the Bishop's Address, prayers and hymns, the procession was reconstituted for the march-past and Bridge Street became packed with people in a spectacle never likely to be repeated. The large flat roofs of the surface shelters along the centre of the roadway were all congested with people - men, women and children. How they got up there was not quite clear; how they got down after the ceremony provided much amusement, as women and children mostly dropped into the safe and gallant arms of Tommies.

Shelters will be Rubble

Now that the threat of German air attack was completely over, the issue of dismantling the city's air raid shelters came to the fore. Due to their construction, it would take some time to dispose of all of the street, and other public shelters in the city. Domestic shelters were all to be closed, and people having keys were asked to keep the shelters locked where possible. They would be stripped of equipment and made "foolproof" to the fullest extent.

Demolition would be on a priority basis, but it would be some time before any work could be undertaken. The shelters were built with strong cement and steel reinforcement. It would not be easy to break them up, and the material would be suitable only for rubble. Some of it might be usable as a basis for the new riverbank development which was already underway, or as hardcore for road making.

Where shelters were on private property, they could be taken over by private citizens on application to the City Engineer's Department. The shelters in the recreation grounds and open spaces would be filled in when labour was available for the purpose. Here also, it was doubtful if the concrete would be of any use for other purposes.

Morrison indoor shelters issued in the area numbered 3,011. Of these, 364 were sold to householders, £7 being charged for single shelters and £9 15s for those with double tiers. When the demand came for shelters for southern England during the V1 and V2 blitz, 1,236 were collected. Of these 70 had been sold, and for these a refund of £5 each was made. Free issue Morrisons remaining in houses would be collected – some day. No further refund was promised for purchased shelters. The free issues could be bought by their holders, if desired, for 30s. Two tenants had already taken them at that price.

More Ration Books Ready

Food at this time was still being strictly rationed and arrangements had now been made for the distribution of 73,000 new ration books in Peterborough. The issue would be made from the Corn Exchange, beginning on Monday, June 4th to Friday 8th. Mr. Frank Smith, the City Treasurer, who was Deputy Food Executive Officer, was responsible for much of the work. He was hoping as many people as possible would collect their books and he had no reason to believe it would not go smoothly.

From Monday, June 11th to Wednesday 13th distribution would be made from the Council Offices at Old Fletton. Later issues would be made from the villages. There would be no alphabetical order of collection for the books in Peterborough, and people were free to collect at their convenience.

Emergency Pipes Going

Towards the end of May, National Fire Service personnel were making good progress with the removal of emergency water pipes which were laid in anticipation of the heavy air raids, which fortunately did not materialise. Outlying areas and a good part of the city centre had been cleared, the only exception being short stretches where the pipes had been laid below ground. These would have to be made good by the Council.

The removal gang was now working its way from the Stanley recreation ground along St. John's Street, towards the river. The pipes were being stored for the time being at the Dogsthorpe fire station. The dangerous water basins and steel tanks were being emptied, and some of the latter were in the process of demolition.

Home at Last

A forced march of 400 miles in a fortnight, such was the harrowing experience described by Private Bert Ludlow, who had now flown home from a prison camp in Germany, and arrived in Peterborough on Friday 18th May. Private Ludlow was the son of Mr. A.J. Ludlow, a railway porter, North Station Road.

Private Ludlow was captured in a wood near Arras when his battalion was surrounded by heavy enemy tanks and artillery during the great German offensive that began on May 10th, 1940. The prisoners in Ludlow's group were forced to march 400 miles to Poland in a fortnight, resting in temporary, ramshackle camps in all weathers.

In Poland the prisoners had to do heavy demolition work and trench digging in the course of a 12-hour day, during which all they had for food was two slices of bread and a half-pint of cabbage and potato soup. "Were it not for the Red Cross parcels that we received once in two or three months, I don't know what we should have done," said Private Ludlow.

He had a particularly rough time in the last four months of the Allied advance into Germany, when the Germans marched prisoners round in a circle in front of the advance. In this way he covered some 600 miles in ten weeks. Thanks to his strong constitution, Pte. Ludlow was in good health, but he had lost a great deal of weight.

Paratrooper, Corporal George Jackson, son of Mr. and Mrs. G. Jackson, 12, Allen Road, had been reported missing after the airborne operation at Arnhem in September 1944. He was eventually reported wounded, and a prisoner of war in German hands. He had now been liberated from Stalag XIB and was in hospital near Burnley, where his wife and child lived. His back and right leg were injured and he had temporarily lost the use of his right arm, following dislocation of the shoulder.

Gunner Bernard Redman, of 'All-Ways,' Thorpe Park Road, was now home. The ship taking him to North Africa was torpedoed, and he was rescued after swimming for two hours. Then at Sidi Nsir, Tunisia, he was taken prisoner when the 155th Battery was overwhelmed by Panzer forces after a gallant stand on February 26th, 1943. Gunner Redman was taken to Italy and from there to Stalag 4C in Czechoslovakia, where he worked in a coalmine.

Another Peterborian home was Gunner Dennis Derry, who escaped from a prison camp in Germany and was hiding in a farm house near Rheims when he heard on the wireless about VE Day. Gunner Derry was captured at El Alamein and sent to Italy. Then when Italy capitulated, he was taken to Germany where he was in Stalag IVA, near Dresden, for three years, living on black bread and soup and working 12 hours a day digging trenches.

421

Other prisoners of war to have reached home in the city in the past week were:
Gunner Harold Glover, 38, Wellington Road, Dogsthorpe.
Private Herbert Leonard Hall, 165, Star Road.
Lance Corporal Lewis Godfrey, 1, Reform Street.
Private Arthur Bayford, 94, Russell Street.
Sapper Edward J. Tomkins, Orton Waterville.
Leading Aircraftman Eric Smith, 1, Geneva Street.

Wardens Stand Down

Peterborough A.R.P. Wardens "stood down" from their duties on the evening of Tuesday 29th May. More than 300 paraded on King's School field, where they were thanked for their services by the Deputy Mayor, the Chairman of the A.R.P. Committee, the Deputy Chief Warden and other dignitaries.

The Deputy Mayor said, "We in Peterborough were fortunate that the enemy did not single us out, but we were also fortunate, in that had he done so, we had a Wardens Service competent to deal with any emergency."

Mr. F. Skevington, the former Deputy Regional Commissioner, said, "I shall have to put on my hat, because I would like to take it off to the Wardens' Service at Peterborough."

Mr E. Ross, the Chairman of the A.R.P. Committee said, "I hope we may never require a Wardens' Service again."

The Army Cadet Force Band attended, and the Wardens stood to attention as they sounded "Last Post."

Planes Collide

Eleven Airmen lost their lives when a Halifax bomber and a Wellington bomber collided over Gunthorpe, at 1.15am on Sunday 3rd, June. At first it was believed that the Halifax had caught fire in the air and exploded. Then a wing of the Wellington was found, and this proved to be the only identifiable part of that plane discovered. Police and others who hurried to the scene found a number of fires blazing fiercely over an area of some fifty acres. The fuselage of the Halifax was in Mr. Coles' wheat field, off Gunton's Road, Newborough. Other parts were as much as 800 yards away. Though most were in a hayfield and a beet field owned by Mr. G.W. Speechley, of Grange Farm, Gunthorpe.

Six bodies were found in the fields, and it was understood that the others were trapped in the wreckage of the two planes. The N.F.S. attended from Dogsthorpe and Oundle Road, with Company Officer C.S.W. Gee in charge, and two foam tenders arrived from an aerodrome. Inspector J.T. Feild controlled police operations, and with him were P.C. Lancaster, P.C. Blackwell and War Reserve P.C. Atmore. Assistance was also given by Mr. F.W. Wright and Mr. Richard Harris of Newborough. When the flames were subdued, all the bodies were removed in ambulances to the mortuary at an air station. RAF personnel mounted guard over the wreckage.

A Werrington resident who heard what she described as a muffled explosion, jumped out of bed in time to see, "a rain of fire." "There was a great light in the sky," she said. "It looked so very near; it might have been in our back yard. I saw the burning mass hit the ground, after the burning bits and pieces had broken up in the sky and come down like flares. There were so many bits and pieces on fire strewn over a wide area." A member of the N.F.S. said, "Our chaps hardly knew where to start at first. But we finally managed to get all the fires under control by about 3.20 in the morning. The fires were extinguished by covering them with soil, water and foam."

Many Evacuees Unable to Return

In just under a month 127 local evacuees had returned from Peterborough to London, making their own arrangements. No Special trains had been run from the city, and no free travel vouchers issued. Special consideration was, in respect of billeting allowances given to mothers unable to return to London owing to a lack of accommodation. As a result of a survey it had been ascertained that, at the beginning of June, there were only around 40 mothers and children in a position to return, the remainder having no homes left. The majority of the evacuees who were unable to return were living in requisitioned houses for which no rent was being charged.

An analysis of evacuees in Peterborough on Monday 4th June, showed the following figures:

• Mothers in private billets	42
• Children (accompanied) in private billets	74
• Other adults in private billets	53
• Children (unaccompanied) in private billets	44
• Children (unaccompanied) in hostels	10
• Mothers in requisitioned houses	32
• Children (accompanied) in requisitioned houses	100
• Other adults in requisitioned houses	39
Total	394

The Deputy City Treasurer explained that the procedure adopted by his department was set out by the Ministry of Health. Circulars were sent out informing adult evacuees that the Government evacuation scheme was in the process of being terminated, and parents who had homes to return to were asked to notify them of the fact.

In the case of unaccompanied children, lists were sent to the Ministry of Health, who passed them on to the London City Council. The latter made enquiries as to whether or not the parents of the children were in a position to have them back. Lists of evacuees who had accommodation in the London area had been sent to the Ministry by the City Treasurer, and it was expected that special travelling arrangements would become available shortly.

Military Medal Awarded

The Military Medal had now been awarded to Gunner Robert William Bennington, Royal Regiment of Artillery, of Peterborough, for services in North-West Europe. The citation stated: "On February 20th, 1945, Gunner Bennington was acting as observation post assistant. He and his officer were travelling in a 'Kangaroo' (open topped armoured vehicle, basically a tank with its turret removed), with the forward company of 2nd Glasgow Highlanders in an attack on the wooded area west of Udem.

At about 12.00 hours the 'Kangaroo' was hit by an enemy shell, wounding the driver and co-driver and Gunner Bennington. At this particular juncture it was essential to establish an observation post as soon as possible. Gunner Bennington

423

assisted his officer to do this in a house nearby, fitting up a wireless set and maintaining communications. Then under heavy shelling, he went back to the 'Kangaroo,' attended to the wounded drivers and arranged for their evacuation.

Although again hit in the leg, Gunner Bennington refused to be evacuated himself, returned to the observation post, and continued with his job. A little later, although neither he nor his officer had ever driven a 'Kangaroo' before, he assisted his officer to manoeuvre and drive it to the next rendezvous.

Only when it got dusk and the observation post was withdrawn did Gunner Bennington agree to return to the regimental aid post for medical attention. By his outstanding endurance and practical ability Gunner Bennington's observation post team was enabled to influence the battle to excellent effect at a time when artillery support was urgently required."

City's Salvage Figures
Mr. F.J. Smith, City Engineer and surveyor now provided the city's salvage figures from November 1939 to December 1944, which were as follows:

- Paper   2,620.2 tons
- Metals   920.6 tons
- Bones   91.95 tons
- Kitchen Waste   1,314.45 tons
- Other Materials 36,987.15 tons

This made a total of 41,934.35 tons, and Mr. Smith said that whilst congratulating the public on the success of their efforts, he wanted to point out that further collection of paper, bones and kitchen waste was still essential in the national interest. The position regarding paper in particular was causing grave concern to the Ministry of Supply.

Prisoner's Russian Bride
Private Reginald John Marriott, Royal Warwickshire Regiment, and his Russian bride arrived home in the city on Sunday 10th June. Private Marriott who had been a prisoner of war in Germany, was the eldest son of Mr. and Mrs. J.W. Marriott, 38, Windmill Street, Peterborough, and was formerly in the Co-operative Society Bakery department. He was attached to the "Desert Rats," and fought in Libya and Greece before he was captured by the Germans in Crete in June 1944.

He was taken to Stalag IVC and there became acquainted with a Russian girl – now his wife – who risked death by taking him parcels, letters and occasionally food. The Russian girl, Maria Sirk, aged 21, was a native of Poltave, and was taking university teaching degrees when the Germans seized her. She was placed in a farm working party and suffered considerable hardship, like all other Russians in German hands. She escaped three times and when Private Marriott made his second escape they found their way to a Czech village and remained in hiding for seven weeks.

Searching S.S. troops came perilously near to them, and they left their hiding place to join the Czech partisan forces. They took part in many raids organised by the Czechs, and were still fighting nine days after VE Day had been proclaimed.

Private Marriott and Miss Sirk were married in Prague and made their way to Lyons, through the Russian lines. A French officer gave them cigarettes and food, and they were flown to Paris, where Private Marriott contacted the British Consul and made arrangements for his bride to be brought to England.

The new Mrs. Marriott had received no news of her parents for two and a half years, and did not know whether they were alive or dead. She could speak five languages but English was not one of them, and for the time being she and her husband spoke to each other in German. Asked for her impression of England, she replied in German, her husband interpreting: "Everybody has made me most welcome and from what I have seen of England, I am sure I will enjoy it."

Another man who had also now arrived home was Craftsman Kenneth S. Trimmings, R.E.M.E., son of Mr. and Mrs. F. Trimmings, 36, Windmill Street, Peterborough. He had been a prisoner of war in Stalag VIIIB, in Eastern Germany, for almost five years, and had been taken prisoner at Dunkirk. While captive he acted as interpreter, and he was released by General Patton's Third Army. Craftsman Trimmings had been a former member of the 5th Hunts. Battalion Band, and before the war was an engineering apprentice at Westwood Works.

More Casualties
Even at this stage of the war, the casualties continued. Bombardier Walter Alec Mears, 135 (The Hertfordshire Yeomanry) Field Regt, Royal Artillery, of 110, Cromwell Road, Peterborough, had been reported missing since the fall of Singapore. An escaped prisoner had now provided the information that he had died at Kuala Lumpur, but no further details were known. We now know that he died, aged 25, on the 6th July 1942, and is buried in Kuala Lumpur Civil Cemetery, Malaysia. Before the war he had been in the Soke County Council offices, and his widow was in the Joint Education Board office.

Private Roland Edward Turner, 1st Oxfordshire and Buckinghamshire Light Infantry, was now reported killed as a result of an accident in Western Europe on May 5th, three days before VE Day. Aged 19, he was the son of Mr. and Mrs. Edward Turner, 12, Wake Road, Peterborough, and joined the Army 12 months earlier. He is buried in Hamburg Cemetery, Germany.

In July it was reported that Private John Thomas Alfred Howard, 4th Suffolk Regiment, 29, Silver Street, Fletton, Peterborough, had died, aged 25, of avitaminosis (a deficiency of vitamins) on September 8th, 1943, whilst a prisoner of war in Japanese hands. His mother lived in Yaxley and his father had been killed in the First World War. Private Howard is buried in Kanchanaburi War Cemetery, Thailand.

Boy Drowned in Water Basin
Fishing for tadpoles in the static water basin in the Park on the morning of Saturday 7th, July, John David Meek, aged seven, of 37, Lincoln Road East, Peterborough, fell into 5ft. of water and was drowned. His younger brother, Colin, aged six, was with him, and ran to fetch a park ranger. It was some minutes before the body was located, and death had then taken place. John was born on September 1st, 1937, and was the son of Mr. and Mrs. David Paxton Meek.

It was explained at the inquest on Monday 9th that the N.F.S. had not emptied the tank because they had been working to a programme – emergency pipe lines first, followed by the basins in the streets, and then those in recreation grounds. The child was identified by his father, David Paxton Meek, a lorry driver for Frank Perkins Ltd.

Dr. W. Michael, Dogsthorpe Road, said that at 10.40am, on the Saturday he was called to the Park, where he saw the body of a boy on the grass by the side of the static water tank. Life was extinct and examination revealed that drowning had been the cause of death. The body was removed to the hospital.

Mrs. Winifred Meek, mother of the dead boy, said that about nine on Saturday morning he left home with his younger brother, Colin, aged 6, to go to the Park. Usually their elder sister took them, but she was unable to go that morning. As a rule they played on the swings and in the sand in the children's corner; they did not tell her they intended to do anything else that morning. She did not see them take a glass jar or a butterfly net.

Percy William Brown, 83, Harris Street, foreman gardener at the Park, said that at 10.30 on Saturday morning he received a report and went to the static water tank, Colin Meek was there, and said his brother had fallen in. Mr. Brown tried to locate the body and found it in five minutes, in 5ft. of water – one of the deepest parts of the tank. By the appearance of the body it had been in the water for some minutes, because the lips and nose were blue. Mr. Brown tried artificial respiration for a long time, but there was no sign of life. He informed the police, and Sgt. Unsworth arrived, followed by the ambulance.

The Coroner said that there was no doubt that the deceased lad and his brother got into the enclosure to attempt to extract tadpoles from the tank, and that the lad slipped in and was drowned. The verdict was accidental death. The fence was of a type which had been approved by the authorities and it was deemed to be sufficient for most purposes but as the Coroner said, "the fence which will keep out small boys has yet to be designed."

Casualties in August
In August it was reported that Gunner George Frederick Hornsby, 70th Medium Regiment, Royal Artillery, 9, Orton Avenue, Woodston, Peterborough, son of Mrs. Helen Hornsby and the late Mr. G. Hornsby, and husband of Dolly Hornsby, had died aged 28 on July 28th, 1945. Gunner Hornsby died of oedema in Belden hospital, Austria, following an abscess on his neck. Before joining the Army he had been employed by the London Brick Company. He is buried in Klagenfurt War Cemetery, Austria.

Lance Corporal Ronald Cecil Bee, Royal Marines, son of Mrs. F. Bee, 5, The Crescent, Peterborough, was now reported as having died on the 18th of August, of injuries received when hit by a lorry in a road accident in England. There were three others hitch-hiking with L/Cpl. Bee, who was going to Bramshott, Surrey, from Portsmouth. The other men were not seriously injured. Lance Corporal Bee was formerly employed by the London Brick Company, Ltd., and his wife and three year old son lived at Coventry. He is buried in Woodston Cemetery, Peterborough.

JAPAN SURRENDERS
The long awaited announcement of the Japanese surrender was officially broadcast by the Prime Minister, the Rt. Hon Clement Attlee, at midnight on Tuesday 14th August. The city was asleep but the normal quiet of the night didn't last for long. The Prime Minister's announcement was followed almost immediately by the blowing of railway works hooters and the sounding of railway engine whistles.

This awoke a good many citizens who immediately guessed the reason for the noise, then people began to rouse their neighbours who had slept on by banging on front doors and throwing stones at windows. It was not long before fireworks which had been stored up for 'The Day' were brought out and used to herald the glad tidings. Local crowds gathered round gates, and some mothers started searching for bunting at one o'clock on Wednesday morning! Just a few people had decorations out since the news was given on the previous Friday that the Japanese collapse was expected.

The more intrepid spirits sped off to the Market Place and made merry. The wooden fittings for the stalls were there ready for Wednesday's market. These were fair game, and soldiers and civilians, gathering them up, soon had a fire going in the middle of the square. Similar scenes took place at the cattle market, and outside the American Red Cross Club in Midgate.

At the cattle market the fire was made up of a selling ring and various wooden oddments. Similar bits and pieces were used for the blaze in Midgate. The N.F.S. was called out and they stood by "until all was quiet." The men saw that no damage was done to nearby property, but pumps were kept near in case they were needed.

All the City Police were on duty, some being called from their beds. They remained on duty until 5am, and some of them went on duty again an hour later. This arrangement of practically continuous duty was expected to continue throughout the celebrations.

To keep the rejoicing on the Market Place on more orthodox lines, Messrs. Stokes' 'Panatrope' was brought out at 2.45am for dancing, and this continued until about 4.30am, (a panatrope was a large gramophone record player designed for the theatre). There they were, civilians and troops of this, and other Allied countries, dancing and singing away for two hours. Everyone was having a lovely time, which ceased quite happily, if a little reluctant at bringing the party to a close, with the singing of the National Anthem.

Wednesday morning found housewives already hurrying home with baskets containing the fruits of early queuing for essential food stuffs to tide their families over the two days holiday (Wednesday and Thursday). Long queues were a feature at all of the shops and it was no holiday for the ladies out harvesting for the larder! Bakers were open, and milkmen delivered on both days. Grocery shops were open for an hour or two on the Wednesday. The Market Place presented a strange scene. There were no stalls following the bonfires of the previous night, and those who would have held stalls made emergency arrangements. Fruit, fish and meat were sold from carts or trailers, and there were long queues for all of these and the tradesmen soon sold out.

One enterprising young man was selling red, white and blue ribbons from the steps of the Henry Gates Memorial. The town was thronged with people, mainly housewives in the early part of the morning, and later on with people waiting "for something to happen."

Members of the City Engineer's Department were early on the job of decorating Bridge Street and Long Causeway with flags and bunting. Tradesmen in the centre of the city and nearby streets, and residents on the outskirts, all hung out their flags and decorations. There were flags of all sorts and sizes, with tributes to all allied countries and services. More appeared as the day went on and the whole made a striking blaze of fluttering colour.

There were crowds in the Market Place throughout Wednesday afternoon, listening to the relayed music, and they grew as the day went on as people flocked in from the outskirts and surrounding villages.

Girls wore red, white and blue hats, boys waved streamers and blew toy trumpets, and there was an almost continual bang of fireworks. As soon as darkness crept on, the Cathedral West Front was flood-lit, and people poured into the Precincts. The police formed a solid line in the centre of the gateway, so that the crowd entered on one side and came out on the other.

The Market Place was again the focal point and as 9pm drew near the notes of Big Ben relayed through loudspeakers echoed around the Square. Then the crowd gathered round to listen to the King's Speech. Afterwards the National Anthem was played and everyone stood erect and cars stopped. Then everyone really got down to the job of "letting their hair down!" Dancing began in the Market Place and in time the dancers overflowed into Church Street, Exchange Street and Bridge Street. Soldiers and civilians climbed shelters to watch and throw "crackers" into the crowd. Cars made their way laboriously through the throng, with boys clinging to the luggage racks.

Many milled about on the river embankment and watched bonfires blazing merrily away. Back on the Market Place news buzzed around that someone was bringing something. Members of the City Police Force then brought a rather gruesome looking figure purported to be an effigy of the Emperor of Japan, and this was burned from an air raid shelter in Bridge Street. It was filled with fireworks and they burst and whizzed as the fire reached them, the crowd roaring and clapping with excitement as the Emperor's end drew near. Soon afterwards members of the 'Standard' works staff brought their own Emperor and he was hoisted up onto a lamp standard and ended up in similar circumstances.

By this time young people had collected in gangs and tramped the streets arm-in-arm singing and yelling at the tops of their voices. One group was headed by a man dressed as a woman and draped with a Union Jack head-dress, and another man was vigorously leading the singing with a trumpet. These scenes were repeated over and over again until 1am Thursday morning when a hectic night was brought to a close by the rousing singing of "There'll always be an England," "Land of Hope and Glory," and the National Anthem. The crowd then dispersed, and people travelled north, south, east and west, singing as they went.

The Bonfires

A police officer stated that when he arrived in the Market Place at 12.45am, a bonfire was already burning and soldiers and civilians were adding to it with portions of wood from the stalls which were up in readiness for the day's market. Other policemen arrived and they were able for a time to restrain the crowd from taking any more of this wood.

By 1.30am however, the crowd had grown so large that the police were unable to intervene effectively. "As fast as we stopped them in one place, they grabbed wood from another, and people well back from the bonfire passed pieces of fuel forward over the heads of the crowd." A while later some of the late-turn policemen, and leave-men came to the scene. At 2.15am a constable phoned Mr. Stokes, and he came with his apparatus and relayed music from the Guildhall. Civilians and Allied servicemen all took part in throwing pieces of wood on to the fire.

Another policeman said a hurricane lamp was overturned on the fire by some unknown person and the paraffin caught light. He confined his efforts to preventing more damage to Corporation property. Mr. Hann of Albert Place, Mr. Smith, Eastfield Road, Mrs. Leveridge of Albert Place, and an unknown railwayman, gave help in keeping the "Victory mischief" from getting too far out of hand.

A constable who was in Midgate said that at 2.40am he went there and saw the N.F.S. dealing with a bonfire in the roadway outside the ex-Servicemen's Club. The materials burnt consisted of wood fencing, doors, poultry cages and other items, the majority of which had been brought out of the cattle market. The police officer kept observation in the vicinity until the fire burnt out, and the people had dispersed. American troops were also expressing their jubilation.

Sergeant Poole now Confirmed Killed
Mr. and Mrs. Stafford G. Poole of Church House, 28, Cromwell Road, Peterborough, received the official news in August 1945 from the Air Ministry, that their younger son, Sergeant Christopher John Stafford Poole, had been killed in action on May 10th, 1940.

Sergeant Poole had been a fully trained airman when war broke out and was in a squadron which formed part of the Advanced Fighting Air Force, which bore the brunt of the fighting before Dunkirk. Sergeant Poole died, aged 20, on bombing operations against German troops invading Luxembourg. He was an Observer in a Fairey Battle, serial number K9270, code letters PM. The aircraft took off at 13:45 hours from Betheniville and the plane was shot down 9km north east of Marche-en-Famenne, Belgium. The pilot became a prisoner of war and the other two crew members were killed. Sergeant Poole is buried in Hotton War Cemetery, Belgium.

Soldier Drowned
Mr. and Mrs. T.C. Bonsor, 4, Fengate Close, Peterborough, now received the sad news that their eldest son, Private James Arthur Bonsor, aged 23, had been accidentally drowned in the Indian theatre of war on August 10th. No details had been forthcoming in the official notification from the Northamptonshire Regiment Records Office, but a friend, Private George Hooke, 76, Fengate Close, wrote home saying, "Jim Bonsor and another M.T. driver were going back to camp on the night of Friday, August 10th. They had to cross a river bed, and it was raining hard. They were crossing when a big wave of water hit their three-ton lorry, and sent it down the river 200 yards. They found the bodies about four days later."

Private Bonsor left a widow, formerly Miss Muriel Brough, A.T.S., of Blaby, Doncaster. When he was with Fairways Ltd., he and his employer Mr. W.V. Spink were involved in the arrest of a German spy near London. Private Bonsor is buried in Kirkee War Cemetery, India.

First Cablegram from the Far East
What was thought to be the first cablegram from a liberated prisoner in the Far East was received on Monday 3rd September by Mrs. S. Dewberry, 197, Gladstone Street, Peterborough. It was from Gunner Leonard John Dewberry, son of Mr. and Mrs. Dewberry. He went to the Far East with the Peterborough Territorial Battery and was captured at Singapore, after which he was transferred to a camp in Thailand.

The cablegram read: "Arrived safely in India. Hope to be home soon. Address letters and telegrams c/o Recovered P.W. Mail Centre, Bombay India Command." It was dated September 2nd (Sunday), and had been despatched from Colombo, Ceylon. Before the war Gunner Dewberry had been employed in the Co-operative Society's coal department.

Later on Monday Councillor A.W. Viney, M.B.E. of "Charnwood" Park Road, Peterborough, received a cablegram from his younger son, Captain Douglas G.

Viney, who also went out with the Peterborough Battery. The cablegram was worded exactly the same as Gunner Dewbery's. Before the war Captain Viney had been a solicitor with Dr. Hunt of Westgate.

Terrible Suffering in Siam

A moving letter had now reached Mr. and Mrs. W. Granger, of 'Sharsted,' Thorpe Road, Peterborough, from Mrs. Granger's youngest brother, Sergeant W. Wesley, an ex-prisoner of war in Thailand. Sergeant Wesley was brought up by Mr. and Mrs. Granger and was expected to return to them when he reached England. He had been in the Regular Army and out in Malaya when the war broke out. He wrote home as follows: "At long last I am able to write to you. Really, we are all in such a bewildered state, we simply cannot yet realise we are free from a terrible bondage. I don't want to waste this letter by telling you all that happened. That will keep, but I must break this news to you.

In the last month of 1942 I was struck blind, by cause of lack of vitamins; I also got that dreaded disease Beri-Beri. For three years I have been blind and paralysed in both legs, but during the last eight months I have made a marvellous recovery. I have regained my eyesight and can now walk normal nearly, so don't worry. By the time I get home I should be about right.

We have been rescued from the terrible jungles of Siam and I am writing this on the bank of the river at Bangkok. In a few hours we are being flown by the RAF to Rangoon, and then to India. Everything here is in a tremendous state of excitement. Thousands of ex-pows are here from the jungle camps. The Thais are doing everything for us. We are even smoking Players. I am allowed to write one letter a week; so the next one I write will be from India. Thank God.

For three and a half long years I have constantly thought, prayed and wished for you all. I received fourteen of your letters – some from Edna, Charlie and Jock.

I don't wish to tell you the grim tale: I can tell you when I get back. Suffice to say that we had to build the Thai-Burma railway, and in three years 50,000 of our comrades died of cholera etc. I am the luckiest man to be alive; I have been looked after by an Aussie M.O., Major Fisher.

I am anxiously waiting for a great reunion with you all. Please don't worry about me because in a few hours I shall be soaring in the clouds leaving this terrible nightmare behind. I can assure you our reunion must be worthily celebrated. Well I'll close now by hoping you are alright at home, and, for myself all I can say is 'Thank God for our deliverance.' So please send my regards to all at Wigston. I am dying to see everyone. God bless you all."

More Cablegrams Arrive

Many more cablegrams were now arriving in the middle of September from liberated Far East prisoners of war. News had been received in Peterborough from the following men:

Captain John Neal, Royal Artillery, elder son of Mr. and Mrs. A. Marcus Neal, Lathbury House, Lincoln Road.

Major Hugh Peacock, Royal Artillery, Longthorpe.

Captain Samuel Egar, Royal Artillery, only son of Mr. and Mrs. S.M. Egar, Melrose, Park Crescent.

Captain Maurice Crick, Royal Artillery, son of Mr. C.W. Crick, Lincoln Road.

Lieutenant J.B. Green, only son of Canon G.A. Green, Fletton Rectory.

Lieutenant T.R. Miles, Cambridgeshire Regiment, son of Mr. and Mrs. W. Miles, Rockbourne, Oundle Road.

Lance Sergeant T.G. Haskayne, 135, Field Regiment, Royal Artillery, 132, Lincoln Road, Walton.

Corporal Edward Lane, Suffolk Regiment, 47, Dogsthorpe Road, son of Mr. and Mrs. Lane, Milton Street.

Bombardier Gordon D. Austin, Royal Artillery, son of Mr. and Mrs. Austin, 34, Westwood Street.

Corporal Kenneth Smith, Suffolk Regiment, youngest son of Mrs. and the late Mr. T. Smith, 130, Walpole Street.

Bombardier Harry Neave, Royal Artillery, fifth son of Mrs. L. Neave, 4, School Place, Albert Place.

Lance Corporal Walter Leonard Sharpe, Army Catering Corps, youngest son of Mr. and Mrs. J.R. Sharpe, 95, G.N.R. Cottages.

Private Herbert William Chattell, Suffolk Regiment, youngest son of Mr. and Mrs. J.H. Chattell, 45, Bamber Street.

Private Leonard Carnell, Suffolk Regiment, 13, Russell Street.

Private Horace Jones, Bedfordshire and Hertfordshire Regiment, 68, Cromwell Road.

Gunner William R. Wells, Royal Artillery, second son of Mrs. W.M. Wells, 48, Burmer Road.

Gunner Lawrence W. Ruff, Royal Artillery, 41, St. Paul's Road.

Gunner William Wadsley, Royal Artillery, 15, Milton Terrace, eldest son of Mrs. E. Wadsley, 6, Woodland Terrace, Wood Street.

Gunner K.W. Wood, Royal Artillery, only son of Mr. and Mrs. W. Wood, 164, Mountsteven Avenue.

Gunner Thomas H. Pinion, Royal Artillery, youngest son of Mr. G.H. Pinion, and the late Mrs. Pinion, Ashlea House, Werrington.

Driver Walter Wilson, 560th Field Company, Royal Engineers, son of Mr. and Mrs. A. Wilson, 735, Lincoln Road.

Gunner C.A. Finch, Royal Artillery, 33, York Road.

Private Donald Poole, Cambridgeshire Regiment, only son of Mr. and Mrs. P.J. Poole, 171, High Street, Fletton.

Gunner W.J. Hall, Royal Artillery, second son of Mr. and Mrs. L. Hall, 201, Fletton Avenue.

Gunner R.A.E. Walker, Royal Artillery, eldest son of Mr. and Mrs. A.E. Walker, 51, Silver Street.

Gunner Jack Henry Walker, Royal Artillery, eldest son of Mr. and Mrs. W.H. Walker, 12, Eastfield Road.

Private Reginald Butler, Royal Norfolk Regiment, son of Mr. and Mrs. W. Butler, 121, Wellington Street.

Private F.A.W. Reynolds, Suffolk Regiment, eldest son of Mr. and Mrs. A.V. Reynolds, 5, Haddon Road.

Gunner G. Pacey, Royal Artillery, youngest son of Mr. E. Pacey, 68, Wootton Avenue.

Tearful Scenes at the Station as Prisoners Return
On Monday 8th October, a number of liberated ex-pows arrived in the city, including many mentioned above. Captain Douglas G. Viney said, "The first sight of the

431

English Coast near Swanage in the mist of an October morning was lovelier to our eyes than all the splendours of the tropics. He went on, "On the whole the Japs treated the officers somewhat better than the men, except when it came to railway building. Then anybody and everybody was treated as a coolie.

The officers were prisoners in separate camps. As soon as the Dakotas came (Allied transport aircraft), dropping their mercy loads of comforts, and the officers knew that they would soon be free, they approached the Japs for permission to send out parties of officers to look after the men. The men got into Dakotas at Bangkok and then were flown to Rangoon at the rate of some 600 a day.

At Rangoon they were assembled at field hospitals to pass out the fit, then to Insen, a transit camp outside Rangoon, where they embarked. After that it was one grand welcome all the way, at Colombo, at Adabaya, at Southampton and in London."

At Adabaya they were fitted out with winter clothing which Captain Viney described as "a triumph of efficient quartermastering."

Lieutenant J.B. Green arrived home on the Tuesday, and asked to speak of his experiences he replied, "I am sorry but I can't, we have all been asked not to say anything as it might harass relations still waiting for news."

Gunner L.W. Ruff arrived home on the Monday and said, "treatment was rather bad, but it varied with the different camps and different Japanese commandants." Gunner Ruff was engaged on railway building from 1942 until 1944, and after that on aerodrome construction. Speaking of conditions in the camp he said, "About 330 of us were housed in large bamboo huts, about 300 ft long. We were lucky to get 3 ft. A concert party put on shows and all the costumes were made from odd articles of clothing as we were very poorly clad. I for one wore no boots or shoes for two years. For shaving we used table knives and tobacco consisted of old pieces of newspapers.

Gunner Dewberry also said they were under orders not to talk about the treatment they suffered under the Japanese. He did however say he had been put on road-making in Thailand. Most of his mates and he had malaria. Fifty percent of the letters home were lost, and most of the Red Cross parcels were mis-appropriated by the Japanese.

Gunner Finch said, "We aren't supposed to tell you any atrocity stories. But there was nothing good about the treatment we received." While a prisoner he received 21 letters and cards, the first being two years old. The only Red Cross parcel received during three and a half years was divided amongst ten men. He said the Japanese kept the Red Cross parcels to feed their own troops.

More Cablegrams Bring News
In the third week of September, more families in the city received news from liberated Far East prisoners of war who were on their way home. The following had made contact:

Driver Kenneth H. Uttley, son of the Rev. Frank and Mrs. Uttley, Peterborough.
Sergeant Llewellyn Hughes, son of Mr. and Mrs. J. Hughes, 144, Dogsthorpe Road.
Sergeant E. Pammenter, St. Margaret's Place, Fletton.
Lance Sergeant J.R. Grubb, Royal Artillery, second son of Mr. and Mrs. R.H. Grubb, 50, All Saint's Road.
Lance Sergeant R.A. Smith, Royal Artillery, son of Mr. and Mrs. A. Smith, 46, Shakespeare Avenue.

Lance Sergeant Richard Beales, Suffolk Regiment, eldest son of Mr. and Mrs. P. Beales, 92, Fulbridge Road.

Lance Sergeant William Gripton, youngest son of Mr. and Mrs. G. Gripton, 218, Clarence Road.

Bombardier A. Smith, Royal Artillery, son of Mr. and Mrs. J.F. Smith, 166, Clarence Road.

Bombardier Jack Truss, Royal Artillery, 20, Granville Street.

Lance Bombardier C. Rouse, Royal Artillery, son of Mr. and Mrs. W. Rouse, 189, Westwood Street.

Lance Bombardier F.E. Roy Phillips, only son of Mr. and Mrs. G.E. Phillips, 22, Charles Street.

Lance Bombardier William Baxter, Royal Artillery, 1, South View, Westwood Street.

Lance Corporal E.A. Davis, Suffolk Regiment, son of Mr. and Mrs. A.E. Davis, 27, Midland Road.

Private W. Gripton, Royal Norfolk Regiment, 52, Star Road.

Private Harold Peach, Cambridgeshire Regiment, 206, Walpole Street.

Private G.T. Platt, Suffolk Regiment, only son of Mr. and Mrs. G.W. Platt, 21, Grange Road.

Gunner Maurice Stacey, Royal Artillery, 218, Clarence Road.

Private Cyril Walter Longfoot, Royal Norfolk Regiment, son of Mr. and Mrs. W. Longfoot, 29, George Street.

Private Horace Dilks, Suffolk Regiment, only son of Mr. and Mrs. Dilks, 81, Bishop's Road.

Gunner Alan Morton, Royal Artillery, 67, Gilpin Street.

Gunner James Frisby Gilbert, Royal Artillery, Longthorpe.

Private Fred Stallebrass, Cambridgeshire Regiment, son of Mrs. Stallebrass, 31, North Street, Stanground.

Private G. Cottom, 5th Suffolk Regiment, eldest son of Mr. and Mrs. G. Cottom, 158, Star Road.

John Meeds, son of Mr. and Mrs. Meeds, Longthorpe.

Private Jack Nicholls, son of Mr. and Mrs. J. Nicholls, 30, Celta Road, Woodston.

Driver Douglas Gray, Royal Engineers, 3, Albert Place.

Signaller James Wicks, 4, Keeton Road.

Death of a Sailor

It was now announced that Telegraphist William Allan Greig, HM Motor Gunboat 78, Royal Navy, of 14, Craig Street, Peterborough, had died on January 31st, 1945, after two and a half years of captivity in Germany. News was received that he had made a forced march of 250 miles and died shortly afterwards. Telegraphist Greig was formerly with the G.P.O. at Peterborough, and was the only son of Mr. and Mrs. J.C. Greig, of Aberdeen. He married Miss V.G. James, only daughter of Mr. A. James, 135, Harris Street, Peterborough, at St. Paul's Church on July 19th, 1941.

Motor Gunboat 78 was attacked on 2/3 October 1942 off Holland which resulted in the crew abandoning her. Telegraphist Greig has no known grave and he is commemorated on the Portsmouth Naval Memorial.

Confirmed Dead

It was now confirmed that Lance Corporal John Thomas Henry Hilson, 5th, Bedfordshire and Hertfordshire Regiment, Belle Vue, Stanground, Peterborough, had died in a Japanese prison camp on 20th July, 1944. He was the son of Mr. Joseph Thomas Henry Hilson and Mrs. Ellen Hilson, and husband of Mrs. Ada Jane Hilson. He is buried in Kanchanaburi War Cemetery, Thailand.

Removal of Street Shelters Begins

What had been described as "a real start" had been made with the demolition of the air raid precaution shelters that clogged up the city streets. By the end of November 1945, Bridge Street was almost cleared. Long Causeway would be next and other districts would follow in planned rotation. It was thought that it would take a year to get the streets back to normal again.

Housing was the post-war priority and this determined the first shelter demolitions. These were trench and surface shelters, as distinct from those underground, which stood in the way of house erection. The numbers removed were eight trench shelters and twenty surface shelters, of various sizes and all of extremely strong construction.

Work now began in the streets in the following order: Bridge Street, Long Causeway and Gladstone Street. After these, work was to proceed on the main roads and bus routes where the shelters were on the carriageway. Those which stood on grass verges and other unobstructive sites would be left until later.

Next it was intended to deal with the rest of the shelters by districts, taking whole roads and picking up backyard and other shelters off the main routes. Demolition would also include protective walls and all static water basins (the City Council having taken responsibility for those of the N.F.S.). Attacking the shelters by district had the advantage of avoiding the delay and expense of transferring plant and machinery unnecessarily from one place to another.

Shelters standing on private property could be retained by the owners if desired, although a small charge would probably be made. There were also regulations relating to town planning to be considered. Employment of direct labour by the City Engineer had been found to be the most economical, and heavy plant had been hired. The method of breaking up a shelter was to use a swinging weight called a "Tup." A blow from this was said to be devastating. Compared with a hand drill it was cheaper and quicker, and more effective when there was room to swing it. In back gardens and where shelters adjoined other buildings, this equipment could not be used, but in open spaces it was ideal. Also, it had not caused broken windows close by or damaged water mains which were just below the concrete floors of the shelters.

The progress of the work in Bridge Street was a daily source of interest to passers-by. The steel reinforced tops and walls would fall under the Tup's "titanic" blows, and then cranes lifted the masses of rubble and brickwork onto the backs of lorries. These then transported their loads to the sites of new houses where it was used for sites and new roadways. A small charge was made to the contractors for the material. The old bricks were of no use for building purposes.

In the middle of November the work was not proceeding at full pace, as there had been some breakdown of the machinery. The proper system was to work in pairs, one machine breaking up and the other removing the rubble. In addition one of the lorries had also broken down, but it was hoped Bridge Street would be finished

434

by the end of the month. Operations were suspended on Wednesdays and Saturdays due to market day traffic. This would not apply when work moved to other parts of the city.

The cost of demolition would work out at from £12 to £15 for small shelters, and up to £35 for the large ones. These amounts were approved by the Government, but how much they would actually contribute had still not been stated.

Faster Progress

A week later, on the last day of November, it was reported that headway had been made faster than anticipated. With all available machinery now at work, Bridge Street had been cleared of shelters by 5.30pm on Friday 23rd, Long Causeway was tackled on the Monday and by Tuesday evening the last load of rubble had been cleared.

The Tups and lorries moved on to Gladstone Street to face what was probably the biggest problem of all. From Westgate to the New England recreation ground there was a continuous succession of shelters. It was estimated that with good going, and the machinery standing up to the weather conditions, the street could be cleared by Christmas. A start was made on Tuesday 27th November.

Two other bus routes were next on the list, Eastgate and Palmerston Road, Woodston. In both streets the shelters left a carriageway of less than fifteen feet. Then other bus routes would be tackled and after that, districts would be taken in turn and cleared of all obstructions.

German Prisoners Work

In December, via the offices of the Ministry of War Transport, the City Council was making use of a gang of 26 German prisoners from the Thorney camp, for road works. Some had been clearing up after shelter demolition in Bridge Street and Long Causeway, and all had then moved on to Lincoln Road, between Church Walk and Manor House Street, replacing paving stones with concrete.

The Council paid the Ministry the full rate for labour, and the men were paid prisoners' wages.

Last Casualty of the Year

On December 28th, 1945, more than four months after V.J. Day, the 'Advertiser' carried a report of a city man who had been killed in 1942. Lance Sergeant Harry Belt, 135 (Hertfordshire Yeomanry) Field Regiment, Royal Artillery, 7, Fengate Close, Peterborough, died, aged 22, on the 27th January 1942. He was the son of Mr. John Belt and Mrs. Mary Belt (nee Cooper) of 75, Bishop's Road, Peterborough, and, like so many other city men, is buried in Kranji War Cemetery, Singapore.

Learning to Live again

The war had now come full circle. It started with the rapid building of air raid shelters, and it had now ended with their destruction in equal haste. Rationing would continue well into the 1950s so there would be little relief there for some time. Hundreds of Peterborough men were dead (and some women), and the pain of their loss would take a long time to heal. Many families would never see their loved ones return, and parents, wives and children would find a gap in their lives that could never again be filled.

Many men had returned from captivity and their suffering as captives of both the German and Japanese forces would haunt them to the ends of their days. Some would never get over their deprivations but at least they had their families to comfort them, and their return from oblivion was priceless to those who had been waiting in Peterborough, never giving up hope.

This was the story of our city – the people we were – and the people we are. There are none better.

MACER, Arthur William – Orton Waterville, Peterborough. Sapper 14345993, 654 Artisan Works Coy, Royal Engineers. Died, aged 31, on the 3rd January 1945 of head injuries received in the course of his duties on the Shetland Isles. The son of Mr & Mrs E. B. Macer of Fletton, Peterborough. Buried in Woodston Cemetery, Peterborough. Sec. 6. Grave 17.

STIMPSON, Peter – 60 Hall Lane, Werrington, Peterborough. Sergeant (Wireless Operator / Air Gunner) 1875441, Royal Air Force Volunteer Reserve. Died, aged 19, on the 11th January 1945. The son of Edgar and Constance Stimpson of Werrington and the husband of Alice Stimpson of Werrington, Peterborough. Commemorated in Werrington Churchyard, Peterborough.

NORRIS, Elsie Kathleen – 295 Oundle Road, Peterborough. Corporal W/127632, Auxiliary Territorial Service, attached 139 (mixed) H.A.A. Regiment, Royal Artillery. Died, aged 24, on the 13th January 1945 in hospital in Belgium from injuries received in an accident. No known next of kin. Buried Heverlee War Cemetery, Leuven, Belgium. Grave 1.A.5.

GOODWIN, Laurence Frederick Bransby – Peterborough. Sergeant R/225325, Royal Canadian Air Force. Died, aged 21, on the 14th January 1945. The son of Laurence and Phoebe Goodwin of Peterborough. No known grave he is commemorated on the Runnymede Memorial, Panel 282.

HILL, John William Rowland – Princes Gate, Peterborough. Flying Officer (Nav) 149695, Royal Air Force Volunteer Reserve. The holder of the DFC. Died, aged 22, on the 22nd January 1945 in Rauceby hospital of heart failure after an appendicitis operation. The son of Rowland and Hannah Hill of Wroxham. Buried in Wroxham (St Marys) Churchyard.

HYLAND, John Henry – Peterborough. Lance Sergeant 5882807, 5th Northamptonshire Regiment. Died, aged 30, on the 28th January 1945. The son of John and Rachel Hyland and the husband of Marjorie Hyland of Old Fletton, Peterborough. Buried in the Old Fletton Cemetery, Peterborough. Grave 92. Sec 7.

WARDLE, Arthur Percival – 32 Huntley Road, Woodston, Peterborough. Able Seaman C/JX 376742, HMS Vengeance, Royal Navy. Died, aged 21, on the 29th January 1945. His twin Ezra also died. The twins both died of alcoholic poisoning after celebrating their 21st birthday drinking what was called 'navy neaters' on board ship in Greenock, Scotland. 'Navy Neaters' to the best of my knowledge is undiluted Pussers Rum. The son of Harry and Lillian Wardle of Woodston, Peterborough. Buried in Woodston Cemetery, Peterborough. Joint Grave 59, Section 7.

WARDLE, Ezra Frank – 32 Huntley Road, Woodston, Peterborough. Able Seaman C/JX 355408, HMS Vengeance, Royal Navy. Died, aged 21, on the 29th January 1945. His twin Arthur also died. The twins both died of alcoholic poisoning after celebrating their 21st birthday drinking what was called 'navy neaters' on board ship in Greenock, Scotland. The son of Harry and Lillian Wardle of Woodston, Peterborough. Buried in Woodston Cemetery, Peterborough. Joint Grave 59, Section 7.

GREIG, William Allan – 14 Craig Street, Peterborough. Telegraphist P/JX 263916, H.M. Motor Gun Boat 78, Royal Navy. Died, age unknown, on the 31st January 1945. Motor Gunboat 78 was attacked on 2/3 October 1942 off Holland which resulted in the crew abandoning her. Death is believed to have been as a result of a 250 mile forced march as a German prisoner of war. No known next of kin. No known grave he is commemorated on the Portsmouth Naval Memorial, Panel 92.

SEXTON, George – 75 Church Street, Werrington, Peterborough. Private 11264629, Army Catering Corps, attached Royal Artillery. Died, aged 23, on the 3rd February 1945. The son of Samuel and Sarah Sexton of Werrington, Peterborough. Buried in Taukkyan War Cemetery, Myanmar. Grave 27.E.23.

COLEMAN, John Arthur – 73 Vere Road, Peterborough. Flight Sergeant (Navigator) 1600603, Transport Command, Royal Air Force Volunteer Reserve. Died, aged 21, on the 6th February 1945. The son of Charles and Olive Coleman of Peterborough. Buried in Oundle Cemetery. Grave 23. Sec L.L.

GREEN, Reginald Horace – Private 5775930, 2nd Royal Norfolk Regiment. Died, aged 28, on the 8th February 1945. The son of William and Edith Green of Stanground, Peterborough and the husband of Lilian Green of Stanground, Peterborough. Buried in Taukkyan War Cemetery, Myanmar. Grave 18. B. 19.

SHELTON, John Barber – 73 Garton End Road, Peterborough. Lance Corporal 5831905, 5th Seaforth Highlanders. Died, aged 31, on the 11th February 1945. The son of Charles and Beatrice Shelton of Peterborough. Buried in Reichswald Forest War Cemetery, Germany. Grave 61.E.19.

HALL, John Derek – 4 Williamson Avenue, Peterborough. Sergeant, Flight Engineer 1869558, 186 Squadron, Royal Air Force Volunteer Reserve. Died, aged 20, on the 14th February 1945. He was the Flight Engineer in Avro Lancaster Mk I, Serial No NG353, Code letters AP-X that took off from Stradishall as part of operation Thunderclap to attack Dresden. All seven crew died. The son of Ernest and Gladys Hall of Peterborough. Buried in Berlin 1939-45 War Cemetery, Germany. Grave 8.C.14.

TEANBY, Thomas Edward – 34 Brook Street, Peterborough. Sergeant 1809870, 640 Squadron, Royal Air Force Volunteer Reserve. Died, aged 23, on the 14th February 1945. He was a gunner in Handley Page Halifax Mk III, Serial No MZ856, Code Letters C8-S that took off from Leconfield to attack Chamnitz. All seven crew died. The son of George and Mabel Teanby of Peterborough. Buried in Durnbach War Cemetery, Germany. Collected grave 5.A.7-10.

EVANS-EVANS, Anthony Caron – Peterborough. Group Captain (Pilot) 19108, 83 Squadron, Royal Air Force. Died, aged 43, on the 21st February 1945. He was the pilot of an Avro Lancaster Mk III, Serial No NE165, Code Letters OL-Y, which took off from Coningsby to mark the Mittelland Canal near Gravenhorst in Germany for bombers from Number 5 Group to attack. This was a very experienced crew, four of whom were decorated. Evans-Evans had the DFC, which was announced on 16th February, five days previously. The aircraft was shot down by a night-fighter and crashed in Holland. All seven crew died. At 43 he was one of the oldest senior officers to die on bombing operations during the war. He was, at the time, also Station Commander of RAF Coningsby. The son of Anthony and Margaret Evans and the husband of Joyce Evans-Evans of Peterborough. His brother Roland Gwynne Evans-Evans was killed in action in 1944. Buried in Mierlo War Cemetery, Holland. Grave VIII.D.5.

BOLLARD, Benjamin – 2 Fengate Close, Peterborough. Private 14722274, 2nd Welch Regiment. Died, aged 35, on the 22nd February 1945. The son of Benjamin and Sarah Bollard. No known grave he is commemorated on the Rangoon Memorial, Myanmar, Face 14.

REYNOLDS, Walter Frederick – 84 Mayors Walk, Peterborough. Private 5834766, 5th Black Watch (Royal Highlanders). Died, aged 32, on the 25th February 1945 attacking farmhouses close to the crossing of the Rhine. The son of George and Emily Reynolds of Peterborough and the husband of Eva Reynolds of Peterborough. Buried in Rheinberg War Cemetery, Germany. Grave 12.E.21.

CLOSE, Bertie – Signalman 2124616, 79th Armoured Division, Royal Corps of Signals. Died, aged 34, on the 3rd March 1945. The son of George and Alice Close and the husband of Annie Close of Peterborough. Buried in Reichswald Forest War Cemetery, Germany. Grave 54. C. 3.

LEACH, Frank – 32 Park Street, London Road, Peterborough. Driver T/193187, Royal Army Service Corps. Died, aged 24, on the 7th March 1945. The son of Alec and Minnie Leach of Peterborough. Buried in Aleppo War Cemetery, Syria. Grave 2.D.7.

BEALES, Ronald – 176 Crown Street, Peterborough. Sergeant Flight Engineer 1868744, 576 Squadron, Royal Air Force Volunteer Reserve. Died, aged 38, on the 8th March 1945. He was the Flight Engineer in Avro Lancaster Mk I, Serial No PD363, Code Letters UL-K2 and named 'Mighty Atom' that took off from Fiskerton to attack Dessau. All seven crew died. The son of Fanny Beales of Peterborough and the husband of Kathleen Beales of Peterborough. Buried in Choloy War Cemetery, France. Collected grave. 4. C. 1-7.

BROOKER, Bernard Chapman – Peterborough. Flight Lieutenant (Navigator) 172486, DFC and Bar, 156 Squadron, Royal Air Force Volunteer Reserve. Died, aged 25, on the 11th March 1945. He was the Navigator in Avro Lancaster Mk III, Serial No PB669 that took off on a training flight from Warboys. At the time he was attached to the Pathfinder Force Navigation Training Unit. The aircraft crashed at high speed at Old Weston near Spaldwick, Huntingdonshire. All eight crew died. He received his DFC in May 1944 as an acting Warrant Officer and the Bar in October 1944 as an acting Flight Lieutenant. Both were awarded while serving with 35

Squadron. The husband of Joan Brooker of Peterborough. Buried in Eastfield Cemetery, Peterborough. Grave 6618.Div.1. Block 16.

HERSON, Eric Cyril – 200 Walpole Street, Peterborough. Private 1533533, Army Catering Corps. Died, aged 28, on the 13th March 1945. The son of Mr and Mrs William Herson of Peterborough and the husband of Dorothy Herson of Peterborough. Buried in Bologna War Cemetery, Italy. Grave II.B.8.

RIPPON, William Ewart – 125 Park Road, Peterborough. T/Captain, War Correspondent for the Peterborough Citizen and Advertiser. Died, age unknown, on the 16th March 1945, believed as a result of a road accident. The son of the Revd. John Rippon and Margaret Rippon and the husband of Edith Rippon of Peterborough. Buried in Venray War Cemetery, Holland. Grave VIII.E.6.

COLLIN, Henry Oswald – 211 Dogsthorpe Road, Peterborough. Sergeant 1880273, 207 Squadron, Royal Air Force Volunteer Reserve. Died, aged 23, on the 21st March 1945. He was the Mid Upper Gunner in Avro Lancaster Mk I, Serial No PA196, Code Letters EM-D that took off from Spilsby to attack a synthetic oil plant at Bohlen. The aircraft was lost without trace. All seven crew died. The son of Arthur and Martha Collin of Peterborough. No known grave he is commemorated on the Runnymede Memorial, Panel 274.

DURHAM, James – 22 Searjeant Street, Peterborough. Lance Sergeant, 8th Parachute Regiment, A.A.C. Died, aged 28, on the 24th March 1945 in Germany. No known next of kin. Buried in Reichswald Forest War Cemetery, Germany. Grave 32.D.9.

HONEYBALL, Thomas William – 138 Newark Avenue, Peterborough. Private 5828943, 5th Suffolk Regiment. Died, aged 25, on the 25th March 1945 while a Japanese prisoner of war. He died, of Acute Enteritis, at the Fukuoka No 24 Branch Camp (Senryu Coal Mine). The son of Alfred and Beatrice Honeyball of Peterborough. Buried in Yokohama War Cemetery, Japan. Grave N.A.6.

BUTLER, John Alfred Francis – Private 5961102, 1/7th Middlesex Regiment. Died, aged 21, on the 25th March 1945. The son of Mr and Mrs John Butler and the husband of Gwendoline Butler of Peterborough. Buried in Reichswald War Cemetery, Germany. Grave 52. A. 11.

MINERS, Alfred James – 37 Taverners Road, Peterborough. Lance Corporal 5883215, 2nd Northamptonshire Regiment. Died, aged 34, on the 28th March 1945. The son of Mr and Mrs J. Miners of Peterborough. No known grave he is commemorated on the Dunkirk Memorial, France. Column 110.

WILSON, William Harry – 5 Manor House Street, Peterborough. Lance Corporal 5834841, 1st Royal Dragoons, Royal Armoured Corps. Died, aged 32, on the 1st April 1945. The son of Harry and Beatrice Wilson of Peterborough. Buried in Diepenheim General Cemetery, Holland. Grave 5.

PARTRIDGE, Percy Ambrose – 32 Westwood Row, Westwood Street, Peterborough. Warrant Officer Class II, 5880594, C.S.M. 2nd Royal Norfolk Regiment. Died, aged 35, on the 2nd April 1945. Awarded the Distinguished Conduct Medal for action in Burma (London Gazette 24/05/1945). The son of Charles and Lily Partridge and the husband of Maud Somme Partridge of Peterborough. Buried in Taukkyan War Cemetery, Myanmar. Grave 21.J.21.

WRIGHT, Frank – 5 Hurn Road, Werrington, Peterborough. Sergeant 1897971, 49 Squadron, Royal Air Force Volunteer Reserve. Died, aged 32, on the 4th April 1945. He was the air gunner in Avro Lancaster Mk III, Serial No ME308, Code Letters EA-F that took off from Fulbeck to attack German barracks in the town of Nordhausen to support advancing Allied troops. The aircraft exploded over the target and all seven crew died. The son of John and Sarah Wright of Peakirk near Peterborough. No known grave he is commemorated on the Runnymede Memorial. Panel 277.

MARTIN, George Robert – 20 South Street, Stanground, Peterborough. Corporal 5831525, 1st East Surrey Regiment. Died, aged 25, on the 17th April 1945. The son of Sydney and Mary Martin of Stanground, Peterborough and the husband of Ada Martin of Stanground, Peterborough. Buried in Faenza War Cemetery, Italy. Grave II.D.11.

EARL, John William – 16 Cambridge Avenue, Peterborough. Sergeant 840190, 53rd Heavy Regiment, Royal Artillery. Died, aged 30, on the 19th April 1945. No known next of kin. Buried in Reichswald Forest Cemetery, Germany. Grave 61.B.18.

ELLIOTT, Kenneth George – 76 Clarence Road, Peterborough. Private 14808472, Dorsetshire Regiment. Died, aged 19, on the 20th April 1945. No known next of kin. Buried in Hanover War Cemetery, Germany. Grave 7.H.5.

JOHNSON, Arthur – 80 Walpole Street, Peterborough. Warrant Officer Class II, B.S.M. 785471, 135 (The Hertfordshire Yeomanry) Field Regiment. Died, aged 33, on the 20th April 1945 while a Japanese prisoner of war. He died, of croup pneumonia, at the Fukuoka No 17 Branch Camp (Omuta) where the prisoners were used by the Mitsui Mining Company working at the Miike Coal Mine. The son of Arthur and Ethel Johnson and the husband of Lily Johnson of Peterborough. Buried in Yokohama War Cemetery, Japan. Grave P.A.13.

SIDEBOTHAM Frederick – Peterborough. Gunner 1827679, 48 Lt. A.A. Regiment, Royal Artillery. Died, aged 28, on the 20th April 1945 while a Japanese prisoner of war. No known next of kin. Buried in Labuan War Cemetery, Malaysia. Grave M.C.3.

TURNER, Roland Edward – 12 Wake Road, Peterborough. Private 14756553, 1st Oxfordshire & Buckinghamshire Light Infantry. Died, aged 19, on the 5th May 1945. The son of Edward and Harriet Turner of Peterborough. Buried in Hamburg Cemetery, Germany. Memorial Plot.

WATSON, Frederick George William – 82 Russell Street, Peterborough. Gunner 913640, 135 (The Hertfordshire Yeomanry) Field Regiment. Died, aged 24, on the 4th June 1945 while a Japanese prisoner of war. No known next of kin. Buried in Kanchanaburi War Cemetery, Thailand. Grave 6.E.12.

BRANKER, Ronald – 39 Croyland Road, Walton, Peterborough. Leading Aircraftman 1723550, Royal Air Force Volunteer Reserve. Died, aged 23, on the 15th June 1945. No known next of kin. Buried in Paston Churchyard, Peterborough. Grave D.15.

LAW, Albert Edward – Woodston, Peterborough. Corporal 5181284, 1st Oxfordshire & Buckinghamshire Light Infantry. Died, aged 35, on the 16th June 1945 in Peterborough Memorial Hospital from an ulcer caused through starvation while being a German prisoner of war. The son of Denis and Frances Law. Buried in Woodston Cemetery, Peterborough. Grave 391. Section 6.

MARTIN, Cyril Ernest – 3 St Martins Road, Fletton, Peterborough. Lieutenant, HMS Byrsa, Royal Naval Volunteer Reserve. Died, aged 40, on the 9th July 1945 in an accident in Naples, Italy. Since February 1945 he was in Naples on the staff of the Commander-in-Chief, Mediterranean. No known next of kin. Buried in Naples War Cemetery. Grave IV.J.17.

STEWARD, Kenneth – Peterborough. Rifleman 14455167, 10th Kings Royal Rifle Corps. Died, aged 18, on the 17th July 1945. The son of Henry and Doris Steward of Peterborough. Buried in Eastfield Cemetery, Peterborough. Grave 6317. Div. 4. Block 16.

HARLOCK, Thomas – 210 St Pauls Road, Peterborough. Private 5833580 2nd Cambridgeshire Regiment. Died, aged 25, on the 23rd July 1945 at Nakon Pathom of tuberculosis while a Japanese prisoner of war. The son of Thomas and Laura Harlock of Peterborough. Buried in Kanchanaburi War Cemetery, Thailand. Grave 8.A.48.

HORNSBY, George Frederick – Woodston, Peterborough. Gunner 966191, 70th Medium Regiment, Royal Artillery. Died, aged 28, on the 28th July 1945 of oedema in Belden hospital, Austria. The son of Helen Hornsby and the husband of Dolly Hornsby of Woodston, Peterborough. Buried in Klagenfurt War Cemetery, Austria. Grave 3.G.1.

BARLOW, Arthur Charles – Private 5823535, 1st Cambridgeshire Regiment. Died, aged 39, on the 31st July 1945 while a Japanese prisoner of war. The son of Samuel and Emma Barlow and the husband of Ivy Barlow of Peterborough. Commemorated in Kanchanaburi War Cemetery, Thailand, Special Memorial 9. M. 9.

BONSOR, James Arthur – 4 Fengate Close, Peterborough. Private 14371337, 1st Northamptonshire Regiment. Died, aged 23, on the 10th August 1945. The son of Thomas and Jane Bonsor and the husband of Muriel Bonsor of Balby, Doncaster. Buried in Kirkee War Cemetery, India. Grave 1.E.12.

FISHPOOL, Leonard Henry – 97 Wellington Street, Peterborough. Private 5945841, 5th Beds & Herts Regiment. Died, aged 42, on the 15th August 1945 while a Japanese prisoner of war at Mountain Camp, Formosa. The son of John and Mary Fishpool of Peterborough. Buried in Sai Wan War Cemetery, Hong Kong. Grave VI.N.1.

BEE, Ronald Cecil – 5 The Crescent, Woodston, Peterborough. Lance Corporal PO/X 3807, Royal Marines. Died, age unknown, on the 18th August 1945 from injuries received when hit by a lorry in a road accident in England. The husband of E. Bee of Coventry. Buried in Woodston Cemetery, Peterborough. Grave 366. Section 6.

PEARCE, Gordon – Leading Air Fitter FAA/FX 81582, Royal Navy. Died, aged 25, on the 19th November 1945. The son of Mr and Mrs Sydney Pearce of Peterborough. Buried in Eastfield Cemetery, Peterborough. Div. 4. Block 16. Cons. Grave 6318.

ROLL OF HONOUR 1946

PEARSON, Walter Hubert – Private 5957718, 8th Beds & Herts Regiment. Died, aged 46, on the 6th February 1946. The son of Phillip and Florence Pearson of Peterborough and the husband of Ida Pearson of Peterborough. Buried in Woodston Cemetery, Peterborough. Grave 484. Section 6.

NORRIS, Frederick William – 22 Fulham Road, Peterborough. Gunner 905118, 336 Battery, 135 (The Hertfordshire Yeomanry) Field Regiment, Royal Artillery. Died, aged 24, on the 25th March 1946 after ill treatment as a Japanese prisoner of war. The son of John and Annie Norris of Peterborough. Buried in Eastfield Cemetery, Peterborough. Grave 6319. Div. 4. Block 16.

ASHBY, Diana Margaret – Second Officer, HMS Victory IV, Women's Royal Naval Service. Died of illness, aged 26, on the 20th April 1946. The daughter of George and Janet Swain of Peterborough. Commemorated at Cambridge Crematorium, Column 1.

TITMAN, Leonard – 453 Gladstone Street, Peterborough. Leading Aircraftman 1872912, 28 Squadron, Royal Air Force Volunteer Reserve. Died, aged 21, on the 30th April 1946. The son of Walter and Ada Titman of Peterborough. Buried in Kuala Lumpur Civil Cemetery, Malaysia. Grave 876.

WRIGHT, Douglas William – Flying Officer (Navigator) 167956, 84 Squadron, Royal Air Force Volunteer Reserve. Died, aged 22, on the 9th August 1946. The son of William and May Wright of Peterborough. Buried in Rangoon War Cemetery, Myanmar. Grave 2.J.1.

BENCH, James – Millfield, Peterborough. Private 14069939, 1st Kings Own Royal Regiment (Lancaster). Died, aged 19, on the 20th December 1946. The son of William and Hilda Bench of Millfield, Peterborough. Buried in Eastfield Cemetery, Peterborough. Grave 6616. Div 2. Block 16.

ROLL OF HONOUR 1947

CRACKNELL, K. E. – Lieutenant 362927, Gordon Highlanders attached King's Own Scottish Borderers. Died, age unknown, on the 14th April 1947. The son of Ernest and Ivy Cracknell of Peterborough. Buried in Karachi War Cemetery, Pakistan. Grave 3.C.12.

SETCHFIELD, George William – Private 19081621, Royal Pioneer Corps. Died, aged 19, on the 17th August 1947. The son of John and Gladys Setchfield of Peterborough. Buried in Eastfield Cemetery, Peterborough. Grave 6523. Div 4. Block 16.

A.R.P. SUPPLEMENTARY FIRE PARTIES

SECTOR	LOCATION	No. OF PARTIES
1A	St. Leonards St. (1), Wood St.-Milton St. (1)	2
1B	Long Causeway (1), Queen St. (1)	2
1C	Cowgate (1), Priestgate (1)	2
1D	Bridge St. (1), Priestgate (1)	2
1E	Westgate (2), Sites to be fixed each end.	2
1F	Albert Place (1), Princes Court (1)	2
1G	Bridge St. South (1)	1
1H	South St.-Hereward Road (1)	1
1I	Eastgate (1), St. Johns St. South (1)	2
1J	Fengate (1), Star Road South (1)	2
1K	North St (1), Geneva St (1), Park Road South (1)	3*
1L	Westwood St-Bright St (1), Cromwell Rd-Bright St (1)	2
2A	Glebe Road-Fairfield Road (1), Fletton Avenue (1)	2
2B	Queens Walk (1)	1
2C	Park Street (1)	1
2D	Silver St (1), London Road (1), Shortacres (1)	3
2E	Orchard St (1), Palmerston Road South (1)	2
2F	Palmerston Road North (1), New Road (1)	2
2G	Jubilee St (1), Wharf Road (1)	2
2H	Oundle Road-George St (1)	1
2I	Tower St (1), Grove St (1)	2
3A	Kent Road (1), Percival St (1)	2
3B	Almoners Lane (1), Williamson Avenue (1)	2
3C	Aldermans Drive (one at each end)	2*
3D	Muswell Road (1), Nicholls Avenue (1), Priory Road (1)	3
3E	Westfield Road (1), Moorfield Road (1)	2
3F	Thorpe Road (1), Woodfield Road (1)	2
3G	At each end of Longthorpe Village (2), Thorpe Ave (1)	3
4C	Russell St-Gladstone St (1), Cobden St-Gladstone St (1), Beech Avenue-Cromwell Road (1)	3
4D	Russell St-Cromwell Road (1), Near Craig St (1), St. Marks St (1)	3
4E	Church Walk-Park Road (1)	1
4F	Cromwell Road between Lime Tree Ave-Cobden Ave (1)	1
4G	Cobden St west of Gladstone St (1), Norfolk St (centre) (1), Lime Tree Avenue near Lincoln Road (1)	3
4H	Westwood St near Hankey St (1), Junction of Hankey St-Cromwell Road (1)	2
4I	Westwood St-Bamber St (1)	1
4J	Taverners Road-Westwood St (1)	1
4K	Taverners Road-Cromwell Road (1)	1
4L	Clarence Road (1), Gladstone St near Cambridge Ave (1)	2
4M	Summerfield Rd-Cambridge Ave (1*) Silverwood Road-	2

445

	Springfield Road (1)	
4N	Lincoln Road near St Martins St (1), Lincoln Road near Green Lane (1)	2
5A	Midgate (1), New Rd (1), near Brook St, Burghley Sq. (1)	3
5B	Broadway near Church Walk (1), Crawthorne Road centre (1)	2
5C	City Road (1), Pipe Lane (1), Chapel St (1)	3
5D	Wellington Street (1), Morris Street (1)	2
5E	Monument Street (1)	1*
5F	Huntley Grove East (1), Bedford Street (1)	2
5G	Whalley Street-Eastfield Road (1)	1
5H	Cavendish St-Eastfield Road (1), Cavendish St near Padholme Road (1)	2*
5I	Whitsed St (1), Padholme Rd near Cavendish St (1)	2
5J	Flag Fen-Saxon Rd (1), Padholme Rd near Dyke (1)	2
5K	Star Road-Dickens St (1), Star Road-Burton Street (1)	2
5L	Charles Street-Dickens Street (1)	1
6A	Green Lane-Dogsthorpe Road (1)	1
6B	Lincoln Rd East-Henry Street (1), Granville Street (1)	2
6C	Huntley Grove West (1), Princes Street (1)	2
6D	All Saints Road (1), Park Crescent near Park Road (1)	2
6E	St Martins Street-Highbury Street (1)	1
6F	Broadway-Broadway Gardens (1), Broadway-Princes Gardens (1)	2
6G	Eastfield Rd south of Broadway (1), Eastfield Rd off Broadway (1)	2
6H	Newark Village (1), Eye Road (1)	2
6I	Garton End (1), Sallows Rd (1), Newark Avenue (1)	3*
6J	Elmfield Road (1), Grange Avenue (1)	2*
6K	Dogsthorpe Rd-Queens Drive (1), Queens Gardens, Park Road end (1)	2
7A	Windmill Street-Harris Street (1)	1
7B	Clarence Rd-Searjeant St (1), Harris St-Occupation Rd (1)	2
7C	Lincoln Rd near Searjeant Street (1)	1
7D	Clarence Road between Searjeant St and English St (1), Windmill St near Occupation Road (1)	2
7E	Walpole Street near Occupation Rd (1), Walpole Street near English Street (1)	2
7F	Alma Road (1), Waterloo Road (1)	2
7G	Dogsthorpe Road near Brownlow Road (1), Dogsthorpe Road towards Alexandra Road (1)	2
7H	Peveril Road near Exeter Road (1), Peveril Road near Brownlow Road (1)	2
7I	Oxford Road (1), Alexandra Road between Waterloo Road-Oxford Road (1)	2
7J	Northfield Road (2)	2

7K	Near Blue Bell, Dogsthorpe (1), Welland Rd half way (1)	2
8A	York Road-Alexandra Road (1), Allen Road (1)	2
8B	Clare Road (1), Vere Road near Exeter Road (1)	2*
8C	St Pauls Road near Warbon Avenue (1)	1
8D	Fulbridge Road near Shakespeare Avenue (1)	1
8E	Tennyson Rd-Wilberforce Rd (1), Portland Ave-St James Ave (1)	2
8F	Crown Street (1), Scotney Street (1)	2*
8G	Thistlemoor Road (1), Burmer Road (1)	2
8H	Lincoln Rd near church (1), G.N.R. Cottages (2)	3
8I	Lincoln Road near Crown Street (1)	1
9A	Lincoln Road-Paston Lane (1), Willesden Avenue-Churchfield Road (1)	2*
9B	Lincoln Road-South View Road (1), South View Road-Churchfield Road (1)	2
9C	Marholm Road (1), Lincoln Road near Mountsteven Avenue (1)	2
9D	Fulbridge Road near Hadley Road (1), centre of Mountsteven Avenue (1)	2
9E	Paston Ridings (1)	1
9F	Werrington near Mill (1), over railway bridge (1)	2
9G	Werrington Village (1), Gunthorpe Village (1), Fox Covert Road (1)	3

*Parties have already been formed and pumps issued to those marked with asterisk.

Each Fire Party will consist of from three to six householders living in close proximity, and having no other Air Raid Precautions commitments.

One member of each party will be responsible for the custody of the stirrup pump, which will be issued by the City Council.

The necessary training consisting of a demonstration and lecture, lasting in all about an hour, will be given to volunteers.

All persons wishing to volunteer should enroll in parties for a particular street at the Old Town Hall, where further information will be supplied.

Arthur J. Reeves, A.R.P. Controller. Town Hall, Peterborough, 8th August, 1940.

GENERAL INDEX

450

SHIPS INDEX

A

ACHERON HMS, 98
AJAX HMS, 139
ANTELOPE HMS, 42, 47
ARK ROYAL HMS, 166, 251
ARROW HMS, 315
AUCKLAND HMS, 146
AVENGER HMS, 265

B

BEDOUIN HMS, 244

C

CHARYBDIS HMS, 321, 322
CURACOA HMS, 260

D

DARKDALE RFA, 165
DORSETSHIRE HMS, 221
DUNEDIN HMS, 177

E

EAGLE HMS, 250, 251

F

FORT LA MONTEE SS, 315

G

GLOWWORM HMS, 49, 50

H

HOOD HMS, 133

K

KACHIDOKI MARU, 405
KASHMIR HMS, 179
KELLY HMS, 179
KHEDIVE ISMAIL SS, 348, 349

L

LACONIA HMT, 275, 355
LINARIA SS, 178

M

MALAYA HMS, 256
MANCHESTER BRIGADE SS, 103
MASTA MARU, 327

N

NAVASOTA SS, 35
NEWFOUNDLAND SS, 289, 290

O

OLYMPUS HMS, 161, 168, 169, 192, 234, 237, 257

P

P512 HMS, 237, 238, 257, 260, 281
PALADIN HMS, 349
PAMPANITO USS, 405
PARTRIDGE HMS, 277
PENELOPE HMS, 101, 384
PETARD HMS, 349
POLYANTHUS HMS, 318
PRINCE OF WALES HMS, 172, 173, 221

R

RAKUYO MARU, 212, 403, 405
REYNOLDS SS, 276
ROYAL SOVEREIGN HMS, 103

S

SEAHORSE HMS, 39, 56
SEALION USS, 212, 403, 405
SEAWOLF HMS, 267
SIKH HMS, 256, 290
SOUTHAMPTON HMS, 20, 48
SOUTHDOWN HMS, 391
STARFISH HMS, 39
SUFFOLK HMS, 133

NAMES INDEX

This is a general index of the names of people who are mentioned in the text.

H

I

J

K

L

M

460

ROLL OF HONOUR INDEX

There are many stories relating to these men and the circumstances of their deaths in the preceding chapters of this book.

HERSON, Eric Cyril, 440
HICKLING, Norman Victor, 330
HICKS, Ronald John Sydney, 388
HILL, Charles Benjamin, 272
HILL, John William Rowland, 437
HILLS, Bertram Sidney, 335
HILLSON, George William, 271
HILSON, John Thomas Henry, 389
HIRST, Tom William, 275
HITCHBORN, Walter Gerald, 277
HODGKINSON, Edward, 277
HODSON, Bernard Stanley, 179
HONEYBALL, Thomas William, 440
HORNSBY, George Frederick, 442
HORNSBY, Harry, 334
HORSTEAD, Alan, 388
HOWARD, John Thomas Alfred, 334
HOWLETT, Thomas Samuel, 383
HYLAND, John Henry, 437

I

IGGULDEN, Humphrey Vint, 275
ILETT, Charles Edward, 276
ILETT, William David, 332
IVES, Augustus Harry, 273
IVISON, John, 181

J

JENKINS, Alfryn James, 386
JENKINS, William, 393
JINKS, Robert Leslie, 103
JOHNSON, Arthur, 441
JOHNSON, Edward Ellis, 277
JOHNSON, Harry Bernard, 103
JOHNSON, Kenneth, 395

K

KAY, Norman Douglas, 104
KENDALL, Victor, 384
KILBY, Ronald, 396
KINGSFORD, Edward Cyril, 182
KINGSTON, Edna, 181
KINGSTON, Frank, 181
KNIGHT, Charles Frank, 332
KNIGHT, Eric, 336

L

LADDS, Herbert Lawrence, 388
LANE, Leslie William, 393
LARKIN, Edward Truman Wyly, 178
LAUD, William Lawrence Henry, 104
LAW, Albert Edward, 442
LAWLOR, Frank Ernest, 390
LAYTON, Sidney George, 180
LAYTON, William, 336
LEACH, Frank, 439
LENTON, Albert Edward, 336
LEVERETT, Ian Donald, 336
LEWIS, William, 273
LIGHTFOOT, Horace, 396
LISTER, Leslie Harold, 336
LOBLEY, Harold Christopher, 335
LONGLEY, George William, 101
LOWE, John Norton, 395
LUCY, William Edward, 329

M

MACER, Arthur William, 437
MALLET, Harold, 388
MANN, A., 182
MANN, Alexander Leonard, 386
MARLOW, Wilfred, 332
MARTIN, Cyril Ernest, 442
MARTIN, George Robert, 441
MCINNERNY, John Leslie, 328
MEADOWS, George, 275
MEARS, Walter Alec, 274
MELLOWS, Thomas Anthony, 391
MEREDITH, George Albert, 276
MILLS, Albert William, 335
MILLS, Harry, 383
MINERS, Alfred James, 440
MITCHELL, Reginald, 394
MITCHEM, Roy Albert James, 337
MUCKLIN, Ronald Eric, 276
MUNTON, Walter Leslie, 329

N

NEVILLE, Edward, 392
NEVILLE, William, 272
NEWELL, Edgar Herbert, 334

NEWMAN, Charles Hugh, 328
NICHOLLS, Charles Ernest, 331
NICHOLLS, Frederick Walter, 335
NIGHTINGALE, George Herbert, 331
NORRIS, Elsie Kathleen, 437
NORRIS, Frederick William, 444
NUNN, Alderman James, 272
NUTT, Arthur James, 274

O

O'DELL, Austin Roy, 278
ORTON, Ronald Henry, 181
OWEN, Joseph Edward, 336

P

PAPWORTH, George Frederick, 387
PARKINSON, Tom Joseph William, 394
PARTRIDGE, Percy Ambrose, 441
PEARCE, Gordon, 443
PEARSON, John Leonard, 396
PEARSON, Walter Hubert, 444
PEET, George William, 327
PHILLIPS, Thomas, 391
PICKERSGILL, Christopher Noel, 275
POOLE, Christopher John Stafford, 101
POPELEY, Alec Charles, 182
POPPLE, Herbert William, 272
POUNTNEY, Howard Owen, 272
PRICE, Stanley Victor, 276
PRIDMORE, Alan Harry, 103
PRITCHARD, Thomas James, 179
PRYKE, Lawrence, 272
PURDY, Thomas Gordon, 178
PYLE, Arthur John, 182

Q

QUIBELL, Stanley La Barte, 390

R

RAE, George, 276
REGAN, Charles, 277
REYNOLDS, Leslie Jack Lane, 395
REYNOLDS, Walter Frederick, 439

RIPPON, William Ewart, 440
RODGERS, George Andrew, 181
ROSE, William Henry, 335
RUFF, George William, 178
RUFF, William, 392
RUSDALE, Cecil Charles, 390
RUSDALE, Jack Kirby, 275

S

SAMPSON, Leonard, 179
SANDY, Eric John, 337
SCARR, Frederick George, 334
SELKIRK, Neil Alexander, 386
SETCHFIELD, George William, 444
SETCHFIELD, Trevor, 389
SEWELL, Frederick John, 102
SEWTER, Colin Archie, 385
SEXTON, George, 438
SHARMAN, Alec James, 335
SHARP, Frederick Leslie, 275
SHARP, William Arthur, 101
SHARPE, Charles William, 384
SHAW, George Ernest, 387
SHELTON, John Barber, 438
SIDEBOTHAM, Frederick, 441
SIMPSON, Langdale Francis, 327
SIMS, Ronald Arthur, 101
SLY, Arthur Ernest, 337
SMART, Robert William, 388
SMITH, Alex James, 103
SMITH, Cyril Reginald, 101
SMITH, Douglas Herbert, 331
SMITH, Harold, 333
SMITH, J.W., 102
SMITHDALE, Alan, 328
SOWMAN, Douglas John, 389
SPRECKLY, Philip George, 329
STANFORD, Horace William James, 102
STANFORD, Raymond Dennis, 273
STEADMAN, Harold Francis, 178
STEDMAN, Walter Ralph, 332
STEELS, Arthur Edward, 271
STEELS, Frederick Leslie, 334
STEELS, Reginald Adolphus George, 271
STEWARD, Kenneth, 442
STIMPSON, Peter, 437